A FRAGILE
RELATIONSHIP

HARRY HARDING

A FRAGILE RELATIONSHIP

The United States and China since 1972

The Brookings Institution | Washington, D.C.

Copyright © 1992 by

THE BROOKINGS INSTITUTION

1775 Massachusetts Avenue, N.W., Washington, D.C. 20036

Library of Congress Cataloging-in-Publication data

Harding, Harry,
    A fragile relationship:the United States and China since 1972 /
Harry Harding.
        p.   cm.
    Includes bibliographical references and index.
    ISBN 0-8157-3466-2 : — ISBN 0-8157-3465-4 (pbk.)
    1. United States—Foreign relations—China.   2. China—Foreign
relations—United States.   I. Title.
E183.8.C5H34   1992
327.73051—dc20   91-44149
                                                                        CIP

9 8 7 6 5 4 3 2 1

ⓑ THE BROOKINGS INSTITUTION

The Brookings Institution is an independent organization devoted to nonpartisan research, education, and publication in economics, government, foreign policy, and the social sciences generally. Its principal purposes are to aid in the development of sound public policies and to promote public understanding of issues of national importance.

The Institution was founded on December 8, 1927, to merge the activities of the Institute for Government Research, founded in 1916, the Institute of Economics, founded in 1922, and the Robert Brookings Graduate School of Economics and Government, founded in 1924.

The Board of Trustees is responsible for the general administration of the Institution, while the immediate direction of the policies, program, and staff is vested in the President, assisted by an advisory committee of the officers and staff. The by-laws of the Institution state: "It is the function of the Trustees to make possible the conduct of scientific research, and publication, under the most favorable conditions, and to safeguard the independence of the research staff in the pursuit of their studies and in the publication of the results of such studies. It is not a part of their function to determine, control, or influence the conduct of particular investigations or the conclusions reached."

The President bears final responsibility for the decision to publish a manuscript as a Brookings book. In reaching his judgment on the competence, accuracy, and objectivity of each study, the President is advised by the director of the appropriate research program and weighs the views of a panel of expert outside readers who report to him in confidence on the quality of the work. Publication of a work signifies that it is deemed a competent treatment worthy of public consideration but does not imply endorsement of conclusions or recommendations.

The Institution maintains its position of neutrality on issues of public policy in order to safeguard the intellectual freedom of the staff. Hence interpretations or conclusions in Brookings publications should be understood to be solely those of the authors and should not be attributed to the Institution, to its trustees, officers, or other staff members, or to the organizations that support its research.

FOREWORD

PRESIDENT Richard Nixon's historic visit to China in February 1972 marked the beginning of a new era in Sino-American relations. For the first time since the Chinese Communist Party took power in 1949, the two countries established high-level official contacts and moved their relationship from confrontation toward collaboration. Over the subsequent twenty years, however, U.S.-China relations have experienced cycles of progress and stalemate, crisis and consolidation. The tensions over the tragic events in Tiananmen Square in June 1989 are the most recent and disruptive example, but they have their precedents in the crisis over U.S. arms sales to Taiwan in 1981–82, and in the stalemate in Sino-American relations in the mid-1970s. Paradoxically, although the political, economic, and cultural ties between the two countries are vastly more extensive today than they were two decades ago, the overall relationship remains highly fragile.

This book is one of the first comprehensive surveys of the U.S.-China relationship during this tumultuous period. In it, Harry Harding, a senior fellow in the Foreign Policy Studies program at Brookings, proceeds chronologically from the initial breakthrough of the early 1970s to the deadlock of today. The book demonstrates how the revolutionary changes in the international environment, the dramatic domestic developments in both mainland China and Taiwan, and the transformation of American economic and political life in the last decades of the cold war have provided a less and less supportive context for Sino-American relations. It also addresses the evolution of each society's perceptions of the other, showing how conflict over such substantive problems as Taiwan, regional security, and human rights has been exacerbated by shifts of mood from euphoria to disillusionment and back.

Harding believes that a return to the economic partnership of the 1980s, let alone to the strategic alignment of the 1970s, is less likely than continued tension or even confrontation between Washington and Peking over trade, human rights, and the proliferation of advanced weapons. But he also explains the importance of maintaining a working relationship with China and avoiding a return to the hostility and estrangement of the 1950s and 1960s. His principal recommendation is that the two countries let go of their outmoded dream of a "special" relationship and work toward achieving a "normal" one.

An earlier draft of this book was reviewed by two study groups that met at Brookings in the spring of 1991. The first was composed of leading American scholars and policymakers interested in China, including Doak Barnett, Mary Brown Bullock, Richard Bush, Ralph Clough, Thomas Fingar, Carol Lee Hamrin, John Holdridge, Arthur Hummel, Lonnie Keene, Richard Kessler, Paul Kreisberg, Thomas Robinson, Alan Romberg, Roger Sullivan, Robert Sutter, Kent Wiedemann, and Eden Woon. That core group was joined in its final session by Alton Frye, Jim Hamilton, Jim Mann, Robert McNamara, Douglas Paal, Edward Ross, Harold Saunders, and Daniel Southerland. The second study group was made up of Chinese scholars of Sino-American relations then in the United States, including Ding Xinghao, Hao Yufan, He Di, Huan Guocang, Jia Qingguo, Tong Yanqi, Wang Jisi, Zhai Zhihai, and Zhu Hongqian. The author thanks all of these colleagues for taking the time to provide extensive and thoughtful comments on his manuscript.

In addition, the author wishes to acknowledge several organizations for invitations to attend conferences in China, the discussions at which yielded many insights reflected in this book. Of special value were meetings sponsored by the Pacific Forum and the Beijing Institute of International Strategic Studies in Peking in October 1988, by the Pacific Forum and the China Association for Industrial Economics in Shanghai in November 1988, by the National Committee on U.S.-China Relations and the Chinese People's Institute of Foreign Affairs in Peking in February 1990, by the National Bureau of Soviet and Asian Research in Peking in June 1990, and by Peking University in June 1991.

The author is also grateful for the hospitality and cooperation provided in China at various times by the Asia Institute, the Beijing Institute of International Strategic Studies, the Center for International Studies under the State Council, the Center for Peace and Development Studies, the Chinese Academy of Social Sciences, the China Institute of Contemporary International Relations, the China Institute for International Studies, the Foundation for International Strategic Studies, Fudan University, the Institute of Global Concern, the Institute for Peace and Development Studies, the National Defense University, Peking University, the Shanghai Academy of Social Sciences, and the Shanghai Institute of International Studies.

Finally, the author appreciates the help of a number of staff members at Brookings who contributed immeasurably to the completion of the book. Research assistance was provided by Andrew C. Scobell and Myles Nienstadt, aided by interns Adam Winegard, David Fong, and Frank Chong. Susan E. Nichols, Yvonne Sabban, Margaret Huang, and Deborah Turner offered secretarial support. Kathryn Breen, Annette Leak, Louise Skillings, and Ann Ziegler typed the final manuscript. Theresa B. Walker edited the book, and Donna Verdier, Yuko Iida Frost, and Michael Levin verified its factual content. Susan Woollen prepared the manuscript for typesetting, and Max Franke constructed the index.

Brookings gratefully acknowledges the financial support provided for this book by the Henry Luce Foundation, the John D. and Catherine T. MacArthur Foundation, the Andrew W. Mellon Foundation, and the Rockefeller Brothers Fund.

The views expressed in this study are those of the author and should not be ascribed to any of the persons or organizations mentioned above, or to the trustees, officers, or other staff members of the Brookings Institution.

BRUCE K. MAC LAURY
President

January 1992
Washington, D.C.

For Jamey

CONTENTS

TABLES

FIGURE

A FRAGILE RELATIONSHIP

Overview

O N February 21, 1972, Richard M. Nixon, thirty-seventh president of the United States, emerged from the door of Air Force One and began walking down the ramp to the tarmac of Peking's Capital Airport. At Nixon's orders, an aide blocked the aisle of the plane to prevent other officials from following too closely.[1] Merely by stepping onto Chinese soil, the president would change the global balance of power in America's favor, helping to extract the United States honorably from Vietnam and to promote the prospects for détente with the Soviet Union. Nixon had determined that such an achievement was not to be shared with others.

Waiting for Nixon at the bottom of the ramp was Zhou Enlai, the only man ever to serve as prime minister of the People's Republic of China since its establishment in 1949. For Zhou, too, this was a pregnant occasion. Ever since his government had been created, the United States had refused to formally acknowledge its existence. There had been sporadic ambassadorial-level contacts but nothing higher. The United States had embargoed all trade with China and persistently worked to exclude it from the United Nations. The arrival of the president of the United States acknowledged the failure of that strategy and thus was a vindication of Zhou, his government, and the entire Chinese Communist movement.

Nixon, having noticed Zhou clapping lightly and remembering that polite Chinese always return applause, began clapping his hands as he descended the steps of his plane. When he saw that none of the other Chinese officials waiting for him on the tarmac were applauding, he stopped, and although still quite far from the bottom of the ramp, extended his hand toward Zhou Enlai. When he reached the ground, he grasped Zhou's hand for a bit longer than usual. By demonstrating, clearly and dramatically, his willingness to shake hands with the Chinese premier, Nixon meant to compensate for John Foster Dulles's pointed refusal to do so at the Geneva Conference on Indochina in 1954, a slight that a wounded Zhou had always resented.[2]

Despite the gratification that both men must have felt at their first encounter, the moment was still awkward. Extensive advance work for the visit, including lengthy meetings between Henry Kissinger and Zhou Enlai and Mao Zedong, had given the Americans little confidence about how Nixon would actually be received in China. Kissinger had fretted over the danger that, in the end, the Chinese might fall victim to the temptation to humiliate the president. Back home, according to one poll, a plurality of the public worried that Nixon might be "fooled and trapped" by visiting China.[3]

At first, these apprehensions seemed vindicated. The arrival ceremonies were scheduled so that they could be televised live in prime time in the United States. And yet, to the dismay of the American advance men, there were no crowds of Chinese gathered at the airport to greet the president. There was only a Chinese military honor guard—larger than usual, to be sure, but still according a welcome that Kissinger described as "stark to the point of austerity."[4] The ride from the airport through the heart of Peking to the Diaoyutai Guest House also disappointed the Americans. The Chinese not only had failed to turn out any crowds to welcome the president but had actually kept curious onlookers well away from the motorcade route. There were none of the "photogenic Chinese multitudes" that Nixon's staff had hoped to show television viewers in the United States.[5] Moreover, to the chagrin of his Secret Service detail, the president was forced to ride in the premier's Red Flag limousine rather than in a car from the White House fleet sent over for the occasion, for the Chinese refused to allow Nixon to use an American car when riding with Zhou Enlai.[6]

The awkwardness that imbued such a momentous occasion reflected the enormous gaps that separated the two countries in 1972. All along China's eastern periphery were traces of an American military presence, aimed one way or another at containing China's influence. Chinese and American military officers still met at meetings of the armistice commission at Panmunjom, witnesses to the inconclusive war the two nations had fought on the Korean peninsula twenty years before. The United States maintained diplomatic relations and a security treaty with the Nationalist government in Taipei, the rival regime that the Communists had forced into exile in 1949, and which still issued periodic calls to recover the mainland. American troops were still stationed on Taiwan, in part to deter a potential Communist assault. Further to the south, in Vietnam, the

United States was waging war against one of China's allies: American planes were bombing Chinese troop concentrations and supply routes, while Chinese antiaircraft batteries were firing back at them.

Gaps in history and culture also separated the two countries. The United States was the world's richest capitalist country; China, one of the world's poorest Communist states. More than any other Western nation, America embodied concepts of individual liberty, political pluralism, and economic opportunity alien to China. China was just past the high-water mark of its Cultural Revolution, a utopian yet futile effort to inculcate its population with the ideals of collectivism, asceticism, and continuous class struggle. The Chinese still vividly remembered the encroachment of Western imperialism in the nineteenth century and regarded the United States as one of the principal beneficiaries of economic and political privilege in China. Many Americans perceived China as an aggressive and irrational power whose support for revolutionary movements around the world made it an even more dangerous adversary than the Soviet Union.

Nor was there yet a firm consensus in either country on the wisdom of a mutual accommodation. In China, whose leaders were increasingly embroiled in an intense struggle over the coming succession to Mao Zedong, two principal political factions—one composed primarily of military officers, the other of radical civilian leaders—were opposed to any opening to the United States, questioning America's intentions and doubting its sincerity. According to some later Chinese accounts, the restrained greeting at the Peking airport reflected the insistence of some of those leaders that it would be wrong to conduct "propaganda for Nixon" on Chinese soil.[7] In the United States, two previous administrations had resisted proposals to broaden contacts with China for fear of a storm of domestic opposition, especially from conservative anti-Communists with strong ties to Taiwan. In 1967, just two years before Nixon came into office, more than 90 percent of the American public held unfavorable images of China, and about 70 percent saw China as the greatest threat to the security of the United States.[8]

And yet, despite the gaps between the two countries and the awkwardness of the first few hours of the Nixon visit, the president's stay in China proceeded remarkably smoothly. Within hours of his arrival at the state guest house at Diaoyutai, the president was summoned to a meeting with Mao Zedong, where the chairman announced that he "liked rightists" and was pleased to deal with the leading representative of American conservatives.[9] Perhaps to their mutual surprise, the two leaders, both of whom had international reputations as committed opponents of each other's political philosophy, found that their ideological differences would have little relevance to the conduct of their relationship. Whatever their public postures, Mao and Nixon were practitioners of realpolitik and, as such, wanted to engage in an accommodation if they could identify areas of common interest.

The shared interest that brought the two countries together was their apprehension about the Soviet Union. The Soviet Union had, under Leonid Brezhnev, undertaken a sustained expansion of its military power, conventional and nuclear. Much of that power was being deployed along the Sino-Soviet frontier, in ways that posed a direct threat to the security of China. At the same time, the Soviet Union was clearly gaining an advantageous position in the global balance against the United States, whose will to continue the rivalry was being steadily sapped by the inconclusive war in Vietnam.

Such circumstances provided a compelling motive for a rapprochement between the United States and China. At a maximum, the two countries could find ways of coordinating their strategic postures, or even pooling some of their military assets, in a united front against Soviet expansion. At a minimum, ending the Sino-American confrontation would mean that neither the United States nor China would have to be worried about a two-front war. Instead, that burden would be shifted to their adversaries in the Kremlin. Thus, simply by shaking hands at the Peking airport, Zhou Enlai and Richard Nixon had fundamentally altered the contours of global geopolitics. From a strategic perspective, it was indeed, as Nixon would later claim, "the week that changed the world."[10]

Although less prominent than containing Soviet expansionism, a second common interest was bringing the United States and China closer together. Chinese leaders, including Mao, were more and more interested in resuming the economic and cultural ties with the United States that had been suspended since the outbreak of the Korean War in 1950. Unlike their successors, Mao and Zhou were not prepared to see China fully integrated into the world economy, let alone to launch a program of vigorous economic reform. But they had determined that their country should end the self-imposed isolation of the Cultural Revolution and turn outward again to acquire the foreign technology necessary for China's economic modernization. An improved relationship with the United States would be an important part of this strategy, not only because it would be a prerequisite for the purchase of advanced American equipment, but also because it would facilitate the import of similar technology from American allies in Western Europe and Japan.

Many in the United States were also aware of the advantages of renewing cultural and economic ties with China. Scholars, missionaries, and ordinary tourists had long been fascinated by China and would welcome the opportunities to teach, study, preach, and travel there. American business would benefit from regaining access to a market that, at its peak in 1946, accounted for 5 percent of total American exports.[11] Although not a part of Henry Kissinger's calculations in planning the opening to China, these considerations would help gain domestic support for the reorientation of American China policy that he and Nixon envisioned.

Thus, when Nixon met Zhou Enlai at the foot of the ramp to Air Force One in February 1972, their encounter reflected the vast differences between the two countries and the potential rewards from a more cooperative relationship. This complex blend of common and competitive interests, memories of a rancorous past, and hopes for a more favorable future provided an uncertain footing for the new ties that the two leaders were inaugurating. What kind of relationship could be built on such unsteady ground and how enduring would it be?

TWENTY YEARS' EVOLUTION

An oscillating pattern of progress and stagnation, crisis and consolidation has characterized the relationship between China and the United States during the past twenty years. The Kissinger and Nixon visits of 1971 and 1972 constituted the initial breakthrough, transforming the U.S.-China relationship from confrontation to collaboration and reestablishing high-level official contacts for the first time since 1949. On this basis, it was possible to expand economic and cultural ties between the two countries, although they were hampered by the absence of formal diplomatic relations and the relatively closed nature of late Maoist China. Trade grew rapidly, but direct American investment in China was still impossible. Exchanges of short-term cultural and academic delegations also grew quickly, but there were as yet no avenues for scholars, journalists, or students to spend extended periods in either country.

The inability of the Nixon and Ford administrations to complete the normalization of diplomatic relations, together with their interest in pursuing détente with the Soviet Union, introduced severe strains into the Sino-American relationship in the mid-1970s. So did the resurgence of radicalism in Chinese domestic and foreign policies in 1975 and 1976, as the Gang of Four made their final bid to remove more moderate adversaries in the struggle to succeed Mao Zedong. Trade and cultural exchanges diminished and high-level contact became more contentious. By 1976, the initial advance in U.S.-China relations had given way to a sense of stagnation.

The establishment of formal diplomatic ties between the two countries at the end of 1978 marked the revival of a relationship in decline. The normalization of Sino-American relations was made possible by the emergence of new leaders in Peking and Washington who possessed the flexibility and commitment to strike a bargain that could push the relationship forward. In the United States, the Carter administration had enough political capital to agree to terminate official relations with Taiwan, remove American forces from the island, and end the mutual defense treaty with Taipei, thus meeting China's conditions for the establishment of official relations. In China, Deng Xiaoping had consolidated his political position sufficiently to tolerate the continuation of an extensive unofficial American relationship with Taiwan that would include an ongoing program of U.S. arms sales to the island.

This compromise attracted criticism in both countries. The terms of normalization were denounced by many in Congress, which added language to the Taiwan Relations Act reiterating an American commitment to the security of Taiwan. The Taiwan Relations Act, in turn, was condemned by many Chinese as a betrayal of the agreement on the normalization of Sino-American relations. But despite the criticism, the deal struck by Carter and Deng remained in effect.

With normalization complete, Sino-American relations entered their second cycle of progress and stalemate. Cultural, economic, and strategic ties scored steady breakthroughs between 1978 and 1980: the first wave of Chinese students and scholars, the first direct air links between the two countries, the first American commercial tourists, the first dispatches by American correspondents permanently stationed in Peking, the establishment of the first American joint ventures in China, the first exchanges of military delegations, and so on. The eagerness with which citizens of each country approached each other, and the unanticipated speed with which Sino-American relations expanded, produced a mood of excitement and elation on both sides of the Pacific.

Then came disenchantment, as each country backed away from the other's embrace. During the presidential race of 1980, Ronald Reagan declared his desire to restore some officiality to American relations with Taipei, a big departure from the concessions on the Taiwan issue that had been made by the Carter administration at

the time of normalization. China, seeking to avoid excessive dependence on the United States, subsequently announced it would follow
a more independent foreign policy, thus abandoning its earlier allu-
sions to a united front with America against the Soviet Union. American journalists and students returned from China dismayed that the
country did not live up to the utopian expectations generated by the
rhetoric of the Cultural Revolution. Peking chose to criticize the
defects in American society as part of its effort to set limits on
political liberalization at home.

This mutual disillusionment was reflected in a steady drumbeat
of irritants on almost every dimension of the relationship between
1981 and 1983: the surge in Chinese textile exports to the United
States, the restrictions on American technology transfer to China,
the potential sale of advanced American jet fighters to Taiwan, the
defection by the Chinese tennis star Hu Na, and the attempt of
American speculators to force the Chinese government to pay principal and interest on the bonds issued by the Qing dynasty just before
the Revolution of 1911 to finance the construction of the Huguang
Railway in southern China. Mocking the Chinese penchant for nu-
merology, American observers gave these seemingly small issues the
facetious label of the "three T's" (textiles, technology, and Taiwan)
and the "two Hu's" (Hu Na and Huguang). But this combination of
problems, spanning the entire spectrum of Sino-American relations,
did much to remove the goodwill that had been engendered by the
normalization agreement of 1978. Indeed, at some points in 1981
and 1982, Sino-American relations seemed to be on the verge of
unraveling altogether.

Fortunately, Chinese and American leaders at the highest levels
intervened to prevent a serious rupture of the relationship. In 1982,
the two countries reached an understanding on the parameters of
American arms sales to Taiwan; and, the following year, the United
States announced a further relaxation of its restrictions on the transfer of advanced technology to China. With those two issues at least
partially settled, Washington and Peking found it easier to deal more
flexibly with the other irritants in their bilateral relationship. The
Hu Na issue was set aside; the Huguang case was resolved; and a
new textile agreement was concluded. The recovery of Sino-American ties was symbolized by the extraordinary exchange of summit
meetings within a four-month period in early 1984: Zhao Ziyang's
visit to the United States in January, followed by Ronald Reagan's
journey to China in April.

The intensification of Chinese political and economic reform beginning in 1984–85 inaugurated yet another cycle in the contemporary Sino-American relationship. A more open China greatly facilitated the quantitative and qualitative expansion of the relations between the two countries. Once again, there was an exciting series of firsts: the first wholly American-owned ventures in China, the first agreements on the coproduction of military technology, the first offices of American foundations in China, and the first truly collaborative research projects by Chinese and American scholars. The overall mood became even more euphoric than it had been at the beginning of the decade. For the first time, Chinese officials began to express their satisfaction with the state of the relationship. Some Americans were convinced that China was on the verge of capitalism and perhaps even democracy. Despite differences over human rights, commercial relations, and China's arms sales abroad, the mutual perception of a more stable and mature relationship between China and the United States lasted until June 1989.

Then, the tragedy in Tiananmen Square sparked the most severe crisis in Sino-American ties since the rapprochement between the two countries had begun some twenty years earlier. Horrified at the signs of repression in Peking, and dismayed at the seeming reversal of political and economic reform, Americans demanded that their government impose diplomatic and economic sanctions against China. Chinese leaders, angered at what they saw as intervention in their internal affairs, responded with countersanctions. As a result, U.S.-China relations suffered on almost every front: American exports to China dropped, American investment in China declined, the number of American tourists and scholars visiting China plummeted, the military ties between the two countries were suspended, and official contacts between Peking and Washington were severely attenuated.

As in the two previous cycles, the leaders of the two countries sought to prevent the relationship from collapsing entirely. In China, Deng Xiaoping and the Ministry of Foreign Affairs beat back calls for a fundamental reorientation of Chinese foreign policy away from the West and toward the socialist bloc and the third world. In the United States, the White House and the State Department tried to maintain direct contact with Peking, moderate the impact of sanctions on Sino-American relations, and preserve China's most-favored-nation trading status. But other powerful interests in each country were skeptical about the desirability of continuing the previous pattern of relations. Conservatives in China accused the United States of attempting to destabilize the Chinese government and to encourage the nation's "peaceful evolution" from socialism to capitalism. A broad cross-section of the American Congress wanted to impose tougher sanctions to punish Peking not only for violations of human rights, but also for arms sales to the Middle East and mounting trade surpluses with the United States.

As Sino-American relations approached the twentieth anniversary of the Nixon visit of 1972, therefore, they embodied a seeming paradox. On the one hand, they were vastly more extensive than they had been two decades earlier. Trade had risen nearly twenty times, from $100 million in 1972 to $20 billion in 1990. Investment, which had been nonexistent when Nixon met Zhou Enlai, amounted to more than $2 billion. One hundred thousand Chinese students and scholars had received visas to visit the United States, and about two and a half million Americans had traveled to China as tourists. The sale of American military equipment through commercial channels, added to agreements reached on a government-to-government basis, totaled more than half a billion dollars.

On the other hand, this extensive relationship remained highly fragile. In each country, the domestic consensus supporting the relationship had collapsed. Important elements of both societies viewed the other with suspicion and dismay. The two governments confronted each other on issues ranging from human rights to economics. Although the intense crisis that had developed after the June 4 Tiananmen incident had eased somewhat, the Sino-American relationship had not experienced a full consolidation, let alone a new breakthrough. Indeed, there was no confidence in either country that their relationship would not deteriorate further.

CHANGING CONTEXTS

The rise and fall of Sino-American relations in the 1970s and 1980s can be traced, in large part, to the deteriorating international and domestic contexts for the relationship. At first, the common threat from the Soviet Union pushed the two countries together. When the Sino-American rapprochement began, leaders in Peking were deeply concerned about the Soviet military deployments along the disputed Sino-Soviet frontier while China was still divided by the ravages of the Cultural Revolution. By the end of the 1970s, the direct Soviet threat to Chinese security had abated somewhat, but Chinese leaders still believed that Moscow had embarked on an equally alarming global geopolitical advance, with the containment of Chinese influence in Asia an essential element of the plan. The United States also worried about Soviet strategic gains in Asia, the Middle East, Africa, and Latin America as it sought to heal the domestic wounds created by the war in Vietnam. This common interest enabled the two countries to overlook the stark differences in their economic systems and ideologies in the quest for common ground against Moscow.

By the late 1980s, however, the strategic rationale for Sino-American relations had become much less compelling for either country. The peaking of Soviet power in Europe and Asia and Moscow's growing preoccupation with internal affairs made it less of a threat in the eyes of Washington or Peking. As a result, both countries were able to seriously reduce tensions with the Kremlin. The United States made conventional and nuclear arms control agreements with the Soviet Union and secured Moscow's cooperation in addressing a wide range of regional issues. China reestablished high-level official contact with the Soviet Union, expanded bilateral economic and cultural ties, and made great progress toward a resolution of its border dispute with Moscow. The Kremlin addressed all of the issues of concern to China by reducing its forces along the Sino-Soviet frontier, withdrawing troops from Afghanistan, and persuading Vietnam to seek a negotiated settlement in Cambodia. As a result, neither China nor the United States felt any longer that it urgently needed the other to bolster its geopolitical position against the Soviet Union.

For a time, the domestic situation in China provided another favorable context for Sino-American relations. Under the leadership of Deng Xiaoping, China embarked on a program of economic and political reform, first tentatively in the late 1970s, and then with greater vigor in the mid-1980s. To a much greater degree than in the late Maoist era, China's leaders were interested in gaining access to advanced technology, export markets, financial capital, and educational opportunities in America. Younger Chinese intellectuals, some of whom served as advisers to reform-minded Party and government officials, looked to the United States as a model for the restructuring of their country's political and economic institutions.

These developments made China even more attractive to Americans than it had been in the 1970s. Political and economic reform produced a more promising environment for American trade and investment, provided more opportunities for academic and cultural exchanges, and narrowed potential differences over human rights. In addition, it reactivated the long-standing American interest in converting China to American values and remolding the Chinese economic and political systems along American lines. What the Chinese saw as a partnership to promote their country's socialist reform, Americans perceived as an effort to encourage China's political and economic liberalization.

The political crisis in China in mid-1989 suddenly and drastically transformed this setting for Sino-American relations. For Americans, the sight of troops in Tiananmen Square tearing down the statue of the *Goddess of Freedom and Democracy* dashed any hopes that China would soon be adopting American values or emulating American institutions. The wave of repression that subsequently swept the country shattered the image of a progressive Chinese leadership undertaking a concerted effort at political and economic liberalization. The appearance of an unstable and illegitimate government made China a much less attractive location for American investment, scholarship, or tourism.

The Tiananmen crisis also intensified the long-standing fears of Chinese conservatives of the subversive effects of extensive contacts with the United States. The huge popular protests calling for greater democracy were seen as the consequences of the opening to the West. The critical commentary in the American press, the sanctions imposed on China by the U.S. government, and the pressure from Congress for even harsher retaliation convinced Chinese conservatives that the United States was engaged in a program of "peaceful evolution" aimed at the overthrow of the Chinese Communist Party.

Changes in the international environment in the late 1980s and early 1990s exacerbated the impact of China's domestic crisis on Sino-American relations. The collapse of communism first in Eastern Europe, and then in the Soviet Union, reinforced the American tendency to perceive Peking as a recalcitrant government rather than a progressive one. Once seen as undertaking the most radical reforms in the Communist world, Chinese leaders were now regarded as reactionary gerontocrats who were resisting inevitable trends toward free markets and democracy.

These same developments intensified Chinese concerns about the future of their relationship with the United States. The surprisingly easy American military victory against Iraq in early 1991 and the equally startling disintegration of the Soviet empire in Eastern Europe rendered the United States the world's only military superpower and threatened to create a unipolar world centered on Washington. The breakdown of communism in Europe and the apparent spread of democracy throughout parts of the third world gave the United States greater confidence in its ideological values. In Chinese eyes, this turn of events increased the odds that Washington would embark on a policy of peaceful evolution, aimed at encouraging the collapse of the few remaining Communist states, and meant that the spearhead of this policy would be pointed squarely against China.

To China, the only reassuring international phenomenon was the decline of American economic power, especially in comparison with that of Japan and Germany. But although this gradual development alleviated Chinese anxiety that the United States would be able to achieve a dominant position in the post–cold war era, in other ways it undermined Sino-American relations. Even before the Tiananmen crisis, domestic budget deficits had limited Washington's ability to give Peking economic assistance or even to help finance U.S. firms exporting to China. In addition, a nation that was now chronically concerned about its international balance of payments was not willing to tolerate surges of Chinese imports, barriers to American exports to China, and a burgeoning Chinese trade surplus with the United States.

The only positive developments to occur in the context of Sino-American relations in the late 1980s were events in Taiwan. Changes in the island's leadership, associated with the emergence of a new generation of political leaders and the rise of a powerful class of Taiwanese entrepreneurs, transformed Taipei's attitude toward the mainland. Chiang Kai-shek's successors—first Chiang Ching-kuo, and then Lee Teng-hui—were willing to tolerate the rapid expansion of cultural and economic ties across the Taiwan Strait. Lee Teng-hui also took a more flexible attitude toward political contacts with Peking and sketched out a more realistic position on national reunification, while still banning any talk of formal independence from the mainland. As relations between Taiwan and the mainland expanded, the United States could disengage itself from the Taiwan issue to a degree unprecedented since 1950. As a result, the Taiwan question became less significant in Sino-American relations than it had been in the past.

But even this welcome circumstance may not be lasting. Greater political liberalization on Taiwan will steadily erode the taboo against discussions of formal independence for the island. Even if the proponents of independence remain a small fraction of Taiwan's population, as is presently true, they will certainly play a more vociferous and visible role in Taiwanese politics than they have in the past. Moreover, their numbers may begin to grow, particularly if the breakup of the Soviet Union legitimates demands for self-determination in other parts of the world and if continued repression or instability on the mainland causes reunification to lose its appeal. Whatever the fate of the Taiwan independence movement, the calls for enhancing Taiwan's role in the international community, including readmission to the United Nations, are already beginning to increase and could well receive growing support in the United States. This development could spark a renewed crisis not only in Peking's relations with Taiwan but by extension in Sino-American relations as well.

SUBSTANTIVE ISSUES

These changing contexts have affected the way in which China and the United States have addressed the chief elements in their relationship: Taiwan, human rights, strategic relations, and economic and cultural ties. Although these four strands have been woven into Sino-American relations throughout the two decades under discussion, their salience and contentiousness have changed over time. The principal obstacle to U.S.-China relations has gradually shifted from Taiwan to human rights and has become larger and more sensitive. The main cornerstone has shifted from strategic relations to economics, a less compelling but more controversial issue. Just as the context for Sino-American relations has evolved in unfavorable directions, in other words, so too have the various important elements in the relationship become less harmonious and more contentious.

The enduring dispute between Washington and Peking over Taiwan reflects a basic difference in perspective between the two countries. Ever since the outbreak of the Korean War, the United States has insisted it has a legitimate interest in a peaceful future for Taiwan and its people. In keeping with this interest, Washington gave Taipei substantial economic aid in the 1950s and 1960s, formed a military alliance with Taiwan in 1955, and supplied it with vast quantities of military equipment. China, in contrast, has insisted that the future of Taiwan is China's internal affair, in which no foreign country has the right to intervene. Ever since 1950, therefore, China has consistently demanded that the United States remove its military forces from Taiwan and recognize the Communist government in Peking as the sole legitimate government of the country.

The rapprochement between Washington and Peking in the 1970s required both sides to make difficult concessions on this sensitive issue, which were reflected first in the agreement on the normalization of Sino-American relations in 1978 and subsequently in the 1982 communiqué restricting the sale of American weapons to Taiwan. After 1982, Taiwan became a much less contentious issue in U.S.-China relations. One reason, as suggested earlier, was the growing economic and cultural contacts across the Taiwan Strait. But another was that Peking and Washington had gained a better appreciation of each other's interests on the island and of the limits to each side's flexibility. After 1982, the United States no longer talked about major new arms sales to Taiwan or about restoring official relations with Taipei—measures that Peking would have regarded as violating the understandings that the two countries had reached on the Taiwan question. Conversely, China no longer vigorously demanded that the United States repeal the Taiwan Relations Act, reduce arms sales to Taiwan more rapidly, or put pressure on Taipei to reach an accommodation with Peking—initiatives that it now understood Washington would reject out of hand.

As the Taiwan issue receded, human rights began to replace it as the most controversial aspect of Sino-American relations. Until the mid-1980s, most Americans paid little heed to the repressive features of the Chinese political system. The desire to join China in an alignment against the Soviet Union, a lack of confidence in the applicability of American values to China, and a willingness to take Maoist rhetoric at face value dampened potential American criticism of China's human rights record in the mid-1970s. Thereafter, the conviction that post-Mao China was undertaking concerted political and economic reform also insulated Sino-American relations from the focus on human rights otherwise so prominent in discussions of American foreign policy during the Carter and Reagan administrations.

Ironically, the very real, if limited, process of political liberalization that occurred in post-Mao China began to erode China's exemption from human rights concerns. The emergence of a small but visible dissident movement in China's principal cities in the mid-1980s gave graphic evidence that Chinese intellectuals wanted to create a more just, open, and democratic society. The massive antigovernment demonstrations that swept across China in the spring of 1989 suggested that those sentiments were shared by a growing number of ordinary urban residents. And the violent suppression of those protests on June 4, followed by the tightening of political controls over Chinese scholars, artists, writers, and journalists, elevated the human rights issue to a central position in Sino-American relations.

At the same time, what Americans saw as the promotion of human rights was perceived by many Chinese leaders as an attempt to undermine the Communist government. Viewed from Peking, previous American intervention in China's internal affairs had been primarily directed against China's territorial integrity: support for insurgents in Tibet in the 1950s and, above all, a commitment to the security of Taiwan. Now, American intervention seemed to be directed against the very stability of the Chinese national government. American support for protest, American espousal of political liberalization, and American sanctions against the suppression of dissent were regarded as evidence of a concerted American campaign to subvert the socialist system in China and to encourage its evolution into a capitalist order.

One of the victims of the 1989 crisis in Sino-American relations was the expanding military and strategic ties between the two countries. Despite their common interest in opposing Soviet expansionism, Peking and Washington had found it difficult to build a strategic relationship in the 1970s and early 1980s. There was some sharing of intelligence and some coordination of foreign policy on issues such as Cambodia and Afghanistan. But military ties proved problematic. Peking was unwilling to purchase American weapons or engage in extensive exchanges of military personnel until the two countries resolved their differences over Taiwan. The United States was, at this point, more eager to move forward than China, but even Washington was reluctant to transfer advanced weapons or technology to China, especially those that might alarm U.S. allies in Asia.

After the successful conclusion of the negotiations over American arms sales to Taiwan in 1982, the military relationship between China and the United States began to expand. The sharing of intelligence and the consultations on regional and global issues continued. Peking and Washington developed programs whereby the United States would assist China in the production of several types of weapons, including antitank missiles, artillery shells, antisubmarine torpedoes, and advanced avionics for jet fighters. The two countries also conducted an ambitious program of military exchanges, including reciprocal visits by Chinese and American defense ministers, chiefs of staff, and service commanders, as well as working-level technical delegations.

Although Peking was willing to conduct military exchanges with the United States and was eager to acquire American military technology, it was not prepared to coordinate its broader foreign policy with that of the United States. In the late 1980s, differences between the two countries emerged on several global and regional issues, most notably China's arms sales to the Middle East, its apparent violation of the norms against the proliferation of nuclear weapons, and its continuing assistance to the Khmer Rouge in Cambodia. As the reorientation of Soviet foreign policy under Mikhail Gorbachev reduced the Soviet threat to China and the United States, these

divergent perspectives assumed greater prominence in the overall
strategic relationship between the two countries. By the time the
Tiananmen crisis of 1989 led the United States to suspend high-level
military exchanges and the coproduction of military equipment, the
Sino-American strategic relationship had more negative elements
than positive ones.

As the strategic rationale for Sino-American relations slowly faded,
analysts on both sides of the Pacific looked for an alternative foundation for the relationship. In the mid-1980s, at the high point of China's
reform program, it seemed that bilateral economic, educational, and
cultural exchanges might play such a role. And, indeed, during this
period this aspect of U.S.-China relations experienced some of its
most rapid growth, in quantitative and qualitative terms. American
investment in China increased and diversified. Trade between the two
countries expanded, and its composition became more sophisticated.
American and Chinese scholars began collaborative research on topics in the humanities, social sciences, and natural sciences.

But virtually every aspect of these linkages proved controversial.
American academics were frustrated by the continuing obstacles to
research opportunities in China, particularly on politically sensitive
subjects. Their Chinese colleagues were dismayed by the many Chinese students and scholars who were extending their residence in the
United States and the difficulties in effectively absorbing those who
did return home. The American business community complained
about the poor investment climate in China, the barriers to American
exports to China, and the flood of Chinese imports entering the American market. Chinese leaders criticized the United States for maintaining tight controls over American technology transfer to China
and limiting the export of Chinese textiles to the American market.
As a result, it soon became apparent that the expansion of economic
and cultural ties could not provide a completely stable underpinning
for the broader Sino-American relationship.

THE SHIFTING POLITICAL BASE

As the domestic and international contexts for Sino-American
relations changed, and as their bilateral interactions expanded
and became more contentious, the political foundations for the U.S.-
China relationship shifted as well. From 1972 to the mid-1980s, the
trend seemed to be the strengthening of political support for Sino-
American relations in both countries, as more and more sectors of
Chinese and American society acquired a stake in the relationship

and as ideological opposition slowly faded. Beginning in the mid-1980s, however, that favorable trend was reversed. The expansion of the substantive relations between the two countries produced various frictions, and an ideologically based opposition began to reassert itself in both societies. By the beginning of the 1990s, the political base for the relationship had been severely eroded, although not completely destroyed, on both sides of the Pacific.

Ideological considerations have been a constant source of ambivalence and opposition to Sino-American relations in both societies for more than forty years. Many Chinese Communist leaders have had a lifelong aversion to capitalism and imperialism and saw the United States as the principal embodiment of both evils in the postwar world. Conversely, many Americans found any variety of communism repugnant and regarded Chinese communism as even more brutal than its Soviet counterpart. These considerations obstructed the moderation of each country's policy toward the other throughout the 1950s and 1960s. Even after the Nixon visit of 1972, conservatives in China forced first Mao and then Deng to impose tough conditions on the establishment of diplomatic relations with the United States. For their part, Richard Nixon, Gerald Ford, and Jimmy Carter recognized that the full normalization of Sino-American relations would engender sharp criticism from the conservative wing of the Republican Party, because of the damage it would necessarily inflict on formal American ties with Taiwan.

From the mid-1970s through the mid-1980s, these ideological obstacles to U.S.-China relations seemed to be shrinking. The threat from the Soviet Union enabled conservatives in both countries to set aside their ideological differences and support a united front against a common enemy. Equally important, the dramatic changes in China following the death of Mao Zedong in 1976 also reduced the impact of ideology on the relationship. The death of Mao, the purge of the Gang of Four, and the rise of Deng Xiaoping steadily weakened the influence of China's ideologues over their country's foreign and domestic policies. The relaxation of controls over the academy and the press and the reorientation of Chinese foreign policy toward promoting economic contacts with the West fostered more favorable images of America. At the same time, the inauguration of political and economic reform in China alleviated the reservations that many American conservatives had previously held about forging friendly relations with Peking. Indeed, some members of the American conservative community persuaded themselves that China would be the first Communist country to renounce Marxism, embrace capitalism, and possibly even adopt democratic reforms.

Developments in the late 1980s, however, led to a resurgence of the ideological factor in the relationship. Chinese conservatives saw the growing American economic and cultural presence in China as a dangerous intervention in their internal affairs. Some began to accuse the United States of trying once again to remake China in its own image, this time by exporting a secular philosophy rather than religious teachings. The interest that many younger urban Chinese showed in American popular culture, economic institutions, and political theory, and the rise of dissent among the Chinese intellectual and student communities, intensified the concern of Chinese conservatives that the relationship with the United States was becoming a destabilizing element in Chinese society.

Similarly, as Americans gained more contact with China, what they learned reignited some of the ideological reservations of the past. Peking's coercive birth control program, harsh control over Tibet, and periodic campaigns against dissident intellectuals united liberals and conservatives in mounting criticism of China's human rights record. The Tiananmen crisis of 1989 spread these concerns throughout American society, sparking an upsurge of revulsion at the repression of what was viewed as a nonviolent student movement in favor of democracy.

Ideological considerations aside, the growing interdependence of China and the United States also had a complex effect on the political base for the relationship between the two countries. As bilateral economic and military ties expanded, a growing number of institutions and localities in both nations gained direct benefit from U.S.-China relations and that became a stabilizing factor in the relationship. The presence of more American diplomats, journalists, and scholars in China provided a better, although still imperfect, understanding of Chinese interests, calculations, and strategies. Similarly, greater access to the United States, coupled with some financial support from American universities and foundations, helped produce a community of Chinese America-watchers that was able to give their leaders more accurate analysis of developments in America and more sensible advice about policy toward the United States. The development of institutional mechanisms for official and unofficial dialogue between the two countries also produced better mutual understanding.

But while growing interdependence strengthened Sino-American relations in some ways, it weakened it in others. The burgeoning economic, strategic, and cultural ties between the United States and China began to arouse competitive interests, as well as complementary ones, and therefore began to stimulate powerful interest groups in both countries to challenge some aspects of the relationship. In the United States, for example, American policy toward China began to attract the attention of the textile industry (which sought tighter restrictions on the import of Chinese fabrics and garments), organized labor (which regarded Chinese working conditions as a form of unfair competition with American industry), the right-to-life lobby (which opposed coerced abortions and other mandatory birth control measures in China), and the nonproliferation lobby (which questioned China's commitment to halting the spread of nuclear weapons). In China, the pattern was less visible to foreign observers, but it is highly likely that state industry sought protection against American imports, that some groups in the military rejected American criticism of Chinese arms sales to the Middle East, and that some elements of the academic establishment felt threatened by the prospect of better-trained young scholars returning to China from research or training in the United States.

At first, the interaction of these two considerations, ideological and pragmatic, strengthened U.S.-China relations. The decline of ideologically based opposition in the two countries in the late 1970s and the emergence of more institutions and localities with a stake in the relationship in the early 1980s made the Sino-American relationship seem more mature and stable than ever before. For the first time since the Second World War, China was not a significant issue in the American presidential election campaigns in 1984 or 1988. In China, too, the national leadership seemed safely under the control of those who saw benefit in strategic, economic, and scientific ties with America.

Toward the end of the 1980s, however, the situation began to reverse, as an ideologically based opposition reappeared in each country and various institutions and interests in each society began to challenge certain aspects of the relationship. The crisis in Sino-American relations after the Tiananmen incident of 1989 catalyzed the formation of powerful coalitions in both countries, drawing together the various opposition elements that had previously acted in relative isolation. In the United States, a grouping of liberal human rights organizations, conservative anti-Communist leaders, and Chinese students and scholars in exile came together to advocate tougher sanctions against Peking. The American trade deficit with China and concerns over Chinese arms sales to the Middle East added the nonproliferation lobby and the protectionist wing of American industry and labor to that coalition. In China, the American sanctions provided powerful ammunition to conservatives who had long argued that China should keep its distance from the United States and gave them common cause with state industrial interests who wanted protection from American imports.

But in neither country did the opposition coalition that emerged after the Tiananmen incident completely dominate policymaking. In the United States, the call for harsher sanctions against China was resisted by a combination of foreign policy strategists, business organizations, and China specialists, with strong support from the Bush administration. In China, the demand for a more hostile policy toward the United States was rejected by the Party's central leadership, with the encouragement of various military, commercial, and academic interests that had developed a stake in the relationship with America. Like the substantive base of the relationship, the political basis for U.S.-China relations was severely weakened, but not completely destroyed, by the crisis of 1989.

PROSPECTS AND RECOMMENDATIONS

The future of Sino-American relations is extraordinarily difficult to predict. All of the contexts that helped shape that relationship over the past twenty years are in a state of flux. With the collapse of the Soviet Union, the main contours of the international system are uncertain and how much Chinese and American interests will coincide or diverge remains to be seen. China is grappling with vexing social, economic, and political problems and could over the next decade witness renewed reform, tighter repression, continued decay, or even national disintegration. The United States is debating its national priorities and policies in the post–cold war era, with no consensus in sight. And Taiwan and Hong Kong are engaged in more vocal domestic disputes over their future relationships with the People's Republic, with a strong possibility that Taiwan could insist on a more active international role and even formal independence, and that Hong Kong could begin to demand more guarantees of autonomy and faster progress toward democracy.

Thus, there are at least five possible scenarios for Sino-American relations in the 1990s:

—There could conceivably be a renewed strategic alignment between China and the United States against a resurgent Russia or an ascendant Japan, which would enable the two countries once again to overlook their bilateral economic and ideological differences to meet a common threat to their interests.

—If the central government in Peking were to collapse and China disintegrate, the United States would be forced to forge distinct relations with multiple Chinas, which would probably range from the friendly to the distant.

—If political and economic liberalization should revive as China enters the post-Deng era, one might well see resumed American support for China's modernization and reform, together with renewed Chinese interest in close economic, military, and cultural ties with the United States.

—Another possibility is a descent into a more confrontational relationship. In the short run, Americans could lose patience over China's failure to improve performance on controversial bilateral issues. Over the longer term, this scenario could occur if China were still governed by a repressive government after the succession to Deng Xiaoping, if there were a crisis in Peking's relationship with Hong Kong or Taiwan, or if China adopted a more hostile foreign policy that ran counter to the interests of the United States or its allies.

—Finally, present trends could continue, featuring a complex blend of congruent and competitive interests and a relationship that would remain strained but would not collapse.

In the short run, the last scenario is the most likely, with the fourth remaining a significant possibility. Over the middle term, the third scenario, a return to reform, would become more probable, although by no means certain. The other two prospects—a revival of a Sino-American strategic alignment or the disintegration of China into regional governments—are currently unlikely but not inconceivable.

In these circumstances, wise American policy toward China should be based on several broad propositions. First, it is desirable to avoid a return to a hostile relationship with Peking. Renewed military confrontation with China, whether over Taiwan or some other regional issue, would be costly, especially at a time of retrenchment in the American defense budget. Even a diplomatic standoff with Peking would be highly undesirable, not only because of the damage it would do to bilateral relations with China, but because it would introduce serious strains into relations with Asian friends and allies, none of whom wants to see Peking and Washington become adversaries again. Obviously, if Peking chooses to adopt a foreign policy that directly confronts important American interests or decides to use force to compel the reunification of Hong Kong or Taiwan on its own terms, a hostile relationship may be unavoidable. But it would be foolish for the United States to push differences with China over trade or human rights to the point of a complete collapse of diplomatic and economic relations with Peking.

It would be equally unwise for the United States to anticipate a

second Sino-American honeymoon in the post-Deng era, characterized by the false euphoria and unrealistic expectations that imbued
the relationship in the mid-1980s. To be sure, the United States can
hope for the renewal of political and economic reform in China,
especially after the death of the country's present elderly leaders and
the emergence of new generations of younger and more pragmatic
men and women. But the revival of reform is not the only conceivable
scenario for post-Deng China. And, even if it should occur, the process of economic and political liberalization is likely to be protracted
and difficult, possibly punctuated by crises comparable to the ones
that swept the country in 1989. Moreover, the success of reform is
no guarantee that China and the United States will always see eye
to eye on global and regional issues. Indeed, successful economic
reform may exacerbate, rather than eliminate, the current imbalance
of trade between the two countries.

Finally, Sino-American relations are too important to warrant a
strategy of benign neglect. To be sure, China is not as important to
the United States today as it was in the 1970s, when manipulating
the strategic triangle was a critical element in global American diplomacy. But China remains relevant to various international issues in
which the United States has interests: maintaining the balance of
power in the Asia-Pacific region, preserving stability on the Korean
peninsula, protecting the global environment, encouraging an open
international economy, and preventing the spread of weapons of
mass destruction. In all these areas, China can make matters much
worse or can contribute to making them better. Moreover, the two
countries already have an extensive bilateral relationship that needs
to be skillfully managed and would benefit from further economic
and cultural exchanges.

What this picture suggests is the need for a more realistic and
mature relationship with China than has existed in much of the
recent past. U.S. leaders should recognize that they share both common and competitive interests with China. They should see China
as a major regional power with global influence, rather than perceive
the People's Republic either as central to American interests or
irrelevant to American calculations. They should acknowledge that
the relationship between the two countries must be based on hard
bargaining, in which the United States mobilizes positive and negative incentives to pursue its agenda of interests. This relationship
would, in fact, be a normal one, of the kind that most countries have
with one another. But for two countries that have for so long sought
a "special relationship," achieving that normalcy may require a
wrenching adjustment in familiar ways of thinking.

Breakthrough

RICHARD Nixon's visit to Peking in 1972 ended twenty years of confrontation and isolation between the United States and China. Throughout the 1950s, the two countries inhabited two different camps in a rigidly polarized world. The United States was the leader of a global alliance of capitalist states created to prevent the spread of communism. China, its Communist revolution victorious, cast its lot with the rival bloc headed by the Soviet Union, which viewed its mission as promoting the victory of socialism over capitalism.

The relationship between China and the United States was severely constrained by this ideological confrontation. Even at the best of times, diplomatic, cultural, and economic contacts between the two countries were minimal. Trade and investment were embargoed, travel prohibited, and diplomatic relations restricted to episodic contacts at the ambassadorial level. Moreover, the Sino-American conflict occasionally flared into military hostility. The two countries engaged in costly and inconclusive combat in Korea, experienced periodic crises in the Taiwan Strait, and waged an intense proxy war in Vietnam. Although Washington and Peking occasionally showed some flexibility toward each other, neither side seemed eager to improve the bilateral relationship.

Interestingly, one of the most important changes in world politics in the 1960s—the emergence of the Sino-Soviet dispute—did not immediately bring the two countries closer together. At first, the Chinese saw the Soviet Union and the United States as posing equally serious challenges to their military security and ideological integrity. Moreover, they felt confident of their ability to oppose both superpowers simultaneously. For its part, the United States regarded China, rather than the Soviet Union, as possessing the more radical ideology and the more revolutionary foreign policy, and thus presenting the more severe menace to American interests. To the extent that the United States thought of taking advantage of the Sino-Soviet split in the early 1960s, it considered forming an alignment with the Soviet Union against China, rather than with Peking against Moscow.

In time, however, the Soviet threat caused China and the United States to view each other more sympathetically. For both countries, 1968 was the turning point. The Soviet invasion of Czechoslovakia that spring offered a disturbing precedent for a possible military strike against Peking, at a time when China was wracked by the turmoil of the Cultural Revolution. Hanoi's Tet offensive in Vietnam that same year and Lyndon B. Johnson's subsequent decision not to run for reelection in the November presidential elections demonstrated the fragility of the American strategic position in Vietnam. Perceiving each other's weakness, Washington and Peking began to regard the Soviet Union as the greater threat to their security. In 1969, therefore, Nixon and Mao began to explore the possibility of forming a Sino-American rapprochement as an effective counterweight to the Soviet Union.

Despite the successful Nixon visit of 1972, domestic problems in both countries continued to constrain Sino-American relations throughout most of the 1970s. Weak Republican presidents—including Nixon in his second term and Gerald Ford during his interregnum—proved unable to make the compromises on Taiwan necessary to achieve full diplomatic relations with China. In the absence of full diplomatic ties with the United States, Peking banned many normal interactions, refusing to open direct air or shipping service, permit American journalists to be permanently stationed in China, or allow exchanges of students and scholars on anything but short-term group visits. Chinese domestic and foreign trade policies, in turn, remained mired in the Maoist era, providing further restrictions on foreign investment, trade, and cultural exchange.

Moreover, the two countries still eyed each other warily. The American public, although intrigued by China and eager to use it to gain diplomatic leverage against Moscow and Hanoi, still regarded it as an unsavory Communist dictatorship. Many Chinese leaders, although willing to use the United States as a counterbalance against the Soviet threat, still viewed it with mistrust, especially because it had not yet decisively broken diplomatic and military ties with Taiwan. Neither government was completely confident that the other would not abandon it in favor of an exclusive détente with the Soviet Union. Despite the breakthrough symbolized by the Nixon visit, therefore, Sino-American relations remained tender and tentative.

HOSTILITY

The successful Communist revolution in China, culminating in the establishment of the People's Republic in 1949, effected a chasm between China and the United States that neither government was able to bridge for the next twenty years.[1] To many Americans the new government in China seemed dangerously radical and irresponsible, precisely the sort of regime against which the new postwar containment policy was meant to be directed. To the majority of Chinese Communists, who had come to power on the basis of an anti-imperialist and nationalistic program, the United States was not only the country that had given the most economic and military assistance to Chiang Kai-shek and the Nationalists, but had also become as a result of the Second World War the leading capitalist power, and thus the greatest threat to the consolidation of their revolution.

From these vastly different perspectives, both governments viewed each other with suspicion and uncertainty. Some American officials, particularly Secretary of State Dean Acheson, were willing to "let the dust settle." In their view, the United States was best advised to acquiesce to the seemingly inevitable fall of Taiwan to the Communists. Then, after the passage of the proverbial decent interval, Washington might be able to open diplomatic relations with Peking. Although later denounced as a policy of appeasement, this strategy hardly envisioned a warm or enthusiastic relationship with Communist-run China. Even those who advocated the eventual establishment of official ties with Peking anticipated that they would be little more than cool and correct.

Moreover, not even Acheson was prepared to argue for immediate recognition of the People's Republic as long as the Nationalist government still existed in exile in Taipei. The Truman administration's need to secure domestic support for the Marshall Plan made it imperative to appear to be resisting the spread of communism in Asia, as well as in Europe. Thus, pending the eventual collapse of Nationalist resistance in Taiwan, the United States adopted a cold, even hostile, policy toward the new government in China. It suspended economic aid to the mainland, restricted the export of strategic goods, and opposed seating Peking in the United Nations. It also moved its embassy from Nanjing to Taipei and rebuffed feelers from the Communists about establishing diplomatic dialogue.

Likewise, the Chinese Communist Party was ambivalent about policy toward America. On the one hand, many members of the new

Chinese leadership—particularly Mao Zedong and Zhou Enlai—wished to maintain relations with the United States and other
Western countries, both to acquire a wider range of commercial
ties and to maintain a diplomatic counterweight against the Soviet
Union. On the other hand, they also decided, for reasons of ideology
and strategy, that they would have to "lean to one side," joining the
Soviet Union in military and economic alliance.

In effect, the Chinese Communists decided to let American policy
determine the balance between these two considerations. Since the
United States insisted on maintaining diplomatic relations with the
Nationalist government on Taiwan and imposed economic sanctions
on the new Communist regime, Peking chose to respond in kind. It
took several hostile steps toward the United States in 1949–50,
including the detention of Angus Ward, the American consul in
Shenyang, on espionage charges, the seizure of the American military
barracks in Peking, the harassment of U.S. diplomats seeking to
leave China, and the arrest of American missionaries working in the
country.

Some Americans, and even a few Chinese, have argued that there
was a "lost chance" in 1949—that greater flexibility and realism on
the American side could have avoided a hostile relationship between
the new People's Republic and the United States. Increasingly, however, the scholarly consensus on both sides of the Pacific is that the
differences between the ideologies and foreign policies of the two
governments were too wide to be quickly amended. Given the ideological preconceptions of both sides, the Chinese alliance with the
Soviet Union, the residual American connections with the Nationalists, and the emerging American policy of containment, forging even
a cool and proper relationship would have required a flexibility and
maturity that neither side possessed.

The Korean War ended any hope that the passage of time would
allow the dust to settle. Although the outbreak of armed conflict on
the peninsula in June 1950 was not the result of decisions made in
either Peking or Washington, Sino-American relations were still one
of the war's principal victims. In August 1950, the United States
broadened its objectives to include the liberation of North Korea and
ordered its own military forces and those of its South Korean allies
to cross the 38th parallel and drive north. The prospect of a pro-
American, non-Communist regime on China's northeastern frontier
was unacceptable to Peking, which viewed the American decision as
a harbinger of a much broader effort to overthrow all the Communist
governments that had emerged in Asia after the Second World War.

Peking therefore threatened to intervene if American forces approached the Yalu River. When, out of a misreading of Chinese intentions and capabilities, Washington ignored his warnings, Mao Zedong decided to intervene in force, despite the reservations of his military and civilian lieutenants and the unwillingness of the Soviet Union to provide direct military support. The result was nearly three years of military conflict between China and the United States, in which about 150,000 Chinese, and approximately 50,000 Americans, lost their lives.[2]

The Korean War deepened and institutionalized the confrontation between China and the United States. With the outbreak of the conflict, Washington imposed even tougher sanctions against Peking than it had adopted earlier. It froze mainland China's financial assets in the United States, placed a full embargo on American trade with China, and banned American ships and aircraft from calling at Chinese ports. It also successfully persuaded the United Nations General Assembly to name China an aggressor in the conflict, the same label that had previously been applied to North Korea. Peking retaliated by expropriating some American firms in China, harassing others until they went out of business, and then blocking the financial claims that resulted.

In addition, the Korean War also occasioned a very significant change in American policy toward Taiwan. In early 1950, the Truman administration had acknowledged that Taiwan was part of China and excluded the island from the American defense perimeter in the western Pacific, the logical consequence of the State Department's assessment that the fall of Taiwan to the Communists was inevitable and that there was no compelling reason for the United States to prevent it. Immediately after the onset of hostilities in Korea, however, the administration changed its policy to accord with the preferences of the Defense Department. The Pentagon had long viewed Taiwan as an essential part of the "island chain" of positions that it was building across the western Pacific and wanted to ensure that it would not fall into Communist hands.

In June 1950, therefore, President Truman ordered the Seventh Fleet to patrol the Taiwan Strait, nominally to prevent the Korean War from expanding southward but actually to reestablish an American commitment to the security of Taiwan. The American naval patrols were soon followed by the resumption of military assistance to Taipei, and then, in 1954, by a mutual defense treaty with the Nationalist government. The subsequent Formosa Resolution of 1955 extended American protection, if only implicitly, to the major groups of offshore islands still controlled by the Nationalists, as well as to Taiwan and the Penghus. Secret American undertakings to Chiang Kai-shek confirmed that commitment. At the same time, in order to deny the Communist government in Peking any claim to sovereignty over the island, the United States also adopted the position that the legal status of Taiwan was undetermined.

After the Korean War the United States began to construct its overall strategy in the western Pacific around the containment of China. Policy planners in Washington regarded China's invasion of Tibet in 1950, its support for the Communist revolution in Vietnam, its involvement in the Korean conflict, and its ties with revolutionary Communist parties in Southeast Asia as evidence enough that Peking's ultimate goal was the Communist seizure of power across Asia. Thus, in addition to its mutual defense treaty with Taiwan, the United States forged military alliances with Japan, South Korea, the Philippines, Thailand, Australia, and New Zealand, and deployed its own forces to the western Pacific. Although some of these alliances were formally justified as efforts to deter the reemergence of a military threat from Japan, their real objective was to contain the expansion of Chinese influence in Asia.

Interestingly, the American policy toward China was not based on any assumption of an enduring Sino-Soviet partnership. Although the conclusion of the treaty of alliance between China and the Soviet Union in February 1950 and the Chinese participation in the Korean War eight months later ended any hopes of a quick rupture between Moscow and Peking, American policymakers consistently assumed that a Sino-Soviet split was inevitable and that the objective of American policy should be to hasten its emergence. Many in Washington were convinced that Chinese political tradition would, in the end, prove incompatible with either a commitment to Marxism-Leninism or an alliance with the Soviet Union. Thus American policy, as stated in a National Security Council document in May 1951, was not just to contain China, but to detach it from its alliance with Moscow and to "support the development of an independent China which has renounced aggression."[3]

That overall assessment still left the question of the most effective strategy for promoting a split between Peking and Moscow. Some American officials and China specialists advocated seeking to lure China away from the Soviet Union through an accommodative policy toward Peking by such gestures as establishing diplomatic contacts and relaxing the trade embargo. The British also consistently urged such a position on the United States, and even President Dwight D. Eisenhower flirted with it from time to time. But the prevailing view in the Truman and Eisenhower administrations was that a wedge could more readily be placed between China and the Soviet Union through pressure rather than accommodation. An unyielding American posture would force China to obtain all its economic and security requirements from Moscow, with a strong probability that Moscow would weary of Chinese demands or that Peking would begrudge the level of Soviet assistance. As John Foster Dulles explained in 1952: "My own feeling is that the best way to get a separation between the Soviet Union and Communist China is to keep pressure on Communist China and make its way difficult so long as it is in partnership with Soviet Russia."[4]

The American "wedge" policy did not involve an active effort to liberate China from Communist rule. Admittedly, the Eisenhower administration adopted the rhetoric of liberation from time to time, with Secretary of State Dulles defining the objective of American policy in 1957 as hastening the passage not only of the Sino-Soviet alliance but of the Chinese Communist government itself. And the United States devoted limited resources to such an endeavor, helping the Nationalists undertake periodic raids against the mainland, providing supplies to remnant Nationalist forces in northern Burma, and training anti-Communist refugees from Tibet. But, other than these steps, the United States was extremely cautious about provoking renewed military conflict on the Asian mainland. One of the prices Taiwan had to pay for the mutual defense treaty was an agreement that it would launch military operations against the People's Republic only with American consent. And when, in 1962, the Nationalists sought permission to take advantage of the economic crisis on the mainland produced by the abortive Great Leap Forward through an attack on the Chinese coast, the Kennedy administration rejected the initiative out of hand.[5]

Instead, the main thrust of American policy was the deliberate and sustained isolation of the People's Republic. Washington not only refused to establish diplomatic relations with Peking, to support China's admission to the United Nations, or to relax its ban on trade with the mainland, but also urged its allies to follow suit. The most famous example of the American policy of isolation was the pointed refusal of John Foster Dulles to shake Zhou Enlai's hand during the Geneva negotiations on Indochina in 1954. Interestingly, Dulles's sister, Eleanor Dulles, subsequently explained that Dulles had feared that acknowledging Zhou's presence would suggest that the American policy of nonrecognition was weakening and might therefore cause "confusion" among U.S. allies in Europe and Asia.[6]

By the early 1960s, there were clear signs that the Sino-Soviet alliance was indeed collapsing, although little evidence this was the result of American pressure. But with its principal objective in sight, the United States still did not quickly shift toward accommodation with Peking. Instead, contrary to earlier expectations, Washington now concluded that China, rather than the Soviet Union, was the more aggressive and dangerous adversary. Both the Kennedy and Johnson administrations began very tentatively to consider some kind of military action against China's nuclear capabilities, possibly in conjunction with the Soviet Union.[7] Rather than forming an alignment with Peking against Moscow, the United States first appeared to be exploring a united front with the Soviet Union against China.

The hostile American policy toward China in the 1950s and 1960s was echoed by a hostile Chinese policy toward the United States. One important aspect of China's strategy was to use military pressure against the offshore islands held by the Nationalists to disrupt the growing strategic links between Washington and Taipei and to force diplomatic contacts between Washington and Peking. There is now persuasive evidence that China intended the Quemoy crisis of 1954–55 to deter the conclusion of the mutual defense treaty between Washington and Taipei, which was then in the final stages of negotiation, by illustrating the risks inherent in a commitment to the security of Taiwan.[8] Although unsuccessful in achieving that objective, the crisis did persuade the United States to open ambassa-dorial-level contacts with China in Geneva in 1955, which continued for two years until they were suspended in 1957. The later crisis over Quemoy and Matsu in 1958 was also largely intended to force Washington to resume the ambassadorial discussions and to reduce its military support for Taiwan, as well as to defuse the threat to China's coastal security posed by the Nationalists' reinforcement of the offshore islands.

A second element in Peking's strategy was to undermine the U.S. policy of containment and isolation by encouraging some of America's allies to adopt a more flexible approach toward China. For example, Peking's assault on the offshore islands in 1954–55 produced serious strains between the United States (which was willing to use force to defend Quemoy and Matsu) and Great Britain (which favored a more conciliatory policy toward Peking). At various times, China also tried to form diplomatic relations and economic ties with third world countries oriented toward the West (as in the mid-1950s), provided material and moral support to national liberation movements and Communist insurgencies directed against governments with close ties to the United States (as in the late 1950s and early 1960s), and expanded relations with such American allies as France and Japan (as in the early and mid-1960s). Although Chinese foreign policy was motivated by many objectives, including the acquisition of foreign capital and technology and the spread of Chinese influence throughout the international Communist movement, one significant theme throughout the two decades from 1949 to 1969 was weakening the international position of the United States by splitting it from its allies.

Finally, China also tried to manipulate the Sino-Soviet alliance to its advantage. Throughout the 1950s, Peking looked to Moscow for advanced military technology, including a sample atomic bomb, so that it could develop an ability to deter American attack. China also sought Soviet support for military undertakings against the offshore islands in 1954–55 and 1958, attempting in the latter instance to capitalize on the perceived shift in the international balance of power occasioned by the first Soviet Sputnik in the autumn of 1957. Eventually, however, the alliance between the two Communist giants became strained: Peking came to resent Soviet efforts to subordinate Chinese strategic policy to its own interests; Moscow was offended by growing signs of Chinese political, economic, and ideological independence. But, just as the Sino-Soviet split did not immediately lead to a moderation of American policy toward China, it did not quickly produce a more accommodative Chinese stance toward the United States. Mao regarded American liberalism and Soviet revisionism as equally pernicious ideological threats to the vitality of the Chinese revolution. Through most of the 1960s Peking therefore adopted a dual adversary posture, confident of its ability to resist both superpowers simultaneously.

Although each country adopted a hostile policy toward the other, there were occasional signs of flexibility. In the mid-1950s, for example, Peking proposed the resumption of trade, an exchange of students and journalists, and a meeting of Chinese and American foreign ministers. But the Eisenhower administration, still committed to a policy of isolating Peking, rejected these initiatives. Although it agreed to ambassadorial discussions with China, the United States regarded them as a substitute for, rather than a preliminary step toward, a foreign ministers' meeting. Washington also consistently used the ambassadorial negotiations to press China for a renunciation of force against Taiwan, a pledge that Peking equally consistently refused to provide. Washington accepted the idea of sending American journalists to China but refused to welcome Chinese journalists in return—a nonreciprocal approach that Peking promptly turned down.

In other areas, however, the Eisenhower administration showed some flexibility. At various times, Washington urged Chiang Kai-shek to withdraw his forces from Quemoy and Matsu so that they might be transformed from highly exposed garrisons to lightly armed outposts. The Eisenhower administration also began internal discussions of an eventual two-China policy, according to which both Taipei and Peking would be admitted to the United Nations and receive diplomatic recognition from the United States. But neither initiative was welcomed by either Taipei or Peking, who regarded them as an effort to institutionalize the division of China into two separate political entities.

Although the few instances of Chinese and American flexibility achieved little result, the two countries did find ways of avoiding further conflict by exercising mutual restraint. Although eschewing formal diplomatic relations or even high-level official contacts, the two governments did engage in regular ambassadorial-level discussions, first in Geneva from 1955 to 1957 and then in Warsaw after the Taiwan Strait crisis of 1958. Although this forum made little progress on any of the issues separating the two countries, except for reaching agreement on the repatriation of civilians in 1955, it did provide a channel for regular communication. Joint participation in multilateral conferences, including the Geneva conference on Indochina in 1954 and the negotiations on Laos in the early 1960s, offered similar opportunities for diplomatic contact.

Partly as a result of this dialogue, the two sides were able to avoid subsequent military confrontations on anything like the scale of the war in Korea. There were periodic crises between them, but each ended without a resumption of open conflict. In 1954–55, and again in 1958, the two sides were able to end the crises over Quemoy and Matsu without engaging in armed hostilities, with President Eisenhower rejecting proposals to employ nuclear weapons against China or to authorize a Nationalist counterattack against Chinese military installations opposite the offshore islands. In 1961–62, as already noted, the Kennedy administration made it clear that it would not support any Nationalist military operations against the mainland. And, during the Vietnam War, although the United States bombed Chinese troop concentrations in Vietnam and Chinese anti-aircraft batteries fired on American planes, the two sides were able to reach tacit agreement to limit the extent of military engagement: the Chinese would not enter the war in force as long as the United States refrained from invading China or North Vietnam and bombing the dikes along the Red River.[9]

In the final analysis, however, these occasional signs of flexibility and restraint represented little more than marginal adjustments to an essentially confrontational relationship. Trade between the United States and China in the early 1960s—two countries with a combined population of nearly one billion people—amounted to less than $500,000 a year.[10] Investment, cultural relations, and scholarly exchanges were nonexistent. Even at the height of the cold war, Moscow and Washington enjoyed formal diplomatic relations, conducted limited cultural exchanges, and maintained high-level contacts, including summit meetings. These interactions were absent between the United States and China. Indeed, in Michel Oksenberg's graphic comparison, before April 1969 more Americans had been to the moon than had received the permission of the U.S. government to travel to China.[11] As Doak Barnett has summarized Sino-American relations during that period: "There were no formal diplomatic ties, no trade, no legal travel back and forth, and virtually no mutual contact between ordinary citizens of the two countries. . . . Probably never in the modern period have two major societies been so isolated from each other for so long in peacetime—if the cold war could be considered peace. . . . China and the United States confronted each other, at a distance, as implacable adversaries."[12]

RAPPROCHEMENT

Despite their mutual confrontation, the logjam between China and the United States began to shift slightly in the early 1960s. Faced with severe domestic economic problems because of the Great Leap Forward, and with a growing security threat from the north as a result of the Sino-Soviet dispute, some Chinese officials responsible for foreign policy began to contemplate major adjustments in their country's diplomatic posture. They advocated easing tensions with all three of China's principal adversaries (the United States, the Soviet Union, and India), and attenuating China's support for Communist insurgencies and national liberation movements overseas. The Party leadership ultimately decided to reject this approach in favor of an adversarial posture toward both superpowers, the foreign policy most consistent with the ideological fundamentalism that Mao was beginning to revive at the time. But the option of improving Sino-American relations had once again entered high-level Party discussions.

Meanwhile, a more open discussion of Sino-American relations was under way in the United States. After the Taiwan Strait crisis of 1958, a growing number of Americans began to question the low level of contact and the high level of tension between China and the

United States. In 1959, Congress commissioned a San Francisco research firm, Conlon Associates, to reassess American policy toward Asia. The Conlon report proposed abandoning the policy of isolating China in favor of a two-stage approach. In the first stage, China and the United States would expand unofficial cultural exchanges and conduct informal discussions on the future of their relationship. If those discussions were fruitful, the United States could, in a second stage, relax restrictions on trade with China, support Peking's admission to the United Nations, and establish some form of official relationship with China.[13]

Although not immediately adopted, these proposals set the stage for the most searching reassessment of U.S. China policy since 1949. In the early 1960s, as American involvement in Vietnam escalated, the Council on Foreign Relations sponsored a major series of study groups and publications on Sino-American relations, clearly intended to stimulate a reconsideration of American policy toward China. Similar efforts were undertaken by the new National Committee on U.S.-China Relations, formed in 1966, and by major hearings in both houses of Congress that same year.

In the course of the debate, a new consensus began to emerge on China policy in the community of American foreign policy analysts and Asian specialists. Rhetoric aside, it was now argued, Chinese foreign policy was much more defensive and cautious than adventurous and aggressive, presenting an opportunity for a significant reduction of tension with Peking. Moreover, given the burden imposed on the American strategic position by the Vietnam War, some kind of accommodation with China would clearly be in the American interest. Accordingly, although continuing to deter any aggressive or subversive behavior on China's part, the United States should no longer attempt to isolate Peking. The policy suggested by such an analysis was best summarized by Doak Barnett before the Senate Foreign Relations Committee as "containment but not isolation."[14]

To a limited degree, the Kennedy and Johnson administrations began to adjust their China policy in response to these ideas. New policy proposals began to circulate inside the government. Some officials proposed the recognition of Mongolia to show that the United States was willing to establish diplomatic relations with an Asian Communist regime. Others, like Adlai Stevenson, suggested that the United States support the admission of both Taipei and Peking to the United Nations. And still others, such as Marshall Green, then the American consul-general in Hong Kong, recommended a significant relaxation of U.S. trade and travel restrictions.[15]

But these more radical proposals were never accepted, in part because there was no consensus in the government over their desirability and in part because, in contrast to the view being expressed by specialists, general public opinion was slow to support a more flexible policy toward China.[16]

Instead, the United States undertook only a few small gestures toward China between 1961 and 1966: calling the capital Peking rather than Peiping, offering at various times to permit the sale of grain and pharmaceuticals to China, inviting Chinese journalists to cover the 1968 election, proposing scientific exchanges, and allowing Americans to purchase Chinese publications. Also, American officials began to promise an even more forthcoming policy if Peking would only moderate its rhetoric and behavior. In the past, Washington had argued that isolation would force China to change; now, the Johnson administration reformulated that policy to note that once China changed, the United States could end its policy of isolation.

Predictably, such limited American initiatives were rejected by Peking. The various American offers to expand bilateral relations were ridiculed; the expressions of hope for changes in Chinese behavior were denounced as Washington's plan to encourage China's peaceful evolution from communism to capitalism. The harsh Chinese response to the U.S. overtures gradually dampened the American official enthusiasm for the enterprise, as did Chinese support for Hanoi as American involvement in Vietnam deepened.[17]

Eventually, however, international developments encouraged Peking to reconsider a more conciliatory policy toward the United States. The Soviet invasion of Czechoslovakia in August 1968, accompanied by the enunciation of the Brezhnev Doctrine, suggested that the Kremlin was prepared to use military force to defend socialism in neighboring Communist states. Soviet descriptions of China during the Cultural Revolution as having abandoned socialism, the sustained buildup of Soviet military forces along the Sino-Soviet frontier, and especially the vigorous Soviet escalation of the clashes that broke out along the border in 1969, implied that Moscow had the intention and the capability to impose similar military pressure against China, at a time when the chaos of the Cultural Revolution made the country particularly vulnerable to external attack. By the end of 1968, Chinese statements had begun to identify the Soviet Union—now described as "socialist in words, imperialist in deeds"—as an even greater threat to Chinese security than the United States.

To cope with the menace from the Soviet Union, China reinforced its military deployments along the Sino-Soviet frontier. It also resumed negotiations with Moscow, beginning with a meeting between Zhou Enlai and Aleksei Kosygin at the Peking airport in the fall of 1969, aimed at defusing tensions along the border. But these short-term palliatives aside, an accommodation with the United States now appeared to be the most effective way of enhancing China's security against the Soviet threat. Thus, even as they began talking to the Kremlin, the Chinese also proposed resuming the Sino-American ambassadorial negotiations in Warsaw, which had been suspended earlier that year, once the new Nixon administration took office. Even if Peking had not decided how far it was prepared to go with the United States, it was interested in probing the attitudes of the new American government.

International developments also encouraged the United States to consider a rapprochement with Peking. When Nixon entered the White House in January 1969 he was committed to seeking an end to the American involvement in Vietnam and to promoting détente with the Soviet Union.[18] An improvement of relations with Peking could promote both these objectives by raising doubts in Hanoi about the commitment and reliability of one of its principal supporters and by raising alarms in Moscow about the possibility of an accommodation between its two principal adversaries. Over the longer term, Nixon viewed China as one of five emerging international power centers with whom it was imperative that the United States develop greater contact. Thus, one month after taking office, Nixon wrote a memo to Henry A. Kissinger, his national security adviser, asking him to explore the prospects for improved relations with China, and in so doing to create the impression in the Soviet Union that American policy was about to change.

Kissinger viewed China from a somewhat different perspective. Unpersuaded by the China specialists that an improvement of relations with Peking would be beneficial for its own sake, or even by Nixon's conviction that it would help promote a settlement in Vietnam, Kissinger became a convert to Sino-American rapprochement only when he was persuaded that there was a significant chance of war along the Sino-Soviet frontier. This, to Kissinger, presented a challenge and an opportunity. On the one hand, it was necessary for the United States to deter any Soviet military action against China that would significantly disrupt the global balance of power. On the other, it was now possible for the United States to gain the pivotal position in an emerging strategic triangle: the United States would enjoy better relations with both Peking and Moscow than they had with each other and thus America would enjoy superior leverage in dealing with them both.

Shortly after Nixon's inauguration, the United States and China began the cautious minuet that ultimately led to the normalization of their relations.[19] In effect, the Nixon administration adopted a two-track strategy toward Peking. Publicly, it announced a steady series of unilateral gestures toward China—steps that Peking would presumably notice and appreciate but to which it would not have to respond. Privately, the Nixon administration opened several lines of communication with China, not only by reactivating the ambassadorial talks at Warsaw but also by using France, Romania, and Pakistan as intermediaries.

Through these channels, the United States passed several consistent messages to Peking. First, it indicated through many of its unilateral gestures that it no longer wanted an adversarial relationship with China. American officials began using the name "People's Republic of China" when referring to the mainland.[20] The White House gradually relaxed the restrictions on trade with and travel to China. Perhaps most important, the Nixon administration took several steps that suggested a more benign strategic posture toward China. It ended naval patrols of the Taiwan Strait and halted reconnaissance flights over Chinese territory. In early 1970, it revised its strategic doctrine so that the United States would maintain the capability to simultaneously fight only one-and-a-half, rather than two-and-a-half, wars.[21] And the so-called Guam Doctrine, or Nixon Doctrine, implied not only that Washington had decided to begin to withdraw its forces from Vietnam but also that the United States would never again be involved as deeply in ground conflict in Asia as it had been in Vietnam. In all these ways, Washington was signaling to Peking that the United States no longer was envisioning a significant military confrontation with China.[22]

A second and even more pointed message was that the United States would oppose any Soviet military or diplomatic initiatives that threatened Chinese security. According to Chinese sources, one of the first messages that Washington passed to Peking in 1969 was to reject a recent Soviet proposal for a collective security arrangement in Asia on the grounds that it constituted an unacceptable effort to isolate China.[23] Moreover, in response to a spate of rumors in the summer and fall of 1969 that Moscow might be planning some kind of military assault on China, Washington began publicly to express interest in bolstering China's security against a possible Soviet attack. It revealed that it was aware of Soviet feelers about the probable international reaction to a preemptive strike against China's nuclear facilities. And it took several opportunities to state that the United States could not tolerate China's defeat in a Sino-Soviet war.

Third, the United States also proposed the inauguration of an expanded Sino-American dialogue. In 1969, in the same message that expressed American opposition to the Soviet proposal for an Asian collective security system, the Nixon administration said that it wanted to open contacts with Peking.[24] At the Sino-American ambassadorial meetings in Warsaw in January 1970, the Nixon administration explained that it was proposing to send a high-level emissary to Peking or receive a high-level Chinese representative in Washington to discuss a fundamental improvement in the U.S.-China relationship. Seemingly casual public statements by the president, such as an interview in *Time* magazine in October 1970, hinted that he himself might be available for such an assignment.[25]

The two tracks of the Nixon strategy complemented each other well. The private communications with Peking, and especially the offer to send a high-level envoy to China, were necessary to convey the American willingness to consider sweeping changes, rather than simply marginal adjustments, in American policy toward China. But the small steps, taken publicly, were necessary to prepare American and international public opinion and to convince Peking of the Nixon administration's sincerity. Neither course of action would have been as effective without the other. The unilateral redefinitions of American policy and the softening of American rhetoric toward China would have been dismissed as trivial and insincere, as they had been when undertaken by the Johnson administration. Conversely, private negotiations without public preparation would have risked a domestic political explosion and great unease among American allies had they suddenly produced successful results. The blending of secret diplomacy and unilateral gestures evinced an American sincerity and commitment that earlier U.S. overtures had lacked.

China responded to the American strategy in kind, with a combination of private communications and public gestures. Privately, Peking informed Washington on several occasions that it accepted the idea of a high-level American emissary, as long as the discussions would address the "key issues" in U.S.-China relations. The public gestures included the 1969 release of two groups of American yachtsmen detained by the Chinese after straying into Chinese waters and the July 1970 release of Bishop James Walsh, an American missionary arrested for espionage in 1958. These were duly noted by the U.S. government but attracted little public attention.

Then, Peking took two more dramatic steps. In December 1970, meeting with the sympathetic American journalist Edgar Snow, Mao Zedong said that he would be happy to welcome Nixon to China, "either as a tourist or as President."[26] And, in April 1971, the Chinese invited an American Ping-Pong team, participating in an international tournament in Japan, to visit China, where team members were informed by Zhou Enlai that they had "opened the door to friendly contacts between the people of the two countries."[27]

The messages passed back and forth between Washington and Peking through these various channels gradually achieved results. In April 1971, the Chinese formally invited a high-level American envoy to visit China, suggesting that the U.S. delegate might be Henry Kissinger, Secretary of State William Rogers, or "even the President of the US himself."[28] Nixon decided to propose two visits: a public presidential visit to Peking, preceded by a secret visit by a lower-level envoy to arrange the agenda. After considering many possible candidates for the first mission—including George Bush, Nelson Rockefeller, and Thomas Dewey—Nixon decided to send Kissinger.[29] The plan was relayed to Peking in a message in May. When the Chinese replied on June 2 that they were willing to receive both emissaries and that Nixon would be assured a meeting with Mao, the president was so elated that he broke out a bottle of "very old Courvoisier brandy" and joined Kissinger in a toast "to generations to come who may have a better chance to live in peace because of what we have done."[30]

Although successful in the end, the process of Sino-American rapprochement had to contend with political resistance in both countries—outright opposition in China, more subtle ambivalence in the United States. In China, a group of military leaders associated with Lin Biao, then Mao's putative successor, appeared committed to maintaining the "dual adversary" policy of the early 1960s, partly because they distrusted American intentions and partly because they feared that a tilt toward the United States would risk provoking the Soviet Union into retaliatory pressure against China. Not only did Lin and his colleagues apparently argue against Sino-American détente in policy councils, but they also took every opportunity to sabotage it. The attempted interception of an American reconnaissance flight over the Taiwan Strait in June 1970 almost certainly reflected military opposition to an accommodation to Washington, and the periodic interruptions of the Sino-American dialogue may have also been caused by internal political difficulties. The weakening of Lin's position after a major Party meeting in the summer of

1970, followed by Lin's death in September 1971 after allegedly plotting a coup d'etat against Mao, facilitated the consummation of the rapprochement.[31]

In the United States, too, potential opposition had to be dealt with. Conservatives, especially those with close links to Taiwan, were likely to oppose any accommodation with China unless it was undertaken with great care. The public remained highly skeptical about China, with pluralities opposing diplomatic relations with Peking and China's membership in the United Nations.[32] Nixon and Kissinger were therefore obliged to conduct the negotiations with China in the greatest secrecy, refusing until the last possible moment to inform American allies, the State Department, or even the secretary of state of the prospects for a presidential visit. From the beginning, too, Kissinger was acutely aware that any weakening of American commitments to Taiwan would invite sharp criticism, and that perception strongly influenced his approach to the negotiation of the joint communiqué to be issued at the end of the Nixon visit.

This potential opposition aside, the White House also had to confront the ignorance of the rest of the government and what Nixon and Kissinger regarded as the bureaucratic inertia of the State Department. Unaware of the extent of the president's intentions toward China, various officials—including Secretary of State Rogers and Vice President Spiro Agnew—periodically made statements about China policy that differed from the messages that the White House was trying to send to the Chinese. American diplomats sought to preserve Taiwan's seat in the United Nations, even though Kissinger regarded the policy as doomed to failure.[33] Moreover, the State Department consistently warned of the risks of a hasty accommodation with Peking: the Soviet specialists were concerned with the potentially negative impact on Soviet-American relations, while the China specialists cautioned that a presidential trip that did not reap significant Chinese concessions on Taiwan and on other regional issues would be regarded as an American capitulation.[34]

And, indeed, the issue of Taiwan was the most knotty substantive obstacle to the rapprochement between the two countries. Although Kissinger has implied that the issue was always a minor one, readily subordinated to the common strategic interests of the two countries regarding the Soviet Union, in fact there was always hard bargaining between Peking and Washington over the Taiwan question. At the beginning of the negotiations between China and the United States during the Nixon administration, Peking insisted that any higher-level contact should deal primarily with what it considered the most important issue in the relationship: the continuing American relationship with Taiwan. In early 1971, for example, a Chinese message passed through Romania declared, "There is only one outstanding issue between us—the U.S. occupation of Taiwan. . . . If the U.S. has a desire to settle the issue and a proposal for its solution, the P.R.C. will be prepared to receive a U.S. special envoy in Peking."[35] Similarly, in the discussions of the joint statement announcing the Nixon visit, the Chinese proposed that the purpose be defined as "a discussion of Taiwan as a prelude to the normalization of relations."[36] Washington consistently responded with a proposed compromise that the Chinese finally accepted: the United States was indeed prepared to talk about Taiwan, but it would insist on discussing other global and regional issues as well.

But this response still left unresolved the way in which the Taiwan issue would be dealt with. Fortunately, China initially defined the issue in the same way it had for fifteen years: the withdrawal of American forces from Taiwan so as to end the "U.S. occupation" of the island. Other potential Chinese demands, such as the termination of American diplomatic relations with Taipei and the abrogation of the U.S. defense treaty with Taiwan, were deferred until later in the negotiations. As Kissinger has pointed out, in doing so the Chinese posed the question in "a manner most susceptible to solution," since the American forces on Taiwan were not essential either to the island's defense or to the broader pattern of American deployments in the western Pacific.[37] The United States could therefore agree to discuss the withdrawal of U.S. troops and military installations from the island insofar as a reduction of tensions in the Taiwan Strait and a resolution of the conflict in Vietnam permitted it. There were still hard negotiations ahead, but this basic formula permitted an agreement on the agenda of the Nixon visit and provided the framework for addressing the Taiwan question in the Shanghai communiqué.

The rapprochement between China and the United States culminated in Kissinger's secret visit to Peking in July 1971, his subsequent trip in October, and then the highly publicized visit by Nixon the following February. The first of these, Kissinger's mission in July, provided each side an opportunity to present a broad *tour d'horizon* of current international problems and to describe the main outlines of its foreign policy. As on subsequent trips, the Chinese made clear that they welcomed the American disengagement from Vietnam and abandonment of any attempt to establish a hegemonic role in Asia.[38] Equally important, they also indicated that they were concerned about Soviet expansionism in Asia (and to some degree about Japanese and Indian ambitions as well), and hoped that the United States would be prepared to cooperate with China in maintaining a regional balance of power. In turn, the American visitors stressed that the network of U.S. alliances and military deployments and installations in Asia was essential to such a role and therefore deserved Chinese support. Kissinger also apparently hinted at various forms of security cooperation with Peking by showing Chinese leaders American intelligence information about Soviet deployments in the Far East and by promising to inform them of any American understanding with the Soviet Union that might affect Chinese interests.[39]

According to Chinese sources, Zhou and Kissinger also laid out their positions on Taiwan in some detail during their meeting in July 1971.[40] Zhou presented three demands to the United States—that it acknowledge that Taiwan was a province of China, that it set a deadline for the withdrawal of its troops from Taiwan, and that it abrogate the mutual defense treaty—but apparently did not demand that the United States terminate diplomatic relations with Taipei. On the first point, Kissinger replied that the United States now acknowledged that Taiwan belonged to China and no longer considered its status undetermined. On the second, he said that the United States would be prepared to withdraw two-thirds of its troops from Taiwan shortly after the end of the war in Vietnam and would reduce the remainder as Sino-American relations improved. With regard to the mutual defense treaty, Kissinger said only that history would take care of that problem. Kissinger stated that the United States could not acknowledge Peking as the sole legitimate government of China until Nixon's second term but added that Washington could support the restoration of China's seat in the United Nations in the meantime, as long as Taiwan's representatives were not expelled. Although this American position had "serious shortcomings" from a Chinese perspective, it still indicated that Washington was prepared to take a first step toward the improvement of U.S.-China relations.[41]

During Kissinger's October trip, the two sides moved from this general discussion of their respective policies and perspectives to a more detailed negotiation of the text of the joint communiqué to result from the president's visit. At first, Kissinger assumed that such a communiqué would follow standard diplomatic practice, emphasizing areas of agreement and glossing over differences. To his surprise, Zhou Enlai firmly rejected such an approach on the grounds that such a document would have little credibility abroad and would be hard to defend to skeptical audiences at home. Instead, the Chinese insisted on a document that would acknowledge and outline the "fundamental differences" between the two countries.

The draft presented by Zhou couched China's views in such radical language that no American president could have agreed to sign it. But it provided the basis for compromise. Kissinger agreed that the communiqué would follow the format proposed by the Chinese: parallel statements summarizing the two governments' divergent positions on a wide range of global and regional issues. But he successfully insisted that it also include areas of agreement, so that the trip could be said to have achieved some positive results, and that each side's statement of its position be put in language acceptable to the other.[42]

The final version of the communiqué, issued in Shanghai at the conclusion of Nixon's visit to China in February 1972, identified the common interests of the two countries as opposing Soviet expansion in Asia, reducing the prospects of bilateral military confrontation, and expanding Sino-American economic and cultural relations (see appendix B). It committed them to conduct their relations on the basis of China's five principles of peaceful coexistence, including respect for each other's sovereignty and territorial integrity and non-interference in each other's internal affairs. The two countries also agreed to promote the normalization of their relations, a phrase implying the establishment of formal diplomatic relations, with Nixon privately expressing the hope that this could be done sometime during his second term in office.[43]

On the question of Taiwan, both sides made significant concessions, following the basic framework adopted during Kissinger's previous visit in October. The United States implicitly abandoned its previous position held since 1950 that the status of Taiwan remained "undetermined." Instead, it stated that it would "not challenge," although not explicitly accept, the proposition that "there is but one China and that Taiwan is a part of China." It also affirmed that its "ultimate objective" was the complete withdrawal of all American military forces from Taiwan, and that this goal could be realized if there were a peaceful settlement of the Taiwan issue by the Chinese themselves.[44]

Beyond this, in his private conversations with Chinese leaders, Nixon made several other overtures: the United States would accept "any peaceful solution to the Taiwan situation," it would not support a Taiwan independence movement, it would ultimately acknowledge that Taiwan was part of China, and Nixon would "seek normalization and try to achieve it," presumably in his second term. In addition, Washington would try to ensure that Japan would not replace the United States as it withdrew its military forces from Taiwan.[45]

But while these statements must have been reassuring to Peking, Nixon's response to China's most important demands was much less forthcoming. While expressing his willingness to normalize relations with China, Nixon said that he could not abandon Taiwan in doing so. This commitment suggested that he was not prepared to acknowledge Peking as the sole legitimate government of China and that he still hoped to maintain some form of diplomatic relations with Taipei. Moreover, Nixon also said that the United States could eventually remove all its forces and military equipment from Taiwan only if Peking guaranteed that it would use only peaceful means to resolve the Taiwan question. These two issues—the future of American relations with Taiwan and Washington's desire for a renunciation of force from Peking—would continue to complicate Sino-American relations for the next six years.

The agreement on the text of the Shanghai communiqué also required concessions from China. Kissinger insisted on stating an American interest in a peaceful future for Taiwan rather than simply expressing, as the Chinese had preferred, the hope that the problem could be resolved peacefully. He linked the withdrawal of American forces and military installations from Taiwan to a diminution of tension in the area, thus giving Peking a stake in the reduction of tensions in the Taiwan Strait and in a successful conclusion to the ongoing negotiations over Vietnam. In addition, the United States not only managed to exclude from the Shanghai communiqué any Chinese demand for the termination of the mutual defense treaty between the United States and Taiwan, but won Chinese consent for an explicit reaffirmation of that treaty during a press conference in Shanghai at the conclusion of the presidential visit.[46]

The momentum imparted to Sino-American relations by the Nixon visit of 1972 continued for at least another year and perhaps a bit longer. The high point of this phase of Sino-American relations occurred when Kissinger visited Peking in February 1973. At that time, Washington and Hanoi had just signed the Paris accords, providing for a cease-fire in Vietnam. That, in itself, removed a major irritant from Sino-American relations. Indeed, Chinese and American interests in the area now began for the first time to coincide, since neither country wished North Vietnam to establish hegemony over Indochina.

This common perspective permitted increasing cooperation between the two countries on the most pressing issues in Asia, with

China reshaping its policies to parallel those of the United States. Peking suddenly ceased its long-standing criticism of the mutual security treaty between Japan and the United States, especially after Americans began to warn that the termination of the Japanese-American alliance could well encourage Tokyo to develop its own nuclear weapons. China began to offer explicit support to the maintenance of peace and stability on the Korean peninsula, including discouraging Kim Il Sung from launching an attack against the south in the aftermath of the fall of Saigon in 1975. And, most prominently, the two countries began to coordinate their policy on Cambodia, agreeing on the desirability of a neutral coalition government under Sihanouk as a preferable alternative to Lon Nol, the Khmer Rouge, or forces oriented toward Hanoi.[47]

In fact, for the first time since 1949, Chinese leaders were prepared to acknowledge the desirability of a continuing American military presence in Asia, and even strategic cooperation between China and the United States. They recognized that, with the end of the war in Vietnam, a precipitous American withdrawal from the region would leave China vulnerable to Soviet military pressure. Although Zhou Enlai would later deny it, two American congressmen, Hale Boggs and Gerald Ford, insisted he told them that the United States should retain military forces in Asia to preserve a stable balance of power.[48] Reports also appeared that, during Kissinger's visit in November 1973, the Chinese began to inquire about the possibility of arms purchases from the United States.[49] That same year, Chinese military officers stationed at the United Nations began discussing the same possibility with a few American foreign policy analysts whom they had come to trust.[50]

The two countries also made surprising progress in expanding their diplomatic contacts. Two such channels were established after the Nixon visit: normal diplomatic exchanges would be conducted through the Chinese and American embassies in Paris, while more sensitive messages would be passed directly between Kissinger and Huang Hua, the Chinese ambassador to the United Nations, using a "safe house" maintained by the Central Intelligence Agency in New York. This cumbersome process was not ideal, and Kissinger raised the issue with Zhou Enlai in Peking in February 1973, proposing to exchange some kind of official representative offices with Peking, such as a trade office, a consulate, or a liaison office.

Because the Chinese had previously refused to establish a formal diplomatic presence in any capital where Taiwan maintained an embassy, Kissinger did not expect Zhou to accept the proposal to exchange official representative offices. But Kissinger accompanied

his proposal with a much more explicit timetable for the normalization of Sino-American relations than the Chinese had ever been
given before. In the first two years of Nixon's second term, Kissinger
said, the United States would remove all its remaining forces from
Taiwan. In the latter two years, it would complete the normalization
of Sino-American relations along the same lines as the normalization
of Sino-Japanese relations at the end of 1972. Since Tokyo had terminated diplomatic relations with Taiwan and maintained only unofficial ties with Taipei, Kissinger's reference to the "Japanese formula" clearly implied that the United States was now abandoning
Nixon's earlier position that it wanted to maintain official relations
with Taiwan even after establishing diplomatic relations with
Peking.[51]

To Kissinger's surprise, Zhou therefore readily accepted his proposal. In fact, Zhou showed no interest in either a trade office or a
consulate but insisted that the two countries exchange liaison offices, the highest form of official contact short of full diplomatic
relations. So enthusiastic were the Chinese that they were able to
present a detailed plan for such an exchange the following day.[52]

The alacrity with which the Chinese agreed to exchange liaison
offices with Washington led Kissinger to great optimism about the
terms on which formal diplomatic relations between the United
States and China could be established. He began to hope that the
Chinese would accept a continued American official presence on
Taiwan after the normalization of U.S.-China relations and tolerate a
continued American defense commitment to the island—two crucial
concessions that would help the Nixon administration gain public
acceptance for breaking formal diplomatic ties with Taipei. On his
next trip to China, in November 1973, Kissinger therefore told his
Chinese counterparts that the United States was "determined to do
much more and to complete the process [of normalization] we started
two years ago as rapidly as possible," as long as Peking could be
flexible on the terms.[53]

Once again, Kissinger's interlocutors were surprisingly forthcoming. Zhou told him that normalization could be achieved simply on
the basis of confirming the principle of one China and did not insist
on the termination of either the mutual defense treaty or American
diplomatic relations with Taiwan. Somewhat more obliquely, Mao
Zedong noted without disapproval that the Soviet Union tolerated
the existence of legations from the Baltic states in Washington.
Kissinger therefore concluded that China was "indirectly inviting a
proposal that combined the principle of a unified China with some
practical accommodation to the status quo."[54] And in interviews

given to reporters just after he left China, Kissinger expressed the hope that, if the United States accepted the principle of Chinese unity, it would be able to maintain official relations with Taiwan and possibly the mutual defense treaty as well, until the two sides were able to resolve their differences through negotiation.[55] If the Chinese had indeed been prepared to normalize relations on such terms, it would have been an important breakthrough for the United States.

COMPLICATIONS

Unfortunately, by early 1974, the promising momentum in Sino-American relations had begun to dissipate.[56] The American public, which had responded enthusiastically to the Nixon visit of 1972, now began to have second thoughts about China. The percentage of those having favorable perceptions of that country had risen dramatically as a result of the presidential visit, from 23 percent in 1972 to 49 percent in 1973. Within a few years, however, the goodwill toward Peking began to dissipate, such that by 1976 the proportion having favorable images of China fell to 20 percent, and the percentage holding unfavorable perceptions rose to 73 percent—just about the same distribution of opinion toward China that had existed before the Nixon trip (table A-1).

At the same time, several small incidents provided a public indication of Chinese displeasure with the United States. The Chinese press began to run articles critical of things American, including Washington's policy of cooperation with the Nationalist government in the 1940s, the writing of prominent American China specialists, and the Western music performed by the Philadelphia Orchestra during its tour of China. The Chinese government protested the stationing of U.S. Marine guards in the liaison office in Peking and claimed to find smut in a shipment of American wheat destined for China. In 1975, two cultural exchanges were canceled, largely because of the differences between the two countries over Taiwan.

The stalemate in Sino-American relations was also reflected in high-level dealings between the two countries. During the Nixon visit, Chinese and American officials had begun to discuss the issue of blocked claims and frozen assets dating from the Korean War, the resolution of which was particularly important to the normalization of Sino-American economic relations. By April 1974, when Deng Xiaoping visited New York to make a major address to the United Nations, the two sides had reached a broad agreement on the solution to the problem. But the discussions soon bogged down, with the Chinese side unwilling to make the political decision to finalize and implement the agreement. Moreover, although Kissinger continued to travel to China about two times each year, he discovered that, after November 1973, his visits "either were downright chilly or were holding actions."[57]

In November 1974, in the hopes of restoring momentum to their relationship, Washington and Peking agreed that the new American president, Gerald Ford, would visit China by the end of the following year. The Chinese clearly hoped that the new American administration would undertake new initiatives toward Peking that a politically enfeebled Richard Nixon had been unable to make.[58] In the end, however, this visit in December 1975 proved disappointing. The journey was cut from seven days to four, and Ford added stops in Indonesia and the Philippines to give his tour greater substance. Although the Americans wanted to issue a joint statement at the end of the meeting to give the impression of headway, the Chinese refused on the grounds that no concrete progress toward normalization had been made. American officials bravely insisted that Ford had had useful exchanges with his Chinese counterparts. But some of them privately acknowledged a different reality. "I think it [the trip] was very useful," said one, "but I can't suggest why I think that."[59] For their part, the Chinese promptly extended an invitation to Nixon to visit China the following February, in the hopes that he could increase the pressure on the Ford administration to break the deadlock.[60]

What were the reasons for the stagnation in the Sino-American relationship after 1973? Three factors combined to sap momentum from the relations between the two countries: differences over strategy toward the Soviet Union, the inability to find a mutually acceptable solution to the Taiwan issue, and the mounting domestic political difficulties of the Chinese and American governments.[61]

Although Washington and Peking shared a concern about Soviet expansionism throughout the mid-1970s, their policies toward Moscow increasingly diverged. In essence, China wanted an alignment with the United States for confrontation against Moscow, whereas the United States wanted an alignment with China in order to promote Soviet-American détente. Zhou and Mao saw the Soviet Union as a singlemindedly aggressive power that should be contained; Kissinger and Nixon viewed Moscow as a more complicated international actor that, to a degree, could be accommodated.

This difference in perspective, muted at first, soon introduced complications into the Sino-American relationship. The Chinese, seeing the American interest in promoting an accommodation with Moscow, feared they would be abandoned by the United States once détente succeeded, thus permitting the Soviet Union to devote all its resources to the containment of China. Chinese leaders sarcastically described this strategy as standing on their shoulders to reach agreements with Moscow. Thus Chinese leaders were skeptical of American negotiations with the Soviet Union throughout the mid-1970s. As Kissinger puts it, "Whatever our motive for negotiating with the Soviets, however sophisticated our explanations, Peking could see no advantage in deferring a showdown."[62]

The United States had the opposite worry. Whereas Peking feared that it would be sacrificed by the United States for the sake of Soviet-American détente, Washington was concerned that it would be drawn by China into a Sino-Soviet confrontation. To be sure, from the beginning of the Nixon administration Kissinger had been convinced that it was in the geopolitical interest of the United States to guarantee Chinese independence and territorial integrity against Soviet attack. But, at the same time, America did not want to become entangled in the rigidly confrontational policy favored by Peking. Unlike Peking, Kissinger notes, the U.S. government "could not afford to be perceived as courting confrontation," either by its allies or by its own people. As a result, although China "had to be able to count on American support against direct Soviet pressures. . . , it must not be permitted to maneuver us into unnecessary show-downs" with Moscow.[63]

At first, Kissinger believed that this dilemma could be finessed by careful diplomacy. As he reported to Nixon after his February 1973 visit to China, "with conscientious attention to both capitals, we should be able to continue to have our mao tai and drink our vodka too."[64] Over time, however, the divergence between Chinese and American perspectives became too great, particularly as the United States sought to define with the Soviet Union the terms for détente in Europe. Peking described the Helsinki accords of 1975 as the Munich agreement of the 1970s, implying that the agreement would simply give the Soviet Union greater opportunities to build up military strength and expand its influence in other parts of the world. Similarly, the enunciation of the Sonnenfeldt Doctrine in early 1976, by which the United States accepted the status quo in Eastern Europe, convinced Peking that Washington was overly eager to accommodate Soviet interests on Moscow's western front.[65] Closer to home, the inability of the United States to prevent the collapse of the Lon Nol government in Cambodia and its replacement by the Khmer Rouge was also disturbing to the Chinese, for it represented the failure of the Sino-American effort to promote a neutralist government under Sihanouk. All these developments suggested a weak United States committed to appeasement of Moscow and unable to fulfill strategic commitments to China.

The only remaining question was whether there was any possibility that one country might change its Soviet policy to more closely parallel that of the other. In 1974–75 the Chinese did probe Moscow's attitude on border issues to see whether the Kremlin was prepared to accept Peking's proposals for a mutual withdrawal of forces from disputed territory.[66] When Brezhnev rejected or ignored the Chinese feelers, Peking must have concluded that it would receive few benefits from a more conciliatory policy toward Moscow. Indeed, the architects of the Chinese initiatives were subject to a mounting attack from leftist leaders in Peking, who accused them of engaging in capitulation and "national betrayal."[67] Conversely, the internal debates in the Ford administration between Secretary of State Kissinger and Secretary of Defense James Schlesinger may for a time have given Peking some hope that America's policy of détente could be reversed. But the dismissal of Schlesinger in late 1975 suggested that the advocates of accommodation continued to hold sway in Washington.[68] Thus, with each country committed to a different approach to the Soviet Union—the United States to détente, China to confrontation—their overall foreign policies increasingly diverged.

The second issue that hampered the development of Sino-American relations in the mid-1970s was Taiwan. Kissinger's hopes that the United States could normalize relations with Peking while maintaining some kind of official relationship with Taiwan never came to fruition. For one thing, many Chinese officials began to doubt American sincerity on the question, perceiving that the United States was moving backward toward a closer relationship with Taipei, rather than forward toward the establishment of diplomatic relations with Peking. The slow pace at which American troops were being withdrawn from Taiwan, the appointment of a new American ambassador to Taipei, Taiwan's ability to open more consulates in the United States, the establishment of a new American trade center in Taipei, and a continued American program of arms sales to the island were all viewed in Peking as evidence of American reluctance to make the final break with Taipei.[69] One Chinese diplomat complained in the fall of 1974, "We don't know whether your Secretary of State is really sincere about getting out of Taiwan."[70] This perception made it more difficult to pursue the flexible formula that Zhou and Mao had presented to Kissinger in 1973.

Moreover, in 1974–75, Zhou Enlai came under sustained criticism by a radical faction in the Chinese leadership, headed by Mao's wife, Jiang Qing. The main concern of the radicals was that Zhou was systematically rehabilitating more moderate officials who had been purged during the Cultural Revolution and was attempting to return China to a more pragmatic course in foreign and domestic affairs. To counter this strategy, the radicals accused Zhou of seeking to restore the status quo prior to the Cultural Revolution. Although the radicals concentrated most of their fire on Zhou's personnel appointments and his educational policy, criticism of the premier's foreign policy and economic strategy was also a significant theme, and any concessions to the United States on Taiwan would have immediately given the radicals powerful ammunition with which to continue their assault.

With Zhou in failing health and under attack, his ability to move Chinese foreign policy in new directions was steadily declining. Authority over Chinese foreign policy began to pass to Deng Xiaoping, the most powerful and controversial official to be rehabilitated in the mid-1970s. But Deng was even more vulnerable to charges of capitulation to the United States than was Zhou, and Deng soon made it clear he was not prepared to endorse the compromise on Taiwan that Zhou and Mao seemed to have suggested to Kissinger in 1973. In November 1974, Kissinger tried futilely to explore such a possibility with Deng. He said that the Japanese formula could not be adopted mechanically by the United States and that Washington would want to maintain a liaison office on Taiwan after the establishment of diplomatic relations with Peking. Moreover, Kissinger also informed Deng that, if the United States were to terminate defense relations with Taiwan, Peking would have to pledge that it would pursue reunification with Taiwan solely through peaceful means.[71]

Deng flatly rejected such an approach, describing it as a significant retrogression from earlier American statements expressing a willingness to accept the Japanese formula. The proposal to establish a "reverse liaison office," as Deng called it, was not part of a Japanese formula, but rather was the symbol of a "one China, one Taiwan" policy that Peking could not accept. First to Kissinger, and then to a delegation of American newspaper editors in mid-1975, Deng laid out a new and more rigid Chinese policy. To achieve diplomatic relations with Peking, Deng declared, the United States would have to meet three conditions: break diplomatic relations with Taipei, abrogate the mutual defense treaty with Taiwan, and withdraw all troops from the island. China could be patient, Deng declared, but normalization could not be achieved on any other terms.[72]

As the hopes for maintaining either the defense treaty or an official

American relationship with Taiwan faded, the Ford administration now understood that future relations with Taipei would indeed have to be conducted under the so-called Japanese formula, according to which the United States might be able to maintain an unofficial presence on Taiwan, but not diplomatic ties or any other form of official relationship. But here domestic factors came into play on the American side as well. Ford was enmeshed in a tough campaign for renomination against Ronald Reagan. Any hint that the Ford administration was about to "abandon" Taiwan, so soon after the collapse of South Vietnam, would have given Reagan enormous advantage in his challenge to the president, especially when a huge majority of the American public opposed expanding diplomatic relations with Peking if that required breaking ties with Taipei.[73] In addition, China's increasingly shrill attacks on Soviet expansionism gave Washington less incentive to make compromises with Peking over Taiwan, since it was widely believed that the Chinese would have little alternative but to sustain their relationship with the United States. As Ford put it in his memoirs, Deng's preoccupation with the Soviet Union gave the Americans the strong impression that he was in no hurry to resolve the Taiwan question immediately.[74]

During his December 1975 visit to China, all Ford would do, therefore, was "hint [to the Chinese] that he would try to address the normalization issue early in his second term." He added that, when he did so, he would accept the Japanese formula if it were coupled with some credible assurances of a peaceful future for Taiwan. Again, Chinese leaders proved inflexible, reiterating that the United States would have to meet all three Chinese conditions and refusing to make any commitment about a peaceful future for Taiwan.[75]

Realizing that U.S.-China relations were stagnating but unwilling to accept Peking's terms for the establishment of diplomatic ties, some Americans now began to advocate the expansion of Sino-American strategic relations as an alternative. Discussions between Chinese military officers and American analysts had, by this time, entered the public debate in the United States, with the publication in 1975 of an article in *Foreign Policy* advocating American military assistance to China through such measures as exchanging military attachés, conducting joint exercises, initiating joint contingency planning, or making American arms sales.[76] Not only was this move seen as a way of restoring momentum to U.S.-China relations, but it was also viewed as a means of strengthening America's strategic position against the Soviet Union and increasing the chances that moderate leaders would dominate in the forthcoming political succession in Peking.

A strategic relationship with Peking began to attract support from prominent members of the American conservative community. Secretary of Defense James Schlesinger promoted studies of such a proposal from late 1974 until his dismissal in November 1975 and later said publicly that he would not "reject it out of hand."[77] Senator Robert Taft, Jr. (R-Ohio) suggested in early 1976 that the United States supply China with surface-to-air missiles, antitank weapons, F-5s, and even F-16s, to preclude any possibility of a Sino-Soviet alignment.[78] Even Ronald Reagan, in the same article in which he insisted on the United States "honoring our commitments" to Taiwan, advocated not only promoting commercial relations with China but expanding intelligence sharing as well.[79]

These proposals were given greater urgency by the mounting signs of political instability inside China. Zhou Enlai died in the beginning of 1976, and the health of Mao Zedong was clearly fading. As the moment of succession neared, radical leaders seemed to be making a comeback. Jiang Qing and her lieutenants had intensified their attacks on Deng Xiaoping toward the end of 1975, charging him with trying to "reverse the verdicts" of the Cultural Revolution and engage in a "capitalist restoration" in China. When massive popular protests swept Tiananmen Square in April 1976, nominally honoring the memory of Zhou Enlai but actually protesting the "feudal fascism" of the Cultural Revolution decade, the radicals had the pretext they needed. Deng was purged from his leading positions in the Communist Party, and the radicals seemed to be in a strong position to influence the outcome of the impending succession. In this context, argued advocates of a closer strategic relationship with China, it would be highly desirable to find ways of bolstering the Sino-American relationship against an upsurge of radicalism in post-Mao China.

In the end, the Ford administration was unprepared to endorse arms sales to China, either by the United States or its allies. Inside the U.S. government, the idea of expanded military relations with China was opposed by a coalition of Soviet specialists who worried about the impact on Soviet-U.S. détente, and by China specialists who were convinced that progress on strategic matters would not compensate for the American failure to establish full diplomatic relations with Peking. Moreover, the Chinese also began to insist they were not interested in acquiring American arms or in other defense arrangements with the United States, at least prior to normalization. Peking's probes to determine American willingness to sell arms to China, for example, stopped in 1974, even though it continued to explore the possibility of purchasing Harrier fighters from Britain and Mirage jets from France.[80]

But Washington took other, less dramatic, steps to bolster strategic relations with China. The Ford administration insisted that it was still following a policy of evenhandedness, selling China only technology that it would also provide to the Soviet Union. In reality, however, in October 1976 Washington allowed Peking to purchase advanced computers for oil exploration and seismological research that it would not have been willing to sell to Moscow. At the same time, the United States was also encouraging its allies to sell even more advanced dual-purpose technology to China, far beyond that which the United States was prepared to sell, including the transfer of British Spey jet engines in December 1975.[81] Technology transfer aside, the United States also reiterated its commitment to China's security. Shortly after the death of Mao Zedong on September 9, for example, Washington publicly repeated its opposition to any "attack or pressure" on China, so as to forestall any Soviet attempt to take advantage of any instability that might result from the political succession in Peking.

UNOFFICIAL RELATIONS

The Shanghai communiqué committed China and the United States not only to the eventual normalization of their official relationship but also to the promotion of their unofficial cultural and economic ties in the meantime. The two governments agreed to facilitate the development of bilateral trade and of "people-to-people contacts" in such fields as science and technology, culture, sports, and journalism.

To that end, the two governments continued the gradual process of dismantling the barriers to economic and cultural exchange that had been constructed during the period of mutual hostility. They agreed to use U.S. dollars to settle their trade accounts, rather than to insist on the use of some third country's currency.[82] Beginning in the spring of 1972, Chinese officials allowed American businesspeople to attend the Canton Trade Fair, the semiannual convention in Guangdong at which foreign merchants could meet with representatives of China's national import and export corporations. The United States relaxed controls on the sale of technology to China, moving Peking from category Z (which provided for a total embargo) to category Y (which allowed China to import technology at the same level as that sold to the Soviet Union).[83] On a case-by-case basis, Washington also began to license the export of equipment that would not have been sold to Moscow, including the satellite ground stations required to provide live television coverage of the Nixon visit in 1972, a small fleet of Boeing 707s to modernize China's domestic and international air service, and some advanced Cyber computers for geological research.[84]

There also emerged a modest facilitative infrastructure to conduct cultural exchanges and to promote economic relations between the two countries. The National Committee on U.S.-China Relations, which had been formed in 1966 to reassess American policy toward China and to foster public education on Chinese affairs, assumed responsibility for the visit of a Chinese Ping-Pong team to the United States in 1972 and soon became the principal conduit for sending American delegations to China and for receiving their Chinese counterparts. The Committee on Scholarly Communication with the People's Republic of China, also organized in 1966 by the American Council of Learned Societies, the Social Science Research Council, and the National Academy of Sciences, reached an agreement with the Chinese Association of Science and Technology in June 1973 to administer the exchange of academic delegations in the humanities, social sciences, and natural sciences.[85] That same year, a group of American corporations interested in doing business in China formed the National Council for U.S.-China Trade, dedicated to providing information to U.S. business about commercial prospects in China and to lobbying the two governments for improvements in the business climate.[86]

These steps permitted the gradual expansion of academic and cultural exchanges between the two countries between 1971 and 1977.[87] Peking invited a diverse group of American delegations to visit China. At one end of the political spectrum, these visitors included groups from the Black Panthers, the Committee of Concerned Asian Scholars, the U.S.-China People's Friendship Association, and other sympathetic organizations. But the delegations hosted by China also included eighty members of Congress, young political leaders, newspaper editors, officials of world affairs organizations, scientists, scholars, and university presidents.[88] The two countries exchanged trade delegations, performing arts groups, journalists, and athletic teams. And a handful of American films, such as *The Sound of Music* and *Tora, Tora, Tora*, were acquired by the Chinese government for screenings to selected audiences in China.[89]

The pattern for hosting these American visitors was set when the U.S. table tennis team visited China in 1971. The emphasis was on professional exchange: American scholars met with their Chinese counterparts, American musicians gave performances, and U.S. athletes participated in exhibition matches with Chinese teams. In addition, the American visitors were treated to visits to historic and scenic sights, such as the Forbidden City or the Great Wall, and were taken to see model Chinese hospitals, schools, factories, and communes. There, they would be given formal briefings (soon known by the English translation of the Chinese term, "brief introductions") featuring a mind-numbing set of statistics meant to illustrate the accomplishments achieved since 1949 and the transformations undergone during the Cultural Revolution. Most delegations were also permitted to meet with Chinese political leaders, in Peking and in provincial capitals, with the highest-ranking visitors allowed to meet Premier Zhou Enlai. Americans reciprocated with similar programs for their Chinese guests, although with somewhat more informal touches. The National Committee on U.S.-China Relations, for example, often tried to arrange for Chinese visitors to stay with or take meals with American families, so that they could obtain a firsthand look at U.S. society at the grass roots.

Within a few months, however, the limits to these cultural and academic exchanges became apparent. For one thing, the Chinese appeared much more willing to receive American delegations than to dispatch their own. By the end of 1972, for example, between 1,500 and 3,000 Americans had visited China, but by the middle of the following year only about 300 Chinese had traveled to the United States.[90] Those responsible for the exchange program in the United States speculated that the Chinese authorities, still experiencing the Cultural Revolution, did not want to expose large numbers of their citizens to life in the United States. In addition, given the absence of direct air links between the two countries, Chinese delegations had to expend scarce foreign exchange to travel on the airlines of other countries to reach America. This imbalance continued through most of the decade. By the end of 1977, it was estimated that 15,000 Americans had visited China and that 1,000 Chinese had visited the United States.[91]

Peking also placed severe restrictions on the types of cultural and academic exchanges it was prepared to undertake. It received American news correspondents for short-term visits and sent its own reporters to the United States for occasional tours. But China did not permit American news organizations to establish permanent bureaus in Peking, forcing them to rely on Xinhua wire service reports or to cover China from the traditional vantage point in Hong Kong.

Similarly, China did not allow American students and scholars to conduct long-term research projects in China, nor did China dispatch its own students to the United States. Instead, it restricted the bilateral academic relationship to the exchange of scholarly delegations for brief tours. China did not allow individual American tourists to visit the country, requiring would-be visitors to join groups organized by the U.S.-China People's Friendship Association or sponsored by the China International Travel Service. Some of these restrictions reflected the limits on China's physical capabilities to receive visitors, but others were the result of Peking's decision to limit ties with the United States until normalization had been achieved.

The cultural and academic ties between China and the United States were also disrupted by political factors. Radical Chinese leaders, who occupied a powerful place in the cultural and educational spheres, were reluctant to see the flow of Western culture into China, even in the limited amounts entailed by the exchanges of delegations and performing arts troupes. Thus, the visit of the Philadelphia Orchestra to China in 1973 was followed, early the next year, by a series of articles denouncing many pieces in their repertoire as unacceptably bourgeois, making future exchanges difficult.

Chinese foreign affairs officials often succumbed to the temptation to introduce political themes, often centering on the Taiwan issue, into the cultural exchange process. The National Gallery of Art, which hosted an archaeological exhibition from China in 1974, was forced to call off the press preview when Chinese officials insisted on barring journalists from Taiwan, South Korea, South Africa, and Israel.[92] In 1975, two high-level exchange programs were canceled: the visit of a Chinese performing arts troupe to the United States was called off when it refused to drop a song from its program about liberating Taiwan; and a delegation of American mayors planning to visit China was canceled when the American organizers rejected Chinese efforts to exclude the mayor of San Juan, Puerto Rico, from the group. In essence, the second incident was retaliation for the first: if the United States was not prepared to accept Chinese claims to sovereignty over Taiwan, then China was unwilling to acknowledge American claims to sovereignty over Puerto Rico.[93]

Even academic exchanges were hampered by political considerations. Peking canceled a delegation from Harvard University out of pique over a book review written by John King Fairbank, the dean of Harvard's Chinese studies program. It forced three scholars to withdraw from a Yale University delegation because they were allegedly unsympathetic to China. It attempted to secure the replacement of a Princeton University scholar from another academic delegation on similar grounds but was forced to relent when the Americans threatened to cancel their visit.[94]

Sino-American economic ties developed fairly rapidly in the early 1970s before declining sharply in the middle of the decade. Two-way trade, which had amounted to only $5 million in 1971, rose to about $90 million in 1972, fueled largely by rapid growth in Chinese purchases of wheat and other agricultural commodities. Trade increased another tenfold over the next two years, reaching nearly $800 million in 1973 and more than $900 million in 1974, as China began to purchase American machinery (including Boeing aircraft, M. W. Kellogg fertilizer plants, and oil production and exploration equipment) in addition to agricultural products. Such rapid growth proved unsustainable, however, especially because China had experienced a cumulative deficit of $1.4 billion between 1972 and 1974. Peking therefore slashed imports from the United States for the following three years, particularly of agricultural products.[95] American purchases from China continued a gradual increase, but two-way trade fell to $462 million in 1975 and leveled off at around $350 million a year in 1976 and 1977 (tables A-2–A-4).

Although many of the dynamics of Sino-American trade in the 1970s can be explained by the emergence of a large Chinese deficit and by Peking's efforts to reduce it, the overall commercial relationship between the two countries was also affected by the remaining political and institutional constraints on both sides. The flow of American capital and goods to China was restricted by the limits on Chinese foreign economic policy that had first been imposed after the break with the Soviet Union in the early 1950s and were now reaffirmed. China would not accept long-term foreign loans, foreign managers in Chinese enterprises, or joint ventures with foreign firms.[96] This refusal was particularly frustrating to American oil companies, who had hoped to be invited to participate directly in exploration, production, and export of Chinese petroleum.[97]

The flow of Chinese goods to the United States was also limited. The failure to resolve the issue of blocked claims and frozen assets dating from the Korean War made it impossible for China to organize trade exhibitions in the United States, for any commodities belonging to the Chinese government landing on American soil were liable to seizure by Americans with outstanding claims against Peking. The absence of a trade agreement providing most-favored-nation status to China meant that Chinese goods were subject to the high duties established in the Smoot-Hawley Tariff Act of 1930. Chinese foreign trade corporations compounded the problem by raising their prices sharply in 1973, with unique arts and crafts increasing by 1,000 percent and other commodities rising well above world levels.[98]

Moreover, Sino-American commercial relationships, like academic and cultural exchanges, became a subject of controversy within the Chinese leadership. As the health of both Mao Zedong and Zhou Enlai began to weaken in the mid-1970s, the struggle for succession intensified. In the course of that struggle, the radical faction headed by Jiang Qing began to criticize China's burgeoning economic relations with the West, not only warning of the trade deficits that might result but also charging that those who favored expanding commercial ties with capitalist nations were guilty of creating an unnecessary dependence on Western capital and technology. In March 1974, for example, articles began to appear that denounced an "unbridled quest" for foreign imports, followed a few months later by essays attacking the "blind worship" of foreign technology.[99]

The debate intensified in 1975, as Chinese leaders prepared their Fifth Five-Year Plan. More pragmatic officials, headed by Deng Xiaoping, proposed a further expansion of Chinese trade with the West, possibly including a limited welcome for foreign investment in China's petroleum industry, whereas the radicals described such suggestions as "servility to things foreign," prostration before "foreign bourgeois authorities," and "capitulation and national betrayal."[100] The vulnerability of the moderates to these charges, especially after the death of Zhou Enlai in January 1976, contributed to the purge of Deng Xiaoping in April and exacerbated the restrictions on Chinese imports from the United States in 1975 and 1976.[101] Moreover, American firms who did business with Taiwan and who joined the U.S.-Republic of China Economic Council when it was formed in 1976 found themselves the target of retaliatory measures from Peking.[102]

On balance, then, unofficial relations between China and the United States developed in a hesitant and somewhat turbulent manner between 1972 and 1977. One of the most important obstacles to the development of economic and cultural ties between the two countries was the absence of full diplomatic relations between Washington and Peking. Without such a relationship, it was extremely difficult if not impossible for the United States to provide China with most-favored-nation status. Moreover, the Chinese government made clear that without established diplomatic relations, it would not permit the opening of consulates to serve the American business community, the stationing of resident correspondents in Peking, the establishment of direct air or shipping links between the two countries, or the exchange of students and scholars on longer-term visits.

In addition, the nature of the Chinese political and economic system also hampered unofficial exchanges between China and the United States. Until Mao's death in September 1976, and indeed for at least twelve months thereafter, China was governed by the rigid ideological premises of the Cultural Revolution, which implied tight administrative controls over the economy, harsh restrictions on academic and cultural life, and severe limits on interactions with the outside world. These doctrinal presuppositions and administrative restraints forced American firms to deal with their Chinese counterparts through a cumbersome centralized foreign trade bureaucracy, prevented Americans from investing in or extending loans to China, precluded individual Americans from visiting China as tourists, and periodically introduced blatant political considerations into the Sino-American cultural and academic exchange program.

AMBIVALENCE

Several American observers, at the time and in subsequent years, have characterized American public attitudes toward China in the mid-1970s as naive and euphoric. Writing in *Commentary* in June 1973, Sheila Johnson charged that many American travelers to the People's Republic were going "to China, with love" and were swallowing the official line they heard there "with the alacrity of trained seals."[103] More recently, Steven Mosher, an American expelled from China when he was conducting field research there in the early 1980s, has described the 1970s as an age of infatuation, which he has linked to the commitment of leftist scholars to a so-called revolutionary socialist paradigm and to the efforts of the Nixon administration to justify its opening to Peking.[104]

There was indeed some American euphoria about China in the early and mid-1970s, in part from the quarters identified by Mosher. Many early American visitors to China returned from their brief visits with glowing accounts of the country, representing what I have earlier called a "virtual celebration of the goals, programs, and accomplishments of China and its people under Communist rule."[105] China was portrayed as a highly egalitarian society that had provided basic subsistence to all its people, a populist society that ensured direct public involvement in grass-roots politics, and a virtuous society marked by a common commitment to utopian values. James Reston of the *New York Times* likened the Chinese efforts at mass mobilization as "one vast cooperative barn-raising," guided by "many aspects of the old faiths the West has dropped along the way."[106] Reston's colleague, Seymour Topping, reported that the service in the Shanghai and Peking department stores was "certainly faster and more efficient than . . . in many American shops."[107] David Rockefeller declared himself impressed by China's "economic and social progress," "efficient and dedicated administration," and "high morale and community of purpose."[108]

Many in the American academic community expressed similar views about China, although often placing them in a more analytic perspective. Mao Zedong was portrayed as grappling with some of the most important dilemmas inherent in the process of modernization. According to this interpretation, the Cultural Revolution was not an irrational attack on the institutions necessary for economic and political development but rather the reflection of Mao's understanding that "bureaucracy and industrialization do not necessarily lead to an improved quality of life."[109] The violence of the Red Guard movement was either minimized or justified as a regrettable but inevitable by-product of the movement's accomplishments. Indeed, the main shortcoming of the Cultural Revolution was merely its failure to achieve all of its ambitious objectives. "Mao's assault did not succeed in totally eliminating privatism, self-interest, and elitism from Chinese society," one political scientist acknowledged. "But should Mao be condemned for trying?"[110] Indeed, some American sinologists suggested that China's "developmental experience" was so successful that it could serve as a useful reference not only for other developing countries but even for the United States and other Western societies.[111]

For both of these groups—the short-term visitors and the academic specialists—the favorable evaluations of China seemed to spring from similar sources. The Cultural Revolution in China coincided with an American cultural revolution of more modest proportions. At a minimum, the widespread disillusionment in the United States with American racial and economic problems, and particularly with the war in Vietnam, made it less likely that American liberal intellectuals and writers would judge China by Western values. The shortcomings of their own society predisposed many Americans to view favorably a Chinese government that was nominally committed to egalitarianism, populism, selflessness, and harmony. Moreover, the short and carefully orchestrated tours on which virtually all Americans visited China obscured the poverty and repression that characterized the country and displayed China's economic and social accomplishments to best advantage. As a result, China's abuses of human rights, which would become such a prominent subject for Americans in the post-Tiananmen period, were largely ignored in scholarly analysis and journalistic reportage in the mid-1970s.

Other groups of Americans had somewhat different reasons for a positive assessment of China. Some government officials, such as Kissinger, were clearly enamored of Zhou Enlai, seeing him not only as a consummate diplomat but also as "one of the two or three most impressive men I have ever met . . . urbane, infinitely patient, extraordinarily intelligent, subtle . . . [and possessed of a] luminous personality and extraordinary perception."[112] Some business executives were enthralled by the potential size of the China market, with one Monsanto spokesman noting in 1971: "Just one aspirin tablet a day to each of those guys—and that's a lot of aspirin."[113] The world of fashion, always on the lookout for new sources of inspiration, found the combination of traditional styles and proletarian clothing irresistible, with Mao jackets and Chinese-style haircuts attaining a brief vogue in the mid-1970s.[114]

But although it is possible to find examples of favorable American comment about China in the mid-1970s, and although uncritical approval of the political and economic institutions was indeed widespread in the American academic community, there is also much evidence of a far more balanced overall assessment of China than the characterizations of "infatuation" and "euphoria" would suggest. Indeed, there emerged in the United States a very complex and balanced evaluation of China. In virtually every sector of American society, from the press to the business community to the academy, one can find criticism of China as readily as praise.

The press, for example, did not give especially high marks to the Nixon visit of 1972, complaining that the United States had acceded to all of China's demands but had received little in return except vague promises of greater trade and expanded cultural exchanges. Even the *New York Times* said that the trip fell "at the lower end of the diplomatic spectrum" because it did not succeed in opening an official American representative office in Peking and because none of the outstanding bilateral issues between the two countries had been resolved.[115] One headline in a regional newspaper put it even more bluntly: "They Got Taiwan; We Got Egg Rolls."[116]

When Ford traveled to China in 1975 the criticism was even more pointed, especially when he appeared to return empty-handed from Peking. Many complained that it was time for the Chinese to send a high-ranking leader to the United States to reciprocate Kissinger's regular visits and the two presidential journeys. In the words of a columnist for the *New York Post*, "Watching the nightly satellite

reports of the presidential party in China one feels a curious annoy-
ance: 'What's he doing way over *there* when we've got so many
problems *here*?' "[117]

One reason for the press's unhappiness may have been the restrictions it faced while trying to cover the Nixon visit—restrictions that
aroused even more bitterness when they were encountered again
during the Ford trip in 1975. Other short-term visitors had similar
objections, such that, in the fall of 1976, the *Los Angeles Times*
carried a front-page story surveying the complaints of those "frustrated by what they perceive as pervasive Chinese secrecy, rigidly
planned tours and their inability to approach common people."[118]

The business community had also developed a more jaundiced and
realistic view of China by the mid-1970s. The sharp drop in U.S.-
China trade in 1976 and 1977 had punctured, at least for the moment,
any anticipation of a large Chinese market, particularly for American
consumer goods. American merchants were increasingly frustrated
by the high cost, low availability, poor quality, and unfashionable
design of many Chinese export commodities, as well as with the
secrecy, inefficiency, and rigidity of the Chinese bureaucracy. The
American petroleum industry, in particular, was irritated by the
endless series of technical seminars in which Chinese officials and
engineers obtained useful data from U.S. firms, but that resulted in
relatively few orders and no opportunities for direct investment.
Moreover, as the novelty of doing business in China wore off, American businesspeople became increasingly willing to express their
views in unattributed interviews with reporters.[119]

American government officials in the executive and legislative
branches tended to take a balanced, if not skeptical, view of China
in the 1970s. Despite the deep personal respect that Kissinger had
for Zhou Enlai, he simultaneously acknowledged the differences in
perspective between China and the United States, especially on the
question of relations with the Soviet Union, and forecast that Sino-
American relations would often be difficult as a result. Indeed, he
warned that the Chinese "will prove implacable foes if our relations
turn sour."[120] State Department officials spoke frankly of the divergent interests of the two countries on such issues as the Vietnam
War, the situation on the Korean peninsula, and international economic issues and on that basis offered modest forecasts for the future
of Sino-American relations. Although many members of Congress
who visited China returned with positive assessments of China's
economic and political situation, others expressed doubts about the
extent to which China had eliminated poverty and reservations about
the cost to political freedom and spiritual values.[121]

Even in the academic community, analysis of China was some-what more complex than might first appear. Most of the positive assessments of China cited earlier were written by a younger genera-tion of China specialists, who were asserting their professional iden-tity through a sharp attack on the less favorable views being produced by older scholars. Other scholars, in contrast, took a less emotional and more balanced perspective, with at least two of them writing forcefully about the suppression of dissent in China.[122] Academic generalists on international affairs and comparative communism tended to take a more skeptical approach to developments in China than did their colleagues who specialized on China.[123] And laudatory journalistic accounts and trip reports were immediately subject to sharp scrutiny by those with less favorable impressions of China.[124]

Nor did public opinion polls suggest any American euphoria about China. To be sure, Americans welcomed the Nixon visit, presumably as a way of easing tensions with a nation that had previously been America's principal adversary in Asia. A Harris poll taken shortly after the visit showed an overwhelming majority (73 percent) appro-ving of the president's trip, whereas a Gallup poll commissioned by the Taiwan government two years later showed a much smaller plurality (45 percent) in favor.[125] But American attitudes toward China remained highly ambivalent. Although the percentage of Americans viewing China in "fairly favorable" or "highly favorable" terms rose from 5 percent in 1967 to 49 percent in 1973 just after Nixon's visit, it fell to 20 percent in 1976 (table A-1). Indeed, in 1976, a plurality of Americans (45 percent) still regarded China "highly unfavorably."[126]

These figures reveal a pattern that will recur throughout the con-temporary history of Sino-American relations: that the American public does not require a favorable assessment of Chinese society in order to endorse a normal working relationship with the government in Peking. They also suggest that although the Nixon visit produced a burst of positive feeling toward China, it was quite short-lived. The differences between Chinese and American ideological values, economic systems, and political institutions remained too wide for Americans to adopt a favorable impression of the People's Republic. Nor, in the mid-1970s, was there any widespread sense that China was about to abandon the revolutionary values of late Maoism in favor of the more liberal values of the West. Just as the large structural gap between America and China obstructed the development of unof-ficial economic and cultural relations in the mid-1970s, so too did it prevent the euphoria and infatuation present in some quarters of American society from spreading widely through the U.S. public.

An even deeper ambivalence was evident in Chinese attitudes toward the United States during this period. As suggested, several factions in the Chinese Communist Party, including the military leaders associated with Lin Biao and the radical ideologues linked to Jiang Qing, had vehemently opposed any accommodation with the United States, on the grounds that no imperialist nation could be a reliable strategic partner for Peking. Indeed, throughout the mid-1970s, the radicals tended to equate the Soviet Union and the United States as threats to Chinese security. Instead of an unprincipled compromise with Washington, the radicals recommended that China deter a Soviet attack through alignment with the third world. "We do not have any 'white friends,' 'big friends,' or 'rich friends,'" declared Jiang Qing in March 1975, in a veiled reference to the United States. China, she said, should place "the emphasis in our diplomacy on our 'black friends,' 'little friends,' and 'poor friends.'"[127] At the same time, the radicals also criticized proposals for increasing Chinese trade with the West, warning directly and through historical analogy that interdependence with the capital economy would inevitably lead to political subordination and economic crisis.[128]

Not all Chinese leaders accepted this extreme analysis. But even those who advocated a closer and more extensive relationship with the United States did so in highly ambivalent language. The United States was consistently portrayed as one of two imperialist powers against which Chinese foreign policy was directed. The fact that the Soviet Union and the United States were engaged in intense "contention for hegemony" made it possible to envision an alignment with one against the other; the simultaneous fact that the Soviet Union was, in the early 1970s, regarded as the more aggressive and more threatening superpower implied that China's alignment should be with Washington against Moscow. But there was as yet no suggestion that this united front would be anything more than a passing phase in Chinese diplomacy. The Chinese cited Mao's writings on the united front with the Kuomintang against the Japanese during the Second World War to justify an alignment with the declining imperialist power against the stronger. But as late as 1977 they were using an unflattering passage from Lenin to portray the United States as a "temporary, vacillating, unstable, unreliable, and conditional" strategic partner.[129]

These highly equivocal images of the United States were conveyed to the Chinese people by the mass media and the educational system. Although there were periods in the early 1970s (especially in 1972 and 1973) when developments in the United States were reported fairly neutrally, during most of the decade American society was still depicted in the Chinese press as a polarized, oppressive, and racist society, dominated economically and politically by a small capitalist elite. The same image was conveyed in more analytical terms by the textbooks produced for use in Chinese universities.

The way that these messages reached the grass roots is suggested by two poems posted on the bulletin board of a factory in Xi'an, presumably written by the factory's propaganda office, just after the Kissinger visit of July 1971. One, which began by claiming that "blazing fires of revolution burn the world order," noted that "the [American] economy takes a further downward turn every day" and concluded that "a visit to China is the only way out for a brief respite from blazing fires that singe the eyebrows." The other depicted Nixon as obsessed with winning reelection and as realizing that "the key to capture votes is a visit to China." Thus, the poem predicted, Nixon would come to Peking "with painted face-mask, disguised as a beauty. . . . But the demons-demasking mirror in the city of Peking is truly inexorable. A fear grows that his true image will be revealed and his great cause will fail."[130]

To the extent that there was an independent Chinese public opinion during this period, it seems to have shared the view that the United States was an unreliable and dangerous partner for China. Interviews with Chinese refugees reaching Hong Kong from Guangdong and Fujian provinces in the mid-1970s revealed an odd but widespread rumor, according to which Nixon—or one of the officials or reporters in his entourage—stole a valuable nine-dragon cup during his visit to China. Although the details of the rumor varied from place to place, most of them ended with the Chinese leaders commissioning a magician to recover the treasure by substituting a replica in its place. Other rumors circulating at the time also portrayed American visitors to China stealing food, or even baby diapers, from their Chinese hosts. In contrast to later years, when the United States was widely seen as a friendly and prosperous nation that could help China modernize, it was viewed in the 1970s as a treacherous and wily country unworthy of China's trust.[131] If there had been a breakthrough in the official relations between the two countries, there had not yet been a breakthrough in their perceptions of each other.

CHAPTER 3

Normalization

SINO-AMERICAN relations stagnated for another year after the death of Mao Zedong in September 1976 and the election of Jimmy Carter the following November. The new leaders in both countries were preoccupied with other priorities. In China, the succession to Mao Zedong occasioned an intense struggle for power between Mao's nominal successor, Hua Guofeng, and his more senior rival, Deng Xiaoping, that hampered new initiatives toward the United States. In the United States, the Carter administration had to weigh the importance of Sino-American relations against other foreign policy issues that might require the expenditure of political capital, such as the search for peace in the Middle East and the negotiation of a treaty on the future of the Panama Canal. In addition, both governments wished to explore the prospects for improving their relations with the Soviet Union before deciding the price they were prepared to pay to establish diplomatic ties with each other. Although the two countries tentatively probed the terms for the normalization of their relations in 1977, they made no significant progress.

In the middle of 1978, however, U.S.-China relations began to recover some of the vitality that had been lost earlier in the decade. Step by step, Deng Xiaoping established his dominance over Hua Guofeng and secured support for a more pragmatic program of economic development, thus gaining greater leeway to make the compromises necessary to achieve the normalization of relations with the United States. At the same time, the continued inflexibility in Soviet foreign policy provided a renewed impetus to Sino-American cooperation. The Kremlin's failure to make substantial concessions to China's post-Mao leadership, its intervention in the Horn of Africa, its refusal to accept deep cuts in strategic arms, and its support for Vietnamese ambitions in Cambodia, led Peking and Washington once again to view each other as partners in an international alignment against Soviet expansionism.

Gradually, these changes in the setting for Sino-American relations drew the two countries closer together. During a visit to Peking in May 1978, Zbigniew Brzezinski, the national security adviser to President Jimmy Carter, told Chinese leaders that the United States had "made up its mind" to achieve normalization as quickly as possible.[1] After six months of intensive negotiations, the two countries reached an agreement on the establishment of diplomatic relations, under which the United States ended official ties with Taiwan, terminated the mutual defense treaty with Taipei, and withdrew its remaining troops from the island.

The terms of the normalization of Sino-American relations aroused sharp debate in the U.S. Congress. Opinion polls had consistently indicated that the public favored the establishment of diplomatic relations with China but not at the price of breaking American ties with Taipei.[2] Moreover, members of Congress felt that the Carter administration had neither secured a pledge from Peking that China would not use force against Taiwan, nor provided an adequate reiteration of the residual American commitment to the security of the island. As a result, Congress added to the Taiwan Relations Act a series of statements about continuing arms sales to Taiwan and the ongoing American interest in a peaceful future for the island. These provisions were regarded by Peking as a violation of the original normalization agreement.

Despite the continuing controversy over American relations with Taiwan, the establishment of diplomatic relations between Peking and Washington permitted a rapid development of the ties between the two countries. Deng Xiaoping traveled to the United States in January 1979, becoming the first high-level Chinese Communist leader to make a state visit to America. The two countries began to explore the development of military and strategic relations, which included exchanges of military personnel, sharing of intelligence, and coordination of policy, but stopped short of the sale of American arms to China. Normalization also promoted the expansion of economic and cultural ties between China and the United States at a pace that vastly exceeded earlier predictions. These developments produced the first real signs of euphoria in the two countries, generating expectations for progress that would be difficult to fulfill.

CONTINUED STALEMATE

The year 1977 brought new leaders to power in Washington and Peking. Jimmy Carter succeeded Gerald Ford as the American president in January 1977, finally ending the long national agony over the Watergate scandal. Faced with a challenge to his nomination from the conservative wing of the Republican Party, Ford had never been able to assign a high priority to the establishment of diplomatic relations with Peking, even though he might have attempted to complete the process had he won reelection in 1976. Carter now had a mandate to make new initiatives in domestic and foreign policy; completing the normalization of Sino-American relations was one of his objectives.

In China, the death of Mao Zedong in September 1976 had been followed almost immediately by the arrest of the radical leaders associated with Mao's widow, Jiang Qing. The purge of the Gang of Four removed from the Politburo the last opponents of an accommodation with the United States. The nominal successor to Mao was Hua Guofeng, a relatively colorless provincial official who had been named heir apparent in the spring of 1976 in a compromise between the radical and moderate factions of the Party. But Deng Xiaoping, who was rehabilitated in the middle of 1977, soon mounted a challenge to Hua's leadership. Within a few months of his political reappearance, Deng had regained substantial control over Chinese foreign policy.

Although nominally committed to the improvement of Sino-American relations, both of these new leaderships wished first to explore the prospects for an improvement in their ties with the Soviet Union. Peking wanted to probe Soviet policy toward China in the post-Mao era, to see whether Moscow might be willing to make any serious concessions to Chinese interests now that the architect of the Sino-Soviet dispute had left the Chinese political stage. In the fall of 1977, therefore, Peking engaged in what one analyst has called a "hundred-day thaw" in its relations with the Soviet Union. China dispatched a new ambassador to Moscow, filling a post that had been vacant for the previous eighteen months. The Chinese addressed their border dispute with the Soviet Union with greater earnestness, reaching an agreement on river navigation in October 1977. And Peking sent its foreign minister to the Soviet embassy to attend National Day celebrations in November, the highest-level official representation at such an event in more than ten years. None of these initiatives represented a major concession on China's part, but they were intended to see if they might evoke a positive Soviet response.[3]

Meanwhile, in Washington, the Carter administration was also exploring the potential improvements in U.S.-Soviet relations. The new secretary of state, Cyrus Vance, was particularly interested in reviving détente with Moscow and in reaching an ambitious strategic arms limitation treaty (SALT). Vance feared that an energetic American attempt to normalize relations with China, particularly if it took on anti-Soviet overtones, might run counter to this objective. Vance's initial strategy, therefore, was to adopt an evenhanded approach to both Communist giants, moving toward China only in tandem with improvements in Soviet-American relations. As a result, although the Carter administration privately committed itself to the normalization of U.S.-China relations, it assigned a lower priority to this objective than to other issues.[4] China policy was not one of the subjects addressed by the first wave of presidential review memorandums (PRMs) commissioned by the incoming National Security Council at its first informal meeting on January 5, 1977, two weeks before the new administration was inaugurated. Indeed, the subject of China was not even discussed at that meeting.[5]

Still, shortly after taking office the Carter administration did begin an internal assessment of policy toward China, including the prospects for the establishment of diplomatic relations with Peking. A formal review of the subject was commissioned in early April and completed the following month. The result, known as PRM-24, reviewed the options for the president with regard to the overall Sino-American relationship, U.S. policy toward Taiwan, and strategic ties with Peking.[6]

The analysis contained in PRM-24 drew on an intense debate over China policy that had raged in the United States ever since the middle of the 1970s.[7] In essence, three principal issues characterized that controversy. The first concerned the urgency of establishing full diplomatic relations with Peking. Some American analysts, observing the stagnation of U.S.-China relations after 1974, attributed the stalemate to Washington's failure to complete the process of normalization. They warned that if the United States did not fulfill the pledge to extend official recognition to China, as implied by the Shanghai communiqué, Peking would continue to impose severe restrictions on economic and cultural ties between the two countries and might even seek an accommodation with the Soviet Union. Others, in contrast, insisted that Peking placed lower priority on the prompt establishment of diplomatic relations with the United States than on continued cooperation with Washington in opposing Soviet expansionism. If China was dissatisfied with American policy, they argued, it was with Washington's naive pursuit of détente with Moscow, not with the United States' failure to normalize relations with Peking.

PRM-24 clearly sided with the first position in the debate. It concluded that some urgency was attached to completing the normalization of Sino-American relations. If the United States did not extend formal diplomatic relations to Peking, the authors of PRM-24 concluded, American cultural and economic ties with China would stagnate, Chinese confidence in American credibility would gradually erode, and China might reorient its foreign policy around a reduction of tensions with the Soviet Union. Conversely, PRM-24 forecast that an improvement in Sino-American relations would increase the pressure on the Soviet Union to be more accommodative toward American interests.[8]

The second issue in the debate concerned the terms on which Washington should normalize relations with Peking, and specifically whether the United States should accept the three conditions for normalization that Peking had set down in 1975: ending official relations with Taiwan, abrogating the mutual defense treaty, and removing the remaining American troops. Some American observers believed that the Chinese conditions were firm and could be accepted by the United States. Others agreed that the Chinese conditions were unlikely to be altered but proposed that the United States ensure a peaceful future for Taiwan through some other means, such as making a unilateral statement of interest in Taiwan's security, continuing American arms sales to the island, or obtaining a firm renunciation of force by Peking. Still others advocated rejecting some of the Chinese conditions by maintaining the mutual defense treaty, official American representation on Taiwan, or both.

In the end, PRM-24 concluded that it would be necessary for the United States to work within the three conditions for normalization that Peking had laid out in 1975. It was held unlikely that Chinese leaders would have the political flexibility at home to abandon any of their previous positions on the subject, especially given the forcefulness with which they had been expressed. Moreover, a careful examination of the record of Sino-American negotiations during the Nixon and Ford presidencies led the Carter administration to determine that the United States had already accepted all three of Peking's conditions, at least tacitly.[9] The Shanghai communiqué had committed the United States to the withdrawal of American military forces and installations from Taiwan; Ford had agreed that the United States would maintain only unofficial relations with Taipei after normalization; and Kissinger had concluded that the mutual defense treaty could not be maintained in the absence of formal diplomatic ties with Taiwan. PRM-24 argued that the United States could not take a different approach to normalization without violating the commitments to Peking undertaken by previous administrations.

But the Carter administration also concluded that the United States could reasonably demand a quid pro quo for each of the Chinese conditions. PRM-24 probably identified several options in this connection, all of which were under consideration in Washington at the time.[10] The United States, for example, could continue arms sales to Taipei or make a statement reiterating interest in a peaceful future for Taiwan. It could seek an accommodative Chinese declaration on the future of Taiwan, such as an outright renunciation of force or a statement of peaceful intentions. At a minimum, it could urge the Chinese to stop threatening the use of force and to speak of "reunification" with Taiwan rather than continuing to use the more bellicose phrase, the "liberation" of the island. Washington could also refuse to abruptly abrogate its defense treaty with Taiwan but could insist on providing the one year's notice of termination provided for in the treaty.

President Carter accepted this general approach to the problem of normalization. He and some of his advisers recall that in mid-1977, just after the completion of PRM-24, the president established minimal American conditions for normalization, including the continued sale of defensive weapons to Taipei, the maintenance of extensive unofficial relations with Taiwan, and a U.S. statement—uncontested by the Chinese—of continued concern for the peaceful settlement of the Taiwan dispute.[11] But the details of each of these conditions remained to be worked out with Peking. Moreover, the Carter administration would subsequently add other conditions to its negotiating position, either to see how flexible the Chinese would be or else to improve the attractiveness of normalization to domestic American audiences.

The third issue addressed by PRM-24 involved the desirability of arms sales to China. As noted in chapter 2, some American analysts and officials had begun in the mid-1970s to advocate a more extensive security relationship with China to prevent the erosion of Sino-American relations in the absence of normalization and to bolster both countries' strategic position compared with the Soviet Union's. Some advocated sharing of intelligence, exchanges of military delegations, and provision of advanced technology to China. Some even proposed the supply of American weapons to Peking. Others, in contrast, considered plans for such a relationship with China premature. They warned that extensive military ties with Peking would not be appropriate before the development of a sound official civilian relationship, and they cautioned that a decisive strategic tilt toward

China might provoke an aggressive, rather than an accommodative, response from the Soviet Union. They also felt that the prospects for a Sino-Soviet rapprochement were not so great as to warrant undertaking military cooperation with Peking as a preventive measure.

Both these views of an American security relationship with China were reflected in the Carter administration. From the beginning, Brzezinski had been enthusiastic about the strategic benefits of a military relationship with China and had even seen such a relationship as a substitute, at least in the near term, for the complete normalization of diplomatic relations. He and Harold Brown supported the addition of what they called "security enhancements" to Sino-American relations, such as looser restrictions on technology transfer, the exchange of military attachés, and American support of European arms sales to China, even before full diplomatic ties had been achieved.[12] Vance, in contrast, had been among the officials most skeptical of an alignment with Peking because of concern for the consequences it might have for Soviet-American détente.[13]

PRM-24 adopted the more cautious and skeptical position. A minority of the working group that drafted it, including officials from the Central Intelligence Agency and the Department of Defense, believed that there could well be diplomatic and military advantages from a program of security cooperation with China. But most of the group, including key officials from the China and Soviet desks of the State Department, concluded that the risks outweighed the benefits. The report warned that the sale of military technology to China might compel the Soviet Union to "make a fundamental reassessment of its policies toward the U.S.," to "stiffen [Soviet] positions on even the major issues of U.S.-Soviet relations such as SALT," and even to engage in a more intense confrontation with China.[14] In the end, the president sided with Vance and the State Department on arms sales, ruling against the sale of American weapons to Peking. But other aspects of the Sino-American strategic relationship—including Washington's policy on the transfer of advanced American technology to China and its attitude toward European arms sales to Peking—remained undecided.[15]

With PRM-24 completed and reviewed, the next step for the United States was to begin negotiations with the Chinese over the terms of normalization. Secretary of State Vance scheduled a trip to Peking in August 1977, with Carter originally instructing him to "lay it all out on the line" and to carry with him a draft of the communiqué that would announce the establishment of diplomatic relations between the two countries. At the last minute, however, Carter and

Vance had second thoughts. They were concerned that the achievement of normalization on these terms might cost the president some of the support he would need in the Senate to secure the ratification of the treaty on the future of the Panama Canal.[16]

Thus, on the eve of Vance's departure for Peking, the purpose of his visit was defined more modestly. Rather than to begin formal negotiations with Peking over the terms of normalization, his objective was to probe the limits of the Chinese position to see what concessions China might make in exchange for American acceptance of its conditions for normalization.[17] Partly as a test of Chinese intentions, and partly as a way of slowing down the pace of the discussions, Vance was also instructed to present what he later described in his memoirs as the "maximum" American position. He told the Chinese that the United States intended to assign government personnel to the unofficial organization that would represent American interests in Taiwan after the withdrawal of diplomatic recognition. And Vance also explored Peking's willingness to commit itself to a peaceful future for Taiwan, if not through an unequivocal renunciation of force, then at least through a stated preference for peaceful reunification and the cessation of "new statements about liberation by force."[18]

Although Vance expected Peking to reject this ambitious American negotiating position,[19] the Carter administration was not prepared for the vehemence of the Chinese reaction. In Vance's proposal that American governmental employees remain on Taiwan after normalization, the Chinese saw an American intention to establish an official liaison office on the island, fully comparable to the American liaison office that was then operating in Peking, and thus, in Deng's words, an embassy without a sign or a flag at its door.[20] This intention, they felt, was a significant retrogression from the position taken by Gerald Ford during his visit to China in December 1975, when he had accepted the proposition that American relations with Taiwan would remain wholly unofficial, and a retreat to an idea that Deng Xiaoping had already rejected when Kissinger first presented it in November 1974. Perhaps most irritating of all to Chinese leaders were subsequent American press reports that they had been "flexible" in their discussions of the Taiwan issue with Vance. At a time when he had not yet fully consolidated his power, Deng could not afford any suggestion that his approach to the Taiwan question was not firm and principled. Thus Deng was disappointed by the Vance visit, telling subsequent American visitors that it had represented a step backward in Sino-American relations.

Other aspects of the visit also may have troubled the Chinese, particularly Secretary Vance's commitment to détente with the Soviet Union. At that point, American policy toward Moscow was guided by another presidential review memorandum, PRM-10, which had concluded that the United States enjoyed long-term economic and technological advantages in its competition with the Soviet Union, thereby implying that Washington need not be overly concerned about any short-range military imbalance between the two countries. In addition, the Chinese were doubtless aware that PRM-24 had recommended against American arms sales to Peking and had counseled that the United States not sacrifice the prospects of improved relations with the Soviet Union for the sake of a strategic relationship with China.[21]

Sensing that the Chinese had been deeply disappointed—even irritated—by the Vance visit, the United States postponed any further consideration of normalization for the time being. Carter and Vance decided to return the issue to the back burner, where it had been placed earlier in the year. Once again, the administration assigned lower priority to China policy than to other issues, including the Panama Canal Treaty, SALT, the Middle East, energy policy, and an "overloaded domestic agenda." The press of other business "did not leave much time for us to pursue the China question," Carter has recalled. "Besides, it was not the right moment to tackle another highly controversial issue."[22] By February 1978, some observers were forecasting that normalization could not be achieved during Carter's first term.[23]

PROGRESS TOWARD NORMALIZATION

Increasingly, however, signs of continued inflexibility in Soviet policy drove the two countries closer together. The Carter administration was disturbed by Moscow's reluctance to incorporate deep reductions of strategic arms into a SALT agreement, by continued Soviet and Cuban activity in western Africa, and especially by the Kremlin's intervention in Ethiopia in early 1978. These Soviet decisions, coupled with Moscow's ongoing augmentation of its conventional and nuclear forces, gradually led the president away from Vance's policy of renewed Soviet-American détente and toward the strategy of vigorous containment advocated by Brzezinski. That inclination was reflected in a presidential speech at Wake Forest University in March 1978 in which Carter decried the "ominous inclination on the part of the Soviet Union to use its military power . . . to intervene in local conflicts" and announced his determination to match the Soviet military buildup. It was also manifest in Carter's commencement address at the U.S. Naval Academy in Annapolis three months later, in which he told the Kremlin that it could "choose either confrontation or cooperation" but warned that the "United States is adequately prepared to meet either choice."[24]

Peking, too, grew increasingly frustrated with Soviet foreign policy. By the spring of 1978, Chinese leaders were deeply disappointed with the Kremlin's reaction to the "hundred-day thaw" of the previous autumn. In response to China's overtures, Moscow had proposed higher-level negotiations and had suggested a joint declaration renouncing the use of force and agreeing to conduct bilateral relations in the spirit of peaceful coexistence. But Moscow had not made any substantive concessions on the issues of greatest concern to China. At about the same time as Carter was announcing a firmer line toward the Soviet Union at Wake Forest, therefore, Peking began to insist on concrete Soviet gestures of goodwill, including the reduction of Soviet forces along the Sino-Soviet and Sino-Mongolian frontiers and a mutual disengagement from disputed territory. The Soviet response—including huge military maneuvers in the Far East personally witnessed by Leonid Brezhnev—suggested that the Kremlin was not prepared to meet any of these new Chinese demands.[25]

China was also concerned about new and unwelcome Vietnamese initiatives in Southeast Asia. In 1975, with the southern half of Vietnam finally under its control, Hanoi began to evince interest in Cambodia as well. At the same time, Hanoi requested more economic assistance from China both to support its own economic recovery from a decade of war with the United States and to finance its ambitions in Indochina. Peking, increasingly preoccupied with its own economic development program and unwilling to subsidize a government that appeared to seek a hegemonic position on China's southern border, denied the Vietnamese request.

Accordingly, the Sino-Vietnamese alliance began to unravel. In rapid succession, the two countries engaged in thrust and counterthrust, each hoping to force the other to yield to its pressure. The Vietnamese government expelled ethnic Chinese from the country. China closed its consulates, withdrew its economic and technical advisers, and suspended its aid program in Vietnam. Hanoi began to deepen relations with the Soviet Union, entering into a virtual military alliance with Moscow in November 1977, joining the Council of Mutual Economic Assistance, and granting Soviet military forces base rights on Vietnamese soil. Border clashes between China and Vietnam broke out in 1978 and, by November, Deng Xiaoping was traveling through Southeast Asia seeking diplomatic support for a coming confrontation with Hanoi.[26]

Thus, each in its own way, China and the United States came to doubt the feasibility of an early détente with the Soviet Union. As the prospects for accommodation with the Kremlin dimmed, both countries again began to see each other as partners in an international strategic alignment against Moscow, and to view the normalization of Sino-American relations with greater urgency. Encouraged by some officials in the White House, the Chinese embassy began to develop contacts with Brzezinski, seeing him as more sympathetic than Vance to their views on the Soviet Union and more eager to achieve the normalization of Sino-American relations. In the winter of 1977–78, Peking formally invited Brzezinski to visit China; and in March 1978, over the objections of the State Department and after much pressure from Brzezinski, Carter permitted his national security adviser to accept.[27]

Brzezinski was instructed to tell his Chinese hosts that the United States had "made up its mind" not only to accelerate the establishment of formal diplomatic relations with Peking but also to accept all three of the Chinese conditions for normalization.[28] Brzezinski also informed the Chinese that the United States was prepared to proceed simultaneously toward a SALT agreement with the Soviet Union and an agreement on normalization with Peking, rather than delay the establishment of diplomatic relations with China until the SALT negotiations had been concluded.[29]

At around the same time, the Carter administration also reached a firmer conclusion about the concessions it would demand from the Chinese in exchange for establishing diplomatic relations with Peking on China's terms. The president established several conditions as America's bottom line: the United States would continue to provide Taiwan with defensive military equipment, it would make a unilateral statement calling for a peaceful settlement of the Taiwan issue and the Chinese would agree not to contest such a statement, the United States would maintain extensive unofficial relations with Taiwan, Washington would terminate its defense treaty with Taipei after one year's notice rather than summarily abrogate it, and all other treaties and agreements between the United States and Taiwan would remain in force.[30] Some of these conditions were conveyed to the Chinese by Brzezinski, but others were withheld until the negotiations had gained greater momentum.

This new American formula for negotiation was, in several ways, a retreat from the maximum position broached during the Vance visit. The president abandoned the earlier proposal, relayed by Vance, that the United States keep some governmental officials stationed on Taiwan after normalization. Instead, American interests on the island would be handled by a completely unofficial body, comparable to the one created by the Japanese in 1972. The United States also stopped seeking a renunciation of force from Peking, a pledge that Washington had attempted unsuccessfully to extract from China throughout the ambassadorial negotiations in the 1950s and 1960s, or even a statement of peaceful intentions toward Taiwan, once Peking made clear that it would demand the termination of American arms sales to Taiwan in return. The administration correctly calculated that the supply of American weapons to Taiwan would be a more credible guarantee of the island's security than would a Chinese statement of goodwill.[31]

In addition to resuming discussions of the normalization of Sino-American relations, the Brzezinski visit was also intended to reassure the Chinese that the United States assigned great strategic value to its ties with Peking. Carter instructed Brzezinski to inform Chinese leaders that his visit was not a tactical expedient to gain temporary advantage in negotiations with Moscow, but rather an expression of a "strategic interest in a cooperative relationship with China . . . that is fundamental and enduring." Carter also authorized Brzezinski to raise the possibility of "political collaboration" with Peking on issues on which the two countries had "shared perspectives." Formally, Brzezinski relayed these messages to the Chinese in toasts in which he expressed an American interest in a secure and strong China and in which he called for cooperation in the face of a common threat. Brzezinski made the same point in a more colorful and less formal fashion when, during a brief break for sightseeing, he challenged his hosts to a race up the Great Wall: "Last one to the top fights the Russians in Ethiopia!"[32]

Despite the ebullient goodwill engendered by the Brzezinski visit, Washington was keenly aware that difficult negotiations lay ahead. The Carter administration was convinced that the conditions it had laid down for the normalization of Sino-American relations were necessary if an agreement were to obtain political support at home. It was also persuaded that—unlike Vance's earlier suggestion about stationing American government officials in Taipei—such conditions were fully in keeping with the prior negotiating record. But it acknowledged that some of those conditions, especially the continuation of U.S. arms sales to Taiwan, would be difficult for the Chinese to accept.

To deal with this dilemma, the United States devised a three-pronged strategy for establishing diplomatic relations with China, each element of which involved a separate channel for negotiations with Peking.[33] First, the discussions of normalization were conducted in Peking between Leonard Woodcock, the head of the U.S. liaison office, and Huang Hua, the Chinese foreign minister. This was done in the belief that negotiations conducted in such a manner would be less pressured and more discreet than if they were undertaken by special emissaries dispatched from Washington in a kind of "shuttle diplomacy."[34] Moreover, the Americans decided to deal first with some of the easier issues, such as the maintenance of unofficial relations with Taiwan after normalization, and to postpone until later some of the harder questions such as American arms sales to Taiwan and the unilateral U.S. statement on a peaceful future for Taiwan. The aim of this tactic was to build a successful record of negotiations, create a sense of momentum, and foster mutual trust between the American and Chinese interlocutors to facilitate the resolution of the more difficult issues at stake.[35]

The second element in the American strategy was conducted primarily by Brzezinski through his dealings with Chai Zemin and Han Xu, the ranking officials in the Chinese liaison office in Washington. It involved various unilateral gestures, to be discussed in greater detail below, that expanded American diplomatic, military, and technological cooperation with China. The goal was to assure Peking that the United States sincerely desired a long-term strategic partnership with China, although still within the limits set by the president after his review of PRM-24. It was hoped that such initiatives would encourage Peking to deal with the Taiwan question in a flexible and forthcoming manner.

Finally, a third line of communication was established between Richard Holbrooke, assistant secretary of state for East Asian and Pacific affairs, and Han Xu, Chai Zemin's deputy at the Chinese liaison office, to receive any Chinese protests over bilateral issues, especially Taiwan. The purpose of establishing this channel of negotiation was to prevent other controversial issues from complicating the discussions of normalization being conducted by Woodcock and Huang Hua in Peking. At the same time, the United States took care to avoid any initiatives toward Taiwan that might arouse Chinese displeasure, as the Ford administration had done unintentionally. Thus, the Carter administration refused to allow Taipei's ambassador in Washington to contact high-level American officials and denied Taiwan's request to purchase either advanced F-4 fighter-bombers or F-5G, F-16, or F-18 fighters.[36]

As the Carter administration had predicted, the most delicate part of the negotiations occurred in September, when the United States finally informed the Chinese that it intended to continue arms sales to Taipei after normalization, that it planned to make a unilateral statement on a peaceful future for Taiwan, and that the mutual defense treaty with Taiwan would remain in effect for one year after normalization. To soothe the angry Chinese, Washington introduced a fresh carrot and a new stick into the discussions, inviting either Hua Guofeng or Deng Xiaoping to visit the United States immediately after diplomatic relations were established, and informing Peking that the SALT treaty was almost complete and that a Soviet-U.S. summit was therefore imminent. The message was clear: if the Chinese could accept the American formula for negotiation, they could have their summit before the Russians. But if they delayed, Soviet-American relations would experience the breakthrough before Sino-American ties were firmly knit.[37]

Other factors also were making it easier for Chinese leaders to be flexible. The growing signs of Vietnamese designs on Cambodia, and particularly the conclusion of the Soviet-Vietnamese alliance in November, increased Peking's interest in securing a strategic alignment with the United States. At the same time, Deng Xiaoping was steadily consolidating his political power in Peking—an achievement confirmed by important Party meetings in November and December—which gave him greater leeway to make necessary concessions to Washington when he took personal charge of the Sino-American negotiations in December.

Thus, in order to complete the normalization process by the end of 1978, the Chinese finally accepted all of the most sensitive conditions for normalization presented by the United States, just as Washington had earlier accepted the three conditions set down by Peking. But the Chinese did so with varying degrees of finality. In agreeing that the American defense treaty with Taiwan could remain in effect for one more year while Washington gave Taipei notice of its termination, Deng Xiaoping successfully insisted that the United States sell no arms to Taiwan in the interim.[38] Although the Chinese also tolerated a unilateral statement that Washington expected a peaceful future for Taiwan, they repeatedly warned American negotiators that, while they would not openly contradict the U.S. declaration, neither would they corroborate it. Perhaps most important, Peking did not accept a continued program of American arms sales to Taiwan but simply decided not to allow the issue to prevent the completion of normalization. In effect, it set the issue aside temporarily but reserved the right to raise it later.

The agreement on the normalization of Sino-American relations, issued on the evening of December 15 in the United States and on the following morning in China, took the form of three sets of statements (see appendix C). In a joint communiqué, the two countries announced that they would establish diplomatic relations on January 1, 1979, and would exchange ambassadors at the beginning of the following March. In a formulation slightly more explicit than the one in the Shanghai communiqué, the United States also acknowledged the Chinese position that Taiwan is part of China. Unilateral American statements, made in a formal pronouncement and in press briefings, announced that the United States would withdraw its remaining military personnel from Taiwan within four months, terminate its mutual defense treaty by the end of the year, and maintain relations with Taiwan "without official government representation and without diplomatic relations."[39] But the American statements also contained a reassertion of a continuing interest in the peaceful resolution of the Taiwan issue and its intention to sell limited quantities of defensive arms to the island after the one-year moratorium it had promised to Deng Xiaoping. In response, unilateral Chinese statements, also made in an official declaration and in press briefings, disclosed China's opposition to continued American arms sales to Taiwan and reiterated that the method of reunifying Taiwan with the mainland would be "entirely China's internal affair."[40]

One other facet of the normalization agreement was China's willingness to send a senior leader to visit the United States for the first time since the rapprochement of the early 1970s. One month after the conclusion of the agreement on normalization, Deng Xiaoping arrived in Washington for a triumphal visit.[41] In addition to meetings at the White House and on Capitol Hill, Deng was the honored guest at a gala performance at the Kennedy Center in Washington, where he was entertained by performers ranging from John Denver to the Harlem Globetrotters. In Atlanta, Deng visited a Ford automobile plant, where he posed admiring a yellow four-door LTD; in Houston, he attended a rodeo and barbecue, where he rode around the arena in a miniature stagecoach, waving a new ten-gallon hat out the window. The visit produced a spate of bilateral agreements to establish consular relations and to expand scientific and cultural exchanges. But Deng's main message—expressed in mild terms in official settings, but in blunt language in unofficial forums—was to encourage the United States to work with China to contain Soviet expansion, and to warn that, as a first step, Peking might have to undertake some kind of military action against Vietnam to "teach it a lesson" for its intervention in Cambodia.

CONGRESS REVISITS TAIWAN

Six months of negotiations between China and the United States produced complex compromises over American relations with Taiwan. In 1975, Peking had set out three conditions for normalization, on which it consistently refused to yield. In 1978, when the negotiations over normalization got under way, the United States accepted China's three conditions but presented several counterconditions. Peking, in the end, yielded to the American position but often without fully accepting it. The result was a patchwork of joint communiqués, unilateral statements, and unresolved issues that enabled the two countries to establish diplomatic relations but that did not fully resolve the Taiwan issue.

The status of American relations with Taiwan was the subject of one of these bargains. The United States agreed to terminate diplomatic relations with Taiwan and gave up any hope of maintaining an official presence there. To replace its embassy, it would create an unofficial agency, known as the American Institute in Taiwan (AIT), to be staffed by officials who had temporarily retired from government service. A similar organization, to be known as the Coordination Council for North American Affairs (CCNAA), would be permitted to represent Taiwan's interests in the United States. Washington also agreed that, while its treaties with Taiwan would temporarily remain in force, they would be replaced by unofficial arrangements once they had expired. In return, Peking acknowledged continuation of extensive unofficial American economic, cultural, and scientific relations with Taiwan.

On the issue of the American commitment to Taiwan's defense, an even more complicated compromise was reached. The United States agreed to end the mutual defense treaty with Taipei but insisted on doing so by giving one year's notice rather than accepting China's demand that the treaty be immediately abrogated. The United States also made a unilateral statement reiterating its interest in a peaceful future for Taiwan and declaring its expectation that the Taiwan issue would be resolved peacefully. As Washington insisted, the Chinese refrained from contradicting that statement. Moreover, Peking stopped references to the liberation of Taiwan and began instead to speak of the peaceful reunification of the country. It also ended the largely symbolic artillery bombardment of the offshore islands and transferred some of its air and ground forces away from the Taiwan Strait.

Still, Chinese leaders never acknowledged the American interest in a peaceful future for Taiwan, nor did they reassure the United States that its expectation of a peaceful resolution of the issue would eventually be met. Indeed, in its unilateral statement issued at the time of normalization, Peking continued to insist that the methods it would use to reunify the country were its own internal affair. Moreover, although Deng expressed a preference for peaceful reunification during his visit to the United States, he also identified two conditions under which Peking would employ force against Taiwan: if the Kuomintang persisted in refusing to negotiate with the mainland or if the Soviet Union established a military presence on the island.[42] And Deng warned that continued American arms sales to Taiwan would bolster Taipei's refusal to negotiate with Peking and thus would make the use of force more likely.

Finally, the United States agreed to withdraw its remaining military forces from Taiwan by the end of April 1979. But, as another way of symbolizing interest in Taiwan's military security, it insisted on continuing to sell weapons and other defense technology to the island. To soothe Peking, the United States did not insist on making a formal commitment to arms sales in either the joint communiqué on normalization or in the unilateral statement that it issued at the same time. Instead, it revealed its intentions in the press briefings that were called to provide background information on the agreement.

Moreover, Washington also set certain limits on arms sales to Taiwan. It assured Peking that it would provide only a reasonable amount of defensive weaponry to Taipei. It implied that arms sales to Taiwan could be reduced as tensions in the Taiwan Strait declined and could even be terminated if the Taiwan issue were peacefully resolved. As Brzezinski had told the Chinese in May, the United States envisioned arms sales to Taiwan as continuing through a "historically transitional era," presumably meaning until Taipei and Peking resolved their differences; moreover, within that transitional period, the quantity and quality of American arms sales would be linked to Peking's policy toward Taiwan. In so doing, the Carter administration dealt with arms sales to Taiwan in much the same way as the Nixon administration had addressed the question of the American military presence on the island in the Shanghai communiqué.[43]

Although the establishment of formal diplomatic relations with the People's Republic of China was widely welcomed in the United States, the specific terms of the agreement aroused severe criticism, especially in Congress.[44] The reaction from conservative Republicans was particularly scathing. Barry Goldwater called the agreement cowardly; Bill Brock, chairman of the Republican National Committee, termed it disgraceful; and Jesse Helms charged that the Carter

administration "proposed to sell Taiwan down the river." Even officials from the previous Republican administrations who had been
deeply involved in developing relations with China either joined in
the criticism or were lukewarm in their support of the president.
Nixon would say only that he would not second-guess Carter's decision; Ford limited his support to those parts of the agreement of
which he had been informed, implying that there might be other
secret undertakings that he could not approve; and George Bush, the
head of the American liaison office in Peking in the mid-1970s, said
that the U.S. concessions on Taiwan had "darkened the prospects
for peace."[45]

In part, congressional leaders were angered by what they regarded
as the Carter administration's refusal to consult them in advance on
the terms of normalization. Over the summer of 1978, it had become
clear from press reports that Washington was engaged in active negotiations with Peking over the normalization of Sino-American relations and that the termination of the mutual defense treaty with
Taiwan was one price that the United States might have to pay to
establish diplomatic ties with China. Barry Goldwater thereupon
introduced a concurrent resolution demanding that the Senate have
the opportunity to advise and consent on the termination of the
treaty. The Goldwater resolution was not voted on, but Senators
Robert Dole and Richard Stone introduced a bipartisan amendment
requesting that the president consult with Congress before making
any change in the treaty's status. That amendment, which passed the
Senate unanimously, was attached to the annual security assistance
authorization act, which in turn was signed into law by the president.

Vance, along with Holbrooke and Deputy Secretary of State Warren
Christopher, proposed accepting the congressional request. But both
Brzezinski and his assistant for Chinese affairs, Michel Oksenberg,
disagreed.[46] Oksenberg argued that Congress already knew the broad
parameters of the U.S. position and that any further consultation
might generate so much domestic opposition that the administration
would be unable to conclude the negotiations successfully. In addition, Oksenberg warned that any public revelation of the American
terms for normalization would confound the Carter administration's
strategy of revealing its negotiating position to the Chinese only
gradually.[47]

After hearing both sides of this debate, Carter concluded that it
would be best not to consult with Congress: "I decided that these
[negotiations] should be conducted in secrecy in order not to arouse
concerted opposition from Taiwan's supporters [in the United
States], as well as to avoid building up excessive expectations."[48]

The Carter administration anticipated that, presented with a fait accompli, Congress would not be able to reverse the normalization of relations with China, and that, in the end, public opinion would be supportive. But this decision meant that many members of Congress, perceiving that their request for consultation had been rejected, were reluctant to give quick or automatic support to the president who had slighted them.

Congressional dissatisfaction was exacerbated because many members of Congress were displeased with the terms of the normalization agreement. Some believed that the United States should have insisted on retaining some official representation in Taiwan, such as a consulate or a liaison office, even though such a proposal had been rejected by China during Vance's visit to Peking in August 1977. Others asserted that Washington should have demanded a binding commitment by Peking that it would not use force against Taiwan, even though China had consistently refused for more than twenty years to make such a statement. Still others noted that China did not even state an unequivocal preference for a peaceful solution to the Taiwan question. As Senator Dale Bumpers (D-Arkansas) put it, "It made me wonder how much the President left on the negotiating table."[49]

Perhaps most important of all, Congress was not satisfied with the way in which the White House had reiterated its commitment to Taiwan's security. Originally, the administration had planned to submit two pieces of legislation to Congress: a bill that would create the American Institute in Taiwan and provide the legal framework for continuing unofficial relations with Taiwan, and a resolution that would express the continuing American interest in a peaceful future for the island. In the end, however, the White House put forward only the first item of legislation, known as the Taiwan Enabling Act,[50] embodying the residual security commitment to Taiwan solely in the unilateral presidential statement that "the United States continues to have an interest in the peaceful resolution of the Taiwan issue and expects that the Taiwan issue will be settled peacefully by the Chinese themselves." Nor did the draft of the Taiwan Enabling Act provide any specific mechanism or provision for continued American arms sales to Taiwan.[51]

Members of Congress explored two possibilities for either rejecting or modifying the terms of the normalization of relations with China. Goldwater filed suit in U.S. district court, challenging the administration's right to terminate the mutual defense treaty with Taiwan without Senate approval. After an initial victory, the Goldwater suit was overturned on appeal.[52] The more successful approach was to alter the terms of the Taiwan Enabling Act to provide a more explicit American commitment to Taiwan's security. Although the White House originally opposed this idea as well, it agreed, in the end, to consider moderate changes in the legislation once it realized that some form of congressional action was inevitable.

The debate over the content of the Taiwan Enabling Act—soon renamed by Congress as the Taiwan Relations Act—focused on two issues. First, several members of Congress introduced amendments that would have upgraded future American relations with Taiwan.[53] The administration successfully resisted any proposals that would have specified, or even implied, an official quality to U.S. ties with Taipei, including amendments by Senator Gordon Humphrey (R-New Hampshire) and Representative Dan Quayle (R-Indiana) that would have transformed the American Institute in Taiwan into an official liaison office. But the White House agreed to accept other amendments, including those that allowed the Overseas Private Investment Corporation to continue work on Taiwan, permitted the transfer of nuclear technology to the island, enabled the AIT to perform consular functions, and authorized the CCNAA to have as many offices in the United States as Taiwan had previously had consulates.

Second, Congress also wanted a firmer and more explicit American commitment to Taiwan's security than the one contained in the unilateral presidential statement of December 15. The administration prevented the inclusion of some formulas that it found too provocative to Peking, such as one by Senator Jacob Javits (R-New York) that would simply have incorporated much of the language of the mutual defense treaty into the Taiwan Relations Act, or one by Senator Charles Percy (R-Illinois) and Representative Quayle that would have described an attack on Taiwan as a "threat" to American security interests. Instead, the White House accepted a somewhat milder statement that American recognition of the PRC rested on the expectation of a peaceful future for Taiwan, that any use of force or coercion against Taiwan would be a threat to the peace and security of the western Pacific and "of grave concern" to the United States. The language also provided that the United States would "provide defensive arms to the ROC" so as to ensure that Taipei enjoyed a sufficient self-defense capability, and that the United States would maintain the capacity to resist any use of force or coercion that would threaten Taiwan's security.[54]

The final version of the Taiwan Relations Act was so altered from the original bill submitted by the administration that some of Carter's advisers urged him to veto it, on the grounds that it would be unacceptable to the Chinese.[55] But the margin in both houses of Congress was so large—339–50 in the House and 85–4 in the Senate—that a veto could have been easily overridden. Instead, the president decided to sign the Taiwan Relations Act while simultaneously reassuring the Chinese that he had substantial discretion in interpreting and implementing the law, and that he would do so in ways fully consistent with the understandings on normalization that he had reached with Peking.[56] Although the Chinese denounced the act, with Deng Xiaoping telling one group of American visitors that its passage had come close to "nullifying" the normalization agreement, they were sufficiently mollified by Carter's assurances that they did not take any retaliatory action.[57]

In reviewing the reaction to the normalization agreement, Carter said, "The serious opposition we had expected throughout our country and within Congress simply did not materialize."[58] In fact, there was great criticism from the public and Congress. Public opinion polls revealed profound reservations about withdrawing diplomatic relations from Taipei and terminating the defense treaty with the island, although some surveys also suggested that, on balance, the public supported the president's decision.[59] Congress, too, sharply questioned the way in which the administration had treated Taiwan in establishing diplomatic relations with China.

The modifications to the Taiwan Relations Act resolved the issue temporarily. But they were not a lasting solution. Some American leaders, notably Ronald Reagan, would later explore the possibility of restoring some officiality to American ties with Taipei. Some Chinese leaders, in turn, refused to accept the Taiwan Relations Act or the American policy of arms sales to Taiwan and would later demand that the United States repeal the act and reduce its supply of weapons to the island more rapidly. The residual dissatisfaction on both sides of the Pacific with the terms of the normalization agreement of 1978 would, within three years, produce a new crisis in Sino-American relations.

AN EXPANDING STRATEGIC RELATIONSHIP

From the beginning of their rapprochement in the late 1960s, both China and the United States were interested in forming a strategic alignment that would counterbalance the growth of Soviet military power and thus deter Soviet expansionism. Just as the history of Sino-American relations in the 1970s can be portrayed as the two countries' effort to resolve their differences over Taiwan, so too can it be depicted as their common search to define a mutually acceptable program of security cooperation. Over time, that cooperative relationship became more extensive and more explicit.

During the Nixon administration, as noted earlier, strategic cooperation between China and the United States largely took the form of American statements of support for Chinese security against a Soviet attack and Chinese cooperation with American regional policy toward Korea, Japan, and Indochina. Each side also began to explore the possibility of a more concrete military relationship. During both of his visits in 1971, Kissinger shared highly sensitive military intelligence with Chinese leaders, including some obtained from satellite photography and from communications intercepts.[60] Although the Chinese did not immediately reciprocate, they did begin to probe Washington's willingness to export arms to Peking or to allow its Western European allies to do so.

In the Ford administration, the possibility of more extensive strategic cooperation was considered even more seriously, as a way of maintaining momentum in Sino-American relations when neither side could make much progress on Taiwan. In the end, the United States decided neither to sell American weapons to China nor to endorse arms sales by its allies, and the Chinese decided that they would not agree to an expanded military relationship with the United States before the normalization of their diplomatic ties. But the flow of advanced civilian technology from the United States and from Europe continued, with Washington easing export controls on a case-by-case basis to permit the sale of sophisticated American computers to Peking.

As James Schlesinger had been when he was Gerald Ford's secretary of defense, Zbigniew Brzezinski was deeply interested in an expanded security relationship with China, as a way of bolstering America's strategic position against the Soviet Union and reinforcing Sino-American relations before the normalization of their relations was complete. In June 1977, on the basis of the analysis presented to him in PRM-24, President Carter decided against the sale of American weapons to China. But in early 1978, he authorized Brzezinski to upgrade American strategic ties with Peking, in part as an element of the complex strategy for inducing greater Chinese flexibility during the negotiations over normalization and in part as a way of signaling his growing displeasure with continued Soviet expansionism. Brzezinski's visit to Peking in May 1978 conveyed the new spirit of American policy to Chinese leaders.[61]

The increased American willingness to engage in strategic cooperation with China in 1978 took three forms. First, the United States continued making public statements supporting Chinese security interests. During his visit to Peking, Brzezinski endorsed the concept of a "secure and strong China"—a considerable advance over the Nixon formulation that Washington did not want to see China defeated in a Sino-Soviet war. Moreover, he assured Peking that the United States supported China's desire to insert, in the Sino-Japanese treaty of friendship then under negotiation, a clause opposing any country's efforts to establish hegemony in Asia. And, on his way back to Washington, Brzezinski stopped in Tokyo to convey the same message directly to the Japanese government. Worried about the impact on its relations with the Soviet Union, Tokyo had been resisting the inclusion of such terminology. Now, however, faced with coordinated pressure from both Peking and Washington on this issue, Japanese leaders concluded they had no choice but to yield.

Second, the United States continued to relax restrictions on the export of advanced technology to Peking. Over Vance's objections, it indicated its willingness to transfer advanced civilian and dual-purpose technology to China by authorizing the sale of American infrared airborne geological survey equipment to Peking and by launching negotiations on an extensive program of scientific and technological exchanges with China. Washington also approved the sale of a French nuclear reactor, many components of which were manufactured in the United States. Still, at this point the transfer of advanced American technology was conducted very much on a case-by-case basis. Opposition from Soviet specialists within the U.S. government, and above all from Secretary of State Vance, prevented the adoption of an overall policy that would have given Peking greater access to American technology than that enjoyed by Moscow.[62]

Finally, although the ban on American arms sales remained in effect, the inclusion of a Defense Department representative in Brzezinski's delegation to Peking in May 1978 suggested that the United States was prepared to engage in other types of security cooperation with China. Brzezinski briefed the Chinese on PRM-10, which analyzed the Soviet-American strategic balance, and on the Carter administration's policy toward the Soviet Union. He also discussed the outlines of the forthcoming SALT agreement with Moscow and arranged for the Chinese to receive a NATO briefing on global security issues.[63] It is also likely that the two countries discussed the possibilities of further sharing of military intelligence. And, in mid-1978, Washington announced that it would no longer object to Western European arms sales to China.[64]

By the end of 1978, with the normalization of Sino-American relations in sight, Peking began to respond more enthusiastically to these American initiatives. On the eve of his departure for the United States, Deng Xiaoping told visiting American journalists, "If we really want to be able to place curbs on the polar bear, the only realistic thing for us is to unite," and he confirmed that China's "united front" against the Soviet Union was intended to include the United States.[65] Throughout his American tour, although denying any desire for a formal alliance with America, Deng continued to speak openly and sometimes bluntly about his desire for a strategic alignment with the United States to counter Soviet expansion and about his hope that Washington would do more to contain Moscow's ambitions.[66]

Nor was Deng reluctant to reveal some of the details of what he had in mind. While in Washington, he informed his American hosts that China was planning an invasion of Vietnam to "teach Vietnam a lesson" for its intervention in Cambodia, and he hoped that Washington would give China moral support.[67] And, after returning to China, Deng discussed with a delegation from the Senate Foreign Relations Committee three options for an expanded security relationship with the United States: port calls by the American navy, Chinese purchases of American arms, and the establishment of American monitoring facilities on Chinese soil to verify Moscow's compliance with Soviet-American arms control agreements.[68]

In reality, however, both countries refrained from more active security collaboration for the rest of the year. The United States gently dissociated itself from the Chinese invasion of Vietnam. After Deng informed him of Peking's intentions, Carter replied that he would prefer diplomatic measures to isolate Vietnam, fearing that direct military confrontation might generate international sympathy for Hanoi's position. Having made the point orally, he also presented Deng a handwritten message, urging China to exercise restraint.[69] When China ignored the American advice, the United States had to decide how to respond. Vance advocated some form of punitive action against Peking, recommending specifically the cancellation of Treasury Secretary Michael Blumenthal's upcoming visit to Peking. In the end, Carter adopted a more moderate approach, demanding the withdrawal of Chinese forces from Vietnam and Vietnamese troops from Cambodia and warning the Soviet Union not to intervene. Brzezinski is correct in describing the American position as "a slight tilt in favor of the Chinese," but it was hardly the unequivocal moral support that Deng had requested.[70]

China, too, began to have second thoughts about expanding military ties with the United States. Shortly after Deng had raised the possibility of American naval visits to Chinese ports with the Senate

Foreign Relations Committee delegation, Brzezinski discussed the matter with Ambassador Chai Zemin. But an embarrassed Chai now rebuffed Brzezinski's overtures. Chai explained that his government was angered at the content of the Taiwan Relations Act and was not prepared to engage in more extensive security cooperation with the United States in such circumstances. Another reason may well have been China's disappointment with the American reaction to its punitive expedition against Vietnam. Why should China agree to the American vision of how to counterbalance the Soviet Union when the United States was unwilling to endorse Peking's measures?

In addition, China attempted in 1979 to see whether the normalization of its relations with the United States had given it additional diplomatic leverage with the Soviet Union. When, in the spring of that year, Peking announced that it would not renew the 1950 alliance with Moscow when it expired in 1980, Chinese leaders also offered to reopen negotiations on an improvement of Sino-Soviet relations. After a long debate over an agenda, those talks finally opened in Moscow in October. They achieved little success because China insisted on concrete gestures of goodwill—such as a Vietnamese withdrawal from Cambodia and a reduction of forces along the Sino-Soviet frontier—that Moscow was unwilling to provide. Until the prospects for those negotiations were known, however, China preferred not to move rapidly toward military ties with the United States.[71]

Thus, the strategic relationship between Peking and Washington was largely kept in a holding pattern through most of 1979. During Vice President Walter Mondale's visit to China that summer, the two sides agreed that Defense Secretary Harold Brown would also travel to Peking, with the date subsequently set as January 1980. But the vice president reiterated that there were no plans for a more substantive military relationship between the two countries. Although some officials in the Defense Department pressed for a more extensive program of military cooperation with China, the ban on arms sales to China was consistently upheld throughout the year, and the original draft of the president's instructions for the Brown visit, written in December, repeated that there would be no arms sales to China and no "military relationship."[72]

But the Soviet invasion of Afghanistan in late 1979 gave renewed impetus to the Sino-American strategic relationship. At the last minute, the guidelines for the Brown visit were changed to propose a much more extensive strategic relationship with China. Since Chinese leaders had concluded that they could live with the Taiwan Relations Act, at least as it was being interpreted by the Carter administration, the Brown visit inaugurated more extensive and more highly visible military ties between the two countries.

First, the Brown visit launched a regular exchange of Chinese and American military personnel. Agreement was reached on an exchange of visits by high-level defense officials, with Brown's trip followed by Undersecretary of Defense William Perry later in 1980 and reciprocated by Chinese Vice Premier Geng Biao (who was concurrently secretary general of the Party's Central Military Commission) and Deputy Chief of Staff Liu Huaqing, who visited the United States separately in May–June 1980. In addition, exchanges of working-level military delegations on subjects such as health and logistics, institutional ties between the American and Chinese national defense universities, and the placement of military attachés in the two countries' embassies opened further channels of communication between the two defense establishments.

China and the United States also began a more active program of intelligence sharing at this time. During the Brown visit, Deputy Assistant Secretary of Defense Morton Abramowitz gave Chinese leaders a highly classified briefing on Soviet deployments in the Far East, complete with satellite photographs of Soviet installations along the Sino-Soviet frontier. Later that year, following Deng Xiaoping's suggestion in April 1979, the two countries established, on Chinese soil, two stations for monitoring Soviet nuclear and missile tests to replace similar facilities in Iran that had been closed after the overthrow of the shah.[73]

The transfer of American technology to China was also liberalized.[74] During his January 1980 visit to Peking, and as another direct result of the Soviet intervention in Afghanistan, Brown announced that the United States would be willing to sell nonlethal military equipment to the Chinese armed forces, including a ground station to receive data from Landsat satellites, transport aircraft, military helicopters, and communications equipment. Licenses would be granted, on a case-by-case basis, for items of technology that were not combat arms or weapons platforms, that would be available to any other friendly country, and that would not contribute to China's chemical, radiological, bacteriological, nuclear, or missile programs.[75]

In midyear, Washington removed China from the same category of export controls as the Soviet Union and placed Peking in its own classification (category P). This step had no immediate practical effect, for the level of restrictiveness and licensing procedures in the new group was the same as in the old classification. But the decision did make it administratively possible for the United States to treat

China differently from the Soviet Union.[76] The following September, William Perry, the undersecretary of defense for research and engineering, informed Chinese leaders that the United States had approved export licenses for four hundred items of dual-purpose technology and nonlethal military equipment and expressed U.S. willingness to participate in a joint assessment of China's civilian and military technological capabilities. In return, Peking offered to increase its sale of rare metals to the United States.

The Chinese were still disappointed, however, by the continued ban on the sale of American arms to Peking. Before leaving China for Washington in late May 1980, Vice Premier Geng Biao said that China wanted to be permitted to purchase American weapons, just like Egypt, Saudi Arabia, and other friendly but nonallied countries that the United States considered strategically important.[77] Geng also brought with him a list of more than fifty items of advanced military technology, including some lethal weapons such as Hawk ground-to-air missiles and TOW antitank missiles. Given Chinese financial constraints, he did not necessarily intend to place orders for any of this equipment. Instead, his goal was to see how forthcoming the United States was prepared to be. He was again informed, however, that Washington had no intention of selling lethal equipment to China.

Finally, China and the United States also discussed ways of coordinating their security policies in 1980. They agreed on the desirability of undertaking parallel or complementary actions on key regional disputes. The two worked together to deny the new pro-Vietnamese government in Phnom Penh a seat in the United Nations and discussed ways of supporting the Cambodian resistance to the Vietnamese intervention. They also agreed on the need to oppose the Soviet invasion of Afghanistan, with the United States reimbursing Peking for some of the costs of transporting Chinese arms and equipment to the Afghan rebels.[78] But some American ideas went too far for Peking to accept. A proposal to establish a hot line between the two capitals was rejected, apparently because the Chinese viewed such a communications channel as the symbol of an adversarial rather than a cooperative relationship. Peking allegedly also turned down a proposal to permit American planes carrying military supplies for Pakistan to fly through Chinese airspace.[79]

More broadly, there were increasing signs that Chinese foreign policy objectives and strategies were conforming with those of the United States. Peking downplayed earlier calls for a new international economic order and argued instead that the third world should be more concerned with resisting Soviet expansionism than with demanding better terms of trade and investment from the West. China terminated, or at least greatly attenuated, ties with revolutionary Communist parties in the third world and demonstrated an eagerness to form friendly relations even with those governments closely aligned with the West. It expressed support for an American military presence abroad, as long as it could be justified as part of a strategy to contain Soviet hegemonism. On issue after issue—from the unity of NATO to the strengthening of the Association of Southeast Asian Nations—Peking's positions came to resemble those of the United States.[80]

In these ways, the strategic relationship between China and the United States did make a qualitative breakthrough in the late 1970s, the result of the normalization of diplomatic relations and the continued expansionism of the Soviet Union and its allies. But the two countries still defined their strategic interests somewhat differently. Each was eager to obtain the other's support for its undertakings but was often reluctant to endorse the other's initiatives. Thus, American proposals for hot lines, overflight rights, and port visits were rejected by the Chinese, because they appeared to violate Chinese sovereignty or to compromise Peking's freedom of action. China's invasion of Vietnam, in turn, received only lukewarm support in the United States because of Washington's concern about possible Soviet retaliation. And China was always seeking approval to purchase more advanced military technology than the United States was prepared to provide. Although much progress had been made in finding a common framework for strategic cooperation, at the end of the Carter administration the process was not yet complete.

THE GROWTH OF ECONOMIC
AND CULTURAL TIES

For the next two years, normalization enabled rapid and dramatic growth in the economic and cultural ties between China and the United States. The establishment of formal diplomatic relations permitted the removal of the barriers to trade and academic exchanges between the two countries and then the creation of a new facilitative infrastructure for bilateral relations. These institutional changes, in turn, encouraged the qualitative and quantitative expansion of the entire spectrum of civilian relations.

As noted in chapter 2, the Korean War had led both Peking and

Washington to construct many legal and institutional barriers to Sino-American relations. Some of these restrictions, especially on economic relations, had been removed during the rapprochement of the early 1970s. But the full institutional normalization of Sino-American relations had to await the establishment of diplomatic relations in 1979. From a legal point of view, many aspects of normal intercourse between the two countries—consular protection, most-favored-nation status, economic assistance, and the like—required formal diplomatic ties. Equally important, Peking had insisted it would refrain from certain kinds of relations with the United States—such as the long-term exchange of students, scholars, and journalists—until Washington had completed the process of normalization.

With diplomatic relations established in early 1979, the two sides were able to clear away many more of the restrictive laws and institutions associated with the cold war. In May 1979, they resolved the issues of blocked claims and frozen assets dating from the Korean War on terms relatively favorable to the United States.[81] Washington subsequently made China eligible for reimbursable technical assistance programs, investment guarantees from the Overseas Private Investment Corporation (OPIC), and trade credits from the Eximbank. It relaxed restrictions on the export of advanced technology to China several times between 1979 and 1980.

Perhaps most important, the Carter administration decided in mid-1980 to sign a trade agreement with Peking that would extend most-favored-nation treatment to China. Without MFN status, Chinese exports to the United States were subject to the high tariffs provided by the Smoot-Hawley Act of 1930. Although many commodities that China had sold to the United States in the 1970s were not particularly handicapped by this fact, the export of light manufactured goods—an area of potential comparative advantage for Chinese industry—was significantly restricted.[82] Granting China MFN status was therefore a prerequisite for expanding commercial relations between the two countries.

The extension of most-favored-nation treatment to China had to overcome both political and legal calculations. Politically, it required an American decision to provide China with a commercial benefit that was not yet granted to the Soviet Union. Legally, the provision of MFN status to "nonmarket economies" was covered by the Jackson-Vanik amendment to the trade act of 1974, which stipulated that the president certify that the governments in question provided freedom of emigration to their citizens or that the extension of MFN treatment would encourage them to do so. The political question

was resolved by the Soviet intervention in Afghanistan; the legal
issue was settled, at least for the time being, by Deng Xiaoping's
jocular offer to provide the United States with as many as 10 million
Chinese, if necessary, to demonstrate his commitment to freedom
of emigration.[83]

During this same period, Peking opened the way for American
scholars, journalists, and businesspeople to undertake longer-term
visits to China. For the first time, it encouraged the development of
routine commercial tourism in the country. It also began in the fall
of 1978 to send students and scholars to the United States for lengthy
courses of study and research. More generally, China began to inter-
act economically with the rest of the world, including the United
States, in ways that had been precluded during the Maoist era. It
accepted long-term loans from foreign banks, governments, and international organizations, permitted direct foreign investment
through an increasing range of organizational formats, established
four special economic zones along its southern coast, and decentral-
ized its foreign trade system to permit Chinese cities and provinces
to conduct imports and exports directly.[84] All these decisions expanded the opportunities for American business to conduct commercial activities in China.

Besides paring away the restrictions of the past, it was also necessary to create a new infrastructure that could actively facilitate Sino-
American relations. Here, too, rapid and substantial progress was
made in the two years following normalization. By the end of 1980,
the two countries had reached bilateral agreements on trade, trade
exhibitions, postal service, commercial air links, shipping services,
and consular matters. An agreement regulating the sales of Chinese
textiles to the United States had been signed, and an agreement on
American grain exports to China neared completion. A bilateral Joint
Economic Committee oversaw the creation of the legal framework
for economic relations between the two countries.[85]

The two countries placed special emphasis on the construction of
an institutional framework for promoting bilateral scientific and
technological exchanges. As part of the Carter administration's effort
to preserve the momentum of Sino-American relations during the
negotiations over normalization in 1978, it had sent a large science
and technology delegation to Peking, led by presidential science
adviser Frank Press. That delegation, described by the White House
as the highest-level delegation on scientific and technological matters ever sent to a foreign country, reached an agreement with the
Chinese on the first exchanges of students and visiting scholars. In
1979, during Deng Xiaoping's visit to Washington, the two countries

signed a further accord on scientific and technological cooperation. Under that agreement, no fewer than fourteen programs were approved by the end of 1980, overseen by an official bilateral commission on scientific and technological cooperation.

The construction of this facilitative infrastructure by the two national governments was echoed by local governments and by the private sector. By the end of 1980, fifteen Chinese provinces and municipalities had inaugurated exchange programs with their American counterparts, sixteen American news organizations had set up bureaus in Peking, and eighty American corporations had opened representative offices in China. Moreover, numerous American universities began to establish exchange programs with their opposite numbers in China. At the beginning, American universities waived their normal admissions requirements and procedures to facilitate the arrival of the first Chinese students and scholars. By December 1981, however, the Educational Testing Service had made arrangements to administer the TOEFL (Test of English as a Foreign Language) and GRE (Graduate Record Examination) in China, thus creating the normal mechanism for evaluating applications from Chinese students and scholars.

The Carter administration was not able to complete the process of building a normal institutional framework for cultural and economic relations with China during its term in office. Most-favored-nation status for Peking was, under the terms of the Jackson-Vanik amendment, subject to annual renewal and conditional on China's emigration policies.[86] Since it was not a member of the General Agreement on Tariffs and Trade, China was not eligible for lower American tariffs under the Generalized System of Preferences (GSP) for developing countries. Although China had been placed in a separate category under U.S. export control regulations, the sale of advanced technology to China was still subject to lengthy and cumbersome review. And the two countries still faced difficult negotiations on agreements to permit the export of American nuclear power–generating equipment, promote direct investment, and protect American intellectual property rights.

Nonetheless, the progress was more rapid than had been anticipated. Writing in 1982, Michel Oksenberg, the National Security Council staff member responsible for Chinese affairs during the first part of the Carter administration, noted that the agreements reached during the Mondale visit to China in August 1979, only eight months after normalization, "essentially completed the agenda which the two sides had set in January 1979 and which both sides estimated would take perhaps 18 months to complete."[87]

The surprising speed with which this facilitative infrastructure was constructed was the result of several factors. To a large degree, it was the result of a deliberate Carter administration strategy: to institutionalize and stabilize Sino-American relations by expanding the points of contact between the two countries to create a relationship as multifaceted and broadly based as possible.[88] This strategy was implemented, in turn, by what became known as "trip-driven diplomacy": a steady stream of Chinese and American officials crossed the Pacific to sign new bilateral agreements or to carry on negotiations on those not yet completed. In 1979 alone, the visitors included Secretary of the Treasury Michael Blumenthal, Secretary of Commerce Juanita Kreps, Secretary of Health, Education, and Welfare Joseph Califano, Vice President Walter Mondale; and, in the other direction, Fang Yi, China's vice premier responsible for science and technology, Kang Shien, vice premier in charge of economic affairs, and Li Qiang, China's minister of foreign trade, among others. Each trip became the occasion for the addition of another building block to the emerging institutional structure of Sino-American relations.

As part of this strategy, the Carter administration was willing to reject the policy of evenhandedness toward China and the Soviet Union championed by Secretary of State Vance and to grant benefits to Peking that were not yet given to Moscow. In 1978, for example, it was decided not to insist on numerical reciprocity in academic exchange programs with China or to channel scholarly exchanges through a single national organization, as was the case with the Soviet Union. Instead, the United States permitted individual American universities, institutions, and exchange organizations to deal directly with their counterparts in China and thereby to allow the number of Chinese studying in the United States to vastly outstrip the number of Americans conducting training and research in China. The decisions to extend most-favored-nation status to China, make Peking eligible for Eximbank credits and OPIC guarantees, and place China in a separate category for American export controls also reflected a decided tilt in China's favor.

The speed of progress also reflected China's simultaneous decisions to proceed with rapid economic modernization, begin a more gradual process of political relaxation, and open its economy to the outside world. At the third plenum of the Central Committee in December 1978, the Chinese Communist Party decided to shift the emphasis of its work from class struggle to modernization and made clear that economic development was henceforth to be achieved through more rational industrial policies, agricultural reform, and technological and scientific advancement rather than through the mass campaigns of the past. Without such a policy decision, China would probably not have been so willing to agree to the rapid expansion of scientific, technological, and academic ties with the United States, and the two countries would probably not have been able to resolve so quickly the issues complicating agreement on trade and financial issues. Indeed, American officials revealed that they were surprised by the number of bilateral agreements Deng Xiaoping was prepared to conclude during his visit to Washington just one week after the plenum and by his eagerness for expanded relations with the United States.[89]

Once the two governments had decided to accelerate the growth of their cultural, scientific, and commercial ties, they could draw on the preparatory work that they had undertaken before normalization. As noted earlier, negotiations on blocked American claims and frozen Chinese assets resulting from the Korean War were conducted during the Nixon administration. Most of the substantive issues were resolved, with a final agreement delayed by the Chinese until after the establishment of full diplomatic relations. Other bilateral agreements—including those on trade, transportation, and consular relations—were negotiated in 1978 as part of the discussions on normalization.[90] Now that the two sides had the will to move forward, these draft agreements could easily be signed, ratified, and implemented.

The dismantling of past restrictions and the creation of a more facilitative infrastructure were reflected in a substantial qualitative and quantitative expansion of Sino-American relations in 1979 and 1980. Bilateral trade between the two countries doubled from $1.1 billion in 1978 to $2.3 billion in 1979, and more than doubled again the following year, to reach $4.9 billion in 1980 (table A-2). This figure far exceeded the original estimates, made just after normalization, that U.S.-China trade might reach $2.5 billion in 1980.[91] At this point, the United States was selling primarily grain, fertilizers, and chemicals to China and was purchasing agricultural products, petroleum, and textiles. Investment remained minuscule, however, because China's legal framework for foreign investment remained incomplete, the Chinese economy was still largely centrally planned, and Chinese policy still favored the creation of equity joint ventures, an organizational format not particularly welcomed by American investors.

The pace of development was even more rapid in the academic and cultural areas. Judging from the number of American visas issued, the number of Chinese students and scholars entering the United States for long-term visits increased from about 500 in 1978 to 4,300 in 1980, for a cumulative total of approximately 7,000 (table A-5). By the end of 1980, between 130 and 140 Chinese delegations were visiting the United States every month, for a total of about 10,000 visitors that year. The number of American students and scholars visiting China was smaller: a cumulative total of perhaps 550 by the end of 1980. But the urge to visit China on holiday seemed nearly irresistible, and the number of American tourists rose from 10,000 in 1978 to more than 100,000 in 1980 (table A-6).

Sometimes the burgeoning cultural ties between the two countries assumed bizarre forms. Chinese television stations and movie houses began showing a motley selection of American programs and films, such as the science fiction television series "Man from Atlantis" and the B-movie *Convoy*, which were acquired more for their low price than their artistic merit. But the Ministry of Culture rejected on political grounds most of the higher-quality films that the organizers of an American film festival had selected.[92] In 1979, comedian Bob Hope led a group of American entertainers to Peking to celebrate the Fourth of July. But most of Hope's jokes failed to surmount the barriers of culture and language, and the Chinese audience was scandalized by the revealing costume worn by one of the female performers.[93]

Nor was the business community immune from similar lapses in common sense. In 1980, the Bloomingdale's flagship store in New York arranged a massive display of Chinese merchandise, together with American goods designed in pseudo-Chinese style, presented in no fewer than thirty separate boutiques on eight floors. A "People's Store" offered clothing with the "authentic worker" look; the beauty salon offered to style women's hair *à la Chinoise*; and the furniture department constructed a model room in the style of "what a Chinese SoHo loft would look like if China had any."[94] The store was tapping an American fascination with China, but it did so in a way that reflected Manhattan more than Peking.

THE SINO-AMERICAN HONEYMOON

The establishment of diplomatic relations and the rapid progress in cultural and economic ties between the two countries produced a profound change in mood on both sides of the Pacific. Attitudes were not completely exultant, but they were more nearly so than they had been earlier in the 1970s. As Michel Oksenberg put it, "The process of rediscovery inevitably produced a public euphoria, and excessive expectations grew on both sides, generated more by sentiment than hard-headed analysis of future possibilities in the economic, cultural, and scholarly realms."[95]

The elation on the American side existed as much inside the government as among the general public. Carter described Brzezinski as being so "overwhelmed with the Chinese" that he had obviously "been seduced," and Brzezinski admitted that he "could not recall a comparable sense of excitement in the White House" as when Deng Xiaoping came to call.[96] But Carter was not exempt from the euphoric mood. In his memoirs, published three years after the event, he described Deng's visit as "one of the delightful experiences of my presidency" and noted that the audience at the Kennedy Center wept when Deng put his arms around some of the American children who had performed for him. He added that his discussions with Deng and other Chinese leaders taught him "why some people say the Chinese are the most civilized people in the world."[97] Walter Mondale, concluding his visit to China in the summer of 1979, announced that the relationship between the two countries had assumed a "maturity and directness" comparable to that between the United States and its European allies.[98]

Even in more serious and less ceremonial moments, American officials tended to portray the benefits of normalization in epochal terms. Administration spokesmen argued there had been a strategic shift of inestimable benefit to the United States: not only was there now a possibility of parallel action against the Soviet Union but a serious potential irritant in Japanese-American relations had been removed. For the first time in the twentieth century, the United States would no longer have to choose between China and Japan in formulating its Asia policy.

The business community was also excited about the new opportunities being created by the American decision to grant diplomatic recognition and most-favored-nation status to China, just as it had been by the more tentative rapprochement of the early 1970s. Even before normalization of Sino-American relations, there were clear signs of China's interest in expanding economic ties with the United States as part of a massive drive to import foreign technology and equipment. Negotiations were conducted, and letters of intent often signed, with the full range of American multinational corporations from Boeing (which sold three 747-SPs in 1978) to U.S. Steel, and from Coca-Cola (which won what it thought would be an exclusive cola franchise in 1978) to McDonald's.[99]

Normalization only increased the excitement. A headline in the Sunday *San Francisco Examiner and Chronicle*, appearing the day after the normalization of relations with Peking was announced, described China as a "gigantic, juicy new plum for [American] business." In the following article, Christopher Phillips, president of the National Council on U.S.-China Trade, was quoted as saying that the potential for commercial ties with China seemed "without limits."[100] Although there were some more cautious voices, they were soon silenced by the basic fact that Sino-American trade was increasing even more rapidly than the optimists had dared hope.[101]

The public mood toward China was also changing. In February 1979, just after the normalization of Sino-American relations, polls still showed that almost half of the American public (44 percent) was neutral in opinions toward China, with the remainder split between those with positive opinions and those with more negative attitudes.[102] But within a few months, there had been what one specialist on polling has called a "colossal shift of opinion." By the end of the year, a Gallup poll showed that fully 65 percent of the American public had a favorable impression of China, and only 25 percent unfavorable. Nor was that simply a temporary response to the excitement of normalization. In 1980, roughly the same results were obtained: 70 percent of the public had favorable images of China, and 26 percent held unfavorable impressions. Indeed, 45 percent now favored defending China against a Soviet attack—roughly the same proportion that supported defending Taiwan against an assault by the mainland.[103]

But amid the euphoria, much evidence of ambivalence toward China remained. Some sectors of the American economy, for example, were not ecstatic about the prospects of a rapid expansion of business with China. According to one account, officials of the AFL-CIO were already haunted by a nightmare in which "hundreds of millions of low-paid Chinese workers report to brand-new factories, fully equipped with the best machines the world has to offer" and then "industriously produce billions of dollars" of consumer goods that are "then shipped to the United States, where they systematically destroy American jobs."[104] These concerns were reflected in tough negotiations over a Sino-American textile agreement, which broke down twice before finally succeeding in July 1980.[105] Congress remained concerned that the security and stability of Taiwan had been seriously damaged by the withdrawal of American diplomatic relations and that the United States was moving too rapidly toward a military relationship with Peking.[106]

Public perceptions of China also remained highly ambivalent. Despite China's high overall approval ratings, the human rights situation there was still regarded as either somewhat unfavorable or highly unfavorable by 60 percent of the American public, and as favorable by only 31 percent. Few Americans regarded China as especially trustworthy. Still, hope seemed to be growing that the changes in post-Mao China—the purge of the Gang of Four, the rise of Deng Xiaoping, the new emphasis on economic modernization, and the signs of opening to the outside world—would gradually produce a China that was more liberal, more dynamic, and more friendly. As one Texan reassured himself during the barbecue hosted for Deng in Houston: "I don't even think this guy Ping is a real Communist anyway."[107]

The evidence on Chinese attitudes during this period is necessarily much more impressionistic, but it points in similar directions. Chinese leaders still had many reservations about American policy, especially the lukewarm response of the Carter administration toward the Chinese invasion of Vietnam in early 1979 and the continued American interest in a peaceful future for Taiwan. The Chinese sharply criticized the Taiwan Relations Act and seem to have delayed signing some early trade and commercial agreements until they could assess American policy more fully.

On balance, however, they characterized Sino-American relations in glowing terms. Deng, on leaving the United States in February 1979, expressed his confidence that "the honeymoon will continue."[108] The Chinese ambassador, Chai Zemin, spoke enthusiastically the following September of the "magnificent prospects" for Sino-American relations. And Geng Biao noted in June 1980 that the two countries had "identical views" on the key strategic issues of the decade.[109]

Chinese press coverage of the United States became more balanced and positive. There were still reports on crime, poverty, racism, and moral decay in the United States, distributed in the open press and through internal channels.[110] But as Sino-American relations improved, the mood changed. Even in the fall of 1978, one American who had scanned the daily Chinese newspapers noted that now more positive stories about the United States appeared, including glowing accounts of Disneyland and laudatory coverage of the immediacy of American television news.[111] The journalists accompanying Deng on his visit to America in January 1979 introduced another set of positive themes: the diligence of American workers, the quality of service in American shops and restaurants, the advanced level of American technology, and the prosperity of the ordinary American family.[112] The television coverage of Deng's visit and the growing number of American films available to ordinary Chinese also inevitably conveyed a powerful visual impression of the United States as a wealthy and advanced society.

At the popular level, too, evidence suggests a euphoric mood toward the United States. Several of the wall posters displayed on Peking's Democracy Wall in late 1978 expressed their admiration for the respect for human rights and the exercise of democracy in the United States. A few weeks before normalization was announced, one young woman in Peking, brushing aside all protests to the contrary, insisted to an American visitor that near-universal ownership of color television sets in the United States proved that "everything in America is good" and declared her determination that China should "learn from you so that we can catch up."

The announcement that the two countries had established diplomatic relations with each other intensified this sense of exhilaration. As one report of urban Chinese attitudes at the time put it, there was an "extraordinary euphoria that swept China in the immediate wake of normalization." The United States had finally decided to treat China as an equal, many Chinese believed. Young Chinese, in particular, were excited by the perceived possibilities of traveling to America to make money, and thousands of university students began exploring the prospects for continuing their education in the United States.[113] Indeed, some of the best evidence of widespread admiration of the United States is provided by articles in the Chinese press that criticized those who blindly worshiped America.[114]

Perhaps the mood among ordinary Chinese was best encapsulated in two letters sent to the *New York Times* in February 1979, hailing the normalization of U.S.-China relations and asking for American help. As one of these correspondents put it,

> I hope the traditional friendship between the people of our two countries will, from today on, be as firm as steel, as everlasting as the sun and moon, and passed on by generation after generation. Everything in my country is far, far behind you. . . . [But] with the help of advanced technology and capital from your country, I am sure we can realize our aim [of modernization]. . . . Dear great and glorious American people, please come to my country for tours, visits or [to give] instructions. We will never forget you; we feel respectful whenever we think of you.[115]

This seeming euphoria on both sides of the Pacific sprang from emotional roots running deep in the cultures of the two countries. For Americans, normalization reawakened what Michael Hunt has called the myth of a "special relationship" with China.[116] This idea built on the deeply held conviction that the United States was itself a special nation, more virtuous than others, committed to the ideals of liberty and democracy, and with the right and the responsibility to convey those values to other countries. This idealistic strain in American foreign policy, in Hunt's phrase, embodied the conviction that "Americans would set about remaking others in their own image while the world watched in awe."[117]

This general purpose tended to find particular resonance in China. There, Americans had found, from the end of the eighteenth century, a society with a glorious past but a dismal present, looking abroad for new ideas, values, and institutions that could save the country. If America was a devoted teacher, then China was widely regarded as an eager student; the special relationship with China envisioned a "golden age of friendship engendered by altruistic American aid and rewarded by ample Chinese gratitude."[118]

Conversely, for Chinese leaders, and to a degree for ordinary urban Chinese as well, American recognition after thirty years was seen as a vindication of the importance of China and the legitimacy of their revolution. The fact that the *People's Daily* was authorized to publish an extra edition announcing the normalization of Sino-American relations on December 16, 1978, and that the broadsheet was printed entirely in red ink, China's traditional color representing happiness, indicates the importance that Chinese leaders attached to their new relationship with the United States and the excitement with which they greeted it. Like many Americans, they felt that a long historical tragedy had finally been ended and that a protracted folly had been rectified.

In addition, the American fascination with reshaping China was paralleled by a long-standing Chinese admiration for the United States. Chinese intellectuals had, from the late nineteenth century onward, seen the United States not only as a more advanced society technologically but also as a relatively virtuous society politically. The American revolution had been a model for many Chinese, who viewed it as a process by which "honest and righteous men" had led "oppressed people to freedom and independence" and thus was a guide for the course that Chinese intellectuals hoped to follow.[119] American politics, with its emphasis on rationality and responsiveness, seemed to embody Chinese desires for "science" and "democracy." For ordinary Chinese, the United States remained, as the Chinese name for San Francisco (*jinshan*, or golden mountain) implied, a country of unimaginable prosperity, which provided relatively abundant opportunities for overseas Chinese to study or make money. Decades of anti-American propaganda during the Maoist era had not eradicated these favorable images of the United States.

The interaction of these two sets of images was enormously powerful for they neatly dovetailed with Chinese admiration of America, coinciding with American self-confidence in the virtues of America's society. But the relationship these images created was also fragile. The history of U.S.-China relations over the previous two hundred years suggested that Chinese attitudes toward the United States could turn angry and bitter, especially when the United States seemed to be interfering in Chinese internal affairs, exporting models of development unsuited to Chinese conditions, or treating China as a subordinate partner. The same history suggested that American attitudes toward China could rapidly turn toward disillusionment and disdain, especially when China adopted foreign policy orientations that ran contrary to American interests, failed to adopt American values and institutions, or appeared insufficiently grateful for American assistance.

A few observers on both sides of the Pacific therefore cautioned that the goodwill between the two countries might be transient. As Deng Xiaoping left the United States, John K. Fairbank, the dean of American sinology, warned that the state of near euphoria Deng had created could soon turn sour. Once Americans realized that China remained an authoritarian system, Fairbank cautioned, "their exuberance could soon change to disillusionment."[120] And during Defense Secretary Brown's visit to China in January 1980, a Chinese intellectual suggested to a delegation of American China specialists that the potential in Sino-American relations should not be overestimated. "You Americans are so charming," he said, "[for] you have such short memories. We can't forget so fast or so easily what happened between us in the past."[121] At the time, such comments seemed rather churlish attempts to dissent from the mood of the moment. In retrospect, however, they appear remarkably prescient forecasts of what lay ahead.

CHAPTER 4

Estrangement

AFTER achieving rapid progress in the first two years after normalization, U.S.-China relations suffered a severe loss of momentum in the early 1980s. Washington and Peking became embroiled in a bitter dispute over continuing American arms sales to Taiwan. China began to criticize American foreign policy in the strongest language in many years and suspended many aspects of military cooperation with Washington. Various smaller issues, ranging from the defection of a Chinese tennis star to the United States to an American court case involving railway bonds issued by the Qing dynasty, enmeshed the relationship in constant controversy. Trade fell for the first time since the mid-1970s, and American investment in China remained low.

Three factors combined to produce this slowdown in Sino-American relations. First, the new Reagan administration came into office apparently committed to upgrading U.S. relations with Taiwan, either by restoring official contacts between Washington and Taipei or by increasing American arms sales to the island. Chinese leaders viewed Reagan's election with alarm. Reagan's statements on the campaign trail suggested that he planned to reverse his predecessor's strategy of gradually distancing the United States from the Nationalists in favor of revitalizing the U.S. diplomatic and military relationship with Taipei. This represented an inconsistency in American policy that Chinese leaders found unacceptable.

Peking was also concerned about other aspects of American foreign relations during the early Reagan years. Although Chinese leaders had previously encouraged the Nixon, Ford, and Carter administrations to take a firm stand against Soviet expansionism, they became noticeably anxious when, for the first time, an American president seemed to be following their advice. Many features of the U.S. military buildup and of Washington's confrontational posture toward Moscow alarmed the Chinese. They were also discomfited by what they regarded as increasing American indifference toward the economic problems of the third world and a growing proclivity to intervene in the internal affairs of developing countries. As its dissatisfaction with American foreign policy increased, Peking adopted a more independent posture in international affairs, abandoning the clear tilt toward the United States that had been the hallmark of its diplomacy from 1972 onward. This change, in turn, aroused concern in Washington that, even if not moving toward accommodation with Moscow, China was at least no longer a reliable partner in American strategy.

Finally, the economic and cultural relations that had developed so rapidly in the 1970s, and especially since normalization, began to experience growing pains. The inherent ideological and structural differences between China and the United States, which were fairly easily ignored when their interaction was modest, became increasingly apparent as their relationship became more extensive. In addition, the economic relations between the two countries were adversely affected by a slowdown in both their economies. As a result of these developments, the Chinese realized that there would be limits to America's willingness to export advanced technology, absorb Chinese exports, or provide financial assistance for China's modernization. In turn, Americans gradually understood that China did not offer the boundless opportunities for business or scholarship that some had earlier anticipated.

Given the unrealistic expectations for Sino-American relations that had developed at the time of normalization, it was inevitable that these developments would have a sobering effect on the mood in both countries. Americans who had been enamored with the Chinese model of development now began to look at Chinese society and politics more skeptically. American political leaders and corporate executives now saw the limits, as well as the promise, in U.S.-China relations. Across the Pacific, the sense of disillusionment was perhaps even more intense. Chinese leaders, if not the general public, began to see the United States as an insincere and patronizing partner, which promised more than it delivered, abandoned previous commitments, and treated China on unequal terms. The result was a mutual disenchantment that stood in clear contrast to the more euphoric mood that had characterized the immediate postnormalization period.

REAGAN AND TAIWAN

The election of Ronald Reagan as president of the United States in 1980 posed a significant challenge to the stability and continuity of Sino-American relations. This is not to say that Reagan was opposed to an extensive economic and strategic relationship with China. Like many conservatives, Reagan viewed China as a valuable counterweight to the Soviet Union. In fact, in his campaign for the Republican presidential nomination against Gerald Ford in 1976, he had charged that the Ford administration was responsible for a troubling stagnation in Sino-American relations. He worried that, unless the United States moved to consolidate its fragile relationship with Peking, "forces that are more pro-Soviet may gain the upper hand after Chairman Mao Tse-tung is dead." To prevent such an outcome, Reagan proposed expanding commercial ties with China, as well as the sharing of additional strategic intelligence with Peking. Perhaps surprisingly, Reagan's concern was that Gerald Ford had been "inattentive" to Peking, not that he had been too accommodating.[1]

Nevertheless, Reagan did not believe that the consolidation of Sino-American ties warranted the sacrifice of the U.S. relationship with Taiwan. In 1976, he insisted that strengthening the relationship between Peking and Washington could be achieved "without making undue concessions" and specifically warned against severing American ties with Taipei. When, in December 1978, the Carter administration announced that it was prepared to do just that, Reagan joined the chorus of critics. He accused the president of having "surrendered" to Peking, and asked, "What was the urgency in doing it now?"[2]

Statements by Reagan and his advisers during the 1980 presidential election campaign suggested that, if elected, he planned a significant change in the U.S. relationship with Taiwan. Speaking at a fundraising event in the spring of that year, Reagan said that he would give official status to the American Institute in Taiwan, the unofficial body that represented American interests in Taiwan after normalization. In May, he said that he could "see no reason why, with an embassy in Peking, we could not now have an official liaison office in Taiwan, the same as we had in Peking before the change occurred," so that Taiwan could have a "government relation" with the United States. The Republican platform of 1980, while calling for the "peaceful elaboration" of Sino-American relations, also declared that Republicans "deplore the Carter Administration's treatment of Taiwan, our longtime ally and friend."[3]

The Chinese immediately protested Reagan's statements, warning that restoration of official ties between the United States and Taiwan would violate the terms of the agreement on the normalization of Sino-American relations. Faced with vigorous protests from China and sharp questioning from American reporters, Reagan's campaign staff began to backtrack. Richard V. Allen, Reagan's chief foreign policy adviser, warned reporters not to exaggerate what the candidate would do for Taiwan if elected and said that Reagan intended no change in American relations with China. To relieve Chinese concerns, the campaign sent Reagan's vice-presidential candidate, George Bush, to Peking. There, the former head of the U.S. liaison office in Peking assured Chinese leaders that Reagan's recent references to the "Republic of China" had been made "out of habit" and that Reagan was not proposing to overturn the American relationship with Peking. "Governor Reagan, if elected, would not set back the clock," Bush declared. "[He] would not go in for some two-China policy."[4]

Unfortunately, the candidate himself did not seem to get the message that his running mate and campaign advisers were trying to convey. Even as Bush was trying to soothe the Chinese, Reagan talked yet again about reestablishing some kind of official relationship with Taiwan. Hearing about Reagan's statements while still in Peking, Bush reportedly "grimaced and put a hand to his forehead, but declined comment."[5] But Reagan's remarks robbed Bush's reassurances of their credibility. As a result, the Chinese media depicted Bush's mission as a failure, saying he had been unable to allay Peking's anxieties about Reagan's intentions.[6]

After Bush returned from Peking, Reagan made a more comprehensive statement of his China policy in an attempt to clear up the confusion his earlier remarks had created. For the first time, Reagan charged explicitly that the Carter administration had "made concessions that Presidents Nixon and Ford had steadfastly refused to make" and that "were not necessary and not in our national interest." He said that, had he been president, he would have insisted on the "retention of a liaison office on Taiwan of equivalent status to the one which we had earlier established in Peking."[7]

But, acknowledging that such a step would no longer be possible, Reagan retreated from his earlier suggestions that he planned to revisit the issue were he elected. Rather than proposing to open an American liaison office on Taiwan, as he had done earlier in the year, he now stated simply that he "would not pretend, as Carter does, that the relationship we now have with Taiwan, enacted by our Congress, is not official." The only concrete change he suggested was to halt "petty practices . . . which are inappropriate and demeaning to our Chinese friends on Taiwan," such as the prohibition on American officials from receiving Taiwan's representatives in their offices. On balance, in the words of the *New York Times*, the Reagan statement "conformed more closely to what Mr. Bush reportedly told the

Chinese than to what Mr. Reagan had been saying on the campaign trail."[8]

In the end, therefore, the possibility of resuming official relations with Taiwan was set aside. Two representatives from Taiwan—one an official in the ruling Kuomintang, the other the governor of Taiwan province—were invited to attend Reagan's inaugural ceremonies, but even those invitations were withdrawn after protests from Peking. The restrictions on contacts between American and Taiwanese representatives were somewhat relaxed. Middle-level American officials, excluding those from the State Department, were now allowed to visit Taiwan. Conversely, middle-level officials from the Coordination Council for North American Affairs, Taiwan's representative office in Washington, were now permitted to call on American officials, except for those in the State Department. But the new secretary of state, Alexander Haig, made sure that these changes were modest, arguing that it "simply did not make sense to lose the People's Republic of China in exchange for the personal or ideological pleasure of having a Taiwanese in for a nonsubstantive chat."[9] The extensive upgrading of U.S.-Taiwan relations that Reagan once envisioned simply did not occur.

Moreover, the new Reagan administration took pains to signal that, despite its sympathies toward Taiwan, it still harbored goodwill toward Peking. In March 1981, two months after taking office, Reagan sent a personal letter to Chinese leaders through Gerald Ford, then on a private visit to Peking, emphasizing his desire to maintain a stable and friendly relationship with China. Reagan also had an early meeting in the Oval Office with the Chinese ambassador, Chai Zemin. That meeting was intended to demonstrate the importance that the new administration bestowed on Sino-American relations. Haig arranged a visit to Peking in June 1981, where he informed his hosts that the United States intended to treat China as a friendly developing nation with which the United States shared many interests rather than as an adversary, and that the White House would therefore seek legislation that would remove all the remaining legal barriers to economic cooperation between the United States and China.[10]

Despite the Reagan administration's decision not to pursue a more official relationship with Taiwan and despite its professions of friendship toward China, Peking's apprehensions about the intentions of the new American government were not assuaged. Increasingly, Chinese leaders and analysts focused on another controversial element in U.S.-Taiwan relations: American arms sales to Taiwan.

As noted in chapter 3, Peking had consistently opposed Washington's intention to sell defensive weapons to Taiwan after the normalization of Sino-American relations. Although Jimmy Carter had decided as early as June 1977 that such arms sales would be a necessary precondition for normalization in the absence of a binding Chinese renunciation of force, this decision had not been conveyed to Chinese representatives in Washington until September. The Chinese promptly responded that they considered continued American arms sales to Taiwan an unacceptable infringement of Chinese sovereignty. But as Deng Xiaoping was eager to conclude the agreement, largely because of the possibility of a war with Vietnam, he was forced to accept the American conditions. Still, the Chinese were neither satisfied with nor resigned to the American policy. Instead, they simply reserved the right to monitor the flow of American weapons to Taiwan and to revisit the issue at a later time.

By the time the Carter administration left office in early 1981, the Chinese were becoming increasingly concerned by what they were seeing. The pattern of American arms sales to Taiwan in 1979 and 1980 was a complex one. The Carter administration had denied renewed Taiwanese requests for more sophisticated weapons systems, such as F-4s, F-16s, or F-18s, Harpoon ship-to-ship missiles, and Standard air defense missiles. In June 1980, however, it authorized two American aircraft manufacturers, Northrup and McDonnell-Douglas, to begin negotiations with Taipei over the possible sale of another type of fighter, the so-called FX, that would be less advanced than the planes Taiwan wanted but more sophisticated than the F-5Es then in the island's inventory. In addition, there were reports that the United States was encouraging its allies to sell weapons to Taiwan that it could not provide itself. At the end of 1980, the Netherlands agreed to build two submarines for Taiwan, amid rumors, later denied by Washington, that it had received official encouragement from the United States to do so.[11]

Nor was the volume of American arms sales to Taiwan encouraging to Peking. Despite the Carter administration's pledge to observe a twelve-month moratorium on weapons transfers in 1979, the final year that the mutual defense treaty with Taiwan remained in effect, the flow of arms to the island continued unabated. The value of new agreements under the foreign military sales (FMS) system did drop somewhat in fiscal 1980. But the actual delivery of American arms to Taiwan was increasing, from $208 million in fiscal 1978 to $267 million in fiscal 1980, as commercial sales continued and as previous FMS contracts were fulfilled.

Peking viewed these developments with considerable disappointment. The United States was providing significant supplies of arms to Taiwan and was considering the sale of a more advanced fighter. Although the mutual defense treaty with Taiwan had now been terminated, the Taiwan Relations Act had, from the Chinese perspective, simply perpetuated the American commitment to the island's security in a slightly different form. As a result, Taiwan had not experienced the crisis of confidence upon the withdrawal of American diplomatic recognition that Peking had hoped for. Taiwan's present leadership showed no willingness to negotiate with Peking. And, with Taiwan's president Chiang Ching-kuo growing older, Chinese leaders were becoming increasingly concerned that future generations of Taiwanese leaders would be even less inclined to accept peaceful reunification with the mainland. By the fall of 1981, therefore, they had decided to make more vigorous efforts to reverse American policy on the subject. Their aim was not simply to prevent the sale of the FX to Taipei but to establish new and more restrictive guidelines for the future transfer of all American weapons to Taiwan.

China first raised its new demands in October 1981, during a meeting between President Reagan and Premier Zhao Ziyang at the North-South summit at Cancun, Mexico. During the negotiations over the establishment of diplomatic relations with China, the Carter administration had hinted to Peking that the "quantity and quality" of American arms sales to Taipei "would be linked to Beijing's posture on the Taiwan issue," implying that those sales would be reduced if tensions in the Taiwan Strait declined.[12] Now the Chinese were invoking that linkage. Zhao described a new nine-point plan for the peaceful reunification of Taiwan and the mainland, first unveiled by Ye Jianying on September 30, that would offer the island substantial autonomy under the sovereignty of the People's Republic. In the context of this new proposal, the Chinese told Reagan, it would be neither necessary nor right for foreigners to continue to sell weapons to Taipei.[13] Instead, the appropriate response was for the United States to reduce arms sales to Taiwan.

The Chinese soon told the Americans precisely what they had in mind. First in Cancun and later in Washington, Foreign Minister Huang Hua requested that the United States promise that its arms sales to Taiwan would not exceed, in quality or quantity, the level reached during the Carter administration, pledge to gradually reduce its supply of weapons to Taiwan, and set a timetable for the complete termination of arms sales to the island. Peking added a further demand: the United States must give China advance notice of its arms sales to Taipei. Otherwise, the Chinese press implied, Peking would reduce its representation in the United States to that of a liaison office or even withdraw it altogether.[14]

The initial American response, according to Chinese accounts, was to reiterate that the United States would continue to sell arms to Taiwan until China was reunified. It would do so in a prudent, restrained, and selective way, and it expected that the quantity and quality of arms sales indeed would not exceed those of the Carter years. But the United States could not unequivocally promise to make such reductions, and it certainly could not agree to stop selling arms to Taiwan within a certain time. Washington agreed to discuss the matter further and pledged to act cautiously while negotiations were in progress, but meanwhile the United States would still "do what it had to do."[15]

The negotiations on the arms sales issue, which proved even more lengthy than those over the normalization of Sino-American relations, opened in Peking in December 1981, conducted by the American ambassador to China, Arthur W. Hummel, Jr., and by two Chinese vice ministers of foreign affairs, Zhang Wenjin and Han Xu.[16] The United States attempted to create a favorable climate for negotiations in several ways. It invited Zhao Ziyang to visit the United States to commemorate the tenth anniversary of Nixon's 1972 trip to China, there to sign a joint communiqué resolving the arms sales controversy. It announced publicly what Haig had already informed the Chinese privately: the administration would ask Congress to repeal or modify the remaining legal restrictions on economic relations between the two countries. And, most important from the Chinese perspective, the United States announced in January that it had decided not to sell either version of the FX to Taiwan, but would simply renew the agreement whereby Taiwan coproduced the F-5E with Northrup.

Despite these conciliatory gestures, the substance of the negotiations proved difficult. The American position was defined by Haig in a memorandum submitted to the president on November 26, 1981. The United States, Haig noted, could meet several of the Chinese demands. It could agree that arms sales to Taiwan would not exceed, in quantity or quality, the level set during the Carter years and could pledge to reduce them gradually. It could praise China's nine-point program for reunification as a "constructive and hopeful sign that the Taiwan issue can, ultimately, be peacefully resolved."[17] But it could not agree to a fixed date for the termination of American arms sales to Taiwan. Moreover, Haig's memorandum also recommended that the United States obtain two statements from the Chinese in return for restrictions on arms sales to Taipei: a renunciation of force against Taiwan to justify the reduction of American arms sales, and a reiteration of Chinese opposition to Soviet expansion to place any American concessions in a broader strategic framework.

The American position was initially unacceptable to Peking. The Chinese continued to insist on a timetable for stopping American arms sales to Taiwan altogether. They also seem to have sought some acknowledgment from the United States that weapons transfers to Taipei were a violation of Chinese sovereignty. In exchange for this concession, Peking would acknowledge that the arms sales program was a problem "inherited from history" and that China was prepared to give the United States time to solve it. But it refused to accept any linkage between the reduction of American arms sales to Taiwan and a peaceful resolution of the Taiwan issue.[18] Nor would it agree to alter the position it had held consistently for nearly thirty years: not to promise the United States that China would never use force against Taiwan.

Thus, the negotiations soon deadlocked. The Chinese refused to make the reduction of arms sales conditional on a peaceful resolution of the Taiwan question; the Americans refused to set a date for the termination of the weapons transfer program. Finally, the impasse was broken by two American initiatives. First, the United States presented what amounted to an ultimatum to the Chinese. It told Peking that it would soon have to make more decisions about arms sales to Taiwan, acknowledging that this issue would produce a further crisis in Sino-American relations if the negotiations were not successful. Moreover, it also warned Chinese leaders that, in the event of such a crisis, Sino-American ties would deteriorate across the board, and the damage could not be limited to those aspects of the relationship that Peking chose to sacrifice. Particularly important in communicating this message to Peking was a visit by Vice President George Bush in May 1982, in which he told the Chinese that the United States could never accept a firm timetable for ending arms sales to Taiwan.

At the same time, the second American initiative contained more conciliatory elements. When Bush went to China, he also told Chinese leaders that, although the United States could not agree to a fixed date for ending arms sales, it did not necessarily intend to sell Taiwan arms forever. The State Department then turned that general position into more specific language in June. The United States could say that it did not seek to carry out a long-term policy of arms sales to Taiwan, thus implying, although not stating explicitly, that it would eventually halt the sales when they were no longer needed.

The final agreement, announced on August 17, 1982, therefore included concessions by both sides (see appendix D). The United States agreed to most of the demands that China had originally raised. It said that its arms sales to Taiwan would "not exceed, either in qualitative or in quantitative terms, the level of those supplied in recent years since the establishment of diplomatic relations between the two countries." It stated that it intended "to reduce gradually its sale of arms to Taiwan" and denied that it sought to carry out a "long-term policy" of arms sales to the islands. But Washington still refused to commit itself explicitly to the termination of arms sales to Taiwan, let alone to a timetable for such a cutoff. Instead, the communiqué merely acknowledged China's position on the issue and spoke vaguely of a "final settlement" or "final resolution" of the question at some later date.

Since the United States did not accept China's demand for a fixed date for the termination of its arms sales to Taiwan, it is understandable that it was unable to secure from Peking the contextual statements it had hoped would cushion the impact of the U.S. agreement to further attenuate its military relationship with Taipei. The communiqué contained no reference to the Soviet Union, only a passing mention of a common opposition to "aggression and expansion." Peking declared it had a "fundamental policy of striving for the peaceful reunification" of China but refused to renounce the use of force against the island or to accept any explicit linkage between that policy and the reduction of American arms sales. It was left up to the United States, in a unilateral statement accompanying the communiqué, to reiterate its interest in a peaceful future for Taiwan and to condition the reductions of arms sales on Peking's adherence to its "fundamental policy" of seeking peaceful reunification (see appendix D).

To ameliorate the reaction of the Taiwan government and conservatives in Congress to the August 17 communiqué, the Reagan administration sought to qualify it through a further series of unilateral interpretations. On July 14, even before the communiqué had been finalized, Washington privately conveyed six points of reassurance to Taipei.[19] In these six points, the United States promised Taiwan that it would not agree to set a date for the termination of arms sales to the island, to alter the terms of the Taiwan Relations Act, or to engage in advance consultations with Peking before deciding on U.S. weapons transfers to Taipei. Washington also pledged not to serve as a mediator between Taipei and Peking or to exert any pressure on Taiwan to engage in negotiations with the mainland.

The six points also implied that the United States would not formally recognize the PRC's sovereignty over Taiwan.

In further statements following the publication of the August communiqué, the Reagan administration also clarified the way in which the restrictions on further arms sales to Taiwan would be interpreted. To begin with, it recalculated the level of arms sales in 1979—the high watermark of the Carter administration—into 1982 dollars, to take inflation into account. Doing so raised the ceiling on American arms sales, and the base from which future reductions would be calculated, from $565 million to $813 million. The White House also hinted that similar adjustments for inflation might be made again in the future. Moreover, administration officials noted privately that the qualitative restrictions on arms sales to Taiwan would also be interpreted in relative rather than absolute terms. That is, the United States would be willing to sell Taiwan more advanced weapons systems as older ones became obsolete or if American production of them ceased. The renewal of the agreement to coproduce the F-5E and the subsequent sales of Chaparral, Standard, and Sparrow missiles to Taiwan indicated that Taipei would still be receiving sophisticated weapons systems from the United States.[20]

Finally, and most important, the administration noted that the August communiqué applied only to "arms sales"—that is, the transfer of actual weaponry—and said nothing about the provision of defense production technology to Taiwan. It later became apparent that the United States would be willing to assist Taiwan in achieving self-sufficiency in a wide range of weapons systems, especially those connected with maintaining air superiority over Taiwan and defending the sea-lanes in the Taiwan Strait.

Like the agreement on normalization in 1978, the communiqué of 1982 on arms sales sparked a flurry of skepticism and opposition in Congress. Many members agreed with Democratic Senator John Glenn that the provisions of the communiqué "contravene the spirit and purpose of the TRA," which had provided that the United States would independently decide on the level of arms sales to Taiwan, without reference to Peking's opinions. Glenn also was concerned that, according to Peking's interpretation, the United States had agreed to cut off all sales to Taiwan eventually, leaving only the question of "when, not if."[21]

But the congressional criticism gradually dissipated as the White House clarified its position. The Reagan administration was able to convince the skeptics that the communiqué was not incompatible with the Taiwan Relations Act. The TRA had committed the United

States to provide Taiwan with enough arms to ensure its own defense, but those objective requirements would be reduced as the
threat from the mainland declined. Congress was also reassured that
the communiqué was not a legally binding agreement but rather a
statement of policy that could readily be revised if the situation
warranted. Thus, should China's policy change and Peking threaten
the use of force against Taiwan, the United States could abandon the
policy outlined in the communiqué and increase its sale of arms to
the island.[22]

Although the August 1982 communiqué defused the immediate
crisis over American arms sales to Taiwan, it did not immediately
end the chill in Sino-American relations that the dispute had created.
One reason was that the two sides had only papered over the basic
differences under dispute. The Chinese insisted that the United
States had agreed to the complete termination of arms sales over a
relatively short period of time, whereas the United States denied any
such thing.[23] The United States claimed that China had announced
an "unchanging and long-term" policy of resolving the Taiwan question by peaceful means, and that the reduction of American arms
sales to the island was "premised on the continuation of China's
peaceful policy." But the Chinese denied that they had undertaken
any commitment to pursue reunification through peaceful means or
that they considered the reduction of American arms sales to Taiwan
to be conditioned on such a policy.[24]

Moreover, China had hoped that the United States could be persuaded to endorse its program for the reunification of Taiwan and
the mainland, as contained in the nine-point plan of September
30, 1981. But here, too, they were disappointed. Haig had publicly
described Peking's proposal as "rather remarkable" and had privately
urged the White House to issue a presidential statement supporting
the peaceful resolution of the Taiwan issue and endorsing the spirit
of the nine-point plan. But with Haig out of office by June, the Reagan
administration was not prepared to go quite so far. Although the
communiqué expressed American "appreciation" for China's more
flexible policy toward Taiwan, the "six points" simultaneously indicated that Washington would put no pressure on Taiwan to negotiate.
Furthermore, in congressional testimony the administration backed
further away from its apparent endorsement of the nine-point plan,
saying that it meant to praise the plan's "peaceful approach," not its
substantive content.[25]

Thus, unlike the agreement on the establishment of diplomatic
relations in 1978, the communiqué on American arms sales to Taiwan did not immediately restore a sense of momentum or goodwill,

let alone euphoria, to U.S.-China relations. The Chinese remained dissatisfied with the terms of the agreement, even though they probably understood that the United States had made as many concessions as it could. In addition, other issues remained in dispute, notably differences over the Reagan administration's broader foreign policy and a host of questions about the economic and cultural ties between the two countries.

CHINA'S INDEPENDENT FOREIGN POLICY

Ironically, even as the Reagan administration was considering upgrading ties with Taiwan in early 1981, it was exploring expanding strategic relations with Peking. To be sure, not all members of the new administration were enthusiastic about such an idea. Secretary of Defense Caspar Weinberger, for example, felt that the United States should make its own independent military preparations against the Soviet Union, rather than rely on any kind of strategic alignment with the Chinese. But Secretary of State Haig was much more favorably disposed. He believed, as he later put it in his memoirs, that China's location at the pivot of the East-West and North-South conflicts made it perhaps "the most important country in the world" for the United States in the early 1980s.[26] Even such pro-Taiwan officials as Michael Deaver were sympathetic to strategic cooperation with Peking, as a way not only of counterbalancing the Kremlin but also of securing China's acquiescence to a closer American relationship with Taipei.[27]

Thus, when Haig visited Peking in June 1981, one of his principal missions was to propose a closer strategic relationship between the United States and China. Haig told the Chinese that for the first time, the United States would consider making commercial arms sales to China on a case-by-case basis and later informed Peking that this would involve some thirty items from the list of fifty-two that Geng Biao had presented in Washington the previous year.[28] He invited the Chinese deputy chief of staff, Liu Huaqing, to visit the United States to discuss the equipment and technology that China wished to obtain.

Haig also informed Chinese leaders that the United States would undertake a further relaxation of its export control system. Although placed in a separate administrative category by the Carter administration in 1980, China was still subject to the same limitations as the Soviet Union. Now, the Reagan administration was willing to make China eligible to purchase technology twice as sophisticated as that licensed for export to the Soviets. Haig believed that Chinese leaders were disappointed in the fruits of their relationship with the United States, and that one of the reasons was the Carter administration's reluctance to transfer advanced technology. At his recommendation, the Reagan administration would rectify this slight.

To make these decisions more palatable to domestic audiences, the Reagan administration began emphasizing the ways in which China was already engaged in security cooperation with the United States. For the first time, through press leaks, Washington revealed the existence of the facilities that had been established in western China in 1980 to monitor Soviet missile tests. The fact that Peking had been rapidly increasing the export of rare metals to the United States was also now openly reported.[29] The message was clear: the strategic relationship between China and the United States was mutually beneficial, and China's cooperative behavior fully warranted a relaxation of American controls on the export of lethal weapons and civilian technology.

Perhaps to Haig's surprise, Peking did not respond enthusiastically to these new American initiatives. Liu Huaqing's visit to Washington was postponed, other high-level military exchanges were suspended, and China did not express any interest in purchasing the weapons that the United States had offered to sell. To some degree, budgetary constraints may have prevented Chinese leaders from approving purchases of expensive foreign weaponry, especially at a time of economic retrenchment. In addition, Washington was proposing to sell finished weapons, not the production technology that Peking desired. And there were still significant constraints on the weapons that the United States was prepared to make available: five or more years behind the state of the art, those not contributing to China's projection capabilities, and in batches worth less than $100 million.[30]

The emerging dispute over American arms sales to Taiwan was an even more important factor discouraging China from expanding strategic cooperation with the United States. Peking quite accurately regarded the offer of American arms as an attempt to win its acquiescence to the continued supply of American weapons to Taipei. Even before Haig arrived in Peking to announce the new American policy, the Chinese began to warn that this kind of bargain would be unacceptable. As the spokesman of the Chinese Foreign Ministry put it, "We would rather receive no U.S. arms than accept continued U.S. interference in our internal affairs by selling arms to Taiwan."[31] And, in explaining to the United States later in the year why they were not willing to continue military exchanges or to purchase American weapons, the Chinese made it clear that they would refrain from such strategic cooperation until the question of American arms sales to Taiwan had been resolved.[32]

Finally, broader international trends also dissuaded Peking from pursuing a military relationship with Washington at this point. Throughout the 1970s, Chinese analysts had regarded the Soviet Union as engaged in a global strategic offensive, with thrusts by land into Africa, the Middle East, and Southeast Asia, and with expansion by sea into the western Pacific and the Indian Ocean. By the early 1980s, however, strategists in Peking had concluded that the situation had changed. The Soviet Union, under the leadership of an ailing Leonid Brezhnev, was bogged down in a war in Afghanistan that was difficult to win. Its support for the Vietnamese intervention in Cambodia and for the Cuban involvement in Angola had done little to decrease the burden on an increasingly ossified Soviet economy. Moreover, Moscow's policies had produced a broad international coalition of states concerned about Soviet expansion, which meant that the Kremlin's relations with its Asian neighbors had, with a few exceptions, reached a low ebb.

The strategic balance between the United States and the Soviet Union, which Peking had previously believed to tilt toward Moscow, was gradually but decisively shifting in Washington's favor. Chinese analysts concluded that a combination of Soviet exhaustion and American revitalization was producing a decisive and lasting change in the global strategic environment. They no longer viewed the Soviet Union as on the offensive. Instead, they saw a long period ahead in which the two superpowers would be relatively evenly balanced, and in which their competition would achieve a fairly stable stalemate.[33]

In this context, Chinese analysts placed particular weight on signs of change in Soviet attitudes toward China. In March 1982, in one of his last major diplomatic initiatives, a dying Leonid Brezhnev signaled a desire for a reduction of tensions with China. In a speech in Tashkent, the Soviet leader announced, in effect, that the doctrine that bore his name would not apply to China. For the first time since the Cultural Revolution, the Soviet leader acknowledged China to be a socialist country, thus obviating any need for Moscow to intervene to restore socialism there. On that basis, he assured Peking that the Soviet Union posed no threat to Chinese security. Brezhnev also reminded the Chinese that the Soviet Union had consistently supported the PRC's position on the Taiwan issue, whereas the United States had never unequivocally accepted Peking's claims to the island. Brezhnev proposed the resumption of the Sino-Soviet negotiations that had been suspended since the Soviet intervention in Afghanistan, as well as offering to resume the economic, diplomatic, scientific, and cultural ties that had been disrupted by the long estrangement between the two countries.[34]

The decline in the relative power of the Soviet Union was, in Chinese eyes, paralleled by the revival of American power. Talk of containing an evil empire had almost completely replaced discussions of détente in Washington. The United States was engaged in its largest military buildup since the Korean War, enlarging its conventional and nuclear forces to deal with a potential Soviet threat in both Europe and the third world. The United States had enunciated, in the form of the Reagan Doctrine, a direct challenge to Marxist regimes in developing countries, and had begun support for the contras in Nicaragua. Through its strong response to the imposition of martial law in Poland in 1981, the Reagan administration had also shown support for the democratization of the Communist states of Eastern Europe.[35]

Although China had long called for more active American resistance to Soviet expansion, Peking regarded many of these policies with dismay. Chinese analysts began charging that the United States was undertaking an excessively interventionist policy in the third world while disregarding the economic needs of the developing nations. American support for democratization in Eastern Europe raised serious alarms in China, many of whose leaders saw direct parallels between developments in Poland and recent trends in their own country. Nor was the American military buildup completely welcomed in Peking, for some of its elements would have done significant harm to Chinese interests. The strategic defense initiative, for example, threatened to emasculate China's own nuclear deterrent, whereas American encouragement of Japanese defense spending promised to hasten the rearmament of a traditional adversary that Chinese leaders still viewed with mistrust.

Some Americans had presumed that a more assertive U.S. strategic posture would reinforce U.S.-China relations by reassuring Peking that the United States was prepared to meet its obligations to contain Soviet expansion. And indeed, in a phrase that would have delighted American conservatives, Huan Xiang, the director of the PRC Institute for International Affairs, bluntly acknowledged in 1983 that the American buildup had "stopped the Soviet Union."[36] But the Chinese drew conclusions opposite to the U.S. forecasts. As the balance of power shifted away from the Soviet Union and toward the United States, China chose to adopt a more independent posture. No longer did it need to tilt toward Washington quite so decisively in order to counterbalance a growing Soviet threat. Instead, it could now act more selectively, supporting some American initiatives while criticizing others. Such a posture would give China more leverage over the United States in dealing with such issues as Taiwan, in that Washington could no longer assume that Peking would acquiesce to a closer U.S.-Taiwan relationship for the sake of preserving a Sino-American alignment against the Soviet Union. In addition, as the United States adopted a more confrontational approach toward the Soviet Union, greater independence would enable China to avoid entanglement in Soviet-American disputes in parts of the world in which it had no real interest.

A more independent policy also carried other potential benefits. Greater distance from the United States would enable China to explore the significance of Brezhnev's overture at Tashkent, probing to see whether the Soviet Union was prepared to make significant concessions to secure improvements in Sino-Soviet relations. At the same time, Chinese leaders were increasingly interested in gaining more direct knowledge of the experience of Eastern European countries in economic and political reform. Although some of the European Communist nations, such as Romania and Yugoslavia, had long been prepared to maintain close relations with China in defiance of the Soviet Union, most of the others would not be able to expand contacts with Peking without Moscow's approval.

Thus, in the late summer and early fall of 1982, Chinese leaders revealed a significant shift in their international posture.[37] They responded to Brezhnev's overtures at Tashkent with a mixture of skepticism and interest. In his address to the Twelfth National Party Congress in September, General Secretary Hu Yaobang said that China would take "deeds, rather than words" to be the truest measure of Soviet intentions. He then identified three issues that China regarded as the most important obstacles to the improvement of Sino-Soviet relations: the stationing of massive armed forces in Mongolia and along the Sino-Soviet frontier; Moscow's support of Vietnam's invasion and occupation of Cambodia; and the Soviet intervention in Afghanistan by force of arms. Hu implied that removing these three obstacles would be the precondition for any improvement in Sino-Soviet ties. But Hu also pledged that Peking would pursue a policy of "peaceful coexistence" with all Communist countries, including the Soviet Union.[38] And, in October Peking announced that it would resume the negotiations with Moscow on the normalization of Sino-Soviet relations that had been suspended since the Soviet invasion of Afghanistan.

Moreover, Peking also announced it was abandoning its alignment with the United States in favor of an "independent foreign policy."

This meant, as Hu explained to the Twelfth Party Congress, that China would "never attach itself to any big power or group of powers" but would henceforth determine foreign policy on the merits of each issue. As one Chinese journal put it, China

> totally opposes hegemony, no matter who seeks it or where it is sought. . . . On the Afghan and Kampuchean issues, both China and the United States oppose the Soviet Union and Vietnam. . . . In another case, both China and the Soviet Union oppose the United States in supporting Israeli aggression and the South African apartheid rule. This does not mean that China "allies" with the United States under some circumstances, or becomes a Soviet partner under other circumstances. [Instead], this precisely proves that . . . China is independent of all the superpowers.[39]

China's new international posture involved more forthright and vocal criticism of those aspects of American foreign policy that Peking found objectionable. The United States was once again described as a "hegemonic" power, and examples of American ambition, particularly in Central America and the Middle East, were now listed alongside instances of Soviet hegemonism in Africa, Afghanistan, and Cambodia. Just as Peking viewed Vietnam and Cuba as regional hegemonists linked to the Soviet Union, so now did Chinese analysts describe Israel and South Africa as regional hegemonists supported by the United States. American policy toward the third world—especially its indifference to the economic needs of the developing countries and its propensity to intervene in their internal affairs—became the subject of increasingly vehement Chinese attack.[40]

The Reagan administration viewed these developments calmly but with undertones of concern. Privately, many American officials welcomed the resumption of Sino-Soviet negotiations, on the grounds that a reduction of tensions between Peking and Moscow would facilitate the management of several major international disputes, particularly those in Cambodia and in Korea. In addition, American policymakers also noted that Peking's terms for improved relations with Moscow, especially a Soviet withdrawal from Afghanistan and a Vietnamese withdrawal from Cambodia, would simultaneously enable an improvement in U.S.-Soviet relations. Still, the anti-American bent of China's new international posture aroused some resentment in the United States. "To put it bluntly," Assistant Secretary of State John Holdridge declared in December 1982, "we take exception to Chinese references to us as 'hegemonists' and expect better from the Chinese than being lumped together with the Soviets as the cause of all the world's ills."[41] Moreover, there was some apprehension that Peking might be exploring an accommodation with Moscow at the expense of American interests.

GROWING PAINS

Although Taiwan was the principal issue separating China and the United States in the early 1980s, other bilateral problems also plagued the relationship between the two countries. The difficulties that arose in Sino-American cultural and economic ties in this period can be seen as growing pains, reflecting the difficulties in enlarging academic and commercial relations between two very different societies, especially when both countries were experiencing economic hardships.

The academic exchanges that had expanded so rapidly in the months immediately after normalization soon encountered obstacles. The American participants in these programs were primarily social scientists and humanists interested in expanding their understanding of China. American scholars of China had been denied access to the Chinese mainland altogether between 1949 and 1971 and had thereafter been able to visit only on short-term delegations. This opportunity had allowed brief surveys of Chinese scholarship and some limited insight into current developments in China but little more. Now, the normalization of Sino-American relations opened the way to long-term research in China, and American sinologists were eager to make the most of the chance.

The reality, however, proved disappointing. Part of the problem was infrastructure. The operation of China's libraries and archives had been severely disrupted—and sometimes their materials and catalogues had been physically damaged—during the Cultural Revolution. Making productive use of such facilities would have been difficult even in the best of circumstances. But the problem was complicated by the reluctance of Chinese officials to make their scholarly resources available to foreigners. Field research in Chinese villages was seen as excessively penetrative and difficult to arrange; the applications of the first American scholars proposing field research were initially rejected as "inconvenient." Many archives and libraries were closed even to Chinese scholars, and yet Americans demanded access to them. And, perhaps most frustrating of all, Americans soon learned that much scholarly analysis was published in "internal," or *neibu*, publications, which were widely read in China but were not supposed to be available to foreigners.

American scholars soon became frustrated by this problem but found that they had little leverage with which to address it. Academic exchanges between the United States and the Soviet Union were designed on the basis of strict reciprocity. All exchanges with the Soviet Union during those years were conducted through a single American institution, which made sure that as many Americans visited the Soviet Union as there were Soviet scholars visiting the United States, and that the United States could deny visas to Soviet scholars from institutions that were relatively inhospitable to Americans. In constructing the academic exchange program with China, in contrast, the United States had not insisted on a similar coordinating institution despite advice from Soviet specialists to do so.[42]

The more flexible approach toward academic exchanges with China had considerable merit. It had the advantage of permitting vastly larger numbers of Chinese to come to the United States than the United States could ever have sent to China. In this way, American universities were able to attract large numbers of talented Chinese students to their graduate programs and could build connections with even more academic institutions and individual scholars in China. But in waiving the notion of numerical reciprocity, the United States had also reduced its ability to seek reciprocity of access. Since the principal organization that dispatched Americans to China, the Committee on Scholarly Communication with the People's Republic of China, did only part of the work of receiving Chinese in the United States, it was not able to gain much leverage against Chinese institutions that imposed barriers to scholarly access. Americans could plead for a more open academic environment, but they could not pressure.

As American academic administrators urged their Chinese counterparts to make more research opportunities available to American scholars, some visiting American academics took more direct action that landed them in trouble with the Chinese authorities. Steven Mosher, then a doctoral candidate in anthropology at Stanford, was accused by the Chinese of engaging in various inappropriate behavior, from bribing local officials to traveling to parts of the country officially closed to foreigners. The Chinese briefly detained Mosher and then expelled him from the country, declaring that his case was closed. But in 1981, after Mosher began publishing articles critical of the coercive features of Peking's birth control program, the Chinese threatened to cut back academic exchanges with the United States unless some

American institution took punitive action against him. Ultimately, Stanford decided to expel Mosher from the doctoral program in anthropology on the grounds that he had engaged in professional misconduct while in China, a decision widely criticized by conservatives in the United States as capitulation to Chinese pressure.[43]

But Mosher was not the only case. In 1982, Lisa Wichser, a graduate student from the University of Denver, was also briefly detained and expelled from China. Wichser had gone to China not as a visiting student but as an English language teacher. While at the Foreign Languages Institute in Peking, however, she had apparently tried to conduct some research on Chinese communes and had received some "internal" unpublished economic and agricultural statistics, presumably from a student who had tutored her and whom she intended to marry.[44] The Chinese government accused Wichser of conducting activities inappropriate to her formal status. But in contrast to the Mosher case, Peking did not insist that the American side undertake any punitive action, largely because, unlike Mosher, Wichser had come to China as a private citizen rather than as part of an official bilateral exchange program.

As a result of the Mosher and Wichser cases, the Chinese Academy of Social Sciences, the sponsor of many visiting American students and scholars, placed a three-year moratorium on further U.S. field research in China. This ban did not affect interviewing, library research, or work in historical archives and in any event was never fully enforced. But it did hamper American research in anthropology, sociology, and local-level politics. And, more important, it offered clear evidence that China was not prepared to be as cooperative in facilitating American social science research in China as many American scholars had hoped.

From the Chinese perspective, there were fewer complaints about the academic and cultural exchange program in those years. The overwhelming majority of Chinese studying in the United States were visiting scholars in engineering and the sciences. The "brain drain" of Chinese students and scholars, which would become so central an issue in later years, had not yet developed, since most Chinese scholars had only just begun their programs of study in the United States. Nor was there yet much concern about the degree to which Chinese visiting scholars were becoming influenced by American values.

But there were minor irritants that bothered the Chinese. Possibly in response to American complaints about limits on access to research opportunities in China, Chinese officials began to point out that their scholars, too, were denied access to advanced scientific laboratories and conferences in the United States for which American or allied nationality was required. An exhibition in China of American painting was threatened when Peking objected to inclusion of thirteen abstract paintings by such artists as Franz Kline and Helen Frankenthaler.[45] And Chinese officials began criticizing the unfavorable stories about their country that appeared under the by-lines of the first American correspondents to be stationed in Peking.[46]

The most serious issue to emerge in the cultural exchange program in the early 1980s concerned a nineteen-year-old Chinese tennis star, Hu Na, who sought asylum in the United States after a tour in July 1982. Hu Na argued that, were she to return to China, she would be forced to become more deeply involved in politics than she preferred. The Chinese retorted that, given Hu Na's age, she could not possibly have made an independent and mature decision on her own and pointed out that Hu Na's lawyer had been paid for by donations from Taiwan. They also insisted that the U.S. government had a moral obligation to return so young a woman to her family in China and promised that she would not be persecuted or punished if she returned home. After much debate, the Reagan administration decided in April 1983 not only to permit Hu Na to remain in America but also to grant her political asylum. In retaliation, the Chinese government canceled nineteen cultural and sports exchanges scheduled for the remainder of the year.[47]

Thus, the academic exchanges between the two countries fell victim to the same sense of stagnation that afflicted other aspects of the relationship. The number of Chinese students and scholars receiving visas to visit the United States, which had risen from 1,330 in 1979 to 5,407 in 1981, now fell slightly, to 4,480 in 1982 and 4,331 in 1983 (table A-5). The main reason seems to have been the financial constraints imposed by Peking's program of economic retrenchment. The cost of the program to the Chinese government was rising rapidly, from $4 million in 1979 to $17 million in 1982.[48] At a time when China was running a large balance of deficits and seeking to stem the drain on its foreign exchange reserves, reducing the flow of students and scholars to the United States may have seemed necessary. But the controversies over Mosher, Wichser, and Hu Na probably played a contributing role.

The economic relationship between the two countries also became increasingly contentious. The principal problem during the early 1980s concerned textiles. Textiles had long been one of the most highly protected sectors in the United States, as the American textile industry fought to limit imports from countries, especially in Asia, with cheaper labor. These limits had been expressed in textile quotas imposed on America's trading partners under the Multifiber Agreement. And yet, textiles were also the industry that China was counting on to produce attractive exports for the American market. Other raw materials were in short supply; the output of heavy industry was not marketable abroad; and other light industries had not yet been reconfigured to produce for foreign markets. Thus, Chinese exports of textiles to the United States rose sevenfold between 1978 and 1982, with the greatest growth occurring in finished apparel rather than in fibers and fabrics (table A-3).

This rapid expansion of Chinese textile exports to the United States guaranteed conflict between the two countries. The first bilateral textile agreement, which expired at the end of 1982, had permitted an annual growth rate of 3 to 4 percent in six categories of imports. When negotiations began in August that year, the American textile industry, struggling not only with a flood of foreign imports but also with a deepening domestic recession, sought to reduce the growth rate to only 1 percent and to extend the agreement to cover more categories of textiles. The U.S. government pressed Peking to accept an increase of 1.5 to 2 percent a year. But Chinese negotiators insisted on an annual growth rate of 6 percent. The gap between these two positions was unbridgeable, and the two sides soon deadlocked.

In January 1983, with the existing textile agreement having ended and without a new one to take its place, the United States imposed unilateral restrictions on imports from China, just as it had done during the original negotiations in 1979 and 1980. This time, however, China retaliated by halting imports of American cotton, soybeans, and chemical fibers and by reducing imports of American grain.[49] The Chinese had learned from the U.S. grain embargo against the Soviet Union that American farmers were a powerful lobby for free trade. Peking was therefore prepared to violate the grain agreement with the United States in order to mobilize pressure from American farmers for more generous quotas for Chinese textile exporters.

The fight over the import of Chinese textiles was echoed in other industries as well. Several American firms filed petitions with the International Trade Commission, charging Chinese competitors with selling products in the United States at less than fair value and seeking relief through increased duties or import restrictions. The American firms did not win all the cases in question. Petitions on the import of menthol, kitchenware, and tableware were dismissed on the grounds that there had been no direct material injury to

American firms. But the cases did indicate that American industry would take advantage of available legal provisions to limit imports from China.[50]

Restrictions on American exports to China also proved controversial. Although China continued to import American grain, cotton, and artificial fibers, just as it had done in the 1970s, it was now principally interested in acquiring advanced American technology. Like the dispatch of Chinese students and scholars to American universities, the purchase of sophisticated U.S. equipment was seen as a way of rapidly overcoming the technological disadvantage caused by the Cultural Revolution and years of relative isolation from the West.

The export of American technology to China was hampered by export controls, both those imposed unilaterally by the United States government and those administered collectively by the Coordinating Committee on Export Controls in Paris.[51] These controls had been somewhat relaxed throughout the period of Sino-American rapprochement. But the procedure remained cumbersome. The Department of Defense, which assumed the responsibility for a strict reading of the national security issues at stake, could obstruct applications for export licenses that had been approved by the Department of Commerce. Both the Chinese government and American exporters were unhappy with the resulting delays in granting licenses, complaining that the Pentagon was hindering the export of equipment (such as advanced computers and a ground station for Landsat satellites) that had been promised to Peking by the White House.

Finally, as U.S.-China trade was partially liberated from bureaucratic restrictions on both sides, it simultaneously became enmeshed in the macroeconomic environment in the two countries. The early 1980s were hard times for the economies of both China and the United States. In China, an overly ambitious investment plan in the late 1970s resulted in a flood of imports, which doubled from $10.9 billion in 1978 to $20.0 billion in 1980. This import surge, described in the West as China's Great Leap Outward, also produced China's first severe balance of payments deficit since the 1950s, with a cumulative deficit of $5.1 billion between 1978 and 1980. Alarmed at the growth of China's gross foreign debt, Chinese leaders clamped down hard on imports, which were permitted to rise only 10 percent in 1981, declined in 1982, and then remained relatively stagnant in 1983.

American exports to China were hard hit by Peking's retrenchment program. Overall, U.S. shipments to China, which had reached $3.6 billion in 1981, fell to $2.9 billion in 1982 and to $2.2 billion in 1983 (table A-4). The greatest reductions involved the raw materials imported by the Chinese industrial sector, which fell by nearly two-thirds between 1980 and 1983. The Chinese cutbacks on purchases of grain and other farm products undertaken in response to the dispute over textiles also had their effect, with the import of American agricultural products dropping from $1.5 billion in 1980 to $547 million in 1983 (table A-4).

The severe recession in the United States in the early 1980s also had a negative impact on American imports from China. Overall, American purchases from the rest of the world fell from $273 billion in 1981 to $255 billion in 1982, before rising to $270 billion in 1983. China was no exception to this general pattern, with sales in the United States falling slightly from $2.3 billion in 1982 to $2.2 billion in 1983. The drop in Chinese exports was most visible in the energy and raw materials sectors, whereas China's sales of clothing and consumer electronics continued to rise (table A-3).

The net effect of these two trends—the great decline in Chinese imports and the more modest reduction in Chinese exports—was that two-way Sino-American trade declined from $5.5 billion in 1981 to $5.2 billion in 1982 and to $4.4 billion in 1983, the first drop in bilateral trade since the mid-1970s (table A-2). Moreover, the uneven pattern of the reduction, with Chinese imports falling faster than Chinese exports, eliminated the trade surplus that the United States had enjoyed with China since the original rapprochement in the 1970s. For the next few years, Sino-American trade would grow but remain in balance. By the late 1980s, however, the United States would begin running sizable and controversial trade deficits with China.

DISENCHANTMENT

These strains in Sino-American relations in the early 1980s were accompanied by significant changes in how the two countries viewed each other. To the extent that it had existed, the euphoria of 1979 and 1980 was rapidly replaced by a mutual sense of disenchantment, verging in some quarters on active disdain.

Many Chinese, in particular, had had high expectations about the benefits to be accrued from their new relationship with the United States. One of the first attempts at a systematic assessment of urban Chinese attitudes toward the United States, conducted in mid-1981, concluded that there was enormous optimism about the prospects for Sino-American relations and thus a significant possibility that

Chinese expectations could be disappointed.[52] And, indeed, by the end of 1982 it was becoming increasingly evident that many of China's hopes were not being met. Bilateral trade, after growing between 1979 and 1981, had now leveled off and begun to decline. American investment in China was still virtually nil. The United States did not provide any economic assistance to China, and little of the $2.0 billion in Eximbank credits that had been promised in 1979 had been expended. Tight restrictions remained on the transfer of American technology to China, and Chinese exports were arousing strong protectionist sentiments in the United States. In October 1982, Foreign Minister Huang Hua described the repeated American pledges to assist the modernization of the Chinese economy as "loud thunder, but little rain."[53]

Furthermore, Peking was dismayed by the continuing American interest in Taiwan. From the Taiwan Relations Act to the August 1982 communiqué, the United States—even as it made concessions to Peking's position—maintained what from Peking's perspective was a dismayingly stout commitment to its "old friends" on the island. The United States continued to express interest in a peaceful future for Taiwan. It continued to sell arms and advanced technology to Taipei. It maintained a vigorous commercial and cultural relationship with the island. And, even though the United States said it favored a resolution of the Taiwan question, it refused to endorse Peking's negotiating position or to press Taipei to negotiate with the mainland. As a result, there were few signs that, despite the loss of diplomatic relations with Washington and the termination of its security treaty with the United States, Taiwan was prepared to accept Peking's proposals for expanding economic and cultural exchanges with the mainland or begin discussions of reunification.

Peking's disappointment with the United States was exacerbated by its failure to understand the complexity of the American political system, especially the separation of powers among the three branches of government and between national and local authorities. Many of the actions that Peking viewed as irritants to Sino-American relations were taken outside the executive branch of the federal government. Several American state and local governments, for example, decided to honor the Republic of China on the occasion of its national day in 1982, occasioning vigorous protests from Peking.[54] Congress periodically considered, and occasionally adopted, resolutions on Taiwan that the Chinese government regarded as unacceptable. And a federal district court in northern Alabama ruled in 1982 that the present Chinese government was responsible for redeeming bonds issued at the end of the Qing dynasty to finance the construction of the Huguang Railway.[55]

Leaders in Peking blamed each of these episodes, directly or indirectly, on the Reagan administration. At a minimum, they seemed convinced that the White House could have prevented the incidents from occurring by issuing a directive to whatever governmental body was acting in a way offensive to China. The failure to instruct a federal court to rule in Peking's favor on the Huguang Railway bonds or to order local governments not to commemorate Taiwan's national day was seen in Peking as a deliberate refusal to uphold Chinese interests. And, at worst, some Chinese leaders may have suspected that these incidents were orchestrated by the White House as a deliberate attempt to embarrass Peking. Living in a country where few aspects of Sino-American relations were independent of central government direction, Chinese leaders were slow to understand the very different principles around which American politics were organized.

As these problems mounted, the Chinese therefore began to question the sincerity with which Washington approached its relationship with Peking. Various issues were invoked to show that the United States was not prepared to fulfill the obligations to China it had assumed. The Reagan administration's early policy toward Taiwan was portrayed as a violation of the agreement on the normalization of Sino-American relations. The failure to relax controls on technology transfer or to provide financial aid to China was regarded as a failure to meet commitments that American leaders had made to their Chinese counterparts. The American offer to sell arms to China was dismissed as "an empty political gesture" because it was presumed insincere: the United States, one Chinese commentator complained, will never sell China "really sophisticated weapons."[56]

Thus, Chinese leaders began repeatedly to complain about the treachery of the United States. In October 1982, Deng Xiaoping explained that it had been necessary to negotiate an understanding on limiting American arms sales to Taiwan because Reagan had been playing "too many cheap tricks" in his policy toward Taipei. A year later, Hu Yaobang similarly charged that the deterioration of Sino-American relations between 1981 and 1983 had been the result of "little tricks" played by the United States.[57] From this perspective, the drumbeat of small issues in 1982 and 1983—what some have labeled the "three T's" and the "two Hu's"[58]—can be interpreted as Chinese probes intended to determine American sincerity and commitment to the relationship. Indeed, asked what would happen if the United States yielded to Chinese pressure on the Hu Na case, one Chinese observer frankly responded that Peking would "find some other issue" to use as a litmus test of American attitudes toward China.

The Chinese also complained in 1981 and 1982 that their relationship with the United States had become less equal and more hierarchical than they could accept. The resurgence of American power, they feared, was leading many in Washington to conclude that China needed the United States more than the United States needed China, and that Peking would therefore be forced to accept American arms sales to Taiwan, U.S. intervention in the third world, and other U.S. foreign policy initiatives that ran counter to Chinese interests.[59] One Chinese scholar said privately at the time that his country was not willing to be treated as the "ward" or "younger brother" of the United States. Deng Xiaoping made the same point more bluntly in August 1981 when he told a visitor from Hong Kong:

> The United States thinks that China is seeking its favor. In fact, China is not seeking any country's favor. . . . China hopes that Sino-American relations will further develop rather than retrogress. . . . [but] if worst [sic] comes to worst and the relations retrogress to those prior to 1972, China will not collapse. . . . The Chinese people . . . will never bow and scrape for help. . . . China and the United States should cooperate on an equal footing. If the United States does not play fair but forces China to act according to the will of the United States, China will not agree.[60]

The Chinese found evidence of inequality in several aspects of their bilateral relations with the United States. The United States, they said, expected support from China for its policy in the third world but had not been prepared to endorse China's invasion of Vietnam in 1979. Washington was willing to sell arms to Peking to create the appearance of a Sino-American military alliance but was not willing to transfer the production technology that China wanted. The trade difficulties between the two countries were also interpreted as suggesting an imbalanced relationship: "The United States' has looked upon its trade as the savior bestowing favors on others. I can impose limitations on your commodities imported to my country, but my commodities will enter your market unimpeded."[61]

Some Chinese, after rehearsing the evidence of American insincerity and arrogance, warned of a fundamental change in their country's policy toward the United States. Even after the issuance of the August 1982 communiqué on American arms sales to Taiwan, the Chinese foreign minister complained that he was not certain whether the United States regarded China as a friend or as a potential adversary, implying that Peking would be reconsidering its foreign policy accordingly. As late as June 1983, one Chinese specialist on the United States noted that "the pile-up of problems . . . have people in the [Chinese] leadership asking whether it is even worthwhile to try and solve them all, or whether it might not be better just to rewrite our foreign policy without the United States."[62]

Many Americans had also held high expectations about their new relationship with China, not only about the benefits to be gained from expanded economic, cultural, and military ties with China but also about the economic and political system that had been created in China by the Communist Party. By 1982, a reassessment had begun to occur along all these dimensions, so as to discount the prospects for American business, to reduce China's place in America's global strategy, and to provide a less glowing account of Chinese society under Communist rule.

Economically, the difficulties of doing business in China and the decline in trade between the two countries greatly eroded the euphoria about commercial relations that had seemed so widespread immediately after normalization in 1978–79. According to one informal poll, less than one-third of American firms involved in trade or investment in China reported that business was good, and nearly half admitted that their activities in China had thus far shown "disappointing results." Few wanted to cut back their efforts, and a great majority felt that China was comparable to other new markets. But the realization was growing that making money in China would take a long time. As one respondent put it, China's potential was "high," but the country was also "slow moving and unpredictable."[63]

Strategically, too, there was a slow reevaluation of China. As noted, Peking's apparent interest in a reduction of tensions with the Soviet Union did not produce any alarm in Washington. But China's promulgation of its independent foreign policy, its new tendency to equate the hegemonic tendencies of the United States and the Soviet Union, and its reluctance to cooperate militarily with the United States did lead to a reconsideration of the prospects for a Sino-American alignment against the Soviet Union. In addition, Haig's resignation as secretary of state in June 1982 removed from the Reagan administration one of the most active proponents of enhanced strategic relations with Peking.

Haig's successor, George P. Shultz, took a noticeably different view of China's role in U.S. foreign policy. In early 1983, a review of American policy toward China undertaken by Shultz concluded that Peking's importance to Washington should be downplayed. China's demands on various bilateral issues seemed excessive, the benefits of meeting them appeared meager, and the risks of rejecting them seemed low. Above all, the growing strength of the United States and its improved cooperation with Japan and its friends in Southeast Asia meant that American policy toward Asia need no longer focus as prominently on China as it had in the 1970s.[64] Accordingly, on the eve of Shultz's first visit to China as secretary of state in February 1983, administration officials declared that China was decades away from becoming a global power and that the United States was not prepared to "pay a high price" to sustain its relationship with Peking. The following month, in a major speech on U.S. policy toward Asia, Shultz gave pride of place to Japan, and he warned that "frustrations and problems" would inevitably characterize Sino-American relations. The implication was clear: China loomed smaller in American strategic calculations than at any time since the original rapprochement in the early 1970s.[65]

American popular attitudes toward Chinese society were also changing during this period. The most important development was the reconsideration of the country undertaken by the first wave of Americans to live as journalists, businesspeople, and scholars in the PRC. Before, Americans had been able to visit China only on short-term visits—perhaps two or three weeks in duration. Carefully controlled itineraries and solicitous treatment made it possible for their Chinese hosts to create extremely favorable impressions of the Communist government and its accomplishments. Now, after normalization, Americans were beginning for the first time to live in China for extended periods of time. Their descriptions of China and the standards they used to judge the country differed a great deal from the euphoric treatment of the PRC in the 1970s.[66]

The reassessment of China occurred along almost every dimension. In the 1970s, China had been depicted as an egalitarian and populist society, in which inequalities were limited, a basic standard of living was guaranteed to all, and ordinary people were directly involved in decisionmaking. Ordinary Chinese were seen as selfless men and women devoted to a common vision of a good society. As Americans got to know China better, they came to realize that the reality was quite different. They learned that some parts of the country were mired in grinding poverty, that there were substantial differences in the standard of living between the elites and the mass of Chinese, and that China was governed by a hierarchical and unresponsive Party bureaucracy. The social psychology of ordinary Chinese was seen not as committed and selfless but as alienated and cynical.

In part, this reevaluation reflected the ability of Americans on longer visits to China to see the flaws of the country more clearly. Paradoxically, too, it also reflected the fact that China was, in the late 1970s and early 1980s, starting to reform. This meant that, compared with the period during the late Cultural Revolution, the Chinese government was more willing to admit the shortcomings of the country's past and that ordinary Chinese were freer to admit their discontent and dissatisfaction. As China gradually evolved from a totalitarian political system to an authoritarian one, its ability to rationalize its flaws decayed, and the visibility of its shortcomings increased.

Moreover, the new descriptions of China were judged with different evaluative criteria than in earlier times. In the 1970s, some Americans were reluctant to apply Western standards to China, either because they were convinced that Chinese culture incorporated different political and social values or because they were dubious of the relevance or appropriateness of American norms to China. By the early 1980s, however, Americans gained a renewed conviction in the universality of their values. Many Americans who lived in China came back convinced that ordinary Chinese sought a comfortable standard of living and individual political rights as much as ordinary Americans did.

Varying results from different surveys make it difficult to assess the impact of this new and less flattering portrait of China on American public opinion. Some polls found little change in popular attitudes toward China in the early 1980s. Surveys conducted for the Chicago Council on Foreign Relations, for example, showed great continuity in the public's evaluation of China between 1978 and 1982. In 1978, China received an average rating of forty-four degrees on a "feeling thermometer" that ranged from zero (very unfavorable) to one hundred (highly favorable). In 1982, China's rating rose slightly, to forty-seven degrees, about the same level as that of Taiwan and India.[67]

But other surveys suggested that the reevaluation of China had a striking if temporary effect on the public mood. Gallup polls indicated that the percentage of Americans having favorable impressions of China fell from 70 percent in 1980 to 43 percent in 1983, whereas the proportion holding unfavorable images of the country rose from 26 percent to 52 percent during the same period. These changes were fleeting, in that the new round of political and economic reform undertaken in the mid-1980s had restored American perceptions of China to postnormalization levels by 1985 (table A-1). But they revealed that the favorable American evaluations of China that emerged after the normalization of diplomatic relations between the two countries were highly fragile, and opinions remained vulnerable to changing economic and political circumstances in the People's Republic.

CHAPTER 5

Reconciliation

THE successful conclusion of the negotiations over American arms sales to Taiwan in August 1982 did not lead to an immediate reconciliation between Peking and Washington. As noted in the previous chapter, Peking was not completely satisfied with the terms of the agreement that the two countries had reached. In the August 17 communiqué, Washington did promise that the volume of arms transfers to Taipei would be gradually reduced. But, much to Peking's disappointment, the United States refused to acknowledge that arms sales to Taiwan were a violation of Chinese sovereignty or to set a timetable for their termination. Nor did the American government explicitly endorse Peking's formula for national reunification.

When Secretary of State George Shultz visited China in early 1983, therefore, the two sides still viewed each other warily. Shultz informed reporters on the eve of his departure that the United States would not make great initiatives to preserve its relationship with China. In contrast with previous high-ranking American visitors, the secretary of state therefore did not bring with him new American concessions—or what one State Department official called a "basket of goodies"—to give to his Chinese counterparts. Peking replied that it still mistrusted American intentions toward Taiwan, and warned that, unless Washington honored its commitment to reduce arms sales to the island, the future of Sino-American relations would be troubled.[1] A month later, Prime Minister Zhao Ziyang told House Speaker Thomas P. O'Neill (D-Massachusetts) that, despite Shultz's visit, Sino-American relations were "unsatisfactory" and had not yet taken a fundamental turn for the better.[2]

By the fall, however, the two countries had successfully addressed some of the other controversial issues in their relationship. In midyear, Peking adopted a new and more effective strategy for dealing with the financial claims presented by American holders of the Huguang Railway bonds, and successfully appealed the previous court ruling against the Chinese government. In August 1983, Peking and Washington finally signed a new textile agreement, ending twelve months of contentious negotiations. And, despite Shultz's declaration that he was not in favor of making new gestures to Peking, each country made timely concessions on matters of concern to the other: the United States further relaxed controls on the export of advanced technology to China, and Peking resumed military exchanges with the United States.

As these problems were resolved, the tone of Sino-American relations gradually changed. In September, a Communist newspaper published in Hong Kong declared that U.S.-China relations had reached their low ebb and begun to improve. One month later, General Secretary Hu Yaobang pronounced the relationship between the two countries to be "not all that bad," the first such characterization since the Reagan administration took office,[3] and a statement in direct contrast to Zhao Ziyang's comments to Tip O'Neill in the spring.

The reconciliation between the two countries was cemented by an unprecedented exchange of visits by Prime Minister Zhao Ziyang and President Ronald Reagan in January and April. These twin summit meetings enabled the two countries to reaffirm their common interest in developing their bilateral relations. With most of the divisive issues of the past—especially Taiwan, textiles, and technology transfer—set aside, the two governments shifted from a relatively confrontational tone, in which they swapped charges and demands, to a more collaborative one, in which they sought ways to enlarge and facilitate their relationship. On that basis, economic, cultural, and military ties between the two countries resumed rapid growth. At the same time, new mechanisms for cooperation began to emerge, making Sino-American relations more extensive, more complex, and more penetrative than ever before.

The quantitative and qualitative improvements in U.S.-China relations in the mid-1980s can be attributed to three developments. First, and perhaps most important, as China gradually recovered from the economic retrenchment of the early 1980s, its leaders began to plan for a period of renewed economic reform and accelerated economic growth. Since the United States was a significant market for Chinese exports, and since it was regarded as the most important potential source of foreign investment capital and advanced technology, Chinese leaders saw the consolidation and improvement of Sino-American relations as an essential component of their long-term economic objectives.[4] In addition, China needed friendly and stable relations with the United States if it were to gain access to technology and capital from America's allies in Western Europe and Asia.

Similarly, the resumption of faster rates of growth and reform made China a more appealing partner for the United States. American merchants could sell more to a market that was growing rapidly. American entrepreneurs could invest more in a country that was introducing market mechanisms into its economic system. And political leaders and ordinary citizens alike could respond more enthusiastically to a nation that seemed to be engaged in a pioneering program of economic and political liberalization. If a renewed commitment to reform made the United States more important to China, it also made Americans more willing to cooperate with Peking.

Second, Peking modified its approach toward national reunification in 1983 and 1984 in ways that helped defuse the Taiwan issue in Sino-American relations. In the past, Peking's primary strategy had been to weaken American political and military links to Taiwan so as to demoralize the island and force Taipei into negotiations. Although China had succeeded in persuading the United States to break diplomatic relations with Taipei and pledge to reduce arms sales to Taiwan, it had not been able to compel an official dialogue across the Taiwan Strait. Now, Peking adopted a somewhat different strategy: to hope that more flexible formulas for reunification and renewed economic reform on the mainland would lure Taiwan into permitting greater contacts. Peking also hoped that successful negotiations with Britain over the future of Hong Kong would persuade Taipei to explore a reduction of tensions with the mainland.

Gradually, this new strategy worked. Under pressure from local entrepreneurs who wanted commercial relations with a growing Chinese economy, and from ordinary citizens who demanded contact with their relatives on the mainland, the Taiwan government gradually relaxed restrictions on commercial and cultural relations across the Taiwan Strait. And as contacts between Taiwan and the mainland expanded, the American role in their dispute was correspondingly reduced. By 1987–88, the United States was no longer perceived as an intermediary between the two sides or regarded as the actor whose decisions would determine the outcome of the Chinese Civil War. This perception, in turn, implied that the Taiwan issue would no longer be so important an obstacle to the development of Sino-American relations.

Finally, still another set of factors contributed to the revival of strategic relations between the United States and China. To begin with, China was disappointed by the evolution of Soviet policy in the early post-Brezhnev period. Neither Yuri Andropov nor Konstantin Chernenko was able or willing to make a decisive break from Brezhnev's policy of refusing to make substantial concessions to Peking or to discuss issues involving a third country. Moreover, as China and the United States found ways of managing the Taiwan issue, the principal obstacle to expanding their military relations was removed. Although China still denied it was interested in a firm alignment with the United States, or even a "comprehensive strategic relationship" with Washington, it was prepared to resume the military exchanges it had suspended during the controversy over American arms sales to Taiwan. The two countries also were able, for the first time, to devise mutually agreeable programs by which the United States assisted China in the development and manufacture of carefully selected defensive weapons systems.

At the same time, however, an unrealistic euphoria about China began to emerge in the United States, as some American observers began to exaggerate the prospects for China's reforms. The restructuring of the Chinese economy was seen in some quarters as nothing less than the repudiation of central planning in favor of free markets and the endorsement of private entrepreneurship in place of state ownership. The initial success of the post-Mao reforms led many Americans to overestimate their irreversibility and to overlook the knotty social and economic problems ahead. To a large degree, therefore, the American relationship with Peking now rested on a fragile base: the assumption that China was becoming the first Communist country to abandon Leninist institutions in favor of capitalism and democracy.

BACK ON TRACK

Throughout 1983, China and the United States dealt in fairly swift succession with most of the problems that had bedeviled their relationship during the previous two years.[5] Peking, eager to obtain American support for its ambitious program of economic development and reform, now proved willing to make the compromises necessary to resolve some of the most controversial issues on the bilateral agenda. The United States, also eager to stabilize its relationship with China, made a crucial concession on technology transfer that regained much goodwill in the eyes of Peking.

On a visit to Peking in May, Secretary of Commerce Malcolm Baldrige informed Chinese leaders of a major liberalization of export controls. China would be transferred from its own separate category (P), where it had been placed in 1980, to the more liberal category (V), which included most of America's friends and allies. This step was significant for two reasons. Substantively, it promised to facilitate the sale of advanced technology to China, in that the levels of equipment available to Peking would no longer be linked to the levels allowed to the Soviet Union. But the symbolic consequences of the new policy were even more important. For the first time, China was in a category that included countries acknowledged to be friendly to the United States, rather than one that implied Peking was a potential American adversary.[6] Chinese leaders had always been especially sensitive about this issue and thus regarded the American initiative as a significant and most welcome concession.

Three months later, the two countries finally concluded a new textile agreement to replace the one that had expired at the beginning of 1983. The new arrangement represented significant concessions by both sides. The annual growth rate of about 3 percent stipulated in the agreement was far less than the 6 percent rate Peking had sought. Moreover, the new agreement was more comprehensive than the old one, placing restrictions on thirty-four categories of textiles rather than fourteen. At the same time, the quotas were far higher than the growth rates of 1.5 to 2 percent a year that had been sought by American negotiators. With this compromise agreement in hand, China lifted the restrictions imposed earlier in the year on the import of American cotton, chemical fibers, soybeans, and grain.[7]

The two countries also adopted a new and more realistic approach to the issue of the Huguang Railway bonds. In the past, the Chinese government had insisted that, under the doctrine of sovereign immunity, it could not be sued in an American court of law. On that basis, it had refused to retain legal counsel to present its case or to appear in court to answer the complaints presented by the bondholders, but simply demanded that the executive branch of the federal government ensure that the courts dispose of the case in China's favor. In mid-1983, however, Peking adopted a more appropriate course of action. While still claiming sovereign immunity, it finally hired lawyers to appeal the original judgment passed down by the federal district court. And, for its part, the Department of Justice filed an *amicus curiae* brief in support of the Chinese government's position that it should not be regarded as the successor to the financial obligations of the Qing dynasty.[8] In the end, the district court reversed itself and ruled that the Chinese government need not pay the American bondholders. That decision was later affirmed by the circuit court, and the Supreme Court refused to hear the case.

With agreements reached on American arms sales to Taiwan and on Chinese textile exports to the United States, and with progress on the case of the Huguang Railway bonds, Peking was prepared to resume the military exchanges with the United States that it had suspended in 1981. In the summer, Chinese leaders agreed to a visit by Secretary of Defense Caspar W. Weinberger—a visit that had been discussed by Secretary of State Shultz in February but had not received Peking's final approval. On that visit, Weinberger added more items to the list of weapons that the United States would be prepared to export to China and indicated that others could also be licensed for sale if Peking provided adequate assurances that the arms would not be turned over to third countries. In return, Peking agreed to resume exchanges of both high-ranking military officers and working-level military delegations and began serious discussions of a program of military technology transfer.[9]

These developments set the stage for the exchange of summit meetings in early 1984. In his visit to the United States in January, Chinese Premier Zhao Ziyang continued to complain that American commitments to the security of Taiwan, including the Taiwan Relations Act, constituted intervention in China's internal affairs. But Zhao was realistic enough to acknowledge that Congress was "not inclined for the moment" to repeal the Taiwan Relations Act and to accept American "friendship" with Taiwan. Rather than demand additional American concessions on the Taiwan question, Zhao took the more conciliatory approach of insisting only that the United States be consistent in its implementation of the several joint communiqués that touched on that issue.[10] As Foreign Minister Wu Xueqian told the Chinese legislature in March, Zhao also asked that the United States not create additional obstacles to the peaceful reunification of Taiwan and the mainland.[11]

In a similar vein, Zhao noted that China's independent foreign policy and its disagreements with the United States on several issues involving the third world precluded what he described as "a strategic partnership between China and the United States."[12] But he also took great pains to deny that China had adopted an equidistant foreign policy between the United States and the Soviet Union, or that it "equated" the two countries' policies in international affairs. The differences between Washington and Peking, Zhao implied, were on secondary questions. Their common views, he said, were on major international issues. And China's refusal to form a strategic partnership with the United States would not prevent the two nations from cooperating on matters on which their interests coincided, continuing military exchanges, or developing a program of American arms sales to China.

Finally, during his visit to America, Zhao emphasized his country's desire for more extensive economic relations with the United States.

He assured his hosts that China wanted to expand commercial and scientific contacts with the outside world, and that China had "opened its door" to the international community and would "never close it again." He urged the American business community to invest in China, assuring it that it would earn reasonable profits at minimal risks. He asked Congress to accept the Reagan administration's recommendations to repeal existing legislation that made China ineligible for American economic aid. And, in his toast at the White House banquet in his honor, Zhao declared that China did not favor the proliferation of nuclear arms and would not assist other countries to develop such weapons, a statement designed to facilitate the conclusion of a nuclear cooperation agreement under negotiation with the United States to permit the export of American nuclear power–generating equipment to China. Zhao's overall message was that, again in Wu Xueqian's words, Sino-American economic relations had great potential, but the two sides were far from realizing it.[13]

President Reagan's visit to China in April 1984, the first presidential visit to that nation since Gerald Ford's trip in 1975 and Reagan's first visit to any Communist country, was also designed to convey the impression of two countries willing to cooperate despite differences.[14] In speeches to Chinese leaders at the Great Hall of the People in Peking and faculty and students at Fudan University in Shanghai, Reagan repeatedly emphasized the dissimilarities in values between China and the United States, noting the importance to Americans of faith, freedom, democracy, and individualism. "It would be foolish," Reagan told his audience at Fudan, "not to acknowledge these differences. There's no point in hiding the truth for the sake of a friendship."[15]

But Reagan went on to deny that those differences would necessarily cripple Sino-American ties. For one thing, he identified common interests that could provide a foundation for cooperation. Both nations had long condemned "military expansionism," and China had recently joined the United States in supporting the principle of nuclear nonproliferation. The two countries would benefit from an expansion of trade, American investment, the transfer of American technology, and exchanges of scientific and managerial expertise. Those common interests, the president insisted, should prevent China and the United States from being "dominated" by their ideological and institutional differences. Moreover, Reagan also portrayed a China that, through economic and political reform, was gradually reducing the gaps that divided it from the United States. Quoting Zhao Ziyang on "emancipat[ing] our thinking" and citing the "fresh breezes of incentives and innovation sweeping positive changes across China," the president implied that China and the United States were now moving in similar directions.[16]

ECONOMIC AND CULTURAL TIES

For China, the mid-1980s were indeed a period of intense economic restructuring, particularly in the country's urban areas.[17] A series of extensive reforms, first introduced in piecemeal fashion in 1983 and 1984, was codified into two more comprehensive packages in 1984 and 1985: an outline of urban economic reform was adopted in October 1984, and the draft of the Seventh Five-Year Plan for 1986–90 was introduced in September 1985.[18] These measures inaugurated sweeping, often spectacular, changes in China's domestic economy, foreign economic relations, and political life.

In the domestic economy, the reforms meant a great relaxation of central planning and a corresponding increase in the role of material incentives and market forces in the production and allocation of goods and services. Prices slowly became more rational, a result of the administrative adjustment of the prices of those commodities deemed essential to the national economy and the decontrol of prices of less important products. The number of commodities directly allocated by the central planning apparatus was sharply reduced. Factories were allowed to retain more of their profits and given greater autonomy over investment and production. Industrial workers received wages and bonuses pegged, at least in theory, to their productivity. Managers were given greater freedom to fire laggard workers, and dissatisfied employees had more opportunities to look for alternative sources of employment. Provincial and municipal governments were permitted to retain a greater share of the revenues generated by the farms, factories, and stores located within their boundaries.

The economic reforms of the mid-1980s also included significant changes in the system of ownership in China. The state relaxed control over the means of production, allowing the virtual decollectivization of agriculture, the emergence of privately or collectively owned enterprises in urban and rural areas, and the leasing or selling of smaller state-owned firms to private entrepreneurs. Since the private and collective sectors grew much more rapidly than the state sector, the result over time was a substantial restructuring of the Chinese economy. In 1978, before the inauguration of reform, the state sector had accounted for 81 percent of industrial output and 91 percent of retail sales. By 1987, less than a decade later, those ratios had fallen below 60 percent and 40 percent, respectively.[19]

At the same time as the domestic economy was being redesigned, the reforms were also opening China to the outside world. The central state monopoly over import and export was relaxed. Factories producing for export were given more opportunities for direct contact with potential customers overseas. Localities and enterprises were allowed to retain a share of the foreign exchange that they earned from foreign trade. Fourteen coastal cities, along with Hainan Island, were permitted in 1984 to offer tax incentives to potential foreign investors, joining the four special economic zones created in 1979. To different degrees, China's provinces and municipalities were also given greater autonomy to approve foreign investment proposals without prior consent from Peking.

And finally, although the reform of the political system lagged behind economic restructuring, some limited political liberalization was nonetheless evident. Political controls were gradually although incompletely relaxed over the universities and the arts, allowing a freer expression of new ideas in culture and scholarship. Although the public security apparatus was being reinforced, other mechanisms of social control—the neighborhood committees, the mass organizations, the political study groups, and even basic-level Party committees—were deactivated or spontaneously decayed. Ideology played a smaller and smaller role in shaping the content of political discourse and artistic expression, and new ideas about political and economic life began to penetrate China from abroad. Tentative steps were taken toward creating a more rational and consultative political system, including experiments with contested elections at the grass roots, a somewhat freer press, reform of the civil service, and greater opportunities for specialists to participate in the formulation of national policy.

These steps toward greater efficiency and openness produced a period of brisk economic growth that, to foreigners and Chinese alike, was a welcome contrast to the retrenchment of the early 1980s. The annual growth of China's gross national product from 1983 to 1987 averaged around 10 percent; the expansion of China's foreign trade, which averaged 15.8 percent a year, was even more impressive.[20] The acceleration of the economy, in turn, sparked a rapid increase in Sino-American trade, which more than tripled within five years, rising from $4.4 billion in 1983 to $13.5 billion in 1988. As a result of these increases, China became the United States' fourteenth largest trade partner, although it still only constituted 1.7 percent of American two-way trade in 1988.[21] The United States remained, after Hong Kong and Japan, China's third largest trade partner, with a share hovering between 10 percent and 13 percent of China's overall foreign trade during the same period (table A-2).

American foreign investment in China also increased rapidly, albeit from a very low base. At the end of 1983, only about $18 million had been invested in China. That figure rose to $280 million by the end of 1984, to nearly $1 billion by the end of 1986, and then to $1.5 billion by the end of 1988 (table A-7). By the middle of 1986, it was estimated that some 250 American firms had established representative offices in China, and about the same number of American investment projects were operating in the country.[22] American investment in 1988 was around 10 percent of the cumulative total of utilized foreign investment in China, making the United States second only to Hong Kong as a source of direct foreign investment.

Changes in American policy also helped stimulate Sino-American economic relations. Of particular importance was the ongoing process of liberalizing controls over the export of advanced technology.[23] The transfer of China from category P to category V in 1983 was followed shortly by the establishment of a three-tiered system of export licenses. For items in a red zone, including primarily technology with direct application to advanced military systems that could pose a clear threat to American security interests, there would be a "strong presumption for denial" of applications for export licenses. Items in a yellow zone would be subject to an interagency review, with approval of export licenses mandated unless a threat to American security interests could be identified. But 75 percent of applications were to fall in a green zone, to be examined solely by the Department of Commerce. Most would receive routine approval, although in some cases the exporter would have to provide assurances about the identity of the end-user in China.

The new system was also intended to facilitate technology transfer to China in other ways. An interagency group working under the National Security Council was supposed to review the boundaries between the zones on a quarterly basis. As the frontiers of technology advanced, the aim was to place more and more items inside the green zone, thus facilitating their export to China. Moreover, the United States also proposed that review by the Coordinating Committee on Export Controls (COCOM) no longer be required for most items in the green zone, an exemption intended to reduce the time for export licensing by as much as a month or two. This step was finally taken in late 1985.

The liberalization of technology transfer to China was not as far-reaching as Chinese officials may have hoped, nor as effective as its

American architects had intended. The Department of Defense soon reasserted its authority to review cases, even for technology in the green zone. The interagency group did not, in fact, expand the green zone on a regular quarterly basis. The export control process still precluded the issuance of distribution licenses for exports to China, which would have allowed large orders to be processed in one batch. Instead, U.S. exporters had to go through the cumbersome process of obtaining individual licenses for each separate item of technology destined for China. And uncertainties about the boundaries of the various zones led companies to file trial applications, in advance of firm export orders, to be certain that they would be able to fulfill a potential sales contract. This, too, vastly increased the paperwork flooding the export licensing offices at the Department of Commerce.

Nonetheless, despite these remaining difficulties, the liberalization of technology transfer controls greatly affected American exports to China. The sale of advanced technology increased from $650 million in 1983 to $1.7 billion in 1985, rising from 30 percent of total exports to nearly 45 percent. Thereafter, the rate of growth slackened, in part because of the complexities of the export licensing system and the temporary suspension of the liberalization of export controls in 1987 and 1988 as a result of disagreements over Chinese arms sales to the Middle East. In 1988, the sale of advanced technology was still around $1.7 billion but had fallen back to approximately one-third of total U.S. exports to China.[24]

One of the most important items on the Sino-American bilateral agenda in the late 1980s was to find further ways of enhancing the economic ties between the two countries. The sense in Washington was that the American share of trade with China was low and stagnant and that the United States was losing out to Japan in the competition for the Chinese market. Those who wanted to assist China's modernization and those who wanted to promote American commercial opportunities in China could find common ground in seeking ways of facilitating American trade and investment in the People's Republic.

The hunt for such mechanisms occurred inside and outside government. In 1986, the two countries finally ratified a bilateral tax treaty, which exempted firms from the burden of double taxation.[25] Chinese and American officials worked on a bilateral treaty intended to promote American investment in China by providing assurances of equitable treatment, provisions for mediation of disputes, and guarantees against expropriation. The two governments were also engaged in a lengthy discussion of China's application for membership in the General Agreement on Tariffs and Trade (GATT), which would have entitled China to participate in multilateral negotiations on trade liberalization issues as well as to join other developing countries in receiving preferential American tariff treatment under the Generalized System of Preferences (GSP).[26] Officials in the Agency for International Development began to consider a small program of aid to China, focusing on technical advice on economic reform and expanded export promotion activities.

Congress also seemed eager to find ways of expanding U.S.-China trade, especially in high technology. A special House subcommittee on U.S. trade with China was formed in July 1983 to remove barriers to U.S. exports and to promote a more stable commercial relationship. The Office of Technology Assessment produced a major report on Sino-American technology transfer, raising for the first time the question about whether export controls might damage American commercial interests even as they sought to protect American security interests.[27] A small China trade caucus was formed in the Senate, some of whose members proposed easing the antidumping laws on the grounds that China had become at least a quasi-market economy.[28]

Outside government, organizations such as the U.S.-China Business Council (formerly the National Council for U.S.-China Trade), the National Committee on U.S.-China Relations, and the Committee for Fair Trade with China also proposed measures for expanding Sino-American trade.[29] The ideas ranged from longer-term waivers of the Jackson-Vanik amendment and greater funding for export promotion to removing China from COCOM and making China eligible for distribution licenses for technology exports. One researcher at the Heritage Foundation even proposed concluding free-trade agreements with the various special economic zones and open cities along the Chinese coast.[30]

Similar patterns were evident in the cultural and academic realms. Official cultural exchanges, suspended as a result of the Hu Na incident in 1983, resumed in 1984 following an agreement reached during the Reagan visit to China. The number of government-to-government protocols on scientific and technological cooperation continued to increase. And, in early 1988, Peking and Washington agreed that the U.S. Peace Corps would send around one hundred Americans to China to teach English.[31] There they were to join the four thousand American teachers who had already taught there since 1986.[32]

These formal agreements, however, represented only the official tip of a much larger iceberg of cultural and academic exchanges. The flow of Chinese and Americans from one society to another kept increasing throughout the mid-1980s, as liberalization made it more feasible for Americans to work in Chinese academic institutions and easier for Chinese to travel abroad. The number of new visas issued annually to Chinese students and scholars to study in the United States increased dramatically in this period, from 4,300 in 1983 to nearly 14,000 in 1988, making America the destination for about half of all the Chinese students sponsored by their government to study abroad (table A-5). By 1988 the total number of Chinese studying in the United States reached 40,000, making the Chinese the largest group of foreign students in American universities. The corresponding number of American students in China grew more slowly but is still estimated to have increased from around 550 in the early 1980s to 1,300 in the 1987–88 academic year.[33]

The flow of tourists and other short-term visitors also increased dramatically. The number of Chinese visiting America—most on delegations, but an increasing number as individual visitors—rose from around 10,000 in 1980 to 50,000 in 1988.[34] The reverse flow of Americans traveling to China, whether on business or for pleasure, is estimated to have grown from around 100,000 in 1980 to about 300,000 in 1988 (table A-6).

The burgeoning economic and cultural relationships between China and the United States were not promoted by an extensive program of official financial assistance to China. Formal bilateral aid programs administered by the Agency for International Development were restricted, first by a legal prohibition against extending aid to Communist countries that was not waived for China until the end of 1985 and later by political and budgetary constraints. But the U.S. government did provide limited financial assistance through three other agencies: trade financing through Eximbank ($349 million through 1988), investment guarantees through the Overseas Private Investment Corporation ($95.5 million through 1988), and trade promotional activities through the Trade Development Program of the Department of Commerce ($22.6 million through the end of fiscal 1988).[35] In addition, the United States lent China some $1.4 billion indirectly, through contributions to the World Bank.[36] And, by the end of 1987, the five hundred joint projects in scientific and technological cooperation, implemented under twenty-seven official protocols and agreements, amounted to $10 million to $20 million more a year.[37]

Private American institutions gave additional financial support to China. By the mid-1980s, foundations, corporations, and especially universities were providing nearly two-thirds of the fellowships for officially sponsored Chinese students and scholars in the United

States, amounting to approximately $80 million a year.[38] Americans complained that the Chinese government gave only minimal support to the students and scholars it was sending to the United States and expected them to acquire fellowships from American sources as soon after arriving as possible. But Americans paid nonetheless, and the fellowships they provided represented the largest source of direct American financial support for China's modernization and reform.

Important as they are, these quantitative measures cannot reflect the qualitative changes occurring in the Sino-American economic and cultural relationship. Ties between the two countries rapidly outgrew the facilitative mechanisms constructed in the 1970s and early 1980s. American trade with China was no longer conducted exclusively through the cumbersome central foreign trade organizations, but was undertaken with a much larger number of provincial and local trading companies, and even more directly with a limited but growing number of Chinese enterprises. Originally, it was anticipated that direct foreign investment in China would be channeled through equity joint ventures, as embodied in the pioneering Chinese legislation establishing such enterprises in 1979. As Chinese officials gradually realized that the equity joint venture was relatively unattractive to Americans and other foreigners, they became more flexible, permitting contractual joint ventures, wholly foreign-owned enterprises, and other more innovative forms of foreign investment.

Many of those American ventures began to have an impact on Chinese popular culture. Coca-Cola and Pepsi-Cola, originally bottled in China for sale to foreign tourists, soon penetrated the Chinese domestic market and became the favored soft drinks of young Chinese. Kentucky Fried Chicken opened, just off Tiananmen Square in Peking, its largest store anywhere, which soon became a social center for the youth of the city. Other American consumer goods manufactured in China, by companies such as Beatrice Foods, Johnson Wax, and Procter and Gamble, also began to establish niches in the Chinese domestic marketplace.

A similar process was occurring in the cultural and academic sphere. Immediately after normalization, as noted in chapter 3, many formal institutional relationships began to spring up to supplement the limited number of national organizations that had previously controlled the relationship. Thus, in the United States, the work of the Committee on Scholarly Communication with the People's Republic of China was supplemented by a growing number of university-to-university exchange arrangements, as well as by the protocols on scientific and technological cooperation signed by the Chinese and American governments. In the cultural realm, the exchanges organized by the National Committee on U.S.-China Relations were complemented by those arranged by an expanding network of relationships linking American state governments, professional associations, and cities with their Chinese counterparts.

In the mid-1980s, even these expanded arrangements began to prove too restrictive. A large proportion of the Chinese students and scholars coming to the United States did so as individuals rather than as part of any formal exchange program. Between 1984 and 1988, for example, of the 56,000 Chinese students and scholars who were issued visas to visit the United States, some 20,000, or 36 percent, were privately sponsored.[39] A growing number of American scholars made their own arrangements with Chinese colleagues to conduct research in the People's Republic of China. And more and more Americans visited China as individual tourists, not as members of organized tour groups.

For the first time since 1949, American foundations and exchange organizations began to establish a physical presence in China. The Committee on Scholarly Communication with the People's Republic of China opened an office in Peking in 1985 to facilitate the research of visiting American scholars and identify promising Chinese for exchange programs with the United States. The Ford Foundation inaugurated its own office three years later, to support Chinese research and training in law, economics, and international studies, and to conduct programs in economic development. In 1986, George Soros, a wealthy American entrepreneur born in Hungary, established a Fund for the Reform and Opening of China, in cooperation with the Chinese Economic System Reform Institute. The fund, with offices in New York and Peking, supported Chinese scholars on research tours abroad, funded conferences on economic and political issues, and gave grants to support research in culture and the social sciences. Soros also helped launch a new journal, *The Chinese Intellectual*, edited in New York but ultimately published in China as well, that provided a forum for young Chinese social scientists to exchange views on academic questions and policy issues.

Americans trained Chinese students and professionals in China, as well as in the United States. The Department of Commerce operated a management training center in Dalian, established in 1980, with formal degrees awarded by the State University of New York. The Johns Hopkins University inaugurated, with Nanjing University, a joint center for Chinese and American studies, providing Chinese students the opportunity to learn about the United States from American faculty teaching in English and offering American students courses on Chinese history, culture, and contemporary affairs taught by Chinese professors in the Chinese language. The Ford Foundation funded one-or two-semester courses on law and economics, conducted in China and taught by American and Chinese faculty. All of this activity was in addition to the thousands of Americans who taught at Chinese institutions, whether hired as foreign experts by the Chinese or supported by the U.S. government's Fulbright program.

As the forms of economic and cultural interactions became more diverse, they also began to penetrate more deeply into the two societies. Some of the Chinese students and scholars studying in the United States began to emerge from their classrooms and libraries to play additional roles: some as interns on Capitol Hill, some as employees of American banks and law firms, and at least one as a pizza deliveryman serving the Old Executive Office Building next to the White House. Other Chinese came to the United States to establish branch offices of Chinese trading companies, and some to make direct investments for firms back home. By 1987, Chinese direct investment in the United States totaled $58 million, in areas as diverse as forestry, steel, computers, restaurants, and real estate.[40]

Americans, too, played new roles in China. As the Chinese political climate became more relaxed, and as Chinese universities and research institutions more fully revived from the devastation of the Cultural Revolution, new opportunities for scholarly collaboration arose. It remained difficult for American scholars to work at local archives and archaeological sites, and anthropological fieldwork was still limited. But access to national archives and libraries improved, the Chinese opened one county in Shandong to sustained fieldwork by American scholars, and Americans with personal contacts with local governments and universities found it increasingly possible to conduct limited independent field research.

Equally significant, collaboration between American scholars and their Chinese counterparts increased. Bilateral academic conferences became more frequent, and the discussions at those meetings became more sophisticated and more open. The proceedings of several of those conferences were published, sometimes in both Chinese and English editions. It was increasingly possible for Americans and Chinese to review one another's manuscripts prior to publication and make suggestions for improvement. And Americans and Chinese began to explore the possibilities of truly collaborative research, in which they would work together on a common research agenda and publish the results jointly.

American culture penetrated China through the mass media, as well as through educational institutions. American popular music, including some in programs packaged by American producers and introduced by Ronald Reagan, filled the Chinese airwaves, with some broadcast in stereo over Chinese FM stations.[41] Cartoons starring *Mi Lao-shu* (Mickey Mouse) and *Tang Lao-ya* (Donald Duck), adventure shows such as "Hunter," and documentaries produced by the Chinese-American journalist Yue-sai Kan became the most popular shows on Chinese television and introduced their Chinese audiences either directly or indirectly to American values and institutions. Thousands of Chinese listened daily to the Voice of America—some to practice English, some to hear about developments in the United States, and some to obtain an outside perspective on developments in their own country. Contemporary American fiction, by such authors as Robert Ludlum, Danielle Steel, and Sidney Sheldon, became wildly popular in translation. Sheldon's *If Tomorrow Comes*, for example, was published in five different translations, sold half a million copies, and was serialized as a program on Radio Tianjin.[42]

For the United States, traditionally an open society, the emergence of a more diverse and penetrative relationship with China was considered a natural and inevitable product of the full normalization of Sino-American relations. For China, however, this kind of relationship was less familiar and less universally welcomed. The introduction of American culture into China gradually became regarded by some conservative leaders as a source of "spiritual pollution" that weakened the commitment of the Chinese people, particularly the nation's youth, to the values promulgated by the Chinese Communist Party. Although the expansion of economic and cultural ties between the two countries strengthened Sino-American relations in some ways, in others it would soon become a source of growing friction.

TAIWAN

Despite the agreement reached in August 1982 on American arms sales to Taipei, the Taiwan issue remained a potentially serious irritant in Sino-American relations. For several years, Chinese officials continued to describe it—sometimes in blunt language—as the principal obstacle to the smooth development of their relationship with the United States.[43] They pushed the United States to promote the reunification of China on Peking's terms, or at least to encourage Taiwan to agree to an expansion of economic, commercial, and cultural ties across the Taiwan Strait.[44] And Chinese specialists on American affairs warned that the differences in perspective between the two sides still made for a "potential crisis" over Taiwan.[45] Gradually, however, the two countries addressed the Taiwan issue with more forbearance and less acrimony. By 1988, the question of Taiwan no longer dominated Sino-American relations, and the two countries seemed to have worked out a modus operandi for dealing with it.

The main reason for this development was the evolving relationship between Taiwan and the mainland. Throughout the early 1980s, Peking unveiled a more flexible policy on the reunification of China that, while still unacceptable to Taiwan, helped create a more relaxed political climate in the Taiwan Strait. Taipei gradually came first to accept and then to promote the rapid expansion of unofficial and indirect economic and cultural ties with the mainland, which gave both sides a greater stake in a less confrontational relationship. Together, these changes in policy brought tensions between Taiwan and the mainland to their lowest level since 1949. And this relaxation, in turn, allowed the United States to disengage somewhat from the Taiwan issue, as Taiwan and the mainland developed a more extensive indirect dialogue than ever before.

China's more flexible policy was first evident in the nine-point program unveiled by Ye Jianying on September 30, 1981, the plan that had been conveyed by Zhao Ziyang to Ronald Reagan in their meeting at Cancun the following month.[46] Peking's proposal called for the inauguration of various cultural and economic exchanges between Taiwan and the mainland, and the initiation of negotiations between the Chinese Communist Party and the Kuomintang. Over the longer term, Ye envisioned a settlement under which Taiwan would accept the sovereignty of the People's Republic but would be permitted to maintain its own armed forces, continue its current economic and social systems, and send representatives to serve in the central government in Peking.

Although Chinese leaders refused to renounce the use of force against Taiwan, seeing the threat of invasion or blockade as one of their principal sources of leverage against Taiwan, they tried to find other ways of signaling peaceful intentions to Taipei. In the August 1982 communiqué with the United States on arms sales to Taiwan they reiterated their "fundamental policy" of "striving for peaceful reunification" of China. And, in less formal settings, Chinese spokesmen specified limited situations in which Peking would feel obliged to undertake military action against Taiwan, including a unilateral declaration of independence by the island, a strategic alignment between Taipei and some unfriendly foreign power (defined originally as the Soviet Union, but later increasingly as Japan), serious political instability on Taiwan, or a "protracted refusal to negotiate." By casting policy in these terms, Peking implied that it would not use force against Taiwan under any other conditions.[47]

Peking's nine-point plan was elaborated by Deng Xiaoping in 1983 in a conversation with a visiting Chinese-American scholar. Taiwan would become a special administrative region of the People's Republic, with a distinct political and economic system and a high degree of autonomy. The central government in Peking would have the authority to represent Taiwan internationally and presumably to guarantee the island's defense. But, under Deng's concept of "one country, two systems," Taiwan would continue to manage its domestic affairs and would enjoy the right to maintain its own armed forces and the right of final adjudication of legal matters. Taiwan would be permitted to send representatives to join the central government in Peking, but the central government would not dispatch any troops or civilian officials to Taiwan. Deng also acknowledged the difficulty of conducting government-to-government negotiations between Taipei and Peking, since Taiwan did not accept the mainland's demand that it be treated as a provincial-level government. To circumvent the problem, Deng again proposed that the reunification of China be discussed on an equal basis between the two great Chinese political parties, Communist and Nationalist.[48]

Moreover, these broad concepts were also embodied in the Sino-British agreement on the future of Hong Kong announced in September 1984. In that agreement, the two sides declared that Hong Kong would become a special administrative region of the People's Republic of China in 1997 but would retain a high degree of autonomy in all areas except defense and foreign affairs. Hong Kong would maintain its social and economic systems, enjoy representation in international economic organizations, preserve its legal and judicial systems, and have an elected legislature and chief executive. Although the Sino-British agreement was primarily intended to solve the problem posed by the expiration of the lease by which Britain held title to most of Hong Kong, it was also seen in Peking as a model for the eventual reunification of Taiwan and the mainland.[49]

The nine-point program did not produce any breakthrough in the political deadlock between Peking and Taipei. Officials in Taipei rejected Deng Xiaoping's notion of "one country, two systems." They insisted that, if China were to be reunified, it would have to be under the constitution of the Republic of China and the "three principles of the people" (the official ideology of the Kuomintang) rather than under any formula specified by the Communist Party. They also refused Deng's proposal for negotiations, saying that they would not engage in "contact, negotiation, or compromise" with Peking.

But in other ways the government on Taiwan proved more flexible, particularly by tolerating the rapid expansion of unofficial cultural and economic ties across the Taiwan Strait. In doing so, Taiwan's two principal leaders in the 1980s—Presidents Chiang Ching-kuo and Lee Teng-hui—responded to pressure from an emerging generation of political and commercial leaders on Taiwan who saw the advantages in building contacts with the mainland. Many of the island's young economic elite regarded the People's Republic as an attractive market for Taiwanese exports and potentially as a site for Taiwanese investment. Younger political leaders concluded that Taiwan's security could most effectively be ensured not simply by a strong national defense or a close relationship with the United States, but by a lasting reduction of tensions with the mainland. Many older Nationalist officials were more fearful of these contacts with Peking, on the grounds that they would give their Communist adversaries channels for subversion or levers of influence. But even they wanted the opportunity to visit the mainland in order to reestablish contact with their relatives or to see their native places before they died.

Thus, Taiwan's restrictions on unofficial economic and cultural ties with the mainland were gradually but steadily relaxed. Indirect trade, conducted principally through Hong Kong, grew from $320 million in 1980 to $1.1 billion in 1985, and then to $2.7 billion in 1988 (table A-8). Investment, also undertaken largely by Taiwanese dummy corporations headquartered in Hong Kong, soon followed, rising to about $450 million in 1988 (table A-9). Although most of these economic relationships involved the flow of capital and manufactured goods from Taiwan to the mainland, there was also a smaller reverse flow of commodities from the mainland to Taiwan, principally of raw materials and agricultural products. In 1984, Taipei agreed to a formula whereby teams from both Taiwan and the mainland could participate in the Olympic games in Los Angeles, with the team from Taiwan doing so under the name "Chinese Taipei." And two years later, the Taiwan government authorized scholars to participate in academic meetings alongside mainland representatives in third countries, particularly the United States and Japan.

Then, in an unusual incident in 1986, a Taiwan-based China Airlines cargo jet flying to Hong Kong was hijacked to Canton by its captain, who wanted to see his aging father on the mainland. The incident not only forced negotiations between officials of the two sides' airlines to secure the plane's return to Taiwan but also dramatized the desire of millions of people on Taiwan to be reunited with family members in the People's Republic. Bowing to such demands in 1987, Taipei authorized its citizens to travel to the mainland for family reunions, an opportunity grasped by 275,000 people by the end of that year, and by another 450,000 people in 1988 (table A-9). Although nominally restricted to this single humanitarian purpose, in reality such visits also provided occasions for economic, academic, and cultural contacts of a much broader sort. By 1988, Taiwanese sports teams were also visiting the mainland for competitions organized by international sports federations, under the same formula used for the 1984 Olympic games.

These developments in the relationship between Taiwan and the mainland did not eliminate Taiwan as an issue in Sino-American ties. The military relationship between the United States and Taiwan remained contentious with Peking. The United States continued to sell great quantities of arms to Taipei. By the measure most commonly used by the U.S. government (the total of commercial deliveries and foreign military sales agreements), the amount dropped by about $20 million a year, from $783 million in 1983 to $700 million in 1988. By a different measure (total commercial and FMS deliveries), however, the volume actually increased, from $473 million in 1983 to $683 million in 1988 (table A-10).

Moreover, as it had implied when the communiqué was issued, Washington reserved the right to sell to Taiwan more advanced equipment than it had provided earlier, especially when the original weaponry was no longer produced. Examples included the sale of Standard antiaircraft missiles in 1983, C-130 transport aircraft in 1984, and Chaparral ground-to-air missiles in 1985, all of which replaced obsolete equipment no longer carried in American inventories. Most important of all, the United States contributed to a program of technology transfer to Taiwan, which helped the island become more self-sufficient in the production of advanced weapons, including the fighter aircraft IDF (indigenous defense fighter) to supplement Taipei's fleet of aging F-104s and F-5Es, frigates, tanks, and surface-to-air, air-to-air, and naval surface-to-surface missiles, to enable it to control the airspace over the Taiwan Strait, secure the sea-lanes to and from Taiwan, and defend against any amphibious assault on the island.

Chinese analysts and officials protested these developments. They calculated that even if Washington reduced arms sales to Taiwan by $20 million a year, as by one measure it had since the 1982 agreement, it would take forty years to terminate arms sales to Taiwan. During the Reagan visit to China in April 1984, therefore, Chinese Foreign Minister Wu Xueqian suggested to Secretary of State Shultz that the annual reduction be increased from $20 million to $100 million.[50] First in press commentary, then in interviews with visiting American scholars, and finally during official visits to Washington, Chinese officials also criticized the transfer of American military production technology to Taiwan.[51] The U.S. government rejected both protests on the grounds that the 1982 communiqué had set no timetable for the reduction of American arms sales to Taipei and had dealt only with weaponry, not with production technology.[52]

Chinese officials were also concerned by what they regarded as tendencies toward independence on Taiwan and by the possibility that those trends might obtain American endorsement. As the liberalization of political life on Taiwan proceeded, and particularly after the legalization of opposition parties in 1986, more and more voices could be heard demanding self-determination for the people of Taiwan. The meaning of such calls, and the degree to which they attracted support, were difficult to judge. For many, the demand for self-determination was more a request for a more representative government on the island than a call for transforming Taiwan into a new sovereign nation, totally independent of the Chinese mainland. Public opinion polls indicated that, whether out of commitment to the principle of a single China or out of fear of the risks of a military response by Peking if independence were formally declared, only about 15 or 20 percent supported the concept of an independent Taiwan. Still, the occasional congressional resolutions expressing support for Taiwan's self-determination, such as the one introduced by Senator Claiborne Pell in 1983, persuaded worried Chinese observers that rising demands for independence would obtain American backing.[53] In late 1988, one of China's leading America specialists worried that, whereas China was committed to a policy of "peaceful reunification," the United States seemed to place greater emphasis on "peace" and less stress on "reunification."[54]

The Kuomintang also faced growing domestic pressure to create a place in international affairs for Taiwan that would be commensurate with its growing economic clout. In response to these demands, the Kuomintang unveiled a policy known as flexible diplomacy, under which Taiwan would, as possible, establish formal diplomatic ties with nations that simultaneously recognized Peking as well as Taipei, build unofficial economic and commercial links with Communist nations in Europe and Asia, upgrade unofficial ties with nations with which it could not establish diplomatic relations, and rejoin international organizations under such names as "Chinese Taipei" or "Taipei, China." This policy of flexible diplomacy alarmed Peking even more than the calls for self-determination, since it was sponsored by the ruling party on Taiwan. Gradually, Chinese analysts began to speculate that Lee Teng-hui, who assumed the presidency of Taiwan after the death of Chiang Ching-kuo in early 1988, was promoting what they characterized as "independence under the leadership of the Kuomintang."

Here, too, Peking was concerned about American intentions. There was little evidence that the United States was considering the reestablishment of diplomatic relations with Taipei. But there were signs that many Americans favored seeing Taiwan keep or regain membership in key international organizations. Congress adopted a resolution in 1983 in favor of Taipei retaining membership in the Asian Development Bank, and the Reagan admininstration informed other ADB members that it would reduce its contributions to the bank if Taiwan were expelled. There was increasing discussion in the United States of the desirability of Taiwan's membership in the GATT.[55] Moreover, the growing economic frictions between Taiwan and the United States, when issues such as expanding access to foreign markets and protecting American intellectual property rights were occupying a more central place in U.S. Asia policy more generally, may have led Washington to consider upgrading contacts with Taipei. According to some reports, shortly after taking office, the Bush administration contemplated holding cabinet-level discussions with Taiwan on economic issues, on the grounds that only contacts at so high a level could convince Taiwanese leaders of the intensity of American concern.

Despite these remaining problems, Taiwan was a remarkably muted issue in Sino-American relations in the late 1980s. The expansion of cultural and economic ties across the Taiwan Strait tended to ameliorate mainland concerns about an independent Taiwan, since that expansion pointed toward the reintegration of Taiwan and the mainland. It therefore reduced Peking's apprehensions about the continuing American commitment to the security of Taiwan, as reflected in U.S. transfer of military production technology to the island. And it obviated the need for Peking to press the United States to support the expansion of civilian contacts between Taiwan and the mainland, as it had done during the Reagan visit to Peking in

1984. Moreover, Lee Teng-hui's consolidation of power in Taipei, together with his commitment to a one-China policy, appeared largely to satisfy Peking that pressures for independence would be kept within limits and that the Taiwanese political system would remain basically stable.

Restatements of American policy in the mid-1980s also enhanced Peking's satisfaction with Washington's attitude toward the Taiwan issue. During his visit to Peking in February 1983, Secretary of State Shultz, in an effort to "rebuild mutual trust and confidence," promised the Chinese the United States would "faithfully carry out the policies" it had enunciated in the August 17 communiqué and the other bilateral communiqués that dealt with Taiwan.[56] In October 1985, in a televised interview provided by the U.S. Information Agency, Defense Secretary Weinberger called for an agreement between Taiwan and the mainland that would be mutually beneficial and mutually acceptable.[57] During a subsequent visit to China in March 1987, Secretary of State Shultz said the United States "welcome[d] developments, including indirect trade and increasing people-to-people interchange, which have contributed to a relaxation of tensions in the Taiwan Strait." He added that the United States also supported a "continuing, evolutionary process toward peaceful resolution of the Taiwan question" and declared that it was American policy to "foster an environment within which such developments can continue to take place."[58] The United States was still not prepared to support Chinese calls for direct postal, transportation, and commercial linkages across the Taiwan Strait or to endorse Peking's concept of "one country, two systems." But Washington was willing to express approval of the growing contacts between Taiwan and the mainland and to reiterate its interest in a peaceful outcome acceptable to both sides.

These statements apparently convinced Peking that the United States was prepared to accept the peaceful reunification of Taiwan and the mainland. They therefore provided a more favorable context for the remaining disagreements between the two countries over American arms sales to Taiwan, congressional resolutions on self-determination, and American endorsement of a more active role for Taiwan in international organizations. Indeed, one Chinese scholar has privately mentioned an internal policy paper, presented in the mid-1980s, that accepted the desirability of continued American arms sales to Taiwan, on the grounds that the Kuomintang would approach negotiations with the Communist Party with greater confidence if it were certain of its defense capabilities and that the termination of American arms sales to the island would reduce

American influence in Taipei and might lead to a resurgence of the Taiwan independence movement.

In short, as China's confidence in the consistency of American policy and its hope for expanded economic and cultural relations with Taiwan grew, it viewed the remaining U.S. ties with Taipei with more equanimity. By 1989, it appeared that the Taiwan issue was no longer an immediate obstacle to stable relations between China and the United States. As President George Bush noted during his visit to Peking in February 1989, the two countries had "found ways to address the Taiwan issue constructively and without rancor."[59] What once had been the principal irritant to Sino-American relations had now become a symbol of the two countries' ability to manage controversial issues successfully.

STRATEGIC RELATIONS

As China and the United States reached a mutual accommodation on the Taiwan question, the prospects for renewing the strategic relationship between the two countries steadily improved. Secretary of Defense Weinberger's visit to Peking in September 1983 marked the resumption of Sino-American strategic cooperation after a two-year hiatus. For the next four years, through 1987, strategic relations between the two countries would experience what one American officer directly involved in military ties with China has described as "steady development."[60]

American officials in the mid-1980s saw a complex rationale for expanding a military relationship with China. A strong China, loosely aligned with the United States, was still viewed as an important counterweight to Soviet power. Peking could reinforce the West's overall deterrent posture if it were willing to endorse NATO's defense preparations, American military deployments in the western Pacific, and the strengthening of the mutual security treaty between the United States and Japan. Cooperation between the United States and China could also help promote a Soviet withdrawal from Afghanistan and the removal of Vietnamese forces from Cambodia, particularly if the two countries could work together to supply resistance forces there.

Furthermore, Sino-American military cooperation would force Soviet planners to face the possibility that a second front would open along the Sino-Soviet frontier if Moscow launched an offensive in another part of the world. In that way, China fit well into the broader

American strategy of horizontal escalation, according to which a war begun by the Soviet Union in one theater (presumably Central Europe or the Middle East) would be extended into another theater (presumably Northeast Asia) so as to overstretch Soviet military capabilities. As one Defense Department official put it in early 1984, "The existence of a stable, long-term US-PRC strategic relationship of itself increases deterrence by making the Soviet Union less confident that it could neutralize China and thus free its Asian forces for use elsewhere."[61]

In addition, a strategic relationship with Peking was regarded as an important way of strengthening American ties with China as a whole. As in the late 1970s, the military was seen as a powerful factor in Chinese politics that would play an important role in determining China's future domestic and foreign policies. For that reason, it would be highly desirable for the United States to give the Chinese army a direct stake in a beneficial relationship with the United States by offering it access to American strategic and tactical doctrine, management practices, production technology, and weapons. Moreover, many American officials argued that a "comprehensive relationship" with China—one that included military as well as civilian components—would be more stable than one restricted to nonmilitary facets. Indeed, to deny Peking access to American military technology could well be interpreted as evidence that the United States still treated China as a potential enemy. And that in turn might become a "self-fulfilling prophecy" if China responded by dealing with the United States in an adversarial manner.[62]

Chinese motives for engaging in a strategic relationship with the United States were never presented in such detail during this period. Peking's public statements on the subject mostly focused on why China would not engage in what Zhao Ziyang called a "comprehensive security relationship" with the Americans. A quasi-alliance with the United States, Chinese leaders feared, might entangle their country in a Soviet-American confrontation. It would run the risk of increasing China's dependence on the United States and thus reduce leverage over Washington on such controversial bilateral issues as Taiwan. By alienating Moscow, it might forestall an eventual reduction of tension between China and the Soviet Union. At the least, even the appearance of an alliance with the United States would cost China its standing in the third world as a major independent power, without strategic ties to either superpower.

But Chinese leaders also indicated that their rejection of a comprehensive security relationship with the United States did not preclude more limited military cooperation. Strategic consultation with the

United States could identify ways in which the two countries could undertake parallel actions to resist Soviet expansion in areas in which China had important interests. Exchanges of personnel could increase China's understanding of American military doctrine, organization, and technology. And, perhaps most important, the purchase of American electronic equipment and weapons systems could help promote the modernization of China's armed forces. Even if no agreements were reached, negotiations of potential arms imports could give Chinese military officers important information about advanced American technology.

Peking's interest in reviving military ties with the United States in the mid-1980s also reflected disappointment in the evolution of Sino-Soviet relations. After Brezhnev's speech at Tashkent in August 1982, the Chinese had responded that the full normalization of their relations with Moscow would require progress in removing what they identified as the "three obstacles" to Sino-Soviet ties: the massive deployments of Soviet forces along the Sino-Soviet frontier, the Soviet intervention in Afghanistan, and the Kremlin's support of Vietnamese ambitions in Indochina. Peking had hoped that a shifting international balance of power in favor of the United States would encourage Soviet leaders to make accommodations on these issues to gain the strategic benefits of an improved relationship with China. But, as in earlier years, the Soviet response proved disappointing. Brezhnev's successors, Andropov and Chernenko, indicated that they would be willing to negotiate various bilateral confidence measures along the Sino-Soviet frontier, including a nonaggression pact, a nuclear-free zone, or an agreement on a mutual reduction of forces. However, like Brezhnev before them, they steadfastly refused to discuss any issue involving a third country, a principle that prevented them from addressing the situation in Afghanistan or Cambodia, or the presence of Soviet forces in Mongolia.[63]

Moreover, in some ways the Soviet threat to China worsened in the mid-1980s. The emplacement of Soviet SS-20 missiles in the Far East placed much of China within range of nuclear attack. The deployment of Tu-16 bombers at Cam Ranh Bay also was viewed in Peking as a significant threat to Chinese shipping, to Chinese positions in the South China Sea, and to Chinese military installations in southern China.[64] And, with Soviet support, the Vietnamese intervention in Cambodia was still escalating. Hanoi's offensives during the winter dry seasons of 1983–84 and 1984–85 led to clashes between Vietnamese and Thai troops along Thailand's border with Cambodia. China responded by pledging support to Thailand, threatening retaliation against Vietnam, and conducting skirmishes along the Sino-Vietnamese frontier. All in all, there was little evidence that China's announcement of an independent foreign policy in 1982 had evoked any conciliatory response from either the Soviet Union or Vietnam.

Based on calculations such as these, Sino-American security relations developed along four dimensions in the mid-1980s. The first involved high-level consultations among military and civilian officials from the two countries. Although there had been exchanges of defense ministers earlier—Harold Brown to China in 1980, Geng Biao to the United States later the same year, and Weinberger to Peking in 1983—the dialogue was carried out with greater intensity after 1983. Defense Minister Zhang Aiping and Yang Shangkun, the ranking vice chairman of the Party's Central Military Commission, reciprocated Weinberger's visit. In addition, the two countries' chiefs of staff, the commanders of the major military services, and the American civilian service secretaries exchanged visits. Regular discussions between the American secretary of state and the Chinese foreign minister in Peking and Washington, supplemented by their encounters at the annual fall meetings of the United Nations General Assembly in New York, also were part of this expanded strategic dialogue.

Results of such consultations are difficult to assess. The two sides certainly reviewed developments in Cambodia and Afghanistan and agreed to continue to use diplomatic channels to demand the withdrawal of Vietnamese and Soviet forces from those two countries. Peking and Washington coordinated military assistance to the Afghan resistance, with the United States beginning around 1983 to purchase Chinese weapons for supply to the *mujaheddin*.[65] The two countries worked together at the United Nations to ensure that Cambodia's seat would continue to be occupied by the anti-Vietnamese coalition headed by Prince Sihanouk. China and the United States also discussed developments on the Korean peninsula, with China helping arrange the inauguration of low-level diplomatic contacts between the American and North Korean embassies in Peking.

Negotiations on intermediate-range nuclear forces (INF) produced even more concrete results. At the beginning of negotiations with the Soviet Union on this issue, the United States seemed willing to envision a solution that withdrew such weapons from Europe but left some of them deployed in Asia. China and Japan objected to that outcome and persuaded the United States to work toward a double-zero formula, whereby the United States and the Soviet Union would dismantle all their INF forces in the European and Asian theaters. This formula was finally part of the INF agreement signed by Moscow and Washington in late 1987.

Second, China and the United States continued to share intelligence on Soviet military capabilities. As noted earlier, two electronic monitoring stations designed to track Soviet missile tests were established in western China in 1980. Thereafter, nine seismographic monitoring sites were constructed in China between 1984 and 1987 to assess Soviet underground nuclear tests, again with the data shared by the Chinese and American governments.[66] Moreover, Peking sold several Chinese F-7 fighters to the United States for training purposes. Since the F-7 was originally modeled after the MIG-21, it could be used to educate American officers about the design and capability of Soviet aircraft.[67]

The third dimension of Sino-American strategic cooperation involved the expansion of working-level exchanges between the two military establishments.[68] The two countries' national defense universities established programs to exchange visiting scholars, professors, and library materials and to host bilateral conferences and visiting delegations to discuss important international issues. China and the United States also traded delegations in specialized fields such as logistics, manpower, and military medicine. The American navy made two port calls to China, one in 1986 and one in 1989, and the Chinese navy reciprocated with a visit to Hawaii in 1989 by one of its training vessels. Although the Chinese would not agree to anything that resembled a joint exercise, they did accept an American proposal for ships of the two navies to pass each other in review on the high seas in January 1986, and Chinese officers paid a visit to an American aircraft carrier, the USS *Nimitz*, operating in international waters in February 1989.[69]

For the most part, these working-level exchanges went smoothly, but the naval port calls occasioned some difficult negotiations. Like several other countries, China was unwilling to allow American ships armed with nuclear weapons to visit its harbors. The American navy, however, maintained its policy of refusing to confirm or deny that specific ships carried atomic devices. The two sides reached an understanding on the issue in early 1985, with the United States proposing to send a small squadron of conventionally powered ships that would be unlikely to carry nuclear weapons. Unfortunately, when asked about the visit prior to a trip to Australia and New Zealand a few months later, Hu Yaobang, failing to distinguish between nuclear-powered and nuclear-armed vessels, declared that the United States had agreed not to send ships armed with nuclear weapons.[70] Washington felt compelled to deny this statement and the vessels' visit was postponed until November 1986.

Finally, the most controversial element of Sino-American military cooperation was the program of American arms sales to China. Before 1984, the two sides had been engaged in inconclusive discussions of the issue, with the Chinese presenting long shopping lists of weapons they wanted to buy and the Americans replying with a shorter list of the items they were willing to sell. Essentially, the Chinese wanted the United States to tell them in advance which weapons systems and defense-related technologies would be approved for export, whereas the United States wanted firm commitments from Peking on what it wanted to buy, after which applications for export licenses could be considered for approval.[71] Moreover, China wanted to acquire American production technology so that it could manufacture its own equipment, whereas the United States wanted to sell finished products to China to minimize the diversion of its technology and to maximize corporate earnings. Given the differences in interests and perspective, the earlier discussions of arms sales had created disappointment and disillusionment on both sides: the Chinese concluded that the Americans would never agree to sell, and the Americans suspected that the Chinese would never decide to buy. Few sales had taken place.

During Weinberger's visit in 1983, Washington and Peking agreed to a new, more productive approach. On the basis of previous Chinese requests, and after consideration of the kinds of weapons the United States would be prepared to transfer to China, the U.S. secretary of defense proposed that the two countries identify several types of military operation to be the focus of their cooperative activities. By the end of 1985, four such mission areas had been agreed to: antitank warfare, artillery and artillery defense, air defense, and antisubmarine warfare. These four areas, all meant to be clearly defensive, provided the parameters within which weapons sales could be discussed.[72] Conversely, the United States made it clear that it would not cooperate with China in six other mission areas, including nuclear weapons and the systems for delivering them, electronic warfare, surface-ship antisubmarine warfare, intelligence, power projection, and air superiority.

In mid-1984, China was made eligible for the FMS program, enabling Peking to purchase American weapons through the U.S. government, with access to official financing. In the next several years the United States and China made several agreements on arms sales and technology transfer. In the category of antitank warfare, the countries agreed to coproduce TOW line-guided missiles, although not the state-of-the-art model. In the area of artillery and artillery defense, they agreed on the export of American counterbattery radar and U.S. assistance in the production of large-caliber fuses and detonators. To strengthen China's antisubmarine capabilities, the United States and China agreed to coproduce an antisubmarine torpedo capable of being launched by surface vessels. And China's air defense was to be modernized by joint development of a more advanced avionics system to be installed in fifty Chinese F-8 fighters. These four programs spurred a rapid increase in American arms deliveries to China, from $8.0 million in fiscal 1984 to $106.2 million in fiscal 1989 (table A-11).

Of all these projects, the largest and most controversial was the project, known as Peace Pearl, to upgrade Chinese interceptor aircraft. Even with the advanced American equipment installed, some critics argued, the Chinese aircraft would still not be a match for the Soviet fighters they were intended to counter. At the same time, other opponents of the program warned that the upgraded Chinese fighters would be able to challenge Taipei's ability to preserve air superiority over the Taiwan Strait unless the United States were willing to provide comparable avionics to Taiwan.[73] In response, the Reagan administration noted that the process of designing, manufacturing, and installing the avionics equipment for the F-8s would require six years, during which Taiwan would be able to reequip its aircraft with similar electronic gear. It also reassured critics by revealing some of the details of its program for assisting Taiwan in the development of a new fighter, the so-called indigenous defense fighter or IDF.[74] In the end, the administration prevailed, and Congress failed to enact proposed legislation disapproving the avionics sale to the People's Republic.[75]

As the strategic relationship between the two countries expanded, some American analysts inside and outside the government began to explore additional avenues for military cooperation with China. The ideas under consideration included agreements for the deployment of American tactical air force units on Chinese bases near Vladivostok, the development of joint early warning and air defense systems, and the right for American aircraft carrying supplies for the Afghan rebels to overfly China and refuel at Chinese bases on their way to Pakistan. Most of these options remained topics for casual discussion rather than proposals for formal presentation to Peking. And, had they been officially proposed to the Chinese, they probably would have encountered resistance from the Foreign Ministry, which feared that such possibilities would tie China too closely to the United States and obstruct a possible improvement of relations with the Soviet Union. But the proposals remain significant because they reflect the mood of the mid-1980s: a sense that Sino-American relations had not yet realized their full potential and that the main task of analysis was to identify the possibilities for further cooperation.

AMERICAN EUPHORIA

Indeed, during the mid-1980s American euphoria about developments in China reached its zenith. Public attitudes about China, which turned positive just after the normalization of Sino-American relations in 1978, continued to improve. In the mid-1980s, according to the Gallup polls, about 70 percent of the public had favorable impressions of China, against 21 percent who did so just before normalization (table A-1). In 1986, according to another survey, nearly two-thirds of Americans said that they "liked" China, compared with only one-third in 1977. The quadrennial polls conducted by the Chicago Council on Foreign Relations showed that the "warmth" Americans felt toward China peaked in 1986 at fifty-three degrees, up from forty-four degrees in 1978 and forty-seven degrees in 1982.[76]

Although these public opinion polls are suggestive, the clearest evidence of the emerging exhilaration about China can be found in American press coverage of the country and occasionally in the statements of American political leaders. Throughout the mid-1980s, each important breakthrough in Chinese economic reform was followed by a new wave of enthusiasm in the American press, and each new sign of relaxation in China's political and social life was avidly chronicled. The conclusion was not only that the prospects for American economic relations with China were good, but that China was rapidly transforming itself in the direction of greater capitalism and democracy. The disillusionment with China so prevalent in the early 1980s was now swept away by a tide of favorable coverage of China's economic and political reform.

One of the first measures of this positive reassessment of China was the newspaper articles on domestic developments in China written as background for the Reagan visit in April 1984. The *Wall Street Journal* described Deng Xiaoping as struggling hard to "modernize China's backward economy" and declared that he had achieved some "stunning changes" at an unexpectedly rapid pace. The *New York Times* added that Reagan would "see a country that little resembles the Spartan Maoist garrison state visited by President Nixon in 1972 and President Ford in 1975." China had already traveled a "startling distance toward prosperity and self-respect," the *Times* reported, and Deng had given notice that "the nation's transformation is barely under way."[77]

A succession of dramatic domestic developments in China in 1984 and 1985 reinforced that image. The urban reform program adopted by the Central Committee of the Communist Party in October 1984 was widely interpreted in the United States as a radical turn toward free markets, material incentives, and private ownership. The *Wall Street Journal* said the plan could be "summarized in five words: You ain't seen nothin' yet. It is laced with enough free-market, supply-and-demand, anti-welfare, get-the-government-off-our-backs rhetoric to sound at times like an old Ronald Reagan campaign speech." Reports such as these acknowledged that the process of economic restructuring would be difficult and that Chinese leaders were still placing some ideological limits on their reforms. But they implied that those doctrinal restrictions were relics that would soon be abandoned. "The most common argument [in China] these days," the *Wall Street Journal* reassured readers, was that "China is a social-ist state; therefore, everything it does is by definition socialist." A few weeks later, the title of a cover story in *Business Week* on China's economic reform drew the obvious and welcome conclusion that Americans were now witnessing the reemergence of "capitalism in China."[78]

At the end of 1984, an editorial in the *People's Daily* acknowledged that ideology could not solve China's present-day problems and advo-cated a more pragmatic approach to economic development and reform. Although the editorial was corrected several days later to state only that ideology could not solve *all* of China's current prob-lems, the original text had already made an impact on American perceptions of China. William Safire wrote in the *New York Times* that the "big event of 1984" was the "rejection of Marxism" and the "embrace of capitalism" by the Chinese Communist Party. The *Wall Street Journal* noted this was "the first time any Marxist government has dismissed Marx so directly," but declared it was "not surprising" that such "practical folk" as the Chinese would be "the first to announce that the commissar has no clothes." *Fortune* implied China had therefore entered not only its post-Mao period but also a post-Marx era, entitling one story "China after Marx: Open for Business?"[79]

In 1985, reports of Chinese beauty pageants, rock music, discos, makeup, fashion, and golf courses—as well as reports of the return of corruption and prostitution—added to the impression that China was undergoing sweeping change. The adoption of new economic reforms in September, embodied in the new five-year plan covering the period 1986–90, produced yet another wave of excitement. To be sure, *Time* magazine noted, the loosening of administrative controls over the economy was creating problems, such as "corruption, large-scale fraud and considerable uncertainty." Nor did the reforms mean "China is about to embrace capitalism full tilt." On balance, however, the assessment of China's future was so optimistic that the magazine named Deng man of the year for 1985, the second time it had done so since his return to power in 1977.[80]

Paradoxically, the country's periodic episodes of economic retrenchment and political consolidation only reinforced the perception that the process of reform in China was irreversible. Each such episode caused some concern in the United States, especially the slower rates of economic growth in 1981 and 1982 and the campaign against "spiritual pollution" in 1983 and 1984. But when each effort at retrenchment was followed by a renewed commitment to economic and political liberalization, the logical conclusion was that China's reforms were tracing an upward spiral in which each reversal would be minor and temporary and in which the principal trend would be continued advance. As Anthony Lewis of the *New York Times* wrote from China in August 1985, "Where will it stop? How can it stop"?[81]

These dramatic developments in China activated American interest of long historical standing and deep emotional resonance. As China proceeded down the path of economic and political reform in the mid-1980s, there was a growing sense in the United States that China might be abandoning communism in favor of freedom. As a postrevolutionary society, America traditionally sought to export its ideas and institutions abroad and often saw China as a promising target for transformation. The tendency, therefore, was to exaggerate the Chinese reforms by concluding that Chinese leaders, without saying so openly, were renouncing Marx, adopting free markets, promoting private enterprise, and even fostering democracy.

Reagan, returning from China in early May 1984, was one of the first prominent Americans to express this conclusion. Stopping over in Anchorage, Alaska, on his way back to Washington, the president denied it was necessary to "impose our form of government" on other countries but implied that political liberalization was already beginning to occur in what he described as "so-called Communist China." The encouragement of market forces and private ownership "has already enlivened the Chinese economy," Reagan pointed out. He claimed that these economic reforms were also having significant political consequences, in that they had "opened a way to a more just society." When asked about Reagan's reaction to the portraits of Marx and Engels that had been erected in Tiananmen Square for the May Day ceremonies on the morning of his departure from Peking, White House spokesman Larry Speakes joked that the president "thought they were the Smith Brothers."[82] Together, these statements left the clear impression that Reagan believed China was beginning to adopt American values, and official invocations of Marxism and communism were now little more than platitudes.

This euphoria about China was not primarily the responsibility of academic specialists on the country. They, like many other Americans, were excited about the potential for change in China, but they tended to underscore the limited vision of Chinese leaders, the resistance to reform generated by the Party and state bureaucracies, and the various problems and contradictions that economic and political liberalization were likely to create. For example, Michel Oksenberg and Kenneth Lieberthal of the University of Michigan, two of the most prominent American scholars of contemporary China, wrote in 1986 that the probability of successful reform, which they defined as the smooth completion of the economic and political reforms then being contemplated, was only about 35 to 40 percent.[83] Jan Prybyla, a specialist at the Pennsylvania State University on comparative socialist economies, consistently warned that ideological preconceptions, political resistance, and economic contradictions could threaten the viability of China's reform program.[84]

Rather, certain conservative American intellectuals and commentators, seeing in developments in China a vindication of their contempt for communism and their faith in free markets, were the people who seemed the most convinced that China was inexorably embarked on the road to capitalism. It was, after all, William Safire and the editorial writers of the *Wall Street Journal*—not liberal China specialists in the universities—who concluded that China had repudiated Marx and embraced capitalism. And, in an article designed to debunk the "fantasies" of the "believing sinologists," one critic unintentionally revealed that the real problem lay elsewhere: "In the Orwellian year of 1984, a Chinese émigré scholar who was invited to an international conservative conference on communism found that his presence was a meaningless formality. For the participants, China was already a solved problem of communism; it was 'going capitalist' and [was] no longer a threat to the West."[85] The view that China had renounced communism in favor of capitalism was indeed a myth. But that myth was a conservative fantasy, not a liberal one.

CHAPTER 6

Storm Clouds

AS Sino-American relations began to recover from the mutual disenchantment of the early 1980s, other changes in the international sphere gave relations between the two countries a new volatility. With the emergence of Mikhail Gorbachev, Soviet policy toward China and the United States began to change rapidly. Although welcomed in Peking and Washington, the "new thinking" in Soviet foreign policy simultaneously removed much of the impetus for a strategic relationship between China and the United States. As the common threat posed by the Soviet Union declined, the differences in perspective between Peking and Washington on global and regional issues—particularly on Cambodia, nuclear nonproliferation, and Chinese arms sales to the Middle East—assumed a larger role in their strategic relationship.

The rapid expansion of the cultural and economic ties between China and the United States also introduced new problems and contradictions into their bilateral relationship. In a way, Sino-American relations began to fall victim to the incomplete character of economic reform. China's economy had been restructured enough to stimulate a rapid expansion of Chinese exports to the United States, but not enough to satisfy American demands for access to the domestic Chinese market or for a more hospitable climate for foreign investment. Chinese educational and scientific institutions had been reformed enough to permit many Chinese students and scholars to engage in graduate studies and conduct advanced research in the United States, but not enough to encourage them to return home once their programs were completed.

The partial quality of political reform in China also began to undermine Sino-American relations. Paradoxically, as China moved slowly and haltingly to liberalize, its remaining violations of human rights became increasingly apparent to foreign observers. At the same time, the relaxation of controls over the press and over academic life permitted the emergence of China's first political dissident community, who began to criticize the corrupt and unresponsive character of the Chinese government and demand more energetic political reform. Together, American human rights activists and Chinese dissidents joined in denouncing various aspects of the political situation in China. As a result, human rights became a serious issue in U.S.-China relations for the first time since normalization.

By late 1988, therefore, the prospects for Sino-American relations were uncertain. Some observers were optimistic, arguing that the great expansion of economic, cultural, and military ties in the mid-1980s had created a much more extensive, much more institutionalized, and therefore much more stable, relationship. There would doubtless be disagreements between Peking and Washington on a wide range of subjects. But the way in which the two countries had successfully defused the Taiwan issue gave confidence that other problems too could be addressed in a calm and pragmatic manner.

However, other analysts, Chinese and American, were less confident of the stability of U.S.-China relations. One of the underpinnings of the relationship, the anti-Soviet rationale, was rapidly being removed. Another, commercial and academic ties between the two countries, was becoming increasingly contentious. To a degree, the Sino-American relationship now rested on the fate of reform in China, but that process too was encountering growing difficulties. As a result, as the two countries celebrated the tenth anniversary of the normalization of their relations in late 1988, there were serious trepidations in some quarters that, over the horizon, the storm clouds were gathering.

THE DECLINE OF THE ANTI-SOVIET RATIONALE

The hostility between China and the Soviet Union in the 1960s was a great stimulus for the rapprochement between the United States and China and the full normalization of Sino-American diplomatic ties. The threat of a Soviet attack on China, implicit in the enunciation of the Brezhnev Doctrine in 1968 and symbolized by the clashes along the Sino-Soviet border in 1969, had encouraged the initial contacts that led to the Nixon visit of 1972. The common perception of an expansionist Soviet Union, extending its influence into Africa, the Middle East, and Southeast Asia in the mid-1970s, had encouraged the completion of Sino-American diplomatic relations in 1978. Soviet support for the Vietnamese invasion of Cambodia, and the Kremlin's direct intervention in Afghanistan, had been an important rationale for the expansion of Sino-American strategic relations in the 1980s.

But leaders in Peking had, at least since the mid-1970s, always been interested in exploring the prospects for a more accommodative Soviet policy toward China. As noted earlier, Chinese officials made overtures to the Kremlin in 1977 and 1978 (when they restored higher-level diplomatic contacts with the Soviet Union), in 1979 (when they reopened negotiations on the improvement of Sino-Soviet relations), and again in 1982 (when they announced an independent foreign policy and forswore an alliance with the United States). In each case, however, they were disappointed by the reluctance of Brezhnev and his successors to make any great concessions on issues of vital concern to Peking. Because of this failure, and because of Soviet expansionism in Asia, Africa, and the Middle East, Sino-Soviet relations never significantly improved.

But China did not give up. To encourage a more accommodating Soviet policy, Peking made another set of conciliatory gestures to Moscow even before Gorbachev's accession to the leadership in 1985. Ever since 1982, China had set three conditions for what it called the normalization of Sino-Soviet relations: the withdrawal of Soviet forces from Afghanistan, an end to the Vietnamese intervention in Cambodia, and a reduction of Soviet military deployments along the Sino-Soviet border. Without departing from this formula, in 1983 and 1984 Chinese officials began to define the term "normalization" more narrowly than in the past. By normalization, they now said, they meant the restoration of party-to-party and military-to-military relations, meetings between the two countries' foreign ministers, cooperation on international issues, and summit meetings between top Soviet and Chinese leaders. Conversely, they would be prepared to revive their cultural, scientific, and economic relations with the Soviet Union without any political conditions.[1]

On this basis, Sino-Soviet relations improved considerably between 1983 and 1985.[2] Trade between the two countries rose rapidly in the mid-1980s, although from a low base, with Peking accepting a Soviet offer to modernize some of the factories that Moscow had helped to construct in China in the 1950s. Exchanges of tourists, journalists, scholars, and even parliamentary delegations gradually revived. Although contacts between Chinese and Soviet officials remained restricted, China found ways of restoring high-level contacts under the guise of resuming economic relations. The establishment of a joint commission on economic and scientific cooperation created a mechanism that permitted Soviet Vice Premier Ivan Arkhipov to visit China in late 1984 and allowed Chinese Vice Premier

Yao Yilin to make a reciprocal trip to the Soviet Union the following year. All these developments seemed related to the broader purpose of expanding China's foreign economic relations to promote the country's domestic development and reform.

Moreover, Peking began to hint that the normalization of political relations with Moscow could occur without the full removal of all three of the obstacles it had earlier identified. By early 1985, Chinese officials were saying they would be prepared to respond positively if the Soviet Union addressed but one of Peking's three conditions. There was, for a time, some confusion about which obstacle was of greatest concern to China: some leaders suggested the buildup of Soviet forces along their common border, whereas others implied that Moscow's support for the Vietnamese invasion of Cambodia most dismayed Peking.[3] Deng Xiaoping, however, stated that Indochina was the critical issue, and he even indicated that China would be prepared to pay a price for a Soviet concession. In April 1985, he said China could accept Soviet bases in Vietnam if the Cambodian issue were settled, and in September he conveyed through Romania the private message that he would be prepared to attend a summit meeting in Moscow if China's terms on Cambodia were met.[4]

China's policy was soon vindicated with the rise of Mikhail Gorbachev in 1985. Strategically, Gorbachev began speaking of a "sufficient defense" and of a purely "defensive defense," in ways that foreshadowed a new willingness to consider arms control agreements with the Soviet Union's military rivals and unilateral reductions of Soviet military deployments. Economically, Gorbachev not only called for *perestroika* in the Soviet domestic economy but also proposed an expansion of Soviet foreign economic relations and a closer integration of the Soviet Union with the rest of the world. Ideologically, Gorbachev and his advisers repudiated proletarian internationalism as the guiding principle of Soviet foreign policy and declared that decisions would henceforth be made without reference to the "class character" of other societies. Together, these new tenets of foreign policy set the stage for a significant reduction of tensions in the bilateral relations between the Soviet Union and the other major powers and for more concerted efforts to resolve the regional conflicts in which the Kremlin had become involved.[5]

In keeping with this general approach, in July 1986 Gorbachev finally began to adjust Soviet policy toward China in ways that met some of China's preconditions. In a speech at Vladivostok, he reiterated his predecessors' proposals for an expansion of bilateral ties, including the acceptance of China's interpretation of the location of the riverine boundaries between the two countries.[6] But, unlike either Brezhnev, Andropov, or Chernenko, Gorbachev promised to take steps that would partially remove two of the three obstacles to improve Sino-Soviet relations. First, he announced the withdrawal of six Soviet regiments from Afghanistan. Although this decision was directed more at domestic audiences and at the United States than at China, it did address one of the three issues that Peking had said were obstructing Sino-Soviet ties. Gorbachev also promised to ease a second obstacle by unilaterally removing a large portion, later set at 75 percent, of Soviet forces from Mongolia, and by offering to negotiate a mutual and balanced reduction of the remaining forces along the Sino-Soviet frontier. More generally, Gorbachev gave China pride of place in his speech at Vladivostok—a rhetorical posture that contrasted with the American tendency to stress Japan, rather than China, in official discussions of Asian policy.

Chinese leaders responded cautiously to Gorbachev's speech at Vladivostok. While welcoming many of the Soviet leader's initiatives, they also cautioned that they would wait to see if his pledges were translated into concrete actions. Peking questioned the importance of several of Gorbachev's concessions, belittling the size of the promised troop withdrawals from Afghanistan and noting that Soviet forces removed from Mongolia could be easily and quickly redeployed. Chinese officials also made clear that the one obstacle on which Gorbachev had failed to make any concessions, Cambodia, remained the one of greatest interest to Peking. Moreover, by receiving Defense Secretary Caspar Weinberger in Peking in October 1986, only two months after Gorbachev's speech at Vladivostok, China emphasized it would not sacrifice its strategic relationship with the United States for the sake of rapprochement with the Soviet Union.

Gorbachev was therefore unable to achieve any further progress in Sino-Soviet relations until he took further initiatives that addressed Peking's interests. In April 1988, in the Geneva accords on Afghanistan, the Soviet Union agreed to the complete removal of its military forces from that country. And finally, in the fall of 1988, Gorbachev began to accept Chinese demands that Moscow press for a full and unconditional Vietnamese withdrawal from Cambodia, in return for Peking's willingness to accept curbs on the role of the Khmer Rouge in a political settlement.[7] These changes in the Kremlin's position permitted a meeting between the Chinese and Soviet foreign ministers in Moscow in December. In the winter of 1988, in a speech to the United Nations, Gorbachev announced the unilateral reduction of Soviet forces; 200,000 men were to be withdrawn from the Far East, and an additional 60,000 would be pulled from central Asia.[8] Within a month, the Vietnamese announced that all their forces would be removed from Cambodia by September 1989. These actions permitted a subsequent foreign ministers' meeting in Peking in February 1989, at which it was announced that Gorbachev would visit China in May.

Initially, many of these developments were viewed with some concern in the United States. By early 1986, noting the improvement in Sino-Soviet relations, American analysts were debating whether Chinese foreign policy had changed and what the implications for the United States might be.[9] Some were sanguine, on the grounds that a reduction of tensions between China and the Soviet Union would contribute to the resolution of several regional disputes in Asia, and that Sino-American relations now rested on a secure political, economic, and institutional base. But others were concerned about the possible resumption of Sino-Soviet military ties or the prospects for coordination of Chinese and Soviet policy on important international issues. Others worried simply that an amelioration of Sino-Soviet relations, even if it took on no overt anti-American overtones, might weaken the U.S.-China relationship by removing its geopolitical rationale.

Significantly, the Chinese were aware of, and concerned by, this American reaction. Throughout late 1985 and early 1986, Chinese analysts and diplomats probed their American counterparts about their reactions to the improvement in Sino-Soviet ties, evincing clear apprehension that an overly rapid rapprochement between Peking and Moscow could damage China's relations with the United States. Even as the final normalization of Sino-Soviet relations was being accomplished, therefore, Peking still took pains to emphasize, to Soviet and American audiences, the limits on its new relationship with Moscow. Even as they made preparations for a summit meeting with Gorbachev, Chinese leaders indicated that Sino-Soviet relations would remain somewhat distant, while Sino-American relations would be unimpaired. Chinese leaders repeatedly emphasized to American leaders—including President George Bush during his trip to Peking in February 1989—that even the full normalization of Sino-Soviet relations would not mean the restoration of an alliance between the two countries or Chinese acknowledgment of Soviet leadership of the international Communist movement.[10] They indicated great reluctance to admit the existence of common interests between China and the Soviet Union on international issues, even though Moscow periodically provided long lists of those subjects on which the two countries' positions coincided.

And, in the end, the Sino-Soviet summit—largely overshadowed by the massive student demonstrations in Tiananmen Square—did nothing to harm American interests. Peking agreed to restore party-to-party ties with the Soviet Union but not to upgrade military-to-military relations. China acknowledged common positions with the Soviet Union on several secondary international issues, such as the role of the United Nations and the need for a reform of the international economic order, but refused to endorse Soviet arms control proposals for the Asia-Pacific region, to admit parallel stands on the Korean question, or to join with Gorbachev in any significant regional or global undertaking. As a result, the United States could take a rather relaxed position toward the normalization of Sino-Soviet ties. In the course of the summit, for example, a State Department spokesman noted that Washington "would welcome any steps that would reduce tensions and we think that these meetings can contribute to that."[11]

Equally important, the rapprochement between China and the Soviet Union took place when Soviet-American relations were also improving. Many of the gestures that Gorbachev was making toward China—such as withdrawing from Afghanistan and promoting a negotiated settlement in Cambodia—helped promote Moscow's relations with Washington as well. In addition, the Soviet Union was adopting a more cooperative approach toward other regional disputes, including Korea and Angola, in which the United States had interests. And the prospects for progress in U.S.-Soviet arms control negotiations were improving, as evidenced by the conclusion of an agreement on intermediate-range nuclear forces (INF) in December 1987, the more frequent exchange of high-level military delegations, unilateral Soviet troop reductions in Europe, and the inauguration of negotiations on the levels of conventional forces in Europe (CFE). Whatever doubts there may once have been in Washington about Peking's intentions were therefore assuaged by the confidence that Gorbachev was basing his foreign policy on a reduction of tensions with the United States as well as with China.

The changes in Soviet foreign policy under Gorbachev therefore did not directly weaken the relationship between China and the United States. None of the participants in the "strategic triangle" seemed to be seeking a tactical advantage over the others. China eschewed any collaborative relations with the Soviet Union—whether an expansion of military relations or coordination of diplomatic initiatives—that might be viewed with alarm in Washington. The United States sought to preserve friendly relations with China even as it worked toward a new détente with the Soviet Union. And Gorbachev wanted to trim, on every front, the commitments of an overextended Soviet empire. From a strategic perspective, the

triangular relationship among Washington, Moscow, and Peking
seemed to be evolving into a ménage à trois in which each capital
sought stable and cooperative relations with the other two. This
state of affairs was in sharp contrast to the situation in the 1970s,
when détente between Washington and Moscow was viewed with
alarm in Peking, or even in the early 1980s, when the prospects of a
Sino-Soviet rapprochement were regarded with concern in the
United States.

GROWING DIVERGENCE ON STRATEGIC ISSUES

Although the changes in Soviet foreign policy did not have a direct
impact on Sino-American relations, they did remove much of
the original strategic rationale for the rapprochement between China
and the United States and thus weakened what had previously been
an important stabilizing element in their relationship. As the threat
from the Soviet Union declined, China became less central to American foreign policy than it had been at the height of Soviet expansionism during the Brezhnev years. It now became less essential for
the United States to make concessions on other issues, such as
Taiwan or technology transfer, to ensure Chinese cooperation in
containing or deterring Soviet adventures abroad. At the same time,
the diminution of the Soviet threat in the mid-1980s revealed the
differences between Peking and Washington on other regional and
global issues. Without a common threat to unify them, the two
countries' foreign policies began increasingly to diverge.

Some of these differences were familiar echoes of the past: China
continued to criticize American policy in the Middle East and South
Africa and ritualistically demanded the withdrawal of American
forces from South Korea. But other themes in Chinese rhetoric were
responses to an evolving American policy. Publicly, Peking opposed
the American strategic defense initiative, even though some Chinese
analysts said privately they were intrigued by the venture.[12] China
supported New Zealand's policy of banning nuclear-armed and nuclear-powered ships from its ports and questioned American pressure
on Japan to increase military expenditures or to assume greater responsibility for its own defense. Peking also criticized the American
intervention in Grenada in 1983, the bombing of Libya in 1986, and
other aspects of American policy toward the third world. Moreover,
American officials sensed a declining willingness by the Chinese to
associate themselves publicly with American policy initiatives or

even to speak positively of the extensive security relationship that the two countries were developing during this period.

None of these areas of divergence posed any serious difficulties for the Sino-American relationship. But three other issues proved more contentious and thus did more damage to U.S.-China ties: China's support for the Khmer Rouge in Cambodia, its policy on nuclear non-proliferation and, above all, Peking's program of arms sales to the Middle East.

Throughout the 1980s, Chinese and American policies on Cambodia had converged for the most part. Both countries opposed Hanoi's intervention in Cambodia in 1978, on the grounds that it threatened to establish Vietnamese hegemony over all of Indochina. China and the United States subsequently refused to recognize the Vietnamese-installed government in Phnom Penh, supporting instead an opposition government, led by Prince Sihanouk, known as the Coalition Government of Democratic Kampuchea (CGDK). Together with the members of the Association of Southeast Asian Nations (ASEAN), Peking and Washington gave the CGDK material assistance, ensured that it occupied Cambodia's seat in the United Nations, and endorsed its 1986 call for a Vietnamese withdrawal, a provisional coalition government of all four Cambodian factions, and free elections to produce a new neutral national government in Phnom Penh. But in other respects Chinese and American policies on Cambodia differed. Jimmy Carter failed to endorse Deng's idea of a punitive expedition against Vietnam when the Chinese leader proposed it during his visit to Washington in January 1979. Moreover, China and the United States supported different elements of the Cambodian resistance movement. Washington was linked exclusively to the two non-Communist factions led by Sihanouk and Son Sann. Peking, while providing aid to all three factions in the CGDK, was most closely associated with the Khmer Rouge, led by Pol Pot and Khieu Samphan.

China's support for the Khmer Rouge troubled many Americans. When it controlled Cambodia between 1975 and 1978, the Khmer Rouge adopted domestic policies that were, in effect, a macabre caricature of the Chinese Cultural Revolution. Urban commercial and intellectual elites were murdered or dispatched to the countryside. Virtually all the private means of production were nationalized, and free markets were eliminated. Such policies were responsible for the deaths of 700,000 to 1 million Cambodians, about 7 to 14 percent of the total population in 1975.[13]

For most of the 1980s, the United States seemed willing to tolerate China's persistent support of the Khmer Rouge. Whatever its record, the Khmer Rouge maintained the largest army of any of the three

Cambodian resistance factions. A policy of guerrilla warfare, aimed at driving the Vietnamese out of Cambodia and destabilizing the Heng Samrin government in Phnom Penh, could not overlook the military assets of the Khmer Rouge. Moreover, for the United States to have raised objections to external support for the Khmer Rouge would have placed it in opposition not only to China but to key members of ASEAN, especially Thailand and Singapore, who wanted to maintain the greatest possible military pressure on Hanoi and its client government in Phnom Penh.

By 1988, however, a negotiated settlement of the conflict in Cambodia, including a full withdrawal of Vietnamese forces, seemed conceivable. Talks had begun in December 1987 between Sihanouk and Hun Sen, the prime minister in the Phnom Penh government, followed by an international conference including all four Cambodian factions in Indonesia in July 1988. This development significantly changed the context in which international support for the Khmer Rouge would be evaluated. It became more difficult to invoke Vietnamese hegemonism as a justification for an alliance with the Khmer Rouge. Indeed, once the issue became the contours of a negotiated settlement, rather than a Vietnamese withdrawal, there was a strong argument for weakening, rather than strengthening, the Khmer Rouge, to prevent it from playing a dominant role in a successor Cambodian government.

Under pressure from members of Congress concerned about the Khmer Rouge's record of gross violations of human rights, the Reagan administration began to press China to change its position on Cambodia. In his visit to Peking in July 1988, George Shultz reportedly urged Chinese leaders to reduce their support of the Khmer Rouge.[14] In September, Washington endorsed an ASEAN resolution in the United Nations that not only called for a Vietnamese withdrawal but also renounced the "universally condemned policies of the past"—a clear reference to the Khmer Rouge. The House of Representatives passed a resolution calling on the U.S. government to urge all nations to terminate assistance to the Khmer Rouge.[15]

In response to the declining international support for the Khmer Rouge, China did adopt a new position on a negotiated settlement in Cambodia. Peking said that, although the Khmer Rouge should be represented in any future Cambodian government, it need not dominate it. Peking also hinted it would accept a significant change in the leadership of the Khmer Rouge—a process indelicately known as "decapitation"—by declaring that the representatives of each faction participating in a successor government should be acceptable to all of the other factions. Still, China did not yield on the underlying issue: it refused to cut off aid to the Khmer Rouge until a comprehensive settlement was made, including a verified Vietnamese withdrawal from Cambodia and an end to foreign assistance to all of the contending factions.

Although the dispute between China and the United States over Cambodia never produced a crisis between the two countries, it was nonetheless significant. First, and most basically, it showed that Chinese and American policies in Asia, although largely parallel, were not congruent. The two countries could still agree on the desirability of peace on the Korean peninsula, and even of the military alliance between Japan and the United States, but they differed on the acceptability of the Khmer Rouge. Moreover, as the threat of a consolidation of Vietnamese control over Cambodia seemed to wane, the commonalities between Peking and Washington also became less significant, and the divergences over the Khmer Rouge assumed greater salience. Just as the decline of the Soviet threat reduced the global rationale for Sino-American strategic cooperation, so did the ebbing of Vietnamese power in Indochina remove some of the regional foundation for a geopolitical alignment between Peking and Washington.

In addition, the growing debate over U.S. policy toward Cambodia began to erode congressional support for the American relationship with China. Some members of Congress began to ask whether the American position on Cambodia—not to provide material support to the Khmer Rouge but not to insist on its exclusion from a negotiated settlement—was shaped by an excessive concern with Chinese interests. In reality, the American position was based at least equally on the preferences of the major ASEAN nations, especially Thailand and Singapore, who believed no negotiated settlement could be successful if the Khmer Rouge were excluded from it. But the perception spread in the United States that American policy toward Cambodia was made in Peking, resulting in tacit American support for a brutal Communist movement with a genocidal record.

A second issue complicating the Sino-American strategic relationship was China's position on nuclear nonproliferation. The issue was raised by the two countries' desire to conclude an agreement on civilian nuclear cooperation, which would have permitted the export of American nuclear power–generating equipment to China.[16] China desired such equipment as a way of increasing its ability to generate electric power, one of the most important bottlenecks in its economy. And American companies, faced with a shrinking domestic market in the aftermath of the accident at the nuclear power plant at Three Mile Island in 1979, were eager to gain access to what appeared to be a large potential Chinese market. In addition, a nuclear cooperation agreement was seen by many American officials as another in the series of bilateral protocols linking various agencies of the U.S. government with their counterparts in China, and as a way of encouraging Peking to join the international regime restricting the proliferation of nuclear weapons.

The process of negotiating the Sino-American nuclear cooperation agreement, which had begun at the start of the Reagan administration in 1981, was complicated by two considerations. First, as a matter of practical politics, it would have been difficult for Washington to gain congressional support for such an agreement in the absence of a Chinese commitment to the principle of nonproliferation. Peking had refused to sign the nuclear nonproliferation treaty of 1968, describing it as an attempt by the superpowers to preserve their monopoly of atomic weapons. Moreover, in the late 1970s and early 1980s there were persistent reports of Chinese cooperation with the nuclear programs of other countries, including sales of heavy water to Argentina, South Africa, and India, and the provision of low-enriched uranium to South Africa.[17] Most disturbing of all were the highly credible reports that China was helping Pakistan develop a nuclear weapons capability by providing information on the design of atomic explosives and by assisting in the construction of an unsafeguarded uranium enrichment plant.[18] Securing explicit Chinese acceptance of the norms of nonproliferation and a termination of questionable Chinese activities abroad was therefore a crucial prerequisite for the successful conclusion of the nuclear cooperation agreement.

A second set of issues stemmed from the provisions of the U.S. Nuclear Non-Proliferation Act of 1978, which governed the transfer of nuclear equipment and materials overseas. Although there were some ambiguities in the law when applied to countries that already had developed nuclear weapons, the act seemed to require that any American nuclear exports to China be subject to international safeguards, including on-site inspections of the raw materials and equipment provided by the United States and American consent to the reprocessing or transfer of spent nuclear fuel. For a country like China, traditionally obsessed with preserving sovereignty against foreign intervention, these American requirements were a controversial intrusion into Chinese internal affairs. Moreover, since China already had nuclear weapons, safeguards on materials and equipment provided by the United States would in themselves provide no guarantee against the further development of Chinese atomic capabilities, nor against Chinese assistance to other nations. Still, the United

States had to insist on such safeguards, not only because of the provisions of the nuclear nonproliferation act, but also because failure to do so might have caused "political damage to the entire nonproliferation norm should other countries deduce a waning of the US commitment."[19]

Thus in December 1983 several members of Congress concerned with nonproliferation, including Senator William Proxmire, wrote to Secretary of State George Shultz about the nuclear cooperation agreement then under negotiation with China. They suggested that the United States demand from Peking an explicit commitment to the principle of nonproliferation and a pledge that it would place all new nuclear exports under the safeguards administered by the International Atomic Energy Agency. They also wanted China to accept IAEA safeguards on its own civilian nuclear installations, similar to those that the United States had accepted after signing the nonproliferation treaty.

Surmounting these two obstacles to a nuclear cooperation agreement proved difficult. Peking agreed to join the IAEA, which implied an acceptance of other elements of the international nonproliferation regime, and began to require IAEA safeguards on exports to nonnuclear weapons states. Moreover, the Chinese government began to make public statements supporting the principle of nonproliferation, one by Zhao Ziyang in a toast at the White House during his visit to Washington in 1984, and another in a report to China's national legislature several months later. Privately, Peking gave Washington oral assurances that it would not assist Pakistan to develop nuclear weapons. The State Department drafted a secret memorandum summarizing its interpretation of the more forthcoming Chinese position on nonproliferation, which Peking declined to sign, but which it did not disavow. Still, China refused to sign the nuclear nonproliferation treaty, citing historical objections to its origins and motivations.

Nor would China agree to accept straightforward safeguards (whether implemented by the IAEA or by the United States) on American materials or equipment or to grant the United States the unambiguous right to review the reprocessing of spent nuclear fuels.[20] Instead, Peking was only willing to insert two highly ambiguous and convoluted passages in the draft nuclear cooperation agreement, one providing for exchanges of information and visits regarding any equipment and materials exported by the United States, and another agreeing that reprocessing of spent fuel would be subject to bilateral discussions, with the United States obligated to "consider such activities favorably."[21] With these concessions in hand, the Reagan administration signed the nuclear cooperation agreement in July 1985 and presented it to Congress.

The Reagan administration insisted that the text of the nuclear cooperation agreement satisfied the legal requirements of the Atomic Energy Act and the political imperative of maintaining the international nonproliferation regime. In the absence of an agreement with the United States, said the White House, China would obtain nuclear materials and equipment from other nations, perhaps on even less stringent terms. Members of Congress, particularly Senators William Proxmire and John Glenn and Representative Edward Markey were not so certain, insisting that the potential commercial benefits to the United States did not justify the weakening of the American commitment to safeguards against nonproliferation. They were concerned that the proposed agreement did not require safeguards on American equipment or materials supplied to China, did not include a written Chinese commitment to the principles of nonproliferation, and seemed to commit the United States to approve the reprocessing of spent fuel.[22]

Like the debate over Chinese support for the Khmer Rouge, the controversy over the nuclear cooperation agreement was fairly moderate. Despite sharp criticism on Capitol Hill, Congress did not attempt to block the agreement altogether.[23] Instead, it adopted a resolution in mid-December 1985 that, before any export licenses could be given, the president would have to certify the following conditions: he had received additional information from China about its nonproliferation policies; China had ceased helping nonnuclear weapons states develop nuclear explosives; technology provided by the United States would be used solely for peaceful purposes; and the United States would maintain control over the reprocessing or transfer of nuclear materials.[24] Since the president was never able to make such a certification, the nuclear cooperation agreement, although technically ratified by the United States, never went into effect.

The altercation over nuclear cooperation again raised serious questions about the solidity of Sino-American relations. As on Cambodia, China did not seem to fully share American perspectives on an important international issue and, while prepared to compromise, was unwilling to completely accommodate American interests. Moreover, the debate further eroded congressional support for the U.S.-China relationship, this time among an influential group of liberal Democrats concerned about the principle of nonproliferation.

The third, and most contentious, geopolitical issue between China and the United States at this time was Chinese arms sales to the Middle East. The provision of weapons to friends abroad, often on highly favorable terms, had long been a feature of Chinese foreign policy. By 1975, for example, China had exported heavy weapons to no fewer than twenty-two countries in Asia, Africa, and the Middle East and had provided light weapons to many other governments and insurgencies. Its arms exports increased significantly thereafter, as Peking began in the late 1970s to reallocate resources from economic aid to military assistance agreements and then in the early 1980s further shifted from military aid agreements to commercial military sales. In the 1980s, China's arms sales were focused on two countries in Asia (Thailand and Pakistan) and five in the Middle East (Egypt, Syria, Libya, Iran, and Iraq). The sale of the most sophisticated weapons systems was probably controlled by the central Chinese government, in line with the objectives of solidifying China's relations with its most important Asian partners and acquiring political influence in the Middle East. But the sale of less advanced arms, perhaps including some missile systems, was controlled by the military and by certain trading companies affiliated with it, whose principal concern was to earn the hard currency with which to purchase foreign technology and weapons systems for China's armed forces.

The Iran-Iraq war offered an ideal opportunity for China to increase arms sales to the Middle East. China showed no reservations about selling weapons to both sides, signing agreements with Iran valued at $3 billion and agreements with Iraq totaling $5.1 billion.[25] At first, Washington paid little attention to this development. But by 1987, with the United States having agreed to reflag and escort Kuwaiti tankers in the Persian Gulf, the sale of Silkworm antiship missiles to Iran attracted American concern. In March of that year, George Shultz raised the issue of Chinese arms sales to Iran (but seemingly did not bring up sales to Iraq) during his visit to Peking, apparently requesting a termination of all weapons transfers to Teheran, and specifically of the Silkworm missiles.[26]

Initially, the Chinese refused to acknowledge that any Silkworms were being sent to Iran, even when shown American reconnaissance photographs.[27] In October 1987, therefore, the United States suspended the liberalization of controls on the export of advanced technology to China.[28] Faced with this American demarche, Peking said it would take measures to stop what it called the diversion of Silkworms to Iran through the international arms market—a veiled reference to China's practice of transshipping the missiles to North Korea. After confirming that China had indeed stopped the delivery of Silkworms to Iran, Washington revealed in March 1988 that it would lift the ban on the liberalization of export controls. The following August, Washington announced the first relaxation of technology transfer restrictions since the dispute began.[29]

These steps did not end the controversy over Chinese arms sales to the Middle East, however. Even as the Silkworm issue was being resolved, Washington received reports of the sale of Chinese C-SS-2 intermediate-range ballistic missiles, valued at $3 billion, to Saudi Arabia. Although Saudi Arabia, unlike Iran, was a close friend of the United States, the provision of a new class of missiles, capable of carrying nuclear warheads and of reaching Israel, was a disturbing development. To reassure Washington, Peking attempted to impose conditions on the transfer of the C-SS-2s: they would not carry nuclear explosives, they would not be used first, they would be employed only defensively, and they would not be transferred to third countries. But verification of the missiles' warheads proved difficult because the Saudi government, irked at American refusals to sell it some of the advanced weapons systems it had sought to acquire, announced it would not permit international inspection of the payloads.[30]

Within a few months, reports appeared that China was also negotiating the sale of medium-range M-9 missiles to Syria, and possibly to Iran, Libya, and Pakistan.[31] During his visit to China in July 1988, Secretary of State Shultz protested to Peking, requesting Chinese officials to begin in-depth consultations with the United States to halt the proliferation of ballistic missiles abroad. At first, Chinese officials refused to admit they were even offering the M-9 for sale. When confronted with a sales brochure for the missile that the Chinese were distributing on the international arms market, those officials responded that the missile was "just a concept" that was not yet in production, and that no sales had been made. China was also reluctant to engage in any broader discussions of the sale of missiles as requested by the United States, on the grounds that it sold far fewer weapons abroad than either the United States or the Soviet Union.[32]

Ultimately, however, without making any firm or explicit commitments, Chinese leaders implied to Defense Secretary Frank Carlucci during his visit to Peking in September 1988 that they would refrain from selling any more missiles to the Middle East. They backed up these private reassurances with the enunciation of the principles governing their arms sales abroad: arms sales should "strengthen the legitimate self-defense capability of the countries concerned" and "help safeguard and promote peace, security, and stability" in the regions in question.[33] Carlucci described himself as "fully satisfied" that China would behave in a "thoroughly responsible way."[34] At the same time, the United States announced it would permit the use of Chinese rockets to launch space satellites manufactured in the United States, with certain economic and technical safeguards. Although both governments formally denied any connection between the two issues, some in Washington suspected this concession had been a quid pro quo for China's reassurance on missile sales to the Middle East.[35]

Like the earlier controversies over Cambodia and nonproliferation, the dispute over Chinese arms sales to the Middle East illustrated the divergences between the strategic interests and perspectives of China and the United States. And, more than the other two issues, China's behavior in negotiations with the United States raised fundamental questions about Peking's credibility and reliability. By denying they were selling Silkworms to Iran, and by refusing to acknowledge they were offering M-9s for sale on the international market, Chinese officials gave the impression they were deliberately deceiving their American counterparts. When the Chinese began to suggest that some arms sales were being made by military trading companies without the knowledge of the Foreign Ministry, they merely introduced new apprehensions that Chinese foreign policy was no longer controlled or coordinated by any single central authority.

In short, as the Soviet threat to China and the United States seemed to recede, and as differences between Washington and Peking over such issues as Cambodia and the Middle East intensified, the strategic underpinnings of Sino-American relations gradually eroded. As early as May 1986, while still insisting that, in Asia, the geopolitical interests of the two countries converged, U.S. Ambassador Winston Lord acknowledged, "The overall global consensus between our nations has narrowed."[36]

ECONOMIC AND CULTURAL PROBLEMS

As the geopolitical foundations of U.S.-China relations slowly weakened, many observers, Chinese and American alike, predicted that commercial ties and, to a lesser degree, cultural exchanges would provide a new and more stable basis for the relationship between the two countries. As noted earlier, dramatic growth indeed occurred in these aspects of Sino-American relations in the second half of the 1980s. Between 1983 and 1988, bilateral trade grew by more than 200 percent, the number of Chinese students and scholars arriving in the United States rose by around 225 percent, and the number of Americans visiting China increased by about 80 percent. Cumulative American investment in China rose from $18 million to $244 million during the same period. But despite these impressive achievements, the economic and cultural relationship between the two countries was, like their geopolitical ties, more and more troubled. Three issues plagued this facet of Sino-American relations: protectionism in the United States, barriers to American trade and investment in China, and the growing brain drain of Chinese students and scholars to the United States.

Throughout the 1980s, the United States grappled with a trade deficit of unprecedented proportions, growing from $26 billion at the beginning of the decade to $126 billion in 1988.[37] The deficit was the result of many factors: a strong American currency until 1985, high interest rates, a low savings rate, stagnant industrial productivity, and barriers to American exports abroad. The consequence was to increase the salience of the bilateral balance of payments with each of America's trading partners and to raise demands at home for protection of U.S. industries threatened by foreign competition.

China was not, in the mid- to late-1980s, a very important trading partner of the United States, nor an especially large contributor to the overall American trade deficit. Nonetheless, it was no exception to the trend. According to American trade statistics, which include as imports from China those commodities transshipped to the United States through Hong Kong, the United States had enjoyed a small trade surplus with China in the late 1970s and early 1980s, as Peking's ambitious program of modernization in the early post-Mao era increased imports of American technology, and as agricultural shortfalls necessitated purchases of American cotton and wheat. By the mid-1980s, however, the two countries' trade was essentially in balance: Chinese imports of agricultural goods slowed as China enjoyed the fruits of rural reforms, and American purchases increased as the United States recovered from the depression of the early 1980s. And by 1986, China had begun to enjoy what seemed to be chronic surpluses with the United States, as exports of textiles, consumer electronics, and other commodities enjoyed rapid and steady growth (tables A2, A3). China's trade surplus with the United States rose from $1.7 billion in 1986 to $2.8 billion in 1987 and to $3.5 billion in 1988.

As Chinese exports to the United States increased, various sectors of American industry began to demand greater protection from Chinese competition. The most vocal was the textile industry, which had long resisted imports from low-cost Asian producers, and which faced, in the mid-1980s, imports of fiber, cloth, and finished clothing from China worth more than $1.4 billion. In 1984, in response to domestic pressure, the U.S. government adopted new regulations redefining the country-of-origin of imported clothing. Previously, garments manufactured in China but modified slightly in Hong Kong could be sent to the United States under Hong Kong's textile quota, leaving room for additional items of clothing produced entirely in China to be exported under Peking's ceiling. Under the new provisions, adopted on an interim basis in July 1984 and finalized the following year, unless garments transshipped through Hong Kong had been "substantially transformed" there, they would be considered of Chinese origin and thus counted against China's quota rather than Hong Kong's.

Still other attempts were made in the mid-1980s to restrict the flow of Chinese textiles to the United States. In 1985, Congress considered a bill, sponsored by Representative Ed Jenkins (D-Georgia) and Senator Strom Thurmond (R-South Carolina) that would have greatly reduced the current import quotas for textiles from twelve principal foreign producers and afterward restricted future imports to an annual increase of 1 percent over the 1984 level. According to Chinese estimates, the Jenkins bill would have meant their country would have had to cut exports by some $500 million in 1985 alone. The legislation was significantly weakened as it passed through Congress, however; the final version exempted China from any deep cuts in its textile quota. Moreover, the bill was vetoed by the Reagan administration, on the grounds that it violated the principles of free trade. In the end, the veto was upheld, but only after the White House promised to use other administrative measures to deal with unfair trading practices by foreign textile exporters.[38] But it was clear that Chinese textile exports were encountering a less hospitable climate in America.

China also faced the regular renewal of its bilateral textile agreement with the United States when the agreement signed in 1983 lapsed at the end of 1987. As in previous years, reaching a new accord required difficult negotiations between the two countries. Despite growing protectionist pressures, the talks concluded successfully, without the United States imposing unilateral quotas on imports from China. Like its predecessor, the 1987 agreement covered a four-year period, from 1988 through 1991, and allowed 3 percent annual growth in Chinese exports to the United States. But it also expanded the range of commodities covered by the quotas to include for the first time natural fibers such as silk and ramie.[39]

In other areas, too, China faced a less accommodating American posture on economic issues. A new maritime agreement signed in December 1988, to replace one that had lapsed in 1983, sought to gain a greater share of cargo for American ships by allowing U.S. shipping firms to establish offices in China and to open feeder service from Hong Kong to Chinese ports. The U.S. decision to permit China to launch American space satellites was accompanied by demands that China charge prevailing world prices and by restrictions on the number of such launches, conditions designed to protect American and European enterprises against Chinese competition.[40] And proposed Chinese acquisitions of American firms were subjected to greater administrative scrutiny, with one deal—a prospective Chinese purchase of an American company that manufactured metal components for commercial aircraft—vetoed by Washington in early 1990.[41]

The rapid growth of China's trade surplus with the United States also fueled criticism of the obstacles to American exports to China. The office of the U.S. Trade Representative (USTR) began issuing annual reports on the subject in 1987. Each year, the reports criticized China for high tariffs and import regulatory taxes, tight foreign exchange controls, restrictive quotas and licenses, and especially inadequate protection of American intellectual property. In 1987, the USTR complained that the impact of such barriers on American exports was "potentially enormous but impossible to quantify." For the first time, the American trade deficit with China became an issue in bilateral negotiations, being a chief topic at the 1987 meeting of the Joint Commission on Commerce and Trade and in subsequent visits by the U.S. trade representative.[42]

Even more concern was expressed in the United States about the obstacles to American investment in China.[43] As a growing number of American firms invested more and more capital in China, they complained about the imperfections in the investment climate there. One of the most important drawbacks was the high cost, low quality, and uncertain availability of various inputs into the manufacturing process, including land, labor, financing in local currency, raw materials, components, and energy. A related problem was the incomplete legal system, a convoluted bureaucratic structure, and a complex set of administrative rules and regulations. Above all, with a few exceptions for projects specially favored by Peking, it was difficult for foreign ventures in China to repatriate any profits that had not been earned in hard currency through exports.

These chronic limitations on American trade and investment with China were compounded by a policy of economic retrenchment adopted by Peking in 1986 to deal with a burgeoning trade deficit of its own. Tighter administrative controls over the expenditure of foreign exchange made it more difficult for Chinese firms to import goods from abroad and complicated the effort of foreign ventures operating in China to acquire foreign equipment, components, and raw materials. A devaluation of the renminbi, announced in July 1986, obstructed imports by raising their price in Chinese currency. And, more generally, a slowdown in the rate of domestic economic growth made it more difficult for foreign exporters overseas or foreign ventures operating in China to find local markets for their goods.

These developments rapidly produced the impression that China was a much less attractive partner for American business than had originally been assumed. The problems of doing business in China were exemplified, in the eyes of many, by the difficulties that American Motors Corporation (AMC) encountered with investment in the Beijing Jeep Corporation, as reported in long stories in the *New York Times* and the *Washington Post* in April 1986.[44] The AMC had planned to assemble the Jeep Cherokee in China, using a mix of imported and domestic components. But technological problems had made it difficult to utilize local parts, and the devaluation of the yuan increased the cost of importing components from the United States. The result was a higher price for the Jeep on the Chinese market, just when many Chinese buyers were reluctant to use scarce foreign exchange to purchase a product manufactured in China, even if by a joint venture.[45] In July, a front-page article in the *Wall Street Journal* summarized the new disillusionment with China by detailing the many "costs and hassles" of doing business there.[46]

Around the same time as the Western press reported the travails of Beijing Jeep, American business and government representatives in China began to express their dissatisfactions publicly. In March 1986, a group of American investors and exporters meeting in Washington explored the possibility of forming a new private U.S.-PRC joint economic council that could press Peking more aggressively for improvements in the Chinese business climate.[47] In April, the International Businessmen's Association in Beijing wrote to Vice President George Bush to warn that American firms might begin withdrawing from China unless the investment climate improved. The commercial section of the American embassy in Peking produced a description of a "model joint venture," outlining the changes in infrastructure, market access, living conditions, and legal framework that would be necessary for Americans to find investment in China an attractive proposition. And in a speech delivered in Washington in May, Ambassador Winston Lord described the American business community as "frustrated by high costs, price gouging, tight foreign exchange controls, limited access to the Chinese market, bureaucratic foot-dragging, lack of qualified local personnel, and unpredictability."[48]

In response, the Chinese government adopted a set of regulations on foreign investment in October 1986 that were intended to improve the climate for foreign business.[49] These regulations were supposed to lower the cost of doing business in China by reducing taxes, wages, rents, and the cost of energy, transportation, and communication. They promised better access to crucial inputs controlled by the planning apparatus, including loans in Chinese currency, water, electricity, and raw materials. And they provided promised foreign ventures greater autonomy for production plans, imports and exports, wages and bonuses, and the employment and dismissal of labor.

Even so, the new regulations touched only a fraction of the problems encountered by foreign investors. Moreover, they embodied certain priorities that limited the attractiveness of the Chinese investment climate to many American firms. While all foreign ventures were to benefit from several provisions, the regulations established two categories of foreign ventures that would enjoy favored treatment. These categories included export enterprises, which were able through exports to generate a favorable balance in their foreign exchange accounts, and technologically advanced enterprises, which used advanced technology to manufacture products that would otherwise be imported. Although these biases were understandable from a Chinese perspective, they did not satisfy the desires of many American entrepreneurs, who wanted to produce goods for the Chinese market, manufacture with fairly simple technology, or export services to China.

As a result, the American reaction to China's investment incentives was skeptical at best, dismissive at worst. American embassy officials said they had expected more comprehensive measures to improve the investment climate, and were therefore "disappointed" in the new regulations. The director of the Peking office of the National Council for U.S.-China Trade described the new provisions as half a sundae: a "really good cherry and whipped cream but no ice cream." And the head of the Japan-China Economic Law Center spoke for many Americans, as well as for many Japanese, when he pointed out that the foreign ventures the new rules sought to attract—particularly technologically advanced enterprises—stood little chance of success given China's poor infrastructure.[50]

Overall, after having been stagnant in 1986, American investment in China scored small increases in 1987 and 1988, mostly because investment in manufacturing projects rose faster than the decline in investment in hotels and real estate. But despite the renewed growth, the fever for investing in China seemed to have ended.[51] China was no longer seen as a land of unlimited opportunity and potential, but rather as a difficult place to do business, where marginal projects should not be attempted. The renewed retrenchment imposed on the Chinese economy in late 1988 and early 1989, reflected again in tighter restrictions on import licenses and reductions in domestic credit, reinforced the impression that China was a more difficult market than had once been naively assumed. One American executive devised what he called the "two plus two equals one-half" formula: "It takes twice as long and costs twice as much as doing business anywhere else, and the return is about half what you get elsewhere."[52]

The economic relationship between China and the United States produced tensions, then, over increasing American protectionism, mounting U.S. trade deficits, and an inhospitable Chinese investment climate. The cultural relationship, too, encountered problems, concerning principally the low rate at which Chinese students and scholars studying in the United States were returning to their home country. By late 1986, Chinese officials began to complain that the United States was encouraging a "brain drain" of talented Chinese intellectuals to America and demanded action to ensure a higher rate of return.

The available statistics give some credence to Chinese concerns. According to the best estimate, as of the summer of 1989 a cumulative total of 80,000 Chinese—47,000 students and 33,000 visiting scholars—had received visas since 1978 to study in the United States. Of these individuals, 43,000 (54 percent) were still enrolled in their degree programs or engaged in research. Eleven thousand (14 percent) had changed their status, either legally or illegally, to remain in the United States. Only 26,000 (32 percent) had completed their studies and returned to China. Of those who had not returned, a few had applied for political asylum or delayed departure, especially after the campaign against "bourgeois liberalization" in China in 1987. But most students stayed on simply by postponing the completion of their studies, applying for a change of visa status, or hiding as undocumented residents.[53]

This seemingly low rate of return needs to be qualified in two ways, however. First, of the total 56,000 Chinese who had received visas as students or scholars, perhaps as many as 30,000 had done so between 1986 and 1988. Given that many master's degree programs in the United States are two years in length, and that the course of study for the Ph.D. is much longer, an overall rate of return of one-third in 1989 is not unreasonable. And second, students from other places had returned to their home countries in even lower numbers. During much of the 1960s, for example, the rate of return for students from Taiwan was less than 10 percent. But it was also true that, in the late 1980s, members of the American scientific community, concerned about the low rate of American enrollment in graduate programs in science and engineering, began to state publicly their interest in seeing foreign students remain in the United States after completing their studies, comments that may have suggested to Chinese officials that the brain drain was the result of deliberate American policy.[54]

Also of concern to the Chinese government was the growing autonomy of many Chinese students and scholars in the United States and their growing interest in Western political values and institutions. As early as 1982, a Chinese medical student studying in Canada, Wang Bingzhang, had moved to the United States and established a dissident journal, *China Spring*.[55] This journal and the organization associated with it served as a forum for those Chinese intellectuals who were dissatisfied with the political conditions in their home country to press for political reform. Other Chinese students used other methods for criticizing violations of human rights in China, sending open letters to the Chinese leadership or writing op-ed essays for American newspapers calling on the U.S. government to press more vigorously for political and civil rights in China.[56] By 1986, Chinese officials were beginning to complain that, if the United States was encouraging some Chinese students to stay on in America, it was encouraging still others to become a "subversive" force to introduce "bourgeois liberal" ideas into China.

Other Chinese students studying history, economics, political science and international studies, and business formed associations in the United States. Most of these students were less radical in their political orientation than those active in the dissident organizations. But they, too, concerned the Chinese government. The student associations, funded by the students' contributions or grants from American foundations, represented a potential political force independent of the Chinese government and the Chinese Communist Party. Moreover, some of the students began writing papers, in English, for presentation at academic conferences in the United States or for publication in American scholarly journals. The views expressed in these essays on Chinese domestic affairs and Chinese foreign policy were not always congruent with the official positions of the Chinese government and were often accorded special legitimacy by American observers. This, from a Chinese perspective, broke their government's monopoly over foreign propaganda and "caused confusion" by presenting Americans with a plethora of Chinese opinions on various issues rather than a single consistent line.

By 1987, the Chinese government seemed to be attempting to restrict the flow of students and scholars to the United States, at least in those categories deemed most politically sensitive, and trying to ensure the return of those who were allowed to study in America. In that year, Peking persuaded Washington to more vigorously enforce the requirement that those who had received J-1 visas as officially sponsored students and scholars should return to China for at least two years after completing their course of study in the United States. It also reportedly gave the U.S. government a list of Chinese nationals whose course of study had been completed and who were therefore obligated to return home. Washington agreed to prevent visiting scholars holding J-1 visas to delay their return by entering formal degree programs.[57]

Also in 1987, Peking issued new regulations for study abroad, requiring that students admitted to a Chinese university complete their full program before applying to study abroad, and that college graduates work for a time in China before traveling overseas. The regulations tried to restrict the number of people eligible for study in the United States by discouraging candidates for B.A. and M.A. degrees, and by imposing upper age limits for students and scholars. They also required all Ph.D. students and visiting scholars, regardless of their source of financial support, to apply for J-1 visas (as officially sponsored students) instead of F-1 visas (as privately sponsored students), making them subject to the U.S. requirement to return home for two years after completing their course of study in the United States.

Additionally, in their most controversial provision, the regulations made Chinese students and scholars going to America sign a contract with their home institutions, requiring them to return after the completion of their studies abroad. In some cases, these agreements stipulated financial compensation to the Chinese institution if the terms of the contract were violated.[58] The regulations were not always rigorously implemented, but they did suggest to many Americans that the Chinese were cutting back, not expanding, their academic exchange program with the United States.

Americans were also troubled by reports in early 1988 that the Chinese government had decided to reduce the number of exit visas for students and scholars traveling to the United States from eight thousand a year to about three thousand, according to one report, or even to six hundred, according to another version.[59] In fact, the rules dealt only with government-sponsored students and scholars and would not have affected privately sponsored individuals. Moreover, if the new regulations did attempt to impose limits on the number of Chinese studying in the United States—an issue still in dispute—those restrictions were modified or violated in the course of implementation, for the number of Chinese students receiving American visas in 1988 increased over the previous year. But reports such as these, even if exaggerated or distorted, did suggest to many Americans that the Chinese government was restricting academic exchanges because it feared the contaminating influence of exposure to American ideas, values, and institutions.

HUMAN RIGHTS

Despite the enormous differences between the Chinese and American political and social systems, human rights was not a principal issue in Sino-American relations until the mid-1980s. In 1969–70, when the rapprochement between Peking and Washington began, China was at the height of the Cultural Revolution—a violent and turbulent period in which several hundred thousand Chinese lost their lives and tens of millions were persecuted. These events did not prevent the Nixon administration from seeking an improvement in relations with Peking, or even from telling Chinese leaders that human rights would not be an important consideration in American policy toward China. As Nixon told Mao, "What is important is not a nation's internal political philosophy. What is important is its policy toward the rest of the world and toward us."[60] Peking seems to have regarded this statement—as well as the American willingness to include the principle of noninterference in China's internal affairs in the Shanghai communiqué—as a tacit commitment that the United States would refrain from official criticism of China's human rights record.

In the early post-Mao period, China was only beginning a process of limited political liberalization and reform, and violations of basic human rights remained widespread. But even the Carter administration, which made the promotion of human rights one of the cornerstones of its foreign policy, did not emphasize human rights in relations with China. Carter claims to have raised the issue in his meetings with Deng Xiaoping in January 1979, but he accepted

Deng's reply that, whatever China's record on human rights, the situation was now changing for the better.[61] Although the State Department issued a mild criticism of the imprisonment of Wei Jingsheng, one of the activists in the Democracy Wall movement of 1979–80,[62] its annual human rights reports did not single out China for condemnation, and it successfully barred the Dalai Lama from meeting any American officials during his visit to the United States in 1979.[63] Continuing restrictions on freedom of emigration did not prevent the Carter administration from proposing, and Congress approving, the extension of most-favored-nation status to China as part of the bilateral trade agreement of 1980.

Nor did private citizens and organizations pay much more attention to human rights than the U.S. government. There were a few books and articles on human rights by scholars, but these works were primarily descriptive and analytical, and none of them called for vigorous American action to promote liberalization in China.[64] One early article on the subject, for example, concluded with the admission, "It is difficult to know the proper time and the most effective way to express our concern so that it would aid rather than harm those we wish to help."[65] None of the principal human rights organizations in the United States made China a principal target of its activities.

Human rights did not play a big role in American relations with China until the mid-1980s for several reasons. In the late 1960s and early 1970s, during the decade of the Cultural Revolution, human rights abuses in China were disguised by a combination of effective repression and utopian propaganda. Moreover, many Americans in those years, dismayed by U.S. involvement in the Vietnam War and preoccupied with domestic problems in the United States, were not disposed to criticize other countries for violations of human rights, least of all those nations that could claim to have been victims of Western imperialism in the past.

In the late 1970s and early 1980s, the tragedy of the Cultural Revolution became better known abroad, if only because Chinese leaders were willing to acknowledge that the late Maoist period had been a catastrophe for their country. But now China seemed to be moving gradually, if sometimes haltingly, in the direction of economic and political liberalization. The grip of the state over Chinese society was being relaxed, the press and intellectual life were becoming freer, channels for political consultation were being opened, and the judicial system was becoming less arbitrary and more predictable. In these circumstances, encouragement seemed more appropriate than denunciation.

Moreover, many American officials responsible for U.S. policy toward China, as well as many American specialists on contemporary Chinese affairs, judged that U.S. pressure on China for its human rights record would prove counterproductive. It was feared that American demands for improvement in China's human rights situation would be regarded by Chinese leaders as unwarranted intervention in China's internal affairs and might thus strengthen the hands of conservatives opposed to a stable relationship with the United States. There was also some apprehension that public association by the U.S. government with particular individuals or groups in China might discredit them, rather than protect them. As a senior Reagan administration official put it in early 1984, "The way to handle issues of that kind with friendly countries is through private diplomacy and private discussion and not through public talk about it."[66]

Finally, and perhaps most important, human rights concerns were seen as only one element in American policy toward China, and a subsidiary one at that. In the early 1970s, an accommodation with China was seen as a way of reducing the American strategic burden in East Asia, extricating the United States from the conflict in Vietnam, and promoting détente with the Soviet Union. Clearly, objections to the state of human rights in China should not have been allowed to interfere with the pursuit of such goals. In the late 1970s and early 1980s, a continuing strategic alignment with China was similarly viewed as a counterbalance against an expansionist Soviet Union. Human rights considerations took second place in such a strategy, especially when the political climate in China seemed to be improving.

By the mid-1980s, however, several of the conditions that had earlier produced what an official responsible for human rights in the Carter administration described as China's "exemption from international accountability" had begun to change.[67] Chinese intellectuals inside China and abroad began to push harder for further political reform, in the name of freedom and democracy. The issue was not simply abuses during the Cultural Revolution, they said, but rather the inadequacies of the Chinese political system a decade after the death of Mao Zedong. Although few of these intellectuals were well known outside China before 1986–87, their protests then attracted international interest and support, and their treatment became an important test of the commitment of the Chinese government to political reform. The protests inside China were echoed by the activities of Chinese students and scholars in the United States, who began writing open letters to the Chinese government urging an end to repression and more rapid political liberalization.

Furthermore, as China opened its doors to greater contact with the rest of the world, other aspects of its human rights record became better known and subject to greater foreign scrutiny. Many observers in the United States were especially concerned about Peking's policies toward Tibet and toward family planning. A few Americans had long been angered by China's forcible occupation of Tibet in 1950, its suppression of an uprising there in 1959, and its refusal to allow the free practice of Tibetan Buddhism. Although the situation in Tibet did improve a great deal after the death of Mao in 1976, it did not satisfy either the Tibetans resident there, those in exile abroad led by the Dalai Lama, or their supporters in the United States. At the same time, there was growing criticism of the coercive aspects of China's birth control program, which imposed economic sanctions, and even abortion or sterilization, on those couples that defied the childbearing quotas set by their local leaders.

Gradually, too, the somewhat naive euphoria that had characterized American perceptions of China's domestic circumstances in 1984 and 1985 began to dissipate. In particular, although the press remained enthusiastic about China's economic reform program, awareness grew that the process of political liberalization was lagging behind. In particular, the rise of student protests in 1986 and 1987—the first serious instance of dissent since the Democracy Wall movement of 1978–79—produced concern that the human rights situation in China was not improving as rapidly as had been hoped. Press accounts began to warn of the dangers of conducting economic reform without political reform. The *Wall Street Journal*, which had seen limitless potential in Peking's reform program in 1984, now portrayed China less effusively as "sitting on the fence" between communism and a democratic market economy.[68]

Finally, changes in the international situation made it more feasible to criticize China for its human rights record. It was becoming apparent that the United States had maintained a double standard, refraining from criticizing China for the same human rights abuses for which it attacked the Soviet Union. One by one, the justifications for such a double standard fell away. The improvement of Soviet-American relations reduced the need for a China card to play against Moscow, and thus made it less necessary to mute criticism of repression in China to preserve a strategic relationship with Peking. As the Soviet Union began to liberalize under Mikhail Gorbachev, in part as a response to Western pressure, it seemed less plausible to argue that similar pressure against China would still be counterproductive or inappropriate. In addition, progress toward political liberalization elsewhere in the world—especially in South

Korea, Taiwan, Chile, and Argentina—placed remaining human rights violations in China in a less favorable light.

The rise of human rights concerns in American policy toward China was evident in three areas during the latter part of the 1980s: family planning, Tibet, and treatment of Chinese intellectuals. Between 1983 and 1985, the American press published several reports about the coercive aspects of China's birth control program, including not only the government's use of economic and psychological incentives to enforce birth quotas, but also the occurrence of forced abortions and compulsory sterilizations.[69] There was also growing concern about the practice of female infanticide, as Chinese women allowed to have only one child sought drastic measures to ensure that their child would be a boy. Since, at the time, the United Nations Fund for Population Activities (UNFPA) was involved in some family planning activities in China, charges were also raised that the fund was actively supporting coercive birth control programs there. Doubts about whether the UNFPA was directly involved in the coercive aspects of Chinese birth control policies, and whether compulsory abortions and sterilizations represented deliberate central policy or distortions by local officials, were swept aside by the revulsion over reports of late-term abortions and mandatory sterilizations.[70]

The Reagan administration, which opposed abortion as a form of birth control in any country, had previously decided to refuse economic assistance to any foreign government or international organization that supported abortion or coercive population control programs. On the basis of that decision, the White House temporarily withheld 50 percent of the U.S. contribution to the UNFPA in 1984 and again in 1985, pending an investigation of the fund's involvement in such programs in China. Further reviews by the U.S. Agency for International Development in both years found no conclusive evidence of any connection between the UNFPA and coerced abortions in China. In 1984, the funds that had been temporarily withheld were then turned over to the UNFPA, on condition that they not be used in China. But in March 1985, the U.S. Agency for International Development still withheld $10 million—the equivalent of UNFPA's entire program in China, and around 20 percent of the budgeted American contribution—because of the Reagan administration's concern about China's family planning practices.

Several members of Congress who were opposed to abortion, led by a junior Republican representative from New Jersey, Christopher Smith, remained dissatisfied with the administration's approach. They decided to use the controversy over China's family planning practices to mandate a total ban on American support for the UNFPA.

Smith's original proposal was to link the two issues by banning American aid to any population program operating in China. After much debate, in August 1985 Congress adopted a somewhat looser amendment jointly sponsored by Representative Jack Kemp (R-New York), Senator Daniel Inouye (D-Hawaii), and Senator Jesse Helms (R-North Carolina), which barred U.S. funds from any organization that, as determined by the president, "supports or participates in the management of a program of coercive abortion or involuntary sterilization."[71] Under pressure from Helms, who had delayed the confirmation of Winston Lord as ambassador to China for five weeks while the population control issue was pending, the Reagan administration finally decided to terminate all funding for the UNFPA in 1986 and did so again in 1987 and 1988.[72]

The debate over China's birth control programs did not directly or immediately affect the bilateral relations between China and the United States. Those members of Congress who criticized coercive population policies in China were not primarily interested in imposing sanctions against Peking but rather sought to use abuses in China as a way of cutting off American support to international population control organizations and of mobilizing resistance to abortion in the United States. The White House and the State Department, even when cutting off all American contributions to the UNFPA, took care not to single out China for criticism or even to identify it as the reason for their decision. Still, the issue was important because, for the first time, human rights in China had become an important issue in American political debate. Those who became aware of Chinese abuses in the early 1980s were more likely to raise the issue again in later years.[73]

Tibet became a consideration in American China policy several years after family planning did. In September and October 1987, Chinese troops and police suppressed three demonstrations in Lhasa, the largest protests since the Tibetan uprising in 1959. At the time, the Dalai Lama was visiting Washington where, in an informal meeting on Capitol Hill, he presented a plan under which Tibet would acknowledge Chinese sovereignty in exchange for a withdrawal of Chinese military forces and a high degree of political and cultural autonomy.[74] In response, the New York Times published an editorial urging the State Department to "stand up for decency in Tibet."[75] And Congress passed several joint resolutions expressing concern about the situation in Tibet, including an amendment to the State Department Authorization Act in December 1987 urging the White House to make the treatment of the Tibetan people "an important factor" in the conduct of its relations with China, and a freestanding

Senate resolution in March 1989 condemning Chinese policies in Tibet.[76]

At first, the Reagan administration not only refused to join in the attacks on Chinese policies toward Tibet, but actually tried to defend Peking from criticism. It opposed the Senate resolution, with one State Department official portraying its description of the situation in Tibet as "inaccurate, incomplete, and misleading."[77] Still, in acknowledgment of the growing public concern, several high-ranking American officials visited Tibet in 1988—first Deputy Assistant Secretary of State J. Stapleton Roy in April, then Ambassador Winston Lord in August, and in September a delegation of three senators headed by Patrick Leahy (D-Vermont)—to express distress over reports of human rights abuses in the region, especially the mistreatment of imprisoned demonstrators.

Finally, Americans began to pay greater attention to Peking's treatment of Chinese intellectuals. Here, the stimulus was the wave of student protests that swept the country in late 1986 and early 1987, which led to the dismissal of Party General Secretary Hu Yaobang, the purge of several prominent intellectuals from the Communist Party, and a renewed political campaign against "bourgeois liberalization," defined as the advocacy of pluralistic political institutions. In response, 160 American scholars wrote to Chinese Ambassador Han Xu appealing for an end to the crackdown against dissent, and Senator Helms introduced a resolution criticizing the campaign against bourgeois liberalization.[78] When Yang Wei, a Shanghai intellectual who had returned to China after studying in the United States, was sentenced to two years in prison for participating in the antigovernment demonstrations, Senators Helms and Dennis DeConcini (D-Arizona) introduced a second resolution, later appended to the Foreign Relations Authorization Act, calling for Yang's release and urging the executive branch to give more sympathetic consideration to applications for political asylum from Chinese students and scholars in the United States who could demonstrate a "well-founded fear of persecution" if they returned home.[79]

As in the case of Tibet, these congressional initiatives forced the White House to react. In February 1989, the American embassy in China proposed, and officials responsible for China policy in Washington approved, an invitation to China's most prominent dissident, Fang Lizhi, to attend the presidential banquet planned for the end of Bush's visit to Peking later that month. Fang, an astrophysicist who served as vice president of the Chinese University of Science and Technology in Hefei, had been an outspoken advocate of political reform and a supporter of the student demonstrations of 1986 and

1987, which began at his campus. For that, he was stripped of his university position and his Party membership in early 1987, but was allowed to move to Peking to assume a research position in the Chinese Academy of Sciences. Some in the Bush administration may have had reservations about inviting so controversial a figure to a presidential dinner, but it was apparently felt that the president would be accused of a double standard on human rights if he failed to do so, especially because Reagan had met Soviet dissidents in the American embassy during the summit meeting in Moscow in May 1988. It was believed that inviting Fang to a large banquet, even one where Chinese officials would be present, would be less provocative to the Chinese government than arranging a private session between the president and a group of Chinese dissidents.

Not surprisingly, Chinese officials vehemently protested the American invitation to Fang, warning that their highest-ranking leaders would not appear at the banquet unless it were withdrawn. After intense negotiations at the working level, U.S. officials believed they had reached an understanding with the Chinese according to which Fang would attend the president's dinner but would not be permitted to greet Bush or any of the senior Chinese leaders attending. But that understanding was not accepted on the Chinese side by the superiors of those who had negotiated it. Plainclothes public security agents prevented Fang and his American escort from reaching the hotel where the banquet was being held. Subsequently, General Secretary Zhao Ziyang pleaded with Bush not to link the United States with those Chinese who advocated multiparty politics or a parliamentary system, because doing so would simply provide "an excuse for reversing the reform and stirring up social unrest."[80] Other Chinese committed to political reform privately agreed with Zhao.

In the end, both sides backed away from a confrontation over Fang. The White House disavowed the invitation, blaming it on Winston Lord and the American embassy staff in Peking.[81] The Bush administration also tried to downplay the issue of human rights, revealing that the subject was not brought up by the president, but only by Secretary of State James Baker, despite pressure from human rights advocates who wanted it placed on the presidential agenda.[82] After denouncing the invitation as "imposing one's own will on others" and showing "disrespect for the host country," the Chinese government said little more about the incident.[83]

Despite these efforts at moderating the confrontation, the flap over Fang had several longer-term consequences. It personalized for Americans the issue of human rights in China as never before. In the words of Aryeh Neier, executive director of Human Rights Watch, Fang was the "first person who has really emerged as a personality who symbolizes the human rights issue in China."[84] It demonstrated how much human rights had supplanted Taiwan, at least for the moment, as the most contentious and emotional issue in Sino-American relations. And finally, it may have suggested to Chinese leaders that, even if Washington raised the issue of human rights with Peking, the White House would back down if China retaliated.

FOREBODINGS

As China and the United States neared the end of the 1980s, the realization was growing in each country that the foundations of their relationship were changing. The moderation of Soviet foreign policy under Gorbachev, and the resulting improvements in Sino-Soviet and Soviet-American relations, was removing some of the strategic impetus from U.S.-China relations. This is not to say that the strategic element in Sino-American relations had completely disappeared. Some analysts in the two countries, especially in the Chinese and American military establishments, still regarded a potential threat from the Soviet Union as a continuing foundation of U.S.-China relations. Others noted the importance of sustained Sino-American cooperation in maintaining peace on the Korean peninsula, ensuring a Vietnamese withdrawal from Cambodia, and addressing other regional issues, especially in Asia. Still others argued that China's standing as a principal regional actor and a potential global power, and the American position as a superpower, made a strategic relationship between them in the national interest of both countries.[85] But almost all analysts agreed that, relatively speaking, the strategic rationale for U.S.-China relations was less compelling than it had been during the 1970s.

Instead, a consensus was emerging that economic ties would provide a new basis for Sino-American ties. As early as 1984, in an essay written on the eve of Reagan's visit to China, Richard Nixon had noted, "Though the threat of Soviet aggression brought us together, we will be kept together by our desire for economic progress for both our countries."[86] In a policy paper published the same year, the Atlantic Council also forecast that the basis of Sino-American relations would shift from security considerations to economic interests and thus become less triangular and more bilateral in character.[87] And a conference of Chinese specialists on American affairs in December

1988 agreed with this assessment. The Sino-American relationship in the coming decade, they said, would be rooted more in "economic relations, trade, and cooperation in science and technology" than in security factors.[88]

Chinese and American analysts debated whether the shifting foundations of U.S.-China relations would affect the stability of the relationship. Some thought a more complex set of bilateral ties would be more stable than one grounded primarily in geopolitics. In May 1984, for example, Paul Wolfowitz, the assistant secretary of state for East Asian and Pacific affairs, suggested that the two countries were creating "neither a predominantly economic nor a predominantly strategic relationship but rather a comprehensive one, in which each element reinforces the others,"[89] implying that the changes would make the U.S.-China relationship more durable than ever before. Four years later, participants in the Chinese academic conference just mentioned also concluded it would be better if Sino-American relations were based on something more than "coping with the threat from a third party." As the "groundwork of Sino-American relations" became "more extensive and varied," they said, the ties between the two countries would be "steady and mature" and would "not be easily affected by transient phenomena."[90]

Indeed, the relationship between China and the United States in some ways did seem more diverse, more institutionalized, more broadly based, and more mature than had been true six or seven years earlier. The rapid growth of economic, cultural, and strategic ties between the two countries was increasing each society's interest in a stable relationship with the other. Those ties, in turn, were being undertaken by more and more institutions and organizations on both sides of the Pacific, as a pluralistic America and a liberalizing China allowed their relationship to be conducted by a much larger range of organizations than in the prenormalization period. In China, various provinces, municipalities, bureaucratic agencies, enterprises, universities, research institutions, and professional associations developed a direct stake in a relationship with the United States. The same was true of the rising number of American corporations, government agencies, institutions of higher education, and cultural organizations that had exchange relationships with China or conducted business in the People's Republic.

The institutionalization of Sino-American relations was evidenced by the regular exchange of government officials at the highest levels. By the mid-1980s, a trip by an American cabinet member to China, or a visit by a Chinese government minister to the United States, was entirely routine. Three joint commissions (one on science and technology, the second on financial matters, and the third on commercial and trade issues), each headed by both an American cabinet secretary and a Chinese minister, convened annually to review the basic components of the relationship. The American secretary of state and the Chinese foreign minister could be expected to meet at least twice a year—once at the fall session of the United Nations General Assembly and once in either Peking or Washington. Even summit meetings had become mundane. The visits of Chinese President Li Xiannian to Washington in 1985, and George Bush to Peking as vice president in 1985 and as president in 1989, received much less press coverage in the United States than had comparable visits at earlier stages in the relationship.

As these institutional bonds between the two countries grew, Sino-American relations seemed to become more stable. Analysts in each country gradually acquired a fuller and more sophisticated understanding of the other. Chinese specialists on the United States became more familiar with the separation of powers between the White House and Congress, and between federal and local governments. They were less likely to overreact, therefore, to congressional measures or local decisions that seemed to violate Chinese interests.[91] American specialists on China gained a better understanding of the dynamics of Chinese politics and were less apt to exaggerate the cycles of economic reform and retrenchment, and political relaxation and tightening, that characterized China throughout the 1980s. The fact that the two countries had successfully weathered a crisis in their relationship in the early 1980s contributed to the sense that Sino-American ties were now durable and strong.

On both sides of the Pacific, Sino-American relations seemed to enjoy greater political consensus. In the United States, the desirability of a durable and stable relationship with China was no longer challenged by any large sector of American society. Public opinion polls showed broad support for friendly ties with China. In a poll conducted in 1986, 60 percent of the American public, and fully 89 percent of American opinion leaders, said the United States had a vital interest in China.[92] In 1985, 71 percent of the public had a favorable view of the People's Republic, compared with only 23 percent in 1972 (table A-1). For the first time since World War II, China policy was not a significant issue in the presidential election campaigns of 1984 or 1988.

In China, too, there seemed to be greater consensus on maintaining collaborative relations with the United States. The purges, rotations, and resignations of the late 1970s and early 1980s had removed many of those who had opposed the opening to the United States and replaced them with leaders who saw clearer benefit in economic, scientific, and even limited strategic ties with America. Some conservative Chinese leaders still expressed reservations about the willingness of the United States to offer genuine and sincere assistance to China's modernization, and others worried about the corrosive or destabilizing impact of American ideas and values on Chinese society. But, in the mid-1980s, these critics seemed to be a group of aging and even irrelevant leaders, whose views represented a distinct minority and whose political power was clearly waning. Moreover, outside Peking, local leaders seemed even more eager for extensive contacts with the United States. They had fewer of the political or ideological reservations that troubled their superiors in the capital.

On this stronger political and institutional base was being built a relationship that many perceived at the time to be more stable and more flexible than before. In December 1986, Gaston Sigur, the assistant secretary of state for East Asian and Pacific affairs, declared that Sino-American relations were "firmly on a stable and durable course," because the two countries could now discuss their differences on a "pragmatic, nonpolemical, case-by-case basis" without permitting them to destabilize the relationship as a whole.[93] In March 1987, American diplomats in Peking described Sino-American ties as marked, as one reporter summarized, by "an impressive breadth, solidity, and sturdiness."[94] And in June 1988, Undersecretary of State Michael Armacost claimed it was "a testament to the maturity of our relationship that we have been able to discuss the most difficult issues without major adverse consequences, while continuing to cooperate and advance our relationship as a whole."[95]

Chinese officials were more reluctant to describe the relationship as mature. Possibly, they defined the term in its biological sense as fully grown or fully developed, and believed that much potential for growth was yet unrealized. But they acknowledged many of the same psychological and behavioral patterns as did their American counterparts. In November 1984, Chinese ambassador Zhang Wenjin said the two governments "now have a good understanding of the importance of our relations. . . . We also understand much better where the difficulties or the differences are. . . . We both understand how to handle those differences so that they will not become unmanageable."[96] A year later, a leading Communist newspaper in Hong Kong, the *Wen Wei Po*, said the differences between the two countries could now be resolved in a "confident and unhurried way."[97]

Other observers were not so sure. In May 1986, American Ambassador Winston Lord, in a speech subtitled "No Time for Complacency," warned that "good relations are not inevitable in the future."

He noted that the strategic alignment between the two countries was fraying, as China's positions on international issues such as Cambodia and the Middle East began to diverge from those of the United States. He also pointed out that China and the United States were "two completely different societies," whose economic and cultural interactions would create contradictions as well as mutual benefit.[98] In January 1988, Huan Xiang, the director general of the Center for International Studies of China's State Council, warned that growing differences over human rights in China and over China's program of arms sales to the Middle East could cause Sino-American relations to "fall back rather than forge ahead."[99] And Roger Sullivan, the president of the National Council for U.S.-China Trade, cautioned that the Sino-American relationship had "run out of road map," and its future was uncertain.[100]

Indeed, despite their seeming maturity and stability, Sino-American relations in the late 1980s were experiencing several changes that gave them a new fragility. In the United States, the consensus on a stable relationship with China was wearing thin. As early as January 1986, staff members responsible for Asian affairs were perceiving an erosion of congressional support for the Sino-American relationship, largely as the strategic rationale for U.S.-China ties began to erode. Conservative members of Congress, such as Jesse Helms, had long been staunch defenders of Taiwan and critics of close ties with Peking. But now these veteran anti-Communists were being joined, on specific issues, by more liberal members who saw advantage in criticizing China on aspects of its foreign and domestic policies, including Senators Glenn and Proxmire on nuclear nonproliferation, Senator Claiborne Pell (D-Rhode Island) and Representative Stephen Solarz (R-New York) on the future of Taiwan, and Representative Solarz on human rights.

Conversely, there were now fewer members of Congress devoted to the preservation of Sino-American relations. A handful, such as Senator Chic Hecht (R-Nevada), were interested in greater liberalization of American trade policy to promote commercial relations with China. But the congressional leadership was no longer as committed to Sino-American ties as Senators Henry Jackson (D-Washington), Hugh Scott (R-Pennsylvania), and Jacob Javits (R-New York) had been in the 1970s. As a talented young Chinese specialist on American affairs concluded in a paper presented in December 1988, "China has few really dependable friends on the Hill."[101]

The situation among American interest groups was roughly similar. The National Council for U.S.-China Trade, now renamed the

U.S.-China Business Council, promoted American commercial relations with China. Former Secretary of State Henry Kissinger, with other former secretaries of state and former presidents, formed the America-China Society in an attempt to create a more secure political base for the relationship. But as U.S. relations with China became more diverse, American China policy attracted the critical attention of several interest groups that had ignored the subject before. Textile imports aroused the opposition of the American textile industry. American human rights organizations became concerned with the status of political and civil rights in China. Those opposed to abortion found, in the coercive aspects of Peking's family planning program, a dramatic illustration of the abuses that abortion could involve. The proponents of nuclear nonproliferation participated in discussions of nuclear cooperation with China. And, to a lesser degree, policy toward China became a subject of ethnic politics as well, with some Taiwanese-Americans promoting (through the Formosan Association for Public Affairs) the cause of self-determination for Taiwan, and with some Chinese-Americans (including students and scholars from China who were not U.S. citizens) doing the same for the cause of human rights on the Chinese mainland.

Even in the executive branch, the erosion of the political base for U.S.-China relations was apparent. In the early postnormalization period, except for the intense debates over forging military ties with Peking, there seemed to be a fairly broad consensus within the bureaucracy in favor of developing a close and extensive relationship with China. By the late 1980s, however, interagency cleavages had begun to develop. Although the Bureau of East Asian and Pacific Affairs at the State Department usually sought to defend U.S.-China relations from domestic political pressures, it increasingly had to battle the Bureau of Human Rights and Humanitarian Affairs over human rights issues, and the East Asian bureau occasionally lost. The Commerce Department, charged with promoting economic relations with China, supported the relaxation of export controls. But in this activity it encountered resistance from some officials in the Department of Defense, especially after the controversy over the sale of Chinese Silkworms to Iran.[102] The Council of Economic Advisers fought against protecting American industries against competition from China, but it encountered some resistance from the USTR, and vigorous opposition from the Department of Transportation to the proposal to allow American satellites to be put into orbit by Chinese missiles.[103]

Perhaps most important, many American officials now viewed

China with far less trust and respect in the late 1980s than had been true a decade before. In 1976, asked by president-elect Jimmy Carter whether Chinese leaders could be trusted, Kissinger had replied, "They will carry out meticulously both the letter and spirit of an agreement."[104] That sense of credibility had largely dissipated by the middle of 1989, as a result of Peking's failure to honor its bilateral grain agreement with the United States in 1983 and 1984, and Chinese disingenuousness about arms sales to the Middle East in 1987 and 1988.[105] Similarly, whereas Nixon and Kissinger saw China as one of the five most important power centers in the international political order, Reagan and Shultz perceived Peking as a regional actor that would acquire global stature only in the distant future.

The result of these developments was a change of tone in the deliberation of American policy toward China. Through the mid-1980s, the principal question addressed in such discussions was, in essence, "What can the United States do to promote Sino-American relations?" By the late 1980s, however, contentions of this sort were being countered by complaints that U.S. policy toward China was excessively accommodative and insufficiently attentive to American interests. Some commentators claimed the United States was too subservient to the Chinese position on Cambodia; others that Washington was too deferential to Chinese sensitivities about human rights; and still others that the White House was not doing enough to promote American commercial interests in China. The common denominator of these various lines of argument was that Americans were no longer asking what they could do for China, but rather what China could do for the United States.

At the same time as these developments were occurring in the United States, some changes were taking place in Chinese attitudes toward America. In the first five years after normalization, the Chinese regarded Taiwan as the principal obstacle to the development of their relationship with the United States. Now, however, a second obstacle was frequently being cited that, by 1988, began to supersede the Taiwan issue in importance. Various Chinese defined the problem differently: some described it as cultural imperialism, others as a cultural invasion, and still others as interference in China's internal affairs. But these different terms referred to the same two phenomena. First, they alluded to the deeper and more penetrative relationship between the two countries that had emerged in the 1980s, through which the United States was beginning to influence—sometimes intentionally, sometimes unwittingly—the political values and attitudes of Chinese citizens, especially younger people in urban areas.[106] And second, the complaints implied that the White

House and Congress—by calling for a more hospitable investment climate for American business, greater respect for human rights, more autonomy for Tibet, or a more liberal system of imports—were demanding basic changes in how the Chinese government managed its economy and governed its people.[107]

By April 1988, these charges were being couched in a new formulation that was at once intriguing and disturbing. The Soviet Union, American visitors were told, posed an external challenge to China, whereas the United States posed an internal threat. The buildup of Soviet forces along the Sino-Soviet frontier, Moscow's intervention in Afghanistan, the Kremlin's support for the Vietnamese invasion of Cambodia, and some improvements in Moscow's military relations with North Korea presented Chinese leaders with a classic threat to their national security. In contrast, American support for Chinese dissidents, pressure for economic and political reform, and contacts with a growing number of Chinese intellectuals threatened to undermine the stability of the Chinese political order and the legitimacy of the Chinese Communist Party.

Throughout their history, the Chinese have always viewed internal threats as more serious than external ones. Traditionally, Chinese rulers have been more concerned about foreign penetration into the heart of Chinese society than about the deployment of foreign military forces along the Chinese frontiers, especially when foreign activities inside China seemed to be winning converts among ordinary Chinese. In the concise formula of John Wills, the real danger to China's rulers has been not the foreign invader but the Chinese traitor.[108] In the early 1930s, Chiang Kai-shek, faced simultaneously with a Japanese invasion in the north and a Communist rebellion in the south, concluded unambiguously that the former represented a "disease of the skin," the latter a "disease of the heart." The use of a similar metaphor in the late 1980s implied that the internal ideological challenge presented by the United States was more severe than the external military threat posed by the Soviet Union.

Some Chinese attempted to defend the United States from this kind of criticism. One of the most knowledgeable and thoughtful Chinese specialists on the United States wrote in December 1988 that China should not fear the consequences of either economic or cultural exchanges with America, no matter how penetrative they might seem, because they were based on a common interest in promoting the modernization of China. Inevitably, some younger Chinese would have a "blind worship" of the United States, some older intellectuals would fear the "loss of China's national identity," and some leaders would develop "worries and doubts . . . about the value of cultural exchanges with the United States." But these problems were less the result of an American desire to infiltrate China than of the fact that "at present China lags too far behind the United States both culturally and economically." The solution, therefore, lay not in trying to insulate China from American influence but in "raising the whole nation's educational and cultural level [and] reestablishing national confidence."[109] Still, voices such as these had to compete with the ones critical of the United States for trying to penetrate, subvert, and control China.

Each of these two forecasts of the future of Sino-American relations—one optimistic, the other more cautious—was illustrated by developments at the end of 1988. In mid-December, the two countries marked the tenth anniversary of the normalization of their diplomatic relations. The two governments exchanged congratulatory telegrams to commemorate the event. Each country's president met with the other country's ambassador: Ronald Reagan with Han Xu, Yang Shangkun with Winston Lord. Each foreign ministry hosted a glittering reception in honor of the relationship, where the accomplishments of the past decade were hailed and the prospects for the future were toasted. A few evenings later, President-elect George Bush and his wife visited Han Xu's residence in Washington to exchange holiday greetings and sing Christmas carols in English and Chinese.[110] At the official and personal levels, these events seemed to be the mark of a stable and friendly relationship.

But even as Chinese and American leaders were congratulating each other on their achievements, a string of incidents illustrated the mistrust with which they still regarded each other. In December 1988, the U.S. government complained that American diplomats in China lacked the same freedom of travel enjoyed by their Chinese counterparts stationed in the United States. When Peking failed to act on the American protests, Washington retaliated by imposing travel restrictions on members of the Chinese consulate in Chicago. China, in turn, placed tighter restrictions on American consular officers in Shenyang and Shanghai.[111] The vituperation occasioned by this incident revealed that, whatever the protestations of friendship and claims of maturity at the highest level, the Sino-American relationship remained fragile and mistrustful. In the words of one American diplomat in Peking, "This dispute calls into question how each side views this relationship. Do we want to treat each other as friends, or . . . with suspicion?"[112]

CHAPTER 7

Crisis

AS the strategic imperative for Sino-American cooperation declined in the mid-1980s, a new rationale for relations between the two countries emerged. Both Chinese and Americans pointed to mutual economic interests as an alternative basis for their bilateral relationship. Natural complementarity existed, it was said, between the world's largest developed country and the world's largest developing nation. Americans wanted more foreign markets for their exports, more sites for overseas investment, and more inexpensive consumer goods, and they could find all those things in China. China wanted access to the vast American market, advanced American technology, and American financial and investment capital. That, along with the two societies' common desire for expanded cultural, scientific, and academic exchange, might sustain Sino-American relations even without a Soviet threat.

Moreover, many Americans, and even some Chinese, saw the United States as a model for the transformation of China. Americans, intrigued by the rapid pace of economic and political change in China, hoped the country's Leninist and Maoist institutions would be reshaped until China, like the United States, became a land of liberty, pluralism, private ownership, and free markets. Some Chinese, especially younger intellectuals, also saw American values and institutions—including the rule of law, multiple political parties, competitive elections, and a free press—as the key to achieving wealth and power for their nation.

The realization of these hopes depended, however, on the future of China's reforms. Despite a decade of impressive change, China's political and economic systems in the late 1980s were far from resembling those of the United States. If Americans demanded evidence that China was moving toward capitalism and democracy, then much more economic and political liberalization would be necessary. Even some of the more modest American economic objec-

tives required further transformation in China. Improving the investment climate, opening the Chinese market to foreign imports, and
maximizing the opportunities for academic and cultural exchange
necessitated a more extensive dismantling of administrative and
ideological controls over Chinese society.

The two countries' ability to manage the Taiwan issue also rested
on the fate of reforms on the mainland. In essence, the growth of
economic and cultural relationships across the Taiwan Strait was
permitting leaders in Peking to overlook the American commitments to the security of Taiwan. The explosion of trade, investment,
and tourism was beginning to bind Taiwan more closely to the
mainland and was encouraging speculation that a gradual process of
reunification might not be so inconceivable after all. But again, these
developments were rooted in the mainland's policies of economic
and political liberalization. Like entrepreneurs in other countries,
Taiwan's business community hoped that a more market-oriented
economy would produce a more hospitable investment climate on
the Chinese mainland. And the people of Taiwan could contemplate
reunification only if the political, economic, and social gaps between
the two societies were narrowed by successful reform on the other
side of the Taiwan Strait.

For all these reasons, if reform proceeded smoothly in China, then
the prognosis for U.S.-China relations was reasonably good, although
the two countries would have to find ways of managing the economic
and strategic issues beginning to plague their relationship. If, however, reform experienced a serious setback, then the new underpinnings for bilateral ties between China and the United States would
be severely undermined. Retrogression in China would make their
economic and cultural relationship less attractive, exacerbate differences over human rights, and possibly complicate the prospects for
the resolution of the Taiwan issue as well.

CRISIS IN TIANANMEN

Through most of the 1980s, the reform program undertaken by
Deng Xiaoping had produced great benefits for most of the Chinese people. The rate of economic growth accelerated, first in agriculture and then in industry. This success permitted great increases in
incomes, with the nominal wages of workers doubling, and the cash
incomes of farmers tripling, during the years between 1979 and 1986.
The greater availability of consumer goods allowed a relaxation of

the rationing systems of the past and enabled ordinary Chinese to translate their higher incomes into improved standards of living. A burst of new housing construction—state sponsored in the cities, and individually owned in the countryside—gave Chinese workers and peasants more room in which to place their new furniture, radios, televisions, and cassette recorders. Although serious inefficiencies remained, reflected in chronic losses by many state enterprises and bottlenecks in energy and transportation, overall the Chinese economy experienced the greatest vibrancy of any period since 1949.

Despite limits on political reform, life for most Chinese improved in the political sphere as well. Ordinary Chinese encountered far fewer restrictions on their choice of friends, hobbies, clothing, and even political opinions than had been true in the Maoist era. Intellectuals enjoyed a more relaxed climate in which to conduct their scholarly research or their artistic activities. Open political dissent and unorthodox literary expression were still occasionally disciplined, but the punishments were less severe and somewhat less arbitrary than during the Maoist period. These developments helped restore some of the faith in the Communist Party that so many Chinese had lost during the Cultural Revolution. The celebration of the thirty-fifth anniversary of the founding of the People's Republic of China in Tiananmen Square in 1984 produced some genuine and seemingly spontaneous expressions of popular support for the leadership, with a group of students carrying a banner with the cheerful slogan, *"Xiaoping, ni hao,"* perhaps best translated as "Hi there, [Deng] Xiaoping."[1]

Toward the end of the decade, however, the less desirable results of reform became more apparent: growing corruption, widening inequalities, surging inflation, and the renewed alienation of broad sectors of urban Chinese from their own government. Many of these problems were the inevitable consequences of the transition from a centrally planned economy to a market-oriented one, and from a totalitarian political order to a more authoritarian system. But they also occurred because Chinese leaders had undertaken reform cautiously and incrementally, with many crucial measures still incomplete.

The relaxation of political controls over society in post-Mao China produced an increase in all kinds of crime, from rape to murder to burglary. From a political perspective, the most dangerous was the rise of corruption. In large part, this upsurge was the result of the uneasy mixture of plan and market, in which private entrepreneurs could encounter a facilitative or restrictive attitude from government officials, depending on how willing they were to bribe them. The existence of a dual price system, in which the same commodities were simultaneously sold at a lower price through the state plan and at a higher price on the open market, gave officials a nearly irresistible temptation to buy cheap from the state and then sell dear on the market. The fact that so many relatives of high officials had access to the cheaper goods available through state distribution channels and engaged in this practice exacerbated resentment throughout Chinese society.

Inequality also began to be a problem, in a society that had become accustomed to egalitarianism during more than three decades of Communist rule. The degree of income inequality in urban areas had fallen somewhat in the first years of reform, but by early 1989 it had risen well above prereform levels. In the countryside, the distribution of income had become steadily less equal ever since the early 1980s as a consequence of the decollectivization of agriculture and the establishment of local industrial enterprises. Regional disparities also widened, as the coastal areas of southeast China took advantage of new foreign trade and investment opportunities to pull far ahead of the provinces in remoter parts of the country.[2]

In essence, economic reform turned the social structure of China on its head. Private entrepreneurs, who had previously been political pariahs, were the ones most able to profit personally from the economic reforms. Conversely, government employees and intellectuals, who had previously constituted China's economic elite, received the least from the new economic policies, even though intellectuals were a prime beneficiary of political relaxation. This turn of events affected the mood on Chinese university campuses, where students questioned the long-term financial consequences of entering careers in which salaries were now, at least in relative terms, lower than before. State industrial workers, another group that had been privileged in the past, still had access to bonuses and wage increases, which enabled them to increase their incomes more rapidly than China's white-collar workers. But even they now had to worry, at least in theory, about the possibilities of layoffs or bankruptcy as inefficient state enterprises were subjected to tighter budgetary constraints and more stringent market discipline.

A third problem, inflation, was probably an unavoidable result of price reform, given the extent to which the prices of key commodities (food, housing, utilities, and transportation) had been administratively set at artificially low levels. But several features of China's incomplete reforms were, by 1988, exacerbating inflationary pressures. In the absence of hard budget constraints on enterprises, industrial wages and bonuses were outstripping increases in labor productivity. The assignment of a greater share of state revenues to local governments and to individual enterprises was creating chronic budget deficits at the central level. Provincial leaders took advantage of greater fiscal and monetary autonomy to stimulate local investment through expanded credit and government subsidies, without much regard to the financial or economic returns. In addition, Zhao Ziyang and some of his lieutenants appeared to hold the convenient assumption that reform would be facilitated by a rapid rate of economic growth, for which inflation would be a reasonably small price to pay.

All three of these problems would have produced growing political pressures on the national government in any event, but in the China of the late 1980s political alienation was being exacerbated by the sluggish pace of political restructuring. The halting progress toward a more rational and institutionalized political system contributed to the perception that the Chinese government was too incompetent to deal with the problems of reform. The discrediting of old doctrinal premises by the Cultural Revolution, the Party's subsequent inability to devise a new and more compelling ideological basis for its rule, and the infusion of controversial ideas from abroad all steadily weakened the legitimacy of the political system. The weakening of the Party's ideological and organizational controls over state employees, and the emergence of private and collective enterprises outside the state sector, created the rudiments of a civil society, independent of the state, which was willing and able to present demands to the government. Unfortunately, the failure to create new mechanisms for hearing and acting upon those demands meant that popular grievances would necessarily be expressed outside institutional channels.[3]

Growing public dissatisfaction with the negative consequences of reform had been apparent for some time. There had been sporadic demonstrations during the 1980s: strikes and slowdowns over economic issues, demonstrations against imported Japanese goods, protests in national minority areas such as Tibet, and especially calls by students for greater democracy in 1986 and 1987, and again in mid-1988. But the protests had never assumed a breadth or intensity that posed a serious challenge to the central government. Those that occurred in Tibet had to be put down by armed force, but those that took place in China proper were fairly easily suppressed by less dramatic measures.

In the spring of 1989, however, the situation was ripe for further protest. Political disorder in China is commonly fostered not only by socioeconomic grievances but also by signs of division within the central leadership, and by early 1989 there were widespread reports of debate among senior Chinese leaders over the pace and extent of reform. One group, led by General Secretary Zhao Ziyang and

supported by Deng Xiaoping, had been promoting more radical economic reform, featuring the complete marketization of the economy,
the drastic curtailment of central planning, and experiments with
the privatization of state industry through stock ownership schemes.
This group had also been entertaining bolder political reform: not
inaugurating full political pluralism but restricting the role of the
Party, promoting a more lively and open press, and increasing the
powers of national and local legislatures. A second group, headed by
Premier Li Peng and senior economic planner Chen Yun, favored
maintenance of mandatory planning, opposed any extensive privatization of industry, and proposed periodic propaganda campaigns to
promote "socialist spiritual civilization."

The economic situation in China was also worsening. Prices in
major cities were increasing at an annual rate of around 30 to 40
percent—not a high rate by the standards of many third world countries, but a level not known in China since the hyperinflation of the
late 1940s. The overheated economy was producing serious shortages
of energy and raw materials. In March 1989, Premier Li Peng told
the National People's Congress that China should be prepared "to
live a hard life for a few years." New restrictions on state investment
raised the possibility that higher prices would now be accompanied
by slower growth, sluggish wage increases, and fewer new employment opportunities.[4]

These economic problems had begun to shift the balance within
the political leadership from more radical reformers like Zhao Ziyang
to more cautious leaders like Li Peng. As early as the fall of 1988,
Zhao admitted that he had been stripped of control over economic
policy, and there were rumors the following spring that he would
soon be forced to resign as general secretary of the Party.[5] There was
speculation that Li Peng's economic retrenchment program would
entail a curtailment of some of the more controversial economic
reforms, particularly in the area of prices and industrial ownership.
The annual meeting of the National People's Congress in March was
marked by a decidedly less open and democratic atmosphere than
the year before, and Li explicitly announced the postponement of
further political restructuring at the provincial and municipal
levels.[6]

These developments sparked plans for a new round of student
demonstrations, originally scheduled to coincide with the seventieth
anniversary of the May Fourth movement of 1919 and Mikhail Gorbachev's summit meeting in Peking a few days later. But an acciden-
tal event accelerated the timetable for protest.[7] On April 15, former
General Secretary Hu Yaobang died in Peking, having suffered a heart

attack at a meeting of the Politburo three days earlier. Hu's forced resignation from office in January 1987, on the grounds he had been too lenient toward prodemocracy demonstrations, had already made him a sympathetic figure in the eyes of many Chinese students. Rumors that he had been stricken at a meeting where he had been defending economic reform against a conservative challenge reinforced Hu's image as a persecuted champion of political and economic liberalization.

Suddenly, the cause of reform had a martyr. Within a few hours, memorial wreaths were placed on several campuses and at the memorial to revolutionary martyrs in Tiananmen Square. Within days, student protesters began daily demonstrations in the heart of Peking. At one point, they staged a sit-in in front of the main gate to the Party and government offices at Zhongnanhai, demanding political reform. At another, a small delegation of student leaders fell to their knees on the steps of the Great Hall of the People, holding a petition above their heads, pleading to engage in dialogue with the officials peering at them through the locked glass doors.

China's central leadership, already deeply divided over a wide range of political and economic issues, now split again over the most appropriate response to these new demonstrations. One group, led by Zhao Ziyang, was willing to hold a dialogue with the students, and may even have sought ways of utilizing the protests as an argument in favor of renewed economic and political restructuring, much as Deng Xiaoping had used the Democracy Wall protests in late 1978 to launch the first wave of reform at the third plenum that December. The rival faction, associated with Li Peng and the municipal leaders of Peking, characterized the protests as counterrevolutionary and proposed that they be suppressed. To them, the demonstrations showed that Zhao Ziyang had failed to pay sufficient attention to ideological education and had allowed subversive ideas to spread through the ranks of Chinese youth.

With the leadership so divided, neither dialogue nor suppression was employed consistently or successfully. A *People's Daily* editorial, published on April 26, accused the students of fomenting turmoil and conspiring to overthrow the government. But the language of the editorial inflamed rather than intimidated the students, and its publication was not followed by effective police action against the demonstrations. Zhao Ziyang, who had been out of the country when the editorial appeared, said upon returning to Peking that the reasonable demands of the students should be accepted and urged extensive consultations and dialogues with all sectors of society. But in the subsequent meetings between Party officials and student representatives, there was no discussion of any political reform, but only patronizing statements by Party leaders on the need for the students to end their demonstrations.

The perception that the central leadership was divided and had been forced to shift from confrontation to dialogue with the students encouraged an escalation of the demonstrations. To gain more support, some students launched a hunger strike on May 13 to underscore their demands for political reform. The earnestness of the students, in sharp contrast to the insensitivity of the Party leadership, produced widespread popular backing for the protests. At their height, the demonstrations attracted around one million people every day to the heart of Peking from virtually every sector of Chinese society, including industrial workers, journalists, and even Party cadres, government officials, and members of the police. As during the Cultural Revolution, Chinese from other cities began to flock to the capital to participate in the protests. Outside Peking, demonstrations on a smaller scale were conducted in scores of other cities, including virtually every provincial capital.

Protests on this scale understandably lacked a clear program. Some participants took part out of curiosity, others out of commitment. Some protested inequality and corruption, while others demanded greater freedom and democracy. Some were not certain about the kind of political system China needed, whereas others called passionately for freedom of the press, freedom of association and assembly, and free elections to the national legislature.[8] Some still supported reform in the Communist Party, while others increasingly came to believe the Party would have to be overthrown. But the common denominator was a call for change and a repudiation of a government that seemed incapable of providing it.

On May 19, with Gorbachev now safely out of China, the protracted deadlock within the elite was finally broken. A group of elderly leaders, many supposedly retired from office, demanded that the protests be ended by force. In their eyes, the ongoing demonstrations in the heart of the capital threatened to throw the entire country into chaos. Of particular concern was the participation of large numbers of industrial workers in the protests, and the emergence of independent labor unions. An alliance of workers and students, each with autonomous organizations, raised the specter of a popular uprising similar to what had occurred in Poland in 1980. And like the leaders of the Polish Communist party, China's gerontocrats believed that the only solution was to impose martial law. Deng Xiaoping personally gave his support to this proposal and lent his prestige to the task of mobilizing enough military force to implement it.

But once again, the authority of the central government was so reduced that what once might have inspired fear and compliance now evoked open criticism and defiance. After the announcement of martial law on May 20, thousands of citizens surged into the streets of Peking to prevent army convoys, which were not yet authorized to use deadly force, from entering the heart of the city. Military commanders, university presidents, and provincial leaders, singly or in combination, wrote petitions to the central leadership calling for restraint and opposing the use of armed force against the demonstrators. Zhao Ziyang resigned from his position as general secretary of the Party rather than give even implicit support to the imposition of martial law. The official press began to criticize the Party leadership, with one English-language journal referring to Deng Xiaoping as a "doddery Chinese leader," reporting that martial law was being "resisted by most of the people of the capital," and acknowledging that most people interviewed "think the action is neither necessary nor justified."[9]

At this point, some student leaders wisely concluded that further protests could provoke a bloody and counterproductive confrontation with the authorities, and proposed calling off the demonstrations. But when the leaders were unable to secure a consensus from their followers on this proposition, the protests continued. In fact, in recognition of the danger that the imposition of martial law might cause the demonstrators to waver, one group of students from the Central Academy of Arts created a powerful new symbol of dissent, erecting a statue of the *Goddess of Freedom and Democracy* in Tiananmen Square on May 29. This gesture created a new wave of public support for the protests.

Finally, on the night of June 3–4, fully two weeks after martial law had been declared, enough troops had been assembled around Peking to permit the final suppression of the demonstrations. But the soldiers in question were from the regular army, equipped with tanks and automatic weapons rather than water cannon and tear gas, and neither adequately trained nor skillfully led in the suppression of urban protests. Perhaps provoked by occasional outbreaks of violence from the crowd, especially from workers and unemployed youth, they opened fire at random on demonstrators on the approaches to the center of Peking, moved forward to retake Tiananmen Square, and then mopped up opposition throughout the city. Although the casualty figures are still uncertain, the best estimates are of perhaps a thousand dead and several thousands injured in a night of brutal carnage.

Thereafter, a wave of political repression began slowly to spread across the country.[10] The demonstrations in Tiananmen Square were officially depicted as a counterrevolutionary riot that resulted from an antigovernment conspiracy. Police combed the country for leaders of the protests, many of whom were seeking to flee abroad. By October, at least 12, and perhaps as many as 100, demonstrators had been executed. Somewhere between 4,500 and 10,000 protesters had been arrested, and an unknown but probably larger number had been subjected to various administrative sanctions.

The repercussions of the Tiananmen incident also extended through the higher levels of China's leadership. On June 24, the fourth plenum of the Party Central Committee announced the purge of Zhao Ziyang from his leadership positions in the Party and the dismissal of three of his lieutenants from the Politburo and the Secretariat.[11] The surviving central leaders began a reshuffling of provincial leaders, central government officials, and military commanders, sometimes targeted at those believed sympathetic to the demonstrations. The victims included the minister of culture, the governor of Hainan province, and the president of Peking University.

Over the subsequent months, the wave of repression spread from the central leadership compound at Zhongnanhai throughout much of the rest of urban China. Political education was resumed or intensified in universities, research institutions, and government agencies. Some of the central mass media were reorganized by military work teams. A reregistration of Party members was conducted in several big cities. Freshmen at some of China's most prestigious universities were subject to as much as a year of military training before beginning classes. Party cells were reestablished in those government agencies where they had been disbanded, and neighborhood committees were resurrected as an instrument of local supervision. A promising period of political and economic reform now seemed to have come to an abrupt and tragic end.

THE BUSH ADMINISTRATION'S RESPONSE

As the demonstrations in Peking mounted in late April and early May, the Bush administration struggled to find an appropriate American response. Its initial position was to support the rights of free speech, peaceful assembly, and nonviolent protest, and to urge restraint on the demonstrators and the Chinese government. In congressional testimony on May 4, the acting deputy assistant secretary of state for East Asian and Pacific affairs, Richard Williams, added that the U.S. government hoped that "the trend towards more openness and more respect for basic human rights will continue." He also warned there would necessarily be a reassessment of American policy toward China if the Chinese government chose to suppress the demonstrations by force.[12] When martial law was imposed later in the month, the Bush administration repeated these statements, noting that it still expected the situation in China to end favorably. Secretary of State James Baker said it was his personal view that the process of reform in China would be irreversible, and a government analyst was quoted anonymously as saying, "The crackdown probably won't work because there is too much support for students in the military and among all elements of society."[13]

These fairly restrained statements reflected the administration's fear that an American overreaction could prove counterproductive. Excessive U.S. support for the demonstrators could inflame the situation in Peking, the White House feared, perhaps leading to prolonged political instability in China, or else provoking the kind of crackdown that would severely set back the cause of political reform. Some American officials said privately that the Bush administration had drawn an analogy between China in 1989 and Hungary in 1956, and it was determined to avoid the previous mistake of encouraging opposition to Communist rule that the U.S. would be unable to support. Thus, as Baker put it at the height of the protests, it was essential that the United States not "be seen to be inciting to riot."[14]

The crackdown in Peking in the predawn of June 4 forced the administration to take bolder action. The White House immediately issued a statement saying the president "deeply deplored the decision to use force against peaceful demonstrators."[15] The following day, the Bush administration imposed its first series of sanctions against China, including a warning against American travel to China, the suspension of military sales to Peking, and the postponement of all high-level military exchanges. The White House announced it was offering humanitarian assistance through the Red Cross to those who had been wounded in the crackdown in Peking. It also said it would make a sympathetic review of requests by Chinese students and scholars in the United States who wished to delay their return home. President Bush met with a small group of Chinese students to express his concern about the situation in their country.[16] And Secretary of State Baker decided that Fang Lizhi, the dissident Chinese physicist who had been prevented from attending the president's banquet in Peking, would be given temporary refuge in the American embassy in Peking.[17]

Beyond these actions, the administration waited to see how the situation in China unfolded, hoping it might not be as bad as the first reports indicated. There was still the possibility that Deng Xiaoping might dissociate himself from the deaths of June 4 and 5, or that the clearing of Tiananmen Square might not lead to any more repression of those who had participated in the demonstrations. Within a few days, however, it was becoming clear that these hopes for an early relaxation of the situation in China would not be realized. When Deng Xiaoping finally reappeared in public on June 9, he met with the commanders of the martial law forces in Peking and endorsed their activities, and accused the demonstrators of wanting to replace the socialist system with a "Westernized vassalage bourgeois republic."[18] On June 15, three workers in Shanghai were sentenced to death for burning a railway train there. Three days later, eight more demonstrators in Peking also received the death penalty for their involvement in what was now officially described as a counter-revolutionary riot.

In response to the deteriorating situation in China, the Bush administration announced a second set of sanctions on June 20. Secretary of State Baker said in a congressional hearing that he was making two recommendations to the president: that the United States request the postponement of all further lending to China by international financial institutions, and that the White House suspend all official exchanges with China at and above the level of assistant secretary. The president accepted both recommendations, thus canceling visits by Secretary of Commerce Robert Mosbacher and Secretary of the Treasury Nicholas Brady that had been scheduled for later in the year, but he redefined the second proposal to exclude only ceremonial exchanges at the cabinet level.[19] It was later revealed that, around this same time, the administration imposed other sanctions against China that were not announced publicly, including the suspension of investment guarantees by the Overseas Private Investment Corporation (OPIC), financing under the Trade Development Program, the issuance of export licenses for American satellites intended to be launched on Chinese boosters, and the implementation of the 1985 nuclear cooperation agreement with China.[20]

The Bush administration recognized that sanctions imposed by the United States alone would be much less effective than sanctions imposed by a broad coalition of Western nations. It therefore actively encouraged allies to follow suit with comparable steps of their own. At its summit in late June, the European Community postponed economic aid to China, suspended high-level official contacts with Peking, and announced opposition to further multilateral lending to

China. This response simply codified the decisions already taken unilaterally by such European nations as Britain, France, and Germany, which had also suspended military contacts, halted arms sales, and offered refuge to Chinese nationals who did not want to return home. The subsequent meeting of the Group of Seven in Paris in July took similar decisions, with Japan now joining the list of nations suspending economic assistance programs to Peking. The Asian Development Bank and the World Bank halted new lending to China, once it became clear that the developed nations would no longer support the continuation of multilateral aid to Peking.[21]

At the same time that it was imposing sanctions on Peking, however, the Bush administration remained deeply concerned that an exaggerated American reaction to the crisis could have severe consequences for China and for Sino-American relations. In two separate statements in early June, the president warned against an "emotional response" to the suppression of the demonstrations, on the grounds that excessive sanctions might produce a "total break in this relationship" or even cause "hardship" to the Chinese people.[22] A few weeks later, the president explained to a group of senators that he shared their revulsion at developments in Peking, but felt that attempts to influence China through public denunciations or through a policy of isolation would be futile at best and counterproductive at worst. The president and his advisers also assigned high priority to the strategic significance of Sino-American relations and worried that precipitous action might "throw China back into the hands of the Soviet Union."[23] Indeed, at this time the administration leaked, to the *Washington Post*, the most comprehensive discussion of Sino-American strategic cooperation yet available, as a way of underlining the importance of China to overall American foreign policy.[24]

Even as it imposed sanctions against China, therefore, the Bush administration tried to defuse the emerging crisis in Sino-American relations so as to preserve as much of the relationship as possible. One approach was to reopen the lines of communication with Peking. Characteristically, the president tried to establish direct contact with the Chinese leadership by placing a personal telephone call to Deng Xiaoping on June 8. According to Chinese sources, Bush was told that the time of the call (early morning in Peking) was inconvenient and that direct phone contacts between Chinese and foreign leaders were not the custom. The president reportedly waited for a return call from Deng, but it never came.[25]

With the direct presidential initiative rebuffed, the U.S. government then attempted to contact Chinese leaders through other channels. Two days after the abortive phone call to Deng, Secretary of

State Baker began a series of meetings with Chinese ambassador Han Xu, aimed at resolving the issue of Fang Lizhi. In those meetings, Baker suggested that Fang and his wife be given safe passage from the American embassy in Peking to asylum in some third country. Baker also continued contacts with his Chinese counterpart, Foreign Minister Qian Qichen, at the Paris conference on Cambodia in late July, and at the meeting of the United Nations General Assembly in September. The administration explained that these encounters between Bush and Qian were not ceremonial exchanges of the sort that had been suspended but rather working meetings taking place either in third countries or in international organizations.

At the same time as Baker was meeting publicly with Han Xu and Qian Qichen, the White House was engaging in private diplomacy with the Chinese. In July, in a step known only to a handful of officials in the administration, President Bush secretly sent National Security Adviser Brent Scowcroft and Deputy Secretary of State Lawrence Eagleburger to Peking to meet with senior Chinese leaders, including Deng Xiaoping. Their message was twofold: to convey the American concern about the suppression of human rights in China after June 4 but to express the president's desire to prevent the collapse of Sino-American relations.

The president and his advisers knew that such a visit would be highly unpopular if it were made public, occurring so soon after the June 4 incident. It appeared to be a violation of the administration's ban on high-level exchanges between Chinese and American officials. But it was also felt that it was necessary to communicate with top-level Chinese leaders directly and privately. As Eagleburger later explained, "Messages delivered below the level of the top leaders often get softened or altered on the way up the chain of command," whereas public statements "often engender public posturing, in which saving 'face' becomes more important than a sober consideration of the issues." Eagleburger insisted that he and General Scowcroft had conveyed an "undiluted message from the President to the Chinese leadership about America's horror over Tiananmen," and he described the visit as "neither easy nor pleasant."[26]

The Bush administration also found ways to define the American sanctions in ways that reduced or moderated their impact. In early July, for example, it permitted the sale of four Boeing 757 commercial aircraft to China. The aircraft were technically prohibited for export under the original sanctions, in that their advanced navigation systems were a type of dual-purpose technology that was on the munitions control list. But the White House argued that the sanctions had never been intended to restrict civilian commerce with China, and so an export license would be granted. In October, the Bush administration also announced it was permitting American engineers and Chinese military officers to continue work in the United States on designing the avionics package for Chinese F-8 fighters under the Peace Pearl program, even though the actual delivery of the equipment would not be permitted so long as the ban on arms sales to China remained in effect. This decision was much more controversial than the licensing of the exports of the Boeing 757s, for it seemed to be a significant exception to the ban on military relations between the two countries.[27]

In short, the Bush administration was walking a very fine line in defining policy toward China in the summer of 1989. On the one hand, it was under great public pressure to impose severe sanctions on China in response to the June 4 incident. But on the other, it was attempting to preserve a viable working relationship with Peking by maintaining channels of communication with the Chinese government. This policy of limited sanctions, muted rhetoric, and continued communication with Chinese leaders was controversial in the Bush administration. The approach was encouraged by Scowcroft and by James Lilley, the American ambassador to China, who believed that Sino-American relations were worth preserving and that a harsher response would severely jeopardize them. Conversely, Secretary of State Baker reportedly feared such a policy would lead to a firestorm in the United States, because it would not satisfy public and congressional demands for tougher measures.[28]

In the end, however, the policy was very much the president's own. Bush had long appeared confident that the experience he had gained as American envoy to Peking in the mid-1970s gave him the background necessary to deal with problems of China policy without much input from the China specialists in the bureaucracy. In 1980, Bush had been offered a State Department briefing before leaving for China to explain Ronald Reagan's campaign statements about restoring official relations with Taiwan. He had declined the offer, saying, "I know these people."[29] Now, nine years later, Bush again took his own counsel on China, soon acquiring the reputation of having become the government's desk officer for Chinese affairs. Moreover, the emphasis on making personal contact with foreign leaders, the absence of emotional rhetoric about the massacre in Peking, and the emphasis on strategic concerns rather than human rights were typical of the president's general approach to the conduct of foreign policy.

THE CONGRESSIONAL RESPONSE

From the beginning of the crisis in China, the Bush administration's restrained approach was very different from much of public and congressional opinion, which favored a more forceful reaction to the events in Peking. In May, at the height of the mass demonstrations in Tiananmen Square, an analysis in the *New York Times* contrasted Bush's "utmost caution" in China with his simultaneous encouragement to the people of Panama to overthrow Manuel Antonio Noriega.[30] Columnists such as R.W. Apple and Rowland Evans and Robert Novak criticized the White House for a lack of vision and a poverty of rhetoric.[31] Representative Stephen Solarz, the chairman of the House Subcommittee on Asian and Pacific Affairs, urged the president on May 21 to "visibly and publicly identify himself" with the demonstrators in China, perhaps by meeting with a group of Chinese students and scholars in the United States.[32]

The gap between the impassive language from the U.S. government and the high emotions felt by the American people produced demands from across the political spectrum for a more vigorous response to the massacre on June 4. Human Rights Watch immediately sent an open letter to the president, urging him to impose a sweeping set of sanctions against China, including recalling the American ambassador, revoking Peking's most-favored-nation status, suspending commercial incentives under the Trade Development Program and the Overseas Private Investment Corporation, terminating all arms sales, prohibiting further technology transfer to China, and opposing international lending to Peking. In a joint appearance on "Face the Nation," Senator Jesse Helms and Representative Stephen Solarz, usually at opposite ends of the political spectrum, agreed that the United States should make a more forceful reaction to the June 4 incident. And Solarz warned, "If the president doesn't take the initiative in changing American policy in this regard, the Congress will do it for him."[33]

At first, the administration's response seemed to satisfy these demands. Although falling far short of the policy recommended by Human Rights Watch, the Bush administration's first batch of sanctions, imposed on June 5, received highly favorable reviews from most domestic audiences. The *Washington Post* called them a "balanced policy" that was not "showy," but "tough." Similarly, in response to the second set of sanctions announced later in the month, the *New York Times* said the president was proceeding in a firm and sensible way that was "far more likely to be constructive than are the merely angry messages proposed by his critics."[34] Public opinion seemed to share this assessment. In mid-June, most of those polled in two separate surveys approved of the president's approach to China. Moreover, a slightly smaller majority agreed that the White House should take the lead in shaping policy toward Peking, with Congress relegated to a subordinate role.[35]

Not that Congress appeared, at this point, to wish to challenge the president. Although many members had pressed the White House to respond more vigorously to the June 4 incident, the administration's actions, once they were announced, received widespread approval. The House and the Senate adopted, by unanimous votes, resolutions endorsing the sanctions announced by the president on June 5. Members of Congress from across the political spectrum expressed their personal support of Bush's approach to China, with Senator Alan Cranston assigning it a grade of A plus.[36]

Just beneath the surface, however, there was an undercurrent of sentiment potentially dangerous to the administration. Although supporting what the president had done so far, the public and Congress seemed ready to impose more extensive sanctions on China if the administration's more cautious approach did not obtain rapid and decisive results. Just after the June 4 incident, for example, Congressman Solarz and Senators Helms, Sam Nunn, and Claiborne Pell warned that further sanctions might prove necessary if the situation in China continued to deteriorate.[37] After the second set of sanctions was announced later in June, the Democratic and Republican leaders in the Senate, George Mitchell and Robert Dole, joined in saying that Congress would demand tougher action if the political situation in China did not improve.[38] Similarly, public opinion polls taken somewhat later, in July, showed the American people were willing to take stronger action against Peking, particularly if the crackdown in China continued.[39]

And, as the days passed, it became clear that the political situation in China was deteriorating rather than improving. In the eyes of many in Congress and in the media, the president had failed to redeem his implicit promise that moderate sanctions, cautious rhetoric, and quiet diplomacy could quickly set things right. As a result, the gap between Congress and the White House, and between the White House and the media, began to widen. Senate Majority Leader Mitchell called on the president to "give voice to the feelings of the overwhelming majority of the American people who are outraged and revolted" by the executions in China.[40] The *New York Times*, which had previously fully endorsed Bush's approach, now began to express reservations. "Unless the President stops speaking so softly," it warned on June 27, "he risks undermining his big stick. . . . Not since a news conference three weeks ago has the President given voice to the public mood. . . . The words are right: his policy is sound. What's missing is the music."[41]

But this time the administration did not yield to the pressure. Vice President Dan Quayle, noting that the president "knows China—he's an expert," said that Bush would not be "pushed into doing something he will regret later down the road." The White House press secretary, Marlin Fitzwater, said the administration had already spoken out, and there was "no need to repeat different words every day of the week" to make the same point.[42]

In the face of the administration's inaction, Congress, which previously had been willing to endorse the White House's policies, now began to push for sanctions of its own. Conservative Republicans and liberal Democrats, acting independently, introduced legislation that would have added new sanctions or written existing sanctions into law. Even before the executions in China, Senator Helms and Representative Benjamin A. Gilman (R-New York) proposed a bill that, among other things, would have ended transfer of advanced technology to China, suspended government-to-government scientific exchange programs, terminated China's access to U.S. government financial assistance and investment guarantees, suspended Sino-American military cooperation, and withdrawn China's most-favored-nation status.[43] By the end of June, other members of the House of Representatives had introduced more specific amendments to the biannual foreign aid authorization bill that would have targeted arms sales, investment guarantees by the Overseas Private Investment Corporation, satellite launches, China's most-favored-nation status, and the like.[44]

These approaches were soon combined into a comprehensive sanctions amendment, which passed the House at the end of June by a vote of 418–0 and passed the Senate in mid-July by a vote of 81–10, and ultimately were attached to the Foreign Relations Authorization Act (Public Law 101–246).[45] In its final form, the amendment codified most of the measures the White House had announced earlier in June: the suspension of OPIC investment guarantees, the Trade Development Program, munitions export licenses, the liberalization of export controls, satellite export permits, and the implementation of the nuclear cooperation agreement. It also endorsed American opposition to further lending to China by international financial institutions. Furthermore, the bill imposed a few additional sanctions beyond those already imposed by the president: it required the suspension of export licenses for police equipment and recommended that any further Eximbank loans to China be postponed. Significantly, however, the bill did not call for the revocation of China's most-favored-nation status at this point. Such a provision would have required additional hearings by a separate set of committees, and the congressional leadership feared that adding it would cost a great deal of time and might even arouse serious opposition.

The congressional legislation required that, before lifting any of these mandated sanctions, the president would have to certify that China had "made progress on a program of political reform," or that it was in the national interest of the United States to relax sanctions. It defined the "program of political reform" to include the lifting of martial law, a halt to executions and other reprisals against participants in nonviolent demonstrations, the release of political prisoners, increased respect for human rights, an end to the jamming of Voice of America broadcasts, and greater access for foreign journalists. It said political reform should occur "throughout the country, including Tibet." Moreover, if repression in China deepened, the legislation recommended (but did not require) that the president impose further sanctions, such as tightening export controls, ending China's observer status in the General Agreement on Tariffs and Trade, opposing full Chinese membership in the GATT, revoking most-favored-nation status and other bilateral trade agreements, and terminating the Sino-American agreements on nuclear cooperation and satellite launches.

This legislation was strongly supported by a new coalition of groups that concluded that the president's cautious policy had failed and a stronger approach to China was necessary. The coalition included human rights organizations, much of the press, and the community of Chinese students and scholars in the United States, who were rapidly organizing to increase their influence on American policy. Initially, it was equally strongly opposed by the Bush administration, which declared itself adamant that China policy should be the prerogative of the White House, rather than of Congress.[46] In an interview with the *New York Times* shortly before the House voted on the sanctions legislation, Bush said it is "for the President of the United States to set what he thinks is right and best. . . . The person sitting in this office has to consider many things that I never had to consider when I was a Congressman."[47] The White House finally agreed to support the legislation, however, after congressional leaders revised the bill to give the president greater leeway to waive sanctions in light of his assessment of the national interest.[48]

The White House did not yield on a second piece of legislation, sponsored by Representative Nancy Pelosi (D-California), regarding Chinese students and scholars in the United States. As just noted, there was a widespread desire to prevent the Chinese in America from being forced to return home after their visas expired, especially if they had participated in antigovernment protests in the United States. The administration's policy, adopted immediately after June 4, required Chinese students and scholars to apply for a one-year extension of their visas, an act that many Chinese feared would be considered in Peking as a kind of self-incrimination. The Pelosi bill, again strongly endorsed by Chinese student organizations, took a much more generous approach, granting Chinese students four years in which to apply for immigrant status or employment visas, exempting them from deportation during that period, and allowing them to work in the meantime.[49]

The White House opposed the Pelosi bill for the same reason that it had originally objected to the comprehensive sanctions legislation: it tied the president's hands in the conduct of foreign affairs. Moreover, some administration spokesmen warned that giving all Chinese in the United States a blanket exemption from existing immigration and visa requirements could set an undesirable precedent and could lead China, which had already complained about the brain drain to America, to retaliate against the entire cultural and academic exchange program.[50] But when Congress adopted the Pelosi bill by overwhelming majorities, the White House realized it could only forestall binding legislation by taking comparable administrative action of its own. It vetoed the Pelosi bill but announced on November 30 that it would issue an executive order with similar provisions.[51]

The president's action inflamed the relations between the White House and Congress, already strained by the debate over the comprehensive sanctions legislation. By promising to issue an executive order, the president signaled that he had no objection to the content of the Pelosi bill and was prepared to modify his original policy to conform with its provisions. But in doing so, the White House simultaneously indicated its only objection to the Pelosi bill was that it was an act of Congress that would reduce the flexibility of the administration. That, in turn, worried Chinese students and scholars, who assumed that, in this case, flexibility implied the president's ability at some future date to rescind the relaxed immigration procedures and force them to return to China against their will.[52] By vetoing the Pelosi bill, the president may have preserved goodwill with the Chinese, but he simultaneously lost much political capital at home.

THE CHINESE RESPONSE

The harsh American reaction to the June 4 incident, and especially the sanctions imposed by the U.S. government, sparked a brief but intense debate in Peking over how to respond.[53] One group of leaders called for retaliation against Washington. Another line of opinion held that Peking should maintain its previous foreign policy, reestablish political stability at home, and wait for the United States and its allies to lift their sanctions against China. In the end, the latter group prevailed, although a few retaliatory measures were taken against the United States in the cultural and academic spheres.

Conservative leaders, long suspicious of American intentions toward China, argued that the Tiananmen crisis and its aftermath proved that the United States had never given up hope of undermining Communist rule in China. In the 1950s and 1960s, Washington had pursued that objective through a combination of diplomatic isolation and military containment. When that policy failed, the United States simply shifted tactics. The new approach, variously described as a "soft offensive" or "peaceful evolution," was to encourage China's gradual transformation from socialism to capitalism in the name of economic and political reform. This strategy was traced back to John Foster Dulles and his concept that the United States should attempt to "hasten the passing" of the Communist regime in China. But more recent American leaders, including some like Richard Nixon and Zbigniew Brzezinski who had previously been regarded as friendly toward China, were also identified as having continued the program of peaceful evolution.[54]

These conservative elements claimed that American institutions had been directly and deeply involved in the political ferment leading up to the protests in Tiananmen Square. According to some accounts, they compiled a list of American organizations active in China, ranging from the Voice of America to George Soros's China Fund, and from the Johns Hopkins Center in Nanjing to the Committee on Scholarly Communication with the People's Republic of China, and charged them with providing financial support and ideological inspiration to Chinese dissidents and activists. They also attempted to identify Chinese leaders and intellectuals who had developed excessively close ties with the United States, portraying them as examples of the preliminary success of the American strategy.

From the conservative perspective, the suppression of the "counterrevolutionary rebellion" by the Communist Party on June 4 had successfully blunted the Americans' soft offensive. But rather than abandoning its strategy of seeking to overthrow Communist rule in China, the United States had simply shifted its tactics. Washington's imposition of diplomatic, military, and economic sanctions against Peking was interpreted by China's conservatives not only as a gross interference in their country's internal affairs, but also as the latest American technique for destabilizing and deposing the Chinese government. In their eyes, the United States continued to pose an imminent threat to the security of the Communist regime.

For a brief period in the summer of 1989, these conservative leaders called for a reorientation of Chinese foreign policy away from the West and toward countries that were presumably more sympathetic to Peking. Jiang Zemin accused his predecessor, Zhao Ziyang, of exaggerating the international tendencies toward economic competition and political détente, and of neglecting the importance of "politics" and "struggle."[55] Others argued that cultural and economic contacts with the West were the instruments used by the United States to conduct its strategy of peaceful evolution, and that China should impose greater restrictions on those linkages if it were to prevent contamination by foreign ideas and values. According to this line of reasoning, China should revitalize its ties to hard-line Communist states, such as Romania and North Korea, as well as develop relations with the third world, as a diplomatic and economic alternative to connections with the West.

In contrast, a second group of officials and analysts called for greater continuity in Chinese foreign policy, despite the Western sanctions imposed after the Tiananmen crisis. In their analysis, the overall international situation had not significantly changed. The relative decline in the power of the United States and the Soviet Union continued, promoting a greater relaxation of international tensions. The emergence of new centers of economic power, including Japan, Germany, and the newly industrialized economies of Asia, was stimulating a more intense round of international economic and technological rivalry. The global competition for "comprehensive national strength" was therefore proceeding unabated.

Chinese foreign policy had, according to this second line of argument, been well designed to adapt to this changing international environment. Peking was taking advantage of the détente between the two superpowers to improve relations with a wide range of nations, especially in Asia, with countries such as Vietnam, Indonesia, India, and the Soviet Union. This policy of peace and development not only allowed China to minimize military expenditures but also enabled Peking to seek capital, technology, and markets from the widest possible range of foreign partners. To change that policy now, by engaging in a confrontation with the United States and its allies, would be extremely dangerous. Neither the third world, Eastern Europe, nor even the Soviet Union could provide a viable alternative to continued interaction with America, Europe, and Japan. Instead, by isolating itself from beneficial economic relationships, China would risk falling behind other countries in the intensifying competition for "comprehensive national strength."

Linked to this second line of argument was also an interpretation of American policy and intentions that was much more benign than that presented by the conservatives. When the conservatives saw a long-term U.S. strategy of subverting China, these reform-oriented leaders saw American actions that were impetuous and short-sighted. When conservatives viewed sanctions as reflecting Washington's hostile intentions toward Peking, their opponents interpreted them as a misguided reflection of a long-standing American sympathy toward China and its people.[56] From this perspective, China would be best advised to avoid retaliation and show patience and forbearance. Gradually, as the situation in China stabilized, and as emotions in the United States calmed, the Americans would come to a renewed appreciation of the importance of China, lift sanctions against Peking, and allow Sino-American relations to return to normal.

The outcome of this debate was a compromise, but one in which the elements of continuity with past policy were far more prominent than the retaliatory measures proposed by the conservatives. Most generally, Chinese foreign policy did not turn, to any significant degree, away from the United States and the West. To be sure, Peking did attempt to demonstrate, both to its own people and to the rest of the world, that it had not been isolated by the Western sanctions. To that end, it successfully established or reestablished diplomatic relations with Singapore, Saudi Arabia, and Indonesia in 1989 and 1990 and sent high-level emissaries on tours throughout the third world. But in expanding relations with other developing countries, Peking did not adopt a hostile approach to the West. China did not increase its criticism of American policy in the third world, nor call for third world unity on global economic issues. Peking's policy toward the developing nations was designed not to confront the West but to demonstrate that China could not be successfully isolated.

China's policy toward the rest of the Communist world was somewhat more complicated. Immediately after the June 4 incident, Peking did try to make contact with other hard-line Communist states, particularly North Korea, Romania, Bulgaria, Cuba, and even Vietnam, in ways that hinted at the reactivation of an alignment of conservative socialist governments. But the collapse of Communist rule in Eastern Europe in the fall of 1989 precluded any reorientation of Chinese foreign policy along these lines. Indeed, by the end of the year, the issue confronting conservative Chinese leaders was not whether to align with Eastern Europe against the United States, but whether to denounce the new governments in Eastern Europe for renouncing Lenin and embracing revisionism.

An accommodation with the Soviet Union posed problems of its own. As the tensions between Washington and Peking over human rights had increased in the spring of 1989, Vice Premier Yao Yilin had reportedly recommended that China expand its economic relations with the Soviet Union as a counterbalance against any deterioration of its ties with the West.[57] And, with the full normalization of Sino-Soviet relations during the May summit in Peking, the door to further political and military ties with the Kremlin had now been opened. But subsequent developments made Moscow a less attractive partner for Chinese conservatives. Gorbachev's statements of support for the student demonstrations in Tiananmen Square, his tolerance of the collapse of Communist governments in Eastern Europe, and his inauguration of more radical political reforms at home persuaded the hard-liners in Peking that the Soviet Union was now as serious a threat to China's internal political order as was the United States. Indeed, some began to call for public criticism of Soviet policies as revisionist and retrogressive, as well as of the American strategy of peaceful evolution.

Peking did impose a few sanctions on the United States, particularly in the cultural and academic spheres. It expelled the two Voice of America correspondents in Peking, accusing the station of broadcasting false reports on the suppression of the protests and of fomenting disorder in China. It jammed some of the VOA's Chinese-language frequencies, although not the English-language service on which many Chinese officials and intellectuals rely for international and domestic news. It suspended the Fulbright exchange program and halted preparations to receive American language instructors through the Peace Corps. Less formally, it took several additional actions to disrupt other exchange activities, including obstructing Chinese participation in the International Visitors Program funded by the U.S. Information Agency and halting several cooperative research programs in the social sciences.

Gradually, too, Peking began to impose more stringent regulations on Chinese wishing to study in the United States. By early 1990, it was clear that the Chinese government would no longer sponsor candidates for academic degrees in American universities but only shorter-term visiting scholars above the age of thirty-five. Privately sponsored students and scholars were unaffected by these regulations but had to cope with other restrictions. They had to receive the permission of their work unit to register for English-language test required by foreign universities and, if they had not worked for five years after graduating from college, they had to repay the state for the cost of their education.[58]

Initially, there were also some indications that local authorities in China had become less accommodating to American exporters and investors than had been true before the Tiananmen crisis, and there were concerns that Peking might also have decided to retaliate against American commercial interests. It soon became evident, however, that these difficulties reflected understandable local caution at a time of great political uncertainty, rather than a coordinated response to any central directives. Sino-American economic relations were indeed disrupted by the crisis in China, but this result was far more because of American uncertainties about the business climate in China than because of official actions by the Chinese government.

Other than placing some restrictions on cultural and academic exchanges, then, Peking's overall policy toward the United States in 1989 was to wait out the crisis in Sino-American relations. The suspension of the Fulbright and Peace Corps programs, and the other limitations on academic and cultural exchanges, gave Peking bargaining chips to use in any negotiation over the relaxation of American sanctions. At the same time, the strictures on sending young Chinese students to the United States to engage in lengthy degree programs helped satisfy the demand of conservative Chinese leaders for decisive measures to combat the American strategy of peaceful evolution. In general, however, China's strategy was to hope that, with the passage of time, Washington would gradually lift the sanctions it had imposed on China in June, with little lasting damage to Sino-American relations.

MUTUAL DISILLUSIONMENT

The Tiananmen crisis had a deep, and probably lasting, impact on American attitudes toward China and toward U.S.-China relations. The massive protests in Tiananmen Square, and then their suppression by the Chinese army, received extensive coverage in the American press. The major television networks, which had already reinforced their bureaus in Peking with reporters and production crews to cover the Sino-Soviet summit, sent even more staff to China to cover the demonstrations. The new technology available to the electronic media, especially minicameras and direct satellite relays, enabled coverage of the protests and their suppression to be broadcast live back to the United States.

The demonstrations in China soon dominated the American media, receiving an extremely large share of time and space. Every day, they were the subject of dozens of articles, filling many full pages in the principal American newspapers such as the *Washington Post* and the *New York Times*. The nightly news programs of the three big commercial networks broadcast nearly six hundred reports on China in the first six months of 1989, compared with less than fifty in all of 1988.[59] At the height of the story, between mid-April and mid-June, China was the subject of nearly 25 percent of the segments shown on the three network evening news programs and was the lead story on more than 50 percent of the broadcasts.[60] At some times, the Cable News Network was devoting nearly all its broadcasts to the dramatic events in China. One study has likened the volume of coverage to that given to an American political convention, a NASA moon shot, or a Soviet-American summit.[61]

Although some complained that the time devoted to China was excessive,[62] most Americans seemed fascinated by the developing story. The massive scale of the protests, the earnestness of the students, the unveiling of the *Goddess of Freedom and Democracy*, the brutality of the suppression, and especially the single demonstrator brave enough to defy an army tank on Changan Boulevard all gave television viewers images at once powerful and enduring. The number of people watching the network evening news programs rose by an average of 14 percent during the week of June 5–9, and subsequent public opinion polls revealed that more than three-quarters of the American people said they were following the story closely or very closely.[63]

American reporters in China covered a complex and emotional story with insight and often with great personal courage. But their work can be faulted on several grounds.[64] For one thing, news reports tended to idealize the antigovernment demonstrators and to suggest that they wanted to transfer American political institutions to China. In fact, many protesters were motivated by economic considerations as much as by politics, and relatively few were calling for the creation of pluralistic political institutions. But the demonstrations were nearly universally portrayed as a prodemocracy movement in the American press. Moreover, the *Goddess of Freedom and Democracy* was often renamed the *Statue of Liberty* by American reporters, even though it drew largely on socialist realist antecedents and bore slight resemblance to the statue in New York harbor.

Conversely, some of the less favorable aspects of the demonstrations were unknown to American reporters or, less forgivably, known but deliberately set aside. The protests were almost invariably described as nonviolent, and yet some demonstrators resorted to violence as Chinese troops moved toward Tiananmen Square on June 4. Student leaders called for a more open and democratic government, and yet their movement was frequently characterized by factionalism and hierarchy, and they viewed the possibility of worker participation in the protests with considerable disdain. Perhaps most spectacular, some student leaders violated their own hunger strike—a fact known by some members of the American news media, but not reported because it ran counter to the favorable image of the mass demonstrations that the journalists wanted to convey.

Finally, American reporting of the suppression of the demonstrations on the night of June 3–4 was often exaggerated. Despite dramatic reports at the time, some deliberately spread by student leaders, there were apparently few if any deaths in Tiananmen Square itself. Instead, the most brutal violence occurred at the approaches to the square, particularly along Changan Boulevard to the west. Accounts of the number of people killed, wounded, or arrested were also overstated. Rumors of deep divisions within the Chinese armed forces, the imminent outbreak of civil war, and assassination attempts on Chinese leaders were occasionally reported as if they were fact, even though they proved inaccurate.

But even had there been no exaggerations or distortions, developments in China unfolded in a way that would have heightened their emotional impact on American viewers in any event. The size, passion, and duration of the protests gave dramatic evidence of the importance of the demonstrations. The Chinese government's delay in responding, coupled with reports of division among the highest levels of the Chinese leadership, gave hope that the political crisis could be resolved through reconciliation rather than by repression. The declaration of martial law shattered those expectations temporarily, but the subsequent inability of unarmed troops to reach Tiananmen Square, together with reports that the military was deeply divided, gave renewed hope that, in the end, the Chinese government would not be willing or able to resort to armed force. Over time, the mass movement in Tiananmen Square began to appear irresistible, and the use of force came to be perceived as unlikely or even impossible. The savagery on June 4 dashed those expectations, with an emotional impact greater than if such hopes had never arisen at all.

What is more, the sense of horror and outrage that Americans felt about what they saw on their televisions, heard over their radios, and read in their newspapers was intensified by the reaction of Chinese students and scholars in the United States, who used public protest and appearances in the mass media to express their fury with eloquence and passion. The comments of articulate Chinese intellectuals tended to reinforce the judgment that the leadership of China had become a brutal and tyrannical government that refused to respond to massive protests by its own citizens.

The impact on American public opinion was sharp and immediate. Within a few weeks—and probably, if one had more precise measures of public opinion, within a few hours—American images of China turned negative (figure A-1). In February 1989, before the protests had begun, nearly three-quarters of Americans held mostly favorable or very favorable impressions of China, the culmination of the gradual improvement in American images of China that had begun with the normalization of Sino-American relations and the initiation of China's economic and political reforms in the late 1970s. But the June 4 incident dramatically reversed this decade of gradual change. Polls reported in July showed that only one-third of Americans still held a favorable impression of China, while 58 percent now held unfavorable images (table A-1).[65]

The shift in public mood was reflected in a change in the language that Americans used to discuss China. Deng Xiaoping, who had been chosen by *Time* magazine to be "man of the year" twice in a decade (in 1978 and again in 1985) for his commitment to economic and political reform, now became one of a group of doddering gerontocrats known collectively as the "butchers of Beijing." Some Americans who had once taken pains to call the Chinese government by its official name, the People's Republic, now referred to it instead as the "Chinese authorities" or the "Chinese regime." The issue had once been how far and how fast China would implement political and economic liberalization. After the Tiananmen crisis, however, the question became the depth and persistence of political repression and economic retrogression in China.

With so dramatic a transformation of public perceptions of China, it was virtually inevitable that American attitudes toward U.S. China policy would also undergo great change. It is worth repeating that the public assessment of Sino-American relations had always lagged far behind popular judgments of China. In May 1988, for example, only around one-quarter of Americans had seen China as a close friend, or even as an ally, of the United States, even though three times as many had a favorable impression of China as a country.

Now, with the deterioration of American images of China, the public's assessment of U.S.-China relations worsened. The percentage perceiving China as a friend or ally of America fell to 16 percent in July 1989, roughly the same as for the Soviet Union. Conversely, the proportion seeing Peking as unfriendly or as an enemy rose from 19 percent in May 1988 to 39 percent, only 9 percentage points behind the Kremlin (table A-1).[66]

This shift in the American mood did not, however, create a new consensus on policy toward China. Instead, it produced a split in American attitudes unprecedented since the great debates over China policy in the 1960s. Americans divided fairly evenly over whether to try to maintain a working relationship with China, or whether to maintain sanctions against Peking as a way of promoting human rights. For example, asked in January 1990 whether they would assign higher priority to criticizing China's suppression of human rights or avoiding such criticism in order to maintain good relations with Peking, the public split into two nearly equal groups: 42 percent favored an emphasis on human rights, 46 percent advocated maintaining good relations with China, and 3 percent proposed giving equal attention to both objectives.[67]

This division was also reflected in public commentary on American China policy. Much editorial opinion called for a harsh stance toward Peking. This view did not necessarily imply tougher sanctions than had already been adopted, but it meant a maintenance of those sanctions already in place, an unyielding rhetorical opposition to violations of human rights in China, and a willingness to impose more sanctions should the political situation in China further deteriorate. Conversely, several prominent former statesmen, including Richard Nixon and Henry Kissinger, called for the restoration of more normal relations with Peking, warning of the negative consequences for China and the United States if confrontation between the two countries continued.[68]

The crisis in China also changed the organizational landscape in which Sino-American relations were conducted. The American organizations that, before the Tiananmen incident, had been calling for greater improvements in U.S.-China relations now largely fell silent, with some issuing condemnations of the Chinese government for its suppression of the demonstrations in Peking. Conversely, human rights organizations that had previously largely ignored the situation in China now began to take up the issue in a sustained way, monitoring developments in China with care, publishing detailed reports on the wave of repression sweeping the country, and calling for tougher sanctions against Peking until the human rights situation there improved. Chinese students and scholars in the United States began to organize to influence American policy, forming a computer network to keep themselves informed on pending congressional legislation related to China and lobbying hard in favor of the sanctions amendment and the Pelosi bill.

Finally, there emerged a deep division between the White House and Congress on China policy. In part, this split reflected simple partisan politics, with the Democrats seeing in China one of the few foreign policy issues on which a popular new Republican president might prove vulnerable. But the criticism of the Bush administration's China policy spanned party lines, suggesting that much more than partisanship was at work. In part, the gap between the White House and Capitol Hill reflected the different weights that the two institutions assigned to competing American interests. In 1979, Congress and the executive branch had diverged over Taiwan, with the Carter administration underlining the desirability of establishing formal diplomatic relations with China, and Congress stressing the need to preserve some form of explicit commitment to the security of Taiwan. Now, the two branches of government differed on human rights in China, with the Bush administration emphasizing the importance of maintaining a normal working relationship with Peking, and Congress underscoring the American commitment to promoting human rights wherever they had been violated.

At the same time, China policy also aroused long-standing differences between the White House and Congress over the relative powers of the two branches of government in the conduct of foreign affairs. The debates over congressional sanctions and over the Pelosi bill dealt only in part with the substance of policy. The sanctions legislation, as already noted, contained few measures that the Bush administration had not already adopted. And although the Pelosi bill did reflect a slightly different approach toward Chinese students and scholars than had originally been taken by the White House, the president quickly agreed to shift his position to accord with that being recommended by Congress. Instead, the issue in each case was whether American interest would be served if foreign policy were embodied in binding legislation. The White House argued that it needed greater flexibility than legislation would provide, but Congress regarded such arguments as an effort to exclude the legislative branch from the formulation of policy toward China. This disagreement transformed the issue into a question of institutional prerogatives, potentially one of the most emotional and knotty issues in the American political process.

Of Chinese attitudes toward the United States after June 4 it is, obviously, more difficult to speak with confidence. The apparent differences within the Chinese leadership over policy toward America have already been noted. For conservative leaders, the Tiananmen incident again aroused long-standing fears over the political consequences of extensive cooperative relationships with the outside world, especially with the United States. Some regarded the threat as a deliberate American strategy of destabilizing China through cultural penetration, ideological subversion, and even economic control. Other conservatives depicted the threat more subtly, not necessarily as the result of an intentional American policy of peaceful evolution, but rather as the unwitting consequence of more extensive interaction with a country with very different values and institutions. In either interpretation, the crisis in Sino-American relations reflected the inherent danger of dealing with a large capitalist power.

This perspective reinforced earlier concerns that the United States was engaged in chronic interference in China's internal affairs but gave those apprehensions a new and even more disturbing dimension. In the past, American intervention had been focused on the peripheral areas of China: support for insurgents in Tibet and assistance to the Nationalist government on Taiwan. These efforts to undermine national unity and prevent the reunification of China under Communist rule had not been directed at the heart of the Communist regime. But now, American intervention had assumed a new and more dangerous form. In the eyes of many conservative Chinese leaders, the United States was exercising strong influence over the values and beliefs of thousands of younger Chinese, who in turn were moved to protest the inefficiency and insensitivity of their own government. This reality constituted an external threat not simply to national unity but to the stability and survival of the central Chinese government.

Moreover, many Chinese leaders probably viewed American policy with a sense of betrayal that paralleled the dismay that Americans felt toward China. The Chinese leaders had based their relationship with the United States on the assumption that American leaders had agreed, in the Shanghai communiqué, that differences between the social systems of the two countries would no longer be an obstacle to a stable and enduring relationship. Nixon and Reagan had personally assured them that ideological differences would not prevent the establishment of friendly and cooperative relations in the economic and strategic spheres. Now, the Tiananmen crisis made it impossible for the American government to fulfill this promise. Instead, it demonstrated the extent to which American policy toward China could still be overturned by the issue of human rights.

Although conservative Chinese interpreted American sanctions as a reflection of continued American arrogance, hegemonism, and even imperialism, the attitude of reform-minded intellectuals toward the United States was much different. To a degree, the student demonstrators in Tiananmen Square had turned to the United States, not only for ideas about political and economic change, but also for assistance. The slogans written in English, and the invocations of Thomas Paine and Abraham Lincoln, reflected some admiration of American institutions and a desire for American moral and political support. American newspaper articles on the demonstrations were faxed or mailed to Peking and posted on bulletin boards at universities, not only as a way for students to learn more about their own movement than was reported in the Chinese press, but also as a sign that the rest of the world cared about their activities and supported them.

Once the crackdown occurred, the expression of outrage by the United States was welcomed by many urban Chinese, including older intellectuals as well as students. As one middle-aged scholar put it privately, "I never welcomed American pressure on China before, but now I realize that we need more such pressure." Still, there was a division of opinion over how far the United States should go in imposing diplomatic and economic sanctions on the government in Peking. Some, perhaps especially younger Chinese, favored a tough American response and reacted strongly against any sign of a relaxation of the American mood toward the government in Peking. Others, including more senior intellectuals, feared that excessive sanctions would indeed offer a pretext for a greater tightening of domestic political controls, as well as cutting off their own contacts with friends and colleagues in the United States. This difference of outlook in China would soon influence debate over policy in the United States, as Americans grappled with whether human rights in China would be promoted, or obstructed, by the withdrawal of China's most-favored-nation status.

Deadlock

BY the end of 1989, China and the United States faced the challenge of "renormalizing" their relationship. Ten years earlier, in the late 1970s, normalization had referred to the establishment of diplomatic relations between the United States and the People's Republic of China. Now, in 1990 and 1991, the renormalization of Sino-American relations implied the lifting of the diplomatic, military, and economic sanctions that the two nations had imposed on each other after the Tiananmen crisis of 1989.

Like the normalization of Sino-American relations in the late 1970s, the renormalization of U.S.-China ties in the early 1990s aroused much controversy in each country. In the United States, China policy became a focal point in a partisan and institutional struggle between a White House led by a Republican president and a Congress dominated by Democrats. The Bush administration, which emphasized the ongoing American strategic and commercial interests in stable relations with China, wished to return, as rapidly as possible, to a normal relationship with Peking. The president's strategy was reflected in several initiatives toward China that were undertaken at the end of 1989 and in early 1990. These moves included sending Brent Scowcroft and Lawrence Eagleburger back to Peking for a second visit in December, as well as relaxing or lifting some of the sanctions that the United States had imposed on China in 1989. The president appeared to hope that these concessions would encourage Chinese leaders to make some conciliatory gestures in response, much in the way that the unilateral overtures made to Peking by the Nixon administration in 1969 and 1970 had led to the subsequent rapprochement of 1971 and 1972.

Many members of Congress, in contrast, favored a more belligerent approach. The president's critics charged that his unilateral overtures to China amounted to unseemly kowtowing to despotic leaders in Peking, and that Chinese officials were not reciprocating the American initiatives with adequate concessions of their own. They were frustrated by the evidence of political repression in China, an increasing American trade deficit with the People's Republic, and Peking's ongoing program of arms sales to the Middle East. Supported by the American human rights community, as well as by many Chinese students and scholars in the United States, they proposed that the annual renewal of Peking's most-favored-nation status be conditioned on political liberalization, a more open economy, and more responsible behavior abroad.

These American initiatives—some conciliatory to China, others more threatening—sparked renewed debate in Peking about how to respond. Conservative Chinese leaders were reluctant to undertake the political relaxation urged on them by the United States, for fear of arousing renewed criticism of the June 4 incident and their role in it. Moreover, many of them viewed the United States as a source of unorthodox ideas and values and charged that some Americans were engaged in a deliberate attempt to subvert and overthrow Communist regimes in Europe and Asia. Thus, they not only were unwilling to pay the price that Congress was demanding for normal Sino-American relations, but also remained skeptical that such an extensive relationship with the United States was in China's interest.

More moderate Chinese leaders, in contrast, were more interested in returning to a more stable and extensive relationship with the United States. They continued to place the highest priority on China's economic modernization in what they regarded as an increasingly dynamic and competitive world. In that context, they saw the United States as a crucial source of markets, technology, and capital—as well as a country that could either retard or facilitate China's purchase of advanced equipment from other Western nations and the acquisition of concessional loans from major international financial institutions. As such, they were prepared to make concessions to help normalize Sino-American relations, even though they had to rebut charges that they were thereby yielding to foreign pressure or were accepting American intervention in China's internal affairs.

In the late 1970s, the international environment—and particularly the common threat from the Soviet Union—had strongly encouraged China and the United States to make the necessary compromises to achieve the normalization of their diplomatic relations. In the early 1990s, however, the international environment was much less conducive to the renormalization of Sino-American relations after the Tiananmen crisis. Developments in the Soviet Union, Eastern Europe, and the Persian Gulf implied that China was less progressive than had once been thought, suggested that Peking was strategically less important to the United States than it previously had been, or else revealed that Chinese leaders defined their domestic and foreign policy interests quite differently than did their American counterparts.

The collapse of the Communist regimes of Eastern Europe in 1989 and 1990, symbolized by the dismantling of the Berlin Wall, the transitions to non-Communist governments in Poland and Hungary, and the execution of Nicolae Ceausescu in Romania, had profound consequences for the ways in which the United States and China viewed each other. Americans, who had previously seen China as standing at the forefront of reform and moving rapidly forward, now saw it as lagging behind the rest of the Communist world and moving backward. Conversely, many Chinese leaders, especially those of a conservative bent, saw the breakdown of communism in Europe as clear evidence of the dangers of political liberalization. Moreover, they also concluded that the American strategy of promoting the peaceful evolution of Communist states would now increasingly focus on China, the largest remaining socialist nation.

The evolution of Soviet foreign policy, together with the internal difficulties of the Soviet Union, also seriously affected Sino-American relations. The end of the cold war between the United States and the Soviet Union—as reflected in regular bilateral summit meetings, the agreement on reductions of conventional military forces in Europe, the intensifying negotiations over the strategic arms limitation treaty (START) in 1990–91, and Gorbachev's participation in the annual Group of Seven (G-7) summit in London in 1991—all implied that the United States no longer needed China as a strategic counterweight against the Soviet Union. Similarly, progress in Sino-Soviet relations, as exemplified by Li Peng's visit to Moscow in 1990, and in Jiang Zemin's subsequent trip to the Soviet Union in 1991, also reduced China's need for American assistance in balancing a hostile neighbor to the north.

At first, the crisis in the Persian Gulf seemed to provide an alternative basis for strategic cooperation between China and the United States. In the late summer and fall, Peking and Washington worked together in the U.N. Security Council to condemn the Iraqi invasion of Kuwait and to impose strict economic sanctions against Baghdad. But once the United States resorted to military force to secure the liberation of Kuwait, the differences in perspective between the two countries became more and more apparent. China, traditionally apprehensive about superpower intervention in regional conflicts, began to describe the war not as a just multinational struggle against an aggressor, but rather as a conflict between a "little hegemonist" in Baghdad and a bigger one in Washington. Moreover, the easy

American victory in the gulf, together with the steady weakening of the Soviet strategic position, aroused Chinese concerns that the United States would redouble efforts to create a unipolar world, centered on Washington.

Conversely, Americans too wondered about China's role in the post–cold war world. China was the only permanent member of the Security Council not to vote in favor of the crucial U.N. resolution authorizing the use of force against Iraq, and it subsequently abstained on other critical votes as well. This decision raised doubts about Peking's willingness to cooperate in multilateral efforts at collective security. Moreover, at a time when strategic planners in Washington were becoming more concerned about regional conflicts than about a global war with the Soviet Union, reports of Chinese arms sales and military technology transfers, especially to the Middle East, were alarming. Rather than helping to moderate regional disputes, many Americans believed, Peking was intensifying them through irresponsible conduct.

In both 1990 and 1991, the annual renewal of China's most-favored-nation status became the occasion for domestic debate and bilateral negotiation over the prospects for Sino-American relations. In the end, both governments made the necessary adjustments in their policy to preserve China's preferential trading status. Each year, Peking made concessions on human rights and on economic issues by releasing political prisoners, lifting martial law, and boosting imports of American goods. In 1991, the Bush administration finally abandoned its policy of swapping concessions with Peking and announced a new strategy of employing carrots and sticks to influence Chinese behavior.

But although these adjustments avoided greater deterioration in Sino-American ties, the relationship between the two countries remained deadlocked, held hostage to skeptical attitudes in both countries and to an overburdened agenda of complex and contentious issues. As China and the United States approached the twentieth anniversary of the Nixon visit and the Shanghai communiqué, their relationship had not yet recovered from the crisis in Tiananmen Square.

WASHINGTON'S YEAR-END INITIATIVE

By the end of 1989, the Bush administration was ready to undertake a new initiative to stabilize the American relationship with

China. This decision may well have been stimulated by the visits to China of Henry Kissinger and Richard Nixon in the fall of the year. Both men had reported that Chinese leaders insisted that "he who tied the knot should untie it." From Peking's perspective, China had not done anything, either on June 4 or subsequently, to harm American interests, but the United States had still imposed unreasonable economic and diplomatic sanctions against China. Accordingly, it was up to Washington to take the first step to undo the damage it had inflicted on Sino-American relations. But Chinese leaders had also told Kissinger and Nixon that, if the United States were prepared to make a conciliatory gesture toward China, they would respond in kind.

In a report to a bipartisan group of congressional leaders, Nixon identified the American interest in preserving a cooperative relationship with China. China, he argued, would be "essential to balance the power of [both] Japan and the Soviet Union in Asia." It would have an indispensable role in controlling the spread of advanced conventional weapons, in preventing nuclear proliferation, in addressing environmental issues, and in managing regional disputes. And in time China would inevitably become an economic and military superpower. It would be foolhardy, Nixon concluded, for the United States to exclude itself from China's huge potential market, let alone for Washington to "run the risk of being an adversary rather than an ally of China in the next century."[1]

Apparently unaware of the secret Scowcroft-Eagleburger visit in July, Nixon proposed the reestablishment of high-level official contacts with Peking. He acknowledged that many steps would have to be taken, by both countries, to restore a more normal relationship. China would have to ameliorate its human rights record, improve the climate for foreign investment, resolve the dispute over Fang Lizhi, and reinstate the cultural and academic exchange programs it had suspended after the Tiananmen incident. The United States would have to lift economic sanctions against China and permit the resumption of lending to China by the World Bank and other international financial institutions. But, as a first step, the former president suggested the resumption of high-level communication with Peking. As he put it, "To leave the present and future leaders of China isolated, nurturing their resentments and even hatred of the United States because of what they consider to be unjustified actions against China, is senseless and counterproductive."

Similar recommendations were coming from other American China experts and foreign policy specialists. In October, the Johns

Hopkins Foreign Policy Institute issued what it called a policy consensus report, endorsed by former members of the Ford, Carter, and Reagan administrations, which also emphasized the "long-term importance of U.S.-China cooperation to American strategic, political, and economic interests."[2] While stressing that the full normalization of Sino-American relations would depend on an end to repression and a return to political liberalization in China, the report also called for the preservation of as much of the infrastructure for a cooperative relationship as possible. The report did not explicitly call for the resumption of high-level contacts with Peking, but such a step would have been entirely consistent with its conclusions.

In this seemingly supportive context, the Bush administration embarked on a new initiative to China at the end of 1989. The most controversial element was a second Scowcroft-Eagleburger mission to Peking, intended to explore the possibility of an improvement in the Sino-American relationship. Through their private statements and public toasts, the two men conveyed the message that President Bush viewed Deng Xiaoping as his personal friend, and that he still viewed China as an important country with whom the United States needed cooperative ties. Indeed, Chinese sources have said that Scowcroft told Deng that China was now more important to the United States than ever before.

But the two American emissaries also indicated that the president would need some sign from the Chinese—on global, bilateral, or domestic issues—that they were prepared to reciprocate his gesture of goodwill. The administration seemed highly optimistic that such a conciliatory response would be forthcoming. In the fall, following the Nixon visit, Chinese officials had begun to acknowledge that both sides, and not just the United States, would have to take steps to improve the relationship. Eagleburger later testified before Congress that this new tone in Chinese statements was a "subtle but distinct signal" that made the trip possible.[3]

It is not known whether Scowcroft or Eagleburger also informed the Chinese the Bush administration was prepared to make additional unilateral gestures to China, in the hope of stimulating such a positive response from Peking. But over the following weeks, the White House lifted or modified three of the sanctions that it had imposed on China in the month after the Tiananmen incident. First, on December 19, it granted export licenses for three American communications satellites to be placed into orbit by Chinese launchers, thus lifting one of the sanctions contained in the comprehensive sanctions legislation still under consideration by Congress. On the same day, the White House also announced it was resuming Exim-bank lending to China, thus removing a sanction Congress had rec-ommended but not mandated in pending legislation. And third, on January 10 the administration said the United States would no longer oppose all World Bank loans to China but would consider on a case-by-case basis those projects that met the basic human needs of the Chinese people.

This American initiative sparked great debate in Peking over the appropriate Chinese response.[4] Some analysts, including many of China's America specialists, apparently urged Peking's leaders to be as flexible and forthcoming as possible. This group argued that the global situation did not especially favor China. In an era of intense international economic and technological competition, China would fall behind its neighbors if it did not maintain cooperative relations with the United States. Moreover, the collapse of communism in Eastern Europe, and the rapid improvements in Soviet-American relations, meant the United States would not be prepared to make many more sacrifices to preserve close ties with Peking. If China wished to restore its relations with the United States, this group argued, some reciprocal gestures to Washington would be necessary. To that end, these analysts very likely recommended such steps as ending martial law, releasing some political prisoners, and allowing the exile of Fang Lizhi—all to signal to Americans concerned about human rights that the political situation in China was gradually relaxing.

Others responded that China could not and should not shape do-mestic policies in response to American pressure, and that the time was not yet ripe to relax political controls. Moreover they insisted that the international environment was not all that threatening to China. Although there was indeed an unprecedented détente be-tween the United States and the Soviet Union, the global competi-tion between the two superpowers had not been eliminated, and Washington could not yet be certain of longer-term Soviet intentions and capabilities. Moreover, Washington was grappling with the rise of new economic powers, especially Germany and Japan, both of whom were engaged in intense economic competition with the United States. America's need for a counterweight against the Soviet Union, Japan, and a unified Europe would give China strategic lever-age. Indeed, this group probably pointed out, the Scowcroft-Eagle-burger visit showed that Washington was eager to improve relations with China, indicating that Peking retained substantial leverage and needed to make only a minimal response.

The outcome of this debate was a compromise, in which China made some conciliatory gestures to the United States but refused to modify policy in other areas important to Washington. Immediately after the Scowcroft visit in December, the Chinese Foreign Ministry denied as "utterly groundless" the reports that it was going to sell M-9 missiles to Syria and for the first time publicly stated the assurances, originally given privately to Frank Carlucci in 1988, that it "has not sold and has no plan to sell any medium-range missiles to any Middle Eastern country."[5] Peking also began to lift some of the restrictions on Sino-American cultural and academic exchanges that it had imposed after the Tiananmen incident. In June, it had expelled both reporters dispatched by the Voice of America; it now agreed to accredit one. It had suspended the implementation of the Fulbright program of academic exchanges; it now agreed to resume the program for visiting professors and scholars, although not for Chinese degree candidates going to the United States. In neither case did the Chinese actions completely restore the status quo ante, but they did take a step in that direction.

Chinese leaders also adopted some modest measures to relax the political climate, especially in Peking. On January 10, they lifted martial law in the capital, which had been in effect since May 20 of the previous year. A week later, they announced the release of nearly six hundred people who had been arrested after the Tiananmen protests. And, at around the same time, they removed the heavy guard that had been placed around the American embassy in Peking and allowed American diplomats better access to Chinese officials. To be sure, with the Chinese New Year holiday approaching, some of these steps may have been undertaken for domestic reasons. But steps such as these had been explicitly identified by American visitors as measures that would help improve U.S.-China relations, and Peking almost certainly adopted some of them for reasons of foreign policy.

Notably missing from the list of the Chinese responses to the December Scowcroft mission, however, was the release of Fang Lizhi from his refuge in the American embassy in Peking. Although involving only two people—a man and his wife—among the thousands denied their freedom in the aftermath of the June 4 incident, the case of Fang Lizhi had become a bellwether of the state of Sino-American relations in the post-Tiananmen period. Unresolved, the matter greatly complicated the conduct of diplomacy in Peking: Fang Lizhi's continued presence in the American embassy prevented the Chinese from conducting normal business there. Moreover, as the Chinese human rights activist best known in the United States, Fang Lizhi's fate now served as a convenient, if somewhat misleading, index as to whether the political situation in China was improving or deteriorating. Conversely, since China's leading dissident had taken shelter in the U.S. embassy, the case of Fang Lizhi was a powerful symbol to conservative Chinese of American intervention in their country's internal affairs.

As noted in chapter 7, Secretary of State James Baker and Chinese ambassador Han Xu began discussions of the issue in Washington within days after Fang was given refuge in the American embassy. The framework of a solution was clear from the beginning: Fang would be allowed free passage to leave China, but he would travel initially to a third country, rather than directly to the United States. Although the Baker-Han negotiations had not produced a final agreement, it was hoped that the Scowcroft-Eagleburger mission would be able to resolve the issue.

In the end, however, no such agreement was reached. American officials believe that Peking was very close to allowing Fang Lizhi to leave the country, but that international events intervened to preclude a final decision. The collapse of the Ceausescu regime in Romania in December sent a shock wave through the Forbidden City, making it an especially difficult time to release a man who might well give renewed impetus to the antigovernment movement at home and abroad. At the same time, the American intervention in Panama may also have temporarily weakened the hand of more moderate leaders who advocated concessions to Washington, and strengthened the position of the conservatives who argued that the United States remained an imperialist power with whom compromise was undesirable. The Chinese therefore apparently concluded the time was not yet ripe for a resolution of the Fang Lizhi problem, and they began to insist that Fang would have to "show a very good attitude of remorse" before he would be permitted to leave the country.[6] From their perspective, there was little cost to maintaining the status quo in the meantime: Fang was effectively in prison where he could not inflame the situation in China, but Americans and not Chinese were responsible for his health and well-being.

On balance, the Chinese response to the Bush administration's year-end initiative suggests that, while willing to make a few conciliatory gestures to Washington, Chinese leaders had concluded they held a relatively strong hand in their showdown with the United States. The fact that Scowcroft emphasized the strategic importance of China to the United States, just as this issue was being intensely debated in Peking, unintentionally reinforced the position of those Chinese analysts who had argued that Peking did not need to do much to restore Sino-American relations. At a time when developments in Eastern Europe suggested the dangers of any significant political relaxation at home, Chinese leaders decided there was no compelling need to respond to the American overtures with many gestures of their own. Indeed, some Chinese implied that their main "concession" to America had been to agree to receive the Scowcroft mission in the first place, and especially to permit American subcabinet officials to meet Deng Xiaoping.

This exchange of conciliatory gestures produced intense controversy in the United States over the wisdom of the Bush administration's initiative. The president had his defenders, including some of the country's most prominent China specialists. Immediately after Scowcroft had returned from Peking, Michel Oksenberg wrote an essay for the *New York Times* describing the mission as an "act of courageous leadership" and urging the Chinese to reciprocate his favor.[7] In a similar vein, Doak Barnett announced that he supported the president's decision to reopen a dialogue with Chinese leaders and said that the initial Chinese response had been encouraging.[8] Some Chinese scholars in the United States also endorsed the gesture, with some saying that the original decision to suspend high-level contacts had been a mistake, and that diplomatic isolation of Peking would only strengthen the hands of Chinese conservatives.[9]

This response was, however, very much a minority view among published opinion in the United States. The response of the leading newspapers and most members of Congress can only be described as apoplectic. The *Washington Post* described the Scowcroft mission as a "placatory concession to a repressive and bloodstained Chinese government"; the *New York Times*, as "hailing the butchers of Beijing."[10] An editorial in the *Wall Street Journal* said that six months after the Tiananmen incident was not enough to provide the "decent interval" needed for a restoration of official contacts with Peking, and that the Scowcroft mission "has to go down as one of the great tin-ear exercises of our time."[11] And Senate Majority Leader George Mitchell (D-Maine) portrayed it as "embarrassing kowtowing" to the Chinese government.[12]

In essence, the critics argued that, in sending Scowcroft and Eagleburger to Peking, the White House had acted deceitfully, given away too much, and received too little in return. At Chinese insistence, the mission was announced publicly only when Scowcroft and Eagleburger were arriving in Peking, which happened to be in the middle of the night, Washington time. At first, the Bush administration insisted that the principal purpose of the trip was to brief Chinese leaders on the outcome of the Soviet-American summit in

Malta, so that Peking would not hear the results from Russian emissaries alone. Only gradually did the White House acknowledge that the mission was charged with a comprehensive review of the entire Sino-American relationship. And the Bush administration also persisted in claiming that the Scowcroft visit was not a violation of the ban on high-level diplomatic exchanges, in that it was not part of regular reciprocal visits by Chinese and American officials. All this gave the trip, from the beginning, an aura of duplicity that the administration was hard put to overcome.

Moreover, the critics emphasized some unfortunate, and probably avoidable, symbolism surrounding the visit. Scowcroft permitted himself to be photographed, at a banquet in his honor, raising a champagne glass in a toast to his Chinese hosts. He was also quoted by the Chinese as thanking Deng for taking the time to see him, and as reporting that Bush "still regards Deng as a friend forever."[13] And in perhaps his most controversial remarks, Scowcroft referred to "negative forces" in both societies that "seek to redirect or frustrate our cooperation." This statement was widely interpreted as equating American critics of human rights violations in China with the conservative gerontocrats in Peking who had ordered the use of force against unarmed demonstrators.[14]

The administration's critics also argued that the United States had received very little for relaxing the ban on high-level diplomatic contact. They were quick to point out that China's vague statement that it had no plans to sell medium-range missiles to the Middle East was simply a public reiteration of the vague reassurances made privately to the United States the year before. They also noted that Peking used a different definition of medium-range than did the West, and that the missile then of greatest concern to the United States, the M-9, was not necessarily covered by the Chinese statement.[15] Moreover, whatever goodwill might have been gained through this gesture was dissipated by reports that, whatever Chinese leaders may have told Scowcroft, Chinese arms merchants were still negotiating with potential customers in the Middle East.[16]

Nor were the other Chinese concessions deemed satisfactory. Renewed negotiations over a Peace Corps presence in China, the accreditation of a Voice of America correspondent in China, the reduction in the number of Chinese guards surrounding the American embassy, and the possible resumption of the Fulbright program were regarded as cosmetic gestures that did not address the central issues in Sino-American relations. As it gradually became clear that Fang Lizhi and his wife were not about to receive free passage from the American embassy, the Bush administration's critics began to charge that the

United States had gotten the worse of the deal. As the *New York Times* commented, "Dividends so meager only mock the Bush policy."[17]

Finally, the critics of the Bush China policy also discounted any signs of a relaxation in the Chinese domestic political climate. Human rights organizations pointed out that martial law was supplanted by tight civil restrictions on political activity, that the military presence in Peking was replaced by a large contingent of uniformed and plainclothes police still organizationally linked to the army, and that possibly thousands of Chinese protesters remained in detention. The State Department's annual human rights report, issued in February, acknowledged that the "crackdown was still continuing" and that "virtually all internationally recognized human rights discussed in this report are restricted, many of them severely." In effect, the State Department appeared to be admitting that, in the critical area of human rights, the White House's China policy had not yet borne fruit.[18]

The criticism of the Bush administration's initiative was intensified when, within a few weeks after the December Scowcroft-Eagleburger mission, a Chinese source finally revealed to the Cable News Network that the same two men had visited Peking the previous July. This revelation reinforced earlier charges that the Bush administration had made gestures to China that had not been adequately reciprocated. Thus, the critics complained, the White House had undermined its sanctions against Peking in ways that severely misled Congress and the American people. Even those who supported the stabilization of Sino-American relations and the maintenance of a normal working relationship with Peking worried that the administration's tactics had given a sensible policy a bad name.

The widespread dismay at the president's China initiative was reflected in the congressional attempt, in January, to overturn his veto of the Pelosi bill to allow Chinese students and scholars to remain in the United States after their visas had expired. The president's critics prevailed in the House of Representatives, which voted 390–25 to override the veto. But they fared less well in the Senate where, after intense lobbying by the White House, they obtained only 62 of the 67 votes they needed. In the narrow sense, the administration had scored an important victory. But from a broader perspective, the president had suffered a serious defeat. The vote on the Pelosi bill had become, in effect, a parliamentary vote of no confidence in the administration's China policy. Given that only 12 percent of Congress—25 in the House, and 37 in the Senate—had voted to support the president, the outcome was a ringing rebuke of his strategy toward Peking. When Nixon and Kissinger had engaged in secret contacts with China in the early 1970s, they had succeeded in securing enough reciprocal gestures from Peking to achieve a major diplomatic breakthrough. Now, when Bush tried a similar strategy, the Chinese did not make a response sufficient to vindicate his gamble.

By February 1990, therefore, the Bush administration's year-end overture had produced a mood of disappointment and disillusionment in Washington and Peking. In Washington, the White House had again been placed on the defensive. Taken together, the Chinese concessions did not seem to justify the relaxation of American sanctions, the dispatch of the two Scowcroft-Eagleburger missions, and the effusive American rhetoric about cooperation with Peking. As a result, the split between Congress and the White House, already widened by the debate over legislative sanctions and the Pelosi bill, was exacerbated, with most Democrats vehemently attacking the president and with few Republicans prepared to come to his support. The president began expressing his disappointment with the Chinese. Some administration officials indicated they felt betrayed because Peking had done so little to reciprocate the American gestures, and suggested that few further initiatives would be forthcoming.[19]

Ironically, Chinese officials and analysts expressed a similar view. In February, they were telling visiting Americans they had expected the United States to have lifted more of its sanctions, and to have done so more quickly. They also pronounced themselves astonished and distressed by the harsh tone of the State Department's depiction of China in the annual human rights report. China, they said, had moderated the criticism of the United States that had appeared in its press in the summer of 1989. But instead of reciprocating, the American government was now denouncing China through its human rights report. In response, Chinese leaders apparently stiffened the conditions for the release of Fang Lizhi, demanding not only that he admit guilt but also that the United States remove the restrictions it had imposed on World Bank loans and the transfer of American technology to China.[20]

In short, an initiative that had been intended to end the impasse in Sino-American relations in some respects intensified the stalemate. Both countries began to warn that the U.S.-China relationship could continue to deteriorate. But each nation also indicated it had made all the concessions it could and that the initiative and the responsibility now rested with the other side.

THE FIRST DEBATE OVER CHINA'S
MOST-FAVORED-NATION STATUS

The sense of disillusionment in Washington was reflected in the first indications since June 1989 that the Bush administration was considering a tightening, rather than a further relaxation, of sanctions against China. The White House began to hint that the president had not yet decided whether to recommend the extension of China's most-favored-nation status, scheduled by chance to expire on the symbolically significant date of June 3, one day before the first anniversary of the Peking massacre of 1989.

Under law, the president had the authority to decide each year whether to renew the most-favored-nation status granted to China and other nonmarket economies. The Jackson-Vanik amendment stipulated that the president was to consider how much freedom of emigration the citizens of such countries enjoyed. According to the amendment's provisions, the president could recommend the renewal of most-favored-nation status to a nonmarket economy only if he could certify that its government permitted the free emigration of its citizens, or if he could assert that such renewal would substantially promote freedom of emigration. In turn, Congress had the right to review the president's decision and adopt a resolution of disapproval. If it did so, however, it would have to be able to sustain such a resolution over a presidential veto. Until 1990, the renewal of China's most-favored-nation status had been a routine event: the president announced his decision to renew it, and Congress, by failing to enact (or usually even to consider) a resolution of disapproval, consented to the president's action. Now, for the first time since this preferential tariff treatment was granted to China in 1980, there seemed to be a possibility that China might lose most-favored-nation status.[21]

Although obviously not as severe as a full trade embargo against China, the denial of most-favored-nation status to Peking would have seriously harmed Sino-American commercial relations. Rather than being subject to normal tariffs, Chinese goods entering the United States would have been assigned far higher duties, which would have risen from an average rate of 8.8 percent to one of 50.5 percent for the twenty-five most important commodities.[22] The U.S.-China Business Council estimated this change would have reduced Chinese exports to the United States by fully 50 percent, or by around $6 billion.[23] Peking would have certainly responded by cutting back on American exports to China, and possibly even by discriminating against all

American investment in China, suspending a wider range of academic and cultural exchange programs, and terminating or reducing strategic and diplomatic cooperation with the United States.

Even at the height of emotion over the Tiananmen incident, the withdrawal of China's most-favored-nation status did not receive serious consideration in the United States. To be sure, some human rights organizations had called on the Bush administration to impose such a sanction against Peking, and several members of Congress had proposed in June 1989 that China's most-favored-nation status be removed. But the White House had not included this sanction in either of the two packages announced by the president in June. Congressional leaders, seeking to craft a sanctions bill that would attract broad bipartisan support and that could be passed by both houses expeditiously, failed to add it to the comprehensive sanctions legislation it assembled in July. Now, more than six months after the Tiananmen incident, the possibility suddenly arose of imposing this sanction on China.

The prospect of losing China's most-favored-nation status occasioned yet another round of debate in Peking, even more intense than the one occasioned by the Bush administration's year-end initiative several months earlier.[24] Given that the United States was one of China's largest trading partners, an increase in American tariffs on Chinese products would have caused severe economic damage to the country, particularly to those sectors (such as textiles) and regions (such as the Southeast) that depended heavily on sales to the American market. Moreover, the economic sanctions already imposed by the West—especially the suspension of lending by international financial institutions, and the cutbacks in commercial credit—were causing alarm in Peking about its ability to service international debt. If China's exports to the United States declined, it would have to find alternative markets for those same goods or else reduce imports by a comparable amount. Chinese officials responsible for foreign trade were fully cognizant of the significance of the issue and the damage that the loss of most-favored-nation status would do. Indeed, the Chinese Ministry of Foreign Economic Relations and Trade estimated the annual loss of export revenues at $10 billion, a figure higher than most of the forecasts being made in the United States.[25]

Moreover, there were many other sectors of Chinese society that would have suffered from a renewed confrontation with the United States. Provinces, municipalities, and enterprises that sought technology or investment from America would have been seriously hurt by a trade war between China and the United States. Chinese scholars hoping to engage in academic exchange with America would have seen their opportunities greatly reduced. More generally, Chinese intellectuals have traditionally experienced a harsher treatment from their government during periods of tension between Peking and Washington, and thus even those who had little chance of studying abroad were apprehensive about the consequences of a greater deterioration of Sino-American ties.

Aware of probable economic costs of the withdrawal of most-favored-nation status, and under great pressure from below to avoid confrontation with the United States, Chinese leaders seem to have sought systematic advice from their foreign policy establishment as to how to respond. At their request, research institutions in Peking and Shanghai presented recommendations on how to stabilize Sino-American relations, including permitting Fang Lizhi to leave China for asylum in a third country, increasing imports from the United States to show China's commitment to mutually beneficial commercial ties with America, releasing more demonstrators detained after the June 4 incident, reducing anti-American propaganda in the Chinese press, and restating Peking's interest in a stable relationship with the United States.[26]

These recommendations were then discussed at a series of high-level meetings in Peking throughout the spring of 1990, including an interagency meeting in March, hosted by the State Education Commission, but attended by representatives from the Ministries of Foreign Affairs, National Defense, Public Security, and State Security as well. This group reportedly came to the pessimistic conclusion that China had relatively few cards to play in negotiations with the United States, other than holding hostage a few cultural and academic exchange programs. The participants also warned that China could not count on substantial differences of opinion between the White House and Congress over policy toward Peking, and that the American attitude could well harden even more if the United States continued to gain the upper hand in its strategic competition with the Soviet Union. They apparently recommended that the release of more political prisoners was one of the few steps that China could take to stabilize its relationship with Washington.[27]

Jiang Zemin, the general secretary of the Communist Party, then personally presided over another round of meetings in June. One was attended by senior Chinese diplomats present in the capital; the other drew together leading analysts from foreign policy research institutions in Peking and Shanghai. Some participants reportedly advocated adopting an "omnidirectional" foreign policy that would further distance China from the United States. But others proposed a more flexible approach designed to stabilize Sino-American relations.

As a result of such deliberations, Peking adopted a multifaceted strategy for dealing with the United States. First, it encouraged America's allies to press Washington to refrain from imposing any more sanctions on China and to return to a more normal relationship with Peking. Second, Chinese leaders made several concessions to the United States on outstanding bilateral issues, without ever undertaking a fundamental reassessment of the Tiananmen crisis or a sustained relaxation of their domestic political climate. And finally, China looked for ways of demonstrating its continued strategic importance to the United States.

As Chinese leaders had anticipated, Japan was the weakest link in the Western united front. As early as September 1989, Deng Xiaoping told a former Japanese foreign minister, Masayoshi Ito, he had noted "some difference" between Japan and the United States.[28] Although Tokyo had imposed its own sanctions against China immediately after the Tiananmen crisis, Japanese leaders never regarded them as the wisest course of action. They believed that attempting to isolate China by imposing diplomatic and economic sanctions against Peking would be a serious mistake. Instead, they advocated a more subtle approach. As one Japanese official responsible for relations with China explained privately, Tokyo would have preferred to express "incomprehension" as to how the June 4 incident could have occurred, let the Japanese business community respond to the heightened uncertainty by reducing investment in China, and then wait for the Chinese government to issue explanations and regrets.

At a time of continued friction over economic issues between Washington and Tokyo, however, officials in the Japanese Foreign Ministry responsible for relations with the United States were unwilling to see additional problems added to the bilateral agenda, especially on an issue arousing such strong emotions in America. Therefore, shortly after the Tiananmen crisis, Japan announced it was not only suspending high-level official contacts with China but also postponing financial assistance to Peking, including the disbursements from a loan package of $2.4 billion for the period 1985–89 and the consideration of new loans from a further package of $5.5 billion for the period 1990–94. Given that Japan gave China more developmental assistance than did any other country, this decision was a severe sanction indeed.[29]

But Japan's support for sanctions against China began to waver at the end of 1989. Tokyo was irritated by the two Scowcroft visits to Peking, concluding that the United States was expecting its allies to refrain from high-level contact with China but insisting on the right to conduct a diplomatic dialogue of its own. In response, Tokyo promptly invited two Chinese officials—Zou Jiahua, the head of the State Planning Commission, and Li Tieying, the chairman of the State Education Commission—to visit Japan in the first half of 1990. In April, Japan also restored foreign office contacts at the vice-ministerial level.

Moreover, Japan began to encourage a broader relaxation of Western sanctions against China. At the annual meeting of the G-7 in Houston in July, Tokyo finally explicitly stated the policy it had been quietly recommending all along. "We have consistently appealed to the international community that it is not the right thing to isolate China," a Japanese Foreign Ministry official explained. Instead, Japan's policy was to "see China reintegrated or returned to normal relations with the international community." His government felt it would be "quite difficult," he said, to introduce "such a Westernized notion as democracy" to China quickly. The only hope was to promote political reform gradually, through a program of economic assistance intended to help China raise its standard of living.[30]

In response to these urgings from Japan, the G-7 summit agreed to a partial relaxation of sanctions against China, including consideration of World Bank projects that could promote economic reforms or address environmental issues, gradual resumption of Japan's bilateral aid program, and restoration of official contacts between China and the West. Within a few months, the consequences of that decision were apparent. Britain, Germany, and Spain sent high-level envoys to China; a Chinese vice foreign minister visited Australia and New Zealand; and the Japanese resumed disbursements of earlier loans and began discussions about their third package of aid to China.[31] In this context, any American decision to revoke China's most-favored-nation status would have created a noticeable discrepancy between U.S. policy and that of its closest allies.

Even as Chinese leaders hoped that pressure from Japan and the rest of the G-7 would persuade the United States to renew most-favored-nation status and to relax its remaining sanctions against China, they also tried a direct approach to Washington. In early May, Peking announced the release of another 211 dissidents, intended to be a sign that the political climate in China was returning to normal. This gesture greatly facilitated President Bush's decision to recommend the renewal of Peking's most-favored-nation status for another twelve months.[32]

In subsequent weeks, the Chinese made even more conciliatory overtures to Washington. Another batch of dissidents, ninety-seven in all, was released in early June. Peking announced it would purchase $2 billion worth of Boeing jetliners, with an option to buy a comparable amount in future years, and would send a high-level

purchasing mission to the United States later in the year.[33] Jiang
Zemin tried his hand at personal diplomacy, conducting a television
interview with Barbara Walters in early May, and sending a long
letter to a group of American university students explaining the
domestic situation in China and expressing his hopes for the normalization of Sino-American relations.[34]

Then, later in June, the Chinese finally agreed to permit Fang Lizhi
to leave the American embassy to travel to Great Britain.[35] Although
Peking had originally insisted that Fang issue a declaration admitting
his guilt and expressing remorse, in the end it settled for much less:
an acknowledgment by Fang that he was opposed to the guarantees
of Party rule contained in the Chinese constitution, and a promise
that he would not engage in activities directed against China after
he had left the country. The Chinese also correctly noted that Fang
had suffered health problems while in the American embassy and
were thus able to employ the face-saving device of claiming that he
was being permitted to go abroad to seek medical treatment.

Although Peking had persuaded Bush to recommend the renewal
of China's most-favored-nation treatment, it had not made enough
concessions to end the debate in the United States over the fate of its
preferential trade status. Not even the release of Fang Lizhi at this
point could prevent the president's decision from coming under intense congressional and public scrutiny. The opponents of renewing
China's most-favored-nation status argued, as critics of the Bush administration's China policy had consistently maintained since June
1989, that the White House had made too many conciliatory gestures
to China, that the human rights situation in China remained basically
unchanged, and that further economic sanctions were therefore warranted. On the other side of the issue stood an equally vocal group of
individuals who were prepared to defend a normal economic relationship with China, on the grounds that the removal of China's most-
favored-nation status would be likely to set back, rather than to promote, the cause of economic and political reform.

The critics of the Bush administration, including many editorial
writers, members of Congress, human rights advocates, and representatives of Chinese students and scholars in the United States, argued
that, despite the release of nearly eight hundred detainees, the political atmosphere in China was still highly repressive. Reports by two
leading human rights organizations, Amnesty International and Asia
Watch, concluded that thousands of dissidents were still imprisoned,
subject to physical and psychological torture and to arbitrary judicial
procedures, and that the overall political atmosphere in China had
worsened rather than improved.[36] Tight political controls remained

on the news media, major universities, the literary community, and social science research organizations. There were press accounts of intimidation of Chinese students by embassy officials in the United States, as well as physical attacks and other forms of harassment of American journalists in Peking.[37] Nor was there much evidence that the climate would soon change for the better. Jiang Zemin's denial to Barbara Walters that the June 4 incident could be regarded as a tragedy, and his insistence that the reaction to it overseas was best described as much ado about nothing, indicated that Chinese leaders were still unprepared to engage in a reconciliation with their own society.

To make matters worse, a steady stream of press reports charged that China was willfully behaving irresponsibly abroad. Accusations were made that China was offering to sell missiles to the Middle East, continuing to supply arms to the Khmer Rouge, and providing Libya with the precursor compounds for the manufacture of chemical weapons. Although some of these reports were of negotiations still under way, rather than of agreements actually consummated, they contributed to the impression that China had adopted a foreign policy that ran counter to American interests, often in direct violation of commitments that had previously been made to Washington.[38]

On the other hand, a strong coalition emerged to defend most-favored-nation status for China. At first, such defenders were reluctant to speak out for fear that they would be perceived as apologizing for China or accepting Peking's interpretation of the Tiananmen incident. Gradually, however, this point of view gained voice and strength, as the various elements of the coalition realized that they were not alone and that their position would receive a fair hearing.

Basically, the coalition made three arguments in support of continuing China's most-favored-nation status. First, they maintained that ending MFN status would inaugurate a trade war with China that would reduce American exports, yield market shares to foreign competitors, threaten the viability of American investments in China, and increase the price of Chinese imports to American consumers. Given that many of China's exports to the United States consisted of low-cost footwear and apparel, it was argued that a disproportionate burden would be placed on lower-income Americans.[39]

Second, they pointed out that most of China's exports to the United States passed through Hong Kong. A reduction of Sino-American trade would therefore seriously damage a friendly market economy already struggling with the transition to Chinese rule in 1997. The Hong Kong government and the American Chamber of Commerce in Hong Kong estimated that the territory would lose between $7 billion and $10 billion in trade, and approximately 20,000 jobs, in the first year after any revocation of China's most-favored-nation status.[40] At a time of increasing uncertainty over Hong Kong's economic viability and political stability as it approached its return to Chinese sovereignty in 1997, it was argued that Hong Kong could ill afford a reduction in rate of growth by 2 or 3 percentage points.

Third, and most important, those opposed to withdrawing China's most-favored-nation status argued that doing so would hurt precisely those people in China whom America was presumably trying to help.[41] Restricting Chinese imports through higher tariffs would hurt small-scale private and collective industry in the coastal regions—the heart of the Chinese economic reforms—while having much less impact on larger-scale state industry that produced primarily for domestic markets. Imposing an additional economic sanction on Peking, especially one of this magnitude, would almost certainly lead to a tightening of political controls in China, in which those with contacts with or sympathy toward the United States would be principal targets. Supporters of renewing Peking's most-favored-nation status also pointed out that, in contrast to Chinese students and scholars in exile in the United States, most Chinese intellectuals still living in China opposed further American economic sanctions, at least unless the human rights situation in China deteriorated.[42]

The coalition that ultimately assembled around these arguments was a diverse one. It included representatives of the American business community—investors, importers, and exporters. The American Chamber of Commerce in Hong Kong and the representatives of the Hong Kong government posted in the British embassy in Washington also lobbied effectively in defense of Hong Kong's economic interests. Some specialists on Chinese affairs spoke in favor of maintaining a normal economic relationship with China. And, perhaps most important, the community of Chinese students and scholars was divided on the issue, the first time it had split openly since the Tiananmen incident. While the most active and vocal members of the community argued for the denial of most-favored-nation status on human rights grounds, others insisted, with equal passion and commitment, that such a step would probably be counterproductive.[43]

As the debate proceeded, a compromise gradually emerged. Although some members of Congress pressed for an immediate withdrawal of China's most-favored-nation status, others began to explore the possibility of a conditional extension: a renewal for one year, with more stringent standards for a further renewal in 1991.[44] Within this approach, however, there were two variants—one harsher, and the other more moderate.

The more moderate approach, sponsored by Representative Don Pease (D-Ohio), would have established additional criteria for determining in 1991 whether most-favored-nation status for China should be renewed for another year. Under Pease's original proposal, the Jackson-Vanik amendment, with its reference to freedom of emigration, would be revised to include objectives such as the termination of martial law in China, the end of Chinese assistance to the Khmer Rouge, and, most important, "the making of substantial and demonstrable progress to reverse the pattern of gross violations of internationally recognized human rights."[45] This supplement was later amended to include even more goals, such as the release of those arrested for nonviolent demonstrations, greater freedom of the press, an end to the jamming of Voice of America broadcasts, the termination of "acts of intimidation and harassment" of Chinese citizens in the United States, and a loosening of restrictions on travel and study abroad. It also requested that the president take into account China's policy toward Hong Kong and its attitude toward Taiwan's membership in the General Agreement on Tariffs and Trade (GATT). As with the original Jackson-Vanik amendment, the president would not necessarily have to declare that these objectives had been realized before he could recommend the renewal of most-favored-nation status. But he would have to certify, in effect, that those goals would be pursued more effectively by continuing MFN status than by revoking it.

The more stringent approach, sponsored in the House by Nancy Pelosi, established similar conditions. But for China's most-favored-nation status to be renewed in 1991, the president would have had to certify that China had fully realized some of the objectives and had made "significant progress" in achieving others. In contrast to the Pease bill, he could not simply present an assessment that the continuation of most-favored-nation status would be more likely than its revocation to promote human rights in China. As the debate continued, other aims were added to the Pelosi bill, including "significant progress toward ending religious persecution" and Peking's adherence to the Sino-British agreement on the future of Hong Kong.

In the end, all three approaches—immediate revocation of China's most-favored-nation status, renewal with tough conditions, and extension with milder conditions—came to a vote in the House on October 18. The Bush administration had opposed all three proposals, and the House Ways and Means Committee had endorsed only the Pease bill. But the White House and the congressional leadership were outvoted on the floor of the House. A simple resolution to disapprove the renewal of most-favored-nation status, the most extreme sanction of all, passed by a vote of 247–174, but not by a large enough majority to override a presidential veto. The Pease approach, which had been favored by the Ways and Means Committee and the House leadership, was then rejected on the floor in favor of the tougher Pelosi bill. That bill, in turn, passed by a vote of 384–30—a larger and seemingly veto-proof majority.[46]

As the congressional session came to an end in December, however, the issue of China's most-favored-nation status had not come to a vote in the Senate, and all three pieces of legislation died, at least temporarily. But the size of the majorities in favor of revoking normal tariff treatment for China, or at least of attaching tough conditions to its renewal, showed that the question would be revisited in future years. Most-favored-nation status, which in the late 1980s had seemed a routine feature of commercial relations with China, now seemed to have a much less certain future.

THE PERSIAN GULF CRISIS

As the third part of their effort to stabilize their relations with Washington, Chinese leaders also attempted to rediscover a strategic basis for Sino-American relations. They were acutely aware that mutual geopolitical interests had been the foundation for the initial rapprochement between China and the United States in the late 1960s and early 1970s, and that the common concern with the containment of the Soviet Union had enabled the two countries to overlook potential differences over human rights, even when China was in the final throes of the Cultural Revolution. Given the recent moderation in Soviet foreign policy and the severe internal problems of the Soviet Union, cooperation against Soviet hegemonism was no longer an immediately compelling rationale for Sino-American relations in the early 1990s. But Chinese leaders and foreign policy analysts still wished to identify some other set of international problems that could provide a new strategic basis for U.S.-China relations, and that might once again persuade Americans to put aside their ideological differences with China.

Through the end of 1990, many Chinese still hoped that the Soviet Union might serve that function. In press commentaries, visits to the United States, and meetings with American visitors, Chinese analysts pointed to what they saw as evidence of continued competition and contention in Soviet-American relations, and they warned that a post-Gorbachev leadership in the Kremlin might revive a more expansionist and less accommodative foreign policy. Chinese military commentators noted that, despite the reduction in the number of troops, the Soviet Union continued to improve the quality of its armed forces in the Far East and maintained them in an essentially offensive deployment. They also began to caution Americans about the implications of the disintegration of the Soviet Union, suggesting that China and the United States might have a common interest in preventing turmoil in a decaying Soviet empire from undermining the stability of the Asia-Pacific region.[47]

Chinese officials also tried to identify other global and regional issues on which they could demonstrate to skeptical Americans that China remained an important actor in international affairs, and that it was willing to find common ground with the United States. Echoing some comments made by Henry Kissinger, Richard Nixon, and George Bush, some began to suggest that the two countries shared a mutual concern in counterbalancing a more assertive and powerful Japan, although they never specified what concrete measures they proposed to adopt to deal with Tokyo.[48] With the prospects of a state visit by Gorbachev to Japan, and with rumors of a resolution of the territorial dispute between the two countries, a few Chinese even began to warn Americans of a possible Soviet-Japanese alignment, against which renewed Sino-American cooperation would be the most logical defense.

Besides warning about the possible evolution of Soviet and Japanese policy, China also took more accommodative positions on more immediate regional and global issues. In late 1989 China began to join with the other permanent members of the U.N. Security Council in developing a comprehensive plan for a negotiated settlement in Cambodia. In 1990, Peking upgraded ties with South Korea, agreeing to exchange trade offices with Seoul and encouraging renewed dialogue on the Korean peninsula. Chinese leaders proposed an international conference on the joint exploitation of the natural resources of the South China Sea, aimed at easing the disputes over which countries possessed sovereignty over the islands and seabeds in the area. China also began to stress its relevance to emerging global issues, promising to cooperate in solving international environmental and drug trafficking problems and warning that chaos in China could create a massive flow of refugees to neighboring countries.[49] Though not all of these overtures directly involved the United States, they were all intended in part to impress Americans with China's flexibility and salience.

The crisis in the Persian Gulf, precipitated by the Iraqi invasion of Kuwait in early August, gave Peking its real breakthrough. China had extensive diplomatic, political, and military contacts in the region as the result of long-standing ties with the Palestine Liberation Organization (PLO) and various Arab states, extensive arms sales to Iran and Iraq, and diplomatic relations with Saudi Arabia. In themselves, these gave China some claim to participate in international negotiations to resolve the crisis. Even more important, as a permanent member of the Security Council, Peking automatically assumed a critical role in any deliberations that might be undertaken by the United Nations. When the Bush administration announced it would seek U.N. sanctions against Iraq, as part of its effort to build a new world order, China's veto power on the Security Council immediately made Peking an important consideration in American strategy. Washington promptly sent an assistant secretary of state, Richard Solomon, to Peking to discuss the crisis—the highest-level American visitor to visit China since the second Scowcroft-Eagleburger mission the previous December.[50]

From the beginning, however, China's response to the crisis in the Persian Gulf contained a serious ambiguity. On the one hand, Peking's ties with Kuwait and Saudi Arabia, its eagerness to demonstrate its strategic importance to the West, and its desire to preserve its reputation as a nation steadfastly opposed to international hegemonism pointed in the direction of strong opposition to the Iraqi aggression. On the other hand, China's links with Baghdad, and its long-standing opposition to superpower intervention in regional conflicts, implied that Peking should oppose the introduction of American military forces in the gulf, let alone the initiation of retaliatory strikes against Iraq. Some Chinese analysts also concluded that a war in the gulf would, in the long run, promote continued instability in the region.

Both horns of this dilemma were evident in Chinese diplomacy in the United Nations during the Persian Gulf crisis. In August and September, China voted in favor of all the Security Council resolutions condemning Iraq, calling for its withdrawal from Kuwait, urging the restoration of the previous Kuwaiti government, and imposing economic sanctions on Baghdad. But, together with the Soviet Union, China worked to remove any reference to the use of military force from the resolution implementing an embargo of Iraq, as a way of signaling opposition to armed retaliation against Baghdad.[51]

In November, the Bush administration concluded that economic sanctions alone were unlikely to achieve timely results and decided to seek Security Council authorization for the use of military force to compel an Iraqi withdrawal from Kuwait. At this point, the most plausible option for Peking was to abstain from the vote on such a resolution. Given China's reservations about employing military power against Iraq, and its recollection that the precedent for such action by the United Nations had been directed against China during the Korean War, it was difficult for Peking to vote in favor of the American-sponsored resolution. And yet, it was equally difficult for China to oppose it, especially if it were the only permanent member of the Security Council to do so. A veto would defy world opinion and enrage the United States. Once the Soviet Union indicated that it would vote in favor of military force against Iraq, therefore, a Chinese abstention was virtually assured.[52]

But the Chinese saw the opportunity of using the vote in the Security Council to gain leverage over the United States. In meetings with Secretary of State Baker, first in Cairo and then in New York, Chinese Foreign Minister Qian Qichen apparently indicated that China's vote was uncertain, hinting that an affirmative vote was still possible if Washington could provide enough incentives, and possibly even suggesting that a veto was conceivable if the United States did not provide China with a sufficient reward. In Cairo, therefore, Baker assured his Chinese counterpart that Peking's support for American policy in the gulf "will not be forgotten."[53] To ensure that Peking would not veto the U.N. resolution, the Bush administration agreed to receive Qian Qichen in Washington once the Security Council meeting had concluded. In itself, this meeting would be the highest-level Sino-American contact since the Tiananmen incident and would make the United States only the second Western country to engage in foreign ministerial visits with China.[54] Moreover, Baker reportedly promised that Qian could meet with President Bush during his visit to Washington, if China decided to vote in favor of the U.N. resolution.[55]

When the final vote was taken in the United Nations, China chose to abstain. According to the agreement reportedly made with the Chinese, Qian should therefore have met only with Secretary of State Baker, and other cabinet-rank officials, during his visit to Washington. At the last minute, however, President Bush decided he still wished to meet with Qian, even though China had not met its part of the bargain. As Qian left the State Department, officials there were still insisting that he was not scheduled to meet with the president but instead would be having lunch with the secretary of commerce. Qian's motorcade, however, headed not for the Federal Triangle but for the White House.[56]

In his meeting with the president, the Chinese foreign minister urged the United States to upgrade diplomatic contacts with Peking. In response, Bush agreed to enlarge the official Sino-American dialogue on bilateral and global questions but insisted that China deal first with two issues important to the United States: human rights and the proliferation of nuclear and conventional weapons. A Chinese proposal that Secretary of State Baker visit China sometime in 1991 was simply parried. Qian also asked the United States to adopt a more accommodating position on World Bank lending to China. Here, the Bush administration soon made clear that, while it could only vote in favor of projects designed to meet basic human needs, it would now be prepared to abstain on other loans rather than oppose them, thereby allowing them to be approved.[57]

The Bush administration subsequently defended the president's willingness to receive the Chinese foreign minister, saying that Bush's meeting with Qian involved a sharply worded statement of the American position on relations with China. Bush strongly criticized China's treatment of dissidents and underscored the importance of human rights as an obstacle to the improvement of Sino-American relations. Nonetheless, it became evident in retrospect that the Chinese had gotten the best of the bargain: without making any significant concessions, they had secured a relaxation of American sanctions against them. Thus, the Chinese press could claim that the meeting between Bush and Qian showed that "the United States has realized . . . that it is impossible to isolate China, a country that Bush describes as very important."[58] In contrast, the Bush administration—particularly Secretary of State Baker, according to some reports—finally began to question whether the strategy of swapping concessions with Peking was achieving the desired results.

If it was disappointed by Peking's decision to abstain in the crucial vote in the Security Council, the Bush administration must have been even more displeased with subsequent Chinese analysis during the course of the war.[59] Chinese observers consistently made erroneous predictions about the outcome of the conflict, all intended to suggest that the American use of force was unnecessary and unwise. Their first prognosis was that international mediation would obviate the need for an attack against Iraq. Then, when the war broke out, they predicted that the United States would become enmeshed in a long ground war with heavy casualties, comparable to the one it had fought on the Korean peninsula in the early 1950s. Moreover, they also forecast that the multinational coalition against Baghdad would rapidly split apart, with Washington's Western allies objecting to the cost of the conflict and the Arab participants defecting as Israel was inexorably drawn into the war.[60]

As a result, Chinese propaganda took on an increasingly anti-American tone as the war escalated. Not only did the Chinese media criticize the heavy losses inflicted on Iraqi troops and civilians by American air strikes, but Chinese spokesmen began to portray the two principal combatants—Iraq and the United States—as equally culpable parties in the war. This depiction, in turn, reflected some internal Chinese assessments of the conflict that were not expressed publicly. He Xin, a younger Chinese intellectual then rapidly becoming the darling of conservative leaders, wrote that the United States was using the war to gain control of the world's energy resources, and he warned that, if it were successful in the conflict, it would then attempt to "tame" China, which would be all that lay "in the way of the American goal of world domination."[61] Deng Xiaoping was said to have described the conflict not as a just war against aggression but as the struggle between a big hegemonic power and a smaller one.[62]

The quick American victory in the Gulf War confounded Chinese predictions about the immediate course of the conflict but intensified Peking's concerns about its implications. The surprising success of American military power, in contrast to the decline of the strategic importance of the Soviet Union, raised the possibility that the world was not evolving toward multipolarity, as Chinese analysts had previously asserted, but was becoming a unipolar system centering on the United States. The Bush administration's call for a new world order, to replace the bipolar rivalry of the cold war era, heightened these apprehensions. Chinese observers feared that such a new world order would be dominated by the United States, perhaps acting together with some of its principal allies. They also worried that the promotion of human rights would become a principal theme in the creation of the new world order, and that China would become the main target of American efforts. Summarizing these concerns, one of China's most senior leaders, Bo Yibo, reportedly told a meeting of delegates to the National People's Congress in April that American proposals for a new world order were nothing less than an effort to achieve "world domination" and to encourage China's "peaceful evolution" from socialism to capitalism.[63]

This pessimistic analysis of American capabilities and intentions did not last long. Within a few months, as it became clear that the American military victory in the gulf had neither succeeded in overthrowing Saddam Hussein nor in solving all the problems of the region, Chinese observers began to adopt a more relaxed view of the international situation. Gradually, they realized that the Gulf War was not the watershed event they had originally feared. They concluded that other trends promoting international multipolarity continued, including the relative decline of the United States, the rise of Japan and Germany, and the emergence of such new regional powers as India and China. Any tendency toward unipolarity, they now judged, would be fleeting. Instead, as this more sanguine analysis put it, the United States lacked the ability to realize its "vaulting ambitions," and the prospects of a "U.S.-dominated 'unipolar world'" were therefore remote.[64]

The perception of a unipolar world, centered on a hegemonic United States, would have virtually required China to try to forge some kind of anti-American united front, just as it had done against the Soviet Union in the 1970s and the United States in the 1950s. But the continuation of trends toward a more multipolar international system recommended a different strategy. Rather than confronting the United States, Chinese leaders concluded, they would be better advised to try to maintain their previous policy of working for the gradual normalization of Sino-American relations through timely but limited concessions, cooperation on international issues, and the maximization of China's diplomatic leverage and maneuverability.

But the developments in Eastern Europe and the Persian Gulf did lead Peking to make one adjustment in that general approach. Rather than focusing on improving relations with hard-line Communist states or the third world, as it had briefly tried to do in 1989, China now focused on improving relations with Asian neighbors. It stopped its criticism of Gorbachev's economic and political reforms and continued to expand diplomatic, economic, and military relations with Moscow. Peking muted criticism of Japanese defense policy, even when Tokyo dispatched a flotilla of minesweepers to the Persian Gulf, and it invited Emperor Akihito on a state visit to China. While still eschewing formal diplomatic relations with Seoul, it agreed, over Pyongyang's objections, to the simultaneous admission of both Koreas to the United Nations. And there were continuing signs of improvement in China's relations with Vietnam, even before the successful conclusion of the negotiations on Cambodia. All these steps suggested that Peking was attempting to reduce tensions with the rest of Asia to gain the diplomatic leverage to deal with the United States from as advantageous a position as possible.

THE SECOND DEBATE OVER CHINA'S MOST-FAVORED-NATION STATUS

Neither Congress's inability to modify China's most-favored-nation treatment in 1990, nor Peking's limited cooperation with the United States during the Persian Gulf War, precluded debate on China's trading status when it next came up for renewal in the middle of 1991. Indeed, the debate was as intense as it had been the previous year, if not more so, because even more bilateral issues were at stake than ever before.

For many Americans the domestic situation in China remained the first and principal concern. By the middle of 1991, evidence was mounting that China had resumed economic reform, through such measures as adjusting prices, phasing out export subsidies, devaluing the renminbi, and experimenting with stock markets and commercialized housing.[65] Admittedly, many of China's post-Tiananmen leaders stayed skeptical of thoroughgoing marketization or privatization. The pace of economic reform was therefore much slower than it had been in the late 1980s, and the rhetoric was more cautious. But even conservatives in Peking recognized that the central budget could not continue to subsidize inefficient state industry or to preserve artificially low prices for food and housing, and thus they accepted the need for further enterprise and price reform.

But there was no comparable evidence of a resumption of political reform. Urban China remained repressive, with universities, research institutions, and the news media subject to sporadic shifts in leadership and to periodic political indoctrination campaigns. Students in some leading universities received twelve months of military training before beginning their freshman classes. The press regularly carried essays insisting on the superiority of socialism and warning against the dangers of peaceful evolution. Chinese leaders reiterated that they would never accept a multiparty system, independent political organizations, or other forms of political pluralism. Dissidents arrested in the aftermath of the June 4 incident slowly worked their way through the Chinese legal system. In January 1991, sixty-six more were released, but others were sentenced through arbitrary judicial proceedings to prison terms of up to thirteen years. Two years after the Tiananmen crisis, there had still been no fundamental relaxation of China's political climate.[66]

Americans also worried that China was selling advanced military technology to volatile regions, especially the Middle East. Two types of medium-range missiles that had previously been under development—the M-9 and the M-11—now moved into production. There were renewed reports that, despite its earlier statements to the contrary, China intended to sell the M-9 to Syria. Launchers for the M-11 were sighted in Pakistan, with the Chinese claiming that, because the range of the M-11 was a few kilometers less than its standard for medium-range missiles, it was not covered by Peking's pledges not to sell medium-range missiles to the Middle East.[67] Critics of the Bush administration also charged that China was still providing arms to the Khmer Rouge and had supplied Iraq with a chemical used in the production of nerve gas, missile fuel, and nuclear weapons.[68]

Most disturbing of all, it was revealed that China was helping Algeria to build a nuclear reactor that was not subject to international safeguards, was too large to be used for research purposes, and yet was not connected to the country's national power grid. The size of the reactor, and the fact that it was surrounded by antiaircraft artillery, strongly suggested it was being used to process weapons-grade fissile material.[69] This discovery reactivated long-standing concerns that, despite the promises made to the United States in the mid-1980s, China was still helping third world countries to develop nuclear weapons.[70]

And the American trade deficit with China swelled, from $6.2 billion in 1989 to $10.4 billion in 1990. Macroeconomic forces, especially a slowdown in the Chinese economy, were largely responsible for these shifting trade patterns. But many American observers attributed the trade imbalance to administrative decisions by Peking. The annual report of the U.S. Trade Representative, issued in late March 1991, noted that the Chinese government had raised tariffs on many imports, tightened controls over import licenses, and increased the allocation of raw materials and financial credits to the export sector in an effort to produce a more favorable trade balance. These observations supplemented longer-standing American concerns that inadequate protection of intellectual property rights and restrictions on foreign service industries reduced the opportunities for the sale of American goods and services to China.[71]

Other aspects of China's international commercial behavior appeared even less defensible. There was increasing evidence that Chinese textile manufacturers were shipping their goods to third countries for relabeling, so as to evade American quotas on imports from China, and that this practice was tacitly condoned by the Chinese government.[72] Concern was also growing that China was using convict labor to produce goods—ranging from tea to textiles to wine—that were subsequently sold to the United States. Although the volume was only a small fraction of China's overall exports, the practice created a powerful political linkage between China's trade surplus and its violations of human rights.[73]

The accumulation of contentious issues—human rights, military technology transfers, and China's trade surplus with the United States—made it inevitable that Congress would use the annual debate over China's most-favored-nation status to express dissatisfaction with Peking. Although some members of the House and the Senate once again proposed revoking China's preferential trading status altogether, the more prevalent approach in Congress was to approve the renewal of most-favored-nation treatment in 1991, but to attach conditions to its renewal in subsequent years. This approach was similar to that proposed by Donald Pease and Nancy Pelosi in 1990. But this time the legislation addressed a longer list of issues, attached stricter conditions, and proceeded through both houses of Congress, rather than just the House of Representatives.

The House measure, again sponsored by Representative Pelosi, would have required the president to certify in 1992 that China had accounted for and released all those arrested or detained as a result of the "nonviolent expression of their political beliefs" during the Tiananmen crisis, that it had taken steps to prevent the export to the United States of goods made with prison labor, that it had ended coercive abortions and involuntary sterilization, and that it had given unequivocal assurances that it would not contribute to the proliferation of nuclear weapons and ballistic missiles. China would also have to adhere to the joint declaration between Britain and China about the future of Hong Kong and moderate its opposition to Taiwan's membership in the GATT. Finally, the Pelosi bill required the president to report that China had made "significant overall progress" on several other human rights, including freedom from torture and inhumane prison conditions, freedom of religion, freedom of the press, and freedom of peaceful assembly and demonstration.[74]

The parallel legislation in the Senate, sponsored by Majority Leader George Mitchell, required the president to certify immediately that China was not transferring M-9 or M-11 missiles or missile launchers to Syria, Iran, or Pakistan, and required him to terminate China's most-favored-nation status at once if he should subsequently determine that such transfers had occurred. The Mitchell bill also stipulated that, for the president to recommend a renewal of Peking's preferential trade treatment in 1992, he would have to report that China had released peaceful demonstrators arrested or sentenced after the June 4 incident, stopped exporting to the United States goods produced by forced labor, ceased supplying arms to the Khmer Rouge, and abided by the Sino-British agreement on the future of Hong Kong. The Mitchell bill also demanded that China make significant progress in protecting human rights, correcting unfair trade practices, and preventing the proliferation of nuclear, chemical, and biological weapons.[75]

As these two pieces of legislation worked their way through Congress, leaders in the Forbidden City and the White House had to decide how to respond. Some Chinese leaders may have been reluctant to make any more concessions to the United States, on the grounds that to do so would encourage the Americans to try to "extort" even more from China in the future.[76] Thus, as the congressional debate proceeded, Chinese officials began to say they would never accept any conditions on their country's most-favored-nation status, suggesting they would renounce their preferential trade treatment if the Pelosi or Mitchell bills became law.[77]

But Deng Xiaoping once again decided that, while China should prepare itself for the loss of most-favored-nation status, it should also make new concessions to Washington to try to preserve it.[78] Thus, in the spring of 1991, a steady series of conciliatory gestures flowed from Peking. China promised to ban the export of goods produced by convict labor and to stop the illegal transshipment of textiles to the United States through third countries. It pledged better protection for American intellectual property. It gave a lengthy explanation of its trade surplus with the United States and promised to make more purchases of American goods.[79] It announced that the suspicious nuclear reactor in Algeria would be placed under safeguards by the International Atomic Energy Agency. It agreed to join the other permanent members of the Security Council in discussing limits on arms sales to the Middle East and said it would consider signing the nonproliferation treaty and participating in the Missile Technology Control Regime.[80] In late June, Premier Li Peng announced that China would make no more concessions to the United States, but he also acknowledged Peking had made "a great deal of efforts" to preserve most-favored-nation status.[81]

The Bush administration also worked hard to defeat the Pelosi and Mitchell bills. In a speech at Yale University on Memorial Day, in which he formally announced he was recommending the renewal of China's preferential trade status, the president charged that his opponents in Congress were adopting a policy of "righteous isolationism." He argued that to "endanger [China's most-favored-nation status] with sweeping conditions" would be tantamount to isolating China, and that isolating China would reduce the ability of the United States to promote peace and stability in Asia and to foster freedom and democracy in China.[82] Despite some speculation that the president might accept a mild set of conditions, the White House showed no willingness to compromise with congressional critics.

But neither the concessions made by the Chinese, nor the arguments made by the president, persuaded the House of Representatives. In hearings on China's most-favored-nation status, supporters of the administration's position repeated the arguments they had made the previous year: further economic sanctions against China would threaten the prosperity of Hong Kong, hurt American consumers and exporters, encourage Peking to tighten administrative controls over the Chinese economy, undermine the vitality of China's most reform-oriented provinces, and offer conservative leaders a ready rationale to intensify their repression of Western-oriented intellectuals. But none of these arguments carried great weight, since none of them were novel any longer. What was new, in 1991, was the mounting evidence of unfair Chinese trade practices, continued violations of human rights, and irresponsible arms sales to the Middle East.

Thus, when the House of Representatives voted on the Pelosi bill on July 10, the Bush administration's China policy suffered yet another setback. Although the president won eighty votes more in 1991 than he had in 1990, the total (313–112) still gave the administration's critics more than they needed to override a presidential veto. The prospects in the Senate were, from the White House's perspective, somewhat better but still not certain. As the Senate vote neared two weeks later, the White House needed to devise a strategy that could ensure that the president's position would prevail.

THE SECOND BUSH STRATEGY

In fact, the White House had gradually become disillusioned with its earlier strategy of making unilateral concessions to Peking and hoping for a reciprocal Chinese response. In general, the gains that the Bush administration had achieved had not been worth the domestic political cost, as Congress and large segments of the American press reacted negatively to the strategy. As early as May 1990, the president had begun to express his dissatisfaction with Peking, saying in a press conference, "Overall, I'm disappointed" with the Chinese reaction to his initiatives.[83] In November, the *Los Angeles Times* reported that members of the Bush administration were "miffed over what they see as a failure of the Chinese leadership to respond to Bush's overtures."[84] Peking's willingness to cooperate with the United States during the early months of the Persian Gulf crisis had earned China some goodwill in the White House, but its failure to vote in favor of the crucial U.N. resolution in late November, and its subsequent criticism of American conduct of the war, had only exacerbated the growing sense of unhappiness with China.

At first, it seemed that the Bush administration was unable to formulate any other strategy for dealing with Peking. Asked in his May 1990 press conference whether he had "anything in mind, other than expressing disappointment, to move things along," the president said only, "We've got some diplomacy in mind." In its report in November, the *Los Angeles Times* noted that the White House had "shelved [its] campaign to patch up the once-cozy U.S. relationship with China," but again could not identify an alternative policy toward China.

Throughout the spring of 1991, however, the elements of a new strategy toward Peking were gradually put into place. Further conciliatory gestures toward China were halted. Instead, the White House took steps—some were formal sanctions, others were symbolic gestures—that together indicated a somewhat tougher position toward Peking. In mid-April, the president met with the Dalai Lama to express his concern for human rights in Tibet, the first such meeting that the Tibetan leader had had with any American president.[85] Approximately one week later, the Bush administration cited China, under section 301 of the trade act of 1988, for denying adequate protection of American intellectual property. Such a designation meant the administration would undertake negotiations with the Chinese government, and that it had the right to impose retaliatory tariffs or other restrictions against imports from China if the issue were not resolved within six months.[86] Finally, at the end of May, at the same time as the president recommended the renewal of Peking's most-favored-nation status, the White House also announced it was denying several licenses for the export of high technology to China because of continuing reports of Chinese weapons exports to the Middle East.[87]

At the same time as it was announcing these punitive measures against China, the United States was also engaging in a more active official dialogue with Peking on all three sets of the most contentious issues in Sino-American relations. The assistant secretary of state for humanitarian affairs, Richard Schifter, visited Peking in December 1990 to begin discussions of China's human rights record and to request information on one hundred fifty protesters known to have been arrested after the Tiananmen crisis. In late February 1991, the assistant U.S. trade representative responsible for China, Joseph Massey, traveled to Peking for negotiations on trade issues, including the Chinese trade surplus, the protection of intellectual property rights, and the export of the output of prison labor. In mid-June, Reginald Bartholomew, the undersecretary of state for international security affairs, conducted talks in China on a wide range of arms control issues. These three visits on specific issues were supplemented by more comprehensive discussions conducted in early May by the undersecretary of state for political affairs, Robert Kimmitt, on the entire spectrum of bilateral and multilateral questions affecting the two countries.[88]

On the eve of the Senate vote on the Mitchell bill, the White House's new strategy was described in detail in a letter from the president to Senator Max Baucus, chairman of the Subcommittee on International Trade of the Senate Finance Committee. During the debate over China's trade status, Baucus had indicated he was concerned about Peking's human rights record and international behavior, but he was also persuaded that revoking China's most-favored-nation treatment would be to "shoot ourselves in the foot."[89] In a letter sent to the White House in mid-June, Baucus and several of his colleagues had asked the president to specify the concrete steps that he proposed to take on such issues as the trade imbalance, human rights, and Chinese military technology transfers. Now, on July 19, just a few days before the Senate was scheduled to vote on China's most-favored-nation status, Bush sent Baucus his reply.[90]

In his response to Baucus, Bush spelled out a new China policy. That new strategy, which had been implicit in some of the initiatives taken by the White House throughout the spring, was the result of the first comprehensive interagency review of American China policy since the Tiananmen crisis, as well as of a lengthy memorandum submitted to the president by Secretary of State Baker.[91] The Bush administration identified a long list of measures it would employ to address the various problems in Sino-American relations. On human rights, the letter noted that many of the economic and military sanctions imposed in June 1989 remained in effect, and it stressed the importance of continued dialogue with China on the subject. The White House called for engaging Peking in multilateral negotiations on arms control measures related to the proliferation of nuclear and conventional weapons and threatened tighter restrictions on technology transfers to China in the event of uncooperative Chinese behavior. On bilateral trade issues, the administration noted it had cited China under section 301 of the trade act for failing to protect intellectual property rights. It also revealed that it was planning to deduct more than $100 million from China's annual textile quota to compensate for goods illegally transshipped through third countries, that it intended to temporarily embargo products believed to be produced by prison labor, and that it would initiate action under section 301 against other barriers to the Chinese market.

Moreover, the Bush letter to Baucus also announced an important change in American policy toward Taiwan. In the past, because of respect for Peking's position, the administration had favored the simultaneous accession of China and Taiwan to the GATT. Now, the White House announced it was prepared to see Taiwan enter the GATT first, although it restated its hope that Peking would undertake sufficient steps toward trade reform so that China's application could also be expedited. For the first time since the 1982 agreement on arms sales to Taiwan, an American president was willing to take a position on Taiwan that departed sharply from Peking's preferences.

The policy described in the president's letter to Baucus differed greatly from the strategy embodied in the Mitchell and Pelosi bills and from the strategy that the Bush administration had followed in 1989 and 1990. Unlike his critics in Congress, the president did not want to discontinue China's most-favored-nation status, nor did he want to attach conditions to its renewal, on the grounds that doing so would "cause serious harm to American interests." But compared with its previous policy, the White House was no longer prepared to make accommodative gestures to China in the hope of a positive response. Instead, it now proposed to undertake detailed, high-level negotiations with Peking on the full range of issues at stake, threaten greater sanctions against China if the questions could not be resolved, and promise more conciliatory actions only if China's behavior improved.[92]

The announcement of this new China policy enabled the Bush administration to win an important victory in the Senate when it considered the Mitchell bill on July 23. The White House did not achieve a majority, but it did win forty-four votes: ten more than it needed to sustain a potential presidential veto, and seven more than it had obtained on the final Senate vote on visas for Chinese students and scholars in January 1990. The Senate's action gave the president some time to demonstrate that his new strategy of carefully targeted incentives and disincentives would be effective. But it did not end the debate over U.S. China policy.

THE BROADER RELATIONSHIP

In the middle of 1991, it was also possible to assess the extent to which the Tiananmen incident, and the crisis in Sino-American relations it had produced, had affected the broader relationship between China and the United States, official and unofficial. In general terms, that relationship had suffered serious setbacks, with measurable reductions in the economic, cultural, and strategic ties between the two countries. And yet, amid the damage, there were islands of activity—sometimes surprising ones—that remained relatively unaffected. Furthermore, despite the remaining uncertainties about China, many of the setbacks were temporary, with most aspects of the relationship beginning clearly to rebound two years after the Tiananmen crisis.

The pattern of bilateral trade between the two countries saw perhaps the most dramatic change. The total volume of trade increased greatly from $13.5 billion in 1988 to $20.0 billion in 1990 (table A-2). Chinese exports to the United States rose sharply, from $8.5 billion in 1988 to $12.0 billion in 1989, and then to $15.2 billion in 1990 (table A-3). Conversely, there was a smaller but significant decrease in American exports to China, which rose from $5.0 billion in 1988 to $5.8 billion in 1989, but then fell back to $4.8 billion in 1990 (table A-4). One result was an increase in each country's share of the other's overall foreign trade. For the first time China's share of American total trade had exceeded 2 percent, and also for the first time, the United States had accounted for more than 15 percent of China's total trade. But a second consequence was more disturbing. As already noted, the trade imbalance between the two countries soared from $3.5 billion in 1988 to $10.4 billion in 1990, making China's surplus with the United States second only to Japan's (table A-2).

The nearly 80 percent increase in Chinese exports to the United States over this two-year period confounded early predictions that signs of political instability in China, and the diplomatic confrontation between the two countries, would lead American importers to turn away from China in search of more reliable suppliers. A country where labor unrest might prevent the fulfillment of export orders, or whose exports might be subject to higher American tariffs, might not seem an attractive partner for many American importers, especially for companies in the fashion industry or the toy business where timely supply is of the essence. In the end, however, few American firms shifted to alternative suppliers. Indeed, the category of trade that grew the fastest in this two-year period was finished apparel, whose exports more than doubled in value between 1988 and 1990.

The surge in Chinese exports to the United States was the result of several factors. The successive devaluations of the renminbi, which had depreciated by 40 percent between 1988 and 1990, were gradually making Chinese products more competitive on the American market. Moreover, the Chinese government offered financial subsidies, concessional credit, and cheap raw materials to exporters, which enabled them to offer their goods to foreign markets at bargain prices. Finally, the improvement of relations across the Taiwan Strait encouraged many Taiwanese firms to shift production from Taiwan (where labor costs were rising) to the mainland (where they remained comparatively low). A similar phenomenon was also occurring in Hong Kong, as entrepreneurs there relocated their factories across the border into Guangdong province. This pattern meant that goods once exported to the United States from Hong Kong and Taiwan were now exported from China. It also meant that the political burden of the resulting trade surplus was shifted from Taipei to Peking.

The 17 percent decline in American exports to China in 1990 also had several causes. Chinese officials claimed it was the result of American sanctions, specifically the restriction of export credits and the tightening of controls over technology transfer. In fact, neither of these explanations is persuasive. The suspension of lending by the U.S. Eximbank was one of the first sanctions to be relaxed by the Bush administration, and the programs that remained deferred (such as the Trade Development Program) had never provided a high volume of financing. Furthermore, although the liberalization of American export controls was halted, the standards were not tightened, and the multilateral controls administered by the Coordinating Committee on Export Controls were actually relaxed.[93] Although there was some decline in the sale of American electronic equipment to China, the reduction in the sale of American chemicals and agricultural products—items not covered by export controls—contributed most to the drop in American exports to China.

More plausible explanations for the decline in American exports to China between 1989 and 1990 must therefore be found elsewhere. To some extent, it was caused by the economic retrenchment program that Chinese leaders had implemented after the Tiananmen crisis to bring inflation under control. The slowdown in the rate of industrial growth was partly responsible for the reduction in imports of machinery and raw materials from abroad. At the same time, a bountiful harvest in 1990 enabled Peking to reduce the import of foreign agricultural goods. Accordingly, American sales of farm products to China, which had risen greatly in 1989, now fell by about 50 percent in 1990.

In addition, as a result of Western sanctions, Chinese leaders now faced a reduction in their access to international financing, precisely when their debt service burden was reaching its peak. This made it imperative to cut back on imports and to promote exports to maintain China's foreign exchange reserves. Through a combination of currency devaluation, the reduction of domestic demand, and the imposition of tighter administrative controls over foreign trade Peking managed to reduce imports by 10 percent in 1990, with American exporters suffering about as much as exporters in other developed countries.[94]

Other aspects of the economic relationship between China and the United States were also affected by the Tiananmen incident. With Americans horrified at the violence they had seen on television, and worried about their personal safety in China, American tourism in China fell off sharply. At the height of the fall travel season in October 1989, for example, the number of American tourists visiting China was 55 percent below the previous year. But tourism rebounded rather rapidly. In May 1990, another peak travel month, the number of American tourists in China reached about two-thirds of those that had visited the country in May 1989. By the end of the year, approximately 230,000 Americans visited China, only about 23 percent below the 300,000 that had traveled there in 1988.[95]

American investment in China showed a similar pattern: a sharp drop followed by a slow recovery. Only a handful of American firms closed their representative offices in China as a result of the Tiananmen crisis, but a much larger number reduced their staff as the uncertainties about Sino-American relations increased and as China's imports from the United States fell. Particularly hard hit by this retrenchment were U.S. firms attempting to sell consumer goods or military equipment to China.[96] New American investment commitments in the first quarter of 1990 were roughly 75 percent lower than in the comparable period of 1989, but then began to rebound in the second quarter. The annual total, at about $400 million, was almost 40 percent less than in 1989, but roughly equal to the investment committed in 1988.[97]

In the cultural sphere, Sino-American relations showed a combination of damage and recuperation by the end of 1991. Peking had partially restored official cultural exchanges with the United States. It continued to jam the Chinese-language service of Voice of America, but not the English-language broadcasts. It reinstated the Fulbright program, although it declined to send any Chinese graduate students to the United States and exchanged fewer faculty members than before.[98] It again permitted some Chinese to participate in the International Visitors Program sponsored by the U.S. Information Agency, and allowed Chinese officials and intellectuals to attend USIA programs at American consulates in China. The number of Chinese participating in official academic and cultural exchanges with the United States declined greatly in 1990, before recovering somewhat in 1991.[99]

In the United States, the National Academy of Sciences and the National Science Foundation suspended all activities in China for one year in June 1989. Since the academy was one of the cosponsors of the official American academic exchange program, conducted by the Committee on Scholarly Communication with the People's Republic of China, this meant that official scholarly exchanges in the social sciences and humanities, as well as in the natural sciences, were canceled for the 1989–90 academic year. By the fall of 1990, however, the academy and the foundation had reactivated their programs with China, the CSCPRC's office in Peking had reopened, and the flow of Chinese and American scholars under its auspices had been resumed.[100] Also, despite an unresolved dispute over the protection of intellectual property rights, the United States and China renewed their bilateral agreement on scientific and technological cooperation, permitting the continuation of the twenty-odd interagency programs of scientific exchange.[101]

Official government-to-government exchange programs had always been a small fraction of the overall cultural and academic relationship between the two countries. The impact of the Tiananmen crisis on unofficial exchanges was much more limited than its effect on official programs. Even as the number of Chinese students and scholars participating in official exchange programs declined, the number coming to the United States under private auspices rose by an almost equal amount (table A-5). As a result, the ranks of Chinese students in American universities swelled, with enrollments rising to more than 33,000 in the 1989–90 academic year. Despite the Tiananmen crisis, the Chinese remained the largest contingent of foreign students in the United States.[102]

Indeed, the flow of Americans to China dropped much more dramatically than the flow of Chinese to the United States. Many prospective students refused to go to China, out of concern for their physical safety or out of revulsion at the June 4 incident. American faculty members and researchers worried that they would be unable to conduct their work effectively, or that their presence would be interpreted as an endorsement of the Chinese leadership. Several U.S. universities—including Yale, Princeton, and Stanford—suspended or reduced the scale of their activities in China.[103]

All these decisions seriously affected the number of Americans visiting China under unofficial exchange programs. One survey of U.S. universities estimated that the number of American students and faculty going to China under formal exchange programs had declined by nearly 57 percent, even as the number of Chinese coming to the United States under comparable programs fell by around only

19 percent.[104] A separate, more comprehensive estimate showed a similar decrease, with the number of American students in China in the 1989–90 academic year fully 56 percent below the number in 1987–88 (table A-6). By the end of 1990, however, virtually all these programs had been restored, although some of them were still operating at a lower level than might otherwise have been expected. Indeed, with the exception of George Soros's China Fund, all the other major American educational and cultural organizations with offices and activities in China were still in operation in the middle of 1991.

A possibly more enduring problem was a decline in the financial resources available to support American exchange programs with China. The American educational community feared that major foundations and contributors, already questioning their continued involvement in China before the Tiananmen crisis, would now divert their contributions to newly emerging opportunities in the Soviet Union and Eastern Europe. Although data on this issue remain sparse, one incident illustrated the danger. In mid-1991, the Department of Commerce decided to stop funding the training program on economic management that it had conducted in Dalian ever since 1984, on the grounds that it wished to divert the funds to launch comparable programs in Eastern Europe.[105]

Academic exchanges suffered from qualitative restrictions as well as quantitative ones. Several collaborative research projects in the social sciences were disrupted, as the Chinese government began to restrict the flow of data, particularly from survey research, to scholars in the United States.[106] It was more difficult now to contemplate research or dialogue with Chinese colleagues on politically sensitive subjects. And yet, by the end of 1990, it seemed that resourceful Chinese intellectuals were carving out some autonomy that permitted them to resume almost all of the activities that had been possible before the Tiananmen incident, save for the dispatch of large numbers of officially sponsored degree candidates to American institutions. It also seemed that many American scholars were still able to conduct useful collaborative research with Chinese counterparts, especially outside of the major institutions in Peking.

The military and strategic relationship between China and the United States was one that was most severely restricted by the American sanctions imposed in 1989. The delivery of American arms through official channels completely stopped, and that through commercial channels fell nearly to zero (table A-11). The Chinese announced their withdrawal from the project to design and produce advanced avionics equipment for their F-8 fighter, in part because cost overruns had made the program prohibitively expensive, and in part because there was now no assurance that the technology in question could ever be exported to China from the United States.[107] The ban on high-level communication between the two countries' military establishments halted the exchange of visits between American and Chinese service chiefs and Defense Ministry officials. Similar sanctions greatly hampered, but did not completely prevent, lower-level contacts: official exchanges of military delegations stopped, but some defense intellectuals continued to travel between the two countries under the sponsorship of other organizations. Moreover, according to some published accounts, the two countries continued to cooperate in monitoring Soviet nuclear explosions and missile tests, using the equipment that had been placed in China in the 1980s.[108]

Finally, in the political sphere, some of the relationships suspended in the immediate aftermath of the June 4 incident also began to revive. In mid-1991, the Bush administration's ban on high-level official contacts was still in effect for most ministerial exchanges, but the secretary of state had met with his Chinese counterpart on many occasions, and exchanges of subcabinet officials to discuss concrete issues in the relationship had resumed. Although no members of Congress visited China for nearly eighteen months after the Tiananmen crisis, the first congressional delegation finally returned to Peking in November 1990.[109] The National Committee on U.S.-China Relations, which had postponed several of the activities it had planned to conduct with the PRC in 1989, resumed its high-level bilateral dialogue with Peking in early 1990 and conducted another session in the United States in the summer of 1991.

On balance, then, much of the broader relationship between the United States and China had recovered by the fall of 1991. Trade was at an all-time high, although it was increasingly imbalanced in China's favor. Investment increased, although new commitments remained below the previous peaks of 1985 and 1989. The flow of Chinese students and scholars to America stayed steady, although fewer Chinese came as degree candidates and more came under private auspices. American tourism in China, after dropping sharply in late 1989 and early 1990, had fully revived. Despite the announced suspension of high-level official contacts, meetings at the subcabinet level had resumed, as had legislative exchanges and dialogue among the broader foreign policy establishments of the two countries. Only the military relationship between the two countries seemed to have been dramatically and permanently affected by the Tiananmen crisis.

On the other hand, just as quantitative indices alone did not adequately measure the growth of Sino-American relations in the mid-1980s, they can not completely portray the transformation of the relationship between the two countries after the June 4 incident. Although commercial and cultural ties between the two countries continued in 1990 and 1991, and in some cases even grew dramatically, in many ways they also assumed a much more truculent tone. The Sino-American dialogue on foreign policy issues was sharply colored by the disputes over the Chinese trade surplus, Peking's arms sales, and human rights, with at least two congressional delegations producing more acrimony than goodwill.[110] Cooperation between Chinese and American scholars was complicated by Peking's reluctance to release data on sensitive social issues, and by its accusations that academic exchanges were a primary instrument of the American policy of peaceful evolution. Commercial relations between the two countries were conducted under the constant specter that Peking might lose its most-favored-nation status in the United States and were now subject to disputes over barriers to the Chinese market.

In short, the third decade of Sino-American relations promised a very different tone than either of the previous two. The 1970s had seen much goodwill, but commercial, cultural, and academic exchanges had been highly restricted before normalization. Good feelings between the two countries had prevailed through most of the 1980s, and the establishment of diplomatic relations between Peking and Washington had allowed economic and cultural ties to expand rapidly. Most of those exchanges were continuing in the 1990s, but with a much higher level of contention than ever before.

THE MOOD

On the second anniversary of the June 4 incident, China and the United States still eyed each other with far less enthusiasm than they had at the height of their collaboration against the Soviet Union in the 1970s or during the apex of reform in the 1980s. Serious splits had emerged in each country between political elites and the ordinary citizenry. Interestingly, the general public in both China and America seemed more willing to support a normal relationship with each other than did large segments of their political establishments.

In the United States, most members of the political elite still regarded China as less important, less admirable, and less cooperative than they had in the past. As Soviet-U.S. relations improved, and as the cold war drew to a close, China lost its previous status as a useful counterweight to Soviet expansionism. Although a few former statesmen, particularly those connected with the original opening to China in the early 1970s, continued to describe China as a potential strategic asset for the United States, most American observers seemed to discount the importance of China to U.S. foreign policy. As Representative Barney Frank (D-Massachusetts) put it during the 1990 hearings on China's most-favored-nation status, "It is hard today to conjure up a major threat to our national security sufficient . . . to dilute our commitment to human rights." Or, in the words of his colleague, Representative Edward Markey (D-Massachusetts): "The Cold War is over. . . . Now, . . . when we turn over the China card, it's a deuce."[111]

The glass through which Americans viewed China was also very different in the early 1990s than it had been in the late 1980s. The earlier prism had belittled the persistence of Leninist economic and political institutions and magnified the trends toward liberalization, creating an image of what the *New York Times* later called "cuddly Communism."[112] The new lens, created by the trauma of the Tiananmen crisis, focused attention on the uncertain future of economic reform, the tendencies toward reasserting administrative control over the economy, the persecution of Chinese dissidents and intellectuals, and the efforts to reimpose political restrictions on Chinese universities and mass media.

This changing perceptual prism meant that the same phenomena were now viewed very differently than they had been before. The Chinese economy, described in the mid-1980s as having virtually gone capitalist, was now portrayed in one typical account as being "rigidly centralized," except for a few enclaves along the coast.[113] Members of Congress had once noted that the human rights situation in post-Mao China was "better now than at any time since 1949," but they now depicted China as the "most repressive nation on earth."[114] The dramatic growth in Chinese exports, once seen as evidence of the spread of private and collective enterprise, was now attributed to a draconian but efficient network of prison factories. Any improvement of political climate or revival of economic reform was explained as the result not of initiatives by pragmatic central leaders, but of pressure from mid-level officials or evasion by local governments.

Moreover, the developments in Eastern Europe in 1989 and 1990 and in the Soviet Union in 1990 and 1991 reinforced these perceptions of a retrogressive China. China had previously been seen as marching at the forefront of reform, but now it was viewed as lagging far behind the rest of the Communist world in its pursuit of economic and political liberalization. As Representative Dan Burton (R-Indiana) asked in early 1990, "If East Germany and Romania can make democratic changes, why can't China?"[115]

Finally, there was growing skepticism among American leaders about the extent to which China's foreign policy interests converged with the United States. The reports that Peking was supplying weapons to the Khmer Rouge, selling missiles to the Middle East, helping countries like Pakistan and Algeria develop nuclear weapons, offering the components for chemical weapons to Iran and Libya, and running huge surpluses with the United States through unfair trade practices seemed to outweigh the evidence that China was prepared to cooperate with the United States on other international issues. For those who followed Chinese statements closely, its treatment of the American involvement in the Persian Gulf War underscored the divergent perspectives of Peking and Washington.

This disenchantment with China extended deep within the American political establishment. Zbigniew Brzezinski, one of the architects of the normalization of Sino-American relations in 1978, and one of the principal advocates of close strategic ties with Peking, announced in April 1990 that he favored the outright revocation of China's most-favored-nation status.[116] Few members of Congress were prepared to speak out openly in favor of a normal relationship with China. Even some members of the business community, which had been among the staunchest defenders of a normal relationship with China, began to waver. Some, warning that "China is fast becoming the South Africa of the world," were reluctant to openly defend most-favored-nation status for China out of fear of arousing public criticism.[117] Others began to express their doubts about the benefits of a commercial relationship with China. "Do we want to continue to be chumps for China?" one American executive asked. "Do we want to continue to sign contracts they don't honor? Do we want to continue to let them steal our technology?"[118]

In some ways, the views of the American public paralleled the opinions expressed by the political establishment in the United States. The public's perceptions of China were just as unfavorable in 1990 as they had been in 1989, suggesting that the dramatic change that had occurred in the aftermath of the Tiananmen crisis was an enduring, rather than a temporary, phenomenon. Moreover, the percentage of Americans having favorable impressions of China in 1990 (approximately one-third) was only slightly higher than the proportion who had held comparable images in 1977 (around one-quarter), revealing that the goodwill generated by a decade of reform and ten years of normal Sino-American relations had been largely eliminated by the June 4 incident and its aftermath (table A-1, figure A-1). Like many editorialists and members of Congress, the public now was more favorably impressed by developments in the Soviet

Union than in China. In a poll taken in June 1990, well before the Russian revolution of 1991, 49 percent of the respondents said they would extend more favorable trade privileges to the Soviet Union than to China, whereas only 16 percent expressed a preference for Peking over Moscow.[119]

Similarly, like American elites, the American public saw China as much less important to the United States than had previously been the case. In 1982, 87 percent of elites and 64 percent of the public regarded China as being "important to the U.S. for political, economic, or security reasons." In 1990, in contrast, the comparable proportions had fallen to 73 percent and 47 percent, respectively (table A-1).[120]

And finally, like their leaders, the American public no longer saw China as sharing common international interests with the United States. To be sure, the percentage of Americans seeing China as unfriendly or as an enemy fell from 39 percent in July 1989 to 30 percent in October 1990, suggesting one area in which the effects of the Tiananmen crisis may have been transient. But the percentage viewing China as a close friend or ally of the United States did not recover, remaining at only 16 percent in both polls (table A-1). In October 1990 only half as many Americans regarded China as a friendly or allied country as saw the Soviet Union in the same way.[121] Moreover, looking to the future, Americans continued to be concerned about the prospects for U.S.-China relations. A separate survey taken at about the same time showed that fully 40 percent of the public regarded China's development as a world power as a critical threat to the vital interests of the United States.[122]

In other respects, however, the American public appeared to take a far different approach to China, in that it was more willing than much of the U.S. political establishment to endorse the restoration of a normal working relationship with Peking. In January 1990, for example, polls suggested that the public was divided fairly evenly over whether to assign higher priority to promoting human rights in China (42 percent) or to maintaining good relations with Peking (46 percent). Similarly, compared with Congress, the public seemed much more sympathetic to President Bush's decision to send Brent Scowcroft and Lawrence Eagleburger on their two trips to China. According to one poll, the public split into roughly equal groups over the timing of the missions, with 47 percent believing that the White House should have waited longer before resuming contact with China, and 40 percent believing that it acted appropriately. On the related issue of the administration's use of secret diplomacy, the public was even more closely divided, with 40 percent saying Bush had been "too secretive about his dealings with China," and 42 percent saying the contrary. Although hardly a ringing endorsement of the president's China policy, the figures still suggested Bush had much stronger backing from the public than he did from Congress.[123]

A strikingly similar situation occurred the following year, as the United States began the second debate over China's most-favored-nation status. Together, the votes on the Pelosi bill in the House and the Mitchell bill in the Senate suggested that the president had been able to gain the support of 156 members of Congress, or about 30 percent of the total. In contrast, in one poll fully 60 percent of both leaders and the public said that they favored the restoration of normal economic relations with China, and nearly 50 percent in another poll supported the extension of China's most-favored-nation status.[124]

On the other side of the Pacific, many Chinese leaders, and a smaller number of intellectuals, continued to view the United States with skepticism, if not hostility. As they had consistently done since the Tiananmen crisis, the Party leadership saw the United States as undertaking a policy of sanction and pressure, attempting to intervene in China's internal affairs, protect the opponents of the Chinese government, and encourage China to renounce socialism in favor of political and economic liberalization. The official press continued to carry articles critical of the American economic and political systems and denying their applicability to China. It also regularly published denunciations of the American policy of peaceful evolution, and charged that American sanctions against China constituted an unwarranted intervention in China's internal affairs. With the collapse of communism in the Soviet Union, Chinese leaders became more convinced than ever that the spearhead of such a policy would now be directed against them. The relatively small amount of American aid extended to China after the disastrous floods in June 1991 reportedly convinced Chinese officials that the United States was hoping that the floods would produce "social unrest," an "economic crisis," and "further turmoil," thus providing a "favorable opportunity for peaceful evolution in China."[125]

The Persian Gulf crisis and the improvements in Soviet-American relations also renewed another strand in Chinese thinking that had been largely dormant since the early 1980s: the concern about the hegemonic tendencies in American foreign policy. The evident American leadership of the international coalition against Iraq, the U.S. willingness to use military force against Baghdad, the calls for a new world order under American sponsorship, and the growing signs of cooperation between Washington and Moscow aroused fears, at least for a time, of a more unipolar world centered around the United States. Although this concern was most openly expressed by conservative Chinese leaders, such as Bo Yibo and even Deng Xiaoping, it was also evident among some older Chinese intellectuals, who warned their American colleagues against a reassertion of American arrogance in the aftermath of its easy military victory in the gulf and its warming relations with the Kremlin.

But Chinese public perceptions of these issues differed greatly from those held by Chinese leaders. While some visitors to China reported that they encountered some anti-American sentiment because of U.S. sanctions against China,[126] it appeared that a much larger number of Chinese understood and appreciated the U.S. condemnation of the actions of Chinese leaders during the June 4 incident. If urban Chinese joined their government in urging the relaxation of American sanctions, it was not because they regarded them as intervention in their country's internal affairs, but because they wished to resume normal political, economic, and cultural exchanges with the United States. Moreover, an even larger number of Chinese urged Washington to preserve their country's most-favored-nation status, on the grounds that its revocation would do great damage to the cause of political and economic reform.[127]

Nor did official Chinese propaganda after the Tiananmen crisis reduce the admiration that many Chinese had for American society. Indeed, the political repression and economic recession that followed the June 4 incident only increased the desire of many Chinese to emigrate to the United States, with some in the south incurring debts of tens of thousands of dollars to Chinese gangs who could arrange for false documentation and transportation to America.[128] As one American correspondent summarized the mood of urban intellectuals in mid-1991: "In their first breath, [they] typically tell their trusted American friends how much they detest their leadership. In their second breath, they express affection for the United States and inquire about getting visas."[129]

Finally, in sharp contrast to their leaders, many ordinary urban Chinese adopted a position toward the Persian Gulf War that one reporter described as "vehemently pro-American." Chinese children invented an updated version of cops and robbers, with the Patriots against the Scuds. A few Chinese volunteered to join in the fight against Iraq, and some even sent financial contributions to support the war effort. One letter to the American embassy praised the United States for "fighting against the devil" and for "protecting democracy, freedom, and human rights from the dictators of the world."[130] Even the Chinese military was reportedly impressed by the American performance in the Gulf War, with one officer quoted as saying, "The American troops are very strong and powerful, and we are no match for them."[131]

To a degree, Chinese perceptions of American conduct in the Persian Gulf War were correlated with age. Some older Chinese, particularly urban intellectuals, shared their leaders' concern that the easy American victory would produce a unipolar world centered on Washington, with other countries such as China reduced to strategic insignificance. Younger Chinese, by comparison, seemed much less worried about the geopolitical implications of the American triumph. At one banquet for some American visitors in Peking in April 1991, a leading Chinese scholar expressed his concern that the United States might begin to show "arrogance" in its relations with China and other developing countries in the war's aftermath. But then, suddenly realizing that his younger colleagues might think differently, he turned to one of his subordinates for his opinion. "Did you and your friends support the United States during the war?" the older intellectual asked. "Of course we did," the younger man flatly replied, his bemused tone suggesting that the answer was so obvious that the question need not have been asked.

All this suggested that potential political support remained in both countries for the stabilization and improvement of Sino-American relations, especially if there were a change of leadership or policy on the Chinese side. In the meantime, however, the relationship was still extremely fragile. In the United States, the Bush administration's second policy toward China was highly vulnerable to new signs of repression in China and to fresh evidence of uncooperative Chinese international behavior. Conversely, the war in the Persian Gulf and the collapse of communism in the Soviet Union made China's leadership even more suspicious of American intentions. More than two years after the Tiananmen crisis, Sino-American relations remained deadlocked.

CHAPTER 9

Prospects

THE relationship between China and the United States has evolved through four phases since the establishment of the People's Republic in 1949. For the first twenty years, the two countries were essentially hostile to each other, as a result of the ideological gap between the American and Chinese leaderships. This initial period was characterized by periodic military confrontation, the absence of economic and cultural ties, and highly limited diplomatic contacts. Over time, relations gradually became more stable, as each country acquired a better understanding of the other's interests and capabilities. Still, it remained an enormously costly dispute. The two countries forsook the benefits they would have gained from normal economic and cultural relationships. Each nation had to maintain sufficient military forces to wage war against the other. Consequently, China and the United States dealt with the Soviet Union from a disadvantageous position.

From 1969 through the early 1980s, China and the United States engaged in a strategic alignment against the Soviet Union. On a few occasions, such as the Nixon visit of 1972 and the normalization of Sino-American relations in 1978, this tacit alliance seemed to generate excitement and goodwill, especially in the United States. But for most of this second period, the Sino-American relationship can be better understood as a marriage of convenience rather than an enthusiastic romance. The united front against the Soviet Union raised the familiar fears of entrapment and abandonment, so common in such relationships.[1] Neither country wanted to become excessively dependent on the other or find itself ensnared in the other's confrontation with Moscow. Each country feared, at various times, that the other might make a secret accommodation with the Soviet Union. Accordingly, Peking worried not only when the United States pursued détente with the Soviet Union during the Nixon, Ford, and Carter administrations, but also when Soviet-American tensions were heightened during the early Reagan years. Analysts in Washington became apprehensive every time Moscow and Peking resumed their sporadic diplomatic dialogue.

The bilateral ties between the two countries remained highly restricted during most of this second phase in Sino-American relations. China retained the constraints on foreign economic and cultural contacts characteristic of the late Maoist era, rejecting commercial credits, barring foreign investment, and engaging in few long-term cultural exchanges. Moreover, Peking circumscribed its relations with the United States pending the establishment of full diplomatic ties. Although there was some increase in trade, the initiation of a modest military relationship, and rudimentary academic exchanges, these aspects of U.S.-China ties remained far below their potential.

And the two countries still had difficulties managing their longstanding dispute over the American involvement with Taiwan. Redefining the U.S. security commitment to the island, such that it meant continuing arms sales and unilateral pledges of support rather than an American military presence and a formal bilateral defense treaty, required hard bargaining on both sides. So did the end of American diplomatic relations with Taipei and their replacement by unofficial representative offices. The negotiations over these issues were punctuated by stalemate (1975–77) and crisis (1981–82), and the resulting compromises were not fully or enthusiastically accepted in either country.

In the mid-1980s, China and the United States entered a third phase in their relationship, perhaps best described as American cooperation in China's modernization and reform. The transition from a strategic alignment to an economic partnership was a protracted process, encouraged by the peaking of Soviet power under Leonid Brezhnev, the reorientation of Soviet foreign policy under Mikhail Gorbachev, and the initiation of China's own program of domestic economic and political reform under Deng Xiaoping. Although there were milestones along the way in the transformation of Sino-American relations during this period, there were no historic turning points comparable in significance to the outbreak of the Korean War in 1950 or the Nixon visit to China in 1972.

The inauguration of this new Sino-American relationship was thus less dramatic than the launching of the united front against the Soviet Union, but the partnership proved to be a much more extensive and enthusiastic bond than was strategic accommodation. The benefits of the strategic alignment had in some sense been negative:

repelling Soviet aggression and preventing the establishment of Soviet hegemony in any part of the world. The advantages of the economic partnership, in contrast, were positive: the rewards that could be reaped when America gained access to the Chinese market and China gained access to American technology and capital. Furthermore, the new relationship tapped deep wellsprings of emotion on both sides. Many Chinese saw in the United States a foreign benefactor that could provide material assistance and technical advice in their quest for national wealth and power. Many Americans saw in China an eager student that could be readily converted to American values and institutions. The idea that China would be remaking itself with American assistance gave the relationship an excitement and electricity that the earlier strategic alignment lacked.

The enthusiasm generated by this partnership enabled growth in bilateral relations that far overshadowed that of the 1970s. Trade, investment, academic relations, and cultural exchanges increased markedly. Despite the diminished direct Soviet threat to China, the strategic relationship between China and the United States reached a level unknown at the height of the united front in the early 1980s. With better mutual understanding, more mechanisms for consultation, and greater trust in each other's intentions, the management of controversial issues such as Taiwan was facilitated.

By the end of the 1980s, however, this third relationship was already beginning to erode. As bilateral ties expanded, complaints grew about the allocation of costs and benefits between the two countries. Americans criticized the terms of trade and investment, charging China with dumping exports, restricting imports, and maintaining an unsatisfactory environment for direct foreign investment. The Chinese countered with their own grievances about barriers to American markets, controls over exports of technology, and the drain of talented Chinese students and scholars to American universities. As the Soviet threat receded, differences emerged on more international issues, especially arms sales, nuclear proliferation, and Cambodia.

Even more important, the growing interpenetration of the two societies reactivated many of the ideological differences that had been set aside in earlier years. Many conservative Chinese became apprehensive that the economic partnership would mean the import of American values as well as American technology. Americans became more cognizant of the areas in which, despite reform, serious violations of human rights still took place in China. As these differences mounted, each country gradually became aware of the divergent ways in which they had defined their common objective. Chinese leaders had pre-

sumed that the United States was prepared to assist in China's socialist modernization and reform. But Americans had assumed that they
would be helping China undertake a more sweeping restructuring of
its Leninist economic and political institutions.

The Tiananmen crisis of 1989 was the single dramatic event mark-
ing the end of the third phase and ushering in a new period of mistrust
between China and the United States. The two governments now
regarded each other very suspiciously. Peking concluded that the
United States was engaged in a deliberate policy of subverting and
overthrowing Communist rule in China, and Washington believed
that China would no longer be willing to accommodate American
interests on bilateral and international issues. The political base
of support for the relationship in the two countries was severely
weakened, with many Americans favoring tougher sanctions against
Peking to secure changes in its policies on human rights, trade, and
arms sales abroad. Partly as a result of the official sanctions imposed
by the two governments after the June 4 incident, and partly because
of the natural reaction of American society to events in China,
some of the cultural, economic, and military ties between the two
countries were seriously attenuated.

The future of Sino-American relations is especially difficult to
predict, since all of the important conditions shaping it are in flux.
The international strategic environment remains highly unsettled.
There is general agreement that the severe internal problems of the
Soviet Union and the collapse of the Soviet empire in Eastern Europe
mark the end of the bipolar era, but there is no consensus on whether
the post–cold war world will revolve around several major powers
or center on the United States alone. The prospects for global war
have surely declined, but with the erosion of bipolarity the possibility
of regional conflicts may now have increased. It is not clear whether
the war in the Persian Gulf will promote more institutionalized
mechanisms for cooperative security or whether nations will rely on
unilateral or collective action to ensure their defense.

The future of the international economy also remains in doubt.
Some believe that the postwar institutions fostering global free trade,
particularly the General Agreement on Tariffs and Trade (GATT),
can be adapted to meet higher levels of economic interaction. Others
foresee the rise of a more competitive and fragmented world economy, with the rules of free trade eroding, economic and technological
nationalism rising, and countries increasingly following neomercantilist and protectionist strategies. Still others forecast the emergence
of powerful trading blocs not only in Europe, but also in the Americas
and in the Pacific. But there is no consensus on the final composition

of any of these possible groupings, let alone on whether in the end they will make international trade and investment freer or more restricted.

These uncertainties surrounding the global strategic and economic environments are echoed in the Asia-Pacific region. Growing interdependence and competition among the various economies of East Asia over the last decade have promoted a great reduction of international tensions and the emergence of regional economic organizations. But the durability of the Asian entente and the extent of regional economic cooperation remain questionable. Unresolved territorial disputes, overlapping geopolitical ambitions, historical enmities, and ethnic rivalries still exist across the region, any of which could spark local arms races or even ignite armed conflict. It is not clear whether the process of regional economic cooperation will evolve into an Asian trading bloc and, if so, how many nations it will include, how closed it will be to outsiders, and how open it will be to commerce within the region.

Moreover, the two partners in the Sino-American relationship are struggling with domestic difficulties. Those in China, of course, are presently the more serious. Power in China is now shifting along at least three dimensions: from an older generation to a younger one, from state to society, and from center to provinces. The mechanisms by which political authority is first redistributed and then exercised remain highly fragile. At the same time, Chinese leaders are grappling with a daunting agenda of domestic issues, including a crisis of political legitimacy, severe environmental problems, intense population pressures, and the instabilities of an economy that seems caught in the transition from plan to market. China could evolve in many possible directions in the 1990s—toward further reform, greater repression, political decay, or even national disintegration—each of which would profoundly affect its relations with the United States.

The United States is debating its national priorities and policies in the post–cold war era. It is confronting the gradual erosion of its economic and educational infrastructure. It is more and more constrained by chronic trade and budget deficits. Its national political system is stalemated by the tendency for different political parties to control the White House and Congress. Moreover, it is trying both to comprehend and to shape the structure of the post–cold war world. Opinions differ widely on the best balance to be struck between isolation and engagement, unilateralism and multilateralism, pragmatism and idealism, and free trade and protectionism in American foreign policy.

Finally, many uncertainties surround the issue of Taiwan, which remains especially important in determining the future of Sino-American relations. The island is entering the most sensitive phase of its political reforms, including the redrafting of the constitution and the recomposition of central legislative bodies. The liberalization of Taiwan's political system has already generated powerful pressures for a more assertive foreign policy and for a more active and respected role in international organizations. As the process continues, it could also result in more vocal demands for independence and could even lead to greater political and social instability. Any of these developments could trigger an angry response from Peking, which may come to fear that Taiwan is drifting inexorably toward a permanent separation from the mainland or even toward formal independence.

Together, these changing circumstances create a highly uncertain setting for Sino-American relations over the rest of the century and suggest several different possibilities for the future of the U.S.-China relationship. Rather than discussing each of these determinants in turn, this chapter is organized around five alternative scenarios, listed in rough order of increasing probability. They include a revived Sino-American strategic alignment, directed against a common enemy; diverse American relations with a fragmented China; a renewed U.S. partnership in China's modernization and reform; a second period of diplomatic confrontation between Washington and Peking; and an extended strained relationship between the two countries.

Like all scenarios, the five possibilities outlined offer simplified portraits of alternative futures. They are intended not to provide detailed forecasts of the decade ahead, but to illustrate the competing tendencies that exist in Sino-American relations and the various contingencies that might produce them. Nor should the scenarios be seen as mutually exclusive. In reality, the future relationship between China and the United States could well involve a blending or sequencing of several of the possibilities outlined here, rather than any single scenario in its purest form.

A RENEWED STRATEGIC ALIGNMENT

One of the less likely scenarios is a renewed strategic alignment between China and the United States, directed against some common adversary. Resurrecting such an alignment has been the dream of Chinese strategists ever since the Tiananmen crisis. They recognize that mutual opposition to Soviet expansionism offered the rationale for the normalization of Sino-American relations in the 1970s, when the internal situation in China was even more repressive and just as unstable as it is today, and when far fewer economic ties and cultural exchanges linked the two countries. As they see it, identifying another common enemy in the 1990s would enable Washington and Peking to set aside their differences over human rights, trade surpluses, arms exports, and other controversial bilateral issues and would restore greater stability to the U.S.-China relationship. A common enemy would also provide the basis for a resumption and expansion of the military relations that were forged in the 1970s and 1980s but suspended in 1989.

For the foreseeable future, however, it is difficult to identify plausible targets for another Sino-American strategic alignment. A resurgent Soviet Union or an assertive Russia is a possibility that Chinese analysts often raise. And it is true that, despite the collapse of the Soviet Communist Party and the breakup of the Soviet Union, the successor national and republican governments in Moscow will still inherit powerful conventional and nuclear forces. But it is difficult to see Moscow, as the capital of either Russia or of a larger Soviet federation, mobilizing the resources or the will for renewed international confrontation with the United States or China. It is much more likely that Moscow would attempt to maintain good relations with both countries. And even if the Kremlin did return to a harder line in foreign policy, it would almost certainly seek to do so in collaboration with China, rather than to alienate Washington and Peking simultaneously. Such a development would, obviously, form little basis for renewed strategic cooperation between China and the United States.

If developments in the former Soviet Union do pose any security challenges for the United States and China, they are likely to be problems that stem from weakness rather than strength. These include the deployment and control of the Soviet nuclear arsenal, an economic collapse that produces many refugees, and the rise of ethnic tensions that spill over international boundaries. Although serious, these problems would be much less compelling than the resurrection of a powerful Soviet military threat or the rise of aggressive Russian nationalism. They might well be the grounds for consultation between China and the United States and possibly even for coordination of policy. But it is improbable that they would be the basis of a new alignment between Peking and Washington.

Another nation that could conceivably provoke renewed Sino-American strategic collaboration is Japan. Some Chinese analysts have raised the specter of a Tokyo resurgent, alienated from the

United States, that seeks to establish the same hegemony over Asia it futilely tried to achieve during World War II. In such circumstances, Peking would indeed turn to the United States to find a counter-weight to Japanese power. And, given its history of opposition to an attempt by any country to establish domination over Asia, America would presumably find such a proposition attractive. If, as some American analysts have recently suggested, there will be a "coming war with Japan"—whether a trade war or a geopolitical confronta-tion—then the United States would want to wage it in cooperation with China.[2]

Although such a scenario is theoretically possible, it remains highly improbable. To be sure, Japanese-American relations are seri-ously strained. The economic relationship between the two coun-tries is becoming more competitive, and elements of confrontation are entering their trade policies. Although the military alliance re-mains intact, the United States is demanding that Japan assume greater responsibility for collective security overseas, as well as for its conventional defense. The end of the cold war in Asia, and espe-cially a settlement of the outstanding territorial disputes between Russia and Japan, will remove much of the strategic rationale for a close U.S.-Japan relationship.

Even so, a complete rupture of the economic and strategic ties between Tokyo and Washington is unlikely, for it would be ex-tremely costly to both sides. Given their economic interdependence neither country could afford an outright trade war. The collapse of the Japanese-American alliance would trigger an arms race through-out the rest of Asia, from which Tokyo and Washington would suffer. Thus, although the U.S.-Japan relationship resembles a marriage from which romance has gone, a divorce remains unthinkable.[3]

As is true of the Soviet Union, there are lesser contingencies con-nected with Japan on which China and the United States can already find common ground. Peking and Washington want to prevent Japa-nese rearmament from increasing tension and instability in Asia. Both want to encourage Japan to open its markets to manufactured goods from abroad. Neither country wants to see China become overly dependent on Japan as a source of capital or technology. Nei-ther wants to be excluded from multilateral security or economic arrangements in Asia, and neither wants to see Japan dominate an emerging Pacific community. But, as is true of the future challenges posed by the Soviet Union, these considerations are more likely to serve as the basis for consultation and cooperation between China and the United States than as a foundation for a firm strategic re-alignment.

DIVERSE RELATIONS WITH A
FRAGMENTED CHINA

Recent developments in the Soviet Union suggest another scenario for China that deserves consideration. The collapse of the
authority of the Soviet Communist Party is leading to the breakup
of the Soviet Union into several successor states. Estonia, Latvia,
and Lithuania have achieved formal independence from Moscow
and have gained membership in the United Nations. Other Soviet
republics have declared their independence from the Kremlin and
may follow the Baltic states in obtaining international recognition
of their status. Although some of the republics may still form a
political or economic confederation under Russian leadership, the
geopolitical status of the Soviet Union has now fundamentally
changed.

A similar scenario for China is improbable, but at least conceivable.
One of the results of China's decade of economic reform and opening
to the outside world has been a redistribution of power from Peking
to the provinces. Provincial governments have obtained much more
authority to attract foreign investment, conduct foreign trade, retain
foreign exchange revenues, make domestic investments, and with-
hold the profits of state enterprises. The declining legitimacy of the
central government has affected the attitudes and behavior of provincial officials, just as it has changed those of urban workers and intellectuals. Peking is much less able to enforce local compliance with its
decisions than in the past, and the provinces are becoming a powerful
lobby in the shaping of national policy. As yet, there has been little
open defiance of the central government. But if Peking's authority
continues to weaken, the line between quiet evasion and outright
insubordination could be crossed more frequently.

Pressures for greater autonomy and even formal independence
are rising in many of China's border regions. The Dalai Lama has
demanded independence for Tibet unless Peking accords Tibet virtual autonomy in its internal political, economic, and cultural affairs.
Calls for independence in Xinjiang have already been heard and could
become more vocal if the Islamic republics of the Soviet Union, such
as Turkestan, secure greater autonomy from Moscow. The upsurge
of democracy, economic reform, and nationalism in the Mongolian
People's Republic could encourage similar demands in the Inner
Mongolian region in China. Although none of these nationalist
movements has yet posed an insurmountable challenge to the central

government in Peking, Chinese military analysts already see them as one of the most important emerging threats to national security.

As China makes the transition to the post-Deng era, the prospects for fragmentation increase. A protracted and inconclusive struggle for power in Peking, the collapse of the Communist Party, the emergence of a divided and indecisive leadership, or the selection of a weak and illegitimate leader could encourage powerful localities to demand greater autonomy from the central government. Just as the faltering Qing dynasty gave way to warlordism in the 1910s and 1920s, so could the decay of the Communist Party conceivably permit the emergence of autonomous provinces in the 1990s. Some of the regions, especially on China's periphery, could declare their independence from Peking. Others in the heartland of China might nominally recognize a weak central government but would act with little regard to its decisions.

Without knowing the details of how it might occur, it is difficult to speculate about the consequences of such an outcome for the future of Sino-American relations. At a minimum, however, it would imply that there would no longer be a single U.S.-China relationship. Washington would presumably retain diplomatic ties with whatever central government emerged in Peking. As with the Soviet Union today, the United States would be especially anxious to ensure that the central authorities in China maintained control over the nation's nuclear weapons. But the United States would also develop a broader range of official relationships with other provinces and regions as they gained their formal independence or their de facto autonomy.

Most of those relationships would fall into two broad categories. Washington would have the warmest and most extensive relations with those parts of China that were committed to economic and political reform and that were prepared to develop wide-ranging ties with the United States. These regions would probably include the areas along the southeastern Chinese coast, from Canton to Shanghai, where most American investment is already located. In contrast, American relations with other parts of China might be cooler and more attenuated. These places might include the interior regions that had less ready contact with the United States or that conducted little political or economic reform. They might also include parts of China that decided to link themselves economically to other countries—the northeast to Korea and Japan, the northwest to Russia—and therefore develop less substantial ties with America.

Could the United States ever have a hostile relationship with any of these pieces of a fragmented China? Severe strains could certainly

develop if there were highly visible and highly objectionable violations of human rights or government interference with normal economic or diplomatic relations with America. Conceivably, as happened in Yugoslavia in the 1990s and China in the 1920s, the breakup
of China could result in open civil war among competing provinces.
If so, the United States might provide diplomatic or material support
of the coastal regions with whom it had established the closest
relations. But military confrontation with any Chinese regional government or direct military involvement in civil conflict in China
would remain highly unlikely.

A RENEWED PARTNERSHIP IN CHINA'S REFORM

A somewhat more likely scenario for Sino-American relations is
the resurrection of the sort of economic partnership between the
two countries that seemed to be emerging in the mid-1980s. The
prerequisite for such a development would be the renewal of both
economic reform and political liberalization, coupled with a more
sympathetic reassessment of the mass demonstrations that produced
the Tiananmen crisis. On that basis, the remaining U.S. sanctions
imposed on Peking after the Tiananmen crisis would be lifted. The
U.S. government would extend enthusiastic moral and material support for China's domestic development programs by relaxing controls
over the export of advanced technology to Peking, and even extending
a modest economic and technical assistance program. American business would increase investment in China, trade would continue to
grow, and academic and cultural exchanges between the two countries would flourish. China would show renewed interest not only in
American capital and technology, but also in Western values and
institutions. And, while not forming a strategic alignment against a
common enemy, Peking and Washington might assume more cooperative postures on various global and regional issues.

This scenario reflects a view of the future that many Americans
have eagerly anticipated ever since the tragic events of 1989. From
their perspective, the suppression of the demonstrations in Tiananmen Square represented a desperate but futile effort by aging dictators
to withstand the inevitable tide of political liberalization and economic reform. As long as senior leaders such as Deng Xiaoping
remain alive, they may be able to control the army, secure the compliance of the Party and state bureaucracies, and repress dissent. But

once the octogenarians begin to pass from the scene, the facade of stability would shatter rapidly. Within a short time, the remaining conservatives would be deposed, younger and liberal leaders would take power, and China would undertake a program of radical reform more ambitious and more successful than anything attempted in the 1980s. On that basis, the shroud of Tiananmen would be lifted from Sino-American relations, and the two countries would resume a close and extensive relationship.

Elements of this picture are, in fact, highly plausible. The evolution of Chinese economic policy since the Tiananmen crisis has shown that the restoration of a centrally planned economy, dominated by collective agriculture and state-owned industry and uninterested in promoting foreign trade or attracting foreign investment, is now inconceivable. The Chinese economy is already too complex to be governed entirely by administrative measures rather than by market forces. A return to collective agriculture would be extremely unpopular in most parts of the Chinese countryside, and the central government lacks the political resources to impose such a system on an unwilling population. The danger of unemployment and under-employment, aggravated by a growing labor force, is too great to permit tight restrictions on the formation of private and collective enterprises. A more autarkic policy would impose great hardship on those industries and regions already producing for overseas markets and would doom the broader economy to lag permanently behind the rest of Asia.

Moreover, there are also strong pressures to proceed toward greater economic reform. The gap between market prices and administered prices continues to produce irresistible opportunities for corruption. Given the complexity of the economy, the only rational way to close the gap is to free virtually all prices, while continuing to regulate the prices of only a few critically important commodities. The failure to impose strict financial accountability on state enterprises is generating staggering government deficits, which constantly pose the threat of renewed inflation. Imposing tighter financial constraints on enterprises would probably require fundamental changes in their ownership, by selling them to individual entrepreneurs, leasing them to their managers, or distributing shares of stock to individual and institutional shareholders. A highly politicized banking system also fosters inflation by offering easy credit to well-connected projects and enterprises, a problem that can be solved only by a full-fledged reform of China's financial system. Even in the absence of further deliberate economic restructuring, the greater dynamism of the private and collective sectors will gradually erode the dominance of central planning and state enterprises over the economy as a whole.

Although some of the senior members of China's present leadership resist such economic reforms, probably most of the country's officials are far more enlightened. The administrative reforms of the 1980s replaced the political generalists of the Maoist era with a new cohort of technical specialists. Younger, better educated, more widely traveled, and more aware of developments in the rest of the world, this new generation of officials is likely to support renewed economic reform once political conditions permit them to do so. The coastal provinces, the new class of private entrepreneurs, and most urban intellectuals would be a powerful constituency for more radical economic reform. Much of the army, too, would favor an economic reform program that would produce a more prosperous state and a more advanced technological and industrial base.

This new generation of leaders might also choose to renew political reform, as they attempted to foster a reconciliation with their society and overcome the crisis of confidence produced by the Cultural Revolution and exacerbated by the Tiananmen crisis. At a minimum, this design would involve a favorable reassessment of the protests of 1989 and a repudiation of the way in which they were repressed. It would also mean a relaxation of controls over intellectual life, the revival of a more consultative policymaking process, further development of the legal system, and further reform of the nation's administrative apparatus. As in Taiwan in the 1970s, signs of greater pluralism might gradually appear: independent social and economic organizations, a more autonomous press, contested elections, and perhaps even a non-Party opposition. Indeed, as in the Soviet Union in 1991, the resumption of reform might entail the collapse of the Communist Party and occur under non-Communist leadership, acting through the existing governmental apparatus.

If it occurred, the revival of economic and political reform would dramatically improve Sino-American relations. A more extensive restructuring of the Chinese economy would offer many more opportunities for American trade and investment. A reversal of verdicts on the June 4 incident and progress toward political liberalization would reduce U.S. criticism of China's human rights record, and open more possibilities for academic and cultural exhange. With a renewed commitment to reform on the mainland, the prospects for the smooth return of Hong Kong to China and for some form of reconciliation between Taiwan and the mainland would be greatly enhanced. A more pragmatic government in Peking would be more likely to find common ground with the United States on important regional and global security issues and more inclined to cooperate with the United States in addressing the emerging agenda of international economic, military, environmental, and social questions.

Why is this optimistic scenario not given a higher probability in this analysis? One reason is that the simultaneous renewal of economic and political reform—the principal prerequisite for the reconstruction of an enthusiastic economic partnership between China and the United States—is not the only course that China could follow after the death of Deng Xiaoping. As already noted, it is possible that China will fragment along geographic lines, with the central government unable to undertake a concerted program of either political or economic restructuring. Alternatively, the pace of political and economic reform could well remain slow in the post-Deng era, particularly if similar effort in the former Soviet Union and Eastern Europe produce further economic dislocation and political turmoil while the Chinese economy continues to perform at reasonable levels. Or future Chinese leaders could choose to accelerate economic reform but move much more cautiously toward any political liberalization. Thus, the resurrection of radical reform in both the political and economic spheres is one possible consequence of the succession to Deng Xiaoping but is unfortunately not the only conceivable outcome.

Moreover, even if it did occur, the revival of economic and political reform would not necessarily produce another Sino-American honeymoon comparable to the short-lived one in the mid-1980s. For one thing, the rebuilding of the economic and cultural ties between the two countries would be influenced by the perceived importance of China in comparison with other international priorities. Already, the attention of American business and American foundations once focused largely on China is being redirected to new opportunities in the Soviet Union and Eastern Europe. The normalization of U.S. relations with Hanoi would also mean an increasing American interest in commercial and cultural opportunities in Vietnam. Even if reform in China revives, in other words, Peking may have to compete with a long list of other reforming socialist societies for a share of American investment capital and philanthropic support.

The resources that the United States could devote to China would be determined by the state of the U.S. economy and particularly by the character of American foreign economic policy. If the American economy can regain vitality by increasing savings and productivity and reducing trade and budget deficits, then it would have more to offer to China's reform and development. A more vibrant economy would present a larger market for Chinese exports and would be less prone to protectionist pressures. If the federal budget can be brought into better balance, and if the "peace dividend" frees monies for other purposes, the U.S. government would have more funds to devote to aid programs for countries like China. A more prosperous economy would generate more money for investment capital, more contributions to philanthropic agencies, and higher returns for foundation endowments, which would form the basis for greater American aid and investment in China.

Conversely, if the American economy cannot overcome structural problems, the economic relations between China and the United States must surely become more contentious. Slow growth in the United States would present China with a smaller market and would absorb fewer Chinese exports. The United States would have fewer financial resources to lend to or invest in China. A sluggish American economy would evoke stronger protectionist measures. China would not only face tougher restrictions on exports to the United States, but it might also encounter tighter controls on American technology transfer, as U.S. firms seek to stem the flow of advanced technology to potential foreign competitors. Even if reforms resume in China, in other words, the extent to which they revitalize the Sino-American relationship would depend on the health of the American economy.

Ironically, successful economic reform in China could exacerbate, rather than resolve, the trade issues that currently divide it from the United States. It is highly likely that a new wave of economic restructuring in post-Deng China would retain a strong neomercantilist cast rather than embody the principles of laissez-faire economics and free trade so familiar to Americans. Like most of the rest of East Asia, China would probably undertake an export-oriented development strategy, supporting it through such government policies as an undervalued currency, export incentives, and various forms of protection against foreign imports. At the same time, the adoption of market-oriented policies and enterprise reforms at home would make Chinese export industries even more efficient and flexible and thus stronger competitors in American markets. The result of greater economic reform, therefore, might well be to increase China's trade surpluses with the United States, rather than to reduce them. Although China would no longer be viewed as another political pariah like Libya or South Africa, it might well be perceived as the next economic rival after Japan or Taiwan. As such, it could become the target of initiatives from Washington designed to open new markets in China or protect existing ones in America. In such a scenario, Sino-American relations might contain highly contentious elements.

Finally, even if reform in China revives, it may not proceed smoothly and successfully. In part, China's domestic crisis of 1989 can be traced to strategic errors by Peking's leadership: an insensitivity to corruption and inequality, an inability to control inflation, an unwillingness to conduct political reform to forestall dissent, and a refusal to engage in meaningful dialogue with disgruntled citizens after the protests began. But the crisis also reflected the dilemmas in reform that no Communist country has yet fully resolved. How can prices be reformed without triggering inflation? How can material incentives be increased without fostering inequality? How can market forces be strengthened without promoting corruption? How can inefficient state industries be rationalized without increasing unemployment? How can political institutions be liberalized without engendering instability?

To be sure, the resumption of more radical reform in China, should it occur, would have a greater chance of success than the first round of moderate reform in the 1980s. The new generation of Chinese leaders would presumably be more pragmatic than their predecessors. They would be more aware of the errors that were made in the urban reforms undertaken by Deng Xiaoping and Zhao Ziyang. They would be advised by knowledgeable Chinese economists, many of whom have been trained abroad, who have been conducting research on more effective strategies of reform. And China would no longer be traveling through uncharted waters when it accelerates reforms. Leaders in Peking would be able to draw on the lessons, positive and negative, learned by the former Communist states of Eastern Europe and the Soviet Union as they experiment with alternative strategies of economic and political restructuring.

Nonetheless, a second wave of reform in China could still encounter serious difficulties, similar to those met by the first round in the 1980s. Indeed, many of China's underlying problems are being exacerbated by the long period of stalemate and indecision that has followed the Tiananmen crisis. The crisis of confidence in government is intensifying, the central government's control over the provinces is weakening, the state's budget deficits are mounting, and environmental and population problems are worsening. A new reform-minded government may have less room for error than Deng Xiaoping did when he first launched China's second revolution in the late 1970s.

Thus the second round of reform could also stall. One possibility, of course, would be retrenchment and retrogression comparable to what China experienced after the 1989–91 period, with tighter controls over domestic economic activity and foreign trade and with harsh repression of internal dissent. Alternatively, a post-Deng government could attempt to sacrifice political liberalization for the sake of economic restructuring, continuing to implement desirable economic reforms but simultaneously suppressing the socioeconomic resentments they engendered. If the resumption of reform created excessively optimistic expectations for China in the United States, much as the initiation of reform did in the 1980s, the stage could be set for another crisis in Sino-American relations. If so, this third scenario, seemingly the most optimistic, could actually evolve into the fourth, the most pessimistic.

A SECOND PERIOD OF CONFRONTATION

More likely than a differentiated relationship with a fragmented China or even a renewed strategic alignment with a unified one is the emergence of an essentially conflictual relationship between China and the United States. Unfortunately, this prospect is also more plausible, at least in the short run, than is the revival of a partnership in support of renewed economic and political reform. Although such a relationship would probably fall short of the openly adversarial one that the two countries experienced in the 1950s, it would still be characterized by a suspension of most cultural ties, an attenuation of economic relations, and even the adoption of confrontational diplomatic postures.

The descent into confrontation could be initiated by several developments. In the short run, the principal danger is growing American impatience with the failure to achieve designed changes in China's domestic and foreign policy. As noted earlier, in the middle of 1991 the Bush administration announced a new strategy toward Peking, featuring the application of various incentives and disincentives against certain aspects of Chinese policy of which the United States disapproved. This new strategy won the administration a short breathing space and reduced the immediate prospects that Congress would be able to rescind China's most-favored-nation status or attach severe conditions to it.

Within a fairly short time, however, American patience with this approach could wear thin. Peking might prove unwilling to modify policies on foreign arms sales, human rights, or trade practices sufficiently to satisfy critics in the United States. Alternatively, the central government in China might seriously try to resolve some of the issues plaguing Sino-American relations, but be unable to impose its will on a domestic textile industry eager to evade U.S. quotas, a defense establishment keen on selling arms abroad, or even a public security organization desirous of earning foreign exchange by exporting the products of prison labor. A protracted failure to solve the problems in the bilateral relationship, let alone another spectacular instance of bloody repression at home or irresponsible arms sales overseas, could trigger congressional and public demands to revoke China's most-favored-nation status that the White House either could not resist or might choose not to challenge.

Whether, at that point, Sino-American relations descended into confrontation would depend on Peking's response. There is a chance that moderate leaders in China would try to limit the damage to U.S.-China relations by acquiescing to the loss of their most-favored-nation status without imposing significant countersanctions in return. But it is far more likely that Chinese leaders would respond in kind, restricting their commercial relations with the United States, cutting off or limiting academic, diplomatic, and political exchanges, and adopting a much less accommodating posture on international issues. They would also probably tighten internal controls, as a way of coping with the disruptive impact of the loss of most-favored-nation status on their domestic legitimacy and on their national economy. These signs of greater repression would further intensify American criticism of the human rights situation in China.

Over the longer term, several other contingencies could also spark a deterioration of Sino-American relations, particularly in the years after Deng Xiaoping's death. One would be the emergence of a repressive government in the post-Deng era that engaged in continuous and severe violations of human rights. There is no great probability that a totalitarian political order could now be created in China. The state is too weak to reimpose close or extensive controls over the society, and the public is too alienated to renew its commitment to Communist doctrine. But it is possible that the Communist Party, or even a non-Communist government controlled by the military, could maintain a "hard" authoritarian regime in China, which continued a program of economic modernization but vigorously suppressed potential political dissent.[4] Indeed, several Chinese intellectuals have already called for the establishment of what they call a neo-authoritarian system in China, patterned on what they view as the successful models of South Korea and Taiwan in the 1960s, in which economic development was achieved while tight restrictions were maintained over political life.

The effect of such a development on Sino-American relations

would depend on how it was perceived in the United States. Conceivably, the United States might by then have adopted a highly pragmatic foreign policy that assigned little weight to human rights concerns. Moreover, if the present trends toward democratization in the Soviet Union and Eastern Europe should somehow be reversed, and if those societies also fell victim to political repression or decay, then the maintenance of a hard authoritarian regime in China might evoke relatively less condemnation. It is more likely, however, that the United States will remain committed to the promotion of democratization and human rights abroad. In that event, renewed suppression of public protests in China or intensified controls over intellectual life would again be regarded as intolerable. If the trends toward economic and political liberalization seemed successful in other parts of the world, while China continued to stagnate or retrogress, then Peking's human rights abuses would seem even more repugnant. Such a situation could produce irresistible domestic political pressure on Washington to impose more economic and diplomatic sanctions against Peking, including the revocation of China's most-favored-nation status.

Developments in Chinese foreign policy could also lead to a deterioration of Sino-American relations. Over the longer term, China might engage in more assertive and disruptive international conduct than it has thus far in the post-Mao era. Admittedly, even if a more repressive government did emerge after the death of Deng Xiaoping, it would probably be preoccupied with internal affairs, remain interested in a peaceful international environment, and therefore be disinclined to initiate a confrontational policy toward the United States. But some possibility remains that a retrogressive Chinese regime could adopt a more aggressive foreign policy, defining its interests in opposition to those of the United States and the West. Such a government might attempt to reactivate radical insurgencies in Southeast Asia and the third world, as in the 1960s. Or it might try to mobilize a coalition of third world governments to oppose American positions on international economic issues, regional disputes, and human rights, as Peking attempted to do in the 1970s.

Other developments, short of a redefinition of China's overall international posture, could also trigger a more hostile relationship between Washington and Peking. Ethnic tensions, territorial disputes, or arms races between China and its neighbors could flare into conflict, with Peking choosing to resolve the issue through military means. The use of American military force against North Korea's nuclear program could produce confrontation with China. China could decide to send troops across its borders for the same reasons as it has in the past: to prevent the collapse of the North Korean government, preclude the establishment of Vietnamese dominance over Indochina, settle its border dispute with India, or seize territory it claims in the South China Sea. It could also intervene in neighboring states such as Turkestan or Mongolia in an effort to discourage or suppress separatist movements inside China. Although a direct American military response would be unlikely, any of these circumstances could set off a more intense diplomatic confrontation in Sino-American relations.

Finally, developments in Hong Kong or Taiwan could also spark a crisis in U.S.-China relations. As already noted, the emergence of a more democratic political system on Taiwan would permit more vocal expression of demands for a formal declaration of independence from the mainland. Moreover, the breakup of the Soviet Union and especially the independence of the Baltic states may encourage independence activists on Taiwan to press for international recognition of a separate Taiwanese republic. Alternatively, the process of democratization on Taiwan could encounter severe difficulties, with mounting social unrest and political instability. In any of these situations, Peking might choose to take forceful action to prevent the permanent separation of Taiwan from the rest of China.

Such a decision would almost certainly have a direct and immediate effect on Sino-American relations. As part of its pressure against Taipei, Peking could demand that the United States reduce arms sales to Taiwan, restrict the transfer of defense-related technology, or oppose Taiwan's membership in international organizations, all as a way of halting the trends toward Taiwanese independence. As in the 1970s, Peking could prescribe economic sanctions against American firms doing business with Taiwan. It could exert economic pressure against Taiwan by cutting off imports of Taiwanese goods or by expropriating Taiwanese investments on the mainland. It could even use force against Taipei by imposing a blockade against Taiwan, attacking some of the offshore islands, or even launching a direct air or naval attack against Taiwan. Any such economic or military coercion against Taiwan would, of course, invoke the American commitment to Taiwan's security contained in the Taiwan Relations Act of 1979.

It is difficult to imagine American acquiescence to such coercion. Public opinion in the United States has always favored a commitment to Taiwan's security, and such sentiment has almost certainly been heightened by the successful struggle of the Baltic states for independence. With the Soviet empire breaking up, there would be little sympathy for any effort by Peking to gain control over Taiwan by force. Moreover, the declining strategic importance of China to the United States and the unfavorable reputation that Peking now has in America would strengthen the tendency to resist any Chinese efforts to resolve the Taiwan question through coercive means. Although a direct military confrontation between the United States and China could be avoided, a severe deterioration in the political relationship between the two countries would be inevitable. Washington could well decide to revoke China's most-favored-nation status, which would lead to a deterioration in the economic relationship as well.

Increasingly, one can foresee circumstances in which Hong Kong would become an equally contentious issue between Peking and Washington, as the territory faces its return to Chinese sovereignty in 1997. Ever since the negotiations between China and Britain concluded in 1984, the delicate balance between China's sovereignty and Hong Kong's autonomy has steadily shifted in favor of the former. In drafting the Basic Law to govern Hong Kong after 1997, Peking left itself important loopholes through which to exercise formal authority over the territory. It has consistently opposed the development of democratic institutions in Hong Kong before or after the transition, because of fears that political liberalization would make the territory less stable and, above all, less susceptible to Chinese control. And in 1991, Peking used a controversy over a plan for a new airport in Hong Kong to establish the principle that no major decision could be taken in the territory without its concurrence. Taken together, these developments suggest that, before and after 1997, China intends not only to exercise broad guidance over public policy in Hong Kong but also to veto decisions of which it disapproves.

The realization that Hong Kong's autonomy will be limited, and that the exercise of local democracy will be restricted, has produced a serious crisis of confidence in the future of Hong Kong, especially among younger professionals, managers, and intellectuals. This uncertainty has been reflected in a mounting outflow of human capital and financial resources from the territory. Moreover, as the 1997 deadline approaches, Hong Kong is likely to experience more difficulties. The brain drain and the flight of capital will increase. The morale of the civil service could well decline, especially in such sensitive sectors as the police, and corruption and influence-peddling could grow. Inflation could surge if large amounts of labor and capital leave the territory, and the growth rate could slow if wages and interest rates rise as a result. If the economic and political situation deteriorated sufficiently, there could be serious social unrest in Hong Kong, before or after the British left the territory. At some point, instability in Hong Kong could trigger direct Chinese military intervention.

Before 1989, Hong Kong was not a serious issue in the relationship between Washington and Peking. Having worked hard to extract itself from the controversy over Taiwan, Washington was not eager to become embroiled in another facet of China's quest for national reunification. But as the crisis of confidence in Hong Kong began to affect American businesses operating in the territory, Hong Kong began to attract greater attention in the United States. When thousands of residents of the territory poured into the streets to protest the massacre in Peking in June 1989, American sympathy for Hong Kong deepened. During the debates over the fate of China's most-favored-nation status in 1990 and 1991, preserving the stability and prosperity of Hong Kong emerged for the first time as an important consideration in the determination of American policy toward China.

Greater deterioration of the situation in Hong Kong would therefore have a deleterious impact on Sino-American relations, conceivably as severe as a confrontation between Taiwan and the mainland. Any use of Chinese military force against Hong Kong, even to quell serious social unrest, would most likely be seen as a serious violation of human rights in the territory and an occasion for another round of American economic and diplomatic sanctions against China. Even less serious actions by Peking, if they were viewed as a violation of the Sino-British agreement of 1984, could create pressure in Washington for the revocation of Peking's most-favored-nation status. In so delicate a period, the imposition of such punitive measures would evoke a harsh Chinese response and would almost certainly trigger a grave confrontation between China and the United States.

Extreme forms of hostility between China and the United States remain unlikely, although not inconceivable, even in this most pessimistic of scenarios. The two countries would doubtless try to avoid a direct military confrontation, since each would be aware of the enormous economic, diplomatic, and human costs of armed hostilities. This reluctance to go to war would deter Peking from using military force to attack or blockade Taiwan and would encourage lesser forms of diplomatic or economic pressure against the island. The same caution would lead the United States to protect Taiwan through diplomatic measures, economic sanctions, and increased arms sales to Taipei, rather than through direct intervention with American military forces. Nor would either side want to return to the isolation of the 1950s, either by breaking diplomatic relations or by embargoing bilateral economic ties.

But each side would engage in lesser forms of confrontation with the other. Americans would come to regard China as a pariah state to be treated in ways comparable to South Africa in the past or Libya today. Economic sanctions against China would be tightened, and official contacts with Peking would be cut back. Although Peking would be unlikely to end all economic and diplomatic ties with the United States, it could well regard American firms as suppliers of last resort, expropriate or harass American investors in China, and drastically reduce cultural and academic links to the United States. As a result, the commercial, cultural, and diplomatic ties between the two countries would be severely attenuated.

Washington and Peking would also adopt much less cooperative approaches to various global and regional issues. Whether or not China reoriented its foreign policy around opposition to American "imperialism" or "hegemonism," it would almost certainly oppose American initiatives on many international questions, including arms control, management of the environment, settlement of regional disputes, and the structure of the world economy. The United States would seek to counter the expansion of Chinese influence in Asia and try to mobilize its allies to join it in imposing sanctions against the Peking government.

A STRAINED RELATIONSHIP

Although a confrontation of this sort is possible, the most likely future for China and the United States for the near- and middle-term future is for a strained relationship, characterized by a complex mixture of conflict, competition, and cooperation. In contrast to U.S.-China relations in the mid-1980s, there would be no overriding sense of common purpose, whether that be a strategic alignment against a mutual adversary or a shared commitment to Chinese reform. But despite strained relations there would also be less chance of military conflict, more intense economic interaction, and more frequent diplomatic cooperation on regional and global issues than would occur in an outright confrontation.

Many of the same factors that could yield a confrontation between the two countries could also produce a strained relationship, especially if they took a more moderate or less vivid form. Domestically, post-Deng China could experience not decisive retrogression but rather protracted political stagnation, in which the central government would maintain control over the country but neither reformers nor conservatives would achieve a clear victory. Economically, there could be modest structural changes, primarily stimulated by the need to address the contradictions of an economy only partially reformed, without a fundamental breakthrough in the direction of marketization or ownership reform. Despite many problems, the economy might perform reasonably well, with adequate rates of growth achieved through the continued operation of a market-oriented economy along the coast. Politically, the status quo would continue, featuring halfhearted efforts to conduct political education campaigns among an alienated population, tight controls over the intellectual and journalistic communities, and periodic suppression of dissent. But if inflation and unemployment could be kept under control, there might not be any more dramatic events, comparable to the June 4 incident of 1989, that would trigger open confrontation between the two countries.

In such a situation, human rights would be a chronic but not acute irritant in Sino-American relations. Private American organizations would monitor and criticize violations of civil and political rights, sometimes in sharp language. Congress would pass resolutions condemning the state of human rights in China, and the White House would press for the release of prominent political prisoners. Washington might adopt new measures intended to promote political liberalization in China, such as establishing new radio stations aimed at the Chinese mainland, requiring American investors in China to respect human rights in their employment practices, and more strictly enforcing the prohibitions on the import of products manufactured by convict labor. But, in this scenario, the United States would stop short of revoking China's most-favored-nation status, and the broader bilateral relationship would not be driven into confrontation.

With Peking's most-favored-nation status still in place, commercial relations between China and the United States would increase. Just as they have since the mid-1980s, however, they would cause ceaseless controversy. American exporters would be frustrated by barriers restricting their access to the Chinese market, and American investors would be irritated by the imperfections in the Chinese investment climate. Administrative measures, such as an overvalued currency and export subsidies, would promote Chinese exports to the United States, but would be regarded as inappropriate trading practices by many Americans. The reaction in the United States would be a function of the state of the American economy and the overall American trade balance. But it would probably include periodic efforts to restrict Chinese imports, especially textiles, through bilateral trade agreements and the imposition of various tariffs and quotas in retaliation against unfair Chinese trade practices.

In foreign policy, China could deal with some global and regional issues more constructively than others. In particular, Peking would be interested in maintaining a peaceful environment in Asia so that it could maximize its access to Asian capital and markets and concentrate resources and energy on internal problems. On the Korean issue, China would encourage Pyongyang to initiate economic and political reform, open its economy to the outside world, refrain from military actions against South Korea, end its nuclear weapons program, and reduce tensions with Seoul. China would support the 1991 settlement in Cambodia even if the Khmer Rouge failed to gain power in the resulting elections, so as to preserve normal relations with Vietnam. Elsewhere in the region, China would pursue its territorial disputes along the Sino-Indian border and in the South China Sea through peaceful means. In so doing, China would avoid any serious difference of opinion with the United States.

On other issues, however, Peking and Washington might engage in tougher bargaining. China might refuse to limit sales of missiles to the Middle East unless the United States accepted similar restrictions on the transfer of advanced fighter aircraft. Peking might resist the establishment of effective international regimes to control the spread of weapons of mass destruction if that meant significant infringements on its national sovereignty. China would demand that multilateral conventions to protect the environment include compensation to third world countries, and it would insist that new regional and global economic arrangements give developing nations preferential treatment. Some of these disputes might lead the United States to impose various economic sanctions against Peking, such as restricting technology transfer in retaliation for Chinese arms sales abroad. In this picture, however, the cycle of sanction and retaliation would not produce a confrontational Sino-American relationship, but it would prevent it from becoming close or harmonious.

Finally, although this scenario would not contain a crisis in U.S.-China relations over Taiwan or Hong Kong, periodic tensions might still plague Washington and Peking over the future of both territories. Controversy could arise, for example, over Taiwan's policy of flexible diplomacy, whereby Taipei applies for membership in various international economic organizations, tries to upgrade its unofficial relations with the developed nations, and seeks formal diplomatic recognition from smaller developing countries. In particular, Taiwan could apply to join international organizations such as the United

Nations, where membership would necessarily imply sovereign status. Taiwan is already exploring the possibility of purchasing arms from several European states, and China's declining political standing in the international community increases the chances that those efforts will succeed. If China chooses to challenge these initiatives and the United States decides to support them, Taiwan would again become a central and controversial issue in Sino-American relations. Military confrontation would be highly unlikely. But Washington and Peking could be drawn into a political contretemps, possibly leading to the imposition of various economic or diplomatic sanctions by both sides.

Relations with Hong Kong could follow a similar pattern. As the 1997 deadline approaches, democratic activists in the territory could press for changes in the Basic Law or even in the Sino-British agreement of 1984. They could propose more binding guarantees of Hong Kong's autonomy from Chinese intervention, insist that Peking waive its right to station military forces in Hong Kong after 1997, or demand more rapid progress toward a directly elected legislature and a popularly elected chief executive. If the political situation on the mainland decayed, they could even propose the indefinite postponement of the implementation of the 1984 agreement on the grounds that Hong Kong should not be forced to revert to Chinese sovereignty against its will.

Given that the 1984 agreement is a valid international convention, it is unlikely that any proposal to scrap it would be endorsed by the British or American governments. But public and congressional pressure could force the White House to make lesser demands on Peking, such as accelerating the process of democratization in Hong Kong or granting Hong Kong even greater autonomy than stipulated in the Basic Law. There could also be efforts in Congress to impose economic sanctions against China if those demands were not met. Although falling far short of insisting that Hong Kong remain beyond Chinese sovereignty, such proposals would inevitably be seen by Peking as intolerable interference in its internal affairs and the occasion for renewed tensions in Sino-American relations.

CONCLUSION

The relative probability of these five scenarios will change over time. In the short run, the last two—a continuation of the present strained relationship or its degeneration into confrontation—are the most likely. The choice between them will depend mainly on the evolution of the situation in China. If the political situation remains stable, without outbursts of protest and repression, the bilateral dispute over human rights may not intensify. If Peking can take effective measures to control arms sales abroad, halt unfair and illegal trading practices, and reduce its trade surplus with the United States, confrontation can be prevented. In contrast, if the human rights situation deteriorates or if other bilateral issues worsen, then patience with China may be exhausted, and a cycle of American sanction and Chinese countersanction may begin.

Over the middle term, the prospects for a renewed partnership in support of China's reform efforts increase. If China's program of economic and political reform revives after the death of Peking's present generation of gerontocrats, such possibilities would be dramatically enhanced. But Americans should not be overly optimistic. The revival of reform is only one of the scenarios that could follow the death of Deng Xiaoping and his colleagues. Reform, if revived, might falter again after a few years. And, most important, even if China resumes economic reform, the commercial ties between the two countries will be competitive as well as cooperative, especially if China replicates the success of its Asian neighbors in running large trade surpluses with the United States. Moreover, as a developing country, China will probably have perspectives different from those of the United States on many aspects of the emerging agenda of global issues.

As with all forecasts, the probabilities of the occurrence of extreme scenarios rise somewhat with the passage of time. In this case, however, they will remain low. It is unlikely that any other country will challenge China and the United States enough to promote a new united front between them, comparable to their alignment against the Soviet Union in the early 1980s. The fragmentation of China, as the result of the collapse of the present central government, is somewhat more plausible. But the breakup of China is far less likely than the collapse of the Soviet Union, given the greater ethnic homogeneity of China, its superior economic performance, and the widespread fear of the consequences of political chaos and national disintegration.

Even over the longer term, therefore, the most probable outcome for Sino-American relations remains some blending of collaboration, competition, and conflict, rather than either cooperation or confrontation in its purest form. It is unrealistic to assume that U.S.-China relations, even in the post-Deng era, will resurrect the economic partnership of the 1980s, let alone the strategic alignment of the

1970s. A return to the military confrontation and diplomatic isolation of the 1950s and 1960s can also be avoided, given wisdom and restraint on both sides. The most likely future is for a difficult relationship, featuring a China that is neither friend nor foe in the international arena, that is neither pluralistic nor totalitarian in its domestic affairs, and that conducts meaningful economic reform without fully embracing capitalism or laissez-faire economics. That complex and ambiguous vision must guide the formulation of an American China policy for the 1990s.

CHAPTER 10

Redesigning American China Policy

AMERICAN policy toward China is now in tatters. Both of the conceptual frameworks that underlay U.S. policy in the previous two decades have been shattered. The original concept, a tacit alignment against Soviet expansionism in Asia and elsewhere, was undermined by the changes in Soviet foreign policy under Mikhail Gorbachev and then destroyed altogether by the breakdown of communism in Eastern Europe and the subsequent disintegration of the Soviet Union. The second framework, American participation in China's economic development and support for its economic and political reform, was weakened by disputes over bilateral trade and investment issues, further eroded by China's record on human rights and arms sales, and then undone completely by the Tiananmen crisis of 1989. If American China policy seemed to be "running out of road map" even before the June 4 incident, the maps themselves now appear to be woefully outdated descriptions of the contours of the U.S.-China relationship.[1]

Moreover, the domestic consensus on China that sustained Sino-American relations from the late 1960s through the late 1980s has broken apart. The American public is sharply and almost equally divided over the best approach to take toward Peking. On one side, many Americans recognize that the end of Sino-American hostility in the early 1970s was one of the most beneficial developments of the postwar era and would prefer not to return to a confrontational relationship with Peking. On the other side, many Americans are deeply disturbed by violations of human rights and disappointed by the failure of China's leaders to sustain their promising program of economic and political reform. Moreover, when communism is in collapse and when American power seems to be on the ascendant, this second group is prepared to risk a deterioration of relations with China for the sake of human rights. This cleavage within American society is readily visible in recent surveys of public opinion, which show that roughly half of the public believes that U.S. policy toward China should be motivated principally by the promotion of human rights, whereas the other half believes that America's main objective should be to maintain a stable relationship with Peking.

The division of American public opinion toward China is paralleled by deep cleavages among various organized interest groups in the United States. Human rights organizations, the protectionist wing of American industry and labor, the nonproliferation lobby, conservative anti-Communist groups, and the organizations representing Chinese students in the United States have pressed for tougher sanctions against China. Conversely, much of the American business community, especially those who trade and invest in China and Hong Kong, have favored the maintenance of normal commercial relations with China. Many specialists in American foreign policy, especially those associated with the tradition of realpolitik, have argued that it would be shortsighted to sacrifice a geopolitical relationship with Peking for the sake of promoting human rights in China. Individual Chinese students and much of the American academic community specializing in China have warned that the attenuation of economic and cultural ties with China would insulate the country from beneficial pressures for economic and political reform.

The public debate over China policy has been echoed in deep divisions between the White House and Congress. American relations with China, one of the most contentious issues between Republicans and Democrats in the late 1940s and 1950s, gradually attracted a bipartisan consensus in favor of a more cooperative relationship with Peking. Richard Nixon's initial visit to China in 1972 was emblematic of the Republican Party's willingness to abandon the anti-Communist policies of the past in favor of détente with Peking. Similarly, Ronald Reagan's issuance of the 1982 communiqué on arms sales to Taiwan symbolized the Republicans' final acceptance of an attenuation of U.S. ties to Taipei. And his subsequent journey to China in 1984 demonstrated that even a conservative Republican had been persuaded to endorse a stable and wide-ranging relationship with China.

The Tiananmen crisis destroyed that emerging consensus. Many Democrats concluded that the president's caution in condemning political repression in China was one of the few foreign policy issues on which the Bush administration was vulnerable to criticism. In a fascinating historical irony, the Republicans now replaced the Democrats as the party accused of being "too soft" on China or of "losing China" to totalitarianism. But although much of the controversy had a strongly partisan tone, some of the criticism of the Bush administration cut across party lines. Many Republicans joined their Democratic colleagues in resenting the White House's reluctance to involve Congress in shaping an American response to developments in China.

Finally, the confusion and controversy surrounding U.S. policy toward China reflects the fact that American foreign policy more generally is also in a state of serious disarray. Just as the prevailing paradigm for Sino-American relations (helping China modernize and reform) was shattered by the events in Tiananmen Square, so has the end of the cold war pulled down the dominant conceptual framework for America's global strategy (deterring Soviet aggression and containing Communist expansion). No alternative has yet filled the policy vacuum. Some champion a reduction of international commitments so as to address domestic issues. Some favor a crusade to bring democracy and markets to countries still dominated by authoritarianism and state planning. Others propose a new world order, in which the United States will build multilateral institutions to deter aggression, protect the environment, and maintain global prosperity. Still others advocate a neomercantilist strategy, in which American foreign policy would be designed to promote the prosperity and ensure the competitiveness of the U.S. economy. Without a consensus on a new national strategy in the post–cold war era, the context for a new American policy toward China will remain uncertain.

Some observers have suggested that these developments represent the true normalization of Sino-American relations, in an even more significant sense than the establishment of formal diplomatic ties between the two countries in 1979. As they see it, incoherent policy frameworks, ambivalent public attitudes, contention among competing interest groups, and periodic confrontations between the White House and Congress constitute a more normal condition in American foreign relations than a relationship rooted in conceptual clarity and domestic consensus.

But even if confusion and conflict are common in American foreign policy, they are not desirable. Without vision, policy lacks purpose and coherence. Important opportunities are overlooked, potential challenges are ignored, and action is shortsighted and may even prove counterproductive. Similarly, without consensus, foreign policy lacks consistency and continuity. Administration programs are overruled by Congress; congressional initiatives are vetoed by the White House. Caught in the vortex between competing interests and institutions, policy is either in stalemate or in flux, and the credibility of

American undertakings is questioned by friends and adversaries alike. Thus, the policy deadlock created by the Tiananmen crisis needs to be broken. American China policy must be redesigned in a way that is appropriate to Chinese realities, can regain domestic support, and is congruent with broader American purposes in the post–cold war world.

Before turning to the more specific dimensions of such a policy, one must first consider the elemental principles that should guide it. Perhaps the most self-evident of these is that China is in a period of transition. At some point in the coming decade, China's most senior elite will pass from the political stage, and a new generation of leaders will replace them. American policy must take into account that coming succession. There is no reason to tie the United States closely to the leadership that now holds power in Peking. Neither morality nor pragmatism suggests a policy that forgets the tragedy of Tiananmen Square or that forgives those who were responsible for it.

But the implications of such a proposition need to be drawn with great care. Although Americans may strongly desire the revival of economic and political liberalization in China, policy cannot be based on the assumption that such hopes can be rapidly realized. It is not inevitable that the reformers will prevail in the struggle for power that will accompany the death or retirement of China's present elderly leadership. Even if they do, the process of reform is likely to be long and tortuous. Neither the collapse of reform after a period of renewed liberalization, the establishment of an even more repressive regime in the future, a continued pattern of political stalemate and immobilism, nor even the fragmentation of China can be fully ruled out.

Moreover, even if reform revives and succeeds, it will not necessarily produce a congruence of interests between the United States and China. Ideological differences between the two countries may fade, but differences based on different cultural perspectives, historical backgrounds, geographic locations, and levels of development will remain. And experience should also warn that successful economic reform in China may intensify the bilateral tensions that are produced when an emerging foreign economy gains a larger share of the American market. It would therefore be foolish to base policy on the anticipation that the revival of reform will be only a matter of time and that it will restore a harmonious relationship between China and the United States.

It would be equally unwise to ignore China during the transition period on the assumption that a repugnant regime warrants only a policy of benign neglect. China may not be as central to American foreign policy as it was in the 1970s, when it seemed to be the key to ending the war in Vietnam and the winning card in the competition with the Soviet Union. Nor should China be the cornerstone of U.S. policy in Asia—the nation to which all other bilateral relationships should be subordinate, or whose interests are given the greatest weight in determining U.S. policy. But China is relevant to many important issues in which the United States has immediate interests, including preserving peace on the Korean peninsula, maintaining a balance of power in the western Pacific, protecting the international environment, managing the global economy, preventing the proliferation of weapons of mass destruction, and building new institutions to maintain global and regional security. In all these areas, China has the ability to make matters marginally better or to make them substantially worse. Whatever we think of its political system, it would be folly to ignore such a nation.

Finally, it is highly desirable for the United States to avoid confrontation with China. The cost of such a hostile relationship would be enormous. Treating China as a potential military adversary would require far larger deployments in the western Pacific than the United States is now envisioning in the post–cold war world. Even a diplomatic confrontation with China would be costly in that it would complicate the ability of the United States to manage the strategic, economic, and environmental issues in which Peking will necessarily play an important role. A hostile policy toward China would also throw broader Asia policy into disarray, for at this point the friends and allies of the United States in that region would not wish to join America in an antagonistic posture toward Peking.

Furthermore, viewing China as an unfriendly nation is not warranted. To be sure, there are once again deep differences in ideology and values between the two countries, as China has turned away from political liberalization and as America has recommitted itself to promoting democratic values. But it is also necessary to appreciate how much economic reform in China has survived the Tiananmen crisis and how far China remains from the dogmatism and totalitarianism of the past. And it is also important to realize that Chinese leaders would be far more likely to respond to an overtly hostile American policy by tightening their controls over their society than by relaxing them. Violations of human rights warrant forthright criticism but not outright hostility.

A hostile policy toward China might be justified if China had adopted a similar policy toward the United States. But China has not done so. It is true that the two nations have divergent perspectives on several international issues, ranging from arms sales to environmental protection. But Peking also acknowledges many common interests with the United States, especially regional security and economic issues. It seeks to maintain beneficial economic and cultural ties with America. And, despite its concern that the United States may try to build a unipolar world centered around Washington, it has not redefined its foreign policy around the containment of American hegemonism. It would not be in the American interest to encourage China to take such a position.

What is needed, therefore, is a realistic and nuanced policy toward China. The United States should see China as neither central nor irrelevant to U.S. diplomacy but rather as a significant actor in an increasingly multipolar and interdependent world, whose policies impinge on the full spectrum of issues important to Americans. U.S. policy should be based on the realization that the interests of the two countries are neither perfectly congruent nor fully conflictual but instead are partly common and partly competitive. China is neither ally nor adversary, but it is a nation with whom America must engage in continuous dialogue and hard bargaining on questions of common concern.

In dealing with Peking, then, the United States needs to employ both rewards and punishments, carrots and sticks. Washington must be creative in rewarding China when its behavior corresponds with American interests and retaliating when China takes actions that conflict with American objectives. Those incentives and disincentives, in turn, should usually be the same as those used with other countries in comparable circumstances. Indeed, one useful guideline for determining U.S. policy toward China is whether it parallels the U.S. approach to other nations. Is most-favored-nation status withdrawn from other countries that violate human rights or run trade surpluses with the United States? Is as much advanced technology or development assistance supplied to China as to other countries with comparable human rights records or similar foreign policies? Treating China in the same way as the United States does other nations would, indeed, make for a normal American relationship with Peking.

How much leverage will the United States bring to such a relationship with China? The United States now deals with Peking from a distinctly advantageous position. With the end of the cold war, America no longer needs China's help in maintaining a balance of power against the Soviet Union. Economically, China depends much more on American markets and capital than the United States relies on China. The United States accounts for nearly 20 percent of China's total foreign trade, whereas China is responsible for a bit more than 2 percent of America's (table A-2). Actual American investment in China at the end of 1989 constituted nearly 10 percent of total foreign investment there, but less than 1 percent of total American direct investment overseas (table A-7). Although both countries benefit from their academic and scientific exchanges, the flow of new knowledge is disproportionately from the United States to China, rather than the reverse.

Still, this familiar accounting of the asymmetries in Sino-American relations can be misleading. For instance, as China continues to conduct an omnidirectional foreign policy, trying to improve its relations with almost every foreign capital, it simultaneously creates alternatives to an economic or scientific dependency on the United States. More and more, the United States is but one of several sources of capital, markets, and technology for China, along with Japan, Korea, Taiwan, Hong Kong, Southeast Asia, the European Community, and even the former Soviet Union. And, although the United States may be able to persuade China to modify its foreign policy and even aspects of its foreign economic policy to correspond with American interests, the United States does not have the leverage to force reform on unwilling leaders, especially those who fear that their political survival would be threatened by a relaxation of their grip over their society.

With these basic principles in mind, the next step toward redesigning American policy toward China is to consider the interests around which it should be constructed. One can then explore the extent to which American interests are likely to coincide or conflict with those of China and come up with feasible guidelines for an American China policy for the 1990s.

SECURITY

China is already a major power in Asia. Its vast landmass, large population, wealth of natural resources, large industrial base, and strategic location give it the raw materials from which national power has traditionally been constructed. China possesses a large standing army, armed with nuclear weapons, whose projection capabilities will probably increase in the years ahead. It has a formal military alliance with North Korea and tacit security arrangements with Thailand and Pakistan. It has latent ties with overseas Chinese communities throughout Southeast Asia, which many governments in the region fear could once again be transformed into a channel for subversion.

Moreover, although it is not a global superpower, China has great influence outside Asia. Primarily through participation in the international arms market, Peking has been able to develop diplomatic leverage in the Middle East. As a large developing country, not closely linked with the United States, China can claim common identity with much of the third world. And as a permanent member of the United Nations Security Council, Peking is guaranteed a place in deliberations of major international issues, as well as a veto over the council's decisions.

The United States obviously wishes to dissuade China from using that influence to oppose the interests of either the United States or its allies. The United States does not want to see China become a disruptive influence anywhere in the world, whether by supporting insurgencies directed at governments friendly to the United States, pursuing territorial or security interests by force, undertaking arms sales that destabilize regional balances, or engaging in a military buildup in ways that would disrupt the balance of power in Asia. Conversely, it is also in the American interest that China use its influence to promote peace and stability in the Asia-Pacific region and in other parts of the world. A cooperative China could help ease international tensions, contribute to the resolution of regional conflicts, support American military deployments and diplomatic initiatives intended to ensure stability in troubled regions, and join constructively in the new international regimes being formed to bolster cooperative security.

Throughout the post-Mao era, Chinese foreign policy has been largely congruent with these objectives. Peking has abandoned a class-based, revolutionary strategy at home and abroad. It is currently preoccupied with the problems of internal modernization and reform and understands that a stable international environment is most conducive to pursuing those objectives. It has now reduced tensions with virtually all of its neighbors, including the Soviet Union and Vietnam, not only to secure more peaceful surroundings but also to maximize access to foreign markets, technology, and capital. It has attenuated ties with Communist insurgencies abroad, taken a responsible position on the resolution of regional conflicts in Asia, and been mostly supportive of American deployments in the western Pacific.

However, China's perspectives on certain regional issues may differ from those of the United States. Although Peking desires peace on the Korean peninsula and wants to expand commercial and political ties with Seoul, it maintains its only military alliance with the North Korean regime in Pyongyang. The reunification of Korea under a non-Communist government, while welcomed in the United States, would doubtless be of great concern to Peking unless it were coupled with credible assurances that Chinese security interests in Northeast Asia were to be respected. Although China has facilitated the negotiated settlement in Cambodia that was reached in 1991, it could well differ with the United States over the implementation of that accord, particularly with regard to residual Chinese ties to the Khmer Rouge. Peking and Washington have some disagreement over the desirability of a greater role for Japan in global and regional security and potentially even greater differences over the appropriateness of direct American intervention in such regional disputes as the Persian Gulf crisis of 1990–91. Chinese arms sales to the Middle East have also proved to be a chronic irritant in Sino-American relations.

Moreover, over the longer term, China's policies could evolve in ways that would pose further challenges to American interests. As noted earlier, a more conservative government in Peking could conceivably return to a more aggressive foreign policy that would be less receptive to American initiatives on regional and global security matters. A future Chinese government might be tempted to use force to resolve outstanding territorial issues or to punish states that sought to expand their influence along China's periphery. Even without any dramatic change of course in Peking, China's present program of military modernization could become a destabilizing factor in the Asia-Pacific region unless it were well understood and accepted by China's neighbors.

These considerations suggest several guidelines for American policy. The most basic is that China should not be seen as a potential ally of the United States, as a partner in some tacit alignment against a third country, or as a card that can be played in some global strategic competition. Instead, in designing the strategic element of U.S.-China relations, Americans should view China as an independent counterpart in a complex balance of power, with which America will often share common interests but whose perspectives will often differ from those of the United States.

The United States should therefore exercise great restraint in any program of military cooperation with China. As the threat to China from the Soviet Union declines, and as Sino-Soviet and Soviet-American relations improve, much of the rationale for the transfer of American weapons systems to China is correspondingly reduced. No longer does China's security with regard to the Soviet Union depend on its acquisition of advanced weaponry from the United States.

Indeed, extensive American arms transfers to Peking in this new context could conceivably be perceived as threatening by China's neighbors and could therefore trigger a round of compensatory deployments on China's periphery. They could also disrupt the balance of power in the Taiwan Strait. There may still be a place for the sale of small amounts of weapons to Peking, once China's behavior with regard to human rights and international arms transfers has improved and if the equipment has well-accepted defensive purposes. But the emphasis in Sino-American strategic relations in the post–cold war era should be on the coordination of policy, not on the transfer of lethal military equipment.

This focus implies the desirability of a continuing and wide-ranging dialogue with China on global and regional security issues. That dialogue must be comprehensive in several respects: it must include representatives of the diplomatic and military communities in each country, it must be undertaken through official and nonofficial channels, it must encompass high-level leaders as well as working-level officials, and it must deal with the full range of international security issues. A good basis was laid for this kind of interaction in the mid-1980s, but much was suspended after the Tiananmen crisis. It is now time to reinstate that dialogue, including further cabinet-level exchanges by officials from both the Defense and State Departments. In the future, halting this dialogue as a sanction against China would be unwise except for the temporary suspension of purely ceremonial contacts.

The principal purpose of such a dialogue would be to explain American policies and objectives, gain a better understanding of Chinese goals and strategies, and secure Chinese cooperation in addressing global and regional security issues. Particular emphasis should be placed on maintaining stability on the Korean peninsula, ensuring the implementation of the Paris accords on Cambodia, preventing conflict between India and Pakistan, and seeking peace in the Middle East. This result cannot be accomplished by American dictation, but it can be achieved through a process of mutual accommodation, with occasional trade-offs and linkages among various bilateral issues. In particular, the level of military cooperation between the two countries and the flexibility of controls on the export of advanced technology to China should be calibrated according to Peking's approach to international security questions.

A further objective of Sino-American dialogue should be to obtain greater transparency in Chinese security policy. Because of the complexity of the balance of power in the Asia-Pacific region, formal arms control mechanisms may be difficult to develop, except perhaps on the Korean peninsula. A more promising approach may be to continue a process of mutual unilateral restraint, according to which each major power limits or reduces military deployments in light of similar actions taken by others. Such a process can be effective, however, only if all the regional powers share with one another their long-term strategic plans. It is therefore imperative that China offer its counterparts, including the United States, a candid and comprehensive understanding of Chinese threat assessments, military deployments, and strategic objectives.

Finally, although the United States will continue to adjust its military burdens in the western Pacific to achieve greater economies, it must do so in ways that do not produce a destabilizing response from China. The United States should avoid pressing Japan—or other regional powers—to develop projection capabilities that China might regard as threatening and that might therefore lead to an acceleration of China's military preparations. Washington should also undertake any reduction of its own deployments gradually and in clear response to a diminution of regional threats to avoid creating a security vacuum that other powers might attempt to fill. Fortunately, the decline of the Soviet threat in the area makes it more feasible for the United States to scale back its military presence in Asia without disrupting the regional balance of power.

COMMERCE

The tragedy in Tiananmen Square notwithstanding, the most important development to occur in China in the 1980s was the program of economic reform and international engagement undertaken under the leadership of Deng Xiaoping. These efforts were rooted in the realization that China could not become a modern and powerful nation, let alone keep up with the rest of the Asia-Pacific region, if it preserved a highly administered economy, insisted on state ownership of industry and commerce, and discouraged foreign investment and trade. Although still far from complete, reform has fundamentally changed the structure of the Chinese economy. An increasing number of enterprises are able to produce directly for export. More and more avenues are available to receive direct foreign investment. Thirty percent of the urban labor force, one-third of industrial production, and 60 percent of retail sales are now accounted for by nonstate enterprise. About half of all commodity prices are set by the market, and another quarter can fluctuate according to market conditions within limits set by the government.[2]

Although criticized by some conservatives after the Tiananmen crisis, China's economic reform program remains largely intact, and is even moving forward.

As a result of these reforms, China's rate of economic growth averaged between 9 and 10 percent throughout the 1980s, compared with 8 percent in the 1970s. At the same time, China's participation in international economic relationships has also increased dramatically. Its two-way trade soared from $20.6 billion in 1978 to $115.5 billion in 1990, representing an average annual growth rate of 15 percent.[3] Since trade grew more rapidly than its gross national product, China's reliance on foreign trade, expressed as the ratio of two-way trade to national output, increased from about 10 percent in 1978 to approximately 30 percent in 1990. The cumulative total of foreign investment commitments in China, virtually nonexistent in 1978, rose to $20 billion in 1990.

Over the same period, China also became more active in the major institutions that form the foundation of the international economy. Peking joined the World Bank and the International Monetary Fund in 1980, the Asian Development Bank and the Pacific Economic Cooperation Conference in the late 1980s, and became a member of the Asian-Pacific Economic Cooperation process (APEC) in 1991. China also applied to become a member of the General Agreement on Tariffs and Trade (GATT) in 1986, but the process was delayed by the uncertainties surrounding China's economic reform program after the Tiananmen crisis.

In many respects, these developments have been beneficial to America. The United States has an interest in China becoming an open, efficient, and prosperous nation, active in the international economic system. A prosperous and efficient China is more likely to satisfy its basic needs than a nation whose economy is in shambles or that squanders its resources. A successfully developing China, whose economic prosperity is largely the result of participating in mutually beneficial foreign economic relationships, is more likely to be a satisfied power than one that is poor or whose achievements result from autarky rather than international integration. An open and vibrant Chinese economy is more hospitable to profitable commercial relationships with foreign partners than an economy that is sluggish, stagnant, and heavily administered. And, not least important, an economy that is dynamic and open to the outside world is more likely over the longer term to produce domestic pressures for political liberalization than one that is not.

Moreover, the United States can benefit from developing extensive economic relations with China. China can be an important source of imports for the United States, from rare metals and minerals to inexpensive consumer goods. Furthermore, in a more competitive international environment, the United States also has an interest in securing and maintaining access to the Chinese market through both exports and direct investments. It would be foolish for any sector of the American economy—agriculture, industry, or services—to abandon the Chinese market to others. A share of the Chinese market yielded to U.S. competitors might not easily be regained.

To a large extent, China's economic interests are consistent with those of the United States. All Chinese leaders would agree on the desirability of a prosperous country: the search for wealth and power has been the one objective shared by all Chinese governments since the late nineteenth century. There is also growing consensus in China on the need to be more engaged in international commerce. One of the great lessons learned from the Maoist period was that an autarkic China, which limited foreign investment and restricted foreign trade, would inexorably fall farther and farther behind the rest of Asia in the competition for comprehensive national power.

The United States is seen by many Chinese economists as a natural partner in economic progress. The American market is large and relatively open; American technology is among the world's most advanced; and American firms are quite willing to share technology with their foreign partners. To be sure, China also has an interest in developing extensive economic relations with Japan. But, like the rest of the world, Peking views the Japanese market as relatively closed and sees Japanese corporations as less eager to transfer technology overseas. Certainly China does not want to become excessively dependent on Japan for markets, financing, or foreign technology. As a result, Peking shows little enthusiasm for the formation of exclusive regional trading blocs, for the creation of such an entity in Asia would increase China's economic dependence on Japan while reducing its access to markets and technology in the United States.

Although sharing these interests with the United States, China will disappoint Americans in some other ways. For ideological and practical reasons, China's strategy of economic development will feature a good deal of state intervention. For the foreseeable future, some prices will be set administratively, financial credit and investment capital will be allocated bureaucratically, exports and imports will be subject to government regulation, and foreign investment projects will receive close official scrutiny. In all these ways, the American business community will find the Chinese economy less governed by market forces and less open to foreign involvement than it would prefer.

Peking is also already emulating the neomercantilist strategies of the other newly industrializing economies of East Asia, using favorable exchange rates and government subsidies to promote exports to the American market, while employing various devices to protect its economy from foreign competition. These policies have contributed to one of the least favorable features of U.S.-China economic relations: the large cumulative Chinese trade surplus, totaling $24.5 billion between 1986 and 1990. Even if economic reform continues, these elements of neomercantilism are likely to endure and to complicate the commercial ties between China and America.

Relatedly, China's position on international economic issues reflects its standing as a developing nation. Ever since the 1970s, China has called for a new international economic order, in which commodity prices, capital flows, and terms of technology transfer would be adjusted in favor of the interests of the third world. At first, Peking took a fairly radical posture on such issues, implying that the creation of a new international economic regime would mean a thoroughgoing restructuring of the existing world capitalist economy centered on the West. Over time, China's position moderated, as it found ways of benefiting from extensive commercial relations with the rest of the world. In recent years, Peking has acknowledged that a more equitable economic order is better achieved through negotiations within existing international institutions than by confrontation with them. Still, as a developing country, China's perspective on international economic issues will periodically contrast, and even occasionally conflict, with that of the United States.

Finally, evidence is mounting that some Chinese exports are arriving in the United States through illegal channels. Despite central government prohibitions, products of factories operated by Chinese penal institutions are entering the American market. Chinese textile manufacturers are evading American quotas by placing false labels of origin on their goods and transshipping them through third countries. Even if the volumes are small, as they almost certainly are in the case of the products of forced labor, exports such as these violate American law and cannot be tolerated.

Taken together, these considerations suggest that the United States should expand its economic relationship with China in the years ahead but should simultaneously insist that it be placed on a more reciprocal basis. Washington must press Peking to reduce its import tariffs and export subsidies, maintain a reasonable exchange rate, protect foreign intellectual property through improved copyright and patent laws, relax administrative controls over imports, and create greater opportunities for foreign investment. These expectations will require not only that the Chinese economy become more open and flexible, but also that its legal procedures become more institutionalized and its administrative regulations become more transparent. The United States should also encourage China to support the maintenance of an open international economy, at both the global and regional levels.

As a preliminary step in these discussions, it is necessary for Peking and Washington to undertake a comprehensive and objective assessment of their commercial relationship. Even as basic a statistic as the balance of trade between the two countries remains in dispute. Following normal international practice, China counts products destined for the American market but transshipped through Hong Kong as exports to Hong Kong rather than as exports to the United States. But American statistics consider all products manufactured in China as imports from China, whether or not they passed through Hong Kong en route. Conversely, U.S. exports to China are higher in Chinese trade accounts than in American ones, because Chinese figures include those that are transshipped through Hong Kong while American figures do not. As a result of these statistical discrepancies, American officials chronically report a much larger bilateral trade deficit with China than their counterparts in Peking are prepared to acknowledge.

Similarly, the two countries need a better understanding of the multilateral aspects of their bilateral trade. Increasingly, China imports components and raw materials from third parties, such as Hong Kong and Taiwan, assembles or processes them in its own factories, and then reexports them to the United States. The Chinese claim that they only retain some 7 or 8 percent of the total value of these transactions.[4] As viewed from the United States, however, the same operations generate huge Chinese sales to America, without any American exports to counterbalance them.

With a better understanding of the contours of Sino-American trade, Washington can use several policy instruments to pursue its economic objectives with Peking. A threat to withdraw most-favored-nation status is not the appropriate mechanism for addressing commercial issues with China, any more than it was in dealing with the trade surpluses generated by Japan or Taiwan. But more precisely targeted retaliatory measures, such as those stipulated in section 301 of the trade act, are an appropriate way of encouraging all American trading partners to accept the principle that free trade can be conducted only on a reciprocal basis. If necessary, higher quotas and tariffs should be imposed on certain categories of Chinese products to retaliate against export subsidies, barriers to American imports, or other unfair trading practices.

The United States must also more vigorously enforce its trade laws when Chinese imports violate them. American importers who knowingly purchase products from Chinese labor camps and mislabeled textiles should be subject to prosecution. Retaliatory tariffs and quotas should be placed on Chinese textiles if false labeling does not stop. If China does not halt shipments of forced-labor products to the United States, then the categories of goods into which those products fall could also be subject to punitive tariffs, quotas, or even prohibitions.

In return, the United States can consider ways of rewarding Peking if it changes its foreign economic policies to correspond with American interests. The further liberalization of the Chinese economy would warrant Peking's membership in the GATT. And once that step was taken, China would be eligible, like other developing countries, to receive more favored tariff treatment from the United States under the Generalized System of Preferences. The American decision on whether to grant GSP treatment to China could be taken in light of the bilateral trade balance and the overall political relationship between the two countries at the time.

If economic reform in China resumes, and if the human rights situation there warrants, the United States could promote China's development through various forms of assistance programs. Credits could be granted on favorable terms to American exporters, to match similar programs offered by the other developed countries. The United States could endorse expanded lending to China by the World Bank, the Asian Development Bank, and other international financial institutions, with an emphasis on those projects that promote China's economic reform and facilitate its integration into the international economic community. And it might be possible for the United States to launch a small aid program to China, focusing not on large loans to Peking, but rather on providing technical advice on such issues as agricultural development, environmental protection, enterprise management, macro-economic regulation, and the problems inherent in transforming a centrally planned economy into a regulated market system.

HUMAN RIGHTS

China is a large and complex society, with a totalitarian heritage, that is undergoing a turbulent process of modernization and liberalization. The Tiananmen crisis of 1989 revealed how unsettling this process can be, especially when the costs of economic reform begin to outstrip the benefits and when the pace of economic change surpasses the restructuring of political institutions. The situation in China after the crisis, together with developments in Eastern Europe and the Soviet Union since 1989, also illustrates the alternatives to successful political reform. In the future China could well experience not further liberalization and institutionalization, but rather retrogression to a more tightly controlled society or even decay into immobility, instability, and turmoil.

The United States gains no advantage from chaos in China.[5] Instability would greatly complicate China's foreign commercial and scientific relationships, resulting in a large decline in trade, investment, and scholarly exchange with the United States. A China in turmoil could well be unable to feed and shelter its people, generating ample flows of refugees to neighboring countries. An unstable China, armed with nuclear weapons and large conventional forces, could disrupt the balance of power in the Asia-Pacific region by threatening its neighbors or by inviting foreign intervention. Past periods of instability, including the warlordism of the 1910s and 1920s and the Cultural Revolution of the 1960s and 1970s, warn unambiguously of the disastrous consequences that instability in China can have on its people and on the rest of the region.

Nor does the United States have an interest in the emergence of a more repressive regime in China. Such a government would be certain to infringe on the political and civil rights of the Chinese people. A more restrictive intellectual climate would hamper academic and cultural exchanges between China and the United States. Although a hard-line Chinese government might attempt to preserve commercial relations with the United States, American investors would in all likelihood find it difficult to manage their Chinese ventures in an atmosphere of intimidation. Moreover, in the end, a government that rules by repression is not likely to be stable. Without legitimacy and without responsive institutions, a repressive Chinese government will constantly be threatened by dissent and protest from below.

This is not to say that China should be expected immediately to copy the political institutions most familiar to Americans. The complex sharing of powers between the executive and legislative branches of government, the equally complex allocation of responsibility between the federal government and the states, and the provisions for judicial review of executive and legislative actions may not be applicable to Chinese circumstances. Nor can the process of political reform in China occur rapidly or uniformly across the entire country. But it is appropriate for Americans to hope that the Chinese political system steadily become more efficient, less corrupt, and more responsive to the demands of its citizens. In particular, it is in the interest of Americans and Chinese alike that the government in Peking respect and protect the internationally recognized human rights of its people by ending arbitrary arrests, lengthy detention, physical and psychological torture, and judicial proceedings without provisions for an active legal defense. America also wants to see greater freedom of speech and the press, greater freedom of assembly and organization, and greater freedom of religion in China as in all other countries.

The American interest does not extend to supporting, let alone actively promoting, the independence of such minority areas in China as Tibet or Xinjiang. If done consistently, endorsing the principle of self-determination for minority nationalities would complicate America's relations with many countries, including many close neighbors and allies, such as Canada. The United States would be better advised simply to define its interest as the extension of political reform and basic human rights to all parts of China, including the minority areas. The accomplishment of this aim would presumably imply a large measure of political decentralization and cultural autonomy, as well as concerted efforts at economic development. But the ultimate question of sovereignty would not be an American concern.

The Chinese will respond to this definition of American interests with much ambivalence. On the one hand, they will welcome an assurance that Americans would prefer to see genuine stability in China rather than chronic unrest. They will also be relieved if the United States abjures supporting independence for Tibet or for other minority areas. On the other hand, Chinese leaders will view American advocacy of human rights and political reform as unacceptable interference in their internal affairs, especially when it includes sharp criticism of their government or economic and diplomatic sanctions against it. The promotion of human rights in China will therefore continue to be a serious—possibly the most serious—irritant in Sino-American relations.

In promoting its interest in a China that is stable and humanely governed, the United States must recognize the limits on its leverage. Quite simply, it is beyond the ability of the United States to prevent disorder or compel political reform in China, any more than it could determine the outcome of the Chinese Revolution in the 1940s.

America can provide economic and technical aid to a Chinese government attempting to undertake modernization and reform but cannot prevent it from falling victim to corruption, inefficiency, and decay. America can encourage liberalization and impose sanctions against repression but cannot force a conservative government to implement domestic reforms. What is therefore required is a sensible human rights policy that simultaneously embodies the American interest in political reform, identifies appropriate methods for promoting it, and acknowledges the limits to American leverage.

The United States can pursue its interests in human rights and political reform in China in several ways. To begin with, dialogue on the subject with the Chinese government should continue, of the sort begun by the Bush administration after the Tiananmen crisis and carried on by other Western governments as well. The basic purpose of such discussions, of course, is to condemn violations of human rights in China, press for improvements, and praise liberalization when it occurs. This process, in turn, will require that public and private organizations monitor human rights in China more comprehensively and objectively. It will be essential to keep an eye on long-term trends, taking care not to exaggerate instances of repression or liberalization. When there are patterns of abuse, they should be honestly and clearly identified. Conversely, when the situation begins to relax, such a development must also be acknowledged even if past violations are not repudiated.

But other objectives can also be promoted by dialogue with Peking. It is important to explain clearly to Chinese leaders what the United States means by human rights. The United States can explain that it is not seeking the violent overthrow of the Chinese government or the immediate adoption of pluralistic political institutions, but rather a gradual but sustained process of political reform. The dialogue with Chinese leaders can also be used to spell out why the United States cares so much about human rights, explaining that Americans are concerned about political developments in China for pragmatic and moralistic reasons, and that attention to human rights is a long-standing and enduring element in American foreign policy.

The dialogue with Chinese leaders must also be conducted in ways that internationalize the issue as much as possible. Peking must come to understand that the human rights being advocated by the United States have not been defined by Americans alone, but represent universal norms that are now embodied in international law and conventions. Chinese leaders must also be persuaded that other governments and not just the United States care about the state of human rights in China and are prepared to take China's domestic political situation into account in formulating their policies toward Peking. Internationalization also implies that the standards of judgment and the sanctions that are being applied to China are the same as those applied to other countries, so as to remove any suspicion that Peking is being treated more harshly or more leniently than similar governments.

The United States can appropriately take several further steps to promote the long-term process of political reform in China. The broadcast of objective news to China about domestic developments and about international events can be increased. In addition, cultural and academic exchange programs need to be continued to promote better understanding of fundamental principles of democratic political institutions and a just legal order. If political reform does resume, then China's governmental agencies and civil organizations may well require extensive technical advice about democratic processes, of the sort that the U.S. Agency for International Development and the National Endowment for Democracy are already providing to other countries committed to democratization.

In cases of a severe deterioration of the political situation in China, such as the Tiananmen incident, it may be appropriate to apply sanctions against Peking. Some of the most effective actions can be symbolic, including sharp criticism of human rights violations in China and temporary suspension of ceremonial contacts with high-level Chinese leaders. In a society where deference by foreigners has traditionally been an important mark of the legitimacy of a government, such symbolic gestures can have a significant impact. Other sanctions can be substantive, such as the interruption or cancellation of certain economic and strategic relationships, especially those involving the provision of weapons or advanced civilian technology. Still other sanctions can be the result not of formal government decisions but of the spontaneous response of the marketplace to instability and repression in China, as individual firms and citizens decide not to conduct trade, investment, tourism, or academic exchange in what appears to be a less hospitable environment.

In all these instances, however, sanctions must be multilateral if they are to be effective. The symbolic impact of a ban on high-level contacts or even of sharp criticism of China's human rights record will be severely mitigated if those measures are undertaken by the United States alone, without the support of its allies. The material effect of unilateral economic sanctions could even be more damaging to the United States than to China if their only effect is to force China to switch from American to European suppliers. It is imperative, therefore, that if sanctions become necessary, they be imposed in a multilateral fashion, as they were by the West in 1989.

Moreover, sanctions must be carefully chosen so that they are not counterproductive. Restricting academic exchanges, even with government research institutions, only limits one of the most important channels through which ideas about political and economic reform can enter China. Untargeted economic sanctions, such as the withdrawal of most-favored-nation status, can also be counterproductive if they give China's government the pretext to tighten administrative controls over the country's society and economy, or if they harm those sectors and regions of the country that remain committed to economic liberalization. Although suspending ceremonial exchanges with high-level Chinese leaders may be appropriate, cutting off normal working relationships with the Chinese government is almost certainly unwise, given the necessity of dealing with Peking on strategic, economic, and environmental issues.

When the human rights situation in China improves, Peking can be rewarded. The ban on high-level ceremonial visits can be lifted, and top Chinese leaders can again be welcomed to the United States. Military cooperation between the two countries can be resumed, subject to the qualifications on strategic relations mentioned earlier. The United States can again support lending to China by multilateral financial institutions and could consider a small bilateral assistance program of its own. Restrictions on technology transfer could be relaxed, as long as Peking is adopting responsible policies on its own sales of weapons and nuclear equipment abroad. In short, Chinese leaders must be reassured that the human rights issue is not simply a pretext for punishing their country but is also a standard for judging when the United States can engage in more cooperative behavior.

TAIWAN AND HONG KONG

More than forty years after the Chinese Revolution of 1949, China remains a divided nation, with Hong Kong and Taiwan (as well as the smaller Portuguese territory of Macao) outside the control of the central government in Peking. Like its predecessors in the imperial era, China's contemporary Communist government has regarded the reunification of the country under its control as an essential mark of its power and legitimacy. Peking has pursued this objective over the years at different tempos and with different strategies. It paid relatively little attention to the goal of regaining sovereignty over Hong Kong or Macao until the 1980s, when it engaged in sustained negotiations with Great Britain and Portugal to arrange their return to Chinese control. It used military force against offshore islands controlled by Taiwan on two occasions in the 1950s but then switched to a more accommodative strategy after the normalization of relations with the United States. Though the tactics have changed, the objective of reunification has been a constant in Chinese foreign policy throughout the Communist era.

Meanwhile, Hong Kong and Taiwan have prospered outside Peking's control. Taiwan's economic development has been one of the true East Asian miracles. The island's economy grew at an average rate of about 10 percent a year throughout the 1960s and 1970s. Its per capita income increased from $387 in 1970 to $7,510 in 1989 and is expected to reach $14,000 in 1996. At the same time, Taiwan has maintained a remarkably equitable distribution of income and generally low levels of inflation. Hong Kong has also enjoyed remarkable economic success. Once a rather sleepy entrepôt for southern China, Hong Kong has become a commercial, transportation, and financial center for much of East Asia. Its rate of growth in the 1970s and 1980s averaged 7 percent a year, and its per capita income has risen from $900 in 1970 to $12,000 in 1990. In inflation and income distribution, Hong Kong has not performed quite as spectacularly as Taiwan, but the territory's overall performance is still highly impressive.[6]

The United States has important economic and moral interests in Taiwan and Hong Kong. A peaceful future for Taiwan has arguably been the single most enduring element in U.S. China policy since 1949.[7] America's relationship with Taipei has involved economic assistance in the 1950s and 1960s, a military alliance from 1955 through 1979, tensions over human rights in the 1970s, and increasing economic frictions in the 1980s. But throughout this entire period, the United States has remained committed to a peaceful resolution of the Taiwan question. That commitment was embodied in the deployment of elements of the Seventh Fleet in the Taiwan Strait after the outbreak of the Korean War in 1950, as well as the mutual defense treaty of 1955. Even after the improvement of relations between Washington and Peking, the United States reiterated its interest in a peaceful future for Taiwan in such policy statements as the Shanghai communiqué of 1972, the joint communiqués of 1978 and 1982, and of course the Taiwan Relations Act of 1979.

Over the past two decades, Taiwan's economic performance has given the United States a greater interest in the fate of the island. Its two-way trade with the United States amounted to $34.3 billion in 1990, 40 percent larger than the People's Republic's trade volume with America that same year, making it America's sixth largest trading partner. American investment has also increased rapidly on the island, reaching a cumulative total of some $3.6 billion in 1990, more than twice that of U.S. investment on the Chinese mainland. Although the growth of these economic ties has introduced new tensions into U.S.-Taiwan relations, the result largely of the huge trade surpluses that Taiwan enjoyed throughout most of the 1980s, the net effect has been to reinforce America's stake in the prosperity of Taiwan.

As noted earlier, the United States has historically had much less interest in Hong Kong, seeing the fate of that territory as in the hands of the British. But the expansion of Hong Kong's dual role as a commercial and financial center for East Asia and as an entrepôt for southern China has increased American economic involvement there. U.S. trade with Hong Kong (excluding goods originating in China) amounted to $16.3 billion in 1990. Cumulative American investment in the territory has now reached about $6 billion. The crisis of confidence in Hong Kong that developed after the 1984 agreement on its retrocession to China and the large demonstrations in support of the antigovernment protests in Tiananmen Square in 1989 began to arouse an American concern with the future of human rights in Hong Kong as well.

The United States therefore wants a peaceful and stable future for Taiwan and Hong Kong. Any use of force by mainland China against Taiwan would directly challenge the commitments made by the United States to the people of the island at the time of the normalization of U.S.-China relations. Any Chinese violation of the Basic Law would run counter to the American interest in seeing Hong Kong's economic and social system remain intact after 1997. Political repression in either place would automatically invoke the American concern for human rights. And social instability or economic stagnation would obviously be detrimental to the growing American economic interests in the two territories.

At the same time, the United States has no reason to oppose the general principle of the eventual reunification of Hong Kong and Taiwan with the rest of China. Hong Kong's return to Chinese sovereignty has already been agreed to by London and Peking, and Washington has no legal basis to dispute it. Similarly, the eventual reunification of China is the stated objective of the Communist government in Peking and the Nationalist government in Taipei, and the United States should have no reason to challenge this outcome, as long as it occurs peacefully and with the mutual agreement of both sides.

Finally, the United States has an interest in seeing Hong Kong and Taiwan more actively engaged in international economic institutions. Both regions are important economic trading entities, constituting a share of international commerce. Both are also increasingly significant sources of direct foreign investment, particularly in China and Southeast Asia. When the shape of the international economic system is the subject of more and more debate, Hong Kong and Taiwan must be represented in major international economic organizations, as befits their standing in the world economy.

China's interest in Hong Kong and Taiwan sometimes corresponds with America's interests and sometimes does not. There is little doubt that Peking would also prefer that the reunification of Taiwan and mainland China occur by peaceful means, but it has consistently refused to categorically renounce the use of force under all circumstances. Like the United States, Peking has a stake in the continued prosperity of Hong Kong, but it will want to restrict the autonomy and democratization that the territory enjoys. Peking increasingly accepts the principle of Taiwan's involvement in the world economy, but it still resists Taipei's membership in major international organizations without its prior approval or participation in ways that imply Taiwan is an independent sovereign state. Moreover, China has consistently described American interest in Hong Kong or Taiwan as unwarranted intervention in China's internal affairs.

Fortunately, the United States has gradually developed a policy toward Taiwan that is appropriate and sustainable. Unlike many other Western countries, which maintained only a minimal institutional infrastructure with Taipei after establishing diplomatic relations with Peking, the United States has, through the American Institute in Taiwan, a highly viable mechanism for consultation and coordination with the Taiwan government. The Coordination Council for North American Affairs performs a similar role for Taiwan in the United States. As the Reagan administration belatedly discovered, there is no need to consider serious changes in these institutional arrangements.

The American commitment to the security of Taiwan is also being adequately promoted. Although the United States is, under the terms of the 1982 agreement with Peking, committed to gradually reduce sales of arms to Taipei, it continues to sell a substantial amount of defensive weapons to Taiwan, providing more advanced equipment as previous designs become obsolete. Washington has also developed a program of technology transfer to Taiwan so that the island can assume greater responsibility for producing the weapons it needs for its defense. This approach, combining arms sales and technology transfer, deserves to be continued. At this point, the United States can begin to encourage its allies to join it in selling appropriate amounts of defensive weapons to Taiwan, a step that, as China's strategic significance declines, more Western European countries may be prepared to take.

Over the longer term, the United States will wish to see a final settlement of the dispute between Taiwan and the mainland, thus ending one of the chief regional conflicts that has threatened the stability of Asia since the onset of the cold war. It would not be wise for America to become closely involved in this process, either by endorsing either party's negotiating position or by serving as an intermediary between them. Nor would such a policy be necessary, for as the cultural, economic, and even political contacts multiply across the Taiwan Strait, the United States can more easily stand back from the process of reconciliation while endorsing its general direction. Washington need only reiterate that it would welcome a peaceful resolution of the Taiwan question, along any lines that are mutually acceptable to Taipei and Peking. This would imply opposition to any attempt by either party to impose its will on the other, whether through use of coercion by the mainland or a unilateral declaration of independence by Taiwan.

The new relationship between Taiwan and the mainland should also facilitate another strand of American policy. The United States has an interest in seeing Taiwan become a member of more international economic organizations, as long as it can do so under formulas that evade the question of sovereignty. The Bush administration was correct in 1991 to endorse Taiwan's membership in the GATT as a separate customs territory. Similar formulas have now been found for Taiwan's membership in the Asia-Pacific Economic Cooperation process and should be sought for the Organization for Economic and Cultural Development. In the future, Taiwan should also be welcomed into the World Bank and the International Monetary Fund, in recognition of its major role in world trade and investment.

The United States must now make clear to Peking that it has an interest in prosperity and stability in Hong Kong, and that it believes that these results can be ensured only by a combination of restraint and flexibility in China and democracy and autonomy in Hong Kong. This interest can be expressed symbolically by increasing the number of high-level American officials visiting Hong Kong both before and after 1997. Conversely, if further economic sanctions against China are ever deemed necessary, it is vital that the United States design them in ways that will minimize the negative effect on Hong Kong and its people. This consideration will continue to be a strong argument against withdrawing most-favored-nation status from China, for Hong Kong will inevitably be one of the principal victims of such a step.

The United States can also take three other steps to promote its interests in Hong Kong. First, it can work with the Chinese and British governments to secure Hong Kong's place in various international agreements and institutions after 1997. It may also be necessary to modify American law to ensure that all agreements between the United States and Hong Kong remain in force after Hong Kong returns to Chinese sovereignty, as well as to guarantee that Hong Kong maintains its separate status for purposes of immigration and import quotas. Second, Washington must find ways to ensure the flow of advanced technology to Hong Kong after it reverts to Chinese sovereignty, provided sufficient safeguards are in place to prevent the diversion of that technology to unauthorized users. It is important to ensure that Hong Kong not suffer if the West should tighten its controls over the export of technology to China, perhaps as part of enforcing international norms on human rights, weapons proliferation, or environmental protection. And third, the United States must be prepared to increase the quota for immigrants from Hong Kong if the situation in the territory warrants, providing a safety net for those who wish to flee repression, instability, or economic stagnation should it occur during the period of transition to Chinese rule.

ACADEMIC AND CULTURAL EXCHANGES

One aspect of China's opening to the outside world since 1978 has been the increase in the flow of Chinese students and scholars abroad. Chinese leaders and intellectuals have become aware that advanced science and technology cannot be studied from a distance but require direct experience abroad. Thus, as many as 100,000 Chinese students and scholars have come to the United States since the normalization of Sino-American relations to pursue advanced training and to conduct research. The number of Americans traveling to China for similar purposes has been much smaller. But thousands of Americans have participated in language study, cooperative scientific projects, archival and field research in the social sciences, and teaching in Chinese institutions of higher learning.

There are at least four reasons why the United States has an interest in sustaining active collaboration with the academic community in China. The first stems from the size of the country and the continuity of its culture. An appreciation of the historical, philosophical, artistic, and literary heritage of humankind would be incomplete without attention to one of its greatest civilizations. Scholars of botany, zoology, seismology, and other natural sciences need access to the unique features found upon China's vast landmass. No generalization about political science, sociology, or economics can possibly be considered universally valid unless it is tested against the experience of one-quarter of the earth's population.

Moreover, despite the shortcomings of its educational and political systems, China is a source of great scientific and artistic talent. Chinese scientists and engineers can make outstanding contributions to finding solutions to problems in the applied and natural sciences. Chinese artists, writers, musicians, and filmmakers can enrich the contemporary international cultural scene. And as their theoretical sophistication and research skills increase, Chinese social scientists can greatly enhance international understanding of their society and of regional and global trends.

Third, academic exchange can promote a more stable relationship between the two societies. A durable relationship with the United States depends on a better knowledge of America at all levels of Chinese society. Conversely, wise American policy toward China requires an understanding of the dynamics of the Chinese economic and political systems and of Chinese foreign policy. Discussion of bilateral and multilateral issues in Sino-American relations—whether strategic, economic, environmental, or human rights—can often be more fruitfully and candidly discussed in unofficial forums than in governmental contexts. For this purpose, academic exchange is also extremely useful.

Finally, to the extent that the United States wishes to promote the modernization and reform of China, academic exchange can play yet another role. China's scientific and technological modernization depends on its access to advanced science and technology abroad. Its program of economic reform can benefit from the study of Western economic theory, management practices, and the experiences of other reforming socialist countries. And the process of political liberalization in China has already been promoted by the exposure of young educated Chinese to other political systems abroad. Obviously, some of this knowledge can be obtained in China or in other Western countries. But academic exchanges between China and the United States can make an important contribution to all these objectives.

Many Chinese intellectuals share virtually all these interests with their American counterparts. They seem eager to learn more about every subject imaginable, engage in collaborative work with foreign scholars, and share with others their understanding of their culture and society. Unfortunately, only a small proportion of them have been able to do so. China's international academic exchange programs, including those with the United States, still draw disproportionately from a few institutions in a few cities, particularly Peking and Shanghai.

In contrast to China's intellectuals, many Chinese leaders are much more ambivalent about academic exchange programs with the United States. On the one hand, they accept the proposition that the Chinese need to study foreign theory and practice in many subjects, including the social sciences as well as the natural sciences and engineering. They are also more and more eager to see Chinese scientists and artists gain international recognition, hoping for Nobel prizes to be awarded to Chinese in science and literature. But they are also apprehensive of some of the consequences of academic exchange programs. As the evolution of Sino-American educational relations since 1979 illustrates, they have been concerned about the brain drain of talented young Chinese abroad and about the unorthodox political and social values of those who return from overseas study. And, unlike their American counterparts, most Chinese leaders seem to have little interest in encouraging foreigners to gain independent and objective knowledge of contemporary Chinese conditions. Instead, they want foreign scholars merely to replicate what the Chinese government has determined to be a "correct understanding" of China's circumstances.

The best policy for the United States is to maintain active cultural and academic exchanges with China, broadening them whenever possible to include participants from a greater variety of Chinese cities and institutions. As with the Sino-American economic relationship, however, the United States should promote reciprocity in its exchange programs with China. The issue is not numbers. It would be impractical to expect the number of Americans studying in China to match the number of Chinese studying in the United States, and it would be unwise to restrict exchange programs administratively to achieve numerical parity. Instead, the issue remains the ability of Americans to conduct collaborative research with Chinese colleagues on a full range of topics in the humanities and social sciences, as well as in the natural sciences and engineering. Peking cannot hope to restrict academic collaboration in the social sciences and still anticipate full American cooperation for Chinese research and study in the natural sciences. American universities, scientific associations, and exchange organizations need to ask whether American objectives are being achieved in the exchange programs and to insist that their Chinese counterparts give adequate attention to American interests as well as to their own.

The United States will also have to grapple with the brain drain of Chinese students and scholars studying in America. Here, the best approach is to address the issue on a global basis. If the United States continues to require officially sponsored students and scholars to return to their native countries after completing their programs in America, then that policy should be applied equally to the Chinese, although possibly with the sort of temporary exceptions that were permitted for Chinese students and scholars after the Tiananmen incident. Conversely, if immigration procedures are relaxed for students and scholars from other countries, then obviously they should be eased for Chinese students as well.

The United States has an interest in making it possible for Chinese students and scholars who have been trained in the United States to carry back to China what they have learned about advanced science, modern institutions, and democratic values. Few are prepared, under present political circumstances on the mainland, to do so permanently. But many would be willing to return for shorter periods if the appropriate arrangements were made. To this end, the United States could develop a program, in cooperation with the Chinese government, whereby Chinese students now living in America could return home frequently for periods of teaching or research, while simultaneously guaranteeing that they could return to the United States at will to resume work here. Private foundations might provide the requisite financial assistance to make such a program viable.

Finally, American institutions should also consider establishing various training programs for Chinese students and scholars to supplement the traditional degree programs in the United States, including courses conducted by American professors in China, joint degree programs offered by Chinese and American universities, and short-term training courses in the United States. In many cases, these programs may prove more effective in reaching larger numbers of Chinese than the previous emphasis on lengthy doctoral study for Chinese graduate students. But adequate selection procedures will have to be put in place to ensure that Chinese participants in such programs are of sufficiently high quality.

THE GLOBAL AGENDA

The new Sino-American relationship must also focus on a growing agenda of transnational issues that directly affect the security, prosperity, and quality of life of virtually every nation. Increasingly, the management of these issues is regarded not solely as a domestic responsibility or even as the subject of bilateral negotiations but as requiring the creation or expansion of international regimes that can specify norms of behavior and impose sanctions on noncompliance.

Two such regimes will be of particular importance in the 1990s. First, there will be growing pressure to construct a more rigorous international regime to control atmospheric pollution, particularly of those gases that are believed to cause global climatic change. And second, the international regime created in the 1960s to prevent the spread of nuclear weapons must gradually be expanded to include other weapons systems, including chemical and biological weapons, ballistic missiles, and conventional weapons of mass destruction. In both these issues, China will be important in exacerbating the problems or in contributing to solutions. It is therefore in the American interest that China participate actively and constructively in developing the international regimes needed to manage this new global agenda.

The effects of atmospheric pollution on the environment have become of rising concern to scientists and national leaders during the past decade. Although the details and their implications are still subject to much dispute, there is growing consensus that the composition of the earth's atmosphere is changing, owing to emission of such gases as carbon dioxide, methane, nitrous oxide, and chlorofluorocarbons. The possible effects of these atmospheric changes include a gradual global warming (the result of the emission of carbon dioxide), greater ultraviolet radiation (the result of the ozone depletion caused by the spread of chlorofluorocarbons), acid rain (the result of the increased production of sulphur dioxide), and the accumulation of various toxic chemicals in the food chain.[8]

The inefficient use of carbon-based energy resources, the absence of effective emissions control technologies, and the growing utilization of chlorofluorocarbons for refrigeration make China a big contributor to atmospheric pollution. China has been estimated, for example, to be the third largest source of carbon dioxide emissions, behind the United States and the Soviet Union. Although China produces relatively little carbon dioxide per capita, the huge size of its population means that total emissions are nearly 50 percent of those of the United States.[9]

Chinese leaders now seem to understand the severity of global environmental problems and, even more important, the extent to which their country contributes to them. They also recognize that a cooperative attitude on environmental issues would help repair the damage to its international reputation inflicted by the June 4 incident of 1989. Some analysts have speculated that Chinese leaders also hope that, by underscoring the severity of their environmental problems, they can win greater foreign tolerance of their coercive birth control programs. Thus, in his addresses to the United Nations General Assembly in September 1990 and again in September 1991, Foreign Minister Qian Qichen emphasized China's commitment to cooperate in the solution of international environmental issues.[10] Subsequently, China has become more active in relevant international organizations and hosted a ministerial conference of developing countries on the relationship between environmental and developmental issues in June 1991.[11]

But China is concerned about the cost of measures to protect the environment. Peking has joined other developing nations in insisting that international dialogue link environmental and developmental issues, and that wealthier nations provide financial support and technical assistance in promoting environmental protection in the third world. China therefore acceded to the 1987 Montreal Protocol on ozone depletion only after an international fund was established in 1990 to subsidize the royalty and licensing fees that accompany the adoption of substitute technologies.[12]

The Montreal Protocol, as modified by the creation of the economic assistance fund in 1990, provides a prototype for the way in which Washington should address environmental issues with China. On the one hand, the United States, along with the other developed countries, should be sensitive to the economic implications of environmental protection measures and should provide bilateral and multilateral assistance programs to ease the burden of compliance with the emerging international regime. On the other, the United States must also support the construction of effective enforcement measures even if they infringe on national sovereignty. The Montreal Protocol's inclusion of barriers to trade in environmentally dangerous materials and its provision of economic sanctions on countries that do not meet its provisions are a model for the management of related environmental questions.

A second part of the emerging global agenda concerns limiting the diffusion of advanced military technology, especially the spread of various weapons of mass destruction. The first international regime to address this issue was established to prevent the proliferation of nuclear weapons, as embodied in the nuclear nonproliferation treaty of 1968, and in the more recent establishment of a fourteen-nation Nuclear Suppliers Group. The strategic arms limitation treaty (START) of 1991 and the unilateral American decision to withdraw and destroy its land- and sea-based tactical nuclear weapons later that year reflect the interest of the two superpowers in reducing the numbers of nuclear weapons deployed. Fledgling mechanisms have also been created to control the export of other very destructive weapons systems, including the twelve-nation Missile Technology Control Regime to limit the spread of ballistic missiles and the twenty-nation Australia Group to prevent the proliferation of chemical weapons.

The Persian Gulf War of 1990–91 increased the interest in all these areas and introduced new concerns. The fact that Iraq was armed with chemical weapons and ballistic missiles, and that it was engaged in a program to develop nuclear weapons, illustrates the necessity of strengthening the international regimes against the proliferation of these three weapons systems. Baghdad's biological weapons capability suggests the need for additional efforts. More generally, the proliferation of highly lethal conventional weapons in the Middle East is producing pressure for tighter controls on the conventional arms trade in the region, as reflected in the Paris meeting of the permanent members of the U.N. Security Council in 1991.

As one of the largest international arms merchants, as well as a nuclear weapons state, China's cooperation will be essential if there is to be a more effective international regime to control the spread of highly lethal weapons systems. As noted earlier, China seems to have provided assistance to Pakistan in the design and production of nuclear weapons, helped countries such as Algeria to design and build nuclear reactors, and exported nuclear materials to still other nations. China's program of conventional arms transfers has been even more extensive. Peking has sold intermediate-range ballistic missiles to Saudi Arabia, discussed the export of shorter-range missiles to Syria and Pakistan, supplied vast quantities of conventional arms to Iran and Iraq during their conflict in the 1980s, and provided tanks and aircraft to several other third world countries. Together, these arms sales have placed China among the top five arms suppliers in the world.

China's attitude toward the questions of arms control and weapons proliferation, like its posture toward international environmental questions, is ambivalent. Beginning in the 1980s, Peking began to take a more flexible and responsible position on the question of nuclear proliferation. Although not a signatory to the partial nuclear test ban treaty of 1963, China halted all atmospheric testing after October 1980.[13] In the middle of the decade, Peking began to express support for the general principle of nonproliferation, abandoning its previous view that all nations should be entitled to develop their own nuclear deterrents. It joined the International Atomic Energy Agency and accepted IAEA safeguards for its exports of nuclear materials and technology. And in the summer of 1991, in a major reversal of policy, Peking expressed its intention to sign the nuclear nonproliferation treaty of 1968.

Although China is gradually acceding to the international regimes to control the proliferation of nuclear weapons, its position on nuclear arms control remains quite different from that of the United States. Although now somewhat muted, Peking's long-standing call for a complete prohibition of nuclear weapons, for binding no-first-use pledges on the nuclear powers, and for recognition of nuclear-free zones around the world have consistently placed it at some distance from Washington. More recently, another issue has emerged: the point at which China would be willing to engage in multilateral negotiations on the size of its own nuclear arsenal. For many years, Peking declared that it would consider participation in such discussions once the United States and the Soviet Union had agreed to reduce their nuclear arsenals by 50 percent. When the START negotiations established such a nominal benchmark, China modified its position to demand that the superpowers make even greater cuts before it would make its own arsenal subject to negotiation.[14] Securing China's involvement in a multilateral regime restricting the size of its nuclear force will become more necessary as the size of the superpowers' nuclear stockpiles decreases, since Peking's arsenal will at some point become a significant consideration in designing American and Soviet deterrents.

China also seems prepared to participate, though grudgingly, in the creation of an international regime to control the spread of other kinds of weapons. Under pressure from Washington, it has engaged in dialogue with the United States on controlling the proliferation of missile technology, chemical weapons, and biological weapons. It participated in the Paris conference of 1991 on controlling the spread of advanced conventional weapons in the Middle East and subsequently agreed to abide by the Missile Technology Control Regime. But Peking has already made clear its concerns about the issue. The Chinese defense establishment relies on the export of weapons not only to earn foreign exchange, but also to acquire diplomatic leverage abroad. China's leaders will not be eager, therefore, to join in an international agreement that would require them to sacrifice lucrative arms sales or political standing abroad. Moreover, China will be looking to see whether international regimes restricting arms transfers will apply to the United States, the Soviet Union, and other major Western powers as strictly as to China and other emerging arms exporters in the third world. It is unlikely to accept restraints on its own arms sales that do not apply equally to others.

The United States should encourage China to take a more active and constructive role in the development of the international regimes to control the spread of highly destructive weapons. It should press China to fulfill its pledge to sign and ratify the nonproliferation treaty, participate in multilateral negotiations to limit the size of its own nuclear arsenal, and cooperate in controlling the proliferation of other weapons of mass destruction. As an incentive, the United States can promise to facilitate China's access to advanced technology if Peking adopts more responsible arms transfer policies and if it joins the emerging international regimes in this area. Conversely, Washington can work with its allies to restrict the flow of dual-purpose technology, as well as weapons systems, to China until Peking's performance improves.[15]

A NEW RELATIONSHIP WITH CHINA

For decades, the United States has sought what many Americans have described as a "special relationship" with China. As noted in chapter 2, this special relationship has had a strongly cyclical character. In its positive phase, it joined America's "dreams of influence and uplift" to China's hope of securing wealth and power from a foreign patron.[16] In its negative phase, it saw China rejecting American influence as disruptive and demeaning and the United States turning away from China in anger and dismay. This cycle, by which hostility gave way to reconciliation, and euphoria yielded to disenchantment, has been repeated several times in the history of Sino-American relations over the last two hundred years.[17] Echoes of that cycle have been clearly evident in the evolution of U.S.-China relations since 1972. But through all the shifts of mood, the common denominator has been high emotion, unrealistic hopes, exaggerated fears, and a mutual preoccupation verging on obsession.

One of the principal theses of this book is that such a relationship is no longer suitable to the objective circumstances surrounding U.S.-China relations. Both the forecast of Sino-American relations in chapter 9 and the analysis of American interests and policies in this one suggest a very different relationship than the hostility of the 1950s and 1960s, the false euphoria of the 1970s and 1980s, or the sense of disillusionment and betrayal of the post-Tiananmen era. That relationship will differ from the past in several ways.

The new relationship is likely to be a less central one for the United States as the result of a more diverse and multipolar world. With the collapse of the Soviet empire and the end of the cold war, China will no longer be regarded as one corner of a strategic triangle, the shape of which will determine the global geopolitical balance. Even in Asia, China will be—along with Japan, Korea, India, Indonesia, Thailand, Taiwan, and Vietnam—but one of several centers of economic and military power around which the United States must construct a sound regional policy. Although China was once at the forefront of reform in the Communist world, it has now been joined by a long list of other countries coping with the legacies of a centrally planned economy and a totalitarian political system. China will continue to be an important player in many international issues, but it will no longer capture American attention as completely as it has in the past.

The new U.S.-China relationship is certain to be much more complex. American policy toward China cannot be constructed on a single unambiguous foundation, be it opposition to communism, containment of the Soviet Union, support for economic reform, or promotion of democracy. Instead, as has been emphasized throughout this study, the relationship between China and the United States will contain elements of cooperation and competition in almost every dimension. The two countries have complementary economies, possess a common desire for stability in Asia, and share the same global environment. But simultaneously they have different ideologies, political and economic systems, levels of development, and geopolitical locations. That makes differences of perspective on these same issues inevitable. Rather than portraying Sino-American relations as a pure convergence or a complete divergence of interests, as was often the case in the past, it will be wiser to portray them as a mixture of complementary and competitive objectives. Such a relationship will be primarily characterized not by antagonism, nor by harmony, but rather by hard bargaining with complicated trade-offs within and between issues.

Partly as a result, Sino-American relations may well be more contentious within the United States than has been true during past periods of hostility or cooperation, as different groups debate the interests they wish to promote in the relationship and the strategy to achieve them. Even if there can be a consensus in the United States about the appropriateness of the policy outlined here, there will continue to be controversy over many of the details, as Americans differ over how to promote human rights in China, how to obtain the benefits of economic relations, and how to address global issues with Peking. A similar situation will occur in China. Tensions will inevitably arise from the long-standing debate between those who want to reach out to the United States for technology, capital, ideas, and institutions, and those who fear that the consequence of such interactions will be economic dependence, strategic subordination, cultural contamination, and political instability.

U.S.-China relations will also be more diverse than in the recent past, as befits the interaction of a pluralistic America and an increasingly varied China. As noted earlier, although China may periodically tighten political controls, the trend toward a weakening of the state relative to Chinese society is unlikely to be completely reversed. Local governments and even individual commercial and academic institutions will gain more leeway to define their own relationships with their American counterparts than in earlier times. American organizations and individuals, in turn, will have the freedom to choose which parts of the country and which counterpart institutions to do business with. This reality suggests that the United States may have more active commercial relationships with cities and provinces that are more active in reform, and richer academic exchanges with universities and research institutions where the political climate is more relaxed. It also suggests that Chinese and Americans seeking cooperative activities may find it possible and desirable to work with a variety of local Chinese institutions, rather than always working through the central government in Peking.

Finally, the U.S.-China relationship should become less effusive and more realistic than it was in the late 1970s or the 1980s. Americans should not look to China as an ally against a common adversary, exaggerate the size of the Chinese market, or assume that a reforming China will soon develop a free-market economy and a pluralistic political system. The exaggerated rhetoric of the past—anointing China as an honorary member of NATO, exalting the purchasing power of one billion consumers, or declaring that China had renounced Marx and adopted capitalism—needs to be replaced by a more objective and balanced portrait. The Chinese need to understand the limits on their relationship with the United States. America cannot be expected to transfer large amounts of advanced military technology to China, provide vast quantities of economic assistance, offer unlimited opportunities for Chinese exports, devise solutions to China's economic and political problems, or ignore violations of human rights.

In redesigning their policy toward China, then, Americans would be best advised to strive not for a "special relationship" but for a normal one. U.S. China policy must be more balanced and less euphoric than it was before Tiananmen and more nuanced and less moralistic than it has been since then. This in turn will require some changes in the ways Americans have traditionally looked at China. In the quixotic search for a special relationship with China, the United States has typically tended toward simplistic, exaggerated, and emotional images of an extremely complex and often engimatic country. To cling to these familiar caricatures of China—as ally or adversary, as willing student or as ideological antagonist—will merely doom the United States to repeat the cycles of euphoria and disillusionment that have been so costly in the past.

Tables and Figure

Table A-1. *U.S. Public Opinion of China*
Percent

Year	Overall perception of China[a] Favorable	Overall perception of China[a] Unfavorable	Those who perceive China as important to United States[b] Elite	Those who perceive China as important to United States[b] Public	Perception of China's policy toward United States[c] Close ally or friend	Perception of China's policy toward United States[c] Neutral	Perception of China's policy toward United States[c] Unfriendly or enemy
1972	23	71	...	...	...	...	...
1973	49	43	...	...	...	...	...
1974	...	...	...	...	...	...	...
1975	28	58	...	...	...	...	...
1976	20	73	...	...	...	...	...
1977	26	52	...	...	...	...	...
1978	21	67	93	70	...	...	...
Normalization of relations							
1979	65	25	...	...	...	...	...
1980	70	26	...	...	...	...	...
1981	...	...	...	...	...	...	...
1982	...	...	87	64	24	39	23
1983	43	52	...	...	21	37	29
1984	...	...	...	...	29	33	25
1985	71	25	...	...	31	34	19
1986	...	...	89	60	...	...	...
1987	65	28	...	...	26	41	19
1988	...	...	...	...	26	35	19
1989[d]	72	13	...	...	...	...	...
Tiananmen crisis							
1989[e]	31	58	...	...	16	29	39
1990	39	47	73	47	16	31	30
1991	35	53	...	...	...	...	...

a. Jaw-ling Joanne Chang, *United States–China Normalization: An Evaluation of Foreign Policy Decision Making*, Monograph Series in World Affairs (University of Denver, Graduate School of International Studies, 1986), p. 126; *Gallup Opinion Index* (July 1972, June 1973, November 1976); *Gallup Report*, May 1989, August 1989); *Gallup Poll Monthly* (February 1990); William Watts, "American Views of the Soviet Union" (April 1987); and Roper Center for Public Opinion Research, *Public Opinion Online* (University of Connecticut, October 1991).

b. John E. Rielly, ed., *American Public Opinion and U.S. Foreign Policy* (Chicago Council on Foreign Relations, 1979, 1983, 1987, 1991).

c. *Roper Reports 90-10* (New York: Roper Organization, January 1991).

d. February 1989.

e. July 1989.

Table A-2. *U.S.-China Bilateral Trade, 1971–90*
Millions of current U.S. dollars and percent of totals

Year	U.S. imports from China	U.S. exports to China	Total bilateral trade	U.S. trade balance	Percent of total U.S. trade[a]	Percent of total PRC trade[a]
1971	4.7	0.0	4.7	-4.7	0.0	...
1972	32.2	60.2	92.4	28.0	0.1	...
1973	63.5	689.1	752.6	625.6	0.5	...
1974	114.4	806.9	921.2	692.5	0.4	...
1975	157.9	303.6	461.6	145.7	0.2	...
1976	201.5	134.4	335.9	-67.1	0.1	...
1977	200.7	171.3	372.1	-29.4	0.1	2.5
1978	324.0	820.7	1,144.6	496.7	0.3	5.4
1979	592.3	1,724.0	2,316.3	1,131.7	0.6	7.9
1980	1,058.3	3,754.4	4,812.7	2,696.1	1.0	12.7
1981	1,865.3	3,602.7	5,468.0	1,737.4	1.1	12.7
1982	2,283.7	2,912.1	5,195.8	628.4	1.1	12.7
1983	2,244.1	2,176.1	4,420.2	-68.0	0.9	10.2
1984	3,064.8	3,004.0	6,068.8	-60.8	1.1	11.8
1985	3,861.7	3,851.7	7,713.4	-9.9	1.4	10.9
1986	4,770.9	3,105.4	7,876.3	-1,665.5	1.3	10.5
1987	6,293.5	3,488.4	9,781.8	-2,805.1	1.4	11.8
1988	8,512.2	5,022.9	13,535.1	-3,489.3	1.7	13.2
1989	11,988.5	5,807.4	17,795.9	-6,181.1	2.1	16.1
1990	15,223.9	4,807.3	20,031.2	-10,416.6	2.2	17.6

Sources: Unless otherwise noted, data aggregated for each of the years shown from annual reports, Bureau of the Census, *U.S. Exports—World Areas, Country, Schedule B Commodity Groupings, and Method of Transportation Report FT 455* and *U.S. General Imports—World Area, Country, Schedule A Commodity Groupings, and Method of Transportation Report FT 155* (Government Printing Office).

a. International Monetary Fund, *International Financial Statistics Yearbook 1982* (Washington, 1982), pp. 67, 71, 149; IMF, *International Financial Statistics Yearbook 1989* (Washington, 1989), pp. 291, 723; and IMF, *International Financial Statistics* (Washington, August 1991), pp. 72–73, 166–69.

Table A-3. *Commodity Composition of U.S. Imports from China, 1971–90*
Millions of current U.S. dollars and percent of totals

Year	Agricultural products		Energy		Chemicals and other raw materials		Textiles: Fibers and fabrics		Finished apparel		Electronics		Other manufactures		Annual total
1971	3.5	74	0.0	0	0.7	14	0.2	5	0.1	2	0.0	0	0.2	6	4.7
1972	12.4	38	0.0	0	9.5	30	3.3	10	1.6	5	0.0	0	5.4	17	32.2
1973	15.3	24	0.4	1	25.1	39	9.9	16	2.6	4	0.0	0	10.2	16	63.5
1974	26.6	23	0.1	0	38.7	34	28.2	25	6.2	5	0.0	0	14.6	13	114.4
1975	25.7	16	0.0	0	71.5	45	32.8	21	10.2	6	0.0	0	17.7	11	157.9
1976	51.3	25	0.0	0	52.3	26	46.8	23	20.8	10	0.0	0	30.3	15	201.5
1977	57.0	28	0.9	0	47.5	24	35.1	17	30.3	15	0.0	0	29.9	15	200.7
1978	69.1	21	0.0	0	79.3	24	62.8	19	68.3	21	0.2	0	44.3	14	324.0
1979	86.6	15	96.4	16	111.3	19	64.5	11	171.8	29	0.4	0	61.3	10	592.3
1980	115.7	11	134.7	13	248.7	23	141.1	13	283.5	27	2.1	1	132.5	13	1,058.3
1981	331.3	18	263.5	14	311.4	17	243.3	13	485.9	26	6.1	1	223.8	12	1,865.3
1982	168.3	7	597.7	26	310.5	14	231.3	10	703.4	31	10.9	1	261.6	11	2,283.7
1983	159.0	7	429.6	19	267.0	12	240.7	11	851.5	38	13.2	1	283.1	13	2,244.1
1984	189.5	6	608.7	20	325.5	11	369.5	12	1,060.0	35	36.6	1	475.0	16	3,064.8
1985	206.4	5	986.0	26	392.4	10	374.2	10	1,165.3	30	55.1	1	682.3	18	3,861.7
1986	252.6	5	639.6	13	367.4	8	474.9	10	1,978.4	41	106.6	2	951.4	20	4,770.9
1987	351.7	6	476.8	8	521.2	8	521.3	8	2,429.1	39	394.0	6	1,599.4	25	6,293.5
1988	572.2	7	427.9	5	680.4	8	570.2	7	2,819.2	33	978.8	11	2,463.5	29	8,512.2
1989	608.7	5	504.0	4	819.1	7	354.7	3	4,457.1	37	1,638.0	14	3,606.9	30	11,988.5
1990	654.7	4	660.9	4	877.0	6	350.0	2	6,000.1	39	1,926.1	13	4,755.1	31	15,223.9

Source: Data aggregated for each of the years shown from Bureau of the Census, *U.S. General Imports—World Area, Country, Schedule A Commodity Groupings, and Method of Transportation Report FT 155.* Percentages may not total 100 because of rounding.

Table A-4. *Commodity Composition of U.S. Exports to China, 1971–90*
Millions of current U.S. dollars and percent of totals

Year	Agricultural products		Chemicals		Other raw materials		Heavy machinery		Electronics		Other manufactures		Annual total
1971	0.0	...	0.0	...	0.0	...	0.0	...	0.0	...	0.0	...	0.0
1972	58.2	97	0.0	0	0.0	0	0.1	0	0.0	0	1.9	3	60.2
1973	474.4	69	7.9	1	137.1	20	63.5	9	0.1	0	6.1	1	689.1
1974	466.7	58	10.2	1	213.4	26	100.2	12	2.2	0	14.2	2	806.9
1975	0.2	0	5.3	2	163.9	54	110.5	36	2.1	1	21.6	7	303.6
1976	0.0	0	10.4	8	50.6	38	61.8	46	1.8	1	9.8	7	134.4
1977	46.5	27	19.6	11	47.7	28	47.9	28	3.7	2	5.9	3	171.3
1978	421.9	51	60.2	7	220.8	27	35.2	4	18.8	2	63.8	8	820.7
1979	638.5	37	125.3	7	647.8	38	86.0	5	78.0	5	148.4	9	1,724.0
1980	1,508.2	40	381.7	10	1,405.4	37	230.7	6	106.6	3	121.8	3	3,754.4
1981	1,493.2	41	405.6	11	1,396.0	39	81.3	2	121.6	3	105.0	3	3,602.7
1982	1,321.2	45	496.7	17	785.2	27	71.2	2	143.0	5	94.8	3	2,912.1
1983	546.7	25	353.4	16	486.6	22	361.3	17	262.0	12	166.1	8	2,176.1
1984	612.3	20	644.3	21	597.9	20	509.9	17	367.0	12	272.6	9	3,004.0
1985	150.7	4	513.7	13	828.2	22	1,088.0	28	622.6	16	648.5	17	3,851.7
1986	70.7	2	441.9	14	515.8	17	811.9	26	710.9	23	554.2	18	3,105.4
1987	370.5	11	810.3	23	544.5	16	829.9	24	535.2	15	398.0	11	3,488.4
1988	736.6	15	1,392.5	28	1,092.6	22	695.2	14	605.3	12	500.7	10	5,022.9
1989	1,210.4	21	928.4	16	1,319.6	23	1,646.7	28	243.9	4	458.4	8	5,807.4
1990	548.4	11	893.4	19	1,082.7	23	1,667.7	35	264.1	5	351.0	7	4,807.3

Source: Data aggregated for each of the years shown from Bureau of the Census, *U.S. Exports—World Areas, Country, Schedule B Commodity Groupings, and Method of Transportation Report FT 455.* Percentages may not total 100 because of rounding.

Table A-5. *Chinese Students and Scholars Entering the United States, 1979–90*

Year	J-1 visas	F-1 visas	Total
CY 1979	807	523	1,330
CY 1980	1,986	2,338	4,324
CY 1981	3,066	2,341	5,407
CY 1982	3,327	1,153	4,480
CY 1983	3,328	1,003	4,331
CY 1984	4,420	1,677	6,097
CY 1985	6,912	3,001	9,913
CY 1986	7,673	5,038	12,711
FY 1987	7,903	4,535	12,438
FY 1988	8,684	5,114	13,798
FY 1989	7,700	6,448	14,148
FY 1990	5,161	8,330	13,491
Total	60,967	41,501	102,468

Sources: Figures for calendar years (CYs) 1979–86 are from Leo A. Orleans, *Chinese Students in America: Policies, Issues, and Numbers* (Washington: National Academy Press, 1988), p. 88. Updated figures for fiscal years 1987–90 (FYs) are from the Visa Office, Department of State, Washington. Between calendar year 1986 and fiscal year 1987 exists a three-month overlap, which may account for some statistically insignificant discrepancies.

Table A-6. *Americans in China, 1980–90*

Year	Sightseeing			Academic study	
	Total foreign tourists	U.S. tourists	Percent U.S. tourists	Academic year	Students
1980	529,100	101,500	19.18	...	...
1981	675,100	130,400	19.32	...	...
1982	764,500	145,200	18.99	...	...
1983	872,500	168,300	19.29	...	...
1984	1,134,300	212,300	18.72	...	...
1985	1,370,500	239,600	17.48	...	...
1986	1,482,300	291,800	19.69	1985–86	ca. 825
1987	1,727,800	315,300	18.25	...	...
1988	1,842,200	300,900	16.33	1987–88	1,300
1989	1,461,200	214,800	14.70	...	...
1990	1,747,000	233,000	13.34	1989–90	566

a. For each year from 1980 through 1987, see State Statistical Bureau, *Statistical Yearbook of China* (Hong Kong: Longman Group, Ltd.); for 1988 and 1989, see SSB, *China Statistical Yearbook* (Hong Kong: SSB); for 1990, see *China Statistical Monthly*, no. 1 (April 1991), p. 57.

b. Data supplied to author by Institute for International Education, based on their annual surveys published under the title, *Open Doors* (New York: IIE).

Table A-7. Foreign Direct Investment in China, 1978–90
Millions of current U.S. dollars and percent of totals

	Annual commitments[a]			Annual utilization[a]			U.S. direct investment overseas	
Year	Total foreign investment	U.S. commit- ments	U.S. as percent of total	Total foreign investment	U.S. con- tribution	U.S. as percent of total	Global[b]	Percent utilized in China
1978–81	4,837	116	2.40	1,121	9	0.80	n.a.	...
1982	700	187	26.71	649	4	0.62	970	0.43
1983	1,917	478	24.94	916	5	0.55	6,700	0.07
1984	2,875	165	5.74	1,419	263	18.53	11,590	2.27
1985	6,333	1,152	18.19	1,956	370	18.92	13,160	2.81
1986	3,330	526	15.79	2,245	326	14.52	18,690	1.75
1987	4,319	360	8.34	2,647	271	10.24	31,040	0.87
1988	6,191	384	6.20	3,740	244	6.52	16,210	1.51
1989	6,294	645	10.25	3,774	288	7.63	31,730	0.91
1990	6,986	400[c]	5.73	3,705	n.a.	n.a.	50,400	n.a.
Cumulative total	43,782	4,413	10.08	22,172	1,780	8.03	180,490	0.99

n.a. Not available.
a. Figures represent actual investment, not merely signed agreements. U.S.-China Business Council, *U.S. Investment in China* (Washington: China Business Forum, 1990), pp. 10–11. For 1990, *Business China* (Hong Kong), May 27, 1991, p. 76. Foreign investment figures include international leasing, compensation deals, and processing and assembly, which may be excluded in reporting by non-Chinese government publications.
b. For 1981, International Monetary Fund, *Balance of Payments Statistics*, vol. 40, pt. 1, *Yearbook* (Washington, 1989), pp. 752–53; for 1982–89, vol. 41, pt. 1, *Yearbook* (1990), pp. 735, 738; for 1990, vol. 42, pt. 1, *Yearbook* (1991), p. 14.
c. *Los Angeles Times*, December 1, 1990, pp. D1, D2. Based on statistics available for the first half of the year.

Table A-8. Taiwan-Mainland Trade, 1978–90
Millions of current U.S. dollars unless otherwise noted

	Trade[a]				Share of each economy's total trade[b]			
Year	Exports to mainland	Imports from mainland	Total bilateral trade	Taiwan's trade balance	Taiwan world trade	Percent of total Taiwan trade	PRC world trade	Percent of total mainland trade
1978	0.1	46.7	46.8	−46.6	23,733	0.20	21,086	0.22
1979	21.3	55.8	77.1	−34.5	30,874	0.25	29,235	0.26
1980	242.2	78.5	320.7	163.7	39,550	0.81	38,041	0.84
1981	390.2	76.3	466.5	313.9	43,655	1.07	43,139	1.08
1982	208.2	89.9	298.1	118.3	40,902	0.73	40,793	0.73
1983	168.6	96.0	264.6	72.6	45,394	0.58	43,539	0.61
1984	425.6	127.7	553.3	297.9	52,441	1.06	51,466	1.08
1985	988.0	116.0	1,104.0	872.0	50,820	2.17	70,450	1.57
1986	811.0	114.2	925.2	696.8	63,984	1.45	74,858	1.24
1987	1,226.8	289.0	1,515.8	937.8	88,622	1.71	82,934	1.83
1988	2,239.3	478.1	2,717.4	1,761.2	110,265	2.46	102,818	2.64
1989	2,896.5	586.9	3,483.4	2,309.6	118,702	2.93	110,295	3.16
1990	3,278.0	765.0	4,043.0	2,513.0	119,417	3.39	113,792	3.55

a. Chung Chin, "Trade Across the Straits," *Free China Review*, vol. 41 (January 1991), pp. 38–45. Includes only trade coordinated through Hong Kong. For 1990, *Far Eastern Economic Review*, June 6, 1991, p. 41.
b. International Monetary Fund, *International Financial Statistics Yearbook 1989* (Washington: IMF 1989), pp. 120–25; and IMF, *International Financial Statistics* (Washington, August 1991), pp. 72–73.

Table A-9. *Taiwan's Tourism and Investment in the Mainland,*
1986–90

Millions of current U.S. dollars unless otherwise noted

		Annual utilization			Taiwan direct investment overseas	
Year	Visits to mainland[a]	Total foreign investment[b]	Taiwan contribution[c]	Taiwan as percent of total	Global[d]	Percent utilized in China
1986	...	2,245	...	...	n.a.	...
1987	275,000	2,647	100	3.78	704	14.20
1988	450,000	3,740	450	12.03	4,100	10.98
1989	540,000	3,774	550	14.57	6,900	7.97
1990	n.a.	3,705	1,350	36.44	n.a.	n.a.

n.a. Not available.

a. For each year, *Almanac of China's Foreign Economic Relations and Trade* (Hong Kong; China's Resources Advertising Co., Ltd.).

b. Figures represent actual investment, not merely signed agreements. U.S.-China Business Council, *U.S. Investment in China* (Washington: China Business Forum, 1990), pp. 10–11. For 1990, *Business China* (Hong Kong), May 27, 1991, p. 76. Foreign investment figures include international leasing, compensation deals, and processing and assembly, which may be excluded in reporting by non-Chinese government publications.

c. For 1987, 1989, and 1990, U.S. embassy reporting based on Chinese and Hong Kong data.

d. Data supplied to author by Chung-Hua Institution for Economic Research, Taipei, Taiwan.

Table A-10. *U.S. Military Sales to Taiwan, 1972–90*
Thousands of current U.S. dollars

Fiscal year	FMS agreements	Commercial export deliveries	Commercial deliveries plus FMS agreements	FMS deliveries	Total deliveries
1972	72,261	5,697	77,958	35,347	41,044
1973	204,241	6,001	210,242	66,264	72,265
1974	72,826	8,086	80,912	92,763	100,849
1975	127,249	44,982	172,231	113,017	157,999
1976	327,353	42,531	369,884	134,269	176,800
1977	143,656	46,140	189,796	139,397	185,537
1978	336,107	73,637	409,744	134,178	207,815
1979	520,632	44,547	565,179	180,752	225,299
1980	455,449	57,770	513,219	209,059	266,829
1981	309,456	66,731	376,187	373,427	440,158
1982	524,155	75,000	599,155	386,343	461,343
1983	698,231	85,000	783,231	388,639	473,639
1984	707,217	70,000	777,217	274,896	344,896
1985	699,786	54,463	754,249	339,413	393,876
1986	510,416	228,400	738,816	247,291	475,691
1987	509,322	210,000	719,322	372,676	582,676
1988	505,062	195,069	700,131	488,068	683,137
1989	526,310	84,753	611,063	349,806	434,559
1990	509,998	149,963	659,961	573,981	723,944

Sources: For each year, see Security Assistance Agency, *Foreign Military Sales, Foreign Military Construction Sales and Military Assistance Facts* (Washington: Department of Defense). Because each year's publication provides an update of the previous ten years, consult the most recent yearbook that contains the year in question to obtain the most accurate figure.

Table A-11. *U.S. Military Sales to China, 1972–90*
Thousands of current U.S. dollars

Fiscal year	FMS agreements	Commercial export deliveries	Commercial deliveries plus FMS agreements	FMS deliveries	Total deliveries
1972	...	4	4	...	4
1973	...	0	0	...	0
1974	...	0	0	...	0
1975	...	0	0	...	0
1976	...	0	0	...	0
1977	...	1,023	1,023	...	1,023
1978	...	0	0	...	0
1979	...	0	0	...	0
1980	...	622	622	...	622
1981	...	0	0	...	0
1982	...	1,000	1,000	...	1,000
1983	...	209	209	...	209
1984[a]	629	8,037	8,666	6	8,043
1985	421	46,247	46,668	424	46,671
1986	36,069	55,243	91,312	547	55,790
1987	254,289	33,933	288,222	3,881	37,814
1988	14,129	48,891	63,020	39,122	88,013
1989	416	16,415	16,831	89,800	106,215
1990	0	3,615	3,615	0	3,615

Sources: For each year, see Security Assistance Agency, *Foreign Military Sales, Foreign Military Construction Sales and Military Assistance Facts* (Washington: Department of Defense). Because each year's publication provides an update of the previous ten years, consult the most recent yearbook that contains the year in question to obtain the most accurate figure.

a. China was made eligible for the foreign military sales (FMS) program in 1984.

Figure A-1. *Percent of Americans Having a Favorable Opinion of China*

Percent

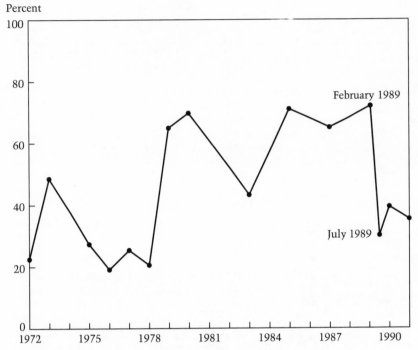

Source: Gallup Organization, Inc. Missing data points indicate years in which question was not asked.

The Shanghai Communiqué
February 27, 1972

Joint Communiqué Between the People's Republic of China and the United States of America

President Richard Nixon of the United States of America visited the People's Republic of China at the invitation of Premier Chou En-lai [Zhou Enlai] of the People's Republic of China from February 21 to February 28, 1972. Accompanying the President were Mrs. Nixon, U.S. Secretary of State William Rogers, Assistant to the President Dr. Henry Kissinger, and other American officials.

President Nixon met with Chairman Mao Tse-tung [Mao Zedong] of the Communist Party of China on February 21. The two leaders had a serious and frank exchange of views on Sino-U.S. relations and world affairs.

During the visit, extensive, earnest, and frank discussions were held between President Nixon and Premier Chou En-lai on the normalization of relations between the United States of America and the People's Republic of China, as well as on other matters of interest to both sides. In addition, Secretary of State William Rogers and Foreign Minister Chi P'eng-fei [Ji Pengfei] held talks in the same spirit.

President Nixon and his party visited Peking and viewed cultural, industrial and agricultural sites, and they also toured Hangchow [Hangzhou] and Shanghai where, continuing discussions with Chinese leaders, they viewed similar places of interest.

The leaders of the People's Republic of China and the United States of America found it beneficial to have this opportunity, after so many years without contact, to present candidly to one another their views

Source: *Public Papers of the Presidents of the United States: Richard Nixon, 1972* (Washington: Government Printing Office, 1974), pp. 376–79.

on a variety of issues. They reviewed the international situation in which important changes and great upheavals are taking place and expounded their respective positions and attitudes.

The U.S. side stated: Peace in Asia and peace in the world requires efforts both to reduce immediate tensions and to eliminate the basic causes of conflict. The United States will work for a just and secure peace: just, because it fulfills the aspirations of peoples and nations for freedom and progress; secure, because it removes the danger of foreign aggression. The United States supports individual freedom and social progress for all the peoples of the world, free of outside pressure or intervention. The United States believes that the effort to reduce tensions is served by improving communication between countries that have different ideologies so as to lessen the risks of confrontation through accident, miscalculation or misunderstanding. Countries should treat each other with mutual respect and be willing to compete peacefully, letting performance be the ultimate judge. No country should claim infallibility and each country should be prepared to re-examine its own attitudes for the common good. The United States stressed that the peoples of Indochina should be allowed to determine their destiny without outside intervention; its constant primary objective has been a negotiated solution; the eight-point proposal put forward by the Republic of Vietnam and the United States on January 27, 1972, represents a basis for the attainment of that objective; in the absence of a negotiated settlement the United States envisages the ultimate withdrawal of all U.S. forces from the region consistent with the aim of self-determination for each country of Indochina. The United States will maintain its close ties with and support for the Republic of Korea; the United States will support efforts of the Republic of Korea to seek a relaxation of tension and increased communication in the Korean peninsula. The United States places the highest value on its friendly relations with Japan; it will continue to develop the existing close bonds. Consistent with the United Nations Security Council Resolution of December 21, 1971, the United States favors the continuation of the ceasefire between India and Pakistan and the withdrawal of all military forces to within their own territories and to their own sides of the ceasefire line in Jammu and Kashmir; the United States supports the right of the peoples of South Asia to shape their own future in peace, free of military threat, and without having the area become the subject of great power rivalry.

The Chinese side stated: Wherever there is oppression, there is resistance. Countries want independence, nations want liberation and the people want revolution—this has become the irresistible trend of history. All nations, big or small, should be equal; big nations should not bully the small and strong nations should not bully the weak. China will never be a superpower and it opposes hegemony and power politics of any kind. The Chinese side stated that it firmly supports the struggles of all the oppressed people and nations for freedom and liberation and that the people of all countries have the right to choose their social systems according to their own wishes and the right to safeguard the independence, sovereignty and territorial integrity of their own countries and oppose foreign aggression, interference, control and subversion. All foreign troops should be withdrawn to their own countries.

The Chinese side expressed its firm support to the peoples of Vietnam, Laos, and Cambodia in their efforts for the attainment of their goal and its firm support to the seven-point proposal of the Provisional Revolutionary Government of the Republic Of South Vietnam and the elaboration of February this year on the two key problems in the proposal, and to the Joint Declaration of the Summit Conference of the Indochinese Peoples. It firmly supports the eight-point program for the peaceful unification of Korea put forward by the Government of the Democratic People's Republic of Korea on April 12, 1971, and the stand for the abolition of the "U.N. Commission for the Unification and Rehabilitation of Korea." It firmly opposes the revival and outward expansion of Japanese militarism and firmly supports the Japanese people's desire to build an independent, democratic, peaceful and neutral Japan. It firmly maintains that India and Pakistan should, in accordance with the United Nations resolutions on the India-Pakistan question, immediately withdraw all their forces to their respective territories and to their own sides of the ceasefire line in Jammu and Kashmir and firmly supports the Pakistan Government and people in their struggle to preserve their independence and sovereignty and the people of Jammu and Kashmir in their struggle for the right of self-determination.

There are essential differences between China and the United States in their social systems and foreign policies. However, the two sides agreed that countries, regardless of their social systems, should conduct their relations on the principles of respect for the sovereignty and territorial integrity of all states, non-aggression against other states, non-interference in the internal affairs of other states, equality and mutual benefit, and peaceful coexistence. International disputes should be settled on this basis, without resorting to the use or threat of force. The United States and the People's Republic of China are prepared to apply these principles to their mutual relations.

With these principles of international relations in mind the two sides stated that:

—progress toward the normalization of relations between China and the United States is in the interests of all countries;
—both wish to reduce the danger of international military conflict;
—neither should seek hegemony in the Asia-Pacific region and each is opposed to efforts by any other country or group of countries to establish such hegemony; and
—neither is prepared to negotiate on behalf of any third party or to enter into agreements or understandings with the other directed at other states.

Both sides are of the view that it would be against the interests of the peoples of the world for any major country to collude with another against other countries, or for major countries to divide up the world into spheres of interest.

The two sides reviewed the long-standing serious disputes between China and the United States. The Chinese side reaffirmed its position: The Taiwan question is the crucial question obstructing the normalization of relations between China and the United States; the Government of the People's Republic of China is the sole legal government of China; Taiwan is a province of China which has long been returned to the motherland; the liberation of Taiwan is China's internal affair in which no other country has the right to interfere; and all U.S. forces and military installations must be withdrawn from Taiwan. The Chinese Government firmly opposes any activities which aim at the creation of "one China, one Taiwan," "one China, two governments," "two Chinas," and "independent Taiwan" or advocate that "the status of Taiwan remains to be determined."

The U.S. side declared: The United States acknowledges that all Chinese on either side of the Taiwan Strait maintain there is but one China and that Taiwan is a part of China. The United States Government does not challenge that position. It reaffirms its interest in a peaceful settlement of the Taiwan question by the Chinese themselves. With this prospect in mind, it affirms the ultimate objective of the withdrawal of all U.S. forces and military installations from Taiwan. In the meantime, it will progressively reduce its forces and military installations on Taiwan as the tension in the area diminishes.

The two sides agreed that it is desirable to broaden the understanding between the two peoples. To this end, they discussed specific areas in such fields as science, technology, culture, sports and journalism, in which people-to-people contacts and exchanges would be mutually beneficial. Each side undertakes to facilitate the further development of such contacts and exchanges.

Both sides view bilateral trade as another area from which mutual benefits can be derived, and agreed that economic relations based on equality and mutual benefit are in the interest of the people of the two countries. They agree to facilitate the progressive development of trade between their two countries.

The two sides agreed that they will stay in contact through various channels, including the sending of a senior U.S. representative to Peking from time to time for concrete consultations to further the normalization of relations between the two countries and continue to exchange views on issues of common interest.

The two sides expressed the hope that the gains achieved during this visit would open up new prospects for the relations between the two countries. They believe that the normalization of relations between the two countries is not only in the interest of the Chinese and American peoples but also contributes to the relaxation of tension in Asia and the world.

President Nixon, Mrs. Nixon and the American party expressed their appreciation for the gracious hospitality shown them by the Government and people of the People's Republic of China.

Documents on the Normalization of U.S.-China Relations
December 15–16, 1978

Joint Communiqué on the Establishment of Diplomatic Relations Between the United States of America and the People's Republic of China, January 1, 1979

The United States of America and the People's Republic of China have agreed to recognize each other and to establish diplomatic relations as of January 1, 1979.

The United States of America recognizes the Government of the People's Republic of China as the sole legal Government of China. Within this context, the people of the United States will maintain cultural, commercial, and other unofficial relations with the people of Taiwan.

The United States of America and the People's Republic of China reaffirm the principles agreed on by the two sides in the Shanghai Communiqué and emphasize once again that:

—Both wish to reduce the danger of international military conflict.

—Neither should seek hegemony in the Asia-Pacific region or in any other region of the world and each is opposed to efforts by any other country or group of countries to establish such hegemony.

Sources: The joint communiqué is from *Public Papers of the Presidents of the United States: Jimmy Carter, 1978*, bk. 2(GPO, 1979), pp. 2264–66; the U.S. statement on diplomatic relations is also from *Public Papers: Jimmy Carter, 1978*, p. 2266; and the statement of the government of the People's Republic of China is from Xinhua, December 16, 1978, in Foreign Broadcast Information Service, *Daily Report: People's Republic of China*, December 18, 1978, p. A2.

—Neither is prepared to negotiate on behalf of any third party or to enter into agreements or understandings with the other directed at other states.

—The Government of the United States of America acknowledges the Chinese position that there is but one China and Taiwan is part of China.

—Both believe that normalization of Sino-American relations is not only in the interest of the Chinese and American peoples but also contributes to the cause of peace in Asia and the world.

The United States of America and the People's Republic of China will exchange Ambassadors and establish Embassies on March 1, 1979.

United States Statement on Diplomatic Relations Between the United States and the People's Republic of China, December 15, 1978

As of January 1, 1979, the United States of America recognizes the People's Republic of China as the sole legal government of China. On the same date, the People's Republic of China accords similar recognition to the United States of America. The United States thereby establishes diplomatic relations with the People's Republic of China.

On that same date, January 1, 1979, the United States of America will notify Taiwan that it is terminating diplomatic relations and that the Mutual Defense Treaty between the United States and the Republic of China is being terminated in accordance with the provisions of the Treaty. The United States also states that it will be withdrawing its remaining military personnel from Taiwan within four months.

In the future, the American people and the people of Taiwan will maintain commercial, cultural and other relations without official government representation and without diplomatic relations.

The Administration will seek adjustments to our laws and regulations to permit the maintenance of commercial, cultural, and other non-governmental relationships in the new circumstances that will exist after normalization.

The United States is confident that the people of Taiwan face a peaceful and prosperous future. The United States continues to have an interest in the peaceful resolution of the Taiwan issue and expects that the Taiwan issue will be settled peacefully by the Chinese themselves.

The United States believes that the establishment of diplomatic relations with the People's Republic will contribute to the welfare of the American people, to the stability of Asia where the United States has major security and economic interest, and to the peace of the entire world.

Statement of the Government of the People's Republic of China in Connection with the Establishment of China-U.S. Diplomatic Relations

As of January 1, 1979, the People's Republic of China and the United States of America recognize each other and establish diplomatic relations, thereby ending the prolonged abnormal relationship between them. This is a historic event in Sino-U.S. relations.

As is known to all, the Government of the People's Republic of China is the sole legal government of China and Taiwan is a part of China. The question of Taiwan was the crucial issue obstructing the normalization of relations between China and the United States. It has now been resolved between the two countries in the spirit of the Shanghai Communiqué and through their joint efforts, thus enabling the normalization of relations so ardently desired by the people of the two countries. As for the way of bringing Taiwan back to the embrace of the motherland and reunifying the country, it is entirely China's internal affair.

At the invitation of the U.S. Government, Teng Hsiao-ping [Deng Xiaoping], vice-premier of the State Council of the People's Republic of China, will pay an official visit to the United States in January 1979, with a view to further promoting the friendship between the two peoples and good relations between the two countries.

Documents on U.S. Arms Sales to Taiwan
August 17, 1982

United States-China Joint Communiqué on United States Arms Sales to Taiwan

1. In the Joint Communiqué on the Establishment of Diplomatic Relations on January 1, 1979, issued by the Government of the United States of America and the Government of the People's Republic of China, the United States of America recognized the Government of the People's Republic of China as the sole legal government of China, and it acknowledged the Chinese position that there is but one China and Taiwan is part of China. Within that context, the two sides agreed that the people of the United States would continue to maintain cultural, commercial, and other unofficial relations with the people of Taiwan. On this basis, relations between the United States and China were normalized.

2. The question of United States arms sales to Taiwan was not settled in the course of negotiations between the two countries on establishing diplomatic relations. The two sides held differing positions, and the Chinese side stated that it would raise the issue again following normalization. Recognizing that this issue would seriously hamper the development of United States-China relations, they have held further discussions on it, during and since the meetings between

Sources: The U.S.-China joint communiqué is from *Public Papers of the Presidents of the United States, Ronald Reagan, 1982*, bk. 2 (GPO 1983), pp. 1052–53; the statement of President Reagan on arms sales is also from *Public Papers: Ronald Reagan, 1982*, pp. 1053–54. The statement from the Ministry of Foreign Affairs of the PRC is from Xinhua, August 17, 1982, in Foreign Broadcast Information Service, *Daily Report: China*, August 17, 1982, pp. B2–B4; and the statement from the Ministry of Foreign Affairs of the Republic of China (Taiwan) is from Central News Agency (Taipei), August 17, 1982, in FBIS, *China*, August 17, 1982, p. VI.

President Ronald Reagan and Premier Zhao Ziyang and between Secretary of State Alexander M. Haig, Jr., and Vice Premier and Foreign Minister Huang Hua in October, 1981.

3. Respect for each other's sovereignty and territorial integrity and non-interference in each other's internal affairs constitute the fundamental principles guiding United States-China relations. These principles were confirmed in the Shanghai Communiqué of February 28, 1972, and reaffirmed in the Joint Communiqué on the Establishment of Diplomatic Relations which came into effect on January 1, 1979. Both sides emphatically state that these principles continue to govern all aspects of their relations.

4. The Chinese government reiterates that the question of Taiwan is China's internal affair. The Message to Compatriots in Taiwan issued by China on January 1, 1979, promulgated a fundamental policy of striving for peaceful reunification of the Motherland. The Nine-Point Proposal put forward by China on September 30, 1981, represented a further effort under this fundamental policy to strive for a peaceful solution to the Taiwan question.

5. The United States Government attaches great importance to its relations with China, and reiterates that it has no intention of infringing on Chinese sovereignty and territorial integrity, or interfering in China's internal affairs, or pursuing a policy of "two Chinas" or "one China, one Taiwan." The United States Government understands and appreciates the Chinese policy of striving for a peaceful resolution of the Taiwan question as indicated in China's Message to Compatriots in Taiwan issued on January 1, 1979, and the Nine-Point Proposal put forward by China on September 30, 1981. The new situation which has emerged with regard to the Taiwan question also provides favorable conditions for the settlement of United States-China differences over the question of United States arms sales to Taiwan.

6. Having in mind the foregoing statements of both sides, the United States Government states that it does not seek to carry out a long-term policy of arms sales to Taiwan, that its arms sales to Taiwan will not exceed, either in qualitative or in quantitative terms the level of those supplied in recent years since the establishment of diplomatic relations between the United States and China, and that it intends to reduce gradually its sales of arms to Taiwan, leading over a period of time to a final resolution. In so stating, the United States acknowledges China's consistent position regarding the thorough settlement of this issue.

7. In order to bring about, over a period of time, a final settlement of the question of United States arms sales to Taiwan, which is an

issue rooted in history, the two governments will make every effort to adopt measures and create conditions conducive to the thorough settlement of this issue.

8. The development of United States-China relations is not only in the interests of the two peoples but also conducive to peace and stability in the world. The two sides are determined, on the principle of equality and mutual benefit, to strengthen their ties in the economic, cultural, educational, scientific, technological and other fields and make strong, joint efforts for the continued development of relations between the governments and peoples of the United States and China.

9. In order to bring about the healthy development of United States-China relations, maintain world peace and oppose aggression and expansion, the two governments reaffirm the principles agreed on by the two sides in the Shanghai Communiqué and the Joint Communiqué on the Establishment of Diplomatic Relations. The two sides will maintain contact and hold appropriate consultations on bilateral and international issues of common interest.

Statement [of President Reagan] on United States Arms Sales to Taiwan

The U.S.-China Joint Communiqué issued today embodies a mutually satisfactory means of dealing with the historical question of U.S. arms sales to Taiwan. This document preserves principles on both sides, and will promote the further development of friendly relations between the governments and peoples of the United States and China. It will also contribute to the further reduction of tensions and to lasting peace in the Asia/Pacific region.

Building a strong and lasting relationship with China has been an important foreign goal of four consecutive American administrations. Such a relationship is vital to our long-term national security interests and contributes to stability in East Asia. It is in the national interest of the United States that this important strategic relationship be advanced. This communiqué will make that possible, consistent with our obligations to the people of Taiwan.

In working toward this successful outcome we have paid particular attention to the needs and interests of the people of Taiwan. My longstanding personal friendship and deep concern for their well-being is steadfast and unchanged. I am committed to maintaining the full range of contacts between the people of the United States and the people of Taiwan—cultural, commercial, and people-to-people contacts—which are compatible with our unofficial relationship. Such contacts will continue to grow and prosper and will be conducted with the dignity and honor befitting old friends.

Regarding future U.S. arms sales to Taiwan, our policy, set forth clearly in the communiqué, is fully consistent with the Taiwan Relations Act. Arms sales will continue in accordance with the act and with the full expectation that the approach of the Chinese Government to the resolution of the Taiwan issue will continue to be peaceful. We attach great significance to the Chinese statement in the communiqué regarding China's "fundamental" policy, and it is clear from our statements that our future actions will be conducted with this peaceful policy fully in mind. The position of the United States Government has always been clear and consistent in this regard. The Taiwan question is a matter for the Chinese people, on both sides of the Taiwan Strait, to resolve. We will not interfere in this matter or prejudice the free choice of, or put pressure on, the people of Taiwan in this matter. At the same time, we have an abiding interest and concern that any resolution be peaceful. I shall never waver from this fundamental position.

I am proud, as an American, at the great progress that has been made by the people on Taiwan over the past three decades, and of the American contribution to that process. I have full faith in the continuation of that process. My administration, acting through appropriate channels, will continue strongly to foster that development and to contribute to a strong and healthy investment climate thereby enhancing the well-being of the people of Taiwan.

Statement of the Spokesman of the Ministry of Foreign Affairs of the People's Republic of China

1. Following discussions, the Government of the People's Republic of China and the Government of the United States of America have reached agreement on the question of United States sale of arms to Taiwan. The two sides have released the joint communiqué simultaneously today.

The United States sale of arms to Taiwan is an issue which affects China's sovereignty. Back in 1978, when the two countries held negotiations on the establishment of diplomatic relations, the Chinese Government stated in explicit terms its opposition to the arms sales to Taiwan. As this issue could not be settled at that time, the

Chinese side suggested that the two sides continue discussions on the issue following the establishment of diplomatic relations. It is evident that failure to settle this issue is bound to impair seriously the relations between the two countries.

With a view to safeguarding China's sovereignty and removing the obstacle to the development of relations between the two countries, Premier Zhao Ziyang held discussions with President Ronald Reagan on this issue during the Cancun meeting in Mexico in October 1981. Subsequently, Vice Premier and Foreign Minister Huang Hua continued the discussions with Secretary of State Alexander M. Haig, Jr., in Washington. As from December 1981, the two sides started concrete discussions through diplomatic channels in Beijing. During this period, U.S. Vice-President George Bush, entrusted by President Reagan, paid a visit to China in May 1982 when he held discussions with the Chinese leaders on the same subject. The joint communiqué released by the two sides today is the outcome of repeated negotiations between China and the United States over the past ten months. It has laid down the principles and steps by which the question of U.S. arms sales to Taiwan should be settled.

2. The joint communiqué reaffirms the principles of respect for each other's sovereignty and territorial integrity and non-interference in each other's internal affairs as embodied in the Shanghai Communiqué and the joint communiqué on the establishment of diplomatic relations between China and the United States. Both sides also emphatically state that these principles continue to govern all aspects of their relations. That is to say, the question of U.S. arms sales to Taiwan must be settled on these principles. Needless to say, only by strictly observing these principles in dealing with the existing or new issues between the two countries will it be possible for their relations to develop healthily.

3. In compliance with the above principles governing the relations between the two countries, the U.S. arms sales to Taiwan should have been terminated altogether long ago. But considering that this is an issue left over by history, the Chinese Government, while upholding the principles, has agreed to settle it step by step. The U.S. side has committed that, as the first step, its arms sales to Taiwan will not exceed, either in qualitative or in quantitative terms, the level of those supplied in recent years since the establishment of diplomatic relations between the two countries, and that they will be gradually reduced, leading to a final resolution of this issue over a period of time. The final resolution referred to here certainly implies that the U.S arms sales to Taiwan must be completely terminated over a period of time. And only a thorough settlement of this

issue can remove the obstacles in the way of developing relations between the two countries.

4. In the joint communiqué, the Chinese Government reiterates in clear-cut terms its position that "the question of Taiwan is China's internal affair." The U.S. side also indicates that it has no intention of infringing on Chinese sovereignty and territorial integrity, or interfering in China's internal affairs, or pursuing a policy of "two Chinas" or "one China, one Taiwan." The Chinese side refers in the joint communiqué to its fundamental policy of striving for peaceful reunification of the motherland for the purpose of further demonstrating the sincere desire of the Chinese Government and people to strive for a peaceful solution to the Taiwan question. On this issue, which is purely China's internal affair, no misinterpretation or foreign interference is permissible.

5. It must be pointed out that the present joint communiqué is based on the principle embodied in the joint communiqué on the establishment of diplomatic relations between China and the United States and the basic norms guiding international relations and has nothing to do with the "Taiwan Relations Act" formulated unilaterally by the United States.

The "Taiwan Relations Act" seriously contravenes the principles embodied in the joint communiqué on the establishment of diplomatic relations between the two countries, and the Chinese Government has consistently been opposed to it. All interpretations designed to link the present joint communiqué to the "Taiwan Relations Act" are in violation of the spirit and substance of this communiqué and are thus unacceptable.

6. The agreement reached between the Governments of China and the United States on the question of U.S. arms sales to Taiwan only marks a beginning of the settlement of this issue. What is important is that the relevant provisions of the joint communiqué are implemented in earnest, so that the question of U.S. arms sales to Taiwan can be resolved thoroughly at an early date. This is indispensable to the maintenance and development of Sino-U.S. relations.

Statement of the Spokesman of the Ministry of Foreign Affairs of the Republic of China [Taiwan]

With regard to the joint communiqué issued on August 17, 1982, by the Government of the United States of America and the Chinese Communist regime, the Government of the Republic of China hereby reiterates its solemn position that it will consider null and void any agreement involving the rights and interests of the government and people of the Republic of China reached between the United States government and the Chinese Communist regime. The Government of the Republic of China makes further declarations as follows:

The supply of adequate defensive weapons to the Republic of China is an established arms sales policy of the United States of America, formulated by and executed within the stipulations of the Taiwan Relations Act.

Now the United States government has mistaken the fallacious "peaceful intention" of the Chinese Communists as sincere and meaningful and consequently acceded to the latter's demand to put [a] ceiling on both the quality and quantity of the arms to be sold to the Republic of China, it is in contravention of the letter and spirit of the Taiwan Relations Act, for which we must express our profound regret.

The Chinese Communists would always justify the means they choose to employ in attaining their aims. The alternating employment of peace talk and military action is their traditional, inveterate trick. The Chinese Communists are exerting all efforts in waging an international united front campaign, with a view to further isolating the Republic of China. They are seeking all possible means to interrupt and discontinue U.S. arms sales to the Republic of China, trying to pave the way for their military invasion of this country.

It is a serious mistake that the United States Government, failing to comprehend the real nature of the trick and fraud of the Chinese Communists, unwittingly issued the above-said document jointly with them.

During the process of discussions of the so-called joint communiqué, the U.S. side has kept the Government on the Republic of China informed of its developments, and at the same time the Government of the Republic of China has presented to the United States its consistent position of firmly opposing the issuance of such a document.

On July 14, 1982, the U.S. side, through appropriate channels, made the following points known to the Republic of China that the U.S. side:

1. Has not agreed to set a date for ending arms sales to the Republic of China.

2. Has not agreed to hold prior consultations with the Chinese Communists on arms sales to the Republic of China.

3. Will not play any mediation role between Taipei and Peiping.

4. Has not agreed to revise the Taiwan Relations Act.

5. Has not altered its position regarding sovereignty over Taiwan.

6. Will not exert pressure on the Republic of China to enter into negotiations with the Chinese Communists.

We earnestly hope that the United States Government will not be deceived by but will see through the Chinese Communists' plot in attempting to annex our base of national recovery and to divide the free world. We also hope that the United States, upholding her founding spirit of freedom and justice, will fully and positively implement the Taiwan Relations Act to continue providing us with defensive arms so as to maintain the stability and prosperity of the Republic of China and to safeguard the peace and security of the Asian-Pacific region.

NOTES

CHAPTER 1

1. Henry Kissinger, *White House Years* (Little, Brown, 1979), pp. 1054–55.
2. *Newsweek*, March 6, 1972, p. 15; Kissinger, *White House Years*, p. 1054; and Richard Nixon, *RN: The Memoirs of Richard Nixon* (Grosset and Dunlap, 1978), pp. 559, 565.
3. Leonard A. Kusnitz, *Public Opinion and Foreign Policy: America's China Policy, 1949–1979* (Westport, Conn.: Greenwood Press, 1984), p. 138.
4. Kissinger, *White House Years*, p. 1055.
5. Kissinger, *White House Years*, p. 1055.
6. Kissinger, *White House Years*, p. 1050.
7. According to one Chinese account, this was the view of Mao's wife Jiang Qing, conveyed to Zhou Enlai by the minister of culture. See Chen Dunde, *Mao Zedong he Nikesun: Zhongmei Jianjiao Jiemi* (Mao Zedong and Nixon: An expose of the establishment of diplomatic relations between China and the United States) (Hong Kong: Jinshi Press, 1989), p. 232.
8. Kusnitz, *Public Opinion and Foreign Policy*, p. 140, table 7; p. 117.
9. Nixon, *RN*, p. 562.
10. Nixon, *RN*, p. 580.
11. William Clarke and Martha Avery, "The Sino-American Relationship," in *China: A Reassessment of the Economy*, A compendium of papers submitted to the Joint Economic Committee, 94 Cong. 1 sess. (Washington: Government Printing Office, 1975), p. 505; and Department of Commerce, Bureau of the Census, *Historical Statistics of the United States, Colonial Times to 1937* (GPO, 1960), p. 537. Even with the spectacular growth in Sino-American trade in the 1970s and 1980s, that ratio has never been achieved again.

CHAPTER 2

1. Among the many works on the history of Sino-American relations since 1949, I have found the following most useful: Gordon H. Chang, *Friends and Enemies: The United States, China, and the Soviet Union, 1948–1972* (Stanford University Press, 1990); Banning N. Garrett, "The Strategic Basis of Learning in U.S. Policy toward China, 1949–1968," in George W. Breslauer and Philip E. Tetlock, eds., *Learning in U.S. and*

392   Notes (pages 27–33)

Soviet Foreign Policy (Westview Press, 1991), pp. 208–63; Nancy Bern-
kopf Tucker, *Patterns in the Dust: Chinese-American Relations and
the Recognition Controversy, 1949–1950* (Columbia University Press,
1983); David Allan Mayers, *Cracking the Monolith: U.S. Policy against
the Sino-Soviet Alliance, 1949–1955* (Louisiana State University Press,
1986); Warren I. Cohen, "The United States and China since 1945," in
Warren I. Cohen, ed., *New Frontiers in American–East Asian Relations:
Essays Presented to Dorothy Borg* (Columbia University Press, 1983),
pp. 129–67; and Harry Harding and Yuan Ming, eds., *Sino-American
Relations, 1945–1955: A Joint Reassessment of a Critical Decade* (Wilmington, Del.: SR Books, 1989).

2. The Chinese casualty figures are drawn from Xu Yan, *Diyici Jiaoliang:
Kangmei Yuanchao Zhanzhengde Lishi Huigu yu Fansi* (The first test
of strength: A review and reflection on the history of the war to resist
America and aid Korea) (Peking: China Broadcast Publishing House,
1990), p. 322. This figure is much lower than American estimates, which
put the number of Chinese deaths at more than one million. See R.
Ernest Dupuy and Trevor N. Dupuy, *The Encyclopedia of Military
History: From 3500 B.C. to the Present*, 2d ed. (Harper and Row, 1986),
pp. 1251–52. This is also the source for the number of Americans who
died in the conflict.

3. Quoted in Garrett, "The Strategic Basis of Learning," p. 215.

4. Quoted in Chang, *Friends and Enemies*, p. 85.

5. For details of the limits imposed on Taiwan by the United States, see
Leonard H. D. Gordon, "United States Opposition to Use of Force in
the Taiwan Strait, 1954–1962," *Journal of American History*, vol. 72
(December 1985), pp. 637–60.

6. Chang, *Friends and Enemies*, p. 321, n. 41.

7. This kind of planning is detailed in Chang, *Friends and Enemies*, chap. 8.
How much serious consideration was given to such plans is still in
dispute. For a criticism of Chang on this point, see the review of *Friends
and Enemies* by James C. Thomson, Jr., in *New York Times Book
Review*, July 29, 1990, p. 25.

8. This point is made by Cohen, "The United States and China since
1945," pp. 149–52; and by Thomas E. Stolper, *China, Taiwan, and the
Offshore Islands Together with an Implication for Outer Mongolia and
Sino-Soviet Relations* (Armonk, N.Y.: M. E. Sharpe, 1985), pp. 37–41.

9. Chang, *Friends and Enemies*, p. 272.

10. Nai-Ruenn Chen, "China's Foreign Trade, 1950–74," in *China: A Reas-
sessment of the Economy*, A compendium of papers submitted to the
Joint Economic Committee, 94 Cong. 1 sess. (Washington: Government
Printing Office, 1975), p. 649, table A.6.

11. Michel Oksenberg, "The Strategies of Peking," *Foreign Affairs*, vol. 50
(October 1971), p. 18.

12. A. Doak Barnett, *China and the Major Powers in East Asia* (Brookings,
1977), p. 178.

13. Stanley D. Bachrack, *The Committee of One Million: "China Lobby" Politics, 1953–1971* (Columbia University Press, 1976), pp. 152, 155–58.
14. "Statement of A. Doak Barnett, Professor of Government and Acting Director of the East Asian Institute, Columbia University, on China and the West," in *U.S. Policy with Respect to Mainland China*, Hearings before the Senate Committee on Foreign Relations, 89 Cong. 2 sess. (GPO, 1966), p. 4.
15. Leonard A. Kusnitz, *Public Opinion and Foreign Policy: America's China Policy, 1949–1979* (Westport, Conn.: Greenwood Press, 1984), pp. 95–130; and Jaw-ling Joanne Chang, *United States–China Normalization: An Evaluation of Foreign Policy Decision Making*, Monograph Series in World Affairs (University of Denver, Graduate School of International Studies, 1986), p. 26.
16. Throughout the early 1960s the public remained vehemently opposed to Peking's admission to the United Nations. See Kusnitz, *Public Opinion and Foreign Policy*, pp. 163–68.
17. Ironically, by the mid-1960s the American public had become more willing to support a flexible policy toward China, in the hope of avoiding conflict with Peking. The explosion of China's first nuclear bomb in 1964 and the escalation of American involvement in Vietnam were key turning points. See Kusnitz, *Public Opinion and Foreign Policy*, pp. 163–68.
18. Even before the election of 1968, Nixon had implied the desirability of some kind of change in American policy toward China. Writing in *Foreign Affairs* in the fall of 1967, he endorsed the emerging consensus by asserting that the integration of China into the "family of nations" should become a major objective of American policy in Asia. Continued isolation of China, he warned, would only encourage Peking to "nurture its fantasies, cherish its hates and threaten its neighbors." Richard M. Nixon, "Asia after Viet Nam," *Foreign Affairs*, vol. 46 (October 1967), p. 121. The interpretation of this article is still a subject of some controversy. Nixon implies that he came to office committed to an opening with China, an interpretation shared by Raymond Garthoff. See Nixon, *RN: The Memoirs of Richard Nixon* (Grosset and Dunlap, 1978), pp. 544ff.; and Raymond L. Garthoff, *Détente and Confrontation: American-Soviet Relations from Nixon to Reagan* (Brookings, 1985), pp. 213–16. Kissinger suggests that Nixon's motivations, at least in the short run, were largely tactical, seeking to give an impression of progress in Sino-American relations so as to gain leverage over the Russians and the Vietnamese, rather than wanting to secure a true détente with China. See Henry Kissinger, *White House Years* (Little, Brown, 1979), pp. 167–71. That interpretation, in turn, is shared by Allen S. Whiting, "Sino-American *Détente*," *China Quarterly*, no. 82 (June 1980), pp. 334–41. In the end, however, Nixon's original intentions are less important than the policy he actually conducted.
19. The account of Sino-American relations during the first Nixon administration (1969–72) is drawn largely from Kissinger, *White House Years*;

Nixon, *RN*, pp. 544–80; Garrett, "The Strategic Basis of Learning"; Garthoff, *Détente and Confrontation*; Marvin Kalb and Bernard Kalb, *Kissinger* (Little, Brown, 1974), chaps. 9 and 10; Jonathan D. Pollack, "The Opening to America, 1968–82," in Roderick MacFarquhar and John K. Fairbank, eds., *The Cambridge History of China*, vol. 15: *The People's Republic*, pt. 2: *Revolutions within the Chinese Revolution, 1966–1982* (Cambridge University Press, 1991), pp. 402–72; and Whiting, "Sino-American *Détente*." The Chinese perspective can be found in Xue Mouhong and Pei Jianzhang, eds., *Dangdai Zhongguo Waijiao* (Contemporary Chinese diplomacy) (Peking: Chinese Social Science Publishing House, 1987), pp. 217–25.

20. A convenient list of the American concessions in the commercial realm can be found in an appendix to Martha Avery and William Clarke, "The Sino-American Commercial Relationship," in Joint Economic Committee, *Chinese Economy Post-Mao*, vol. 1: *Policy and Performance*, 95 Cong. 2 sess. (GPO, 1978), pp. 761–63.

21. In fact, rather than reassuring Peking, this change in policy puzzled the Chinese, who at first regarded it as an unwelcome indication that the United States planned to reduce its ability to counterbalance the Soviet Union. It was only early in the Carter administration that they finally understood that the target of the second large war, which the United States was no longer proposing to fight, was to have been China, not the Soviet Union. See Jimmy Carter, *Keeping Faith: Memoirs of a President* (Bantam Books, 1982), pp. 192–93.

22. For the evidence that China was favorably impressed by the scaling back of American commitments in Asia, see Seymour M. Hersh, *The Price of Power: Kissinger in the Nixon White House* (Summit, 1983), p. 352.

23. Xue and Pei, *Dangdai Zhongguo Waijiao*, p. 219.

24. Xue and Pei, *Dangdai Zhongguo Waijiao*, p. 219.

25. *Time*, October 5, 1970, p. 12.

26. Edgar Snow, "A Conversation with Mao Tse-tung," *Life*, April 30, 1971, pp. 46–48. Interestingly, the Mao interview with Edgar Snow had virtually no impact in the United States: there was no interest in Washington in interviewing Snow, who was seen as excessively sympathetic to the Communists; the State Department did not even report on it until early April, months after Snow had met with Mao; that report did not mention Mao's invitation to Nixon to visit China, and it concluded that Snow felt there was little immediate prospect for any improvement in Sino-American relations. Kissinger, *White House Years*, p. 709; and Whiting, "Sino-American *Détente*," pp. 338–39.

27. *Peking Review*, vol. 14 (April 23, 1971), p. 5. According to one Chinese account, Peking had already decided to invite several foreign teams to visit China after the conclusion of the tournament. The Chinese delegation reported that the American team was very friendly and that its leader expressed an interest in visiting China. The Chinese Foreign Ministry and the State Physical Education and Sports Commission considered this option but concluded that it was premature. Moreover, they

felt that the first Americans to be invited to China should be more prominent than a group of Ping-Pong players. Zhou approved their report but sent it to Mao for his reference. Much to everyone's surprise, Mao overruled both his Foreign Ministry and his prime minister and decided to invite the team to China. See Qian Jiang, *"Bingbang Waijiao" Shimo* (The full story of "ping-pong diplomacy") (Peking: Dongfang Press, 1987), pp. 90–93, 113, 122.

28. Kissinger, *White House Years*, p. 714.
29. Nixon was particularly interested in Dewey, the unsuccessful Republican presidential candidate of 1948, until Kissinger informed him that "Dewey was no longer available, having died a few months previously." Kissinger, *White House Years*, pp. 715–17.
30. Nixon, *RN*, p. 552. Kissinger implies that the toast was not quite so exalted. Kissinger, *White House Years*, p. 727.
31. The signs of opposition in China that were visible to the American government at the time are summarized in Kissinger, *White House Years*, pp. 768–70; and Garthoff, *Détente and Confrontation*, pp. 235–36. For a retrospective overview of the debate in China, see Thomas M. Gottlieb, "Chinese Foreign Policy Factionalism and the Origins of the Strategic Triangle," R-1902-NA (Santa Monica: Rand Corporation, November 1977); and John W. Garver, *China's Decision for Rapprochement with the United States, 1968–1971* (Westview Press, 1982). There is as yet little detail from Chinese sources about differing opinions on the opening to the United States. One account claims that, when the Kissinger visit of July 1971 was announced, Albania, which had not been informed in advance, wrote Peking to complain. Knowing that Lin Biao opposed Zhou's efforts to improve Sino-American relations, Li Zuopeng, the political commissar of the Chinese navy, referred approvingly to the Albanian protest at a Politburo meeting. To his surprise, however, neither Lin nor any of his other associates backed him up, suggesting that they did not choose to openly resist Mao and Zhou at this point. See Chen Dunde, *Mao Zedong he Nikesun: Zhongmei Jianjiao Jiemi* (Mao Zedong and Nixon: An expose of the establishment of diplomatic relations between China and the United States) (Hong Kong: Jinshi Press, 1989), pp. 179–80.
32. Chang, *United States–China Normalization*, p. 124, table 4; and Kusnitz, *Public Opinion and Foreign Policy*, pp. 164–65, table 16.
33. Kissinger, *White House Years*, pp. 770–74.
34. For a summary of the distribution of opinion in the State Department, see the analysis by Harvey Feldman quoted in Chang, *United States–China Normalization*, pp. 107–08.
35. Nixon, *RN*, p. 547.
36. Kissinger, *White House Years*, pp. 751–53.
37. Kissinger, *White House Years*, p. 727.
38. To facilitate the American exit from Vietnam, Peking urged Hanoi to drop its previous demand that the Saigon government under Nguyen Van Thieu be dismantled as part of a negotiated settlement with the

United States. It also transmitted warnings that the United States was prepared to escalate its airstrikes against North Vietnam unless such an agreement could be reached. There is no evidence, however, to support Hanoi's later charges that Peking sought to perpetuate the division of Vietnam. Instead, Chinese leaders seemed to assume that, without direct American military support, the Thieu government would eventually collapse. See John W. Garver, "Sino-Vietnamese Conflict and the Sino-American Rapprochement," *Political Science Quarterly*, vol. 96 (Fall 1981), pp. 445–64; and Jonathan D. Pollack, *The Lessons of Coalition Politics: Sino-American Security Relations*, R-3133-AF (Santa Monica: Rand Corporation, February 1984), pp. 31–32.

39. Garthoff, *Détente and Confrontation*, pp. 232–33.
40. This aspect of the visit is not mentioned in Kissinger's memoirs, but it is discussed in Xue and Pei, *Dangdai Zhongguo Waijiao*, pp. 221–22.
41. Xue and Pei, *Dangdai Zhongguo Waijiao*, p. 222.
42. Kissinger, *White House Years*, pp. 780–83. Kissinger wryly notes that much of the language that he had found to be unacceptable ended up in the maiden Chinese speech before the United Nations General Assembly that fall. See p. 786.
43. Kissinger, *White House Years*, p. 1073. On Nixon's thoughts on the timing of normalization, see also *New York Times*, April 11, 1977, pp. 1, 5; and *Washington Post*, December 17, 1978, pp. A1, A12.
44. Each of these phrases departed subtly but significantly from the wording that the Chinese preferred. Peking wanted the United States to make a firm pledge to withdraw all its forces from Taiwan, but Kissinger insisted on describing this aim merely as an objective to be pursued, rather than a commitment to be fulfilled. China also wanted the United States to acknowledge that Taiwan was a province of China, a much stronger statement than the actual text. For a fascinating and detailed review of the negotiations over this section of the Shanghai communiqué, see Kissinger, *White House Years*, pp. 1077–79.
45. These assurances were later known by the Carter administration as "Nixon's five points." See Zbigniew Brzezinski, *Power and Principle: Memoirs of the National Security Adviser 1977–1981* (Farrar, Straus, Giroux, 1983), p. 198, which sketches out the contents of the five points but does not say when they were presented to the Chinese. The Chinese account reveals that they were put forward during Nixon's visit to Peking but diplomatically leaves out Nixon's reference to Japan. See Xue and Pei, *Dangdai Zhongguo Waijiao*, pp. 223–24.
46. This was because of pressure from the State Department representatives on the Nixon delegation, including Secretary of State William Rogers and Assistant Secretary Marshall Green, who tried unsuccessfully at the last minute to have the United States revise the text of the Shanghai communiqué to reiterate its commitment to the mutual defense treaty. Nixon was so furious at this that he considered firing Rogers. See Chang, *United States–China Normalization*, p. 101; and Hersh, *The Price of Power*, pp. 497–99.

47. This strategy is summarized in Oksenberg, "A Decade of Sino-American Relations," *Foreign Affairs*, vol. 61 (Fall 1982), pp. 178–79, and is described more fully in Kissinger, *Years of Upheaval* (Little, Brown, 1982), pp. 59–60.

48. *New York Times*, July 18, 1972, p. 3. Ford's memoirs do not mention any specific reference to Asia but reiterate that Zhou vigorously criticized any possible reduction of American military spending. Gerald R. Ford, *A Time to Heal* (Harper and Row, 1979), pp. 97–98.

49. *Newsweek*, December 24, 1973, p. 7. This overture, if it occurred, is not mentioned in Kissinger's memoirs.

50. "Statement of Banning Garrett, Research Associate, Institute of International Studies, University of California at Berkeley," in *The United States and the People's Republic of China: Issues for the 1980's*, Hearings before the Subcommittee on Asian and Pacific Affairs of the House Committee on Foreign Affairs, 96 Cong. 2 sess. (GPO, 1980), pp. 96–108.

51. This account is drawn from Xue and Pei, *Dangdai Zhongguo Waijiao*, p. 225; and from Kissinger, *Years of Upheaval*, pp. 44–71, 688. The two accounts differ in several respects. Kissinger agrees that he informed Zhou that, with the end of the Vietnam conflict, the forces supporting American activities there could be removed from Taiwan but does not say that this would have meant the withdrawal of all U.S. troops from the island. Second, Kissinger reports that Zhou reassured him that China "had no intention of liberating Taiwan by force 'at this time' " a statement that does not appear in the Chinese account. (*Years of Upheaval*, p. 47.) Third, the Chinese account claims that Kissinger specifically proposed an exchange of liaison offices, whereas Kissinger says that he casually listed several options, ranging from trade offices to consulates to liaison offices.

52. Kissinger, *Years of Upheaval*, pp. 61–62.

53. *New York Times*, November 11, 1973, p. 1.

54. Kissinger, *Years of Upheaval*, p. 692. Interestingly, this crucial visit is not discussed in the Chinese account, indirectly confirming that the Chinese made initiatives they would later retract.

55. *New York Times*, November 17, 1973, p. 16, and November 18, 1973, p. E4.

56. *New York Times*, March 22, 1974, p. 3, and March 31, 1974, p. E5; and *Newsweek*, October 14, 1974, pp. 21–22.

57. Kissinger, *Years of Upheaval*, p. 698.

58. For this analysis, see *New York Times*, December 2, 1974, p. 2.

59. *New York Times*, December 5, 1975, p. 18. Ford recalls that Mao reiterated his opposition to Soviet-American détente, urging the United States to "remain strong in the Pacific basin" and "be willing to challenge the Soviets everywhere." Ford, *A Time to Heal*, p. 336.

60. For an overview of the Nixon visit of February 1976, see *New York Times*, February 28, 1976, p. 3.

61. The relative weight of these considerations, especially the first two factors, immediately became a matter of some debate among American

observers. Many Democrats and many China specialists insisted that it was because the two countries were unable to find a suitable formula for the United States to redefine its relations with Taiwan and establish formal diplomatic ties with Peking. Henry Kissinger, in contrast, has downplayed the significance of the Taiwan issue in contributing to the stalemate in the mid-1970s, just as he has denigrated the importance of Taiwan as an obstacle to the original breakthrough in Sino-American relations between 1969 and 1972. At the time, he and his lieutenants consistently insisted that the Chinese never expressed any dissatisfaction with American policy toward Taiwan. "If there are any problems," one U.S. official declared in 1974, "they haven't told us about them." (Maynard Parker, "Rising Suspicion in Peking," *Newsweek*, October 14, 1974, p. 21. See also *New York Times*, September 5, 1974, p. 3, and December 2, 1974, p. 2.) Indeed, by late 1975, Kissinger was presenting the thesis that the Taiwan issue was simply a kind of control rod, manipulated by the Chinese to warm up or cool down the Sino-American relationship, but that the decision to do so was based on geopolitical considerations. (*New York Times*, October 20, 1975, pp. 1, 12.) A more dispassionate judgment would be that both issues were of genuine concern to Chinese leaders.

62. Kissinger, *Years of Upheaval*, p. 51.
63. Kissinger, *Years of Upheaval*, pp. 49, 54.
64. Kissinger, *Years of Upheaval*, p. 70.
65. Radio Peking Domestic Service, August 5, 1975, in Foreign Broadcast Information Service, *Daily Report: China*, August 6, 1975, pp. A1–A2. On China's reaction to the Sonnenfeldt Doctrine, see *New York Times*, April 21, 1976, p. 10.
66. According to the Chinese, this was a proposal that Zhou Enlai had made to Kosygin at their meeting at Peking airport in 1969, but that the Soviet Union had never honored. See Harry Harding, "The Domestic Politics of China's Global Posture, 1973–78," in Thomas Fingar and the Stanford Journal of International Studies, eds., *China's Quest for Independence: Policy Evolution in the 1970s* (Westview Press, 1980), p. 103.
67. For a fuller discussion, see Harding, "The Domestic Politics of China's Global Posture," pp. 93–146.
68. On China's reactions to this development, see *New York Times*, November 9, 1975, p. 1.
69. William Shawcross, "Cynicism after a Fleeting Affair," *Far Eastern Economic Review*, May 13, 1974, pp. 30–32.
70. *Newsweek*, October 14, 1974, p. 21.
71. Xue and Pei, *Dangdai Zhongguo Waijiao*, p. 226. Other evidence also suggests that some preliminary planning was done in the final months of the Nixon administration to find a "plausible substitute" for the mutual defense treaty, to include some combination of American statements reiterating Washington's commitment to the security of Taiwan, a Chinese renunciation of force against the island, guarantees that the

Taiwan Strait would be an international waterway open to all, and continued American arms sales to Taipei. This may have been the background to Kissinger's initiative to Deng. See the essay by Eugene K. Lawson, who had served on the Taiwan desk in the State Department during the Nixon administration: "Taiwan: We Forgot Who Held the Trump Cards," in *Washington Post*, December 29, 1978, p. A15.

72. On Deng's response to Kissinger in November 1974, see Xue and Pei, *Dangdai Zhongguo Waijiao*, p. 226. Deng would not allow his remarks to the American Society of Newspaper Editors to be quoted, but the substance of his comments was recorded in an internal memorandum prepared by one of the editors present at the meeting.

73. A Gallup poll in 1975 indicated that only 10 percent favored normalization of relations with China on such terms, whereas 70 percent of the public opposed it. Chang, *United States–China Normalization*, p. 124.

74. Ford, *A Time to Heal*, p. 337.

75. The quotation is from Oksenberg, "A Decade of Sino-American Relations," p. 180. See also Chang, *United States–China Normalization*, pp. 88–89; and Cyrus Vance, *Hard Choices: Critical Years in America's Foreign Policy* (Simon and Schuster, 1983), p. 82. The Chinese account is virtually identical, adding that Ford also promised to cut the remaining contingent of American troops on Taiwan in half in the meantime. Xue and Pei, *Dangdai Zhongguo Waijiao*, p. 226.

76. Michael Pillsbury, "U.S.-Chinese Military Ties?" *Foreign Policy*, no. 20 (Fall 1975), pp. 50–64.

77. *New York Times*, April 12, 1976, p. 10. For contemporary discussion of the issue, see *New York Times*, October 4, 1975, p. 3. For analysis, see Garrett, "The Strategic Basis of Learning," esp. pp. 228ff.

78. *New York Times*, January 1, 1976, p. 16.

79. *New York Times*, July 28, 1976, p. 29.

80. Banning N. Garrett, "The China Card," Ph.D. diss., Brandeis University, 1983, pp. 49–50; and *New York Times*, April 26, 1976, p. 3.

81. On this policy, see *New York Times*, April 25, 1976, pp. 1, 4. On the controversy that it generated within the U.S. government, see *Washington Post*, October 29, 1976, p. A13.

82. For the American decision, see *New York Times*, May 8, 1971, p. 8.

83. *New York Times*, February 15, 1972, pp. 1, 6.

84. *New York Times*, July 6, 1972, pp. 1, 53.

85. *New York Times*, August 27, 1974, p. 13.

86. *New York Times*, March 27, 1973, pp. 1, 61.

87. For an overview, see Douglas P. Murray, "Exchanges with the People's Republic of China: Symbols and Substance," *Annals*, vol. 424 (March 1976), pp. 29–42.

88. The number of members of Congress to visit China is drawn from Robert G. Sutter, *The China Quandary: Domestic Determinants of U.S. China Policy, 1972–1982* (Westview Press, 1983), p. 22. See also table 9 in Chang, *United States–China Normalization*, pp. 140–41.

89. *New York Times*, March 23, 1973, p. 10.
90. *New York Times*, January 22, 1973, p. 1; and August 6, 1973, p. 7. This ratio would soon widen to 15:1. See Sutter, *China Quandary*, p. 21.
91. Sutter, *China Quandary*, p. 21.
92. *New York Times*, December 11, 1974, pp. 1, 5.
93. On the cancellation of the performing arts troupe, see *New York Times*, March 28, 1975, p. 16. For the Chinese perspective on the two incidents, see *Peking Review*, vol. 18 (April 11, 1975), pp. 10, 21, and vol. 18 (September 26, 1975), p. 27.
94. Jerome Alan Cohen, "U.S.-China Relations," *New York Times*, December 18, 1974, p. 45.
95. China's retrenchment efforts included the cancellation of several contracts for the purchase of American corn and soybeans. See *New York Times*, January 26, 1975, section 3, p. 30, January 28, 1975, pp. 1, 54, and February 28, 1975, pp. 43, 47.
96. See the article by Foreign Trade Minister Li Qiang in *China's Foreign Trade* quoted in Xinhua, July 9, 1974, in FBIS, *China*, July 9, 1974, pp. A1–A3.
97. See *New York Times*, January 5, 1975, section 3, p. 3; and November 28, 1975, pp. 1, 63.
98. *New York Times*, May 7, 1973, pp. 61, 63.
99. *China News Summary*, no. 511 (April 4, 1974), and no. 537 (October 2, 1974).
100. *Hongqi*, no. 5 (1976), in *Peking Review*, vol. 19 (June 11, 1976), pp. 8–12; and *Hongqi*, no. 7 (1976), in *Peking Review*, vol. 19 (August 27, 1976), pp. 6–9.
101. See Ann Fenwick, "Chinese Foreign Trade Policy and the Campaign against Deng Xiaoping," in Fingar and Stanford Journal, *China's Quest for Independence*, pp. 199–224; and Kent Morrison, "Domestic Politics and Industrialization in China: The Foreign Trade Factor," *Asian Survey*, vol. 18 (July 1978), pp. 687–705.
102. *Wall Street Journal*, January 25, 1977, p. 15; and *New York Times*, March 28, 1977, pp. 43, 48.
103. Sheila K. Johnson, "To China, with Love," *Commentary*, June 1973, p. 42.
104. Steven W. Mosher, *China Misperceived: American Illusions and Chinese Reality* (Basic Books, 1990), chaps. 6, 7.
105. Harry Harding, "From China, with Disdain: New Trends in the Study of China," *Asian Survey*, vol. 22 (October 1982), p. 936.
106. James Reston, "China Is Building a New Nation," in Frank Ching, ed., *The New York Times Report from Red China* (Avon Books, 1971), p. 246; and Reston, "New China: 'A Sink of Morality'," in Ching, *Report from Red China*, p. 239.
107. Seymour Topping, "Stores Give Customers a Better Deal," in Ching, *Report from Red China*, p. 195.
108. David Rockefeller, "From a China Traveler," *New York Times*, August 10, 1973, p. 31. Rockefeller went on to acknowledge, however, that

these achievements had involved "a stiff price . . . in terms of cultural and intellectual constraint."

109. Michel Oksenberg, "Comments," in Ping-ti Ho and Tang Tsou, eds., *China in Crisis*, vol. 1: *China's Heritage and the Communist Political System*, bk. 2 (University of Chicago Press, 1968), p. 493. Other volumes containing such interpretations include Richard Baum with Louise B. Bennett, eds., *China in Ferment: Perspectives on the Cultural Revolution* (Prentice-Hall, 1971); Victor Nee and James Peck, eds., *China's Uninterrupted Revolution: From 1840 to the Present* (Pantheon, 1975); and John G. Gurley, *China's Economy and the Maoist Strategy* (New York: Monthly Review Press, 1976).

110. Richard Baum, "The Cultural Revolution in Retrospect," in Baum with Bennett, *China in Ferment*, p. 177.

111. That proposition was the premise of Michel Oksenberg, ed., *China's Developmental Experience* (Praeger, 1973). For a further assessment of American views of the Cultural Revolution in the 1970s, see Harry Harding, "Reappraising the Cultural Revolution," *Wilson Quarterly*, vol. 4 (Autumn 1980), pp. 132–41.

112. Kissinger, *White House Years*, pp. 745, 746.

113. *Time*, April 26, 1971, p. 88.

114. See, for example, "The Chinese Look: Mao à la Mode," *Time*, July 21, 1975, pp. 50–51.

115. *New York Times*, March 1, 1972, p. 38; and C. L. Sulzberger, "Judging the Peking Picnic," *New York Times*, March 3, 1972, p. 39.

116. The press reaction to the Nixon visit is summarized in Kissinger, *White House Years*, pp. 1091–92.

117. Harriet Van Horne, "Tourism or Diplomacy?" *New York Post*, December 3, 1975, p. 42.

118. "Euphoria Has Faded for Some Visitors to China," *Los Angeles Times*, October 9, 1976, pp. 1, 26.

119. See, for example, *New York Times*, October 31, 1973, pp. 61, 71.

120. Kissinger, *White House Years*, p. 754.

121. Congressional reports during this period are surveyed in Sutter, *China Quandary*, pp. 22–34.

122. Peter R. Moody, *Opposition and Dissent in Contemporary China* (Stanford: Hoover Institution Press, 1977); and Susan L. Shirk, "Human Rights: What about China?" *Foreign Policy*, no. 29 (Winter 1977–78), pp. 109–27. One should also cite the study produced by Richard L. Walker, *The Human Cost of Communism in China*, published in 1971, that estimated that the Communist revolution had been responsible for between 34 million and 64 million deaths over the previous fifty years. *The Human Cost of Communism in China*, Study prepared at the request of Senator Thomas J. Dodd, Senate Judiciary Committee (GPO, 1971), p. 16.

123. See, for instance, Donald S. Zagoria, "China by Daylight," *Dissent*, vol. 22 (Spring 1975), pp. 135–47; and Edward N. Luttwak, "Seeing China Plain," *Commentary*, December 1976, pp. 27–33.

124. Johnson, "To China, with Love," passim; and Stanley Karnow, "China through Rose-Tinted Glasses," *Atlantic*, October 1973, pp. 73–76.
125. *Newsweek*, March 6, 1972, p. 15; and *A Gallup Study of Public Attitudes toward Nations of the World: The Findings for Nationalist China* (Princeton, N.J.: Gallup Organization, 1974).
126. Kusnitz, *Public Opinion and Foreign Policy*, p. 146, table 7; and The Gallup Opinion Index, *Political, Social, and Economic Trends*, Report no. 136 (November 1976), p. 11.
127. "Chiang Ch'ing's Speech to Foreign Affairs Cadres" (March 1975), *Chinese Law and Government*, vol. 9 (Spring–Summer 1976), p. 53.
128. See Fenwick, "Chinese Foreign Trade Policy," pp. 204ff.
129. Hua Kuo-feng, "Political Report to the Eleventh National Congress of the Communist Party of China" (August 1977), in *The Eleventh National Congress of the Communist Party of China (Documents)* (Peking: Foreign Languages Press, 1977), p. 61.
130. The poems are quoted in Ross Terrill, *The Future of China after Mao* (Delta, 1978), pp. 296, 297.
131. Ivan D. London and Miriam B. London, "Rumor as a Footnote to Chinese National Character," *Psychological Reports*, vol. 37 (1975), pp. 343–49. The Londons suggest the rumor might have been "elaborated upon and processed in some central agency for nationwide distribution," but it is equally plausible that it was transmitted spontaneously.

CHAPTER 3

1. Zbigniew Brzezinski, *Power and Principle: Memoirs of the National Security Adviser 1977–1981* (Farrar, Straus, Giroux, 1983), chap. 6.
2. If forced to choose between establishing formal diplomatic relations with Peking and maintaining the existing diplomatic ties with Taipei, the public chose Taiwan by a five-to-one margin in 1977 and by a three-to-one margin in 1978. Leonard A. Kusnitz, *Public Opinion and Foreign Policy: America's China Policy, 1949–1979* (Westport, Conn.: Greenwood Press, 1984), pp. 143–44. See also William Watts, Ralph N. Clough, and Robert B. Oxnam, *The United States and China: American Perceptions and Future Alternatives* (Washington: Potomac Associates, 1977), pp. 31–33.
3. See Thomas M. Gottlieb, "The Hundred-Day Thaw in China's Soviet Policy," *Contemporary China*, vol. 3 (Summer 1979), pp. 3–14.
4. For contemporary discussions, see *New York Times*, April 11, 1977, pp. 1, 5; and Stanley Karnow, "Our Next Move on China," *New York Times Magazine*, August 14, 1977, p. 38. For retrospective analyses, see Brzezinski, *Power and Principle*, pp. 48–57; and Cyrus R. Vance, *Hard Choices: Critical Years in America's Foreign Policy* (Simon and Schuster, 1983), pp. 76–78.

5. Brzezinski, *Power and Principle,* pp. 51–52, 197.
6. This discussion of the process of normalizing Sino-American relations draws on the memoirs of four of the principal participants on the American side: Brzezinski, *Power and Principle;* Jimmy Carter, *Keeping Faith: Memoirs of a President* (Bantam Books, 1982); Michel Oksenberg, "A Decade of Sino-American Relations," *Foreign Affairs,* vol. 61 (Fall 1982), pp. 175–95; and Vance, *Hard Choices.* It is also based on the following secondary analyses: Raymond L. Garthoff, *Détente and Confrontation: American-Soviet Relations from Nixon to Reagan* (Brookings, 1985); Banning N. Garrett, "The Strategic Basis of Learning in U.S. Policy toward China, 1949–1968," in George W. Breslauer and Philip E. Tetlock, eds., *Learning in U.S. and Soviet Foreign Policy* (Westview Press, 1991), pp. 208–63; Jaw-ling Joanne Chang, *United States–China Normalization: An Evaluation of Foreign Policy Decision Making,* Monograph Series in World Affairs (University of Denver, Graduate School of International Studies, 1986); and Yufan Hao, *Solving the Dilemma in China Policy, 1978–1979: A Case Study of Normalization of U.S.–China Relations and the Taiwan Relations Act,* Ph.D. diss., Johns Hopkins University, School of Advanced International Studies, 1989.
7. The best survey of the debate is Robert G. Sutter, *The China Quandary: Domestic Determinants of U.S. China Policy, 1972–1982* (Westview Press, 1983), chap. 3. See also Chang, *United States–China Normalization.*
8. This section of PRM-24 is summarized in Oksenberg, "A Decade of Sino-American Relations," pp. 181–82.
9. Oksenberg, "A Decade of Sino-American Relations," p. 181.
10. *San Francisco Sunday Examiner and Chronicle,* June 26, 1977, p. A3; and Robert L. Downen, *The Taiwan Pawn in the China Game: Congress to the Rescue* (Georgetown University, Center for Strategic and International Studies, 1979), p. 22.
11. Carter, *Keeping Faith,* pp. 190–91; and Oksenberg, "A Decade of Sino-American Relations," pp. 181–82.
12. Vance, *Hard Choices,* p. 78.
13. Vance, *Hard Choices,* pp. 76–78.
14. The quotations from PRM-24 are drawn from the *New York Times,* June 24, 1977, pp. A1, A3, as is the account of the debate in the Carter administration on military cooperation with China.
15. Vance, *Hard Choices,* p. 113.
16. Vance, *Hard Choices,* p. 79. On the evolving design of the Vance visit, see Oksenberg, "A Decade of Sino-American Relations," p. 182.
17. *New York Times,* August 27, 1977, p. 7.
18. On the Vance visit, see Vance, *Hard Choices,* pp. 79–83; Oksenberg, "A Decade of Sino-American Relations," p. 182; and Xue Mouhong and Pei Jianzhang, eds., *Dangdai Zhongguo Waijiao* (Contemporary Chinese diplomacy) (Peking: Chinese Social Science Publishing House, 1987), pp. 227–28.

19. Vance, *Hard Choices*, p. 79.
20. *New York Times*, September 7, 1977, pp. A1, A2; and Vance, *Hard Choices*, p. 82.
21. On the importance of these issues to the failure of the Vance visit, see Garrett, "The Strategic Basis of Learning," pp. 208–63. Without referring specifically to either PRM-10 or PRM-24, Oksenberg also acknowledges that "the Carter Administration had done little to that point to generate Chinese respect for the firmness of its overall foreign policy" but instead was giving the impression of "an Administration oblivious to the Soviet global design." Oksenberg, "A Decade of Sino-American Relations," p. 183.
22. Carter, *Keeping Faith*, pp. 192–93.
23. *Oakland Tribune*, February 5, 1978, p. 1.
24. Garthoff, *Détente and Confrontation*, pp. 593, 602.
25. The new Chinese position was authoritatively revealed in Hua Guofeng's report to the National People's Congress in February. See Hua Guofeng, "Unite and Strive to Build a Modern, Powerful Socialist Country," February 26, 1978, in *Documents of the First Session of the Fifth National People's Congress of the People's Republic of China* (Peking: Foreign Languages Press, 1978), pp. 112–13. For analysis of the Chinese position, see *New York Times*, March 21, 1978, p. 7; and *Washington Post*, March 21, 1978, p. A18. On the subsequent Soviet military maneuvers, see *Washington Post*, April 6, 1978, p. A9.
26. On the deterioration of Sino-Vietnamese relations, see Robert S. Ross, *The Indochina Tangle: China's Vietnam Policy, 1975–1979* (Columbia University Press, 1988). On Deng's trip through Southeast Asia, see *New York Times*, November 6, 1978, pp. 1, 12.
27. Oksenberg, "A Decade of Sino-American Relations," pp. 183–84; and Brzezinski, *Power and Principle*, pp. 202–06.
28. President Carter's letter of instructions to Brzezinski is reprinted as annex I in Brzezinski, *Power and Principle*, pp. 551–55. See also Brzezinski, *Power and Principle*, pp. 207–08.
29. Oksenberg, "A Decade of Sino-American Relations," p. 185.
30. These American demands are contained in Carter, *Keeping Faith*, pp. 190–91. Vance says that these conditions were based on recommendations he had made in a memorandum to the president on May 10, which was endorsed by Brzezinski and Brown. Vance, *Hard Choices*, pp. 115–16. For the Chinese version of the Brzezinski visit, which differs only in minor details from the American version, see Xue and Pei, *Dangdai Zhongguo Waijiao*, p. 228.
31. Brzezinski, *Power and Principle*, pp. 218–19. But Washington continued to urge the Chinese to speak in conciliatory terms of the "reunification" of Taiwan and the mainland, rather than to use the traditional and bellicose phrase the "liberation of Taiwan."
32. Brzezinski, *Power and Principle*, p. 551; and *Time*, June 5, 1978, p. 19. As Brzezinski remembers, the loser was to fight the Cubans, not the

Russians. (Brzezinski, *Power and Principle*, p. 210.) The Chinese responded in kind. Posing for a photograph with a group of Chinese sailors he encountered at the Great Wall, Brzezinski asked if they knew they were posing with an "imperialist." The sailors rejected Brzezinski's self-description, responding that they were having "a photograph taken with the polar-bear tamer." *Time*, June 5, 1978, p. 19.

33. This strategy is identified in Oksenberg, "A Decade of Sino-American Relations," p. 186.

34. Vance, *Hard Choices*, p. 117.

35. This aspect of the strategy is described in Carter, *Keeping Faith*, pp. 197–99, as well as in Oksenberg, "A Decade of Sino-American Relations," pp. 185–86. The technique was opposed by Brzezinski, who felt it would be best to reveal the entire American negotiating position at the beginning of the talks. (Brzezinski, *Power and Principle*, p. 224.)

36. James C. H. Shen, *The U.S. and Free China: How the U.S. Sold Out It's Ally* (Acropolis Books, 1983), p. 218. Jonathan D. Pollack, *The Lessons of Coalition Politics: Sino-American Security Relations*, R-3133-AF (Santa Monica: Rand Corporation, February 1984), pp. 34–35. See also *New York Times*, July 1, 1978, p. 2, and November 7, 1978, p. 9.

37. Carter, *Keeping Faith*, p. 198.

38. Oksenberg, "A Decade of Sino-American Relations," pp. 187–88.

39. Background briefing distributed by the White House, December 15, 1978.

40. The quotation is drawn from the Chinese government statement found in appendix C. The press conference given by Party Chairman Hua Guofeng was reported by Xinhua, December 16, 1978, in Foreign Broadcast Information Service, *Daily Report: People's Republic of China*, December 18, 1978, pp. A4–A8. (Hereafter FBIS, *China*.)

41. Deng's visit is brilliantly chronicled in Orville Schell, *"Watch Out for the Foreign Guests!" China Encounters the West* (Pantheon, 1980).

42. Carter, *Keeping Faith*, p. 209.

43. Brzezinski, *Power and Principle*, p. 214; and Oksenberg, "A Decade of Sino-American Relations," p. 188.

44. On congressional reaction and on the redrafting of the Taiwan Relations Act, see Hao, *Solving the Dilemma*, pp. 270–74; Louis W. Koenig, James C. Hsiung, and King-yuh Chang, eds., *Congress, the Presidency, and the Taiwan Relations Act* (Praeger, 1985); Ramon H. Myers, ed., *A Unique Relationship: The United States and the Republic of China under the Taiwan Relations Act* (Hoover Institution Press, 1989); Downen, *The Taiwan Pawn*; Jacob K. Javits, "Congress and Foreign Relations: The Taiwan Relations Act," *Foreign Affairs*, vol. 60 (Fall 1981), pp. 54–62; and Lester L. Wolff and David L. Simon, eds., *Legislative History of the Taiwan Relations Act: An Analytic Compilation with Documents on Subsequent Developments* (Jamaica, N.Y.: American Association for Chinese Studies, 1982).

45. Hao, *Solving the Dilemma*, pp. 303–22.

46. Vance, *Hard Choices*, p. 118.
47. Michel Oksenberg, "Congress, Executive-Legislative Relations, and American China Policy," in Edmund S. Muskie, Kenneth Rush, and Kenneth W. Thompson, eds., *The President, the Congress, and Foreign Policy* (University Press of America, 1986), pp. 207–30. Senator Jacob Javits later insisted, however, that "either on the manner and timing of the decision nor on the substance of the understandings reached had there been effective consultation." Javits, "Congress and Foreign Relations," p. 55.
48. Carter, *Keeping Faith*, p. 197; and Hao, *Solving the Dilemma*, pp. 301–2.
49. Hao, *Solving the Dilemma*, p. 312.
50. Moreover, the drafting of the Taiwan Enabling Act did not even begin until after December 15, as part of the administration's attempt to keep secret the details of the negotiations with the Chinese. See Harvey Feldman, "A New Kind of Relationship: Ten Years of the Taiwan Relations Act," in Myers, *A Unique Relationship*, p. 27; and Oksenberg, "Congress, Executive-Legislative Relations, and American China Policy," pp. 215–19.
51. See appendix C. Several members of the Carter administration have said that the White House did not submit the text of a congressional resolution on the future of Taiwan because they knew that Congress would have broadened anything that the president proposed. See Oksenberg, "Congress, Executive-Legislative Relations, and American China Policy," p. 217.
52. *New York Times*, October 18, 1979, p. A1, A6, December 1, 1979, pp. 1, 26, and December 14, 1979, p. A13.
53. Some of these amendments were suggested by representatives from Taiwan's embassy in Washington. Feldman, "A New Kind of Relationship," p. 32.
54. Feldman, "A New Kind of Relationship," p. 28.
55. Feldman, "A New Kind of Relationship," pp. 30–31.
56. On the ways in which the Taiwan Relations Act was drafted to give the president this discretion, see Richard Bush, "Helping the Republic of China to Defend Itself," in Myers, *A Unique Relationship*, pp. 79–118.
57. For the Chinese reaction, see Xue and Pei, *Dangdai Zhongguo Waijiao*, pp. 232–34. The Chinese charged that the TRA amounted to the continuation of the mutual defense treaty and the restoration of official U.S.-Taiwan relations, and thus violated the principles of the normalization agreement.
58. Carter, *Keeping Faith*, p. 200.
59. Kusnitz, *Public Opinion and Foreign Policy*, pp. 145–46.
60. Garthoff, *Détente and Confrontation*, pp. 232–33.
61. The most comprehensive analysis of the strategic relationship between China and the United States in 1978 is in Garthoff, *Détente and Confrontation*, pp. 701–06. See also Garrett, "The Strategic Basis of Learning"; and Pollack, *Lessons of Coalition Politics*. See *New York Times*, May 28, 1978, pp. 1, 6.

62. These issues were debated in the process of drafting PRM-31 on technology transfer to Communist countries. See *New York Times*, January 4, 1978, p. A7, and June 9, 1978, pp. A1, A5. For Vance's recollections of this issue, see Vance, *Hard Choices*, pp. 114, 117.
63. Brzezinski, *Power and Principle*, pp. 203, 206.
64. *New York Times*, June 25, 1978, pp. 1, 7, and November 8, 1978, p. A3.
65. *Time*, February 5, 1979, p. 34.
66. Brzezinski, *Power and Principle*, p. 406; and Carter, *Keeping Faith*, pp. 204–05.
67. Deng's presentation to Carter on this question is described in Brzezinski, *Power and Principle*, pp. 408–14.
68. Pollack, *Lessons of Coalition Politics*, pp. 41–44. For evidence of China's interest in acquiring American weapons, see *New York Times*, March 8, 1979, p. A5.
69. Carter, *Keeping Faith*, pp. 206–09.
70. Brzezinski, *Power and Principle*, p. 413.
71. Chinese analysts are divided on the significance of Peking's overtures in 1979. Some regard them simply as a tactical device for defusing the tensions inevitably generated by the Chinese war with Vietnam and by the termination of the Sino-Soviet alliance of 1950; these analysts think no breakthrough in Sino-Soviet relations was ever anticipated. Others insist that the initiatives were part of a genuine desire for improved ties with Moscow. Both groups agree, however, that the failure of the Soviet Union to respond in a forthcoming manner doomed the negotiations to stalemate.
72. See *New York Times*, October 4, 1979, pp. A1, A8; *New York Times*, January 4, 1980, p. A2; the column by William Safire, "The Chinese Morsel," in *New York Times*, January 21, 1980, p. A23; and *Aviation Week and Space Technology*, April 14, 1980, p. 15. See also Vance, *Hard Choices*, p. 390.
73. *Washington Post*, June 25, 1989, pp. A1, A24.
74. The discussion of the U.S. military supply relationship with China draws on Pollack, *Lessons of Coalition Politics*, pp. 59–72.
75. "Statement of Honorable Richard C. Holbrooke, Assistant Secretary of State for East Asian and Pacific Affairs," in *The United States and the People's Republic of China: Issues for the 1980's*, Hearings before the Subcommittee on Asian and Pacific Affairs of the House Committee on Foreign Affairs, 96 Cong. 2 sess. (Washington: Government Printing Office, 1980), p. 3.
76. Vladimir N. Pregelj, "Normalization of U.S. Commercial Relations with the People's Republic of China: United States Statutory and Regulatory Aspects," in *China under the Four Modernizations, pt. 2: Selected Papers Submitted to the Joint Economic Committee*, 97 Cong. 2 sess. (GPO, 1982), p. 162.
77. Pollack, *Lessons of Coalition Politics*, pp. 63–64.
78. *Washington Post*, June 25, 1989, pp. A1, A24.

79. Pollack, *Lessons of Coalition Politics*, p. 55.
80. For details, see Harry Harding, "China and the Third World: From Revolution to Containment," in Richard H. Solomon, ed., *The China Factor: Sino-American Relations and the Global Scene* (Prentice-Hall, 1981), pp. 257–95; and Harry Harding, "China's Changing Roles in the Contemporary World," in Harry Harding, ed., *China's Foreign Relations in the 1980s* (Yale University Press, 1984), pp. 177–223.
81. The United States unfroze all of China's assets, totaling $80.5 million, whereas China also agreed to pay $80.5 million, or about 41 percent, of American financial claims totaling $197 million. For background on the issue, see Richard T. Devane, "The United States and China: Claims and Assets," *Asian Survey*, vol. 18 (December 1978), pp. 1267–79. On the final agreement and its implementation, see Natalie G. Lichtenstein, "Unfrozen Assets: The 1979 Claims Settlement between the United States and China," in *China under the Four Modernizations*, pp. 316–28.
82. Philip T. Lincoln, Jr., and James A. Kilpatrick, "The Impact of Most-Favored-Nation Tariff Treatment on U.S. Imports from the People's Republic of China," in Joint Economic Committee, *Chinese Economy Post-Mao: A Compendium of Papers*, vol. 1: *Policy and Performance*, 95 Cong. 2 sess. (GPO, 1978), pp. 812–39.
83. Deng's exchange with Carter on this issue is reported in Carter, *Keeping Faith*, p. 209, and in Brzezinski, *Power and Principle*, p. 407.
84. These reforms are analyzed in Harry Harding, *China's Second Revolution: Reform after Mao* (Brookings, 1987), chap. 6.
85. Patricia A. Haas, "The United States–China Joint Economic Committee," in *China under the Four Modernizations*, pp. 368–81.
86. Throughout the 1980s, however, this review was routine. Although the bilateral trade agreement that had extended most-favored-nation (MFN) status to China was opposed in congressional hearings in 1979 by representatives of the textile industry, the mushroom industry, the AFL-CIO, and human rights organizations, after 1980 there was no testimony against continuing MFN treatment to China until after the Tiananmen incident.
87. Oksenberg, "A Decade of Sino-American Relations," p. 190.
88. As Michel Oksenberg described the strategy in June 1979, the goal was that "most government agencies with the legislative mandate and with the budget to do so will have initiated programs with their Chinese counterpart agencies." "A Conversation with Michel Oksenberg," *Rackham Reports*, vol. 5 (June 1979), p. 1. See also Oksenberg, "The Dynamics of the Sino-American Relationship," in Solomon, *The China Factor*, pp. 48–80.
89. *Wall Street Journal*, February 9, 1979, p. 12.
90. Carter, *Keeping Faith*, pp. 198–99.
91. The estimates were made by the National Council for U.S.-China Trade. See *San Francisco Chronicle*, December 21, 1978, p. 21.
92. On the popularity of "Man from Atlantis," see *New York Times*, January

28, 1980, p. A10. On the film festival, see *New York Times*, July 7, 1980, p. A3.

93. The targets of Hope's jokes ranged from California Governor Jerry Brown to Raquel Welch. The hapless Chinese translator confessed several times to the audience that he couldn't understand some of the material, asking Hope at one point, "Who is Billy Graham?" On the Hope visit, see *Washington Post*, July 5, 1979, p. B12; and *New York Times*, July 5, 1979, p. A8.

94. See the description in Randall E. Stross, *Bulls in the China Shop and Other Sino-American Business Encounters* (Pantheon, 1990), pp. 50–52.

95. Oksenberg, "A Decade of Sino-American Relations," p. 189.

96. Carter, *Keeping Faith*, p. 196; and Brzezinski, *Power and Principle*, p. 406.

97. Carter, *Keeping Faith*, pp. 202, 208, 211.

98. *New York Times*, September 1, 1979, p. 5.

99. On the Boeing and Coca-Cola deals, see *New York Times*, December 20, 1978, pp. D1, D12, and December 25, 1978, pp. A1, D12.

100. *San Francisco Sunday Examiner and Chronicle*, December 17, 1978, p. C13.

101. For a typical example of the more cautious views expressed after normalization, see *New York Times*, December 19, 1978, pp. D1, D17.

102. *New York Times*, February 4, 1979, p. 10.

103. William Watts, *Americans Look at Asia: A Need for Understanding* (Washington: Potomac Associates, November 1980), pp. 7, 48.

104. *San Francisco Sunday Examiner and Chronicle*, March 18, 1979, p. A19.

105. *New York Times*, May 31, 1979, pp. D1, D11; *Wall Street Journal*, May 15, 1980, p. 34; and *Wall Street Journal*, July 25, 1980, p. 17.

106. These were reflected in a series of congressional hearings and workshops in 1980. On Taiwan, see Senate Committee on Foreign Relations, *Implementation of the Taiwan Relations Act: The First Year*, 96 Cong. 2 sess. (GPO, 1980); *Implementation of the Taiwan Relations Act*, Hearings before the Subcommittee on Asian and Pacific Affairs of the House Committee on Foreign Affairs, 96 Cong. 2 sess. (GPO, 1981); Senate Committee on Foreign Relations, *Taiwan: One Year after United States–China Normalization*, report of a workshop sponsored by the Committee and the Congressional Research Service, 96 Cong. 2 sess. (GPO, 1980). On the military relationship, see *The United States and the People's Republic of China*; and, somewhat later, Senate Committee on Foreign Relations, *The Implications of U.S.-China Military Cooperation*, report of a workshop sponsored by the Committee and the Congressional Research Service, 97 Cong. 1 sess. (GPO, 1981). See also David M. Lampton, "Misreading China," *Foreign Policy*, no. 45 (Winter 1981–82), pp. 103–14.

107. Watts, *Americans Look at Asia*, p. 36; Schell, "*Watch Out for the Foreign Guests!*", pp. 118–19.

108. *Time,* February 12, 1979, p. 16.
109. Chai Zemin, address at the 13th Annual National Committee Members' Meeting, September 17, 1979, New York. *Renmin Ribao,* June 18, 1980, in FBIS, *China,* June 18, 1980, p. B3. Li Xiannian had also expressed the same view; see Xinhua, April 27, 1980, in FBIS, *China,* April 28, 1980, p. B3.
110. See, for example, *Washington Post,* March 31, 1980, p. A14.
111. *San Francisco Chronicle,* November 11, 1978, p. 10.
112. See, for example, *Beijing Review,* January 26, 1979, pp. 9–22.
113. Ralph N. Clough, *Chinese Elites: World View and Perceptions of the U.S.,* Research Report R-15-82 (Washington: International Communication Agency, August 1982), p. 22.
114. Xinhua, April 20, 1980, in FBIS, *China,* April 22, 1980, p. B1; and Xinhua, April 5, 1980, in FBIS, *China,* April 7, 1980, p. L9.
115. *New York Times,* February 20, 1979, p. A14.
116. See Michael H. Hunt, *The Making of a Special Relationship: The United States and China to 1914* (Columbia University Press, 1983); and Michael H. Hunt, *Ideology and U.S. Foreign Policy* (Yale University Press, 1987).
117. Hunt, *Ideology and U.S. Foreign Policy,* p. 42.
118. Hunt, *The Making of a Special Relationship,* p. 299.
119. Tu Wei-ming, "Chinese Perceptions of America," in Michel Oksenberg and Robert B. Oxnam, eds., *Dragon and Eagle: United States–China Relations: Past and Future* (Basic Books, 1978), p. 93.
120. *Time,* February 12, 1979, p. 16.
121. *New York Times,* January 8, 1980, p. A3.

CHAPTER 4

1. Ronald Reagan, "Expanding Our Ties with China," *New York Times,* July 28, 1976, p. 31.
2. Reagan, "Expanding Our Ties"; and *New York Times,* December 17, 1978, pp. 1, 18.
3. *Washington Post,* April 24, 1980, pp. A1, A2; *New York Times,* August 25, 1980, p. A18; and *New York Times,* July 13, 1980, p. A14.
4. *Wall Street Journal,* July 23, 1980, p. 26; *Washington Post,* August 24, 1980, pp. A1, A3; and *New York Times,* August 23, 1980, p. A9.
5. *Washington Post,* August 24, 1980, pp. A1, A3.
6. *Renmin Ribao,* August 26, 1980, p. 6, in Foreign Broadcast Information Service, *Daily Report: China,* August 26, 1980, pp. B1–B2. (Hereafter FBIS, *China.*)
7. Excerpts from the text of the statement are in *New York Times,* August 26, 1980, p. B7.
8. *New York Times,* August 26, 1980, pp. B7, A1.

9. Alexander M. Haig, Jr., *Caveat: Realism, Reagan, and Foreign Policy* (Macmillan, 1984), p. 200. See also Harvey Feldman, "A New Kind of Relationship: Ten Years of the Taiwan Relations Act," in Ramon H. Myers, ed., *A Unique Relationship: The United States and the Republic of China under the Taiwan Relations Act* (Stanford: Hoover Institution Press, 1989), pp. 25–48.

10. *New York Times*, June 17, 1981, pp. A1, A16.

11. For the rumors, see Xinhua, January 27, 1981, in FBIS, *China*, January 28, 1981, p. B1; for the denial, see *Wall Street Journal*, January 19, 1981, p. 22.

12. Michel Oksenberg, "A Decade of Sino-American Relations," *Foreign Affairs*, vol. 61 (Fall 1982), p. 188.

13. Xue Mouhong and Pei Jianzhang, eds., *Dangdai Zhongguo Waijiao* (Contemporary Chinese diplomacy) (Peking: Chinese Social Science Publishing House, 1987), p. 236.

14. Haig, *Caveat*, p. 210; Xue and Pei, *Dangdai Zhongguo Waijiao*, p. 236; Martin L. Lasater, *The Taiwan Issue in Sino-American Strategic Relations* (Westview Press, 1984), p. 182; and *Ta Kung Pao*, December 31, 1981, p. 2, and *Hsin Wan Pao*, December 31, 1981, p. 2, both in FBIS, *China*, December 31, 1981, pp. W2–W4.

15. Xue and Pei, *Dangdai Zhongguo Waijiao*, p. 236.

16. On the negotiations, see Haig, *Caveat*, pp. 211–15; Xue and Pei, *Dangdai Zhongguo Waijiao*, pp. 236–37; Jaw-ling Joanne Chang, "Negotiation of the 17 August 1982 U.S.–PRC Arms Communiqué: Beijing's Negotiating Tactics," *China Quarterly*, no. 125 (March 1991), pp. 33–54; and Brewer S. Stone and Frederick L. Holborn, "Dealing with China: Negotiating Normalization and Renormalization," unpublished manuscript, August 1988.

17. Chang, "Negotiation," p. 42.

18. *Renmin Ribao*, December 31, 1981, p. 6, in FBIS, *China*, December 31, 1981, pp. B1–B3; and Lasater, *The Taiwan Issue*, pp. 191–92.

19. This fact, and the content of the six points, was revealed in a statement issued by Taiwan after the publication of the communiqué of August 17. The text of Taiwan's statement is in appendix D. The content of the six points was confirmed in testimony before the Senate Foreign Relations Committee on August 17. See "Statement of Hon. John H. Holdridge, Assistant Secretary, Bureau of East Asian and Pacific Affairs, Department of State," in *U.S. Policy toward China and Taiwan*, Hearing before the Senate Committee on Foreign Relations, 97 Cong. 2 sess. (Washington: Government Printing Office, 1982), pp. 13–14, 16–17.

20. Lasater, *The Taiwan Issue*, pp. 203–05, 215–17.

21. *U.S. Policy toward China and Taiwan*, pp. 3–4. Other statements of congressional concern can be found in *China-Taiwan: United States Policy*, Hearing before the House Committee on Foreign Affairs, 97 Cong. 2 sess. (GPO, 1982).

22. See, in particular, "Statement of Hon. John H. Holdridge," p. 13; and "Statement of Davis R. Robinson, Legal Adviser, Department of State,"

in *Taiwan Communiqué and Separation of Powers,* Hearings before the Subcommittee on Separation of Powers of the Senate Committee on the Judiciary, 97 Cong. 2 sess. (GPO, 1982), p. 95.

23. This interpretation was conveyed to Ambassador Hummel by Deng Xiaoping on August 17, just before the communiqué was publicly released. Xue and Pei, *Dangdai Zhongguo Waijiao,* pp. 238–39. It was also contained in the unilateral Chinese statement issued on August 17, which stated that "the final resolution referred to here certainly implies that the U.S. arms sales to Taiwan must be completely terminated over a period of time." See appendix D. The American denial was contained in the six points conveyed to Taiwan.

24. "Statement of Hon. John H. Holdridge," p. 13. The Chinese denial is contained in Deng's remarks to Hummel, in Xue and Pei, *Dangdai Zhongguo Waijiao,* pp. 238–39.

25. *U.S. Policy toward China and Taiwan,* pp. 32–33.

26. Haig, *Caveat,* p. 194.

27. As noted, in 1976 Reagan had urged a closer strategic relationship with China as a way of preventing it from pursuing an accommodation with the Soviet Union after the death of Mao Zedong. But Reagan had said that proposals to sell arms to Peking "should be treated with exceptional care." Reagan, "Expanding Our Ties."

28. Jonathan D. Pollack, *The Lessons of Coalition Politics: Sino-American Security Relations,* R-3133-AF (Santa Monica: Rand Corporation, February 1984), p. 91.

29. *Washington Post,* June 25, 1989, p. A24; and Pollack, *Lessons of Coalition Politics,* p. 88, n. 49.

30. The first two limitations are from Roger W. Sullivan, "U.S. Military Sales to China: How Long Will the Window Shopping Last?" in *China Business Review,* vol. 13 (March-April 1986), pp. 6–9. The last is from John H. Holdridge, "U.S. Relations with China," *Current Policy,* no. 297 (Department of State, July 1981), p. 3.

31. Xinhua, June 10, 1981, in FBIS, *China,* June 10, 1981, p. B1. See also Xinhua, June 11, 1981, in FBIS, *China,* June 12, 1981, p. B1.

32. Pollack, *Lessons of Coalition Politics,* pp. 91–92.

33. For an analysis of changing Chinese perceptions of the global balance of power, see Banning Garrett and Bonnie Glaser, "Chinese Estimates of the U.S.-Soviet Balance of Power," Occasional Paper, no. 33 (Washington: Woodrow Wilson International Center for Scholars, 1988).

34. The text of Brezhnev's speech is in Moscow Domestic Television Service, March 24, 1982, in FBIS, *Daily Report: Soviet Union,* March 25, 1982, pp. R1–R7.

35. For overviews of the foreign policy of the early Reagan years, see Coral Bell, *The Reagan Paradox: U.S. Foreign Policy in the 1980s* (Rutgers University Press, 1989); and Kenneth A. Oye, Robert J. Lieber, and Donald Rothchild, eds., *Eagle Resurgent? The Reagan Era in American Foreign Policy* (Little, Brown, 1987).

36. *Der Spiegel*, December 26, 1983, in FBIS, *China*, December 29, 1983, pp. A6–A13.
37. This declaratory shift was accompanied by important personnel changes, including the replacement of Foreign Minister Huang Hua by Wu Xueqian and the reassignment of two vice foreign ministers, Pu Shouchang and Zhang Wenjin. Chinese sources have said that all three of those removed from their posts were regarded as excessively pro-American.
38. Hu Yaobang, "Create a New Situation in All Fields of Socialist Modernization," in *The Twelfth National Congress of the CPC (September 1982)* (Peking: Foreign Languages Press, 1982), pp. 58–64.
39. *Liaowang*, October 20, 1982, quoted in Xinhua, October 20, 1982, in FBIS, *China*, October 21, 1982, pp. A1–A2.
40. The changes in Chinese foreign policy in this period are reviewed in Carol Lee Hamrin, "Emergence of an 'Independent' Chinese Foreign Policy and Shifts in Sino-U.S. Relations," in James C. Hsiung, ed., *U.S.-Asian Relations: The National Security Paradox* (Praeger, 1983), pp. 63–84; and A. Doak Barnett, *U.S. Arms Sales: The China-Taiwan Tangle* (Brookings, 1982), pp. 38–49.
41. John H. Holdridge, "Assessment of U.S. Relations with China," *Current Policy*, no. 444 (Department of State, December 1982), p. 3.
42. Interestingly, the United States had offered to establish a nongovernmental clearinghouse to facilitate Chinese applications to American universities. This the Chinese had rejected in 1978. They probably did so precisely because they wanted to avoid working through a single American organization that could be used to constrict their ability to dispatch students and scholars to the United States. See Linda A. Reed, *Education in the People's Republic of China and U.S.-China Educational Exchanges* (Washington: National Association for Foreign Student Affairs, 1988), p. 93.
43. On the threats by the Chinese, see *New York Times*, June 18, 1983, p. 22; and *New York Times*, September 17, 1984, p. B10. On Stanford's decision, see the university's *Campus Report*, March 2, 1983, pp. 1, 6, and March 9, 1983, pp. 1, 14. One of the first criticisms of the expulsion, arguing that Stanford was "censuring a scholar for daring to utter unpleasant truths" and was punishing Mosher to "mollify Chinese authorities," was in the *Wall Street Journal*, March 2, 1983, p. 24.
44. *New York Times*, June 6, 1982, p. 15, and July 31, 1982, p. 2.
45. *New York Times*, September 2, 1981, pp. A1, C27.
46. See, for example, the accusations that Michael Weisskopf of the *Washington Post* lacked a "responsible attitude" because of his coverage of labor camps in China. Agence France Presse, September 21, 1981, in FBIS, *China*, September 21, 1981, p. B1.
47. On the Hu Na case, see *New York Times*, August 4, 1982, pp. A1, A4; *New York Times*, March 21, 1983, p. A2; *New York Times*, March 31, 1983, p. A9; and *New York Times*, April 5, 1983, pp. A1, A10. On the Chinese retaliation, see *New York Times*, April 8, 1983, pp. A1, A8.

48. Leo A. Orleans, *Chinese Students in America: Policies, Issues, and Numbers* (National Academy Press, 1988), p. 91, table 5-4.
49. *Wall Street Journal*, January 14, 1983, p. 5; and *Wall Street Journal*, January 20, 1983, p. 29.
50. John J. Sullivan, "U.S. Trade Laws Hinder the Development of U.S.-PRC Trade," *Columbia Journal of Transnational Law*, vol. 22 (Winter 1983), pp. 135–74.
51. The Coordinating Committee (COCOM), then consisting of Japan and all NATO countries except Iceland, reviewed applications for technology transfer to China, the Soviet Union, and other Communist countries.
52. Ralph N. Clough, *Chinese Elites: World View and Perceptions of the U.S.*, Research Report R-15-82 (Washington: International Communication Agency, August 1982), p. 20.
53. Xinhua, October 7, 1982, in FBIS, *China*, October 8, 1982, pp. B1–B3.
54. Xinhua, October 22, 1982, in FBIS, *China*, October 25, 1982, p. B1.
55. Ultimately, after the Chinese government hired legal counsel, the district circuit court reversed itself, ruling that the PRC was not obligated to pay the bondholders. That decision was affirmed by the circuit court in July 1986; the Supreme Court refused to hear further appeals in March 1987.
56. *Banyuetan*, no. 16 (August 25, 1981), pp. 52–54, in FBIS, *China*, September 11, 1981, pp. B1–B2.
57. Kyodo, October 24, 1982, in FBIS, *China*, October 25, 1982, p. B1; and Xinhua, October 9, 1983, in FBIS, *China*, October 11, 1983, p. A3.
58. As noted in chapter 1, the "three T's" referred to textiles, technology, and Taiwan; the "two Hu's" referred to the tennis star Hu Na and the Huguang Railway bonds.
59. *Banyuetan*, no. 3 (February 10, 1981), pp. 16–17, in FBIS, *China*, March 12, 1981, pp. B1–B2.
60. *Ming Pao*, August 25, 1981, quoted in Pollack, *Lessons of Coalition Politics*, p. 89.
61. *Wen Wei Po*, December 20, 1983, p. 3, in FBIS, *China*, December 27, 1983, p. W2.
62. Xinhua, October 7, 1982, in FBIS, *China*, October 8, 1982, pp. B1–B3; *San Francisco Chronicle*, June 1, 1983, p. C3.
63. Henry J. Groen, "U.S. Firms in the PRC Trade (The Sweet and Sour China Market)," in *China under the Four Modernizations*, pt. 2: *Selected Papers Submitted to the Joint Economic Committee*, 97 Cong. 2 sess. (GPO, 1982), pp. 331, 344.
64. *New York Times*, January 9, 1983, p. 6; and Robert Sutter, "The Taiwan Relations Act and the United States' China Policy," in Myers, *A Unique Relationship*, pp. 69–70.
65. *New York Times*, February 2, 1983, p. A3; and Paul Wolfowitz, "Developing an Enduring Relationship With China," *Current Policy*, no. 460 (Department of State, February 1983). The downgrading of China was also implicit in a companion statement by Shultz himself: George Shultz, "The U.S. and East Asia: A Partnership for the Future," *Current*

Policy, no. 459 (Department of State, March 1983). For contemporary analysis of the shift, see Richard Nations, "A Tilt toward Tokyo," *Far Eastern Economic Review*, April 21, 1983.

66. For a fuller discussion, see Harry Harding, "From China, with Disdain: New Trends in the Study of China," *Asian Survey*, vol. 22 (October 1982), pp. 934–58; and "A Romance Turns Sour," *Asiaweek*, April 1, 1983, pp. 40–44.

67. John E. Rielly, ed., *American Public Opinion and U.S. Foreign Policy* (Chicago Council on Foreign Relations, 1987), p. 18, table III-3.

CHAPTER 5

1. On the Shultz visit, see *Wall Street Journal*, February 7, 1983, p. 23; *New York Times*, February 8, 1983, p. A15; Robert Manning, "A Strategic Soft-sell," *Far Eastern Economic Review*, February 17, 1983, pp. 9–10; and Xue Mouhong and Pei Jianzhang, eds., *Dangdai Zhongguo Waijiao* (Contemporary Chinese diplomacy) (Peking: Chinese Social Science Publishing House, 1987), p. 343.

2. *New York Times*, March 30, 1983, p. A2.

3. *Wen Wei Po*, September 2, 1983, p. 2, in Foreign Broadcast Information Service, *Daily Report: China*, September 2, 1983, pp. W1–W2; and Xinhua, October 9, 1983, in Foreign Broadcast Information Service, *Daily Report: China*, October 11, 1983, p. A3. (Hereafter FBIS, *China*.)

4. This was reportedly one conclusion of a conference on foreign policy convened in Peking toward the end of 1985. See *Wen Wei Po*, December 20, 1985, p. 2, in FBIS, *China*, December 20, 1985, pp. W1–W2.

5. A useful overview of Sino-American relations during this period is Robert A. Manning, "China: Reagan's Chance Hit," *Foreign Policy*, no. 54 (Spring 1984), pp. 83–101.

6. On the Baldrige visit, see *Wall Street Journal*, May 26, 1983, p. 30.

7. *Wall Street Journal*, August 1, 1983, p. 3; and *Wall Street Journal*, September 7, 1983, p. 34.

8. On China's retention of legal counsel, see *Wall Street Journal*, August 8, 1983, p. 22.

9. Jonathan D. Pollack, *The Lessons of Coalition Politics: Sino-American Security Relations*, R-3133-AF (Santa Monica: Rand Corporation, February 1984), pp. 117–18.

10. *Beijing Review*, January 23, 1984, pp. 18–22. On the Zhao visit, see *Beijing Review*, January 23, 1984, pp. 22–23; *New York Times*, January 19, 1984, p. A17; *Washington Post*, January 18, 1984, pp. A1, A24; and Xue and Pei, *Dangdai Zhongguo Waijiao*, p. 344.

11. Xinhua, March 8, 1984, in FBIS, *China*, March 8, 1984, pp. K3–K4.

12. *Beijing Review*, January 23, 1984, pp. 18–22.

13. Zhao's statements are drawn variously from *Renmin Ribao*, January 4,

1984, in FBIS, *China*, January 4, 1984, pp. A1–A4; and *Beijing Review*, January 23, 1984, pp. 18–22.

14. As an editorial in the *Washington Post* put it, "The eighth wonder of the world is the spectacle of Ronald Reagan—in his first trip to any communist country—visiting the People's Republic of China." *Washington Post*, April 25, 1984, p. A20.

15. Xinhua, April 30, 1984, in FBIS, *China*, May 1, 1984, pp. B1–B3; and *Public Papers of the Presidents of the United States: Ronald Reagan, 1984*, bk. I: *January 1 to June 29, 1984* (Washington: Government Printing Office, 1986), pp. 603–07.

16. *Public Papers of the Presidents, 1984*, pp. 579–84.

17. See Harry Harding, *China's Second Revolution: Reform after Mao* (Brookings, 1987); and Carol Lee Hamrin, *China and the Challenge of the Future: Changing Political Patterns* (Westview Press, 1990).

18. "Decision of the Central Committee of the Communist Party of China on Reform of the Economic Structure," carried by Xinhua, October 20, 1984, in FBIS, *China*, October 22, 1984, pp. K1–K19; and "Proposal of the Central Committee of the Chinese Communist Party for the Seventh Five-Year Plan for National Economic and Social Development," in *Uphold Reform and Strive for the Realization of Socialist Modernization—Documents of the CPC National Conference* (Beijing: Foreign Languages Press, 1985), pp. 11–62.

19. Harding, *China's Second Revolution*, p. 129, table 5-2; and Guojia Tongjiju (State Statistical Bureau), *Zhongguo Tongji Zhaiyao, 1988* (A statistical survey of China, 1988) (Peking: Chinese Statistical Publishing House, 1988), pp. 36, 78.

20. Author's calculations, based on data in World Bank, *World Tables 1991* (Johns Hopkins University Press, 1991), pp. 184–85; and International Monetary Fund, *International Financial Statistics Yearbook 1991* (IMF, 1991), pp. 121, 125.

21. Ranking information supplied by Department of Commerce, International Trade Administration, Office of China and Hong Kong.

22. On the number of representative offices, see Winston Lord, "Sino-American Relations: No Time for Complacency," address to the National Council on U.S.-China Trade, Washington, D.C., May 28, 1986, p. 6. On the number of investment projects, see Sun Haishun, "Direct Investment in China," in *Ten Years of Sino-U.S. Relations*, ed. Institute of American Studies, CASS, and Chinese Association for American Studies (Nanjing: Yilin Press, 1990), p. 336, table 1.

23. The following discussion of American technology transfer policy draws on *Controls on Exports to the People's Republic of China*, Hearing before Subcommittee on International Economic Policy and Trade of the House Committee on Foreign Affairs, 98 Cong. 1 sess. (GPO, 1985); Madelyn C. Ross, "China and the United States' Export Controls System," *Columbia Journal of World Business*, vol. 21 (Spring 1986), pp. 27–33; and *Washington Post*, December 17, 1985, p. A27.

24. "US Export Controls and China," *Gist* (Department of State, March 1989).
25. "Benefits of the Bilateral Tax Treaty," sidebar to Andrew Ness and Stephanie J. Mitchell, "Taxing US Offices in China," *China Business Review*, vol. 13 (September–October 1986), p. 38.
26. *Far Eastern Economic Review*, March 10, 1988, p. 78.
27. Office of Technology Assessment, *Technology Transfer to China*, OTA-ISC-340 (GPO, 1987).
28. Some provisions along these lines were included in the Trade Act of 1988. See *Congressional Quarterly Almanac*, vol. 44 (Washington: Congressional Quarterly, Inc., 1989), pp. 209–12.
29. See Nicholas R. Lardy, *Economic Policy toward China in the Post-Reagan Era*, China Policy Series, no. 1 (New York: National Committee on U.S.-China Relations, January 1989); "Council Recommendations to the Bush Administration," *China Business Review*, vol. 16 (January–February 1989), pp. 6–8; and *Wall Street Journal*, April 9, 1987, p. 64.
30. Andrew B. Brick, "The Bush Administration and U.S.-China Trade," Asian Studies Center Backgrounder, no. 89 (Washington: Heritage Foundation, March 1989), pp. 3, 11.
31. *Washington Post*, March 10, 1988, p. A41.
32. Linda A. Reed, *Education in the People's Republic of China and U.S.-China Educational Exchanges* (Washington: National Association for Foreign Student Affairs, 1988), p. 100.
33. Leo A. Orleans, *Chinese Students in America: Policies, Issues, and Numbers* (National Academy Press, 1988), p. 80, table 4-2; and *Washington Post*, May 2, 1989, p. A3.
34. Winston Lord, "A Stroll through Tiananmen Square: Tradition, Transition, and the Future in Sino-American Relations," address to the Commonwealth Club, San Francisco, December 2, 1988, p. 4.
35. The $467 million provided by the United States under these three programs compared with the $3.3 billion lent to Peking by Japan between 1979 and 1988. See Japanese aid data from Organization for Economic Cooperation and Development, *Geographical Distribution of Financial Flows to Developing Countries*, for the time periods 1979–82, 1981–84, 1984–87, and 1985–88 (Paris, published annually).
36. World Bank lending to China totaled $7.1 billion from 1979 through 1988, of which the United States provided approximately 20 percent. See *World Bank Annual Report* for each of the years listed (Washington: World Bank).
37. Toufiq A. Siddiqi, Jin Xiaoming, and Shi Minghao, "Joint Study of US-China Government S&T Protocols," *China Exchange News*, vol. 16 (March 1988), pp. 21–25.
38. Orleans, *Chinese Students in America*, p. 91, table 5-4.
39. Orleans, *Chinese Students in America*, p. 88, table 5-1; and, for fiscal 1988, Visa Office, Department of State, Washington.

40. The amount of Chinese direct investment in the United States was extrapolated from data supplied by the Department of Commerce's Office of Trade and Investment Analysis.
41. In describing the package introduced by Ronald Reagan, the executive director of the central Chinese radio station noted that "Comrade Reagan cared for our program and extended friendly feelings to all the people of China." *Korean Herald*, April 21, 1988, p. 9.
42. Shi Xianrong, "American Literature in China during the Last Decade," in *Ten Years of Sino-U.S. Relations*, p. 424.
43. During Vice President Bush's visit in October 1985, Zhao Ziyang's comments on Taiwan were said to have been characterized as "frankness border[ing] on the impolite." *Wen Wei Po*, October 16, 1985, pp. 1–2, in FBIS, *China*, October 16, 1985, pp. W1–W2.
44. This message was, for example, conveyed to Reagan through British Prime Minister Margaret Thatcher in early 1985.
45. See the article by Zi Zhongyun and Zhuang Qubing, "Opportunities and Potential Crisis," in *Beijing Review*, October 14, 1985, pp. 21–24.
46. *Beijing Review*, October 5, 1981, pp. 10–11.
47. Lester L. Wolff and David L. Simon, eds., *Legislative History of the Taiwan Relations Act: An Analytic Compilation with Documents on Subsequent Developments* (Jamaica, N.Y.: American Association for Chinese Studies, 1982), p. 312; *Far Eastern Economic Review*, July 24, 1986; pp. 23–25; Agence France Presse, July 20, 1981, in FBIS, *China*, July 21, 1981, p. G3; and Agence France Presse, June 14, 1988, in FBIS, *China*, June 14, 1988, p. 60. A compilation of statements on the issue made by Chinese leaders has been prepared by the Taiwan government, "A Study of a Possible Communist Attack on Taiwan," 3d ed. (Taiwan: Government Information Office, March 1990).
48. Deng Xiaoping, "A Concept for the Peaceful Reunification of the Chinese Mainland and Taiwan (June 26, 1983)," in Deng Xiaoping, *Build Socialism with Chinese Characteristics* (Beijing: Foreign Languages Press, 1985), pp. 18–20.
49. *New York Times*, September 20, 1984, pp. A1, A10.
50. See the testimony of Paul Wolfowitz, assistant secretary of state for East Asian and Pacific Affairs, "Developing an Enduring Relationship with China," in *United States–China Relations*, Hearings before the Subcommittees on Asian and Pacific Affairs and International Economic Policy and Trade of the House Committee on Foreign Affairs, 98 Cong. 2 sess. (GPO, 1984), pp. 187–92, 230–31.
51. *Liaowang* (overseas edition), no. 30 (July 28, 1986), pp. 22–23, in FBIS, *China*, August 1, 1986, pp. B2–B4; and *Washington Post*, April 25, 1986, pp. A32, A33.
52. *Far Eastern Economic Review*, August 28, 1986, p. 26.
53. The resolution was adopted by the Senate Foreign Relations Committee, but did not proceed further through Congress. For Chinese commentary, see *Renmin Ribao*, November 14, 1983, in FBIS, *China*, November 14, 1983, pp. B1–B2; Xinhua, November 16, 1983, in FBIS, *China*, November

17, 1983, p. B1; Xinhua, November 18, 1983, in FBIS, *China*, November 18, 1983, pp. B1–B2; and Xinhua, November 18, 1983, in FBIS, *China*, November 21, 1983, p. B1.

54. *Renmin Ribao*, December 30, 1988, p. 7, in FBIS, *China*, January 10, 1989, pp. 6–12.

55. The resolution, which referred to Taiwan as the "Republic of China," was included in the Supplemental Appropriations Act of 1984, approved November 1983 (Public Law 98-181). For the Chinese protest, see Xinhua, November 25, 1983, in FBIS, *China*, November 25, 1983, p. B1. Peking appeared satisfied when Washington replied that the resolution did not reflect the position of the Reagan administration and the president's signature of the bill did not represent any change in U.S. policy. See Xinhua, December 6, 1983, in FBIS, *China*, December 6, 1983, pp. B1–B2.

56. The quotations are from Paul Wolfowitz, "Developing an Enduring Relationship with China," *Current Policy*, no. 460 (Department of State, February 1983).

57. *Chung-kuo shih-pao*, October 21, 1985, p. 2, in FBIS, *China*, October 25, 1985, pp. V1–V3.

58. Shultz's remarks were made in a banquet toast, reported by Beijing Domestic Service, March 5, 1987, in FBIS, *China*, March 6, 1987, p. B1. A similar attitude was expressed by President Reagan in a meeting with Chinese Foreign Minister Wu Xueqian in early 1988. See Radio Beijing, March 9, 1988, in FBIS, *China*, March 9, 1988, p. 4.

59. *Renmin Ribao*, February 26, 1989, p. 1, in FBIS, *China*, February 27, 1989, p. 11.

60. Eden Y. Woon, "Chinese Arms Sales and U.S.-China Military Relations," *Asian Survey*, vol. 29 (June 1989), pp. 601–18.

61. James R. Martin, "United States Defense Policy for East Asia and the Pacific and the Strategic Importance of China," speech delivered at Lewis and Clark State College, Lewiston, Idaho, February 10, 1984. Martin was assistant for regional affairs in the Office of the Assistant Secretary of Defense for East Asian and Pacific Affairs.

62. Martin, "United States Defense Policy," p. 6.

63. On Andropov's approach to China, see *Far Eastern Economic Review*, March 3, 1983, pp. 10–11. On Chernenko, see *New York Times*, March 27, 1984, p. A12; and *Wall Street Journal*, May 10, 1984, p. 39.

64. *New York Times*, October 7, 1983, p. A3; *Far Eastern Economic Review*, June 14, 1984, p. 46.

65. *Washington Post*, June 25, 1989, pp. A1, A24.

66. *Washington Post*, June 25, 1989, pp. A1, A24. More generally, see *Far Eastern Economic Review*, November 17, 1983, p. 15.

67. Zhang Jingyi, "The Security Factor in Sino-American Relations: Review and Outlook," in *Ten Years of Sino-U.S. Relations*, p. 74; and *New York Times*, July 3, 1984, p. A6.

68. When first proposed by Caspar Weinberger in 1983, this program was described as a series of training missions by which the United States

would assist in the modernization of the Chinese armed forces. Peking did not appreciate the paternalistic connotations of "training missions," and the program was soon redefined as a series of military exchanges. The Chinese reservations are suggested in *New York Times*, September 30, 1983, p. A3.

69. See *Far Eastern Economic Review*, May 22, 1986, p. 32; and *Far Eastern Economic Review*, March 23, 1989, p. 9.

70. Zhongguo xinwen she, April 10, 1985, in FBIS, *China*, April 11, 1985, p. E2. The issue was particularly sensitive in New Zealand, which had barred nuclear-powered or nuclear-armed ships from entering its ports.

71. *New York Times*, October 11, 1983, p. A11.

72. Edward Ross, "U.S.-China Military Relations," paper presented to the Heritage Foundation Asian Studies Center Seminar on United States–China Relations, Washington, D.C., January 28, 1986.

73. See, for example, A. James Gregor, *Arming the Dragon: U.S. Security Ties with the People's Republic of China* (Washington: Ethics and Public Policy Center, 1987), pp. 100–02.

74. *Aviation Week and Space Technology*, March 31, 1986, p. 31.

75. Such legislation, originally proposed by Martin Lasater of the Heritage Foundation, had been supported by Senators Jesse Helms and Barry Goldwater and by Congressmen Philip Crane and Mark Siljander.

76. Richard G. Niemi, John Mueller, and Tom W. Smith, *Trends in Public Opinion: A Compendium of Survey Data* (Greenwood Press, 1989), p. 66, table 2.20; and John E. Rielly, ed., *American Public Opinion and U.S. Foreign Policy* (Chicago Council on Foreign Relations, 1987), p. 18, table III-2.

77. *Wall Street Journal*, April 23, 1984, pp. 1, 20; and *New York Times*, April 24, 1984, p. A6.

78. *Wall Street Journal*, October 25, 1984, pp. 1, 29; and *Business Week*, January 14, 1985, pp. 53–59. See also *New York Times*, October 21, 1984, pp. 1, 14.

79. William Safire, "Greatest Leap Forward," *New York Times*, December 10, 1984, p. A23; *Wall Street Journal*, December 10, 1984, p. 31; and Louis Kraar, "China after Marx: Open for Business," *Fortune*, February 18, 1985, pp. 28–33.

80. *Time*, September 23, 1985, p. 44; *Time*, January 6, 1986, pp. 24–41; and *Time*, January 1, 1979, p. 12.

81. *New York Times*, August 29, 1985, p. A23.

82. *Washington Post*, May 2, 1984, pp. A1, A8. The bearded Smith Brothers, the trademark of a brand of cough drops in the 1950s, did bear a certain resemblance to Marx and Engels.

83. Michel Oksenberg and Kenneth Lieberthal, "Forecasting China's Future," *The National Interest*, no. 5 (Fall 1986), pp. 18–27.

84. From this period, see Jan S. Prybyla, "The Chinese Economy: Adjustment of the System or Systemic Reform?" *Asian Survey*, vol. 25 (May 1985), pp. 553–86; and Jan S. Prybyla, "China's Economic Experiment:

From Mao to Market," *Problems of Communism*, vol. 35 (January–February 1986), pp. 21–38.

85. Miriam London, "China: The Romance of Realpolitik," *Freedom at Issue*, no. 110 (September–October 1989), p. 11.

CHAPTER 6

1. This was first apparent during the Andropov period. See Nayan Chanda, "A Thaw in Siberia," *Far Eastern Economic Review*, April 28, 1983, pp. 26–27. For an explicit statement by Deng, to the effect that the three obstacles should not prevent "improving or developing ties in certain other fields," see *Beijing Review*, March 5, 1984, p. 6.

2. The following discussion of the evolution of Sino-Soviet relations from 1983 through 1989 draws in part on Herbert J. Ellison, "Changing Sino-Soviet Relations," *Problems of Communism*, vol. 36 (May–June 1987), pp. 17–29; John W. Garver, "The 'New Type' of Sino-Soviet Relations," *Asian Survey*, vol. 29 (December 1989), pp. 1136–52; Steven M. Goldstein, "Diplomacy amid Protest: The Sino-Soviet Summit," *Problems of Communism*, vol. 38 (September–October 1989), pp. 49–71; and William deB. Mills, "Baiting the Chinese Dragon: Sino-Soviet Relations after Vladivostok," *Journal of Northeast Asian Studies*, vol. 6 (Fall 1987), pp. 3–30.

3. See the comments by Foreign Minister Wu Xueqian, in Xinhua, April 5, 1984, in Foreign Broadcast Information Service, *Daily Report: China*, April 5, 1984, p. G1. (Hereafter FBIS, *China*.)

4. Deng's statement on the importance of the Cambodian issue appeared in *Wen Wei Po*, April 25, 1985, in FBIS, *China*, April 25, 1985, pp. W1–W2. The private message conveyed through Ceausescu was first revealed by *Ta Kung Pao*, September 9, 1986, p. 2, in FBIS, *China*, September 9, 1986, pp. C3–C4. On the retention of Soviet bases in Vietnam, see Beijing Domestic Television Service, April 17, 1985, in FBIS, *China*, April 18, 1985, p. G1. It was widely presumed that, once the Cambodian conflict was settled, the Vietnamese would no longer desire a Soviet military presence in their country.

5. One of the best summaries of those changes is Robert Legvold, "The Revolution in Soviet Foreign Policy," *Foreign Affairs*, vol. 68, special issue (1988/89), pp. 82–98.

6. Moscow Television, July 28, 1986, in Foreign Broadcast Information Service, *Daily Report: Soviet Union*, July 29, 1986, pp. R1–R20.

7. *Far Eastern Economic Review*, September 15, 1988, pp. 17–18.

8. Michael MccGwire, *Perestroika and Soviet National Security* (Brookings, 1991), p. 324.

9. See, for example, an article by Frederick Kempe entitled "As Sino-Soviet

Relations Warm, When Should the U.S. Worry?" in *Wall Street Journal*, March 24, 1986, p. 24.

10. *Washington Post*, April 2, 1989, p. A36.

11. *New York Times*, May 17, 1989, p. A8.

12. Bonnie S. Glaser and Banning N. Garrett, "Chinese Perspectives on the Strategic Defense Initiative," *Problems of Communism*, vol. 35 (March–April 1986), pp. 28–44.

13. These estimates are drawn from Kimmo Kiljunen, ed., *Kampuchea, Decade of the Genocide: Report of a Finnish Inquiry Commission* (London: Zed Books, 1984), p. 33. For the caution that no estimate of the human cost of the Khmer Rouge regime can be considered authoritative, see Craig Etcheson, *The Rise and Demise of Democratic Kampuchea* (Westview Press, 1984), pp. 147–49.

14. *Wall Street Journal*, July 14, 1988, p. 23.

15. *Congressional Record*, daily ed., August 8, 1988, pp. H6574–77.

16. On the nuclear cooperation agreement, see Michael Brenner, "The US/ China Nuclear Bilateral Accord," Case Studies in International Negotiation, no. 4 (University of Pittsburgh Graduate School of Public and International Affairs, 1986); Daniel Horner and Paul Leventhal, "The U.S.-China Nuclear Agreement: A Failure of Executive Policymaking and Congressional Oversight," *Fletcher Forum*, vol. 11 (Winter 1987), pp. 105–22; Qingshan Tan, "U.S.-China Nuclear Cooperation Agreement: China's Nonproliferation Policy," *Asian Survey*, vol. 29 (September 1989), pp. 870–82; and Hongqian Zhu, "Congress and American Normal Bilateral Foreign Policy: A Study of Congressional Opposition in the Making of U.S. China Policy during the 1980s, Ph.D. diss., University of Michigan, Department of Political Science, 1991, chap. V.

17. *Washington Post*, July 23, 1981, p. B11; and *New York Times*, September 19, 1982, p. 11.

18. *Washington Post*, June 21, 1984, p. A17; *New York Times*, June 22, 1984, pp. A1, A23; and *New York Times*, June 22, 1984, p. 3.

19. Alan T. Crane and Richard P. Suttmeier, "Nuclear Trade with China," *Columbia Journal of World Business*, vol. 21 (Spring 1986), p. 39.

20. China did, however, agree to standard language granting the United States consent rights regarding the transfer of spent fuel to third parties.

21. *Nuclear Energy Cooperation with China*, Hearings before the Special Subcommittee on U.S.-Pacific Rim Trade of the House Committee on Energy and Commerce, 99 Cong. 1 sess. (Washington: Government Printing Office, 1986), p. 3.

22. For the relevant hearings, see *Nuclear Energy Cooperation with China*; and *United States–People's Republic of China Nuclear Agreement*, Hearings before the Senate Committee on Foreign Relations, 99 Cong. 1 sess. (GPO, 1986).

23. Under existing law, it could have done this in two ways. If the House Foreign Affairs Committee or the Senate Foreign Relations Committee had found that the proposed agreement violated the requirements of the nonproliferation act, it could have insisted that the Congress formally

ratify the agreement before it went into effect. If both committees determined that the proposed agreement was in conformity with the nonproliferation act, Congress could still have tried to pass a resolution of disapproval and then to override a presidential veto. Neither committee chose to label the agreement in violation of the nonproliferation act. And even the opponents of the agreement sought to impose conditions on its implementation rather than to disapprove it completely.

24. *Washington Post,* November 14, 1985, pp. A1, A35; *Far Eastern Economic Review,* November 28, 1985, p. 23; and *Washington Post,* December 17, 1985, p. A27. The best summary of the congressional resolution appears in Robert G. Sutter, "China's Nuclear Weapons and Arms Control Policies: Implications for the United States," Report 88-374F (Washington: Library of Congress, Congressional Research Service, May 1988). An even tougher restriction, sponsored by Senator Glenn and Representative Edward Feighan (D-Ohio), would have also required the imposition of IAEA safeguards on American nuclear exports to China and a written statement by Peking clarifying its policy on nonproliferation. This measure passed the Senate but was not included in the final legislation.

25. Eden Y. Woon, "Chinese Arms Sales and U.S.-China Military Relations," *Asian Survey,* vol. 29 (June 1989), p. 604.

26. *Washington Times,* June 9, 1987, pp. A1, A8; and *Washington Post,* June 11, 1987, p. A29.

27. This followed earlier Chinese denials that they were selling any arms to either Iran or Iraq. See, for example, Xinhua, February 22, 1984, in FBIS, *China,* February 22, 1984, p. A1.

28. *New York Times,* October 23, 1987, pp. A1, A9.

29. *New York Times,* March 10, 1988, pp. A1, A11; *Washington Post,* March 10, 1988, p. A41; and *Asian Wall Street Journal,* August 8, 1988, p. 19.

30. Beijing Television, April 6, 1988, in FBIS, *China,* April 6, 1988, p. 18. For a detailed analysis of the Sino-Saudi transaction, see Yitzhak Shichor, *East Wind over Arabia: Origins and Implications of the Sino-Saudi Missile Deal,* China Research Monograph, no. 35 (Berkeley: University of California, Institute of East Asian Studies, 1989).

31. *New York Times,* June 22, 1988, p. A6; *Washington Post,* June 23, 1988, p. A33; and *Washington Post,* July 14, 1988, p. A22.

32. On the Shultz visit, see *Washington Post,* July 15, 1988, pp. A15, A18; and *Far Eastern Economic Review,* September 8, 1988, p. 24.

33. The third principle was that they would not be used to interfere in the recipient's internal affairs. See Xinhua, September 8, 1988, in FBIS, *China,* September 8, 1988, p. 1.

34. *Washington Post,* September 8, 1988, pp. A31, A35. These assurances were repeated during the Bush visit in February 1989, when the Chinese again promised to "act responsibly." *Washington Post,* February 27, 1989, pp. A1, A11.

35. The linkage was reported in a column by Rowland Evans and Robert Novak in *Washington Post,* October 12, 1988, p. A19. For the denial, see *Wall Street Journal,* December 20, 1988, p. B3.

36. Winston Lord, "Sino-American Relations: No Time for Complacency," address to the National Council on U.S.-China Trade, Washington, D.C., May 28, 1986, pp. 17, 21–24.

37. International Monetary Fund, *International Financial Statistics Yearbook 1989* (Washington, 1989), p. 140.

38. Jerome Turtola, "Textile Trade Tensions," *China Business Review*, vol. 13 (September–October 1986), pp. 26–31; and Zhu, "Congress and American Normal Bilateral Foreign Policy," chap. VI.

39. *Asian Wall Street Journal Weekly*, December 28, 1987, p. 14.

40. *Wall Street Journal*, December 20, 1988, p. B3.

41. *New York Times*, February 3, 1990, pp. 1, 9.

42. *Financial Times*, April 23, 1987, p. 4; *Asian Wall Street Journal Weekly*, February 1, 1988, p. 3; and "USTR Report—Trade Barriers in China," in *AmCham Outlook*, vol. 20 (April 1988), p. 58.

43. This discussion draws on Harry Harding, "The Investment Climate in China," *Brookings Review*, vol. 5 (Spring 1987), pp. 37–42.

44. *New York Times*, April 11, 1986, pp. D1, D4; and *Washington Post*, April 11, 1986, pp. B1, B10.

45. The fullest description of Beijing Jeep can be found in Jim Mann, *Beijing Jeep: The Short, Unhappy Romance of American Business in China* (Simon and Schuster, 1989).

46. *Wall Street Journal*, July 17, 1986, p. 1; see also John F. Burns, "Why Investors Are Sour on China," *New York Times*, June 8, 1986, pp. A1, A3.

47. In the end, this organization was never formed.

48. Lord, "No Time for Complacency," p. 10.

49. *Beijing Review*, October 27, 1986, pp. 26–28.

50. *New York Times*, November 17, 1986, p. D10; and *Japan Times Weekly*, November 29, 1986, p. 5.

51. See Louis Kraar, "The China Bubble Bursts," *Fortune*, July 6, 1987, pp. 86–89.

52. Kraar, "The China Bubble Bursts," p. 89.

53. Leo A. Orleans, "Chinese in America: The Numbers Game," *China Exchange News*, vol. 17 (September 1989), p. 10. For an earlier estimate, see Orleans, *Chinese Students in America: Policies, Issues, and Numbers* (National Academy Press, 1988), p. 112.

54. *Washington Post*, November 15, 1987, pp. C1, C2; and *Washington Post*, September 26, 1988, pp. A1, A8.

55. On the origins of *China Spring*, see Mary Lee, "The Mouse That Roared," *Far Eastern Economic Review*, March 10, 1983, pp. 28–29.

56. For example, one thousand Chinese students in the United States sent an open letter to China's leadership expressing concern over the suppression of prodemocracy protests and the dismissal of General Secretary Hu Yaobang. Portions of the text were in *Wall Street Journal*, January 23, 1987, p. 22. A similar petition was sent in December 1987 to protest the treatment of Yang Wei, an American-trained biologist who had been

arrested for participating in antigovernment protests in December 1986. See *New York Times*, December 21, 1987, p. A5. Another open letter was sent in March 1988 to Li Peng, chairman of the State Education Commission, protesting a decision, discussed later in the text, to restrict the flow of students to the United States. See *China Times* (Taipei), March 30, 1988, p. 2, in *Inside China Mainland*, May 1988, p. 25. One of the first op-ed essays was written by a Harvard graduate student, M.X. Pei in the *Washington Post*, February 10, 1987, p. A21.

57. *Asian Wall Street Journal Weekly*, October 19, 1987, p. 20.
58. See *Asian Wall Street Journal Weekly*, October 19, 1987, p. 20; and Linda A. Reed, *Education in the People's Republic of China and U.S.-China Educational Exchanges* (Washington: National Association for Foreign Student Affairs, 1988), pp. 91–92.
59. *New York Times*, March 24, 1988, pp. A1, A5; and *New York Times*, April 4, 1988, p. A5.
60. Richard Nixon, *RN: The Memoirs of Richard Nixon* (Grosset and Dunlap, 1978), p. 562.
61. Jimmy Carter, *Keeping Faith: Memoirs of a President* (Bantam Books, 1982), pp. 203, 207.
62. *New York Times*, October 18, 1979, p. A3.
63. *Washington Post*, September 12, 1979, p. D8.
64. See Peter R. Moody, *Opposition and Dissent in Contemporary China* (Stanford: Hoover Institution Press, 1977); Merle Goldman, "Human Rights in the People's Republic of China," *Daedalus*, vol. 112 (Fall 1983), pp. 111–38; and Susan L. Shirk, "Human Rights: What about China?" *Foreign Policy*, no. 29 (Winter 1977–78), pp. 109–27.
65. Goldman, "Human Rights," p. 137.
66. "Background Briefing by Senior Administration Official on the President's Visit to China," White House, Office of the Press Secretary, March 21, 1984, p. 17.
67. Roberta Cohen, "People's Republic of China: The Human Rights Exception," *Human Rights Quarterly*, vol. 9 (November 1987), pp. 447–549.
68. *Wall Street Journal*, October 2, 1986, p. 30; and *New York Times*, December 24, 1986, p. A14.
69. These reports included those by Michael Weisskopf in the *Washington Post*, January 6, 1985, pp. A1, A30; January 7, 1985, pp. A1, A20; and January 8, 1985, pp. A1, A10; and by Steven W. Mosher, in *Broken Earth: The Rural Chinese* (Free Press, 1983); *Wall Street Journal*, July 25, 1983, p. 11; *Wall Street Journal*, May 13, 1985, p. 23; and *Washington Post*, April 10, 1988, pp. B1, B4.
70. The birth control issue is analyzed in Zhu, *Congress and American Normal Bilateral Foreign Policy*, chap. 7; and Barbara B. Crane and Jason L. Finkle, "The United States, China, and the United Nations Population Fund: Dynamics of US Policymaking," *Population and Development Review*, vol.15 (March 1989), pp. 23–59.

71. *Congressional Quarterly Almanac,* vol. 41 (1985), p. 112.
72. The policy of withholding U.S. contributions from the UNFPA was upheld by the Bush administration.
73. There was a debate about whether Chinese citizens subject to the coercive abortion policy would thereby be qualified for political asylum in the United States, should they be able to reach America. Attorney General Edwin Meese issued such an interpretation in August 1988. But the Immigration and Naturalization Service resisted, on the grounds that asylum was restricted to those who were persecuted on the basis of their race, religion, nationality, social group, or political opinion. The issue was resolved after the Tiananmen incident by the Bush administration, which reiterated Meese's ruling. See *Washington Post,* August 6, 1988, p. A14; *Washington Post,* February 5, 1989, p. A16; and *New York Times,* April 3, 1989, p. A13.
74. *New York Times,* October 7, 1987, pp. A1, A9.
75. *New York Times,* October 8, 1987, p. A38.
76. On the 1987 resolution, see *New York Times,* October 7, 1987, pp. A1, A9. The 1989 resolution was in response to the suppression of a renewed proindependence demonstration in Lhasa, in which at least twelve people were killed, more than one hundred injured, and at least three hundred arrested, and to the subsequent imposition of martial law in Tibet. *Far Eastern Economic Review,* March 16, 1989, pp. 10–11; *New York Times,* March 20, 1989, p. A8; and *Washington Post,* April 1, 1989, p. A17.
77. *New York Times,* October 7, 1989, pp. A1, A9.
78. On the letter, see *New York Times,* February 24, 1987, p. A7. On the resolution, see Robert Delfs, "Sino-US Links Are Solid Despite Occasional Storms," *Far Eastern Economic Review,* March 19, 1987, pp. 65–68.
79. *Far Eastern Economic Review,* January 7, 1988, pp. 14, 15.
80. *Renmin Ribao,* February 27, 1989, p. 1, in FBIS, *China,* February 27, 1989, pp. 22–23.
81. *Washington Post,* March 3, 1989, p. A9; and *New York Times,* March 3, 1989, p. A3.
82. *Washington Post,* February 27, 1989, pp. A1, A11.
83. Xinhua, March 1, 1989, in FBIS, *China,* March 1, 1989, p. 1.
84. *Asian Wall Street Journal Weekly,* March 27, 1989, p. 11.
85. See, for example, Huan Guocang and Corinna-Barbara Francis, "Sino-American Ties and Asian Security," *Millennium,* vol. 14 (Winter 1985), pp. 272–91; and Zhang Jingyi, "The Security Factor in Sino-American Relations: Review and Outlook," *Ten Years of Sino-U.S. Relations* ed. Institute of American Studies of the Chinese Academy of Social Sciences and the Chinese Association for American Studies (Nanjing: Yilin Press, 1990), pp. 65–89.
86. Richard Nixon, "The New China Card," *Newsweek,* April 30, 1984, pp. 32–33.

87. U. Alexis Johnson, George R. Packard, and Alfred D. Wilhelm, Jr., eds., *China Policy for the Next Decade* (Boston: Oelgeschlager, Gunn and Hain, 1984), pp. 5–6.

88. *Renmin Ribao*, December 21, 1988, p. 7, in FBIS, *China*, December 28, 1988, p. 5. The point was elaborated in one of the papers presented at the conference. See Li Guoyou, "The Next Dimension in Sino-U.S. Relations," in *Ten Years of Sino-U.S. Relations*, pp. 269–302.

89. Paul D. Wolfowitz, "The U.S.-China Trade Relationship," address before the National Council for United States–China Trade, May 31, 1984, in *Department of State Bulletin*, September 1984, p. 26.

90. Zi Zhongyun, "Convergence of Interests: Basis for Relations among Nations," in *Ten Years of Sino-U.S. Relations*, p. 39; and *Renmin Ribao*, December 21, 1988, p. 7, in FBIS, *China*, December 28, 1988, p. 5.

91. See, for example, Xinhua, December 6, 1983, in FBIS, *China*, December 6, 1983, pp. B1–B2.

92. John E. Rielly, ed., *American Public Opinion and U.S. Foreign Policy* (Chicago Council on Foreign Relations, 1991), p. 19.

93. Gaston J. Sigur, Jr., "China Policy Today: Consensus, Consistence, Stability," *Current Policy*, no. 901 (Department of State, December 1986), pp. 1, 3.

94. *Far Eastern Economic Review*, March 19, 1987, pp. 65–67.

95. Michael H. Armacost, "China and the U.S.: Present and Future," *Current Policy*, no. 1079 (Department of State, June 1988).

96. *Washington Post*, November 9, 1984, pp. A37, A38.

97. *Wen Wei Po*, September 6, 1985, p. 2, in FBIS, *China*, September 9, 1985, pp. W2–W3.

98. Lord, "No Time for Complacency," pp. 2, 17, 9.

99. *Liaowang* (overseas edition), no. 2 (January 11, 1988), pp. 22–23, in FBIS, *China*, January 15, 1988, pp. 2–5.

100. Roger W. Sullivan, "China, the United States, and the World: Beyond Normalization," *China Business Review*, vol. 15 (May–June 1988), p. 20. See also the cautious articles in *Far Eastern Economic Review*, September 8, 1988, p. 24; and in *Business Week*, January 30, 1989, p. 47.

101. Zhang Yi, "U.S. Congress and Sino-U.S. Relations in the Last Decade," in *Ten Years of Sino-U.S. Relations*, p. 185.

102. *Far Eastern Economic Review*, March 24, 1988, p. 19.

103. *Washington Post*, October 12, 1988, p. A19.

104. Carter, *Keeping Faith*, p. 188.

105. On the effect of the violation of the grain agreement on China's credibility, see *Washington Post*, September 28, 1984, p. A27.

106. *Ming Pao* (Hong Kong), April 15, 1987, in FBIS, *China*, April 15, 1987, p. B1.

107. For a survey of Chinese criticism of the United States during this period, see James L. Huskey, "America as Scapegoat: Chinese Media

Anti-Liberalization Campaign Focuses on U.S.," Research Memorandum (Washington: U.S. Information Agency, Office of Research, March 4, 1987).

108. John E. Wills, Jr., "Chinese and Maritime Europeans in the Late Ming and Early Qing," in Harry Harding, ed., *China's Cooperative Relationships: Partnerships and Alignments in Chinese Foreign Policy* (forthcoming).

109. Zi Zhongyun, "Convergence of Interests," pp. 55–57.

110. *Washington Post*, June 28, 1989, p. A23.

111. *Washington Post*, December 29, 1988, p. A17.

112. *Wall Street Journal*, December 28, 1988, p. A4.

CHAPTER 7

1. Xinhua, October 1, 1984, in Foreign Broadcast Information Service, *Daily Report: China*, October 1, 1984, p. K10. [Hereafter FBIS, *China*.]

2. For contemporary accounts of growing inequality in China, see *Guangming Ribao*, March 4, 1989, p. 3, in FBIS, *China*, March 17, 1989, pp. 36–39; and *Liaowang* (overseas edition), no. 9 (February 27, 1989), pp. 5–7, in FBIS, *China*, April 10, 1989, pp. 37–43.

3. For an excellent discussion of the relationship between economic reform, the creation of a civil society, and the emergence of political crisis in China, see Yanqi Tong, "Economic Reform and Political Change in Reforming Socialist Societies: The Cases of China and Hungary," Ph.D. diss., Johns Hopkins University, Department of Political Science, 1991.

4. Li Peng's report was carried on Radio Beijing, March 20, 1989, in FBIS, *China*, March 21, 1989, pp. 11–31. Quotation on p. 14.

5. On Zhao's loss of control over economic policy, see Xinhua, September 6, 1988, in FBIS, *China*, September 6, 1988, pp. 35–36. On the rumors of an impending change in leadership, see, *inter alia*, *Cheng Ming* (Hong Kong), no. 38 (April 1, 1989), pp. 6–8, in FBIS, *China*, April 3, 1989, pp. 39–41; and *South China Morning Post* (Hong Kong), April 12, 1989, pp. 1, 10, in FBIS, *China*, April 12, 1989, pp. 11–12.

6. On the atmosphere of the National People's Congress, see Xinhua, March 28, 1989, in FBIS, *China*, March 29, 1989, pp. 19–20; and Xinhua, March 30, 1989, in FBIS, *China*, March 30, 1989, pp. 27–28. On the postponement of political reform, see Li Peng's political report to the Congress, cited in note 4.

7. The account of the Tiananmen crisis has benefited from the following analyses by others: Robin Munro, "Who Died in Beijing, and Why," *The Nation*, June 11, 1990, pp. 811–22; Nicholas D. Kristof, "China Update: How the Hardliners Won," *New York Times Magazine*, November 12, 1989, pp. 38–41, 66–69, 71; *People's Republic of China:*

Preliminary Findings on Killings of Unarmed Civilians, Arbitrary Arrests and Summary Executions since June 3, 1989 (New York: Amnesty International USA, August 1989); International League for Human Rights and the Ad Hoc Study Group on Human Rights in China, *Massacre in Beijing: The Events of 3–4 June 1989 and Their Aftermath* (New York: International League for Human Rights, n.d.); Lowell Dittmer, "The Tiananmen Massacre," *Problems of Communism*, vol. 38 (September–October 1989), pp. 2–15; Andrew J. Nathan, "Chinese Democracy in 1989: Continuity and Change," *Problems of Communism*, vol. 38 (September–October 1989), pp. 16–29; Andrew G. Walder, "The Political Sociology of the Beijing Upheaval of 1989," *Problems of Communism*, vol. 38 (September–October 1989), pp. 30–40; Yi Mu and Mark V. Thompson, *Crisis at Tiananmen: Reform and Reality in Modern China* (San Francisco: China Books and Periodicals, 1989); and Chu-Yuan Cheng, *Behind the Tiananmen Massacre: Social, Political, and Economic Ferment in China* (Westview Press, 1990).

8. In one oft-quoted remark in late April, a student demonstrator admitted that he did not know precisely what democracy meant but insisted that China needed more of it. *New York Times*, April 28, 1989, p. A6.

9. *Beijing Review*, vol. 32 (May 29–June 4, 1989), pp. 7, 10.

10. The most objective account is the Asia Watch report *Punishment Season: Human Rights in China After Martial Law* (New York: Asia Watch, March 1990).

11. For the communiqué of the plenum, see Radio Beijing, June 24, 1989, in FBIS, *China*, June 26, 1989, pp. 15–16.

12. *The Wave of Protest in the People's Republic of China*, Hearing before the Subcommittee on Asian and Pacific Affairs of the House Committee on Foreign Affairs, 101 Cong. 1 sess. (Washington: Government Printing Office, 1990), pp. 11, 15–16.

13. *Washington Post*, May 21, 1989, p. A32.

14. *Washington Post*, May 21, 1989, p. A32.

15. *Washington Post*, June 5, 1989, p. A24.

16. *New York Times*, June 6, 1989, pp. A1, A15; and *Washington Post*, June 6, 1989, pp. A1, A18.

17. *New York Times*, June 13, 1989, pp. A1, A10.

18. Radio Beijing, June 27, 1989, in FBIS, *China*, June 27, 1989, pp. 8–10.

19. *New York Times*, June 21, 1989, pp. A1, A8.

20. These further sanctions were noted in the text of the congressional sanctions legislation, introduced on June 29. *Congressional Record*, daily ed., June 29, 1989, pp. H3455–56.

21. A useful summary of the sanctions imposed by the West after the June 4 incident can be found in *Business As Usual. . . ? The International Response to Human Rights Violations in Beijing* (New York: International League for Human Rights, May 1991).

22. *New York Times*, June 6, 1989, pp. A1, A15; *New York Times*, June 9, 1989, p. A22.

23. *Washington Post*, June 25, 1989, p. A25.

24. *Washington Post,* June 25, 1989, pp. A1, A24.
25. *New York Times,* June 9, 1989, p. A22.
26. "Statement of The Honorable Lawrence S. Eagleburger, Deputy Secretary of State, before the Senate Committee on Foreign Relations," February 7, 1990.
27. On the sale of the Boeing 757s, see *New York Times,* July 8, 1989, pp. 1, 32; on the Peace Pearl project, see *Washington Post,* October 29, 1989, p. A7.
28. *Washington Post,* June 25, 1989, p. A25.
29. Philip Geyelin, "Reagan's China Syndrome," *Washington Post,* August 25, 1980, p. A19.
30. *New York Times,* May 22, 1989, p. A11.
31. R. W. Apple, Jr., "The Capital," *New York Times,* May 24, 1989, p. B6; and Rowland Evans and Robert Novak, "Bush's Beijing Caution," *Washington Post,* May 24, 1989, p. A25.
32. *New York Times,* May 22, 1989, p. A11.
33. *Washington Post,* June 5, 1989, p. A24.
34. *Washington Post,* June 11, 1989, p. C6; and *New York Times,* June 22, 1989, p. A22.
35. Sixty-seven percent in a Gallup poll and 54 percent in an ABC News-*Washington Post* poll approved of the way Bush was dealing with events in China. *New York Times,* June 14, 1989, p. A17; and Roper Center for Public Opinion Research, University of Connecticut (poll of June 15–19, 1989). Fifty-one percent in a *Los Angeles Times* poll opposed further congressional action, whereas 33 percent said that Congress should take the lead in legislating further sanctions. Roper Center for Public Opinion Research, University of Connecticut (poll of June 14–15, 1989).
36. *Washington Post,* June 6, 1989, pp. A1, A18.
37. *Washington Post,* June 6, 1989, pp. A1, A18.
38. *Washington Post,* June 22, 1989, pp. A1, A32.
39. See "Americans' View of China Shifts in Wake of Beijing Crackdown," press release issued by the Gallup Organization, August 1989. If the crackdown continued, 62 percent favored a complete embargo on trade with China, and 59 percent favored the recall of the U.S. ambassador.
40. *Washington Post,* June 23, 1989, pp. A1, A30.
41. *New York Times,* June 27, 1989, A22.
42. *Washington Post,* June 23, 1989, pp. A1, A30.
43. *Congressional Record,* daily ed., June 8, 1989, pp. S6409–11; and *New York Times,* June 23, 1989, p. A5.
44. Representatives Mel Levine (D-California) proposed suspending all exports of advanced technology for a period of six months; Benjamin A. Gilman, prohibiting the export of items on the munitions control list; Theodore S. Weiss (D-New York), banning OPIC investment guarantees; Gerald B. H. Solomon (R-New York), halting export licenses for American satellites slated for launching by Chinese boosters; and Tom Lantos (D-California), withdrawing China's most-favored-nation status. In the

Senate, Daniel P. Moynihan (D-New York), Dennis DeConcini (D-Arizona), and Alan Cranston separately introduced legislation that would have repealed China's most-favored-nation status. See Thomas L. Friedman, "Congress, Angry at China, Moves to Impose Sanctions," *New York Times*, June 23, 1989, p. A5; and *Congressional Record*, daily ed., June 22, 1989, p. 57250, and June 23, 1989, p. 57504.

45. *United States Code Service, Lawyers Edition*, no. 3 (March 1990), pp. 296–301.
46. *Washington Post*, June 27, 1989, p. A18.
47. *York Times*, June 27, 1989, p. A21.
48. The House version of the amendment provided that the president could relax or lift sanctions only if he certified it to be in the "national security interest" to do so. The Senate version, which proved acceptable to the White House, referred less restrictively to the "national interests" of the United States. For details on the sanctions amendments, see *Congressional Quarterly*, November 11, 1989, pp. 3083–84.
49. The right to change status was particularly important. Existing immigration law required that officially sponsored students and scholars with J-1 visas had to return to China for two years after completing their course of study or research, and prohibited from changing to a less restrictive status until they had done so.
50. In this, the administration was supported by the Institute of International Education and the National Association for Foreign Student Affairs.
51. *Washington Post*, December 1, 1989, p. A45.
52. These feelings were intensified when it was revealed, several months later, that the White House had never issued the formal executive order it had promised, but had instead relied on an administrative order from the Department of Justice. The administration explained that executive orders were required only on subjects that came under the purview of several departments, and that immigration policy was under the sole jurisdiction of the Department of Justice. But this was widely regarded as another example of the White House's duplicity on China policy. See *Washington Post*, April 5, 1990, p. A25; *Washington Post*, April 6, 1990, p. A26; *New York Times*, April 7, 1990, p. A3; and *Washington Post*, April 12, 1990, p. A34.
53. This section draws on earlier analysis in Harry Harding, "The Impact of Tiananmen on Chinese Foreign Policy," in National Bureau of Asian and Soviet Research, *China's Foreign Relations after Tiananmen: Challenges for the U.S.*, no. 3 (Seattle, December 1990), pp. 5–17.
54. Two publications, Xin Can, ed., *Xifang Zhengjie Yaoren Tan Heping Yanbian* (Western political personages on "peaceful evolution") (Peking: Xinhua Publishing House, 1989), and Qi Fang, ed., *"Heping Yanbian" Zhanluede Chansheng ji qi Fazhan* (The origins and development of the strategy of "peaceful evolution") (Peking: Oriental Publishing House, 1990), provided handy compendia of statements by American

statesmen, including Dulles, Kennedy, Nixon, Reagan, Bush, Kissinger, and Brzezinski.

55. *Liaowang* (overseas edition), no. 31 (July 31, 1989), pp. 6–8, in FBIS, *China*, August 8, 1989, pp. 1–4.

56. See the speech by the departing Chinese ambassador to the United States, Han Xu, in *Beijing Review*, vol. 32 (September 18–24, 1989), pp. 30–33.

57. *Wen Wei Po*, May 28, 1989, in FBIS, *China*, May 31, 1989, pp. 2–3.

58. *Washington Post*, February 7, 1990, p. A1, A20. Exceptions were made for students with relatives overseas.

59. *Media Monitor*, vol. 3 (Washington: Center for Media and Public Affairs, September 1989).

60. Suzanne Huffman, Tai-en Yang, Liqun Yan, and Keith P. Sanders, "Genie Out of the Bottle: Three U.S. Networks Report Tiananmen Square," unpublished paper, University of Missouri, School of Journalism, August 1990.

61. Michael Berlin, Ross Terrill, and Akira Iriye, *Tiananmen Two Years Later –How Did the Media Perform: A Study of American Media Coverage of the Beijing Spring of 1989* (Harvard University, Barone Center on the Press, Politics and Public Policy, draft dated May 20, 1991). Berlin's study is also the source of the items cited in footnotes 59 and 60.

62. An elderly couple in Palo Alto, California, wrote to Ann Landers to complain that "stale news about China," which could have been left to regularly scheduled news programs, was interrupting their favorite soap operas. *Washington Post*, August 15, 1989, p. E2.

63. For the ratings of the network news programs, see *New York Times*, June 19, 1989, p. D6. For the polling data, see "Americans' View of China Shifts."

64. One particularly thoughtful, thorough, and balanced effort to evaluate American press coverage of the Tiananmen incident is Berlin and others, *Tiananmen Two Years Later*.

65. Although a substantial minority in one poll said that they did not have enough information to judge the protests, 63 percent said that they supported the demonstrations, and 79 percent said they opposed the government's use of force to suppress them. Poll conducted by ABC News–*Washington Post*, June 15–19, 1989, reported by the Roper Center for Public Opinion Research, University of Connecticut.

66. *Roper Reports 90–10* (New York: Roper Organization, January 1991).

67. Undated press release for a CBS–*New York Times* poll conducted January 13–15, 1990.

68. Henry Kissinger, "The Drama in Beijing," *Washington Post*, June 11, 1989, p. C7; Richard M. Nixon, "China Policy: Revulsion Real, Reprisal Wrong," *Los Angeles Times*, June 25, 1989, pp. 1, 2; and especially Henry Kissinger, "The Caricature of Deng as a Tyrant Is Unfair," *Washington Post*, August 1, 1989, p. 24.

CHAPTER 8

1. Richard Nixon, "The Crisis in Sino-American Relations," sent to Senators Lloyd Bentsen (D-Texas), Robert Byrd (D-West Virginia), Robert Dole (R-Kansas), and Alan Simpson (R-Wyoming), and to Representatives William Broomfield (R-Michigan) and Dante Fascell (D-Florida), November 1989. Excerpts appeared in *Time*, November 20, 1989, pp. 44–49.
2. "U.S.-China Relations," Policy Consensus Report (Washington: Johns Hopkins Foreign Policy Institute, Paul H. Nitze School of Advanced International Studies, October 1989).
3. "Statement of The Honorable Lawrence S. Eagleburger, Deputy Secretary of State, before the Senate Committee on Foreign Relations," February 7, 1990, p. 16.
4. The following paragraphs draw on Harry Harding, "The Impact of Tiananmen on China's Foreign Policy," in National Bureau of Asian and Soviet Research, *China's Foreign Relations after Tiananmen: Challenges for the U.S.*, no. 3 (Seattle, December 1990), pp. 5–17.
5. Xinhua, December 11, 1989, in Foreign Broadcast Information Service, *Daily Report: China*, December 11, 1989, p. 11. (Hereafter FBIS, *China*.)
6. This statement of Jiang Zemin was quoted in *Wen Wei Po*, December 22, 1989, p. 3, in FBIS, *China*, January 19, 1990, pp. 1–2. See also Xinhua, January 11, 1990, in FBIS, *China*, January 11, 1990, p. 1.
7. *New York Times*, December 13, 1989, p. A31.
8. *New York Times*, January 21, 1990, p. E21.
9. *Los Angeles Times*, January 15, 1990, p. B7.
10. *Washington Post*, December 11, 1989, p. A14; and *New York Times*, December 12, 1989, p. A24.
11. *Wall Street Journal*, December 12, 1989, p. A20.
12. *Washington Post*, December 12, 1989, p. A22.
13. Xinhua, December 10, 1989, in FBIS, *China*, December 11, 1989, pp. 1–4. For his part, Deng seemed confused as to who had dispatched Scowcroft. He began the meeting by saying that he was "so glad President Carter sent you." *New York Times*, December 11, 1989, p. A9.
14. As the *Washington Post* asked editorially: "Just what does that mean? That the Chinese who massacred the students and the U.S. government that imposed sanctions were merely victims of a misunderstanding and of malevolent prodding from troublemakers in each of their realms?" *Washington Post*, December 11, 1989, p. A14.
15. The M-9 is a missile with a range of 600 kilometers, or 375 miles. This is within the American definition of a medium-range ballistic missile, which is 160 miles or more, but outside the Chinese definition, which is between 1000 and 3000 kilometers. See John W. Lewis, Hua Di, and Xue Litai, "Beijing's Defense Establishment: Solving the Arms-Export Enigma," *International Security*, vol. 15 (Spring 1991), pp. 86–109.
16. *New York Times*, March 30, 1990, p. A7.

17. *New York Times,* January 11, 1990, p. A22.
18. *Country Reports on Human Rights Practices for 1989,* report submitted to the Committee on Foreign Relations, U.S. Senate and the Committee on Foreign Affairs, House of Representatives, by the Department of State, 101 Cong. 2 sess. (Washington: Government Printing Office, 1990), pp. 802–25.
19. *Washington Post,* March 7, 1990, p. A30; and *New York Times,* March 11, 1990, pp. A1, A16.
20. *New York Times,* April 4, 1990, p. A12.
21. For an overview of the issue, see Vladimir N. Pregelj, "Most-Favored-Nation Status of the People's Republic of China," Issue Brief IB-89119 (Washington: Library of Congress, Congressional Research Service, March 1991). Pregelj points out that resolutions to disapprove the renewal of China's most-favored-nation status had been introduced in the House in 1982 and 1983, but either died in committee or were defeated on the floor. As noted, bills to revoke China's most-favored-nation status were also proposed in 1989 but had not been included in the comprehensive sanctions legislation adopted by Congress.
22. "Testimony of Joseph A. Massey, Assistant U.S. Trade Representative for Japan and China, before the Subcommittee on Trade of the House Ways and Means Committee, June 21, 1990," *United States–People's Republic of China (PRC) Trade Relations, Including Most-Favored-Nation Trade Status for the PRC,* Hearings before the Subcommittee on Trade of the House Committee on Ways and Means, 101 Cong. 2 sess. (GPO, 1990), pp. 369–72.
23. Other estimates ranged from $2 billion to $10 billion. See *Los Angeles Times,* May 22, 1990, pp. A1, A12; and *Christian Science Monitor,* May 21, 1990, pp. 1–2.
24. For overviews of the debate, see *Cheng Ming,* no. 152 (June 1, 1990), pp. 18–19 and 20, in FBIS, *China,* June 4, 1990, pp. 34–35 and 38–39; *Cheng Ming,* no. 153 (July 1, 1990), pp. 12–13, in FBIS, *China,* July 3, 1990, pp. 19–20; and *Ching Pao,* July 10, 1990, pp. 36–37, in FBIS, *China,* July 9, 1990, pp. 21–22.
25. *Journal of Commerce,* May 16, 1990, p. 4A.
26. According to Chinese scholars, such reports were submitted by the Institute of American Studies at the Chinese Academy of Social Sciences and by the Shanghai Institute of International Studies.
27. *New York Times,* May 11, 1990, p. A6; and *Tangtai,* no. 24 (May 12, 1990), pp. 7–9, in FBIS, *China,* May 23, 1990, p. 6.
28. Xinhua, September 19, 1989, in FBIS, *China,* September 19, 1989, p. 8.
29. On the first loan package, see Allen S. Whiting, *China Eyes Japan* (University of California Press, 1989), pp. 121–26. On the second, see Lowell Dittmer, "China in 1989: The Crisis of Incomplete Reform," *Asian Survey,* vol. 30 (January 1990), p. 37.
30. *Washington Post,* July 6, 1990, p. A25.
31. Still, in fiscal year 1990, China received only $590 million from the World Bank, compared with $1.7 billion in fiscal year 1988 and $1.3

billion in fiscal year 1989. Before the Tiananmen incident, it had been estimated that the World Bank might lend as much as $2.5 billion in fiscal year 1990. See *Far Eastern Economic Review*, June 7, 1990, pp. 56–57; and *World Bank Annual Report 1989*, p. 158.

32. To make this initiative more palatable to domestic audiences, the White House made it part of a broader package of measures, including a relatively restrained statement on the first anniversary of the June 4 incident, and an hour-long meeting between Vice President Dan Quayle and the Chinese student leader Chai Ling. See *Los Angeles Times*, June 5, 1990, pp. A16, A17; *Washington Post*, June 5, 1990, p. A21; and *Washington Post*, June 8, 1990, p. A14. The idea of placing the recommendation to renew China's most-favored-nation status in a broader package of policy initiatives was suggested by the former U.S. ambassador to China, Winston Lord, in early May. But the package ultimately assembled by the Bush administration included few of the specific components that Lord had advocated. *New York Times*, May 9, 1990, p. A31.

33. *Los Angeles Times*, June 1, 1990, pp. A1, A18; and *Wall Street Journal*, June 1, 1990, p. A16.

34. The text of the interview with Barbara Walters is in *Beijing Review*, June 4–10, 1990, pp. 16–18; the text of the letter to the students at California Polytechnic State University is in Xinhua, June 18, 1990, in FBIS, *China*, June 18, 1990, pp. 8–11.

35. *Wall Street Journal*, June 26, 1990, p. A14; and *Washington Post*, June 26, 1990, p. A18. On the debate among Chinese leaders over Fang's release, see *Kuang Chiao Ching*, no. 214 (July 16, 1990), pp. 6–11, in FBIS, *China*, July 25, 1990, pp. 1–5; and *Cheng Ming*, no. 153 (July 1, 1990), pp. 6–7, in FBIS, *China*, July 3, 1990, pp. 16–18.

36. Amnesty International, *Amnesty International Report 1990* (New York: Amnesty International Publications, 1990); and the Asia Watch report *Punishment Season: Human Rights in China After Martial Law*, (New York: Asia Watch, March 1990).

37. *Washington Post*, May 11, 1990, pp. A1, A34; and *Los Angeles Times*, June 5, 1990, pp. A16, A17.

38. The negotiations over possible Chinese missile sales were difficult to evaluate for they involved weapons systems that were not yet in production in China. See *New York Times*, March 30, 1990, p. A7. The reports of the provision of arms to the Khmer Rouge and components of chemical weapons to Libya appeared more credible. See *New York Times*, May 1, 1990, p. A13; *Washington Post*, June 7, 1990, p. A34; and *New York Times*, June 7, 1990, p. A15.

39. See, for example, "Statement of Roger W. Sullivan, President, United States–China Business Council," in *United States-People's Republic of China (PRC) Trade Relations*, pp. 43–49.

40. *Washington Post*, May 12, 1990, p. A17; and "Statement of John T. Kamm, President, American Chamber of Commerce in Hong Kong," in *United States–People's Republic of China (PRC) Trade Relations*, pp. 50–102. The estimates of the economic loss to Hong Kong in 1991

were even higher: the Hong Kong government forecast that the territory would lose up to $12 billion in trade, and some 43,000 jobs, if China's most-favored-nation status were revoked. See Xinhua, July 10, 1991, in FBIS, *China*, July 11, 1991, p. 6.

41. See the editorial entitled "Don't Punish the Wrong China," *New York Times*, April 27, 1990, p. A34.

42. *Wall Street Journal*, March 1, 1990, p. A13; and *New York Times*, May 13, 1990, p. A16.

43. The Independent Federation of Chinese Students and Scholars called for the revocation of China's most-favored-nation status in 1990 and for the imposition of conditions in 1991. See "Statement of Yang Ye, Ph.D., Adviser to the President, Independent Federation of Chinese Students and Scholars, and Assistant Professor, Bates College, Lewiston, ME," in *United States–People's Republic of China (PRC) Trade Relations*, pp. 131–57; and the "Statement of the Independent Federation of the Chinese Students and Scholars on Conditioning Most-Favored-Nation Status for China," presented by Haiching Zhao, Ph.D., before the Sub-committees on Asian and Pacific Affairs, Human Rights and International Organizations, and International Economic Policy and Trade of the House Committee on Foreign Affairs, May 29, 1991. For the contrary opinion, see *Los Angeles Times*, January 15, 1990, p. B7; and the testimony at the House hearings in June 1990 by Xiaoxia Gong, Xianglu Li, Shi-Jiang Li, and Lin Yu Deng, all in *United States–People's Republic of China (PRC) Trade Relations*, pp. 158–61, 173–79, 314–19, and 338–43, respectively. Similar statements were made in the second round of debate over China's most-favored-nation status in 1991. See *Washington Post*, June 4, 1991, p. A23; and *New York Times*, July 23, 1991, p. A21.

44. These resolutions were introduced in the House by Representatives Gerald Solomon (R-New York) and Tom Lantos (D-California) and in the Senate by George Mitchell. The Mitchell bill would have required that the president make a certification of China's compliance with certain human rights standards before most-favored-nation status could be restored.

45. H.R. 4939, 101 Cong. 2 sess. (GPO, 1990).

46. *New York Times*, October 19, 1990, pp. A1, A8.

47. Examples of these lines of argument can be found in *Shijie Zhishi*, no. 24 (December 16, 1989), pp. 2–3, in FBIS, *China*, January 26, 1990, pp. 1–2; *Jiefangjun Bao*, March 23, 1990, p. 3, in FBIS, *China*, April 18, 1990, pp. 8–9; *Liaowang* (overseas edition), no. 16 (April 16, 1990), pp. 4–6, in FBIS, *China*, May 1, 1990, pp. 1–5; and *Liaowang* (overseas edition), no. 39 (September 24, 1990), p. 28, in FBIS, *China*, September 27, 1990, pp. 8–9.

48. For an overview of Peking's invocation of a threat from Japan, see *Christian Science Monitor*, February 15, 1990, p. 19. Kissinger's views on the subject were stated most concisely in an interview published in early June, in which he argued that the loss of America's "special relationship" with China would remove "one of the assets the United States has had

in its relations with Japan" (*Los Angeles Times,* June 3, 1990, pp. M2, M8). Nixon's views were contained in his report to congressional leaders, "The Crisis in Sino-American Relations," in *Time,* November 20, 1989, pp. 44–49. A statement by Bush in a news conference in January alluded vaguely to the way in which the maintenance of working relations with China would provide a way of preserving American leverage over Japan. See *New York Times,* January 25, 1990, p. B8.

49. On China's willingness to cooperate in dealing with global issues, see Qian Qichen's address to the U.N. General Assembly in September 1990, *Renmin Ribao* (overseas edition), September 29, 1990, p. 4, in FBIS, *China,* October 1, 1990, pp. 1–4. The warnings that emigration from China could become a "big problem" to the rest of the region were made by Deng Xiaoping personally. See *Wen Wei Po,* June 16, 1990, p. 1, in FBIS, *China,* June 18, 1990, pp. 29–30.

50. *Los Angeles Times,* August 5, 1990, p. A8.

51. *New York Times,* August 30, 1990, p. A15.

52. Soviet intentions were discussed by Foreign Minister Eduard Shevardnadze during a visit to China in November. See Xinhua, November 23, 1990, in FBIS, *China,* November 26, 1990, p. 13; and *Washington Post,* December 2, 1990, pp. A1, A33.

53. *New York Times,* November 28, 1990, p. A8.

54. The first had been Spain, whose foreign minister had visited China the previous November.

55. *Washington Post,* December 1, 1990, p. A14.

56. On the last-minute change in Qian's schedule and the confusion surrounding his departure from the State Department, see *Washington Post,* December 1, 1990, p. A14.

57. *Far Eastern Economic Review,* December 13, 1990, pp. 10–11. This shift in American policy reflected the fact that the United States no longer had the votes in the World Bank to block renewed lending to China.

58. Beijing International, December 4, 1990, in FBIS, *China,* December 7, 1990, pp. 7–8.

59. The following discussion of Chinese attitudes toward the United States during and after the Persian Gulf War is drawn from Harry Harding, "China's American Dilemma," *The Annals of the American Academy of Political and Social Science,* vol. 519 (January 1992), pp. 13–26.

60. See, for example, *Ta Kung Pao,* January 16, 1991, p. 3, in FBIS, *China,* January 16, 1991, pp. 3–4; and *Ta Kung Pao,* February 1, 1991, p. 2, in FBIS, *China,* February 1, 1991, pp. 2–3.

61. *South China Morning Post,* February 27, 1991, p. 15, in FBIS, *China,* February 27, 1991, pp. 5–7.

62. *New York Times,* February 20, 1991, p. A14.

63. *South China Morning Post,* April 4, 1991, p. 11, in FBIS, *China,* April 4, 1991, p. 3.

64. These quotations are drawn, respectively, from *Liaowang* (overseas edition), no. 19 (May 13, 1991), pp. 9–10, in FBIS, *China,* May 21, 1991, pp. 3–6; and *Liaowang* (overseas edition), no. 14 (April 8, 1991),

pp. 26–28, in FBIS, *China*, April 17, 1991, pp. 7–9. Some Chinese analysts also privately discounted the notion that Washington even sought "world domination," noting that the United States was increasingly preoccupied with its domestic problems.

65. The case that economic reform in China had resumed was made by Nicholas R. Lardy, *Redefining U.S.-China Economic Relations*, NBR Analysis, no. 5 (Seattle: National Bureau of Asian and Soviet Research, June 1991). For a more skeptical view, see "The Chinese Economy in 1990 and 1991: Uncertain Recovery," EA 91–10022 (Washington: Central Intelligence Agency, July 1991).

66. For a similar conclusion, see Asia Watch, *Two Years After Tiananmen: Political Prisoners in China, Cumulative Data* (New York: Asia Watch, May 1991).

67. *Wall Street Journal*, April 5, 1991, p. A16; *Washington Post*, April 6, 1991, p. A-15; and *New York Times*, June 10, 1991, pp. A1, A8.

68. For a summary of all these accusations, see "China: Weapons Proliferation and the Question of Continued Unconditional MFN Status," DPC Special Report, SR-19-Foreign Policy (Washington: Democratic Policy Committee, June 1991).

69. *Los Angeles Times*, April 12, 1991, pp. A1, A18; and *Washington Post*, April 20, 1991, p. A17.

70. The evidence to support this proposition was reviewed in an influential article in the *Washington Post*, May 12, 1991, pp. C1, C4.

71. Office of the United States Trade Representative, *1991 National Trade Estimate Report on Foreign Trade Barriers* (GPO, 1991), pp. 43–52.

72. *Wall Street Journal*, November 23, 1990, p. A5b; *New York Times*, August 23, 1990, p. D15; and *Washington Post*, July 23, 1991, pp. A1, A5.

73. The subject of China's export of the products of convict labor first arose in the late 1980s and began to receive attention from labor unions and members of Congress in 1989. At the request of Senator Jesse Helms, the General Accounting Office produced a report on the subject in July 1990. Asia Watch issued a study in April 1991. See *Washington Post*, July 15, 1990, p. B5; and *Washington Post*, April 19, 1991, pp. A14, A18.

74. This description is of the Pelosi bill (H.R. 2212) as amended after deliberation in the Ways and Means Committee. *Additional Objectives Which The People's Republic of China Must Meet in Order to Qualify for Nondiscrimination Treatment in 1992*, H. Rept. 102–141, 102 Cong. 1 sess. (GPO, 1991).

75. This description is of a second bill (S. 1367) introduced by Mitchell in June, which was somewhat milder than an earlier piece of legislation (S. 1084) that he submitted in May.

76. *Wen Wei Po*, May 11, 1991, p. 2, in FBIS, *China*, May 13, 1991, pp. 10–11.

77. *South China Morning Post*, April 6, 1991, p. 6, in FBIS, *China*, April 8, 1991, pp. 7–8.

78. On Deng's role, see *Cheng Ming*, no. 163 (May 1, 1991), pp. 14–15, in FBIS, *China*, April 30, 1991, pp. 6–7.

79. The text of the explanation, prepared by the Ministry of Foreign Economic Relations and Trade, was carried by Xinhua, May 9, 1991, in FBIS, *China,* May 10, 1991, pp. 10–14. A similar statement on human rights was published toward the end of the year. See Information Office of the State Council, "Human Rights in China," *Beijing Review,* vol. 34 (November 4–10, 1991), pp. 8–45.
80. These initiatives were summarized in a lengthy pamphlet issued by the Chinese embassy in Washington at the height of the debate over MFN, awkwardly titled "Facts about Some China-Related Issues of Concern to the American Public" (Washington: Embassy of the People's Republic of China, May 1991).
81. *South China Morning Post,* June 26, 1991, p. 10, in FBIS, *China,* June 26, 1991, pp. 3–4.
82. "Remarks by the President in Commencement Address to Yale University," Office of the Press Secretary, White House, May 27, 1991. The president had made similar comments two weeks earlier, when he informed Senate Republicans that he intended to recommend the renewal of China's most-favored-nation status. See *Washington Post,* May 16, 1991, pp. A1, A35.
83. *Washington Post,* May 4, 1990, p. A22.
84. *Los Angeles Times,* November 19, 1990, pp. A1, A18.
85. *Washington Post,* April 17, 1991, p. A3.
86. *New York Times,* April 26, 1991, pp. D1, D6.
87. The administration action deferred licenses for several computers, denied China permission to launch several American-made satellites for foreign customers, and prohibited the sale of missile technology and equipment to one Chinese state corporation. *New York Times,* May 28, 1991, pp. A1, A8. The administration had previously barred the export of American components for a Chinese satellite on similar grounds. See *New York Times,* May 1, 1991, p. A15.
88. On the Schifter visit, see *Washington Post,* December 20, 1990, pp. A25, A36; on the Massey visit, *Los Angeles Times,* March 4, 1991, pp. D1–D6; on the Bartholomew visit, *Los Angeles Times,* June 19, 1991, p. A11; and on the Kimmitt visit, *New York Times,* May 8, 1991, p. A7. Unlike the earlier Scowcroft-Eagleburger visits, or the meeting with Qian Qichen in the White House, none of these trips attracted much public criticism, although Representative Donald Pease did complain in May that "we've had far too many high-level contacts and not much result." *New York Times,* May 16, 1991, pp. A1, A10.
89. "Statement of Senator Max Baucus, MFN for China, May 21, 1991."
90. *Congressional Record,* daily ed., July 22, 1991, p. S10519, vol. 137, no. 112. Three lengthy attachments to the letter to Senator Baucus were not included in the *Congressional Record.*
91. On the Baker memorandum, see *New York Times,* May 28, 1991, pp. A1, A8.
92. These more conciliatory actions were implicit in several passages in the president's letter to Baucus: when he implied that some sanctions could

be lifted if the "human rights climate in China improved," when he noted that "our policy mix of sanctions and cooperation at any given time" is dependent on the pattern of Chinese military technology transfers to third countries, and when he suggested that further trade reforms in China could accelerate Peking's accession to the GATT.

93. *New York Times*, June 8, 1990, p. A6.

94. See the annual report of the State Statistical Bureau, Xinhua, February 21, 1991, in FBIS, *China*, February 27, 1991, pp. 45–52.

95. The annual figures are drawn from table A-6. The monthly figures for October 1988 and 1989 are from *China Statistics Monthly*, no. 9 (December 1990), p. 57; those for May 1989 and 1990 are from *China Statistics Monthly*, no. 4 (July 1990), p. 59.

96. "Testimony of Joseph A. Massey"; and *Los Angeles Times*, April 24, 1990, p. H2.

97. *New York Times*, June 4, 1990, pp. D1, D6; and *Los Angeles Times*, December 1, 1990, pp. D1, D2.

98. *Washington Post*, April 7, 1990, pp. A10, A14.

99. Data from the Visa Office of the Department of State show that the number of Chinese receiving J-1 visas for official exchange programs fell from 8,684 in fiscal year 1988 to 5,161 in fiscal year 1990. A survey of American colleges and universities with formal exchange relationships with China suggested that Chinese participants in such programs declined by 19 percent in the 1989–90 academic year. See Carol Strevy, "Current Status of Academic and Cultural Exchanges Between US and PRC Institutions A Year After Tiananmen" (New York, Institute of International Education, November 1990), p. iii.

100. *Chronicle of Higher Education*, September 12, 1990, p. A37.

101. Mary Brown Bullock, "The Effects of Tiananmen on China's International Scientific and Educational Cooperation," *China Exchange News*, vol. 19 (Spring 1991), pp. 3–7.

102. Strevy, "Current Status of Academic and Cultural Exchanges," p. iii; and *Chronicle of Higher Education*, November 28, 1990, pp. A1, A36.

103. One major exception to this trend was the Johns Hopkins University, which continued its program in Nanjing throughout the 1989–90 academic year.

104. Strevy, "Current Status of Academic and Cultural Exchanges," p. iii. On the reluctance of American faculty to go to China to teach, see *Washington Post*, March 10, 1990, p. A10.

105. *New York Times*, July 27, 1991, p. 33. This step had also been considered the previous year. See *New York Times*, February 21, 1990, p. B8.

106. *Washington Post*, May 18, 1991, p. A16.

107. *Los Angeles Times*, May 15, 1990, pp. A1, A7.

108. *Washington Post*, June 25, 1989, pp. A1, A24.

109. *Washington Post*, November 15, 1990, p. A26.

110. *Los Angeles Times*, September 5, 1991, p. A16; and *Washington Post*, April 23, 1991, pp. D1, D8.

111. "Statement of Hon. Barney Frank, A Representative in Congress from

the State of Massachusetts," in *United States–People's Republic of China (PRC) Trade Relations*, p. 9; and *Los Angeles Times*, October 19, 1990, p. A1. See also Nicholas D. Kristof, "Suddenly, China Looks Smaller in the World," *New York Times*, March 27, 1990, p. A15.

112. *New York Times*, March 27, 1990, p. A15.

113. *Washington Post*, May 30, 1991, p. A19.

114. The first comment is from Representative Gus Yatron (D-Pennsylvania), *Congressional Record*, May 7, 1986, p. E1559. The second is from Representative Steny Hoyer (D-Maryland), *Washington Post*, July 11, 1991, p. A6. This extreme statement was not included in his official remarks as published in *Congressional Record*, daily ed., July 10, 1991, vol. 137, no. 105, pp. H5348–H5349.

115. *New York Times*, January 12, 1990, pp. A1, A3.

116. *Washington Times*, April 23, 1990, p. A8.

117. The quotation is from William Abnett, executive director of the Washington State China Relations Council, *Washington Post*, April 18, 1990, p. 32.

118. *Wall Street Journal*, May 3, 1991, p. A8.

119. *New York Times*, June 12, 1990, p. A12.

120. John E. Rielly, ed., *American Public Opinion and U.S. Foreign Policy, 1991* (Chicago Council on Foreign Relations, 1991), p. 19; and John E. Rielly, ed., "American Public Opinion and U.S. Foreign Policy, 1987," Chicago Council on Foreign Relations, 1987, p. 17.

121. *Roper Reports*, no. 90–10 (New York: Roper Organization, Mid–January 1991), pp. 38–39, 106.

122. Only 16 percent of elites shared the same perception. Rielly, *American Public Opinion, 1991*, p. 20.

123. The two polls are reported respectively in *Wall Street Journal*, January 19, 1990, p. 1; and undated press release on a CBS News–*New York Times* poll conducted January 13–15, 1990, p. 10.

124. Rielly, *American Public Opinion, 1991*, p. 24; and *New York Times*, June 11, 1991, p. A16.

125. Zhongguo Tongxunshe (China news service), July 31, 1991, in FBIS, *China*, August 1, 1991, pp. 13–14.

126. On reports of this sentiment, see *Ming Pao*, August 5, 1991, p. 7, in FBIS, *China*, August 7, 1991, p. 6.

127. *New York Times*, March 1, 1990, p. A13; *New York Times*, May 13, 1990, p. A16; *New York Times*, May 15, 1991, p. A10; and *Washington Post*, May 29, 1991, pp. A21, A23.

128. *New York Times*, September 12, 1990, p. A12; and January 3, 1991, pp. B1, B2.

129. *New York Times*, May 15, 1991, p. A10. He added that, "in their third breath, they worry that harsh American sanctions would hurt the Chinese people rather than their leaders."

130. *Los Angeles Times*, February 19, 1991, pp. A1, A16–A17.

131. *Cheng Ming*, no. 166 (August 1, 1991), pp. 14–15, in FBIS, *China*, August 5, 1991, pp. 46–48.

CHAPTER 9

1. See Charles Lipson, "International Cooperation in Economic and Security Affairs," *World Politics*, vol. 37 (October 1984), pp. 1–23.
2. George Friedman and Meredith LeBard, *The Coming War with Japan* (St. Martin's Press, 1991).
3. This metaphor is from Ellen L. Frost, *For Richer, For Poorer: The New U.S.-Japan Relationship* (New York: Council on Foreign Relations, 1987), esp. p. 163.
4. The distinction between hard and soft authoritarianism is made in Edwin A. Winckler, "Institutionalization and Participation on Taiwan: From Hard to Soft Authoritarianism?" *China Quarterly*, no. 99 (September 1984), pp. 481–99; and Robert A. Scalapino, "The United States and the Security of Asia," in Robert A. Scalapino, Seizaburo Sato, and Jusuf Wanandi, eds., *Internal and External Security Issues in Asia*, Research Papers and Policy Studies, no. 16 (Berkeley: University of California, Institute of East Asian Studies, 1986), p. 76.

CHAPTER 10

1. Roger W. Sullivan, "China, the United States, and the World Beyond Normalization," *China Business Review*, May–June 1988, p. 20.
2. Nicholas R. Lardy, "Redefining U.S.-China Economic Relations," NBR Analysis, no. 5 (Seattle: National Bureau of Asian and Soviet Research, June 1991), p. 8.
3. Data for 1978 are from Harry Harding, *China's Second Revolution: Reform after Mao* (Brookings, 1987), p. 139, table 6-1. Data for 1990 are from the annual communiqué of the State Statistical Bureau, Xinhua, February 21, 1991, in Foreign Broadcast Information Service, *Daily Report: China*, February 27, 1991, pp. 45–52. (Hereafter FBIS, *China*.)
4. See the statement on Sino-American commercial relations by the Ministry of Foreign Economic Relations and Trade in FBIS, *China*, May 10, 1991, p. 11.
5. This section draws heavily on the conclusion to Harry Harding, "China in the 1990s: Prospects for Internal Change," NBR Analysis, no. 1 (Seattle: National Bureau of Asian and Soviet Research, September 1990), pp. 20–24.
6. Council for Economic Planning and Development, *Taiwan Statistical Data Book 1985* (Taipei, 1985), p. 25; Asian Development Bank, *Asian Development Outlook 1991* (Manila, 1991), p. 279, and *Asian Development Outlook, 1990* (Manila, 1990), p. 222; and International Bank for Reconstruction and Development/World Bank, *World Tables 1991* (Washington, 1991), p. 300.
7. On the origins of that policy, and its persistence through subsequent

decades, see Harry Harding, "The Legacy of the Decade for Later Years: An American Perspective," in Harry Harding and Yuan Ming, eds., *Sino-American Relations: A Joint Reassessment of a Critical Decade* (Wilmington, Del.: SR Books, 1989), pp. 325–26.

8. See Kenneth Bush, "Climate Change, Global Security, and International Governance: A Summary of Proceedings of a Conference on Climate Changes and Global Security," Working Paper 23 (Ottawa: Canadian Institute for International Peace and Security, June 1990).

9. *New York Times*, September 10, 1991, p. C9.

10. For Qian's 1990 address, see *Renmin Ribao* (overseas edition), September 29, 1990, p. 4, in FBIS, *China*, October 1, 1990, pp. 1–4; for the 1991 address see Renmin Ribao, September 26, 1991, in FBIS, *China*, October 2, 1991, p. 1.

11. Yufan Hao, "Environmental Protection and Chinese Foreign Policy," paper presented to the Conference on the Foreign Relations of China's Environmental Policy, sponsored by the American Enterprise Institute for Public Policy Research, August 1991.

12. Armin Rosencranz and Reina Milligan, "CFC Abatement: The Needs of Developing Countries," *Ambio*, vol. 19 (October 1990), pp. 312–16.

13. John Wilson Lewis and Xue Litai, *China Builds the Bomb* (Stanford University Press, 1988), p. 285, note 48.

14. The actual START agreement of 1991 provides for a 15 percent reduction for the United States and a 32 percent reduction for the Soviet Union in the number of warheads from existing levels: from 12,225 to 10,360 for the United States, and from 10,702 to 7,310 for the Soviet Union. Arms Control Association, Fact Sheet, Washington, September 25, 1991.

15. On the use of technology transfer policy to promote the development of an arms transfer regime, see John McCain, "Controlling Arms Sales to the Third World," *Washington Quarterly*, vol. 14 (Spring 1991), pp. 79-89; and National Academy of Sciences, Committee on Science, Engineering, and Public Policy, *Finding Common Ground: U.S. Export Controls in a Changed Global Environment* (Washington: National Academy Press, 1991).

16. Michael H. Hunt, *The Making of a Special Relationship: The United States and China to 1914* (Columbia University Press, 1983), p. 304.

17. See the tabular chronologies in Harold R. Isaacs, *Scratches on Our Minds: American Views of China and India* (M.E. Sharpe, 1980), p. 71; and Warren I. Cohen, "American Perceptions of China," in Michel Oksenberg and Robert B. Oxnam, eds., *Dragon and Eagle: United States-China Relations: Past and Future* (Basic Books, 1978), p. 55.

INDEX

Abramowitz, Morton, 92

Academic exchanges, 55, 97; autonomy of Chinese scholars resulting from, 196–97; "brain drain" of Chinese scholars, 127, 195–96, 353; Chinese restrictions on, 197–98; collaborative programs, 153; decline in early 1980s, 128; expulsions of U.S. scholars, 126–27; increase in 1979–80, 99–100; increase in mid-1980s, 149–50; in 1990s, 350–53; political factors, 57–58; political reform and, 344; reciprocity issues, 98, 126, 352–53; research by U.S. scholars in China, 125–27, 153; Tiananmen crisis and, 238–39, 287–88; U.S. funding for Chinese scholars, 150–51; U.S. interest in sustaining, 350–51

Academics' views on China, 61, 64

Acheson, Dean G., 25

Acid rain, 354

Afghanistan, Soviet invasion of, 91, 93, 121, 165, 177

AFL-CIO, 102

Agency for International Development (AID), 149, 150, 202

Agnew, Spiro T., 40

Akihito, emperor of Japan, 275

Algeria, 277, 279, 356

Allen, Richard V., 109–10

America-China Society, 210–11

American Institute in Taiwan (AIT), 82, 85, 86, 109, 348

American Motors Corporation (AMC), 193

Amnesty International, 265

Andropov, Yuri, 140, 164

Apple, R. W., 230

Argentina, 184

Arkhipov, Ivan, 175

Armacost, Michael, 209

Arms control, 165, 179; in 1990s, 355–58

Arms sales to China, 88, 143; aircraft upgrades, 168; ban on, 73, 89, 91, 93, 119; Chinese proposal for, 45, 93; Chinese rejection of, 120; in 1990s, 333–34; rapprochement and, 52–54; Tiananmen crisis and, 288–89; types of weapons, agreement on, 167–68

Arms sales to Middle East by China, 186–89, 250, 254, 257, 276–77, 321

Asian Development Bank, 227, 336

Asian issues, U.S.-Chinese cooperation on, 44–45. *See also* Cambodia

Asia-Pacific Economic Cooperation (APEC) process, 336, 349

Asia-Pacific region, future of, 301

Asia Watch, 265

Association of Southeast Asian Nations (ASEAN), 181, 182, 183

Atlantic Council, 206

Atmospheric pollution, 354–55

Australia, 264

Authoritarian regime in China, prospects for, 314–15

Baker, James A., III, 205, 255; Persian Gulf crisis, 272; renormalization of relations, 273, 282; Tiananmen crisis, 225, 226, 227–28, 229

Baldrige, Malcolm, 141

Baltic states, 305